THE WORLD ENCYCLOPEDIA OF

SWORDS AND SABRES

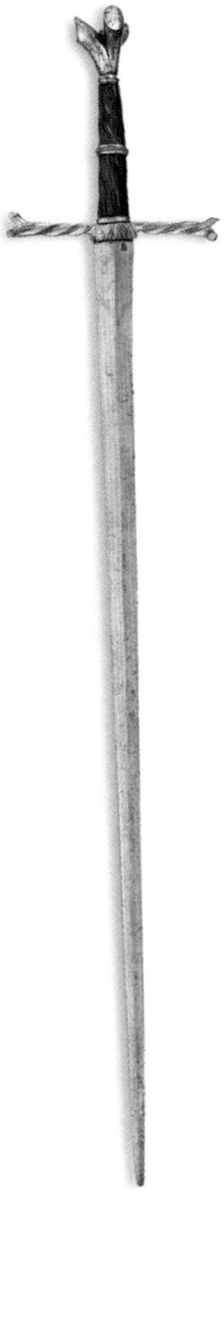

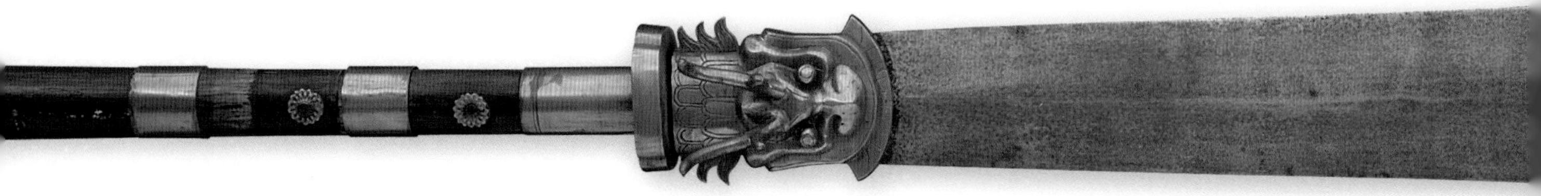
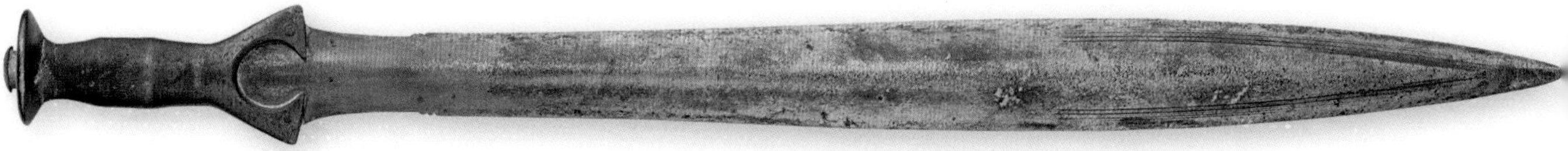

THE WORLD ENCYCLOPEDIA OF

SWORDS AND SABRES

AN AUTHORITATIVE HISTORY AND VISUAL DIRECTORY OF EDGED WEAPONS FROM AROUND THE WORLD, SHOWN IN MORE THAN 800 OUTSTANDING PICTURES

HARVEY J. S. WITHERS

LORENZ BOOKS

This edition is published by Lorenz Books
an imprint of Anness Publishing Ltd
info@anness.com
www.lorenzbooks.com
www.annesspublishing.com

Anness Publishing has a new picture agency outlet for images for publishing, promotions or advertising. Please visit our website www.practicalpictures.com for more information.

Publisher: Joanna Lorenz
Editorial Director: Helen Sudell
Project Editor: Sarah Doughty
Photography: Gary Ombler (Armouries) and David Cummings (Berman)
Designer: Alistair Plumb
Art Director: Lisa McCormick
Production Director: Ben Worley

With special thanks to the Royal Armouries, in Leeds, England, and the Berman Museum of World History, in Anniston, Alabama, USA. Also grateful thanks for the assistance of Hermann Historica Auctioneers, Munich.

Designed and produced for Anness Publishing by
THE BRIDGEWATER BOOK COMPANY LIMITED.

A CIP catalogue record for this book is available from the British Library.

Publisher's Note:
Although the information in this book is believed to be accurate at the time of going to press, neither the authors nor the publisher can accept any legal responsibility or liability for any errors or omissions that may have been made.

Contents

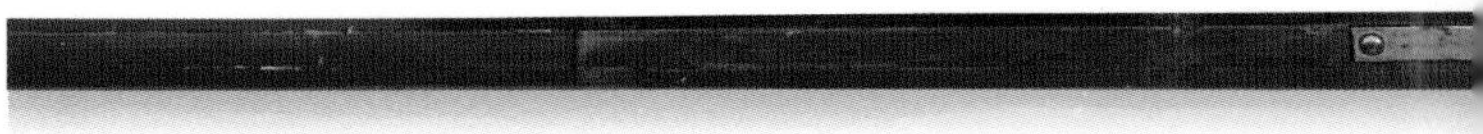

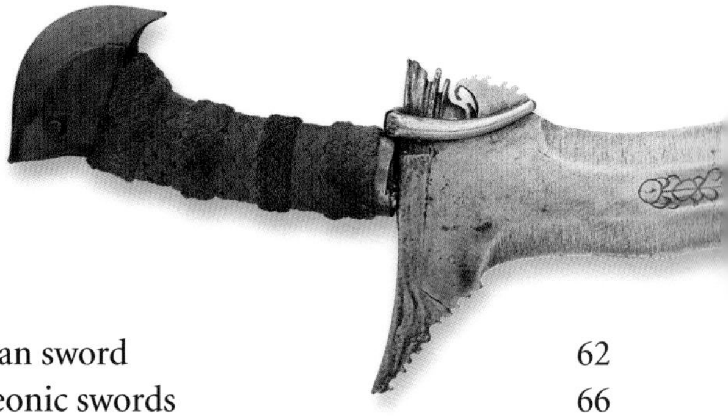

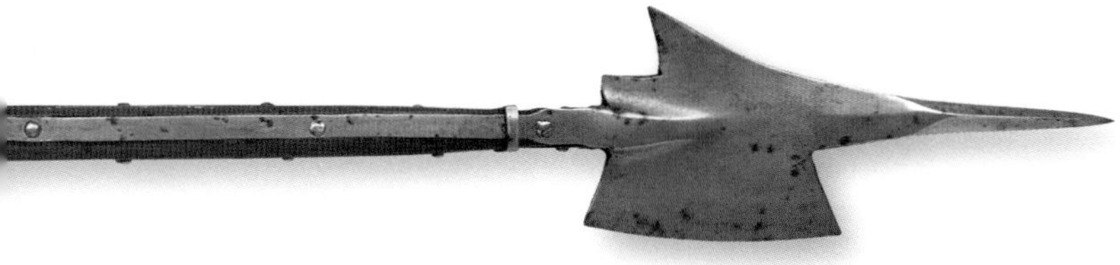

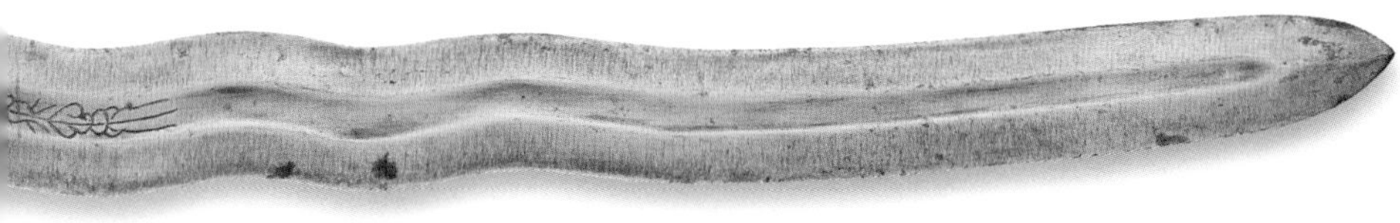

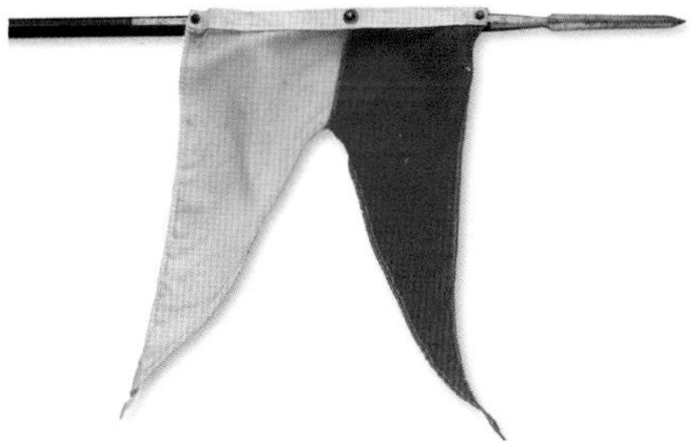

Introduction

From the primitive edged weapons used by early humans through to those of the modern world, the history of the sword is a truly fascinating story. It has been used as a fighting weapon, a symbol of authority, a mark of social rank and as a ceremonial object. For centuries, the sword remained the first weapon of choice for the military soldier and its pre-eminence was secured by a combination of continuous technological improvements and adaptation to ever-changing battlefield conditions.

Early swords and sabres

The historical background to the development of the sword and other edged weapons starts with an examination of the simple tools of Stone Age people, including hand-held flint points and the first axes, which date from 1.4 million years BC. We then move ahead in time to focus on such ancient civilizations as Sumeria and Mesopotamia, where metalworkers began to combine bronze and copper alloys to produce reliable spears, axeheads and swords.

In ancient Egypt, the countless invasions and subsequent assimilations led to the introduction of bronze- and iron-bladed weapons. Although noted for their reliance on the spear and shield, the Greek infantryman or "hoplite" also carried a straight, double-edged, leaf-shaped short sword known as the "xiphos" and it became the model for the more recognizable Roman "gladius". At this time, Celtic swordsmiths were also producing swords of unique beauty and robustness.

11th- to 17th-century European swords

In Europe, the wide-bladed and double-edged Saxon and Viking broadsword would become the inspiration for the early medieval "knightly" sword of the 11th to the 14th century. In both Europe and Asia, polearms (pole-mounted weapons) were used on the battlefield, and in the jousts of the medieval and Renaissance periods, public displays of horsemanship and fighting skills were performed using the lance and the sword.

Sword design changed during the Renaissance and, from around 1400, the emphasis shifted from a sword that had cutting and slashing capabilities to one that could pierce plate armour. Around 1500, the rapier appeared and soon became the sword of choice for a gentleman and the ultimate weapon for trials of honour, such as the duel. German and Swiss mercenaries ("Landsknechte") roamed across Europe, carrying their own huge, two-handed swords and waded into massed rows of enemy infantry, cutting and hacking a passage through for the cavalry.

During the 16th and 17th centuries, more accurate firearms and artillery were developed, and swords were relegated to a secondary role, although they were still regarded as the preferred weapon during close combat with the enemy.

17th- to 20th-century world swords

The introduction of the smallsword in the late 17th century highlighted the new requirement for both practicality and fashion. On the battlefield, the seasoned soldier knew that a more robust broadsword would always be required, such as the distinctive broadsword of the Scottish Highlander. Wide-bladed and double-edged, this broadsword had an enclosed basket hilt and was devastating when used at close quarters.

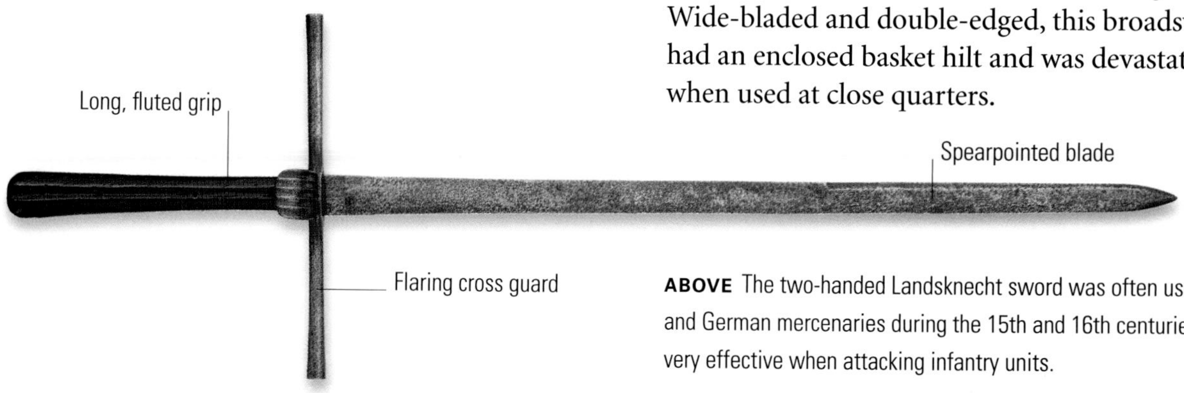

ABOVE The two-handed Landsknecht sword was often used by Swiss and German mercenaries during the 15th and 16th centuries and was very effective when attacking infantry units.

ABOVE The Battle of San Romano in 1432. The medieval battlefield normally comprised a mass of polearms and poleaxes which were used to inflict injuries both from horseback and on foot.

ABOVE A 19th-century Japanese print depicting a Samurai warrior with his sword. Their swords were often given names as a mark of devotion and a belief that their warrior spirit was contained within them.

During the late 18th and early 19th centuries Europe and the outside world were rocked by countless wars and momentous battles. The swords carried by the major nations at war, particularly the French and British, are studied, as are the swords that were carried during one of the bloodiest conflicts outside Europe, the American Civil War.

However, by 1914, the sword had become obsolete in battle and, after the First World War, it was relegated to a purely ceremonial role. Indeed, during the rise of Nazi Germany, we see the sword worn simply as a dress accessory.

Asian and African swords

In Japan, the rise of the Samurai warrior class during the 12th century saw the development of the Samurai sword. These swords had a complex and ritualized process of manufacturing. China also has a long history of sword making that stretches back over 3,000 years and includes such indigenous swords as the famous straight-bladed "jian" and the curved-bladed "dao". In addition, a wide variety of polearms was carried by the Chinese foot-soldier.

The Indian sword was almost totally unaffected by the influences of the West. Even when the British Empire had established virtually complete control over this vast country, Indian swordsmiths continued to produce unique indigenous swords of superb artistry and quality, including the "talwar" and the "khanda". In Africa, there was a dramatic division in sword styles between the Muslim-influenced north of the continent, and the central and southern areas.

The sword directory

There is a comprehensive list of swords, spears, axes, lances and polearms in the directory of swords and sabres. The development of the sword from ancient to modern times includes an enormous variety of styles found within specific time periods and geographical regions. Each weapon is described in detail and listed according to country of origin, chronology and type. Sword dimensions are included to give an accurate idea of scale. Each entry also has a short description detailing both the function and historical context of the weapon. The directory follows the progression of the sword from the Stone Age to the modern-day.

ABOVE This British Army officer's sword, *c.*1870, was not used in fighting but carried as a dress sword and only worn on dress occasions. It was a regimental sword of the Border Regiment, based in the north of England.

This section traces the fascinating history of swords, sabres, spears and lances through to the 20th century.

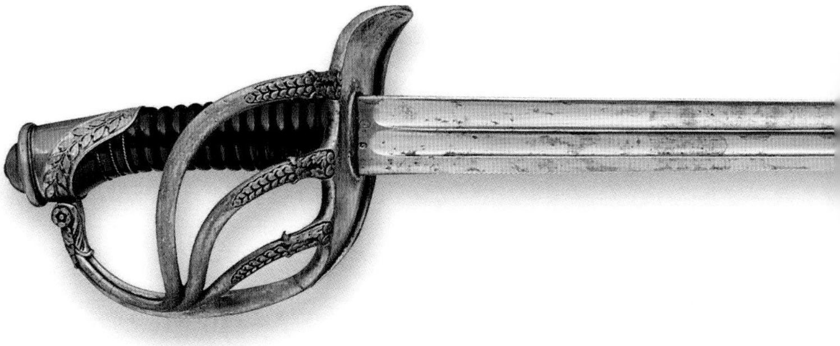

A history of swords and sabres

Since the first flint spearheads emerged at the dawn of humanity around 600,000 years ago, edged weapons have played an incredible role in the shaping of human history. Used by people as diverse as the ancient Egyptians, medieval knights and American civil war soldiers, these weapons have become some of history's most powerful status symbols.

TOP French dragoon officer's sword, Model 1854.

TOP RIGHT German Luftwaffe sword, *c.*1941.

MIDDLE Spanish swept-hilt rapier *c.*1650.

BOTTOM RIGHT French cavalry officer's sword *c.*1780.

The origins of edged weapons

Around 2.5 million years ago, the first recognized edged tools were developed when so-called "Stone Age" peoples began to fashion simple hunting tools from flint and obsidian. The impact of prolonged droughts and the constant territorial battle for a reliable source of food inevitably led to conflict between neighbouring tribes. The weapons of hunting, including the axe and spear, were soon readily transformed into weapons of combat.

LEFT The Neolithic period is known as the New Stone Age. This ancient cave painting depicts a hunting scene in Libya.

Early use of tools

The first widespread use of tools occurred during the Palaeolithic Age (the Old Stone Age), between *c.*2.5 million and 8500BC. The hand axe was the most important tool of this period and would have been designed to provide both a cutting edge and a sharp point. It is impossible to assign to these axes a purely combative role as their primary function would have been either to attack animals or to remove their flesh and hide, but the axes would no doubt have been effective as both slashing and thrusting weapons. Flint and stone were shaped and tied to a wooden handle, and then bound with animal sinew and tendons. Later, in the Neolithic period (the New Stone Age), 13,000–8500BC, an opening was developed in the axehead to accept a handle.

The Stone Age spear was one of the earliest weapons used for hunting animals. Like the hand axe, the spearhead would have been secured by tying it with sinew or leather strips to a longer handle.

Hand-held flint and stone tools were gradually replaced by finely sharpened flint blades. The process of manufacturing such blades involved a technique known as pressure flaking, which involved skilfully knapping the flint with a pointed piece of hard wood or antler horn. Finely crafted examples of these laurel-leaf points were unearthed in the 1860s at the prehistoric site of La Solutré, near Mâcon in Burgundy. Sources of good flint were highly prized; it is thought that some communities would travel up to 160km (100 miles) in order to obtain suitable working materials for tools and weapons. Such advanced tools were first used by Neanderthal man, and then *Homo sapiens,* around 35,000BC. *Homo sapiens* and later sub-groups (such as

The Clovis Spear point

Clovis flint points are the oldest known flint projectile points found in North America. They date to around 13,500 years ago and were used by the ancient peoples of the Americas, the Paleo-Indians. The first Clovis flint point was excavated in Clovis, New Mexico, in 1931. Many points were excavated alongside the remains of hunted Ice Age animals, particularly mammoths. The points are thin, fluted in shape and created from pressure flaking. Due to their small size, they were easily carried and became one of the first highly mobile edged tools, or possibly weapons, in human history. Inhabitants of the Americas in the Archaic period (8000–1000BC) are believed to be direct descendants of Paleo-Indians.

ABOVE This is an Archaic period Clovis spear point from the Americas. The Archaic period preceded the adoption of farming.

Cro-Magnon man) began to create semi-permanent agricultural settlements in the Old World between 35,000BC and 10,000BC.

From hunting to farming (7000–6000BC)

Following the end of the Ice Age (10,000BC), humans began to make the transition from semi-nomadic hunters to creators of established farming communities. The practice of agriculture began in the then fertile plains of Mesopotamia (comprising present-day Iraq, Turkey, Syria and Jordan). The natural requirement for defence of these settled areas also coincided with the development of more robust, edged weapons. One of the earliest excavated farming settlements can be found in the village of Çatal Hüyük (*c.*6700–5650BC) in central Anatolia (present-day Turkey). Numerous pressure-flaked projectile points and simple flint daggers were found during excavations, and indicate that the use of tools, whether for domestic or defensive purposes, had become an important part of daily life.

The Americas (8000BC–AD1000)

Paleo-Indians are believed to be the first people to have inhabited a large number of areas in the Americas about 11,000 years ago. It is thought that they were nomadic hunter-gatherers. Paleo-Indians are understood to have hunted with both fluted, stone-pointed wooden spears and the atlatl (a leveraged weapon that fired short spears). In addition, they probably foraged for edible plants. The Archaic period (8000–1000BC) is characterized by subsistence economies supported through the exploitation of nuts, seeds and shellfish. Between 1000BC and AD1000 Woodland Indians hunted small game and foraged in the forests.

The atlatl – Stone Age machine gun

Archaeologists believe that during the Palaeolithic Age, points or darts were attached to short wooden shafts and then mounted into sockets on heavier spear shafts. This created a form of reloadable, hand-held spear, or *atlatl* (taken from the Aztec language, Nahuatl).

The back end of the spear was fitted into the atlatl. The thrower would hold the atlatl and its flint dart in place, with the elbow bent and the hand resting beside the ear. A forward motion with the shoulder straightened the elbow and the wrist flicked the atlatl forward, creating the necessary momentum to propel the dart at great speed – an action which has been compared to that of a fly fisherman casting his line. Atlatl weights, commonly called "banner stones", are wide and flat shaped, with a large hole drilled into the centre. This may have been a clever improvement to the design as it made the atlatl quieter when swung, so it was less likely to alert prey or other hunters. However, another theory suggests that the banner stone was carried primarily by hunters as a spindle weight to produce string from natural fibres gathered while hunting.

Atlatls are thought to have originated in North Africa over 25,000 years ago. These weapons have been recreated in modern times and shown to have the potential to kill animals at 40m (131ft). Despite their obvious capability to kill humans, they are more likely to have been used for hunting and bringing down big game. Great skill would have been required to wield such a weapon although its accuracy tends to decrease when used over larger distances.

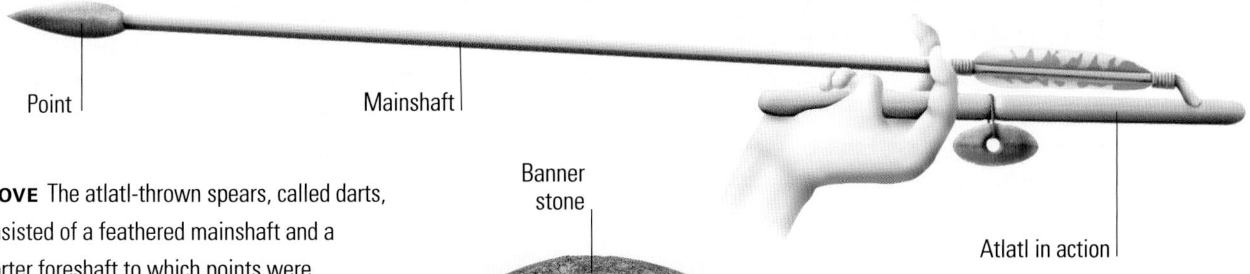

ABOVE The atlatl-thrown spears, called darts, consisted of a feathered mainshaft and a shorter foreshaft to which points were fastened. The spears ranged between 1.2 and 1.6m (4 and 5ft) in length. A refinement was to add a banner stone to increase resistance.

Bronze Age weapons

New technologies to refine, smelt and cast metal ores were first used during the Bronze Age (*c.*3500–700BC). Early civilizations in the Middle East began to combine bronze or copper alloys to produce spears, daggers, swords and axes. Later, swordsmiths started producing finely detailed swords with stronger iron blades. These techniques spread to China, India, South-east Asia and Europe, where they would have a profound influence on future warfare.

ABOVE This short sword was made between 3200 and 1150BC. The decorated hilt and round pommel were later replacements.

Early metal weapons

With the introduction of copper alloys (90 per cent copper and 10 per cent tin), the bronzesmith was able to produce a much harder metal. Its hardness and consequent durability were wholly dependent on the temperature that could be achieved during smelting. The higher the temperature, the harder the metal would become. Iron ore was also discovered and soon became the material of choice for the production of bladed weapons. Iron ore was abundant and, like copper alloys, it could be heated to high temperatures by using charcoal. Immersion of the blade in water and continuous hammering to form a well-tempered blade developed a consistent surface that was less prone to fracture and breakage than bronze or copper. Most blades would have been cast in stone, metal or clay moulds.

The sword in Europe from *c.*2000BC

Although it is difficult to date precisely when the sword was first introduced into Europe, there is general agreement that long-bladed swords were being manufactured around 2000BC. Their appearance in Europe was probably independent of earlier developments in metalworking seen in the Near East and the Aegean. Distinctive flint swords have been found from this date in Denmark and northern Europe, including riveted bronze swords with triangular blades from the early Bronze Age.

In the later Bronze Age, swords were cast in one piece, including the grip and pommel (the knob at the top of the handle or hilt). Many differing pommel shapes also emerged. One of the most common swords is the antenna (or voluted) sword. This had a two-pronged or scrolled, inwardly curving pommel, said to represent the outstretched hands of a human figure. Sword shapes also varied, from broad-leaf shapes to straight forms that featured grooves, sometimes erroneously described as "blood channels", but more likely to have been designed to provide a lighter and more easily wielded sword.

The carp's tongue sword

Common in western and eastern Europe around 1000BC were a group of bronze swords known as "carp's tongue" swords. A significant number of this distinct sword type were discovered at excavations in the Thames Valley and Kent during the mid-20th century. The most notable find was at the Isleham Hoard, in Cambridgeshire, England. It comprised more than 6,500 objects made of bronze, including many swords of carp's tongue design. They had wide, tapering blades which were useful for slashing, with a thinner, elongated end suitable for stabbing. This style of sword is thought to have originated in north-western France.

The socketed axe

Another important military innovation of the Bronze Age Mesopotamian armies in the Middle East, and one that would have an enormous impact on future

ABOVE A complete Bronze Age sword (top) with hilt and leaf-shaped blade (*c.*1100BC) and a large bronze spearhead (bottom) from 700BC.

BELOW These Bronze Age socketed axes were used as both domestic tools and close-quarter combat weapons.

battlefield warfare, was the introduction of the socketed axe. Previously, ancient axe makers had struggled to keep the axehead firmly attached to the haft (the handle), especially when handling the axe with considerable force. The Sumerians devised a cast bronze socket that slipped over the haft and was secured with rivets. Its development was probably a consequence of the introduction of primitive forms of body armour and the need to penetrate this armour with sufficient force. Later axes would have narrower points that could be used to penetrate bronze plate armour. The axe would remain an integral battle weapon for the next 2,000 years.

The sickle sword of Mesopotamia

One of the earliest societies in which organized warfare was waged was the Sumerian culture of southern Mesopotamia (*c.*3000BC). Even at this early stage of human civilization, professional standing armies were being used to defend communities. Although the most common weapons used by the Sumerians, and later the Assyrians (*c.*1100–600BC), included the spear and bow, warriors also carried a sharply curved sickle sword.

Introduced around 2500BC, this all-metal sword had a single-handed grip and a blade of around three grip lengths. A stunning example in the British Museum, London, England, has the following inscription on the blade: *Palace of Adad-nirari, king of the universe, son of Arik-den-ili, king of Assyria, son of Enlil-nirari, king of Assyria.* It is believed that this sword was owned by the Assyrian king Adad-nirari I, who conquered northern Mesopotamia (*c.*1307–1275BC). Mesopotamian art frequently depicts the sickle sword as a symbol of authority, and it is often seen placed in the hands of gods and kings.

BELOW An illustration of a sickle sword, 1307–1275BC, from the Middle Assyrian period (the reign of Adad-nirari I).

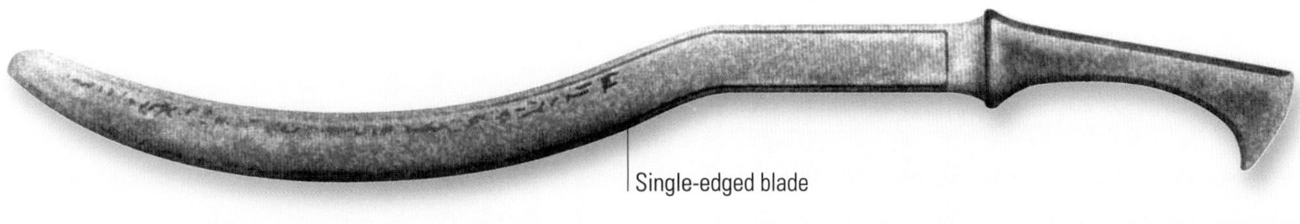

Ancient Egyptian weapons

The Egyptian armies of the Old Kingdom (*c.*2649–2134BC) and Middle Kingdom (*c.*2040–1640BC) fought primarily on foot and in massed ranks. Their soldiers were lightly equipped with shield, bow, spear and axe. The constant wars and invasions of the later dynasties brought with them the assimilation and transference of diverse military technologies. This greatly expanded their range of weapons, which diversified to include plate armour, chariots and, more importantly, the sword.

Introduction of the sword

Following the collapse of central government in Egypt due to internal rebellion, the Hyksos peoples of Palestine took advantage of this instability and invaded Egypt around 1640BC. They ruled Egypt for over 200 years and brought with them striking advances in weapon making, particularly the use of metal in the manufacture of swords and edged weapons.

The adoption of the sword in ancient Egypt was a direct consequence of the introduction of metal. Prior to this, axes and spears were fashioned from flint, and swords were simply not available. Copper had already been utilized for some time, but bronze was the first material consistently used for sword blades, as it was much harder and easier to work. Sickle-shaped swords (originally inherited from the Sumerians) were gradually replaced by swords with slightly curving blades. The "Sea Peoples", invaders from the Aegean and Asia Minor who first attacked Egypt during the reign of Merenptah (1213–1202BC), also introduced straight, two-edged blades with sharp, stabbing points. Contemporary depictions of battles show massed infantry using both jabbing and slashing swords.

The influence of iron

Throughout the Mediterranean during the New Kingdom period of Rameses III (*c.*1186–1155BC), the smelting of iron ore had a direct impact on Egypt, enabling swords to be produced with much longer and sturdier blades. Examples of swords with blade lengths of up to 75cm (30in) have been unearthed from royal tombs.

RIGHT This ancient Egyptian warrior is depicted carrying a long, double-edged and broad-bladed sword. It is probably a one-piece construction.

The spear

Primarily a weapon used for hunting, the Egyptian spear never surpassed the bow and arrow, which remained the standard weapon of the Egyptian Army. During the Old Kingdom (*c.*2649–2134BC) and Middle Kingdom (*c.*2040–1640BC), simple pointed spearheads were constructed from either flint or copper and attached to long wooden shafts by means of a tang (the hidden portion or "tongue" of a blade running through the handle). In the later New Kingdom (*c.*1550–1070BC), stronger bronze blades were secured by a more reliable socket.

Spears were made for either throwing or thrusting, and were especially useful when chasing fleeing enemies and stabbing opponents in the back. They were regarded primarily as auxiliary weapons and called upon by charioteers when they had spent all their arrows and needed some form of close protection. The following description of Amenhotep II's victory at the Battle of Shemesh-Edom *c.*1448BC (in Upper Galilee, now modern-day

LEFT Carved by an unknown Egyptian artist during the 18th Dynasty, *c.*1567–1320BC, this relief depicts two soldiers, one carrying a spear.

The khepesh – sword of the Pharaoh

Originally a throwing weapon of sickle-sword shape, the khepesh could also be used as a conventional slashing or cutting sword. It appears to have been a favoured weapon of the Pharaoh, as he is often depicted wielding it against enemies or during a hunt. The discovery of the tomb of Tutankhamun (r.*c.*1361–1352BC) by Howard Carter in 1922 revealed remarkable insights into the lives of ancient Egyptians. One of the numerous objects found in the tomb included a ceremonial shield, which depicted the young Pharaoh "smiting a lion" with a khepesh.

ABOVE The Tomb of Tutankhamun. The king is depicted in a number of battle scenes, although it is not known whether he actually took part in any campaigns.

ABOVE An Egyptian bronze khepesh sword with a handle inlaid with ivory. The sword comes from El-Rabata and dates to the New Kingdom, *c.*1250BC.

Israel) is recorded at the Temple of Karnak (built over a period of some 1,600 years from around 1500BC), near Luxor in Egypt:

> *Behold His Majesty was armed with his weapons and His Majesty fought like Set in his hour. They gave way when His Majesty looked at one of them, and they fled. His Majesty took all their goods himself, with his spear…*
>
> *Karnak Stele of Amenhotep II*
> from W.M. Flanders Petrie, *A History of Egypt, Part Two.*

The battle-axe

There were two distinct types of battle-axe used by the Egyptian soldier: the cutting axe and the piercing axe. The cutting axe, used during the early kingdoms, had a head attached to a long handle and would have been used at arm's length. The blade head was attached to the handle through a groove and then tightly bound with leather or sinew. This axe was especially effective against opponents who wore little body armour, particularly Egypt's African enemies, like the Nubians. It was usually deployed after the enemy had been routed (often by the archers), rather than as a weapon against massed ranks.

The cutting axe was later superseded by the piercing axe that was designed to penetrate armour. Unlike contemporary Asiatic societies (especially the Sumerians and the Assyrians), who used a blade cast with a hole through which the handle was inserted and firmly attached by rivets, the Egyptians continued to use the antiquated method of a mortise-and-tenon joint (a tenon is a tongue that slots into a hole called the mortise) to fix the blade to the handle. This made the battle-axe inherently weaker. During the invasion by the Hyksos around 1640BC, this obsolete weaponry, coupled with the invaders' use of horse-drawn chariots, long swords and stronger bows, proved fatal for the lightly armed Egyptians.

ABOVE A painted relief of light infantry with standards, battle-axes and palm fronds, from the temple of Hatshepsut in Thebes, Egypt, *c.*1480BC.

Ancient Greek weapons

The ancient Greeks (*c.*750–146BC) regarded the sword as strictly an auxiliary weapon, one that would never supplant their battle-proven reliance on the spear. The spear enabled the heavily armoured hoplites, or infantrymen, to stand together and protect each other within the close formation of their phalanx wall of shields and spears. This allowed them to repeatedly fight and win battles against far superior opposition.

The hoplites

Infantry foot-soldiers, the ancient Greek hoplites (from the Greek word *hoplon*, or armour) formed the military backbone of the Greek city states. Hoplites were recruited mainly from the wealthier and fitter middle classes, and bore the financial responsibility to arm themselves. Bronze armour, sword, spear and shield all had to be provided from solely private means. Hoplites were not full-time professional soldiers whose only life was war. They had volunteered to serve their state only in times of war (usually in the summer), and, if they survived, would return afterwards to their civilian roles. The hoplite was a true manifestation of the classical Greek ideal of shared civic responsibility.

ABOVE Mosaic showing Alexander the Great, leader of the Macedonians, hunting a lion with a doru (spear) in the 3rd century BC.

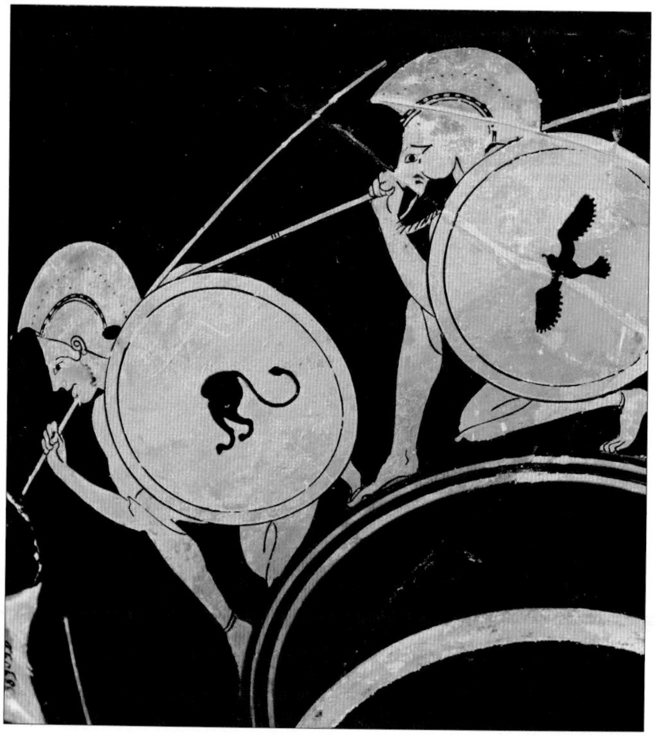

ABOVE Spartan hoplites, *c.*500BC, wearing Corinthian helmets. In addition to the shield and spear, hoplites would have also carried a sword.

The spear

A Greek infantryman's main battle weapon was the spear, or doru. Measuring around 2.7m (8.8ft) in length, it would have been held in one hand, while the shield (aspis) was grasped in the other. The spearhead was leaf-shaped, socketed and made of iron. At the butt of the shaft was a sharp bronze spike, or sauroter ("lizard killer"), which could be thrust into the ground for added stability. In extremis, when the spearhead was broken, the sharp spike could be flipped around and used as a weapon of last resort.

The Macedonians, under the leadership of Alexander the Great (356–323BC), also developed their own spear or pike, the sarissa. Little is known about it, but it is thought to have been up to twice the length (around 4–5m/13–16.4ft) of the doru and had to be wielded underarm with two hands. This meant that the usual protection of the shield-and-spear phalanx could not be utilized, and so a small shield, or pelte, was strapped to the left forearm. The sarissa's great length meant that it could keep the opposing troops at a distance, enabling the Macedonian cavalry to wheel around the flanks of an enemy and strike with devastating effect.

The phalanx – ancient armoured fist

Derived from the Greek word *phalangos* (meaning "finger"), the hoplite phalanx was made up of a tight formation of spearmen, armed with large, concave shields that rested on the soldier's left shoulder and protected the man next to him, thus forming an all-enveloping, locked curtain of defence. The phalanx was typically about eight men deep, with the front ranks projecting their spears forwards. The key to the success of the phalanx was the ability of the soldiers to keep together and not break the formation. This was not always easy, especially for the first few ranks, who were the main combatants, as the rear ranks' main purpose was to continually push their phalanx forward and maintain its shape.

There has been much debate as to how the spear was used while in the phalanx: was it held aloft or under the arm? Some authorities believe that it had to be held aloft, as it would have been impractical for a hoplite to hold his spear underarm, in case the sharp butt spike injured the man behind him. The use of the sword by the hoplites in the phalanx would have been regarded as a highly dangerous manoeuvre, because it necessitated breaking up the shape and, consequently, the defensive cohesion of the phalanx.

LEFT A stone depiction of Greek hoplites standing in phalanx formation, from *c.*400BC.

The sword

There is great irony in noting that the most successful sword design of the Ancient World was developed by the Greeks, who were ostensibly spearmen. The sword was never regarded as a main battle weapon and played a purely secondary role. Once the spears had been thrown or lost in battle, swords were then engaged to finish the conflict in a decisive manner.

The main battle sword of the ancient Greek military was the xiphos. Introduced around 800–400BC, it comprised a straight, double-edged, leaf-shaped blade of around 65cm (25.6in), and was particularly effective at slashing and stabbing. The Spartans carried a slightly shorter sword of the same design as the xiphos. This design probably influenced the later Roman gladius, or short sword.

Mounted Greek cavalry used a curved sword, or makhaira (meaning "to fight"). It had a large, slightly curved falchion-type blade and was designed to deliver a heavy slashing blow at speed.

The use of a curved blade for mounted horsemen would remain a constant feature of cavalry swords for the next 2,500 years.

ABOVE A frieze from the Mausoleum of Halicarnassus, *c.*350BC, depicting a mythical battle between the Greeks and the Amazons.

Ancient Celtic weapons

The warrior Celts (*c.*600BC–AD50) were famed for their ferociousness and tenacity in battle, and even received grudging respect from their Roman adversaries. The early Celts fought mainly on foot (later in chariots and on horseback), and relied heavily on the awesome psychological and physical impact of a massed charge of their warriors. Armed with either sword or spear and protected with little more than a shield or helmet, they defeated the mighty Roman legions and, in 390BC, even sacked Rome itself.

Symbolism of the Celtic sword

The Celtic sword symbolized to its owner power, strength, honour and ultimate glory in battle. The fine quality and extraordinary skills required to produce these swords meant that they were extremely expensive and normally reserved for nobles and chieftains. The sword was often buried with its owner amongst his many other possessions, or symbolically thrown into water as a gift to the gods or spirits.

The falcata

With a large inwardly curving, single-edged blade rather like a kukri (heavy, curved Nepalese knife), the falcata was an extremely devastating weapon. Hilts were iron, hook-shaped and sometimes decorated with stylized horse or bird-head pommels. The origin of the falcata was pre-Roman and it is likely to have been a development of the ancient Greek sickle-shaped sword, or kopis. The sword could deliver a very powerful blow, something akin to an axe strike but with the slashing capabilities of a conventional sword. Contemporary Roman writers often describe how the falcata had the capacity to split both shield and helmet. The Celts of Hispania (Spain) were said to be the most feared exponents of this sword and it was a common weapon encountered by Roman forces during the early years of the Roman Republic (509–124BC).

The manufacture of the falcata

During this possibly unique process of manufacture, various forged steel plates were buried in the ground, usually for more than three years, and allowed to corrode. They would then be dug up and any weak or spurious metal would be separated and discarded. Any remaining good steel was reforged again through the traditional Celtic method of pattern welding – the practice of forming a blade from several metal pieces of differing composition. The blades were then forge-welded together and manipulated to form a pattern, making it considerably harder. In response to these much tougher blades, the Roman legions redesigned their shields and armour to give them more protection. The introduction of the Roman gladius, or short sword, was said to be a direct reaction to the Roman soldiers' battlefield experience of the falcata.

Longer Celtic swords

The growing use of cavalry and, later, the war chariot meant that Celtic warriors needed a longer sword to effectively reach down and strike at an opponent.

LEFT Relief plaque, made from copper with silver and gold plating, of a warrior wielding a long-bladed Celtic sword from the 1st century AD.

These long swords, with an average blade length of around 70cm (27.5in), had wood, bone or horn hilts, with blades manufactured in iron or steel. Scabbards were normally constructed from plates of iron and suspended from a belt of iron links.

The Celts were one of the first European peoples to discover how to smelt iron, and by the time they made contact with the Romans they had developed consistent methods of producing better balanced swords that were more resilient and longer. It is therefore curious that the Roman writer Polybius (*c.*203–120BC) reported that, at the Battle of Telamon (225BC), the Gauls had carried inferior iron swords which bent at the first stroke and had to be straightened with the foot against the ground. This is also mentioned by Plutarch (*c.* AD46–127), but it seems more likely that this was Roman propaganda, as subsequent archaeological testing of excavated Celtic sword blades indicates that the quality of the iron and steel was quite exceptional.

The spear

A standard battlefield weapon for the Celtic warrior, the Celtic spear or javelin normally comprised an ash wood pole around 2m (6.5ft) in length, fitted with a large iron, leaf-shaped and socketed spearhead.

The swords of the La Tène culture

Archaeological finds from the La Tène settlement on the north edge of Lake Neuchâtel in Switzerland, dating to around 500–1BC, highlight the Celtic genius for creating swords with complex abstract and organic decoration on both the hilt and the scabbard. Blades were double-edged and straight, and made from pattern-welded iron or steel. They are found in both long and short versions. Many finely worked hilts also feature human heads and other anthropomorphic and zoomorphic motifs.

RIGHT A 1st or 2nd century BC sword and scabbard from La Tène in Switzerland.

ABOVE Three Celtic spearheads from the La Tène period, each with a leaf-shaped, finely ridged, slightly bent blade. Two of the examples have holes in the socket for attaching the head to the shaft.

Following military experience gained after initial contact with the Roman armies from the 1st century AD, the Celts changed the design of their spearheads so that they possessed a narrower profile. This was a reaction to the Roman use of protective body armour and the need to find a spear that could effectively puncture their plate. Spears and javelins were also carried in bunches by young warriors, or "gaesatae". These were paid mercenaries who had gained a fearsome reputation for their bravery. Once they had thrown all the spears at the enemy, they would retrieve them from the ground or their opponents' bodies.

Ancient Roman weapons

The army of ancient Rome (800BC–AD476) was a formidable fighting force – well disciplined, organized and supplied with an array of effective and battle-proven weapons. The sword and spear were the infantryman's main weapons, and the spectacular military successes of the Roman legions throughout Europe and the Near East lay in the disciplined battlefield application and relentless training in the use of these weapons.

The gladius

A short stabbing weapon with a blade length of around 50–60cm (19.6–23.6in), the gladius was the primary fighting sword of the Roman soldier. Its origins are somewhat uncertain, simply because very few examples have been unearthed by archaeologists and the only identifiable gladii have come not from Italy but from Germany. This sword was described by the ancient Romans as the "gladius hispaniensis", in recognition of a similar type of Celtic design encountered by the Romans during their conquest of Hispania (modern-day Spain) during the Second Punic War (218–201BC). Before this, Roman soldiers would have used swords of Greek origin.

The hilt, or capulus, of the gladius featured a rounded grip, moulded with four finger ridges to allow a comfortable and firm hold upon the sword. Pommels were bulbous and normally of plain form. The scabbard was made of wood, covered with leather and strengthened by a rigid frame of brass or iron.

Wearing the gladius

Although in later centuries most swords would be worn traditionally on the left side, the gladius was worn on the right side. This allowed the wearer to draw with the right hand and at the same time carry a heavy shield in the left hand. This can be confirmed from the depictions of Roman soldiers on tombstones, wall paintings and friezes. The tombstone of Annaius Daverzius, an auxiliary infantryman who served with the Cohors III Delmatarum, a Roman garrison stationed in Britain during the 1st century AD, shows his sword attached on the right side of his belt by four suspension rings. As an acknowledgement of his status, a centurion was allowed to wear his sword on the left.

RIGHT Legionaries, carrying gladius swords, are depicted during battle in a relief carving from the base of a column found at Magonza, Italy.

The gladius in battle

If used with enough force and directed at the most vulnerable parts of the body, particularly the stomach, the stab of a gladius blade into the flesh of an opponent was nearly always fatal.

Roman soldiers fought as a single fighting unit within an organized and massed formation. This fighting block comprised hundreds of men standing

ABOVE A battle between Roman and Germanic armies, depicted as a relief on a marble sarcophagus, *c.* AD180–190.

shoulder to shoulder. They had to keep this formation solid and it was crucial, therefore, that all soldiers fought with the gladius placed in their right hand. Any left-handed recruit would have this hand strapped behind his back during training, and it would be kept tied until he learned to fight with the right hand as well as he would have done with the left. Wearing the gladius on the right also meant that the drawing of the sword would not interfere with soldiers on either side, and would also not restrict the use of the Roman scutum (the shield).

The Roman line would wait for the enemy to come right up to it and then await the order to advance. Upon receiving this order, all soldiers would take one step forward and thrust their shields, or scuta, into the bodies and faces of the enemy, causing them to lose their balance and so render them temporarily vulnerable. The shield was then quickly withdrawn and the gladius thrust into the body of the opponent. The Roman soldier was taught to deploy the gladius horizontally, so piercing the enemy's ribs and penetrating to his vital organs.

BELOW A gladius and scabbard, which belonged to an officer of Tiberius (42BC–AD37), the second Emperor of Rome.

ABOVE A stone depiction of the Emperor Hostilianus in a Roman battle scene, 251AD. He is carrying a gladius, of which the blade is broken.

The spatha

By the middle of the 1st century AD, the gladius had been replaced by the spatha (*spada* is the modern-day Italian word for sword). It had a much longer blade (60–80 cm/23.6–31.5in) and shorter point. The sword was Celtic in origin and it is probable that Gallic cavalry (from Gaul, in modern-day France), in the employ of Rome, introduced the sword to the Roman Army during the time of Julius Caesar (100–44BC) and Augustus (63BC–AD14). It was a slashing weapon and designed to be used by both the Roman cavalry and infantry.

ABOVE Found in Spain, this is the only known actual example of a spatha with an eagle-headed hilt. It would have been used by a tribune in the early 4th century AD.

The manufacture of swords

By the time of the Roman Republic (*c.*509–44BC), the use of steel in the manufacture of swords was well advanced and Roman swordsmiths smelted iron ore and carbon in a bloomery furnace (the predecessor of the blast furnace). The temperatures in these furnaces could not achieve the high levels required to fully melt the iron ore, so the swordsmith had to work with pieces of slag (residue left after smelting) or bloom (mass consisting mostly of iron), which were then forged into the required blade shape. These pieces or strips of cooling metal were welded together for increased blade strength. During this process the owner's initials or full name were sometimes engraved onto the blade.

The pilum

Around 2m (6.5ft) in length, the main heavy spear or javelin used by the Roman Army was the pilum. It consisted of a socketed iron shank with a triangular head. The pilum weighed in at around 3–4kg (6.6–8.8lb); later versions produced during the Empire (27BC–AD476) were lighter. The pilum would have been thrown by charging legionaries and could easily penetrate shield and armour from a range of around 15m (49.2ft). A lighter, thrusting spear, the hasta, was also used for close-combat situations.

The narrow, spiked shape of the spearhead meant that when it became stuck in the wood of an opponent's shield it was extremely difficult to dislodge, so disrupting the opponent at a critical moment of battle. He might have to relinquish his shield, leaving himself extremely vulnerable to the oncoming Roman infantry. Even if he was able to remove the spear, he couldn't throw it back at the Romans because the soft iron of the spear shank meant that it bent on impact and so became useless as a weapon. In the aftermath of a Roman victory, used pila were gathered from the battlefield and sent back to the Roman Army blacksmiths for straightening. The Roman military strategist Vegetius (*c.* AD450) comments on the effectiveness of the pilum:

> *As to the missile weapons of the infantry, they were javelins headed with a triangular sharp iron, eleven inches or a foot long, and were called piles. When once fixed in the shield it was impossible to draw them out, and when thrown with force and skill, they penetrated the cuirass without difficulty.*

from *De Re Militari* (*c.* AD430)

Later, a further development of the pilum was introduced: the spiculum. Vegetius notes its power:

They had likewise two other javelins, the largest of which was composed of a staff five feet and a half long and a triangular head of iron nine inches long. This was formerly called the pilum, but now it is known by the name of spiculum. The soldiers were particularly exercised in the use of this weapon, because when thrown with force and skill it often penetrated the shields of the foot and the cuirasses of the horse.

from *De Re Militari* (*c.* AD430)

The contos

A long, wooden cavalry lance which was 4–5m (13.1–16.4ft) in length, the contos derived its name from the Greek word *kontos*, or "oar", which probably gives some indication as to the length of the lance. It took two hands to wield, so the horseman had to grip his mount by the knees. To be able to do this effectively would have taken considerable strength and training.

ABOVE Made in the Roman provincial style, this contos lance head dates from the 2nd century AD.

LEFT Roman soldiers carrying light spears (lancea) and shields. Detail of a relief from the Antonine Column, Rome, erected *c.* AD180–196 in recognition of the Roman victory in battle over a Germanic tribe.

BELOW Dating from AD70, this inscribed Roman commemorative stone depicts a horseman (Vonatorix) wielding a spear.

Saxon weapons

Around AD400, the Saxons came to England with a reputation for warlike ferocity and a strong reverence for the sword as a potent symbol of both strength and martial spirit. The mass of Anglo-Saxon warriors normally carried a shield and dagger (seax) and fought with spears and axes. More sophisticated members of the nobility and professional soldiers carried spears (similar to the Roman pilum) and swords.

The Saxon sword

Through excavating numerous graves in England, archaeologists have learnt that the Anglo-Saxons often chose to bury their dead with a full array of weapons and armour. These grave weapons are normally of great beauty and artistry, highlighting the belief that a warrior needed to take with him into the afterlife (or in later Christianized Anglo-Saxon society – heaven), material proof of the great status afforded to its owner while alive.

Ownership of both sword and spear defined the Anglo-Saxon warrior as a free man, compared with slaves (oeows) who were forbidden from carrying any arms. The great cost of acquiring a serviceable sword would also have shown the owner to be a man of means and rank. A typical Anglo-Saxon sword had a long, straight, double-edged blade with an average length of around 90cm (35.4in).

ABOVE A winged Saxon spearhead (top) with double wings to prevent an opponent's blade travelling down the spear. A slim spearhead (bottom) to allow penetration through armour.

The Saxon spear

In Anglo-Saxon burial grounds, the spear is by far the most common type of weapon unearthed and is regarded as the primary armament of the Anglo-Saxon warrior. All ranks of society carried the spear, from king and eorl (earl), to the lowly ceorl (free man of the lowest rank) or conscripted peasant. Comprising a leaf-shaped iron spearhead and wooden shaft, traditionally made of ash, a typical spear measured around 1.5–2.5m (4.9–8.2ft) in length.

The spear would have been held in one hand while a shield was grasped in the other. It was extremely effective when used in a mass formation, most notably the famous Anglo-Saxon "shieldwall" or shildburh. It was this shildburh that faced William the Conqueror at the Battle of Hastings. It was only compromised when

BELOW In a detail from the Bayeux Tapestry, 1082, the English soldiers, who are all on foot, protect themselves with a shield wall while the Normans mount a cavalry attack.

The Saxon battle-axe

Anglo-Saxon warriors inherited the two-handed "bearded" battle-axe from earlier generations of Danish Viking invaders who had employed it with great effect to board enemy ships. The Anglo-Saxons soon became extremely proficient at using the battle-axe. With its 1.2m (3.9ft) haft and large honed axehead of around 30cm (11.8in), it had the capacity to shatter shields and inflict grievous wounds. Swung from side to side, it could cut down a mounted soldier and his horse in a single blow.

These long axes were wielded by the huscarls (King Harold's personal bodyguards) and described as cleaving "both man and horse in two". One of the drawbacks of using the two-handed axe is that while raised above the head it momentarily left the user dangerously exposed at the front to sword or lance thrusts. Despite this, the sight of a mass of axe-wielding Anglo-Saxon warriors approaching the enemy's ranks normally had the desired psychological effect, with many contemporary accounts noting that the opposition simply fled from the battlefield.

RIGHT A later depiction of the felling of King Harold II (*c.*1022–1066) by a Norman arrow at the Battle of Hastings (1066).

the Normans feigned a cavalry retreat, deliberately allowing themselves to be chased, whereupon they suddenly wheeled back and charged the openly exposed Anglo-Saxons. This was a fatal error by the pursuers and dictated the eventual outcome of the battle.

In contemporary descriptions of the Battle of Maldon in AD991 (situated on the modern-day Essex coast in England), the Anglo-Saxon Eorl Byrhtnoth is depicted as throwing two types of spear or javelin, both long and short. It is interesting that it was only when injured by a Viking spear, and finally exhausting his supplies of spears, that he eventually resorts to using his sword.

Anglo-Saxon women warriors

It was not only men who fought and became respected heroes during the Anglo-Saxon period. Recent archaeological discoveries have raised the possibility that women also took part in warfare.

In the village of Heslerton, in North Yorkshire, England, two female burials were unearthed in 2000. Dated to around AD450–650, both women had been buried with spears and knives. Just outside Lincoln, a town in eastern England, the skeleton of another Anglo-Saxon woman warrior (*c.* AD500) was found with a dagger and shield.

Procopius (*c.* AD500–565), the late Roman Byzantine scholar, notes in his history of the Gothic Wars (AD535–552) that an unnamed Anglo-Saxon princess, from the tribe of Angilori and described as "the Island Girl", led an invasion of Jutland (western Denmark) and captured the German King Radigis of the Varni.

Aethelflaed, eldest daughter of Alfred the Great of England (*c.* AD849–899), was known as the Lady of Mercia and was at the forefront of many battles against the invading Vikings. Aethelflaed was also responsible for the construction of a number of Anglo-Saxon fortifications.

The Sutton Hoo sword

The sword is part of a magnificent hoard of royal Anglo-Saxon treasures found in a huge ship grave, in Suffolk, England, in 1939; its design is based on the earlier Roman spatha, or cavalry sword. Its decoration includes a hilt comprising a beautiful gold and cloisonné garnet pommel and gold cross guard. The iron blade is heavily corroded but the original pattern welding is still identifiable and includes eight bundles of thin iron rods hammered together to form the pattern. This would have given the sword exceptional strength, although it is more likely that it was produced solely as a sumptuous grave gift.

Viking weapons

The Vikings were Scandinavians who colonized parts of Europe from the 9th to the 11th century. Vikings revered the sword above all weapons. The passing of a family sword from father to son was considered a major event. Even better was the knowledge that a sword had been wielded in battle or in a feud by a great warrior or nobleman. This gave the sword added status and was thought to imbue the blade with special powers. The Viking armoury also included the spear and battle-axe, the first-line weapons launched against an enemy.

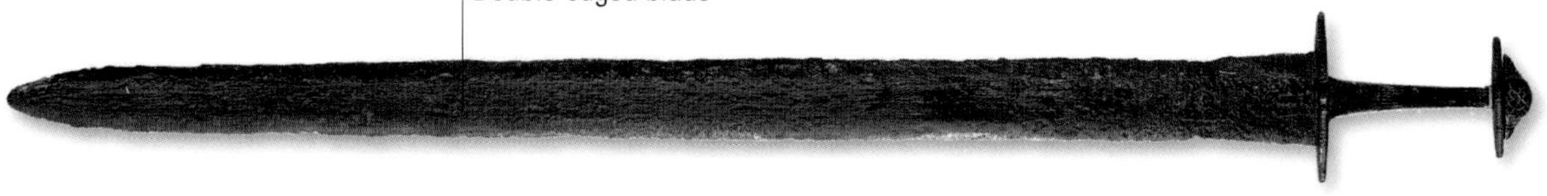

ABOVE A Viking sword from the 10th century with lobed pommel. The wide, double-edged blade would have made it a very powerful weapon.

Viking weapons

The main Viking battlefield weapons employed during first contact with the enemy were the spear and battle-axe. One of the reasons why the sword usually took a secondary role in the initial phase of a battle was that the continual striking of one sword edge against another would have inflicted large nicks to the blade and eventually removed the consistency and effectiveness of its finely sharpened edge.

Because of this, once the spear or axe had done its work, the Viking warrior would then draw his sword and look for exposed and softer areas of the body to attack. Skeletons of Viking battlefield victims unearthed by archaeologists consistently exhibit more spear wounds than sword cuts, highlighting the selective use of Viking swords in battle.

The Viking spear

A Viking warrior's most common battlefield weapon, the spear, comprised a simple iron, broad-leafed or spiked point on a wooden (normally ash) shaft, with a total length of around 1–2m (3.2–6.5ft). Spearheads with wings were called barbed spears. The spear was extremely effective and used for both thrusting and throwing, with larger-headed spears being used for cutting. There is evidence that the spears used to cut through chainmail were used one-handed as well as two-handed. A skilled Viking spearman was reputed to be able to throw two spears at once, using both hands, and also to catch a spear in flight and hurl it back at the opposition. A sword was then used in close-combat fighting.

LEFT A 9th-century Viking-decorated stone carving from Gotland, Sweden, depicts two soldiers fighting with swords.

Pommels and scabbards

The Viking sword pommel (located at the end of the hilt) is one of the most distinctive characteristics of a Viking sword. Most pommels were cast in solid iron (its weight providing a counterbalance to the weight of the blade), but there are also fine examples in bronze and also of iron inlaid with sheets of silver. Pommels ranged from the early pyramidal shapes of *c.* AD800 to the later, more complex pommels that were formed from triangular segments.

The great artistry and imagination of the Viking metalworker is clearly evident in these pommels and cross guards, with complex interlaced and geometric patterns worked in both silver and bronze gilt.

A scabbard (sheath or case) was made of two carved pieces of wood, glued at the sides and sometimes covered in leather or fur. The mouth and chape (the metal plate at the point) of the scabbard were sometimes mounted with decorated silver or bronze gilt. The sword would have been carried using a baldric (waist or shoulder belt).

ABOVE A Viking sword hilt with a cocked hat or lobed pommel. The decoration includes stamped abstract cartouches.

The Viking battle-axe

When wielded with appropriate force, the Danish long-handled or "bearded" battle-axe was a devastating weapon. Its design was based on domestic Viking wood-splitting axes found throughout Scandinavia during the Viking period and evolved for use in battle. The battle-axe had a much larger head of either crescent or convex shape, which favoured downward blows, with a long wooden haft measuring 1–2m (3.2–6.5ft) in length. Sometimes blades were forged with an especially hardened double edge. They could also be forged quite thinly to give the user a lighter, more easily handled weapon.

The Viking sword

About 70–80cm (27.5–31.5in) long, the wide, double-edged blade of a Viking sword had shallow fullers, or so-called "blood grooves". The grooves were not actually designed to allow the blood to run down easily but rather to reduce the weight of the blade and give it added flexibility. The Vikings had a very close relationship with their swords, borne out by the personalized names they gave them, including Gramr ("Fierce"), Fotbitr ("Leg-biter") and Meofainn ("Decorated down the middle"). Swords were not common or inexpensive weapons and it is likely that they were mainly carried by persons of rank and wealth.

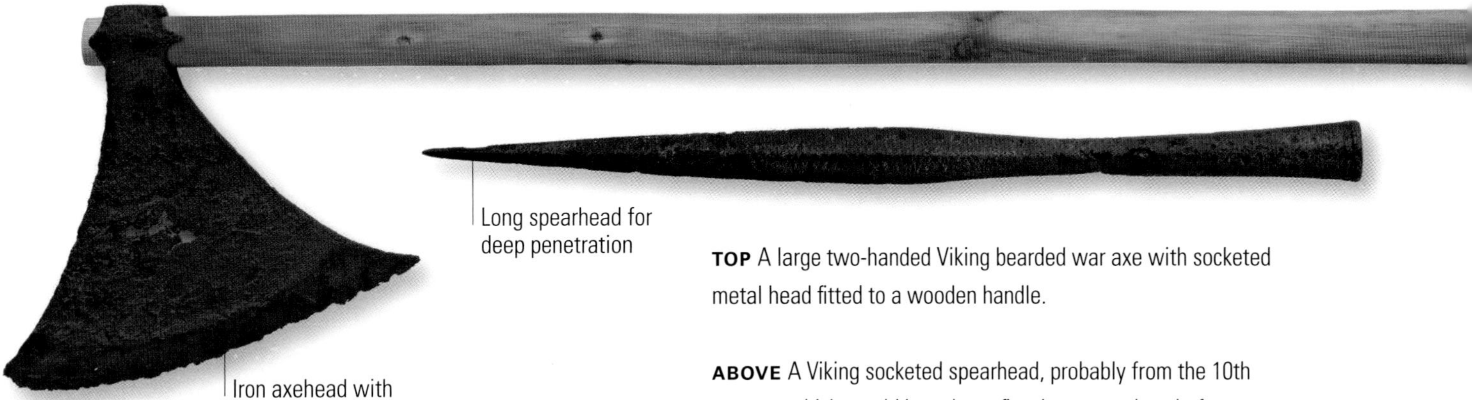

Iron axehead with hardened convex blade

Long spearhead for deep penetration

TOP A large two-handed Viking bearded war axe with socketed metal head fitted to a wooden handle.

ABOVE A Viking socketed spearhead, probably from the 10th century, which would have been fitted to a wooden shaft.

Viking sword manufacture

The smelting of iron ore with carbon to produce fine steel was well known to the Vikings and contributed to their reputation for producing blades of superb quality. They are best known for the complex process of pattern welding employed in their manufacture.

Modern X-ray technology of surviving blades now enables us to see how Viking smiths produced patterned blades by welding long strips of iron and steel together, forging them into square rods then finally twisting or folding these rods into small bunches, so creating the hard inner core of the blade. The outer cutting edge of the blade was welded to this inner core, using the best steel. Finally, the blade was carefully ground and polished with acid to reveal the extensive patterning.

Smiths worked hard to produce their own distinctive patterns. Their pride in such skilled work resulted in many blades being engraved with their makers' names, notably "Ulbehrt", "Lunvelit" and "Ingelri".

RIGHT A 12th-century carving from a wood panel in a church in Setesdal, Norway, depicts a scene from the Norse legend of Sigurd (Siegfried). Here, the dwarf Regin and his helper are shown forging a sword on an anvil.

Viking sword duels

The Vikings engaged in formal duels, or holmganga, to settle feuds. Holmganga roughly translates as "island going" and indicates that most duels took place on small islands where limitations of space (and, consequently, options for retreat), could be strictly enforced. The area of combat was determined by the laying out of a square cloth. Furrows were marked out around the cloth and the space was enclosed by a rope. Each of the combatants was allowed a second whose role was to hold the warrior's shield. Swords were the weapon of choice.

The duel did not commence with both warriors rushing at each other. Instead, each man took his turn at making one strike against his opponent. If a combatant chose this opportunity to back off and in so doing placed his foot outside the cloth, he was deemed to have run away and the fight would be stopped. If a strike was effective and incapacitating, the wounded party was allowed to stop the fight but was then obliged to forfeit a sum of money to his winning opponent.

RIGHT Two swords that display the distinctive punched and geometric decoration that was common on Viking sword pommels.

Orkneyinga Saga

Settling a feud by single combat with swords is a common theme in Viking sagas. One of the most famous accounts of the bloody use of a sword in such a feud is retold in the *Orkneyinga Saga* (*c.*1200), a unique historical narrative of the Orkney Islands that covers the period from its capture by Norwegians in the 9th century until the early 1200s.

The saga recounts how Rognvald, a Norwegian chieftain who ruled Orkney in *c.* AD860, was burnt to death in his own home by two of Harald Fairhair's sons. Bent on revenge, Rognvald's son Einar struck down and killed one of Harald Fairhair's sons, Halfdan Halegga. The victim's body was found the next day on the side of a hill, and the shape of an eagle had been cut into his back with a sword. More gruesomely, the ribs had been removed from the backbone and his lungs splayed out to represent the eagle's wings. Einar believed this display a worthy sacrifice to the Norse war god, Odin.

RIGHT The Norse god Odin with his sword and two ravens. He was the god of war and battle and the bringer of victory.

The sword in Viking sagas

The Vikings were great storytellers and believed that recounting tales was a gift, handed to them by the all-powerful war god, Odin. Without any means of writing them down, the Viking storytellers or skalds prided themselves on recalling epic stories and passing them on to others. Through these tales, the Vikings ensured that details of their religious beliefs and adventures were passed on from one generation to the next. Skalds were often employed by kings who wanted to be revered throughout their kingdoms. Although the stories were likely to have been exaggerated by the skalds, there is probably some truth in their telling of the events that occurred.

ABOVE A detail from a stone carving from Gotland representing Valhalla, the great hall of the god Odin. Here warriors enjoyed a glorious afterlife awaiting the final battle against the forces of evil.

The ancient sagas of both the Vikings and the Anglo-Saxons frequently refer to the great strength of a sword blade and its apparent capability to hew a man in two. Sword strokes were aimed primarily at the head and neck, and were calculated to be killing blows. The following description from a later Icelandic text, describing events in the 10th and 11th centuries, underlines the devastating effect of a single sword blow:

Then Thorbjorn rushed upon Grettir and struck at him, but he parried it with the buckler in his left hand and struck with his sword a blow which severed Thorbjorn's shield in two and went into his head, reaching the brain.

from *Grettir's Saga* (*c.*1400)

Medieval weapons

Feudal armies in Europe from the 11th to the 14th century produced a core group of premium fighting men – the mounted knights. Over time, they became more heavily armoured and reliant upon the shattering force of horse, lance and wide-bladed sword. In their wake, massed ranks of foot-soldiers engaged the enemy with long polearms (essentially weapons mounted on the end of a long pole), hoping to dismount and finish off any enemy knight. The fighting was brutal and bloody, conducted in a crush of jabbing, thrusting weapons.

1066 – the battlefield

The Battle of Hastings (1066) saw William of Normandy (*c.*1028–1087) unleash the devastating power of his heavily armoured knights for the first time on British soil. During many hours of hard fighting, King Harold II (*c.*1022–1066) and his fellow Anglo-Saxon defenders were constantly harried by repeated Norman cavalry charges. This type of mounted and mobile warfare was unknown to the Anglo-Saxons, who were predominantly foot soldiers, and it was only their fortunate selection of superior and defensible terrain prior to the battle that stopped them from being immediately overwhelmed.

The Norman war sword

A double-edged, razor-sharp broadsword with an average length of around 75cm (29.5in), was the main battle weapon of the Norman knight of the medieval period. It was ideal for swinging at speed and downward slashing. It would be used one-handed and in conjunction with a large, kite-shaped shield.

LEFT In this detail from the Bayeux Tapestry, Harold II's Anglo-Saxon troops, led by an armoured standard bearer and a warrior with an axe, confront a Norman cavalryman armed with a lance.

BELOW This sword is a "transitional" piece between the Viking and medieval period. It has a distinctive "brazil nut" pommel that was common in the early medieval period and the cross guard has increased considerably in width, while the blade is also more finely tapered.

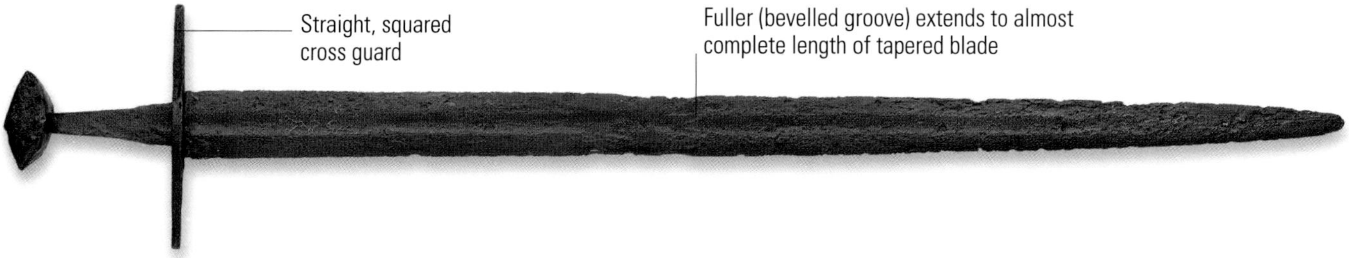

LEFT A 13th-century French soldier. He carries a double-edged broadsword with brazil nut pommel and down-sloping cross guard.

BELOW RIGHT William the Conqueror, accompanied by knights and soldiers, from a page of illustrated Latin text from the 14th century.

The Norman lance

Although it is called a lance, Norman knights used what could more accurately be described as a long, wooden spear with a simple, spiked end. It would be held firmly under the arm in order that the maximum force of both man and horse could be transmitted into the charge. Once the enemy had been engaged, the lance could also be transformed into an effective close-combat thrusting weapon, or simply thrown.

The "knightly" or "arming" sword

During a period when there was a practical need for a substantial and sturdy fighting weapon on the battlefield, the medieval "knightly" or "arming" sword was carried. Most battles in Europe took the form of two heavily armed and armoured scrums locked in a frenetic life-or-death struggle to push the enemy back, coupled with the added difficulty of trying to kill or maim as many enemies as possible in a very limited amount of space. It was quite common for soldiers to be literally crushed to death by their own side as the battle moved along.

Sword manufacture

Before the 9th century good sources of quality iron ore were not always available and many swords were often forge-welded from a selection of smaller iron pieces, thus reducing the inherent strength of the blade. Conversely, swordsmiths also forged high-quality swords using a process known as pattern welding, using rods of superior iron. The process required that the rods be tightly twisted together, so creating a much stronger and more durable blade with great qualities of tempering. The interlocking of these rods under great heat, and their sudden cooling and hammering, created distinctive forging patterns on the blade's surface. This diversity of swirling patterns was highly prized by an owner.

By the 9th century in Europe, the blast furnace became widespread and the need for pattern welding diminished. During the centuries that followed, the technique was slowly lost, and by 1300 there are few examples of its use. The technique survived, however, in Scandinavia, where good-quality iron ores and charcoal were widely available.

ABOVE The knights Galahad and Gawain are pictured taking part in a tournament, from *La Queste el Saint Graal*, *c.*1316. The knights wield wide-bladed, slashing swords typical of this period.

The typical style of the "knightly" or "arming" sword was firmly established by the 12th and 13th centuries. In general terms, it comprised a long, broad-bladed cutting and thrusting sword with double fullers (bevelled grooves); a plain crossbar hilt; and a wheel, brazil nut, ovoid or mushroom-shaped pommel. This sword design had remained virtually unchanged since the Viking invasions (AD793–*c.*1066), and over the next three centuries there was to be little innovation. Most blades and hilts were plain, although some surviving blades are found with inlaid decoration, mostly in the form of large, punched lettering or symbols, normally of a religious or mystical nature. Pommels of this period can also be found with inset heraldic devices, denoting particular royal or noble families. Rare specimens have pommels of agate, inlaid gold or rock crystal.

Swords would have been pattern forged or "braided" in the manner of earlier Viking swords, making them excellent fighting weapons – very strong and not prone to breakage. Swords were normally combined with either a large shield or buckler (small shield), although there are many contemporary images and written descriptions that describe the use of the knightly sword without a shield. This was thought to enable the free hand to grab or grapple with opponents. A knight would have worn this large sword whether in armour or not. He would have been considered "undressed" without his sword.

Medieval ceremonial swords

Swords produced specifically for use at royal coronations and similar ceremonies began to appear from the 11th century onwards. They were not designed for battle and were kept safely in churches, palaces and state arsenals. Decoration was profuse and the scale was deliberately large and impressive. One of the swords of Charlemagne (or Charles the Great), King of the Franks (*r.* AD742–814), is preserved in the Schatzkammer (Treasury) in Vienna. The blade is single-edged, slightly curved and overlaid with copper decoration, including dragon motifs. Hilt and scabbard are covered in silver gilt. The grip is wrapped in fishskin, set at an angle and very reminiscent of Near Eastern swords of the period. The second sword sometimes attributed to Charlemagne is found in the Louvre, Paris. The ornamentation on the hilt suggests it was carried by him, but it was also known to have been used as a ceremonial sword when Philip the Bold was crowned in 1270.

RIGHT A line drawing of one of two swords attributed to Charlemagne or Charles the Great (*r.* AD742–814). The sword is kept in the Louvre Museum in Paris.

LEFT A knight's sword, *c.*1250–1300, with a narrow blade, light enough to use on foot. This sword has a spear-point blade and impressive cutting and thrusting capabilities.

ABOVE A longsword with a highly tapered blade which could be used to penetrate armour.

The medieval sword in battle

A contemporary Florentine description of the Battle of Kosovo, between the Serbs and the Ottoman Empire in 1389, highlights the "knightly" aspect of the use of the sword and its perceived retributory power.

Fortunate, most fortunate are those hands of the twelve loyal lords who, having opened their way with the sword and having penetrated the enemy lines and the circle of chained camels, heroically reached the tent of Amurat himself…Fortunate above all is that one who so forcefully killed such a strong vojvoda by stabbing him with a sword in the throat and belly. And blessed are all those who gave their lives and blood through the glorious manner of martyrdom…

Response from the Florentine Senate (1389)

ABOVE A 14th-century French battle scene. The chaotic nature of a medieval battle is very evident.

The medieval longsword

A natural progression from the two-handed "arming" or "knightly" swords of the early to mid-medieval period was the first longswords, with the main difference being an increase in blade length. The double-edged blade was 80–95cm (31–37in) long and weighed in at approximately 1–2kg (2.2–4.4lb). This was very much a sword of the late medieval period and was used from around 1350 to 1550. The length of the grip was also extended to allow a more powerful and directed use of two hands, but the traditional cruciform hilt was still retained.

The longsword was a new departure in sword design and this innovation was soon witnessed in its battlefield application. It had the usual cutting functions expected of a broadsword but the blade profile had become thinner and was now designed (through stiffening of the blade tip) to thrust and penetrate plate armour. The longsword would come to prominence during the Renaissance, when the battlefield became a testing ground for new forms of penetrative edged weapons. The terms "hand-and-a-half sword", "greatsword" and "bastard sword" are different classifications of swords of this period.

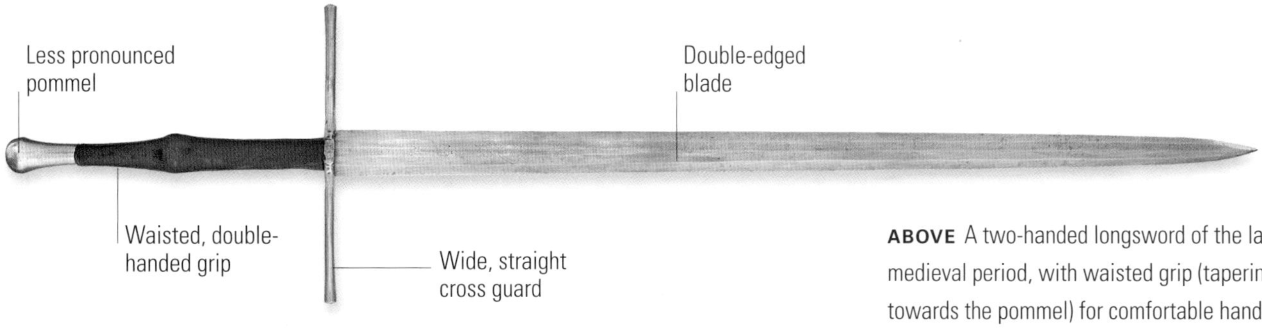

ABOVE A two-handed longsword of the later medieval period, with waisted grip (tapering towards the pommel) for comfortable handling.

Medieval polearms

Massed formations of infantry soldiers carrying polearms was a common sight on the battlefields of Europe from the medieval period right through to the early 1700s. The fighting part of the polearm was placed on the end of a long shaft and they were specially designed to disable and inflict crushing injuries upon knights. Cheap to produce in large numbers and versatile on the battlefield, these weapons became the mainstay of the European medieval foot-soldier when engaged in close combat.

The bardiche

A particularly brutal polearm used extensively in medieval and Renaissance Europe, the bardiche found particular favour in eastern Europe and Russia. Blade design varied considerably from country to country, but the main characteristic was a substantial cleaver-type blade and attachment to the pole by means of two widely spaced sockets. Blade length was around 60cm (23.6in), although the haft was unusually short at approximately 1.5m (4.9ft). This weapon appeared top-heavy and impractical, but the bardiche was regarded more as a heavy axe and wielded accordingly.

The bill

With a tradition going back to the Viking Age, the bill is commonly regarded as the national weapon of the English both during and beyond the medieval period, although it was used elsewhere in Europe, particularly Italy. As with many polearms, the bill developed from an agricultural tool, the billhook, and displayed a hooked chopping blade with several protruding spikes, including a pronounced spike at the top of the haft, resembling a spearhead. The bill also had a strong hook for dismounting cavalry. Used skilfully, it could snag onto any loose clothing or armour and wrench

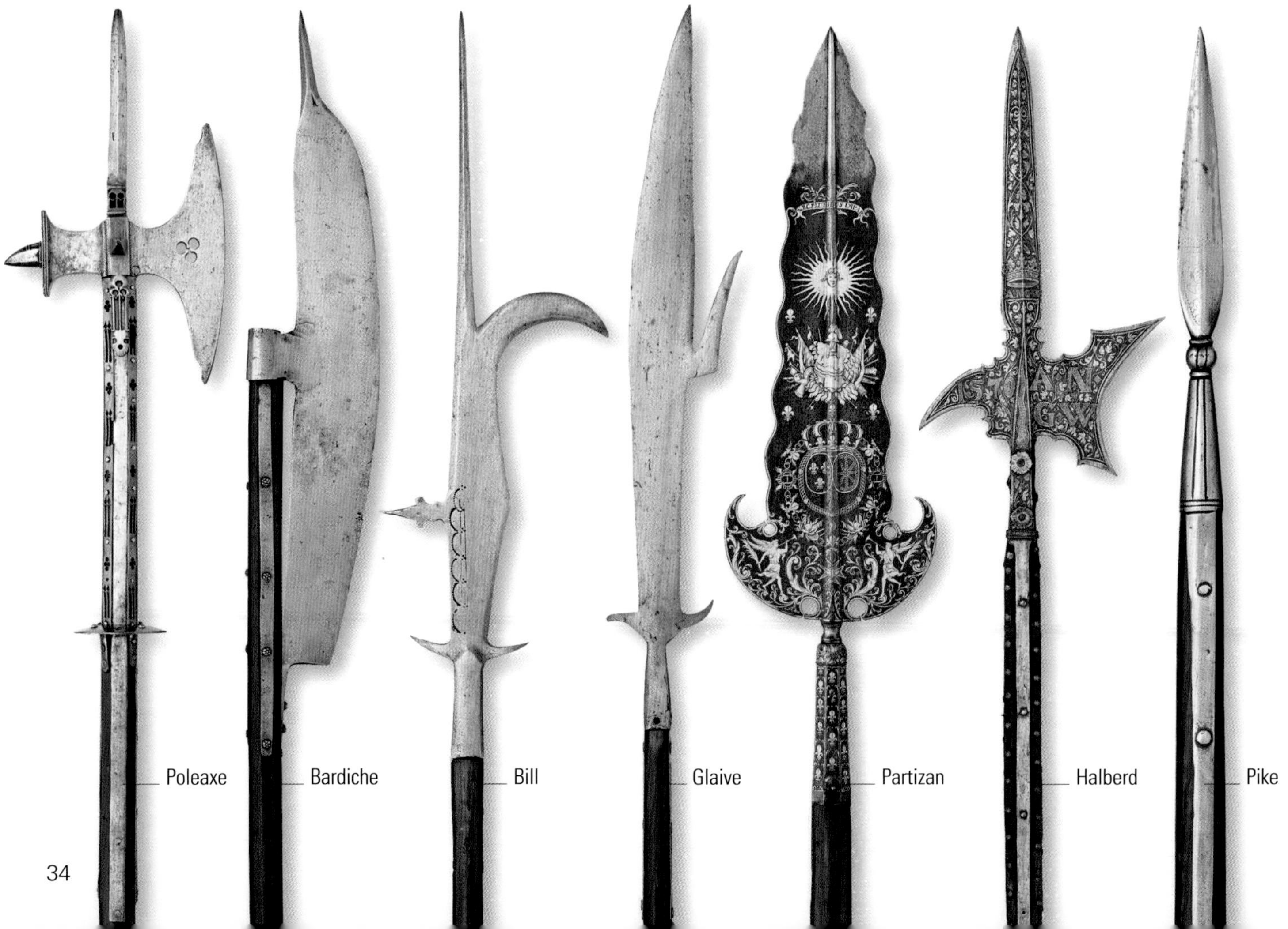

ABOVE The battle of Pavia, 1525, between the Holy Roman Emperor Charles V and Francis I of France. Note the pikes and halberds (right).

the target from his horse and throw him to the ground. English bills tended to be shorter with the emphasis more on the chopping action of the blade, while Italian bills had a very long spiked end, resulting in its use as a thrusting weapon.

The glaive

Similar in design to the Japanese naginata, the glaive originated in France, and its single-edged blade was attached to the haft by means of a socket shaft. Blade length was typically around 55cm (21.6in), with a wooden pole 1.8–2.1m (5.9–6.8ft) long. Medieval Swedish infantry adapted the glaive by fixing a double-edged sword blade to the haft. Glaives with small hooks are known as "glaive-guisarmes".

The halberd

The halberd is a crude, rectangular blade, shaped to a point at the top; the earliest known use of the halberd comes from an excavated example from the battlefield at Morgarten (1315) in Switzerland. The word "halberd" originated from the German halm (staff) and barte (axe). Over time, the halberd's spear point was improved to allow it to be used to repel oncoming horsemen. The haft of the halberd was also reinforced with thick metal rims, making it more effective and durable when blocking blows from an enemy sword or axe.

The partizan

Smaller than normal polearms at 1.8–2m (5.9–6.6ft), the partizan was constructed from a spearhead or lancehead, with an added double axehead at the bottom of the blade. It proved not to be as effective as other polearms and it was gradually withdrawn from frontline use. It remained as a ceremonial weapon and many have elaborately decorated blades. Partizans were carried right through to the Napoleonic Wars (1804–15).

The pike

A ubiquitous battlefield weapon during the medieval period, the pike was simply a very long, thrusting spear employed by infantry as both a static defensive weapon against cavalry attacks and as an attacking polearm, when used in massed ranks and close formation. The combined length of both haft and head rose over time to a staggering 3–4m (9.8–13.1ft), sometimes even 6m (19.6ft), and it was this very length that was both its strength and also its inherent weakness. The pikeman could stand at a relatively safe distance from close combat, but the weapon's unwieldiness could also prove dangerous for him. A pikeman was armed with sword, mace or dagger in case his pike was lost in battle.

Medieval and Renaissance jousts

Jousts and tournaments took the form of individual combat between armoured knights, mounted or on foot, using lances, swords, axes and maces. Jousting was first practised in the early Middle Ages. During these colourful public events, two knights fought to enhance their martial reputation. The melée, a tournament (or tourney), provided the audience with the spectacle of many knights involved in mass trials by combat. Compared with warfare proper, this form of organized "entertainment" was only one step away from the real thing.

Origins of the tournament

The first written record of a formulated set of tournament rules is usually credited to a Frenchman, Geoffroi de Purelli, in 1066. Unfortunately, his guidelines were of limited use to him as he was killed at the very tournament for which he had composed the rules. Despite this early setback, the popularity of jousting was firmly established in western Europe by the 13th century and it continued as a public sport well into the 1600s.

Military service in the medieval period

Medieval knights were obliged to provide military service to their king, lord or liege on a regular basis. Warfare during this period, although perhaps exciting to a young knight on his first campaign, was, for most of those involved, extremely unpleasant. Living conditions were usually poor and, if the knight was not killed or badly wounded in battle, the combination of disease or hunger would normally carry him away. But there could be an opportunity for redemption amidst this state of wretchedness. By showing valour and courage on the battlefield, he had the opportunity to establish a martial reputation with the consequent possibility of great financial and social rewards from his master, or even the king.

On the other hand, equivalent fame and fortune, combined with regular practice in the use of weapons, could also be gained in peacetime and without embarking on a long and possibly fatal campaign of war. This alternative avenue was to be found in the joust and tournament.

RIGHT A knight is unhorsed with a jousting lance. The illustration is taken from the *Codex Manesse* by Walther von Klingen, Zurich, *c.*1310–40.

The individual joust

A joust was a horseback encounter between two knights with lances. The object was to unhorse the opponent. If a combatant struck either rider or horse with his lance, he was automatically disqualified. This was known as "tilting". If the opponent was not unhorsed but a clean hit was made to the centre or "boss" of his shield, points would be awarded.

LEFT A knight with jousting lance, *c.*1500. His plate armour includes an extra protective layer near his vulnerable left side.

The melée or tourney

Taking the form of massed trials by arms in a public arena, the melée or tourney was a popular part of the tournament in the 12th and 13th centuries (jousting became popular later on). It was a savage and brutal fixture, with many lives lost and serious injuries sustained. Upon hearing the call to charge, rival knights rode or ran onto the tournament field and proceeded to unhorse or attack their designated opponents with a selection of weapons, including broadsword, war axe, club or mace.

In some competitions, the melée was more organized, with combat restricted to a series of three strokes per weapon: for example, three tilts of the lance or three strokes of the sword, and the same for both battle-axe and mace. To actually kill an opponent during a tournament was considered morally wrong, although the ferocity of the combat sometimes inevitably led to fatalities.

RIGHT In this French 14th-century illumination the knight Lancelot is depicted in single combat, watched by King Arthur and Guinevere.

The jousting lance

Jousting lances were made of solid oak and it would have required considerable strength, force and accuracy to unseat an opponent. It would certainly have taken a significant strike to shatter a lance. Knights practised their technique against a specially constructed target, or quintain, a life-sized re-creation of an opponent's lance, helmet and shield. In modern-day re-creations of the joust, a lightweight, wooden lance is used in order that it can break more easily and so lessen the impact on an opponent.

Two types of horses were used during the joust. Warmblood chargers were selected for their stamina and quickness in the charge, whereas heavy warhorses or coldblood destriers were chosen for their large bulk, which made them deliberately slower but able to pack a heavier punch upon contact. Horses were trained to canter at an ambling pace to give their riders stability and enable them to focus and aim better with their lances.

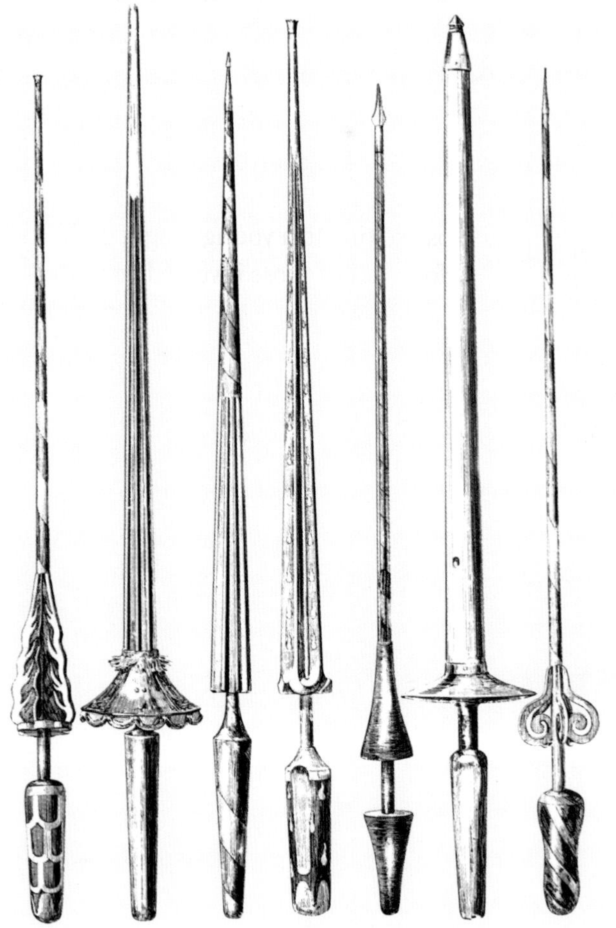

RIGHT A selection of jousting lances. At the end of each lance was a coronal (crown-shaped metal cap) consisting of three or more metal prongs, designed to catch onto the opponent's shield.

Swords of the Renaissance

The soldier of the mid-1500s witnessed dramatic advances in military technology. Swords, bows and pikes were now being challenged by early artillery, hand-held guns and complex siege weapons. In response, combatants became more heavily armoured. The sword evolved from being a purely slashing weapon to one that could pierce and break through plate armour. New sword types also appeared, from the huge two-handed broadsword of the Landsknecht to the handy short-bladed falchion of the ordinary infantryman.

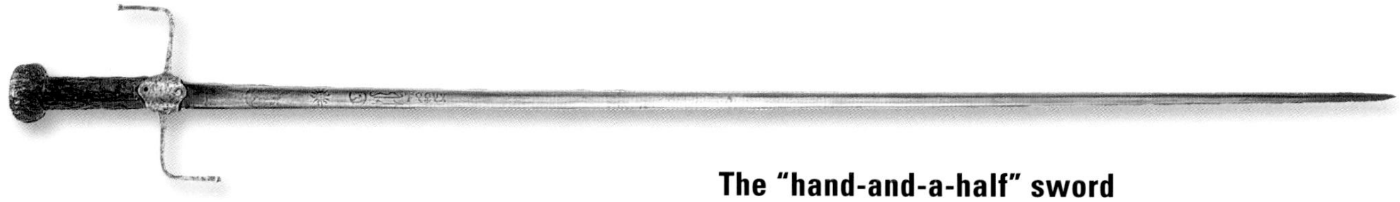

ABOVE A Polish estoc, which would have been used by the cavalry. The needle-like blade was ideal for penetrating armour.

The estoc or tuck sword

Stiff, lozenge or diamond-shaped thrusting blades were now replacing the wide-bladed and cruciform-hilted swords typical of the medieval period. This new type of sword was known to the French as an estoc and to the English as a tuck.

The estoc featured a long, two-handed grip, enabling the bearer to achieve maximum effect as he thrust the sword downwards into armour. This sword was particularly effective at splitting chainmail and piercing gaps in armour. Due to the narrowness of the blade, it had no discernible cutting edge but a very strong point. Opponents who had lost the protection of their armour during the heat of battle were still dispatched by the traditional double-edged cutting sword, held in reserve for just such an eventuality. Versatility and a range of weapons to hand was still an important and practical factor.

The "hand-and-a-half" sword

Common throughout Europe from the beginning of the 15th century, the "hand-and-a-half sword" is also referred to as a "longsword". The contemporary term "bastard sword" derives from it being regarded as neither a one-handed nor a two-handed sword. Despite these perceived drawbacks, it possessed a reasonably long grip and shorter blade, which allowed one hand to hold the narrow grip firmly, while a couple of fingers placed strategically on the forte gave the soldier extra leverage and manoeuvrability when wielding. The length of these swords was around 115–145cm (45.3–57in).

The falchion

Although the falchion's design had originated in ancient Greece, the sword experienced a widespread revival during the Renaissance, particularly in Italy, France and Germany. This short-bladed sword had a straight or slightly curved blade, with cross guards either absent or very simple.

BELOW The "hand-and-a-half" sword has a short grip that accommodates one hand, while the fingers of the second hand are placed on the blade forte to allow extra leverage and control when swinging the blade.

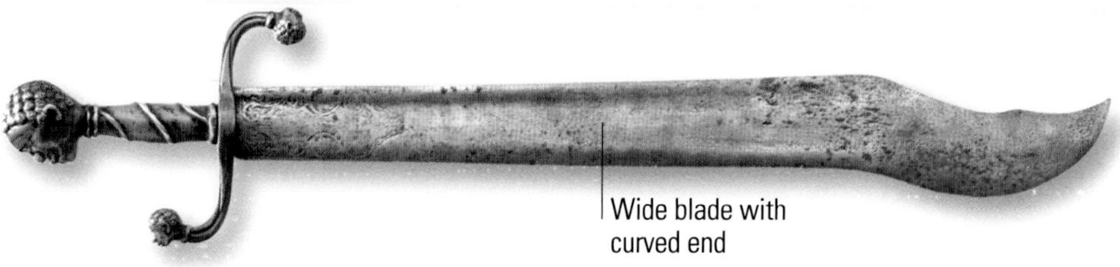

RIGHT This Milanese ceremonial falchion, *c.*1600, features a strong, broad blade with curved, double-edged point.

Two-handed (Zweihänder) swords

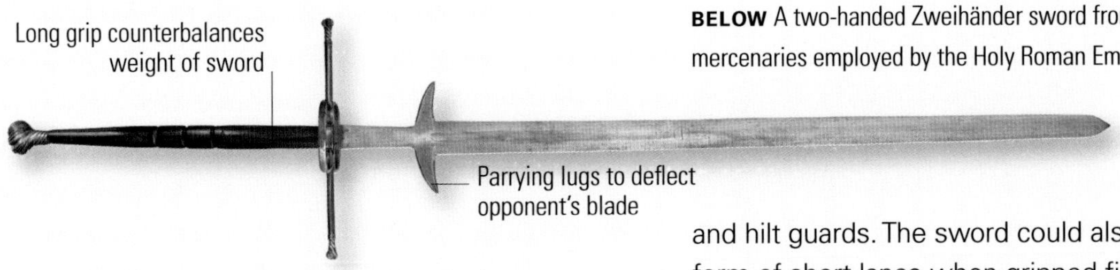

BELOW A two-handed Zweihänder sword from *c.*1550, used by mercenaries employed by the Holy Roman Emperor.

Very large broadswords called Zweihänder or two-handed swords, became very popular during the 15th and 16th centuries, and are probably best known for their association with the famed Landsknechte, or mercenaries. Established during the reign of the Holy Roman Emperor, Maximilian I (1459–1519), and drawn mainly from Germany and eastern Europe, Landsknechte fought in numerous battles throughout the continent, particularly during the Italian Wars of 1494–1559.

Their Zweihänder swords had a length of up to 1.8m (5.9ft) and weighed 2–3.5kg (4.4–7.7lb). The hilt was of massive form, with extremely large pommels and hilt guards. The sword could also be utilized as a form of short lance when gripped firmly at the blade forte. Because of its immense size, the Zweihänder would also have been extremely effective at attacking and breaking up massed ranks of infantry or pikemen.

Another sword favoured by the Landsknechte was the Katzbalger (cat-skinner or brawler), a short sword, or hanger. It was a sturdy, wide-bladed sword, with a distinctive "figure-of-eight" guard. It was 75–85cm (29.5–33.5in) long. The sword's name is thought to derive from the practical reality that it would have been a weapon of last resort and used in close, confined combat, when the soldier would literally have to fight like a cornered feral cat. The Landsknecht carried it alongside his Zweihänder.

BELOW The Katzbalger was a secondary sword of the Landsknecht, and used when his larger, two-handed sword was unavailable.

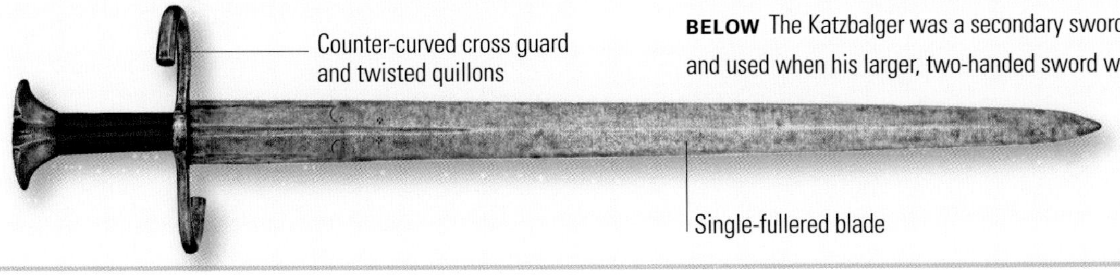

The falchion was primarily a side-weapon and was usually carried by the infantry. Because of its short blade and ease of manoeuvrability, the falchion became the precursor to the hunting sword.

The cinquedea, or "five-fingered" sword

Another distinctive short sword that developed in Italy during the Renaissance was the cinquedea. The shape and form of the cinquedea typifies the Renaissance belief in the importance of artistry, combined with a newly rediscovered passion for the classical world. It was worn mainly with civilian dress and comprised a very wide blade of five-fingered span. The hilt was normally of simple form, with a severely waisted grip. Because of its wide blade, many swordsmiths took the opportunity to embellish the swords with exquisite engraving and gilding. The sword would have been worn in the small of the back in order that it could be drawn laterally.

There is some debate as to whether the cinquedea was actually a dagger rather than a sword. The average length is noted at 40–50cm/16–19in (and there are even two-handed versions known), so this probably indicates that the cinquedea fits more comfortably within the broad family of swords rather than dagger types.

RIGHT A cinquedea sword, with typical pronounced medium ridge, or spine, running down the centre of the blade.

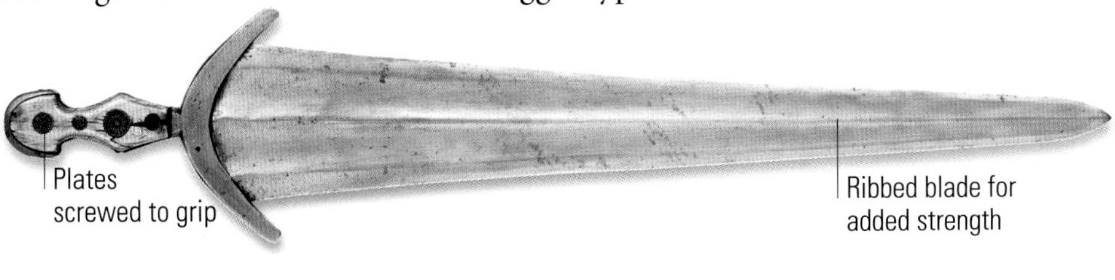

ABOVE Sword and scroll of Anne de Montmorency, 1493–1567, from the *Hours of Constable Anne de Montmorency*.

Ceremonial swords

The increasing power and wealth of the European monarchies and city states during the Renaissance meant that the sword did not only serve a purely military function. It also became a manifestation of the rank and status of the privileged, and its most notable appearances were at royal coronation ceremonies. Although the medieval cruciform-hilted sword had fallen out of favour on the Renaissance battlefield, being superseded by more complex and enclosed-hilt forms, it was still retained for ceremonial purposes – perhaps recalling a more "knightly" time – when a gentleman or courtier swore allegiance to his king by the kiss of a knightly sword. These "bearing" swords were carried before kings, queens and senior clergy. The sword of Frederick I of Saxony, presented to him by Emperor Sigismund I of Germany in 1425, has a cruciform hilt inset with rock crystal and heavily gilded in gold and silver. There is also a massive 15th-century bearing sword, supposedly made for either Henry V of England or Edward, Prince of Wales, which has a total length of over 228cm (88.6in). Ceremonial swords were also presented as symbols of state office. From the 14th century onwards, English mayors were granted the right (usually by the monarch) to carry a great civic sword on ceremonial occasions. This tradition was upheld for centuries and many historic towns in the United Kingdom still retain these swords. The earliest recorded civic sword still in existence is to be found in Bristol and is thought to date from around 1373. Constables of France, including such notables as Bertrand du Guesclin and Anne de Montmorency, carried bearing swords.

In terms of sheer brilliance of decoration and craftsmanship, the ceremonial swords presented by the Renaissance popes must rank as the apogee of 16th-century sword decoration. Given with a richly embroidered belt and cap by the pope each year on Christmas Day, invariably to members of the European Catholic nobility, these great two-handed swords were fabulously ornate and featured a profusion of precious stones and extensive gold and silver metalwork.

The development of hunting swords

Hunting had always been the favoured and exclusive pursuit of the nobility since the early medieval period and Renaissance hunters continued this pastime with vigour. The depiction of the royal hunt was a popular subject for artists and many painters and weavers of tapestry found the drama of the chase and final kill with sword and spear irresistible.

The falchion sword, or short hanger, was well known to the infantry as a side-weapon. It was first adopted during the 14th century, specifically as a dedicated hunting weapon. In later years, a saw-back blade was also incorporated for ease of cutting up the kill, followed by the development of a specialist set of tools for pairing. This combination of sword and skinning tools was known as a garniture, or trousse. As the owners of these hunting swords invariably had great financial means, decoration of the swords became ever more elaborate.

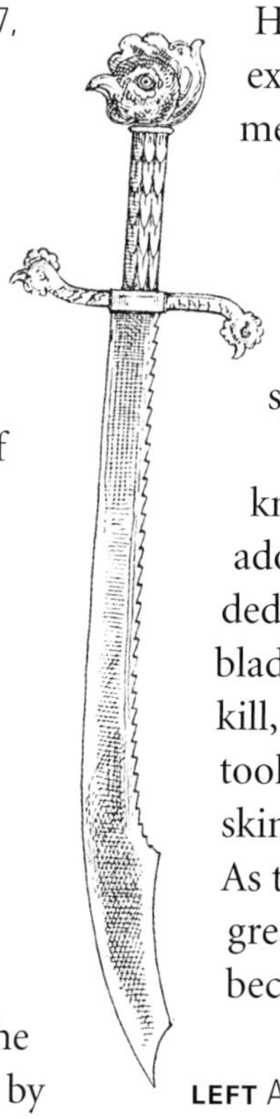

LEFT An illustration of a hunting sword with pommel and crossbar decorated by birds' heads. It has a saw-back blade for cutting the kill.

Swords of justice, swords of execution

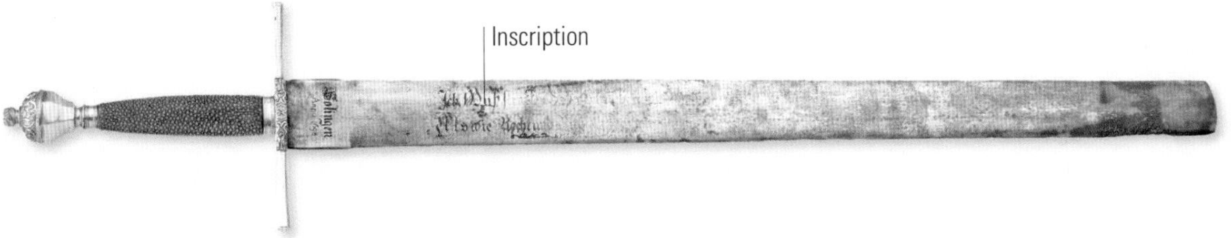

ABOVE This German executioner's sword has a double-edged blade with a blunt, lightly rounded point. Many surviving "execution swords" are actually swords of justice which would be carried before the judge to indicate his power over life and death.

ABOVE In this detail from the above sword, an etched inscription can be seen. In German it reads "*Ich Muß straffen daß verbrechen – Als wie Recht und Richter sprechen*". Translated, this means "I have to punish crime as the law and judge tell me".

Great swords were also employed as both symbols and facilitators of judicial law. Many local courts of justice placed a large bearing or executioner's sword on the courtroom wall. The presence of the executioner's sword was not purely symbolic for it had a practical application in the actual beheading of prisoners. It was often highly decorated and engraved with prayers for the condemned, warnings against transgressions and vivid images of beheadings, hangings and torture.

Executioners' swords were more common in continental Europe from the 1400s, particularly Germany, with England still preferring the axe. The sword hilt was normally of conventional cruciform shape with a large counter-balancing pommel. It was very well constructed, with high-quality steel used for the manufacture of the blade. The blade edge was extremely sharp and it was a requirement of the executioner to keep it well honed so that the head of the victim could be severed in one mighty blow. Blades were broad and flat backed, with a rounded tip. The sword was designed for cutting rather than thrusting, so a pointed tip (as in the case of military blades) was unnecessary.

An executioner's sword in the British Museum, London, has the following words engraved on the blade in Latin. It translates as: "When I raise this sword I wish the sinner eternal life / The Sires punish mischief: I execute their judgement." When no longer used for executions, swords became ceremonial.

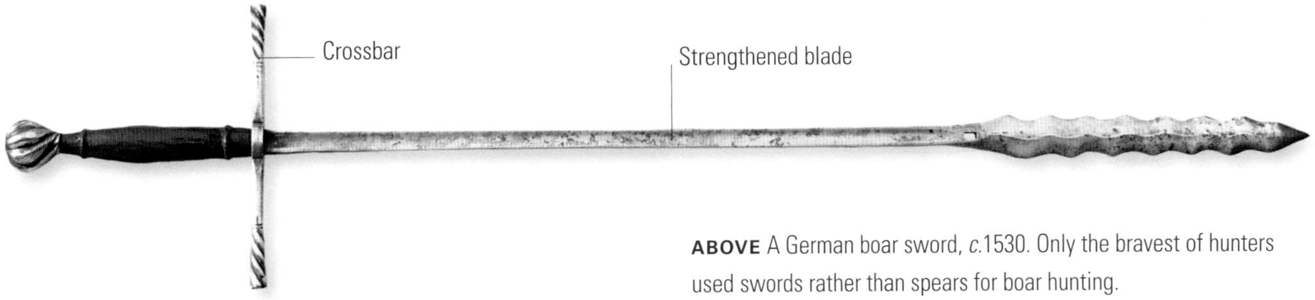

ABOVE A German boar sword, *c.*1530. Only the bravest of hunters used swords rather than spears for boar hunting.

Another sword designed solely for the hunt was the boar sword. Based on the triangular-bladed estoc or tuck, its greatly stiffened blade was designed to withstand the power of a charging boar or other large animal. The boar sword was introduced during the 14th century and by around 1500 it had developed a faceted or leaf-shaped spear point. A crossbar was later added near the end of the blade to prevent an animal running up the length of the blade and so making it difficult to retrieve.

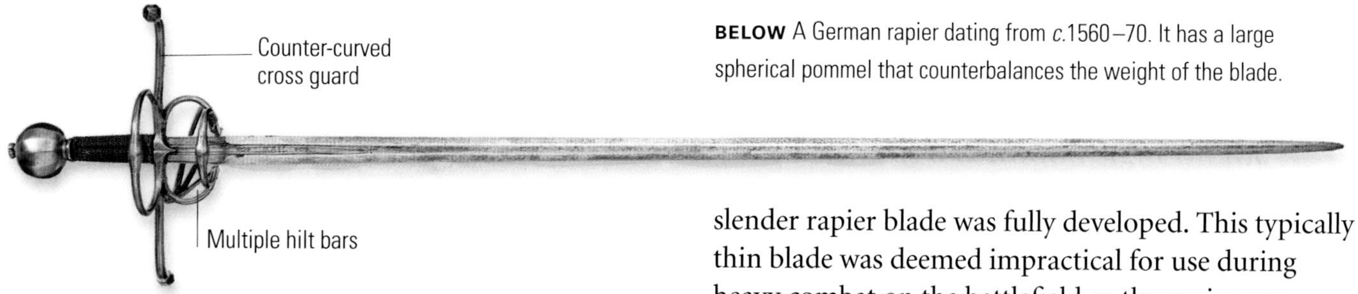

BELOW A German rapier dating from *c.*1560–70. It has a large spherical pommel that counterbalances the weight of the blade.

The rapier

Spain is normally cited as the first country to have introduced the rapier, or *espada ropera* (sword of the robe), during the late 1400s. This designation highlighted the new-found ability for a gentleman to wear these swords with ordinary civilian dress, rather than needing to don his armour. Italy, Germany and England adopted the rapier soon afterwards.

In its most complete and recognizable form, the rapier came into full prominence during the early 16th century. In the mid-1400s, precursors of the rapier (including the standard cruciform-hilted sword) had begun to develop a primitive knuckle guard and forefinger ring or loop. By 1500, a series of simple bars were joined to the knuckle guard to form a protective hilt. At this time, the blade was still a wide, cutting type, and it is only well into the 16th century that the slender rapier blade was fully developed. This typically thin blade was deemed impractical for use during heavy combat on the battlefield so the rapier was viewed primarily as a "civilian" duelling sword. The new rapier hilt, however, was adopted by the military but with the retention of a wider, more traditional broadsword fighting blade.

The blade

Sword blades were manufactured in Toledo and Valencia (Spain), Solingen and Passau (Germany), and Milan and Brescia (Italy). They were sold as unhilted blades and then hilted locally at their eventual destinations throughout Europe. Some blades are marked by their maker, although many are plain. Notable bladesmiths' names include Piccinino, Caino, Sacchi and Ferrara from Italy, Johannes, Wundes and Tesche (Germany) and Hernandez (Spain). Respected names were often stamped on blades by lesser-known rivals to enhance the value of an inferior sword.

BELOW Italian rapier, *c.*1610. Of true swept-hilt form, it has deep chiselling to the knuckle guard.

BELOW A North European duelling rapier, *c.*1635, with a distinctive elongated and fluted pommel.

BELOW A Spanish cup-hilt rapier, *c.*1660. The cup and hilt are extensively pierced. It has very long, straight, slender quillons with finials to each end.

BELOW An English rapier with a finely chiselled cup hilt, *c.*1650. The blade is stamped "*Sahagum*".

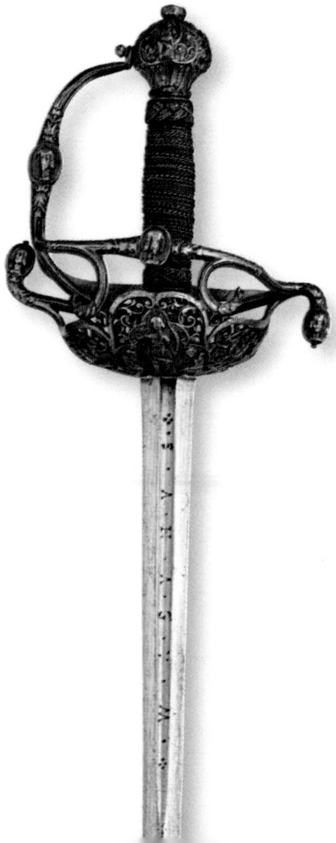

LEFT Two Italians fencing with broadswords. The rapier was later adopted as a cut-and-thrust civilian weapon used for self-defence and duelling rather than heavy combat.

The hilt

Renaissance swordsmen were presented with many differing styles of rapier, which had developed over time and in different areas. This difference was normally displayed in the sword hilt rather than the blade. To make identification clearer, historians have divided the hilt into a series of distinct evolutions from primary, basic, quarter, half, to three-quarter and then full hilts. Some examples have just a simple loop and knuckle guard, while later rapiers exhibit multiple ring guards and S-shaped upswept and downswept quillons (cross pieces at right angles to the blade and hilt). These later, more extravagant rapiers are commonly described as being of "swept-hilt" form. Large ovoid or octagonal pommels were necessary to counterbalance the weight of the long blade.

The development of the rapier

In the 16th century, the first 50 years could truly be called the age of the rapier. This century witnessed the rapier being worn as the ultimate fashion accessory and signifier of rank. Great competition was placed at Court to be the nobleman with the most grandly ornate sword, and contemporary paintings vividly show the wide range of rapiers available to those willing to pay the vast sums needed to purchase such a "trophy" piece.

By the end of the 16th century, blade lengths had reduced, making the rapier more manageable in the hand. Hilt design had now become significantly complex and, with increased blade-to-blade action, more emphasis was laid on protecting the hand. In the 1600s we see the addition of more side plates and shell guards for this purpose.

The rapier and fencing

Modern fencing emerged during the latter half of the 15th century and is directly attributable to the development of the rapier as a weapon of choice for a gentleman. The first fencing manuals were published in Spain in 1471 and 1474. In Germany, the Marxbruder and Federfechter fencing guilds were given a letter of privilege by Emperor Friedrich III in 1478, enabling them to recruit members and teach the art of fencing.

In Italy and central Europe a left-handed dagger (main gauche) was developed and used in conjunction with the rapier, and sometimes also a small shield, or "buckler", would be used to parry the sword blows. More noblemen died during the 16th century from duelling than conventional warfare.

RIGHT A sword fight with rapiers. This illustration was taken from a woodcut, *c.*1656.

17th- and 18th-century swords

A dramatic change in sword design appeared in the 17th and 18th centuries. The long-bladed rapier of the Renaissance and the great two-handed sword of the Landsknechte had become obsolete as the changing nature of war relegated the sword to a more secondary role, being steadily overtaken by more reliable and destructive firearms. Despite this, the military sword was still regarded as an effective weapon. Civilian gentlemen now carried smaller, lightweight, ornamented swords, as dictated by the changing fashion of the day.

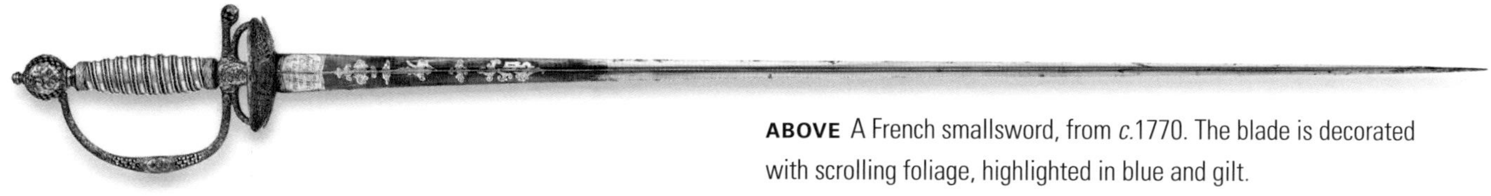

ABOVE A French smallsword, from *c.*1770. The blade is decorated with scrolling foliage, highlighted in blue and gilt.

The smallsword

Towards the end of the 17th century, the need to carry a substantial sword in civilian life diminished and gentlemen began to adopt a sword of smaller proportions. It was described as a "town", "walking" or "court" sword and would later develop into the smallsword proper. In England, this change coincided with a period of relative social stability after the English Civil War (1642–51), and a growing belief that there was less need to be heavily armed when going about one's business.

These early "transitional" or part-rapier smallswords were more practical when used in close order combat (particularly the now-popular duel), and were also considered more comfortable to wear alongside the civilian dress that had now superseded the wearing of armour in public.

The traditional rapier hilt was also replaced by new hilt styles from the 1700s, including a stylized shell guard and smaller quillons, thinner knuckle guards and a wider range of pommel styles. Extra *pas-d'âne* rings (the inwardly curving quillons that reached the base of the shell guard) were added to the hilt. *Pas d'âne* literally means "a donkey's steps".

LEFT In *Portrait of a Gentleman, c.*1640 (oil on canvas), the subject carries an early form of basket hilt, combined with a backsword blade.

BELOW An ornate French smallsword hilt, *c.*1760. The pommel, knuckle guard and shell guard are deeply embossed. The blade is engraved with numerous decorative motifs.

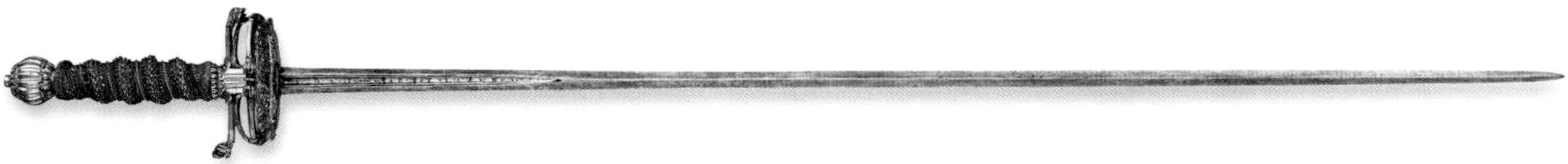

ABOVE Probably French with a Spanish blade. It is likely that this duelling rapier, *c.*1670, would have been used in conjunction with a gauntlet and cloak in the left hand, acting as a distraction to the opponent.

The function of the sword also changed. It had now become not just a weapon of defence or attack but also a distinctive signifier of rank and very much influenced by the vagaries of fashion. The smallswords worn at European courts were soon copied within society's more fashionable circles. During the late 17th and early 18th century, the dominant decorative influence in European society was French design and this became a powerful stimulus in smallsword design and decoration. The Rococo movement was at its height and the incorporation of shell-like curves, foliage and classical imagery is very evident in hilt design. Advances in technology and metalworking meant that smallswords were more easily manufactured in combinations of iron, steel, brass, silver and, occasionally, gold. The craftsmen who produced these smallswords were only limited by the depth of the client's purse and their own imagination. Consequently, the swords displayed a stunning range of quality, ornamentation and sheer creative elegance.

Military influence

As the 18th century progressed, the smallsword entered the military arena and was adopted by officers. Ordinarily, they tended to purchase more than one sword, and the smallsword, with its less robust, yet elegant proportions, was deemed more suitable for formal or "walking out" occasions, particularly parades and balls where it was seen as a status symbol. A more practical fighting sword of larger dimensions and wider blade was still carried into battle although some hilts were of smallsword design.

The colichemarde blade

In the late 1600s the normally flat rapier blade of the late Renaissance was superseded by an important technological breakthrough, when a group of German sword makers developed the colichemarde blade. This radical new blade shape was of trefoil, or three-sided, form and "hollow ground" with a hexagonal or diamond-shaped profile. The forte was also purposely wider and longer, giving the blade more strength. This new-found manoeuvrability allowed the weight of the sword to be concentrated in the hand, so providing more control and precision when thrusting.

The technical knowledge needed to produce these hollow-ground blades was jealously guarded by the German sword makers, despite attempts by the English government to bring over German workers. A rival sword factory was eventually established at Shotley Bridge in County Durham, in 1690. Its attempts at producing hollow-ground blades were not successful and it reverted to manufacturing swords of a more traditional and flat-backed design.

The popularity of colichemarde blades was quite short-lived and by the mid-1700s, blade shape was already changing again. The demise of the colichemarde blade was due partly to its greater suitability for duelling over everyday or military use.

RIGHT Duelling in the 17th century. The antagonist on the right has adopted a typical duelling pose.

LEFT A British dragoon officer, *c.*1795. He carries a curved stirrup-hilted sabre of the "hussar" type.

Cavalry swords

The cavalry sword was still a horseman's most effective weapon of defence and attack up to the 18th century. Unlike the infantry soldier, who began to rely more on musket and pistol, the cavalry soldier carried a firearm only as his secondary weapon of defence. It was therefore crucial that he had a sword capable of producing a devastating effect when combined with his horse's speed and his own strength and skill. The sword needed to be heavy and robust, with a long cut-and-thrust blade, fixed to a large hilt, affording good protection to the sword hand.

The use of a straight-bladed and single-edged cavalry "backsword" had been well established by the 1600s. These swords were carried throughout Europe and became the mainstay for cavalry formations. The early 18th century also witnessed the growing influence of cavalry sabres with curved blades. Their origins are thought to be either Eurasian or Arabic. The Ottoman Turks had carried curved "mameluke" swords for many years. It is likely that the spread of the Ottoman Empire into eastern Europe by the late 1600s created an opportunity for western sword makers to examine captured examples of this new form of sword, eventually interpreting and converting them into more "western" sword styles.

Emergence of heavy and light cavalry

By the mid-1600s, European nations began to establish permanent standing armies, dividing them into designated infantry and cavalry regiments. Cavalry regiments took this transformation a stage further by making a distinction between light and heavy cavalry. The swords issued to these different branches of the army also changed, with the heavy cavalry carrying a long, straight, thrusting blade, and the light cavalry a slightly shorter, slashing, curved blade (although the widespread adoption of a curved blade would appear much later, in the early 1700s).

The backsword

Like most European nations, English cavalry troopers of the 17th century favoured a heavy backsword. Common hilt styles included an enclosed, multi-bar iron basket hilt with a large apple-shaped pommel. This design originated in Germany and northern Europe, and was later taken to a new level of sophistication by the work of Scottish basket hilt makers. The basket hilt, in many different forms, was carried by cavalry

BELOW A French cavalry backsword, dating from *c.*1690. The hilt is made up of a complex series of intertwined bars.

BOTTOM The blade of this English mortuary sword, *c.*1645, is double-edged and multi-fullered (a number of grooves).

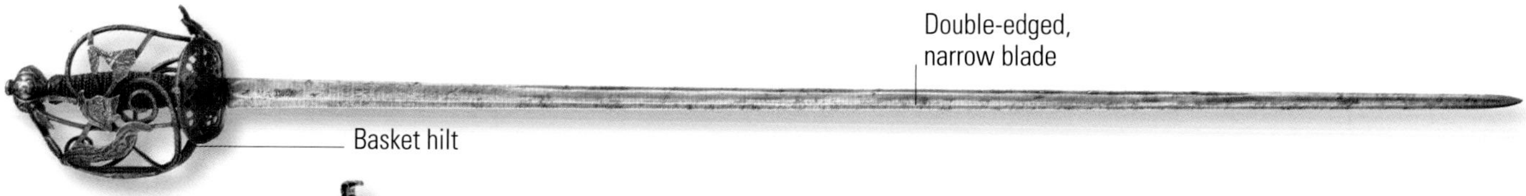

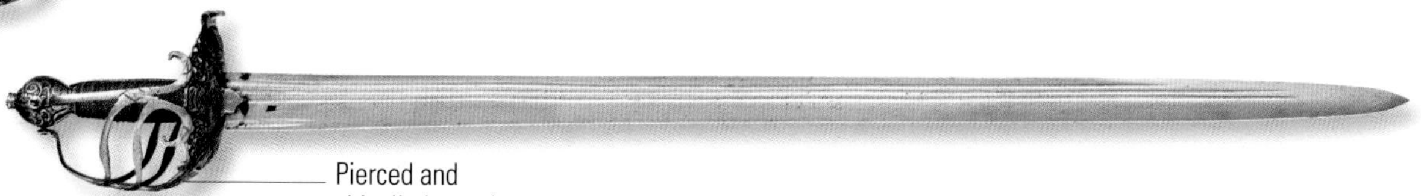

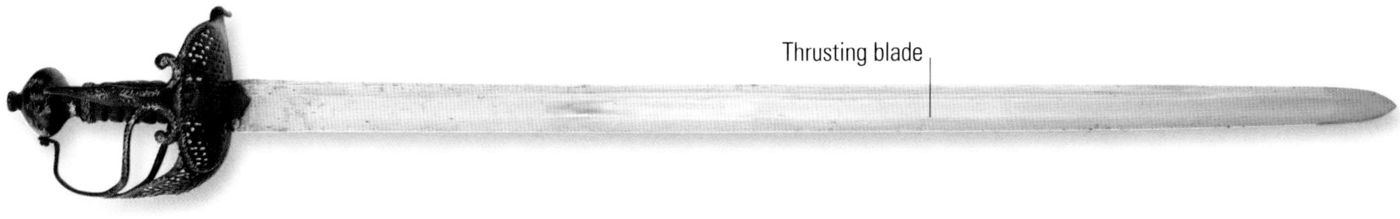

ABOVE A mid-17th century English backsword with a mortuary-type hilt. It was reputed to have been used by Oliver Cromwell during the siege of Drogheda in 1649.

regiments well into the 18th century. Parallel to this was the development of a more robust "military" version of the newly adopted smallsword (normally for officers). It had a bilobate (two-branched) counter-guard, large ovoid pommel and broadsword blade.

The "mortuary sword" of the English Civil War

During the English Civil War (1642–51) the so-called "mortuary" sword was another peculiarly English sword type carried extensively. It was given the erroneous title "mortuary" by Victorian sword collectors because of the application of decorative work to the hilt that featured a series of engraved human faces, supposedly in memory of the beheaded Charles I (executed in 1649) and his wife, Henrietta Maria. Although there is a mortuary sword in the collection of HM The Queen at Windsor that bears a likeness to Charles I and his queen, mortuary swords with human faces were being carried as early as 1635. Not all of them display human faces as the primary decorative motif. Alternative hilt decoration comprises armed figures, coats of arms and extensive engraving, including both fanciful and geometric designs.

The main features of the mortuary sword are a dish- or boat-shaped guard with a wide wrist guard and two branched knuckle bows screwed to the pommel. Shield-shaped langets (to guard the shaft) are found at the top of the blade forte and probably acted to keep the hilt solid into the blade. Blades were normally of backsword type and single or double-edged towards the end of the blade to enable a thrusting capability.

The mortuary sword, which fell out of use around 1670, was carried by both Royalist and Parliamentarian cavalry throughout the English Civil War. Oliver Cromwell was believed to have carried a mortuary sword during the Battle of Drogheda, in 1649, and an example attributed to him still exists in England.

BELOW Oliver Cromwell at the siege of Drogheda, 1649. Instead of starving the Royalist garrison into submission, Cromwell ordered an assault. This was eventually successful and led to a terrible massacre of both the military and civilians.

BELOW A schiavona sword of a type carried by Slavonian soldiers who acted as guards to the Doge of Venice up until the late 18th century.

The schiavona

Slavonic mercenaries from eastern Europe, particularly the Balkan or Dalmatian region, carried distinctive broadswords and are thought to be the originators of the schiavona sword. These mercenaries were vicariously employed by both Spain and the Republic of Venice during the 16th and 17th centuries, but the schiavona is probably best known for its Venetian association. The Council of Ten, or Consiglio dei Dieci, under which the Doge (head of state) administered the Venetian state during the 1600s, hired many of these Dalmatian mercenaries to protect and promote Venetian interests. A large store of schiavona swords is still present in the Armoury of the Doge's Palace, in Venice. Most are stamped with the "CX" mark for the Consiglio dei Dieci.

The schiavona sword has a most distinctive hilt design. Hilt styles differ but they all exhibit the common feature of having a multi-leaf-shaped guard and "cat's-head", or katzenkopfknauf, pommel in either brass, bronze or iron. Early examples are simpler in form with less complex basket hilts, whereas later schiavonas are usually of higher quality, with the hilt bars cast in one piece.

This particular sword proved popular with central and north European cavalry during the 17th and 18th centuries. Its long and wide blade was very effective as a slashing weapon, allowing the horseman both to cut and to thrust.

Hunting swords

The dedicated European hunting sword came into prominence during the mid-1600s. Its rise was attributed to the increasing use of firearms and the changing nature of the hunt. Now the hunting sword was used to dispatch wounded or exhausted game brought to bay by the hounds, rather than being the

BELOW The Council of Ten at the Doge's Palace, Venice, painted in the 18th century. The council hired mercenaries during the 17th and 18th centuries to fight for Spain and the Republic of Venice.

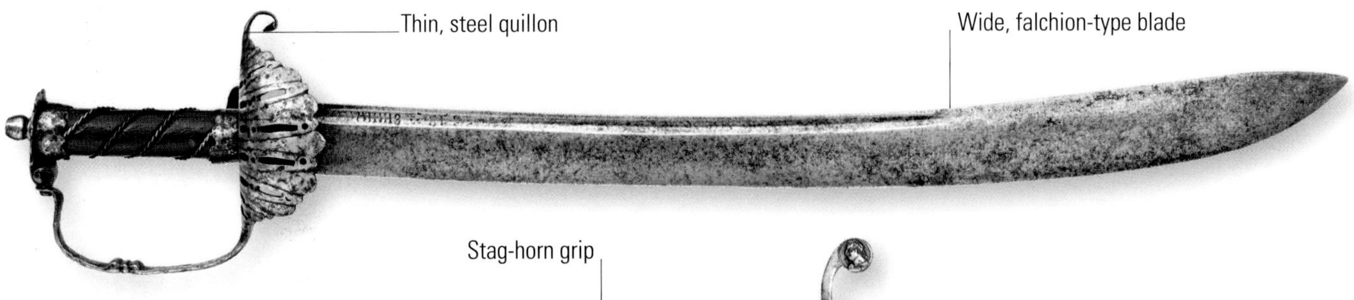

ABOVE A hunting sword or hanger, *c.*1650. The blade is curved and of falchion shape.

ABOVE The hilt of this hunting sword, 1650–75, is English, while the blade is German. The hilt is cast in hallmarked silver.

primary weapon of choice for the outright kill. Later, this sword would become more of an ornament than a functional weapon.

From around 1650, the most common form of hunting sword style was a short, lightweight hanger with a broad, single-edged, straight or sometimes slightly curved blade, typically no more than 64cm (25in) long. Some earlier blades had serrated back edges that could be used for sawing through bone.

Although hunting swords were used throughout western Europe, they were most popular in the German-speaking countries and France. Hunting swords were also referred to as hangers because they hung vertically from a sword belt, or baldric. German hunting swords are more commonly known as hirschfangers, which translates as "deer catchers".

Hunting sword hilts

Many different materials were incorporated into the construction of the hunting sword hilt, with a combination of two or three being quite common. Silver, brass, bronze, steel and later, silver was widely used. In England, silver was a popular metal for the manufacture of hunting sword hilts. The hilt would be cast in silver and then designs worked onto it, with prominent hallmarks stamped on the hilt, enabling identification of the maker and the place of manufacture.

Blade decoration

Although the hilts were furnished from many sources, the blade was normally obtained from Solingen, north-western Germany, which had a virtual monopoly on hunting sword blades from the 17th to the 19th century. Decoration of the blade usually took the form of an etched or engraved design, including scenes of the hunt and related animal motifs. A gold wash or gilt finish would sometimes be applied over these designs. Towards the middle of the 18th century, both blue and gilt were commonly applied to the blades.

Sword scabbards and sword styles

The hunting sword scabbard was in itself a very skilled piece of work. Each scabbard was individually constructed and fitted to its own sword. Scabbards of the 17th century were normally made from thin, shaped pieces of wood, glued together to form a rigid base that would receive an external covering of parchment, calfskin or Morocco leather. Scabbard mounts included a metal locket at the upper end and a chape at the tip. A stud was also fixed to the locket that would be placed in the eye of a belt frog worn around the waist or over the shoulder.

Occasionally, a pocket was constructed in the locket mount, containing either a small knife or a fork. The handles on these tools were matched with the sword hilt and designed to complement the rest of the outfit to form a set, or trousse.

Through the 17th and into the first half of the 18th century, hunting swords became even more ornamental and were decorated in the Baroque style. Based on classical ideals, this was ebullient in spirit and characterized by rich decorative effects, including the use of prolific foliage, rounded contours and heavy symmetrical volutes. By the mid-18th century, the Rococo style had taken over and motifs based on shell and rock forms, foliage, flowers, "C" scrolls and tortuous curves were now in vogue.

Scottish Highlander swords

For centuries the Scottish Highlander fought with a distinctively Scottish range of weapons. Most notable were the broadsword, targe (small shield), dirk (dagger) and polearm. Over time the Highland broadsword eclipsed the others, both in its unique design and in the associated romance that has captured the imagination of many. It took many forms: from the massive two-handed claymore of the 16th century to the agile basket hilt, wielded at the Battle of Culloden in 1746.

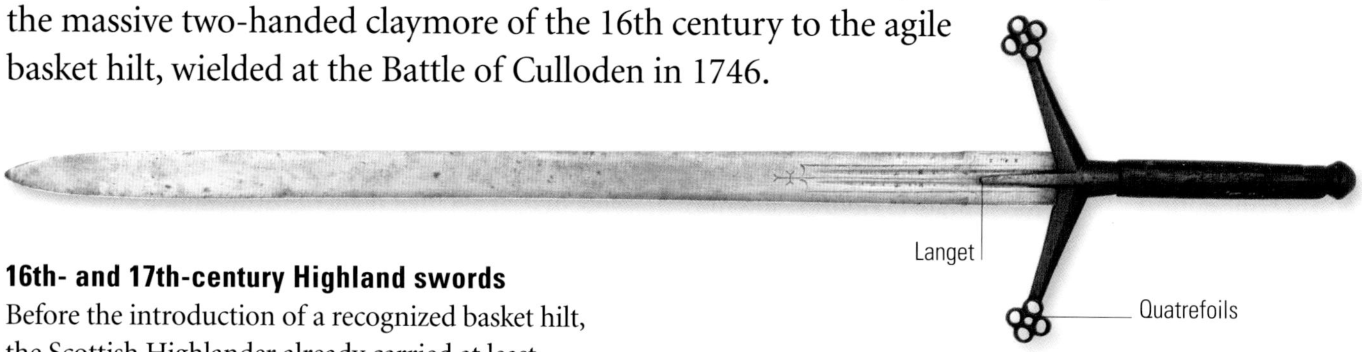

ABOVE A claymore, *c.*1600. This large sword was the mainstay of the Highlander until the late 17th century.

16th- and 17th-century Highland swords

Before the introduction of a recognized basket hilt, the Scottish Highlander already carried at least three distinct sword types. The first comprised the claidheamh mor (claymore), which was a double-edged broadsword. Introduced during the 1500s, it was of hand-and-a-half length, with a long, broad blade of diamond section, with a cross guard angled towards the blade. The end of the cross guard was also decorated with brazed iron quatrefoils (four-leafed flower petals).

LEFT A Scottish Highlander with basket hilt and targe (shield) at the Battle of Culloden, 16 April 1746.

In the late 16th and early 17th centuries, Highlanders also carried the claidheamh da laimh, a two-handed sword. It was similar to contemporary German or Swiss two-handed (Zweihänder) swords used by Landsknechte, or mercenaries. The few surviving Scottish examples have Scottish hilts fitted with German blades. The hilt includes an oval shell guard and long, flattened, downswept quillons. The third sword type is referred to as the "lowland sword". It had a very long blade with a characteristic side ring to the hilt, globular pommel and quillons set at right angles to the blade, terminating in knobs. These great lowland swords were used for many years, and even as late as 1746, after the Battle of Culloden, many examples were subsequently found on the battlefield.

Origins of the Scottish basket hilt

The geographical origin of the distinctly "Scottish" basket-hilted sword was not actually Scotland. Swords with basket hilts are thought to have originated in Germany, Scandinavia and even England, where basket hilts of simple form were already known by the early 1500s. The development of an enclosed hilt was a natural consequence of the need for more protection to the hand at a time when the wearing of armour,

RIGHT In this 17th-century oil painting of Mungo Murray (1668–1700), the fifth son of the Marquis of Athol, the subject is depicted as dressed for hunting in a costume of highland tartan. The sword he carries under his left arm is an early ribbon-hilted broadsword.

and particularly the metal gauntlet, had become less common. Why the sword became associated with Highland use is not clear, although it is known that numbers of Scottish mercenaries fought for the English in Ireland during the 16th century, and it is probable that basket-hilted swords were brought back to Scotland and their design copied by local sword makers. They were then known as "Irish" hilts by their English contemporaries.

The first true Scottish basket hilts

There are very few written or visual sources to enable us to determine exactly when the basket hilt began to be carried in the Highlands. The earliest known painting showing a Scottish clansman carrying this type of sword is recorded *c.*1690. The painting is of a Highland Chieftain by John Michael Wright (1617–94), and shows the subject carrying a broadsword with "beaknose" or ribbon hilt. This comprised a series of welded ribbon-like strips of metal drawn together to form a beak at the front of the basket. The "beaknose" hilt was a uniquely Highland style and differed from English basket hilts in that the pommel was of "coned form" as opposed to the English "apple" shape. Pommel shape is an important indicator of whether a basket hilt is either Scottish or English. A number of characteristic differences between the hilt styles of Scottish and English swords also began to emerge in the 1600s. English hilts tended to have thinner, more spaced, bars, whereas Scottish hilts adopted wider, rectangular plates to either side of the hilt, coupled with decorative heart-shaped piercing.

Highland feuds

The idea of Highland clansmen being compelled to fight each other to the death during a duel is not historically accurate. There were many feuds between rival clans and broadswords were normally employed to settle these quarrels. But they did not always result in the death of one opponent. It was enough for a swordsman to have drawn first blood. Rob Roy MacGregor (1671–1734), the famous Scottish patriot and folk hero, fought a duel with sword and targe just before his death. His opponent, Alasdair Steward of Invernahyle, won the duel with a cut to Rob Roy's arm.

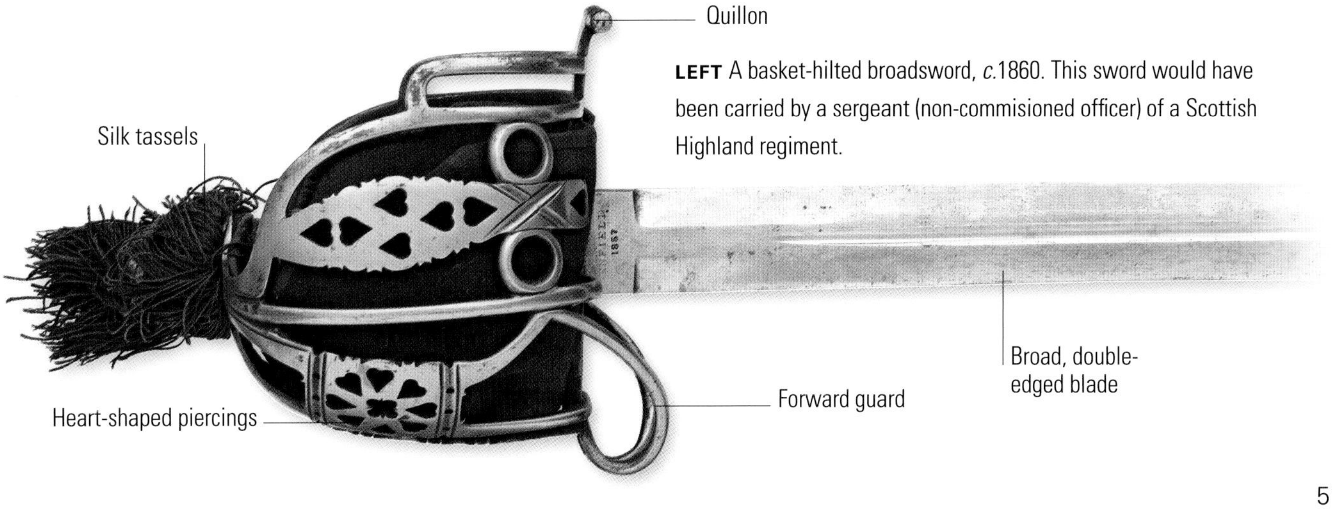

LEFT A basket-hilted broadsword, *c.*1860. This sword would have been carried by a sergeant (non-commisioned officer) of a Scottish Highland regiment.

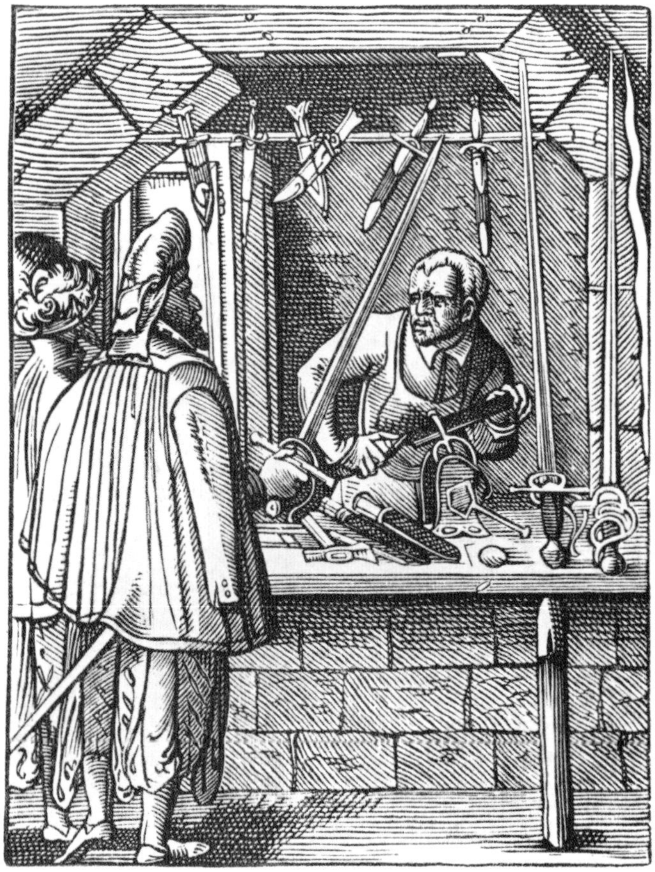

LEFT A European sword maker, *c.*1600. He is working on a sword hilt clamped within a vice. Around him are displayed daggers and rapiers.

Scottish sword makers

We know of specific Highland makers only in instances where the maker has signed the hilt. Most Scottish-made basket hilts are unsigned, adding to the confusion of identification. Scottish sword makers are normally described as falling into two notable schools of basket-hilted sword making – that of either the "Stirling" or "Glasgow" schools. Edinburgh did manufacture basket hilts but not to the extent of Glasgow and Stirling. Swords of these schools are now acknowledged as representing the apogee of Scottish basket hilt sword making during the 18th century. The superb craftsmanship and detailing to the hilts identify them as being of truly historic form. Two sword-making families, the Simpsons and the Allans, predominated during this period.

During the first quarter of the 18th century, father and son hilt-makers (or "Hammermen") John Allan Sr and Walter Allan Jnr from Stirling produced hilts of rare artistry and freedom of style, many with intricately inlaid brass circles, wavy lines and cross hatching.

The Simpson family of Glasgow included a father and two sons, all confusingly named John. In 1683 the father was admitted as a Freeman of the Incorporation of Hammermen of Glasgow and was later conferred the prestigious title of King's Armourer in Scotland (1715), an honour carried on by his eldest son. This family of sword makers produced some very fine basket hilts, noted for their restrained elegance and fine detail.

The wide variety and breadth of quality that we see in Scottish basket hilts indicates that many were produced as part of a "cottage" industry. Most blades were actually imported from the continent, principally Germany and Italy, with the hilts then manufactured and decorated in Scotland. Small workshops in Glasgow, Stirling, Edinburgh and other Highland locations produced the swords with a workforce comprising little more than one or two people.

Post-Culloden and the banning of swords

After the failure of the Highland Scots to restore James Stuart (the Young Pretender) to the English throne at the Battle of Culloden in 1746, the Scottish Highlander lost his right to bear arms, and the carrying of swords was outlawed by the English Government. Most swords were not handed over to the English but hidden. The ban also had a devastating effect on Scottish sword makers, and the production of basket hilts went into steep decline. The subsequent raising of regiments for the newly established British Army in Scotland created a requirement for basic military broadswords. Ironically, most of these were actually

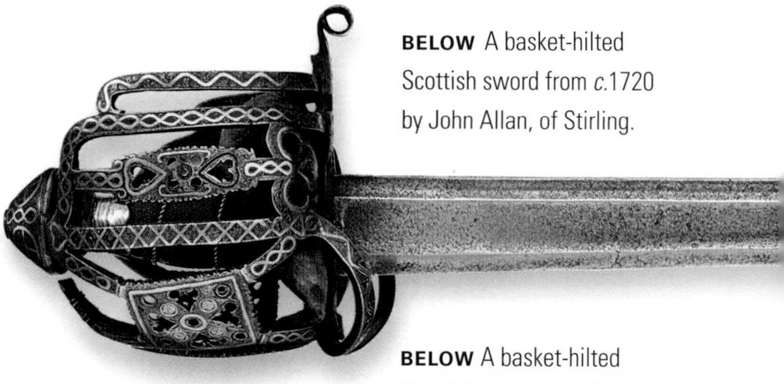

BELOW A basket-hilted Scottish sword from *c.*1720 by John Allan, of Stirling.

BELOW A basket-hilted Scottish sword with liner to protect the swordsman's hand from chafing against the hilt bars, *c.*1720.

The Highland charge

This account was written by Major General Hawley (*c.*1679–1759) before the Battle of Culloden and was meant to give the English soldiers a taste of what it would be like to face a mass charge of Highlanders.

They commonly form their Front rank of what they call their best men or True Highlanders, the number of which being always but few, when they form in Batallions they commonly form four deep...When these Battalions come within a large musket shott or three score yards this front rank gives their fire, and immediately throw down their firelocks and come down in a cluster with their swords and targets, making a noise and endeavouring to pierce the body or battalion before them – becoming 12 or 14 deep by the time they come up to the people they attack.

Records show that in most cases the enemy would have already fled the battlefield before the Highlanders reached them, but in the case of the Battle of Culloden the English forces had established complete military superiority, and could rely on the combined forces of the cavalry, infantry squares (armed with musket and fixed bayonet) and strategically placed artillery pieces.

No amount of heroic brute force could withstand this new form of military warfare. The Highlanders were unsurprisingly cut down in swathes.

ABOVE The Battle of Culloden, 16 April 1746. The army of Charles Edward Stuart (the Young Pretender) was swiftly crushed by William, Duke of Cumberland.

produced in England. A basket-hilted sword for infantry privates in Highland regiments was issued *c.*1750–70. It was of relatively poor manufacture, with a thin sheet-metal guard and crude cut-outs in the junction plates. The grip was leather on wood. Blades were manufactured in London or Birmingham and marked with a royal "GR" crown, and the maker's name of either "Iefries" (Jeffries, London) or "Drury" (Birmingham). Most Scottish-made basket-hilted swords after 1746 are likely to have been made for officers in the newly formed Highland regiments.

In 1798, a regulation pattern of Highland Infantry Officer's basket-hilted broadsword was introduced. Its gilt brass basket hilt mirrored previous Highland designs. This pattern was replaced in 1828 by a basket hilt that is still worn by officers of Highland regiments in the British Army.

The Lochaber axe

First noted in the 1600s, the main polearm of the Highlander was the Lochaber axe. Its name derives from the Lochaber area of the Scottish Western Highlands. Agricultural in origin, it was similar to cropping tools such as the scythe. The pronounced hook at the back of the axe could also have been used to pick up tied bundles. The axes ranged in height from 1.8–2m (5.9–6.5ft), including the haft.

This was a weapon carried extensively by Highland infantry and used primarily against massed cavalry. The axe hook allowed the Highlander to pull the cavalryman off his horse from where he could be swiftly dispatched with the thrusting, spiked end or axe blade.

ABOVE Re-enactors fighting with Lochaber axes and spears. The axes were heavy weapons, used by foot-soldiers for defence against cavalry and as a pike against infantry. The axe consisted of a wooden handle (haft) and a blade.

Napoleonic swords

Sword fighting during the Napoleonic Wars was primitive and brutish, typified by the thundering clash of opposing cavalry regiments and the hacking melee that followed. Unlike modern warfare, where military technology can quickly locate and kill at a distance, the Napoleonic swordsman was alongside his opponent and victim. Ironically, despite this battlefield butchery, the Napoleonic soldier lived in an age of Neo-classical and Romantic revival, in which elegant sword styles were matched by equally opulent uniforms.

British cavalry swords before 1796

Until the introduction of a universal sword for both light and heavy cavalry in 1788, the British Army had left the decision of which swords should be carried to individual colonels of regiments. Unsurprisingly, this led to a chaotic situation, with a plethora of sword types, many varying in both quality and effectiveness. Some unscrupulous colonels purchased cheap, substandard swords in the expectation of pocketing a profit from the deal and some regiments adopted swords that invariably broke on first contact with the enemy. This continual failing of blades during combat forced the authorities to establish a system of official government "proving", or testing, of blades. Eventually, a new series of officially approved cavalry sword patterns was introduced.

At this time, heavy cavalry regiments were issued a large iron or steel basket-hilted broadsword with a long, straight, broad-fullered blade. Military experience soon indicated that it was not a good design, with both officer and trooper versions badly balanced and cumbersome. The official system of blade inspection was still in its infancy and not all the blades were vigorously tested, so poor blade quality was still a major problem. The light cavalry version comprised a slightly curved blade and stirrup-shaped hilt. It was better received by troopers in the field as the curved blade proved effective at slashing on horseback.

The argument of whether a "cut" or "thrust" blade was most effective in battle would be continually debated within the British Army for the next 100 years, and many sword tests undertaken to establish the truth. This conundrum would not be properly resolved until 1908 when, with the introduction of the 1908 Pattern Cavalry Trooper's Sword, the British Army chose a thrusting rather than a cutting sword.

In 1796, two new sword designs were issued to officers and men. Blades were now subject to a more rigid official testing regime. A punched stamp with a crown and inspector's number was placed on the ricasso (the flat of the blade near the hilt) to indicate that a blade had been passed as suitable for use in combat.

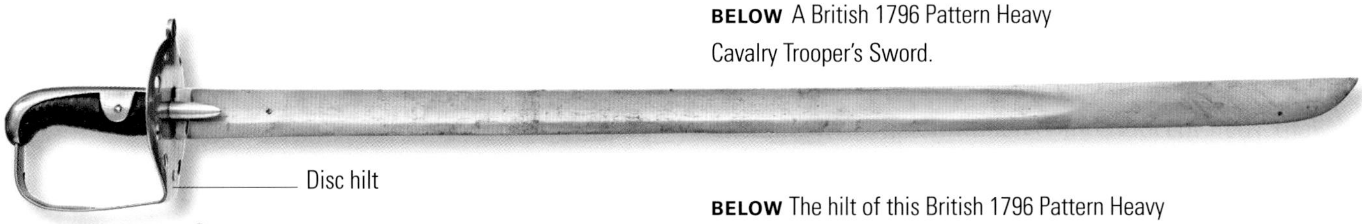

BELOW A British 1796 Pattern Heavy Cavalry Trooper's Sword.

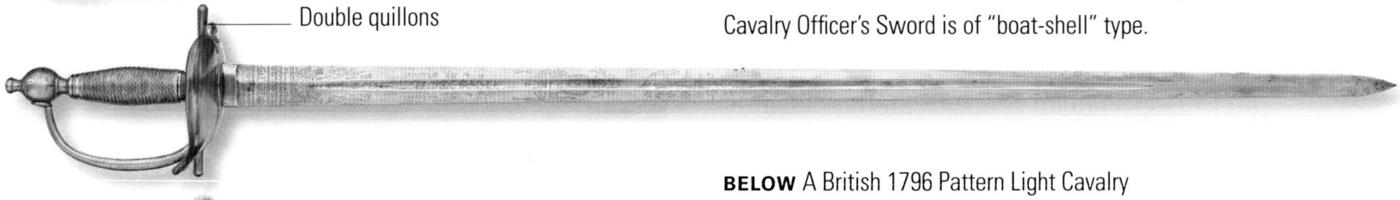

BELOW The hilt of this British 1796 Pattern Heavy Cavalry Officer's Sword is of "boat-shell" type.

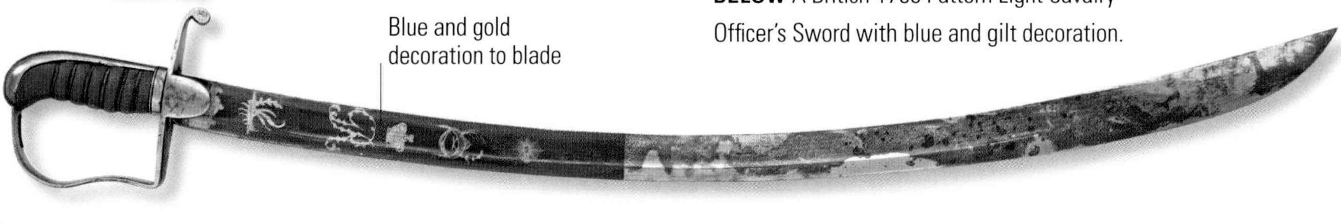

BELOW A British 1796 Pattern Light Cavalry Officer's Sword with blue and gilt decoration.

ABOVE The painting *Scotland for Ever,* by Lady Butler, shows the charge of the Royal Scots Greys at Waterloo in 1815. They are depicted carrying the 1796 Pattern Heavy Cavalry Trooper's Sword.

British cavalry swords after 1796

The 1796 Pattern Heavy Cavalry Trooper's Sword has found modern-day recognition as the sword favoured by Captain Richard Sharpe of the green-jacketed 95th Rifles Brigade, a colourful and dashing fictional character in the novels by Bernard Cornwell. The practical necessity for an infantry officer to carry such a long sword is a little far-fetched as the weapon actually measured around 110cm (43.3in) from blade tip to top of the hilt, which would have made it quite a burden to drag around while on foot. The reality is that most rifle officers carried a stirrup-hilted and curved sabre of much smaller proportions.

One of the most famous real-life exponents of this pattern sword was Sergeant Charles Ewart of the 2nd Dragoons (Scots Greys), who captured the French Eagle at the Battle of Waterloo (1815). His later retelling of the act highlights the effectiveness of a large sabre when used in the right hands.

It was in the charge I took the eagle off the enemy; he and I had a hard contest for it; he made a thrust at my groin I parried it off and cut him down through the head. After this a lancer came at me; I threw the lance off my right side, and cut him through the chin upwards through the teeth. Next, a foot soldier fired at me, then charged me with his bayonet, which I also had the good luck to parry, and I cut him down through the head; thus ended the contest.

Sgt. Charles Ewart, 2nd Dragoons
(Scots Greys), Waterloo, 1815
from Edward Cotton, *A Voice from Waterloo* (1862)

The 1804 Birmingham sword trials

Driven by a heady mixture of technological pride and simple xenophobia, two Birmingham-based sword cutlers, James Woolley and Henry Osborn, were so certain of the superiority of their British-made sword blades that they agreed to a series of tests vying their blades against a number of imported German blades from Solingen that were currently being supplied to the British Army. On 7 November 1804, the tests were conducted under the supervision of a Major Cunningham. Predictably (and no doubt foreknown by Woolley and Osborn), the Solingen blades failed in droves, with many of them snapping immediately upon being struck against iron plates or when bent with any force. Both Woolley and Osborn went on to become major suppliers of military swords to the British Army throughout the Napoleonic Wars.

French cavalry swords

The rise of Napoleon Bonaparte coincided with a great revival and interest in the ancient classical world, particularly its architecture and decoration. This creative mood was not lost on French sword makers and Napoleon, who also understood the morale-boosting effect of appearance in his army. This resulted in many new cavalry sword designs being introduced during this period. One of the most influential designs was the AN XIII Heavy Cuirassier Trooper's Sword. It was a very heavy sword, with a four-bar brass hilt and a long, straight, single-edged blade measuring around 95cm (37.4in). It was a fearsome sword when used as a thrusting weapon (almost like a small spear) causing more fatal injuries than the hatchet-bladed and slashing swords of the British cavalry regiments. A French eyewitness recounts the effectiveness of these spear pointed blades but also acknowledges that when a British blade found its mark it could be equally devastating:

We always thrust with the point of our sabres, whereas they always cut with their blade which was three inches wide. Consequently, out of every twenty blows aimed by them, nineteen missed. If, however, the edge of the blade found its mark only once, it was a terrible blow, and it was not unusual to see an arm cut clean from the body.

Captain Charles Parquin, "*Chasseurs à Cheval of the Imperial Guard*"
from Charles Parquin, *Military Memoirs*, ed. (1969)

The French light cavalry trooper carried an elegant three-bar, brass-hilted sword with slightly curved blade, with hussar regiments favouring a stirrup-hilted sword. Elite regiments such as the Imperial Guard Dragoons carried a fine broadsword with brass basket hilt, cap pommel and a hilt with an inset oval plate and a silver or brass flaming grenade badge. The Mousquetaires de la Garde du Roi, who served as the mounted bodyguard to Louis XVIII (*r.*1814–24) after Napoleon abdicated his throne in 1814, used an equally elegant sword. It was similar to the Imperial Guard Dragoon's sword, but with a cross, fleur-de-lys and sun ray inset within the hilt.

The manufacture of French swords

Swords issued by the government to French cavalry troopers were normally marked on the spine of the blade with the year, month and place of manufacture. From the 1700s, the town of Klingenthal, in Alsace, eastern France, became the official government location for the manufacture of French military

ABOVE In this illustration, *c.*1790, entitled *Officier de Cuirassiers de la Garde Royale*, you can see the sword knot hanging from the sword hilt. It prevented the sword from slipping out of the hand.

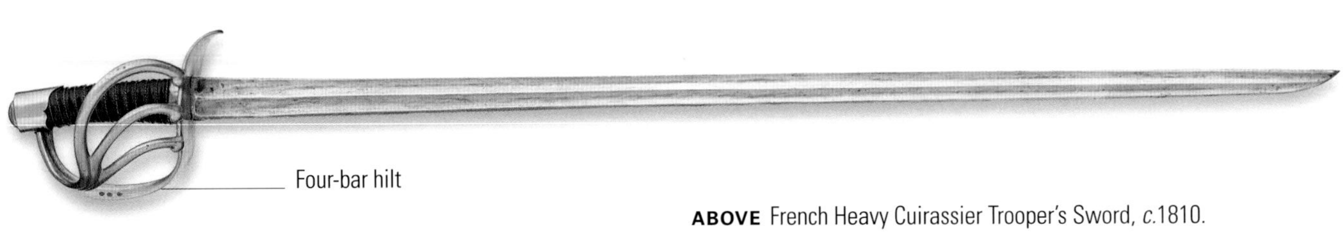

ABOVE French Heavy Cuirassier Trooper's Sword, *c.*1810. It was used primarily as a thrusting weapon.

ABOVE Small officer's sword, dated 1780, presented to Napoleon by a friend and comrade who attended military school with him.

swords. It produced an enormous quantity of swords, both before and after the French Revolution. Blades produced during the period of Louis XVIII's monarchy are marked to the spine with a designation of "Rle" (Royal). Those manufactured during the reign of Napoleon are marked with the designation "Imple" (Imperial). After the Napoleonic Wars (1799–1815), French sword hilts and blades were constantly re-used and many Napoleonic era blades were fitted on new hilts well into the 19th century.

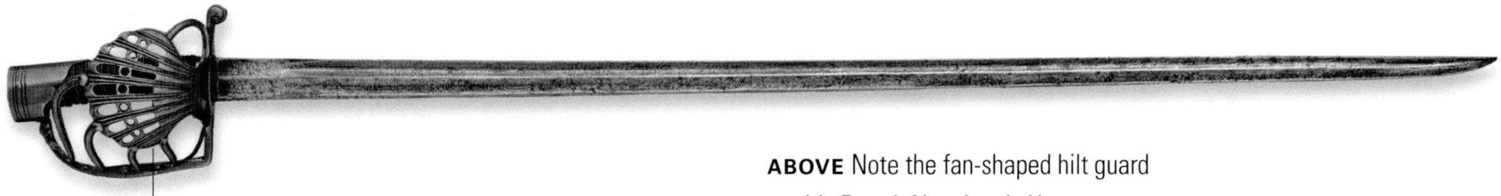

ABOVE Note the fan-shaped hilt guard on this French Napoleonic Heavy Cavalry Officer's Sword from *c.*1800.

The mameluke sword

During the Egyptian campaigns of 1798–1801, the French army was greatly influenced by its military contact with the opposing Mamluk slave troops of the Ottoman (Turkish) Empire. Dressed in colourful robes and armed with pistol, daggers and distinctively curved scimitars, the Mamluks soon caught the attention of many French officers, who quickly adopted their scimitars, now renamed mamelukes, as part of their military uniform.

Evidence of the vogue for mameluke swords amongst French officers is found in the famous painting of *The Battle of the Pyramids* (1810) by Antoine-Jean Gros (1771–1835), in which he depicts *all* of the French officers carrying mameluke swords. Napoleon was so impressed with the fighting spirit of the Mamluks that he went on to purchase 2,000 troops from Syrian merchants, raising a regiment of "Mamelukes", who eventually served in his Imperial Guard. Napoleon also chose a Mamluk (Roustam Raza) to be his personal bodyguard. The mameluke sword was also adopted by British officers, and its influence even spread to the burgeoning United States, where Marine Lieutenant Francis O'Bannion was presented with a scimitar for his capture of Derne (modern-day Tripoli) in 1804, the first recorded land battle of the US Army on foreign soil.

ABOVE The victorious French officers at the battle of the Pyramids, 21 July 1798, are all carrying mameluke swords.

RIGHT The mameluke sword presented to Marine Lieutenant Francis O'Bannion, in recognition of his leadership and success during the capture of Tripoli, 1804.

British infantry swords

Officers did not carry an officially approved regulation sword until 1786. Before this, an officer chose his own sword and most opted for variations of the popular narrow-bladed smallsword. Some also opted for short hangers with flat-backed blades.

1786 Pattern Infantry Officer's Sword

Following an Order issued by George III (1738–1820), the 1786 Pattern Infantry Officer's Sword was introduced. The Order stipulated that this new sword pattern must be:

> *...strong cut and thrust weapon with blade 32in long and 1in wide at the shoulder, the hilt to be steel, gilt or silver according to the buttons of the uniform.*

Grips were composed of either ribbed ivory, ebony or dark horn, with some swords having a metal "cigar band" placed around the centre of the grip. This normally bore an engraved royal crown, the "GR" cypher of George III, or even a regimental badge. Hilts had a cushion-shaped pommel and forward knuckle bow with five decorative balls, or "beads". These beads are sometimes found on the side guard.

BELOW A 1786 Pattern Infantry Officer's Sword, with ivory hilt.

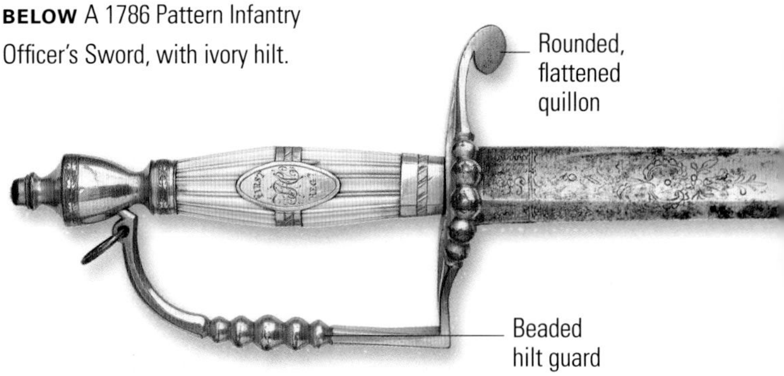

Later versions featured a fixed double-shell guard and "Adam style" urn pommel (from the Neo-classical architect Robert Adam, 1728–1792). Both pommel and quillon were decorated with acanthus leaves.

1796 Pattern Infantry Officer's Sword

The disparate hilt variations were finally standardized in the 1796 Pattern Infantry Officer's Sword, a weapon that epitomized the British Napoleonic Infantry Officer's sword. The original inspiration for the design came from Prussian military smallswords of the 1750s. Upon close inspection, it is clear that this rather flimsy bladed sword would not have stood up to a charging horseman's broadsword or sabre, but these were times

Sword wounds

Ironically, a clean sword cut received during battle probably gave you more chance of survival than a wound caused by a musket ball or artillery. This is because the steel blade was less likely to contain deadly infected matter that could be driven into the body by the discharge of a firearm. Surgeons also found sword wounds easier to treat through cauterization, and consequently patients were less likely to suffer the effects of gangrene and post-operative infection. Although a cut from a sword could undoubtedly inflict dreadful wounds, there are many tales of soldiers receiving multiple sword wounds and still surviving. At the Battle of Waterloo (1815), the French divisional commander, General Pierre-François Durette, of the Fourth Corps, lost his hand to a sword cut and also received life-threatening cuts to the face and head, leading to blindness in one eye. Remarkably, he survived these awful injuries and lived on until 1862.

LEFT The Battle of Waterloo, 18 June 1815. Napoleon is depicted with sword aloft rallying his men, including the Imperial Guard (on the right of the image).

The hussars of eastern Europe

A common image in both British and French art of this period, and also found engraved on many sword blades, is the sight of a dashing hussar, sword held aloft. The word *hussar* is Hungarian in origin and loosely translated means "highwayman" or "brigand", but was later used to describe a lightly armed horseman. Hungarian and Polish-Lithuanian hussars of the 17th and 18th centuries were utilized as shock troops during constant wars with the Ottoman Empire in eastern Europe and the Balkans. They carried both curved and straight-bladed swords. Importantly, Polish hussars also retained the lance and were largely responsible for its re-introduction during the Napoleonic Wars. Napoleon formed his own Imperial Guard regiment of lancers in 1810, known as the Red Lancers. They fought with distinction in the Russian campaign of 1812 and the Battle of Waterloo in 1815. Their lances were around 2.74m (9ft) long with a fluted steel point, mounted on a wooden shaft.

LEFT The swords carried by hussars inspired the curved sabres adopted by British light cavalry regiments of the early 19th century.

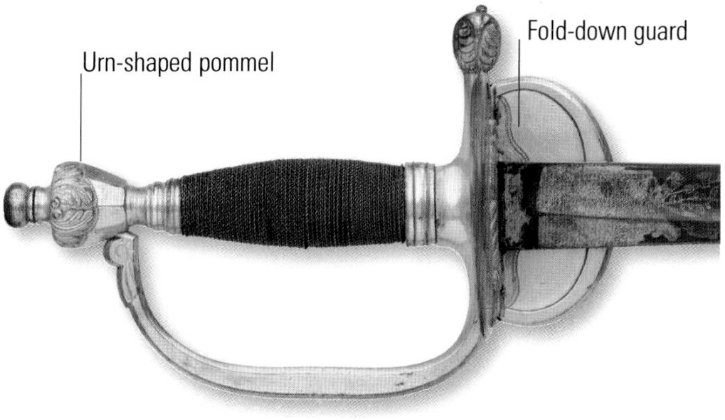

LEFT A 1796 Pattern Infantry Officer's Sword, with folding shell guard.

when elegant appearance sometimes took precedence over practicality. Protection for the hand was minimal, with just a single knuckle guard and double shell guard. One of the shell guards was hinged in order that it could be folded and so prevent chafing by the uniform. The grip was bound in either silver wire or applied sheet silver. Blades were lavishly decorated with blue-and-gilt highlighted engraving.

1803 Pattern Infantry Officer's Sword

The colourful image of the gallant and dashing light cavalryman or hussar had created a strong impetus within British light cavalry regiments to carry a curved or "hussar" sabre that reflected this new *esprit de corps.* Not to be outdone, the infantry regiments introduced a new pattern of sword based on contemporary light cavalry swords.

The 1803 Pattern Infantry Officer's Sword had a single-edged, curved blade with a lion's-head pommel and a gilt brass knuckle bow. A "GR" royal cypher and crown were affixed within the knuckle bow, and above that was a representation of either a strung bugle, denoting use by a rifle company officer, or a flaming grenade, symbolizing a grenadier company officer. The blade was usually decorated in blue and gilt.

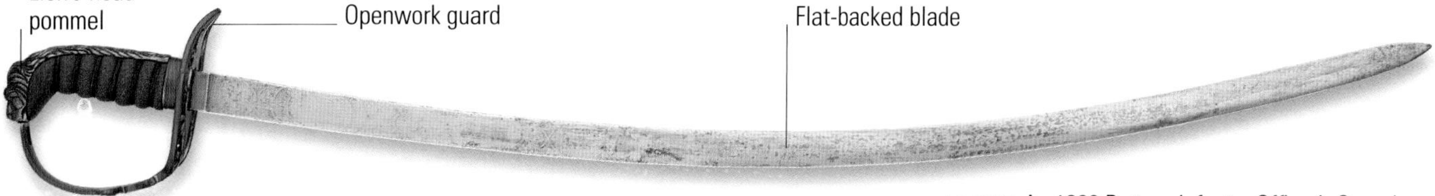

ABOVE An 1803 Pattern Infantry Officer's Sword with a lion's-head pommel.

ABOVE Napoleon bids farewell to the Imperial Guard at Fontainebleau in April 1814, after his first abdication and prior to his exile in Elba. The following year he was to lose the Battle of Waterloo.

French infantry swords

Napoleon Bonaparte's armies displayed a far greater range of infantry swords than most of their European counterparts. The perceived importance of rank and regiment was highly regarded within the French Army and we find that an infantry private, sergeant, captain and general officer all carried their own specific model of sword. The early years after the French Revolution (1789–99) saw the development of many distinctive infantry swords, including those carried by prestigious regiments such as the Garde Nationale and Garde Nationale Chasseur. These unique swords featured Neo-classical helmet pommels and half-basket brass guards with republican emblems (such as the Phrygian cap) placed within the hilt cartouche.

A common type of sword carried by French infantry privates during the Napoleonic Wars was the sabre briquet, which was a short, brass-hilted hanger. It comprised a slightly curved, single-edged, flat-backed blade with brass and leather mounted scabbard. This sword was widely copied throughout Europe and adopted by many countries during the early to mid-1800s. Napoleon also understood the importance of rewarding his favoured regiments with honours or special uniform and equipment privileges. This beneficence also applied to swords. An example of this is the distinctive sword of the Imperial Sappers (Pioneers) of the Old Guard. They were awarded a newly designed uniform including bearskin, felling axe, apron and, more importantly, a striking, cockerel-hilted sword. They were also granted the unique right to grow a beard.

French infantry smallswords and curved sabres

Throughout the 18th century, French infantry officers had always carried a straight-bladed sword. It usually took the form of a traditional smallsword, with pommel styles ranging from plain ovoid to Neo-classical helmet. Shell guards were also classically inspired, with some featuring extensive embossed decoration including victory wreaths, stands of trophies and figures in classical poses.

This style continued throughout the Napoleonic Wars and blades were also frequently finished in blue and gilt. The vogue for Neo-classical hilts and corresponding decoration to the blade influenced the design of other infantry swords, including a wide range of curved infantry sabres, similar to their light cavalry counterparts but with shorter and lighter blades. There was little official pressure formally to regulate these swords and French officers were allowed a great deal of freedom to choose whatever style of sword they wished to carry.

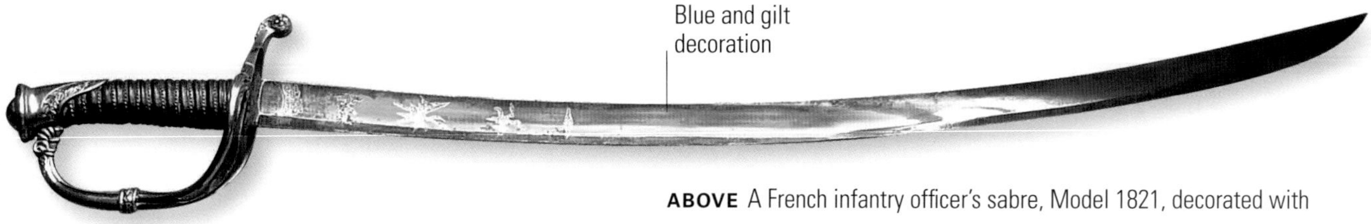

ABOVE A French infantry officer's sabre, Model 1821, decorated with blue and gilt. This form of decoration was beginning to lose favour and later examples have plain blades.

Russian infantry swords

From the mid-1700s, Russia embarked on a sustained period of contact and rapprochement with the West. These new influences hastened changes in civil administration, architectural styles, dress and, most importantly, military organization. The czars had looked with envy at the disciplined troops of Frederick the Great of Prussia (1712–1786) and wanted the same attitude to be instilled within their own ranks. To do this the czars needed to change the whole appearance of the Russian army which, it was hoped, would then improve the military effectiveness of both the officers and rank and file. One of the methods of achieving this goal was to adopt Western military dress and weapons.

By 1800, the Russian infantry officer was carrying a smallsword of European style. The Model 1786 Infantry Officer's Sword had a slightly curved, double-edged blade with a brass, heart-shaped guard and ovoid pommel. It was contained within a leather and brass mounted scabbard. Subsequent patterns (Model 1796 and Model 1798) had straight, single-edged blades with typical Napoleonic double shell guards and pronounced upward quillons.

Lower ranks in the infantry carried simple brass-hilted short swords with shell guards. As the century progressed, the Russian infantry adopted the same style of brass-hilted hanger as that carried by Prussian and English troops.

German infantry swords

The German states of the 18th and 19th centuries normally followed the sword patterns and styles prevalent throughout Europe. In keeping with French and English infantry privates of the mid- to late-1700s, a short, brass-hilted infantry hanger was carried throughout the Napoleonic Wars, particularly by Prussian infantrymen.

By 1800, German officers were already wearing a sword similar in design to the British 1796 Pattern Infantry Officer's Sword (the British had actually copied the pattern from a Prussian design of the 1750s). Hilt design was also heavily influenced by French infantry swords of the period. Sword blades featured engraved decoration, including the coats of arms and royal cyphers of individual states. Blue and gilt were also used extensively. There was no real attempt at uniformity of pattern, and different German states adopted and jealously guarded their own styles of infantry sword.

Austro-Hungarian infantry swords

The Austro-Hungarian infantry officer of the 1800s followed the same path as his British and German counterparts in favouring a smallsword. It included a gilt brass hilt with double boat shell guard and rounded pommel. The blade was straight and double-edged. Blades were normally engraved with the royal cypher and double-headed eagle of the Habsburg monarchy. Austrian infantry officers also carried a wide range of unofficial swords, including wide-bladed and curved "hussar"-type sabres. This type of sword was popular with infantry regiments throughout Europe during the 19th century.

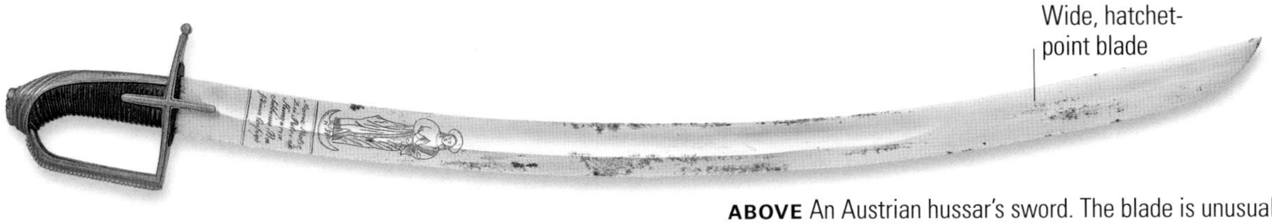

ABOVE An Austrian hussar's sword. The blade is unusually wide, and single-edged with a hatchet point.

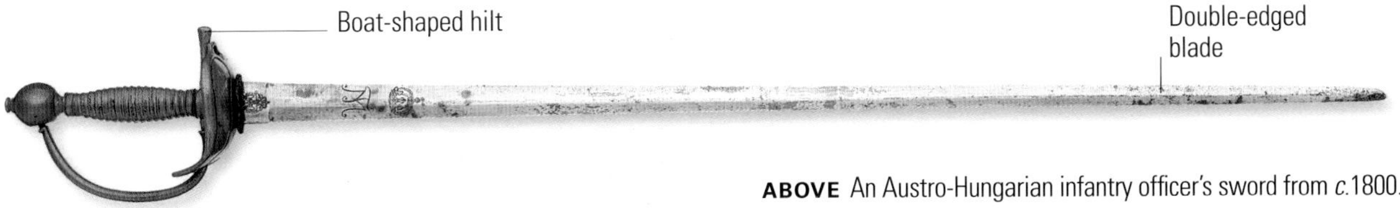

ABOVE An Austro-Hungarian infantry officer's sword from *c.*1800. It has a double-edged blade with a double boat shell guard and rounded pommel.

The American sword

At the start of the American War of Independence (1775–83) the opposing armies carried a very similar range of weapons. This was inevitable because the Continental Army of General George Washington (1732–99) included many former British-trained local militias, armed with both British government and their own privately purchased weapons. As the war progressed and the British blockade of ports such as Boston (1775) began to bite, American forces had difficulty sourcing weapons from overseas. This forced them to rely on simple, locally manufactured swords, leading to the adoption of a distinctly "American" sword style.

Colonists' swords in the 16th and 17th centuries

The early settlers of the 16th and 17th centuries, living in newly established colonies such as Virginia and New England, were predominantly of British stock and brought with them significant quantities of edged weapons, particularly swords. Contemporary records of the period and subsequently excavated examples indicate that rapiers, short hangers and long-bladed horsemen's sabres were the most common sword types of this period. Apart from swords brought directly from England or purchased from passing trading ships, a number of simple, locally forged swords were also manufactured in the colonies.

The American colonies were a crucial part of the expanding empires of both Great Britain and France, so a regular military presence was required to maintain order and promote national interests. During the early 18th century, soldiers from these nations carried the same swords in the colonies as they would have done in their home countries, including short, brass-hilted hangers for infantry troops and short hangers or smallswords for the officers.

The American War of Independence

During the early years of the American War of Independence the colonists fighting against the British and her allies would have carried virtually identical swords to their enemies. Later in the war, when replacements became more difficult to source from overseas, the colonists turned towards domestically manufactured weapons to fill the shortfall. Local American blacksmiths forged simple military blades that were attached to improvised hilts.

Although these blades were never produced to impress (tending to be flat, unfullered and undecorated), they proved quite effective on the battlefield. In the absence of any official style or designated sword patterns for the new Continental Army, American sword makers merely copied or interpreted the British or French patterns available at that time. The main priority of the Continental Army was to produce swords and edged weapons as quickly as possible.

LEFT The surrender of the British General Cornwallis, Yorktown, 1781. It was a tradition that the defeated commanding officer handed over his sword to the victor.

Cavalry swords in the 18th century

American cavalry troops of the 1770s carried an assortment of swords, including long, straight-bladed, basket-hilted broadswords and light cavalry sabres. Many would have been captured from the British. Their armoury also included home-made "D-guard", slotted-hilt, and flat-bladed backswords with simple, turned wooden grips. Typical pommel shapes such as ball, urn, cap, ovoid, high domed, flat or lion's head were also used. Scabbards were manufactured in leather and wood, with crude iron mounts.

Infantry swords in the 18th century

The ordinary American infantry soldier and officer of the 1770s had an extensive range of weapons, many of them captured from the British and some home-produced. The short hanger or hunting sword was favoured by the infantry officer, especially when fighting in the dense forests of North America, where a long-bladed sword was sometimes impractical. Smallswords were also carried by American officers but it is unlikely they would have been the first weapon of choice for combat.

Sword types after the War of Independence

During the War of Independence, the Eagle Pommel Sword became one of the defining "American" sword types of this period. It remained popular after the war. In the 1800s, many of these swords were supplied to American officers by British-based sword makers, most notably William Ketland and Henry Osborn of Birmingham. In America, Frederick W. Widmann, a German-born sword maker, made distinctive and high-quality Eagle Pommel Swords in Philadelphia during the 1830s and 1840s. Indian-head and Neo-classical helmet pommels were also very popular during this period. Blade decoration began to incorporate specifically nationalistic American themes.

The new cavalry sword of 1798

After independence, the new American government began to form its fledgling army into established regiments, and with this reorganization there was the requirement to arm troops with new swords. The American Congress did not want to rely solely on overseas countries for their swords and so a domestic manufacturer was actively sought for a new model of cavalry sword. Nathan Starr, of Middleton, Connecticut, initially produced 2,000 Model 1798 Cavalry Trooper's Swords.

The sword had a simple stirrup guard with a leather and wood-covered grip, and a single-edged, slightly curved blade. The blade was marked "N Starr & Co." on one side and "US – 1799" on the other. Starr produced updated versions of this sword between 1814 and 1818.

The "Eagle Pommel Sword"

A common weapon of the post-Revolutionary War period was the American "Eagle Pommel Sword". During the war, other animal forms were also used for the pommel, including horses', dogs' and lions' heads. The variety of hilt and pommel types produced by American sword makers is numerous, and they were manufactured in silver, brass and iron, with grips of ivory, horn, wood and leather. They also differed widely in terms of quality and construction, reflecting the challenging conditions and the scarcity of basic materials. The sword makers were usually imitating British and continental sword styles of the period, but the relative naivety of design and crude construction of some types can be differentiated as typically "American". Conversely, there were also many American-made swords of this period that exhibited excellent workmanship.

ABOVE The American Eagle Pommel Sword was used by American officers. Early swords were normally produced in England.

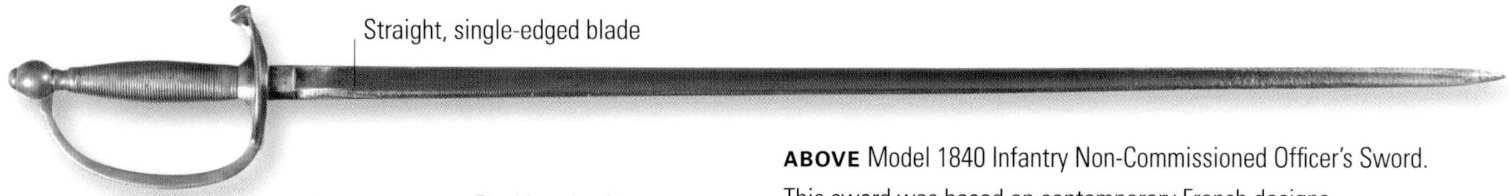

ABOVE Model 1840 Infantry Non-Commissioned Officer's Sword. This sword was based on contemporary French designs.

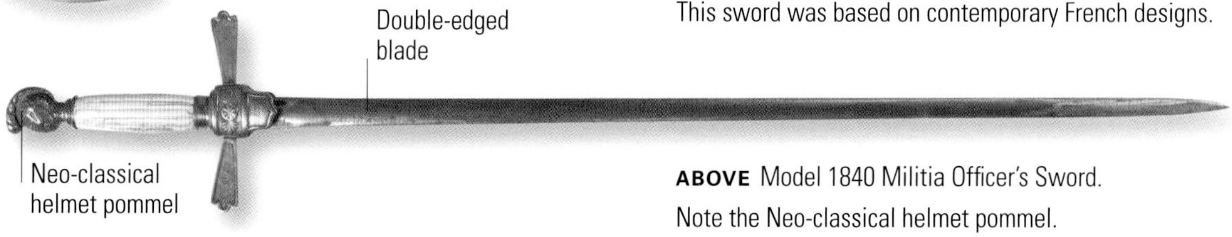

ABOVE Model 1840 Militia Officer's Sword. Note the Neo-classical helmet pommel.

By 1833, the N.P. Ames Sword Company of Springfield, Massachusetts, was manufacturing a robust brass, three-bar hilted cavalry sword with slightly curved blade. It was not well received by soldiers and, in 1840, the company introduced a cavalry trooper's sword of French style. This had a heavy, three-bar, brass hilt and a slightly curved blade with steel scabbard. It was grudgingly known by its users as the "wristbreaker".

This sword was replaced again in 1860 by a much lighter version, which became the standard issue cavalry trooper's sword for Union troops throughout the American Civil War (1861–65). The sword was updated in 1872 and 1906. Officers carried more elaborate versions with etched blades and embossed and gilt-covered hilts.

Infantry swords after 1830

Regulation infantry swords for the US Army began to appear from the 1830s. In 1832, a rather impractical smallsword of English style, with a gilt-brass boat-shell hilt, ovoid pommel and straight blade was introduced for officers of the Infantry, Artillery and Ordnance. There followed a number of other regulation infantry swords including the Model 1840 Foot Officer's Sword, similar to the Non-Commissioned Officer's version. The blade was straight, single-edged, with a double fuller. Decoration included drums, cannons, floral sprays, "US", eagles and crossed military pikes.

During the 1840s, states raised their own militias, and officers were required to provide their own uniform and sword. This gave them the opportunity to choose from a wide variety of swords from private manufacturers. Differences of design normally centred on the pommel type and blade decoration. Some have Neo-classical helmet pommels in the style of contemporary French infantry swords, and other examples feature diverse interpretations of the American eagle-head pommel.

Militia regiments were also keen to present swords to fellow officers, and some presentation-grade swords are truly spectacular, with grips of engraved brass, silver or even gold, with heavy embossed decoration to the hilt and scabbard mounts. A number of swords were decorated over the entire length of the blade. The regular US Army also carried sword patterns specific to individual departments or branches of service. These included the Model 1834 Revenue Cutter Service Sword; the Model 1840 Engineer's Sword; the Model 1840 Commissary Officer's Sword; and the Model 1832 and Model 1840 Medical Staff Officer's Sword.

Infantry swords after 1850

In the mid-19th century and in keeping with the vogue for French-inspired designs, the US Army introduced a completely new sword for infantry officers. The Model 1850 Foot Officer's Sword is an almost exact copy of the French Model 1845 Infantry Officer's Sword. The blade is slightly curved and single edged, with double fullers. Decoration took the form of an outstretched American Eagle, floral and military motifs, "US" and the US government motto

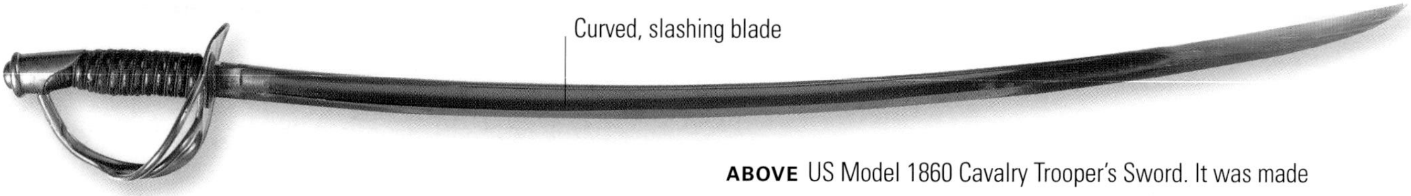

ABOVE US Model 1860 Cavalry Trooper's Sword. It was made by Mansfield and Lamb of Forestdale, Rhode Island.

Confederate swords in the American Civil War (1861–65)

Prior to the American Civil War, the US Army was composed of officers and men from both the Southern and Northern states. In general, they carried the same sword models and this continued until war between the Union and Confederacy was declared on 12 April 1861.

During the early days of the war, many Confederate officers still carried their original Union swords but, as the war dragged on and the Union undertook a successful blockade of southern ports, overseas sword imports to the South began to dry up. Some imports still got through and Confederate agents were constantly busy in Europe, sourcing swords from both Britain and Germany, but this was still not enough to furnish a growing Confederate army and to replace the loss of existing swords due to combat. Confederate officers also wanted to differentiate themselves from the enemy and carry swords that reflected their national aspirations. This meant that the Confederate government was forced to turn to local manufacturers to make up the shortfall.

Southern sword makers usually copied the Union sword patterns, but there were subtle changes. These included the replacement of the standard "US" lettering on sword hilts with a "CS" or "CSA", representing the Confederate States or Confederate States of America. Blade etching also included specifically Southern motifs, including the five-pointed star of the Confederacy or a circle of 11 stars, which represented the 11 Confederate states.

However, most Southern sword makers, working with basic machinery and lacking essential raw materials, were forced to produce rather crudely manufactured swords. The quality deteriorated even further as a number of established Southern sword-making factories were overrun by Union forces towards the end of the war.

ABOVE William Tecumseh Sherman (1820–91) left, Union general, meeting General Joseph E. Johnston (Confederate) to discuss terms of surrender of Confederate forces in North Carolina, 24 April 1865.

BELOW Confederate Cavalry Officer's Sword, *c.*1864. Standards of manufacture in the north were invariably superior.

E Pluribus Unum (Out of Many, One). A large number of these swords were imported from Europe at the beginning of the American Civil War to make up for a shortfall in home production.

The Model 1850 Staff and Field Officer's Sword is similar to the Model 1850 Foot Officer except that it has an additional branch to the hilt, with a "US" set between the hilt bars. This was one of the most popular officer's swords carried by line officers and staff officers between 1850 and 1872.

Cavalry swords in the 20th century

The Model 1913 "Patton" hilt Cavalry Trooper's Sword was based on a design presented by the young Lieutenant George S. Patton (1885–1945) of the US Army, later to become a famous American general during World War II. This sword owes more than a passing nod to the popular British 1908 Pattern Cavalry Trooper's Sword but it differs in having a dove-head pommel, slightly lower basket guard and a wider, double-fullered blade.

Post-Napoleonic swords

The massed cavalry charges of the Napoleonic Wars had been a vital shock tactic, however, as the 19th century progressed, their effectiveness began to be questioned, especially in light of the huge advances being made in military technology. The contest between bullet and blade had now become one-sided. In the American Civil War, only 2 per cent of wounds received were from edged weapons. Nonetheless, the sword was still regarded as an essential combat weapon, and efforts were redoubled to design the perfect sword.

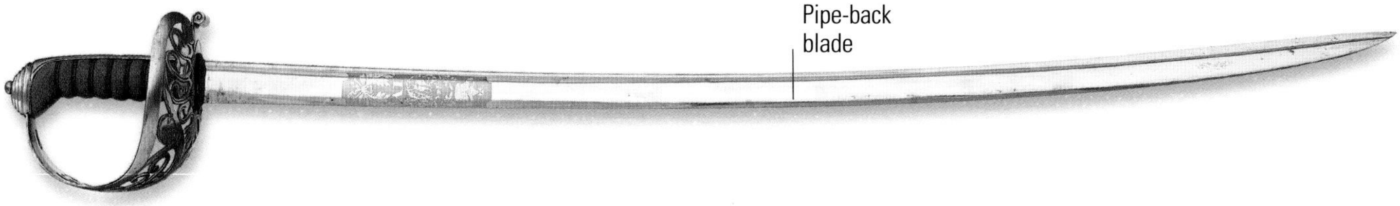

ABOVE British 1821 Pattern Heavy Cavalry Officer's Sword with pipe-back (tubular) blade.

British light and heavy cavalry swords

Following the Napoleonic Wars, the British Army introduced a series of cavalry swords with both cut and thrust capabilities. These included the 1821 Pattern Light and Heavy Cavalry Trooper and Officer's swords. The light cavalry version comprised a steel, three-bar hilt and slightly curved, spear-point blade. Heavy cavalry officers also carried a spear-point blade, etched for most of its length, with a pierced bowl guard of acanthus-leafed decoration. Heavy cavalry troopers had a plain, solid bowl guard. The initial reception of these swords by troops in the field was poor, with frequent complaints that blades were too thin and liable to snap in combat. Soldiers also encountered difficulties when attempting to pierce enemy uniforms with their sword points, especially during the Crimean War (1853–56), when the Russian infantryman's thick greatcoat, combined with a rolled blanket worn on his back, made penetration by the blade extremely difficult.

The British universal pattern of 1853

In 1853, the next major change in British sword design occurred, when the differentiation between heavy and light cavalry troopers' swords was finally dropped in favour of a universal pattern. This was the 1853 Pattern Cavalry Trooper's Sword. It had the same three-bar hilt and blade as the previous 1821 pattern but employed a new "patent" grip, designed by the sword maker Charles Reeves, in partnership with fellow sword maker Henry Wilkinson. It was a revolutionary hilt design as it enabled the full width of the tang to be driven the length of the grip, rather than the previously tapered and potentially weaker tangs. Chequered leather grips were then riveted through this full-length tang, adding more strength and durability.

Thrusting versus cutting swords

From the mid-19th century, British cavalry swords went through a further series of changes. The historic argument concerning the use of either a thrusting or a cutting sword continued, with many official army committees established to consider the question. The eventual result of this "decision by committee" process was a predictably unsuitable compromise, with blades being neither fully straight to enable proper thrusting

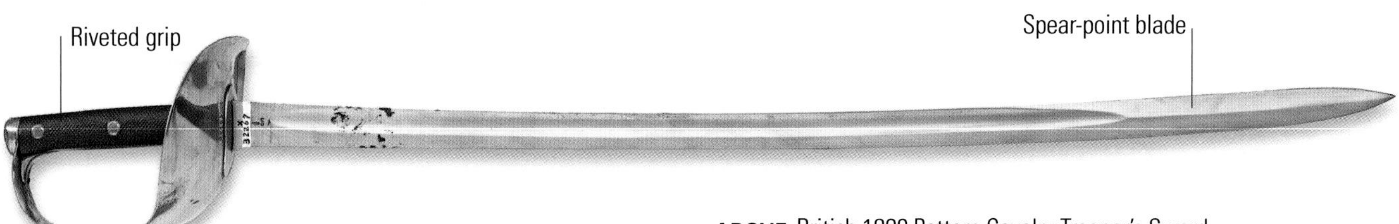

ABOVE British 1899 Pattern Cavalry Trooper's Sword with a slightly curved, spear-point blade.

The charge of the 21st Lancers, Battle of Omdurman, 1898

During the Second Sudan War, the Battle of Omdurman in 1898 was one of the last occasions when massed British cavalry carrying lances charged in force at the enemy. The future British prime minister, Winston Churchill, was present at the battle as a young cavalry officer attached to the 21st Lancers and he later graphically described his first-hand experiences on 2 September 1898. The sight of the 21st Lancers just before the famous charge was caught by Churchill in typically realistic terms:

...a great square block of ungainly figures and little horses, hung all over with water-bottles, saddle bags, picketing gear, tins of bully beef, all jolting and jangling together; the polish of peace gone; soldiers without glitter; horsemen without grace; but still a regiment of light cavalry in active service against the enemy...

from Winston Spencer Churchill, *The River War: An Historical Account of the Reconquest of the Soudan*, 2 Vols., ed. Col. F. Rhodes (Longmans, Green, London, 1899).

Colonel R.M. Martin, commanding officer of the 21st Lancers, initially engaged his 300 lancers with what appeared to be a few hundred Dervishes from the army of Abdullah al-Taashi (successor to the so-called "Mad Mahdi" Muhammad Ahmed, responsible for the death of General Gordon at Khartoum in 1885). But within seconds, over 2,000 spearmen and swordsmen crouching in a nearby shallow depression had risen to meet the advancing lancers. Having committed the regiment to the charge and too close to wheel around, Martin and his lancers crashed into the waiting Dervishes. Later accounts highlight the sheer brutality and bloodshed experienced during these colonial encounters. For their gallant action against impossible odds and driving back the Dervishes, three Victoria Crosses (the highest award for gallantry in the British Army) were subsequently awarded to members of the 21st Lancers. Their losses were five officers, 65 men, and 120 horses.

RIGHT Charge of the 21st Lancers at Omdurman, 2 September 1898. The battle was seen as Britain's revenge for the death of General Gordon at Khartoum, 1885. The charge of the 21st Lancers was regarded as the last full cavalry charge of a British regiment equipped with lances.

nor sufficiently curved for effective cutting. The patterns of 1864, 1882, 1885, 1890 and 1899 highlight the constant changes made to cavalry swords during this period in order to achieve this requirement.

British infantry swords

The Napoleonic 1796 and 1803 Pattern Infantry Officers' swords had a relatively long service life, and it was not until 1822 that a new pattern replaced them. This was very different in design to its predecessors and featured a "pipe-back" blade with a tubular sectioned back, or spine, to provide extra strength, combined with a "Gothic" gilt brass, half-basket hilt. The term "Gothic" refers to the similarity of the hilt profile to medieval Gothic church windows, the design of which heavily influenced the Gothic Revival in Britain during the first half of the 19th century. Within the hilt there was placed a "cartouche", or inset panel, featuring a cut-out royal cypher of the reigning monarch: for example, "VR" for "Victoria Regina".

British infantry swords in the late 19th century

The blue and gilt blade decoration favoured by a previous generation of British infantry officers had now become unfashionable, and blades were acid etched (rather than engraved) on a plain background.

Scabbards were leather and gilt brass mounted (for dress), brass or plain steel. The updated 1845 Pattern removed the folding guard, and the original pipe-back blade was replaced in the 1850s by a single-fullered "Wilkinson", spear-point blade that proved less prone to breaking.

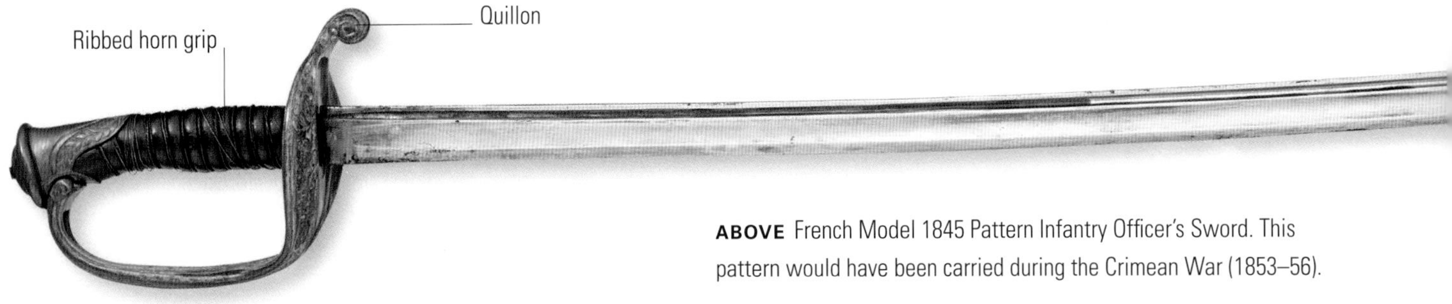

ABOVE French Model 1845 Pattern Infantry Officer's Sword. This pattern would have been carried during the Crimean War (1853–56).

In 1892, the blade changed to a "dumb-bell" profile and became a purely thrusting weapon. There was also a complete redesign of the hilt which now took the form of a solid sheet steel, half-basket guard impressed or pierced with the Victorian royal crown and cypher. In 1895 and 1897, there were minor modifications to the hilt, including the addition of a turned-down inner edge to avoid fraying the officer's uniform.

The Rifle and Foot Guards regiments carried a steel half-basket-hilted sword (1827 Pattern and 1854 Pattern) of similar design to the 1822 Pattern "Gothic" hilt but with the addition of their regimental badges within the hilt. In 1857, the Royal Engineers were designated a pierced gilt-brass, half-basket-hilted sword which they carried until 1892, when they reverted to the standard 1897 Pattern Sword for all infantry officers.

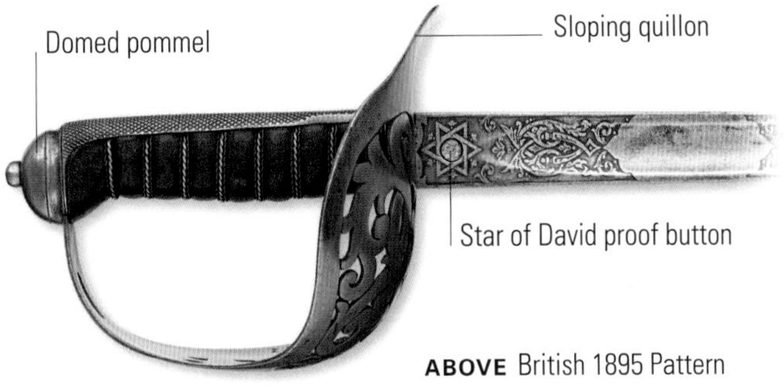

ABOVE British 1895 Pattern Infantry Officer's sword.

French infantry swords

The French Model 1821 and 1845 Infantry Officer's Sword was a radical departure from previous infantry swords, and its elegant design inspired many other countries, particularly the United States. It comprised a decorated brass, half-basket hilt with a single knuckle bow guard and a slightly curved, single-edged, quill point blade. Grips were of ribbed horn and brass twistwire. The later Model 1845 continued the knuckle bow into a pierced shell guard with floral decoration. The blade was also a little straighter and produced in both pipe-back and quill-pointed form. Scabbards were leather and gilt-brass mounted. In 1855, the blade was changed to a single-fullered, spear-point type. This sword was carried until 1882, when the French Army introduced a nickel-plated steel, four-bar hilted sword with a much narrower, straight blade.

French sword design

In 1822, a new light cavalry sword was issued to French cavalry troopers. It comprised a three-bar brass hilt, slightly curved blade, and heavy steel scabbard. It would be adopted by many other countries during the 19th century. This was also true of the French Model 1829 Mounted Artillery Sword that featured a single "D-guard", brass knuckle bow and unusual, slightly domed pommel. This style of sword was copied by the United States (Model 1840 Artillery Officer's Sword) and carried throughout the American Civil War by Union forces. Other European nations such as Spain, Germany, Belgium and even Russia were all heavily influenced by French three or four-bar hilt design and French-designed blades.

BELOW French Model 1822 Light Cavalry Officer's Sword. Unlike the trooper's version, the hilt has been decorated.

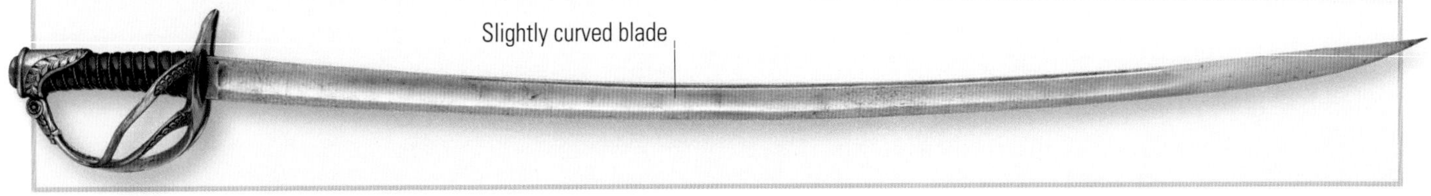

LEFT Falguière's hilt was decorated with patterns of delicate flowing curves and botanical forms around the guard. On the pommel, an open wreath of acanthus and oak foliates surrounds the owner's initials.

French cavalry swords

The Model 1822 Light Cavalry Sword had a long service life, only being replaced in 1896 by a new universal cavalry sword, which served for both light and heavy cavalry. The officer's version of this 1896 Pattern Cavalry Officer's Sword is quite unique with an innovative hilt style. It is very much an example of contemporary Art Nouveau decorative art forms influencing the design of a weapon of war. The hilt ornamentation was designed by the French sculptor and painter Jean Alexandre Falguière (1831–1900), who was a professor at the École des Beaux-Arts in Paris.

Falguière designed the hilt around a pattern of flowing lines and botanical motifs that draped itself around the bowl guard. Symbolism was important to exponents of Art Nouveau (1890s–early 1900s), and we see this with the striking incorporation of the mythological figure of Medusa's head into the curving quillon. The sword has always had an important association in mythology. In this case the designer has focused on the myth of Perseus and Medusa. The sight of the gorgon Medusa would turn men to stone, but Perseus managed to kill her by only viewing her image reflected in his shield. He cut off her head with his sword and gave the head to Athena, who placed it in the middle of her shield to terrify her enemies.

In 1923, a universal model of sword for all officers of the French Army was issued. This was an attractive sword with a gilt-brass, shallow-bowl hilt, and single knuckle bow. The sides of the bowl guard were pierced and decorated with leaf patterns, and its overall appearance was still clearly influenced by the Art Nouveau movement.

ABOVE A professor at the École des Beaux-Arts in Paris, Jean Alexandre Falguière (1831–1900), designed the hilt of the 1896 Pattern Cavalry Officer's Sword in the Art Nouveau style.

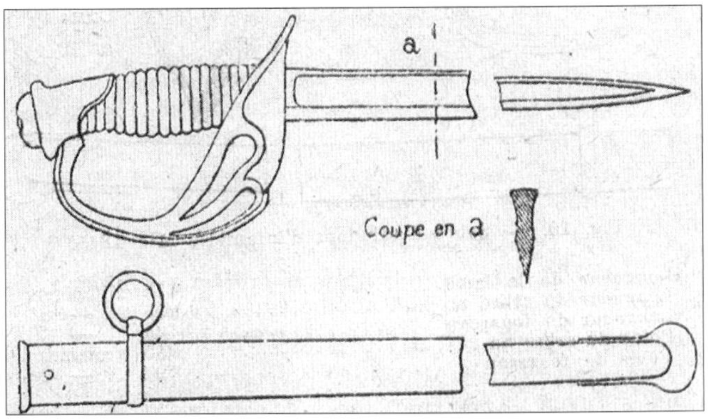

ABOVE An official diagram of the 1896 Pattern Cavalry Trooper's Sword, issued in 1937 by the French Ministry for War.

Naval swords and edged weapons

The truly naval sword probably originated in the 16th or 17th century. Before then, naval officers and sailors carried swords identical to those on land. During this time, navies began to evolve from legalized privateers serving under covert royal patronage into more organized enforcers of a state's military and commercial interests. Ship and crew underwent changes in their administration, equipment and appearance. The emergence of "fighting ships" in the 18th century meant that close hand-to-hand boarding engagements became common. Effective swords, axes and pikes were needed for chaotic, confined naval encounters.

The emergence of the British cutlass

Cutlasses were provided for seamen by the Board of Ordnance. This was a British government authority created in the 15th century with the responsibility for the design, testing and production of armaments for both the British Army and Navy. From the late 1500s, a short-bladed weapon described as a "curtleax", or coute-lace, was carried on British ships. Although this is now thought to have been more of an axe than a sword, the name was established and, by the 18th century, ships' captains began to refer to a specific sword for use on board ship as a "cuttlashe".

British cutlasses in the 18th and 19th centuries

The number of cutlasses carried on board a ship was actually small in relation to the numbers of sailors, and not every seaman was issued with a cutlass. Other weapons such as pikes and axes were employed to fill the gaps. The manufacturing quality of these early cutlasses was quite poor and most cutlass hilts were made from a single piece of thin sheet steel, which opened out into two discs for better hand protection. Blades were flat, single-edged, straight or slightly curved.

Cutlass manufacture for the Royal Navy was undertaken by a number of English sword makers, resulting in a marked variation in both quality and reliability. The official inspection and testing of sword blades was still in its infancy during this period. In 1804, a regulation pattern of seaman's cutlass was adopted. This was the "figure-of-eight", or double disc-hilted, cutlass and is probably the one most commonly associated with British seamen during the Napoleonic Wars. It comprised a blackened cast-iron hilt with ribbed grip and a straight, flat, unfullered blade.

Subsequent patterns followed in 1814, 1845, 1858 and 1889 until 1900, when the last official pattern was introduced. Naval planners of the 1900s realized that boarding actions in the age of the ironclad battleship were unlikely and no more patterns were introduced after this date. In 1936, the cutlass was withdrawn from British naval use except for ceremonial purposes.

British naval officers' swords in the 17th and 18th centuries

Up until the beginning of the 19th century, a Royal Navy officer was given considerable leeway as to which edged weapons he carried. During the latter part of the 17th century, the rapier was abandoned by naval officers in favour of short-bladed, hunting-type hangers. These short swords were far more practical when officers were fighting amongst the rigging and confined spaces of a ship's deck. Many contemporary portraits show British naval officers carrying these swords. Naval officers might also have carried a smallsword, which was similar in design to those carried by civilians or army officers, although some rare examples displayed nautical motifs to the hilt and blade.

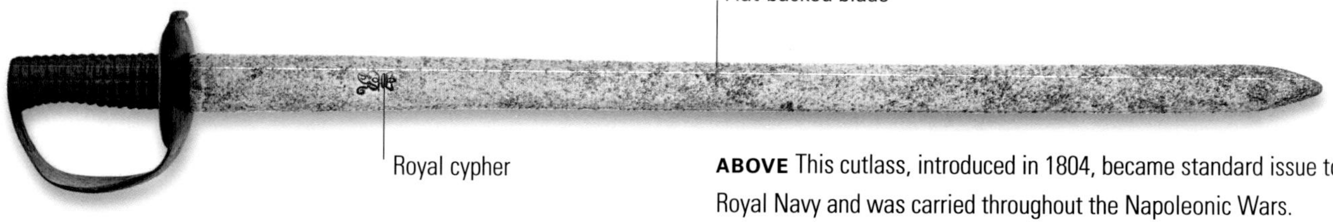

ABOVE This cutlass, introduced in 1804, became standard issue to the Royal Navy and was carried throughout the Napoleonic Wars.

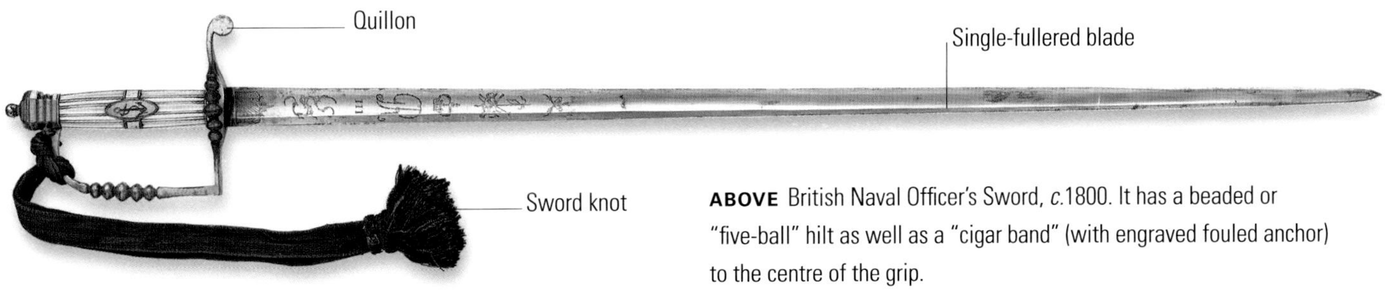

ABOVE British Naval Officer's Sword, *c.*1800. It has a beaded or "five-ball" hilt as well as a "cigar band" (with engraved fouled anchor) to the centre of the grip.

In 1786, the British Army formally adopted a new regulation pattern sword for all infantry officers, and naval officers soon copied this style. The cut-and-thrust blade was straight with a beaded or "five-ball" "D-guard" hilt and cushion pommel. An anchor was also engraved into a gilt-brass "cigar band" that was placed in the centre of a ribbed ivory or ebony grip. Some examples also had a small anchor placed in the centre of a side ring. Other sword types included "S-bar" hilts (which featured an anchor) and stirrup hilts engraved with anchors on each of the hilt langets. These swords imitated contemporary infantry and cavalry swords.

By the late 18th century, the hunting hanger was dropped in favour of a more traditional short infantry sword with "slotted" guard, lion's-head or ovoid pommel and slightly curved blade. To distinguish them from infantry swords, many had a small fouled anchor inserted into the slotted guard or engraved on the pommel.

BELOW A British naval officer's sword, *c.*1815. It has the standard lion's head pommel and the ivory grip indicates that its owner was a high-ranking officer. This is not a fighting sword and would have been carried as a dress weapon, reserved for social occasions.

British naval officers' swords in the 19th century

The 1805 Pattern Naval Officer's Sword was a more recognizably "naval" style of sword. It featured a gilt-brass lion's-head pommel and engraved fouled anchor to the langets (located in the centre of the cross guard). Blades were straight and single-fullered. Many had extensive blue and gilt decoration, including naval motifs such as flags, trophies, anchors and buoys. A Royal Navy midshipman (junior officer) of the early 1800s carried a sword similar in design to senior officers but with black rather that white fishskin or ivory grips. In 1827, officers adopted a solid, gilt-brass, half-basket hilt, a pattern that mirrors the 1822 Pattern Infantry Officer's Sword. The grip was composed of white fishskin (black for warrant officers), and blades were initially of pipeback and quill point profile, changing to a single-fullered "Wilkinson"-type blade in the mid-1850s. The 1827 Pattern is still carried by serving Royal Navy officers today.

Other British naval sword designs included a mameluke sword for flag officers; open rather than solid hilts; "dove-head" pommels (for warrant officers); and a Scottish Highland, or "claymore", blade, which became popular in the late 19th century.

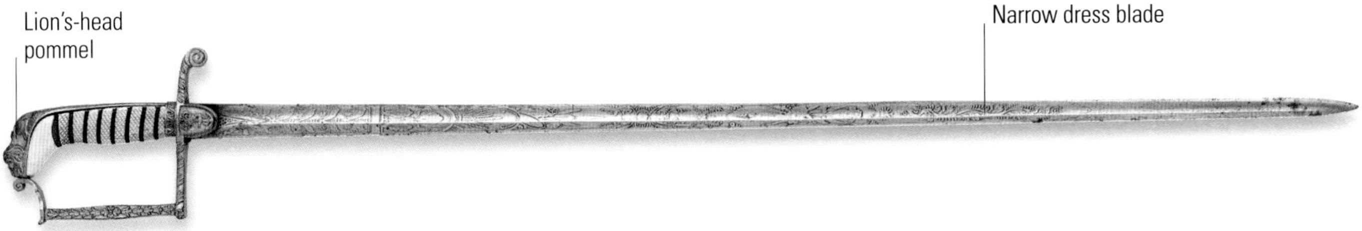

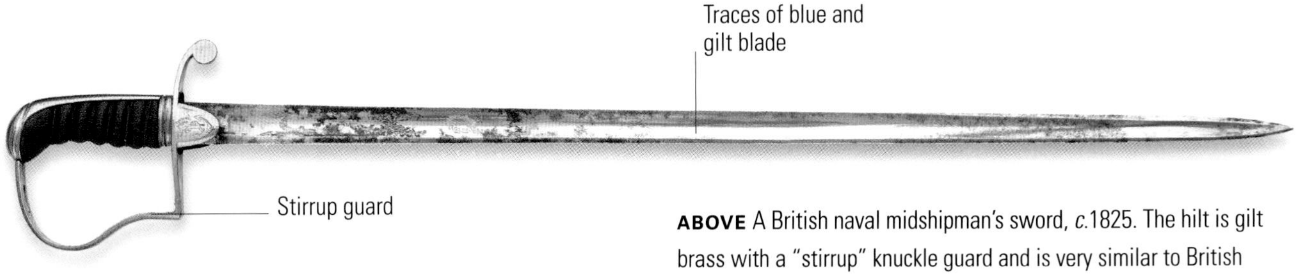

ABOVE A British naval midshipman's sword, *c.*1825. The hilt is gilt brass with a "stirrup" knuckle guard and is very similar to British cavalry hilts of the period.

Presentation swords

It was common practice during the Napoleonic period for British naval officers to receive presentation swords in honour of their gallant acts in the face of the enemy and bodies such as the Corporation of London regularly bestowed presentation or commemorative swords.

The Lloyds Patriotic Fund presentation swords have since become famous for their opulence, craftsmanship and breathtaking beauty. They were paid for and presented by members of the insurance house, Lloyds of London, between 1803 and 1810, and were given in recognition of the recipient's bravery under fire. They were also an acknowledgement of (and a vote of thanks for) the protection afforded by the Royal Navy to British commercial interests, both home and abroad, during the long wars with Napoleon.

The swords were awarded in four categories depending on the cost of manufacture and rose in magnificence as their value increased. They were presented as swords of £30, £50 and £100 value. There was also a special sword of truly epic grandeur awarded to the 29 captains and lieutenants who commanded ships during the Battle of Trafalgar, in 1805.

The Lloyds' swords had heavy, slightly curved blades with lavishly applied blue and gilt decoration, white ivory grips and opulent hilts of fire gilt. The hilt backpiece was decorated in imitation of a lion skin and the quillons displayed ancient Roman fasces (tied bundles of birch rods wrapped around an axe and symbolizing "strength through unity"). The knuckle guard took the form of a stylized interpretation of the club of Hercules entwined by a serpent. Scabbards were even more elaborate, encased in either leather or blue velvet (depending on the value awarded) and decorated with numerous classical reliefs and panels. The production of these swords was a showcase for the artistry and imagination displayed by some of the finest artisans in Georgian London.

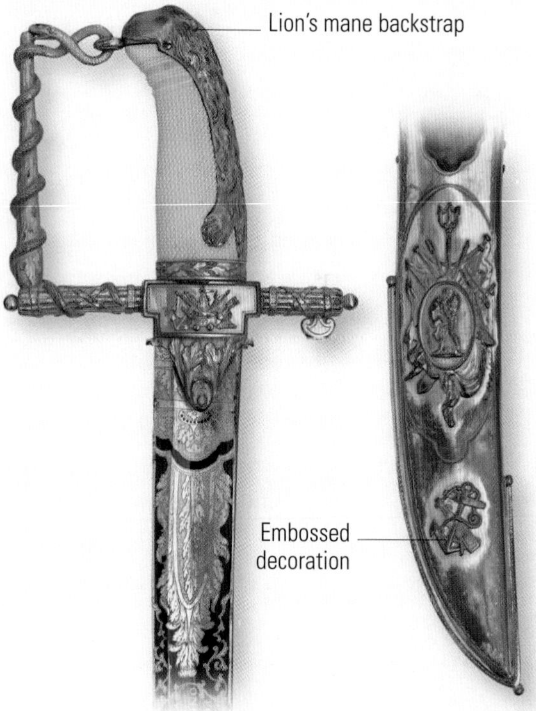

ABOVE From the Patriotic Fund at Lloyds to Lieutenant James Bowen of HMS *La Loire*, who was commader of one of the boats that successfully attacked a French national brig in 1803.

French cutlasses in the 18th and 19th centuries

In the 18th century, cutlasses in the French Navy were formally standardized with the introduction of a Model 1771 Seaman's Cutlass (modified in 1782-83). The hilt was brass with a ribbed grip and prominent pommel cap. It was similar to contemporary infantry grenadier hilts, but differed in having a three-bar hilt rather than a single knuckle guard.

The Napoleonic Model Year XI (1801–02) Cutlass had a large, half-basket guard of blackened iron, with a smooth octagonal grip and a slightly curved and wide-fullered blade. A later model (1833) saw the addition of an engraved anchor to the blade. The Model 1872 was the last regulation pattern French cutlass and comprised a hilt of plate steel, shaped grip and perforated guard.

French naval officers' swords in the 18th and 19th centuries

During the 18th century, French naval officers followed the British practice of carrying swords similar to those in the army. Later, a more uniform sword was introduced based on a French Light Cavalry Officer's sword differing only in having an engraved anchor within the lozenge-shaped hilt langets. In 1805, a new pattern saw the complete removal of langets and the placing of an anchor within the cross guard.

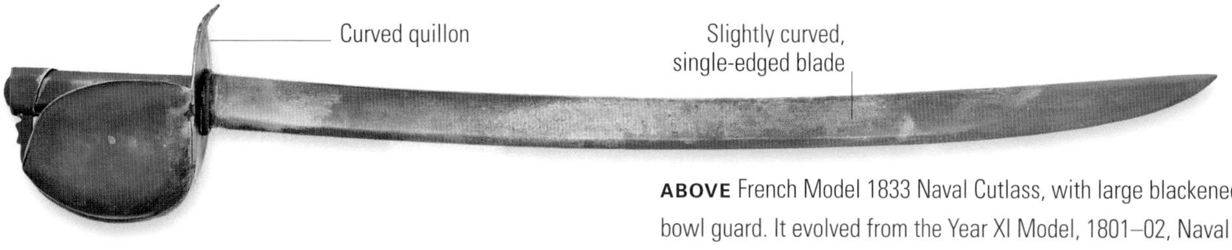

ABOVE French Model 1833 Naval Cutlass, with large blackened bowl guard. It evolved from the Year XI Model, 1801–02, Naval Cutlass, introduced during the Napoleonic period.

In 1837, a completely new sword design is noted. It comprised an elaborately decorated gilt-brass, half-basket hilt, incorporating an anchor, royal crown and display of martial trophies. There followed some slight changes to the hilt decoration in the years 1848 (removal of the royal crown), 1852 and 1870.

BELOW Portrait of Louis-Jean-Marie de Bourbon (1725–1793), Admiral of the French fleet. He is carrying a smallsword favoured by officers.

German cutlasses in the 19th and 20th centuries

During the mid-1800s, Prussian naval seamen carried a cutlass that was almost identical to the French Model 1833 Cutlass, differing only in having a distinctive falchion-type blade. It was the standard naval cutlass for the Prussian and, later, the Imperial German Navy throughout the 19th century. In 1911, a new model was introduced that comprised an open steel, three-bar hilt of cavalry type, with a blade similar to contemporary German "butcher"-type bayonets, featuring a gradually widening and double-edged blade.

German naval officers' swords in the 19th and 20th centuries

It is difficult to present an accurate picture of German naval officers' swords before the unification of the country in 1871, as there was no dedicated "German" Navy until the formation of the mainly Prussian Imperial Fleet (Reichsflotte) during the revolutionary period of 1848–52. No tangible attempts were made to standardize sword patterns, and, before 1871, German naval officers carried swords that were similar to contemporary British naval officers' swords, including solid half-basket hilts and lion's-head pommels.

With the establishment of the Kaiserliche Marine, or Imperial Navy, after reunification in 1871, naval officers' swords took on a more specifically "German"

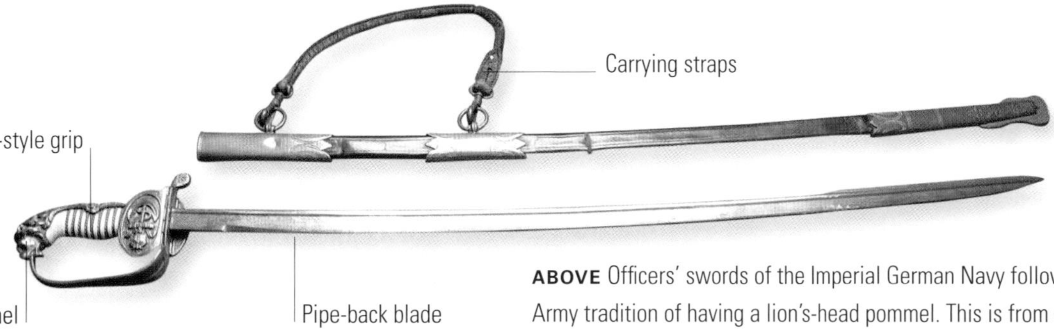

ABOVE Officers' swords of the Imperial German Navy followed the Army tradition of having a lion's-head pommel. This is from *c.*1914.

The boarding pike

For many centuries the simple spear or javelin was a weapon that had been carried on land and at sea. It was only when European nations began to formalize their navies in the 17th and 18th centuries that a designated polearm for boarding ships begin to emerge.

The polearm had many other names, including half pike, strong pike or short pike, and comprised a drastically reduced traditional infantryman's pike. The boarding pike was particularly effective at thrusting and fending off enemies in the confined and restricted spaces of a ship's deck. Pikes were normally kept in racks on board ship.

Early 17th century examples had a pick-style point, square or triangular in cross-section, with long langets, and were designed to deliver a thrusting blow. Later pike heads of the 18th century were more streamlined in profile and so avoided snagging in the rigging of the crowded upper decks of sailing ships. An account by an American, Jacob Nagle, serving on a British sloop of war off the coast of Spain in 1800, gives a dramatic illustration of the primitive effectiveness of a pike when used in trained hands.

In the smoke I purceiv'd the French capt. drawing a pistol from his belt to fire at our capt. that was giving command. I drew a pistol at the same time and let him have the contents. At the same time a stout Frenchman made a blow at me with a large hangar, from the netting, but the man behind me saw the blow and covered my head with his boarding pike, which was cut that it fell and the bare point struck me in the head and I fell, but the man ketch'd up the pike and run it into his body and he fell between two vessels...

from the *Nagle Journal*, 1775–1841, (Weidenfeld & Nicolson, New York, 1988).

BELOW A boarding pike with tomahawk head.

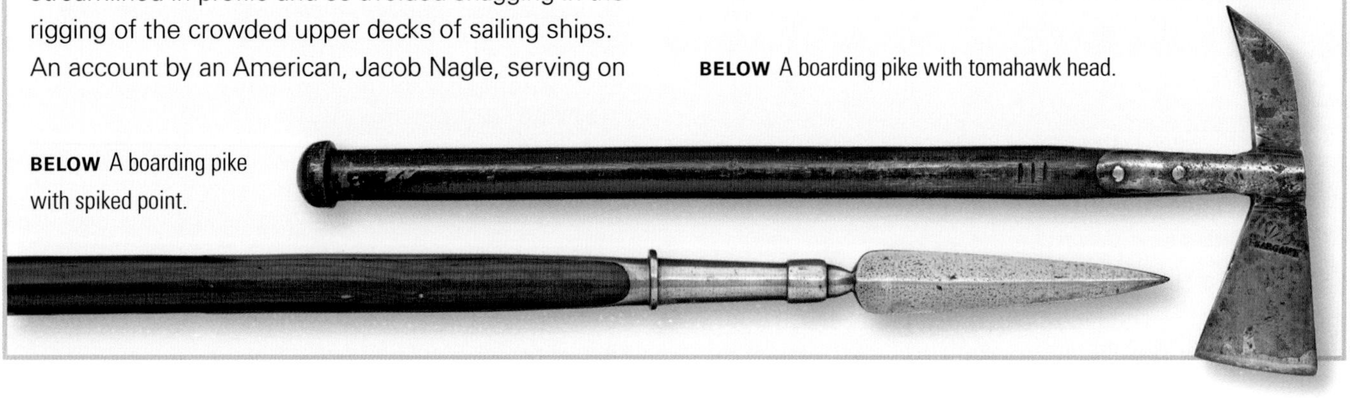

BELOW A boarding pike with spiked point.

style. The solid, gilt-brass hilt and lion's-head pommel remained but became flatter in profile, with the addition of a fold-down guard and Imperial Crown cartouche (a tablet within the hilt). Grips were bone or ivory. This style remained until Germany's defeat in 1918 when the Imperial Crown was removed. During the Nazi period (1933–45), naval officers' dirks, but not swords, bore an eagle and swastika.

Imperial Russia in the 19th and 20th centuries

Like most European navies, Russia did not attempt to formally regulate its naval swords until the 1800s. Russian naval officers of the early 1800s would have carried swords similar to the British 1796 Pattern Infantry Officer's Sword. The 1811 Pattern Naval Officer's Sword set the trend for future Russian naval officers' swords, comprising a brass three-bar hilted sword with a distinctive canted or curved backpiece and pommel. This is a style also found on many French and German military swords of the period. The pattern was updated in 1855 and 1914.

Naval swords remained unchanged until the Russian Revolution of 1917. Thereafter, all Imperial designations to both blade and hilt were erased, and the sword became plainer in design, although some naval officers were known to place Soviet hammer-and-sickle or red-star devices on the blade pommel.

Russian cutlasses

A formal pattern of naval cutlass for Russian seamen was not issued until 1810. Before then, naval ratings carried a short hanger of French "briquet" form. The 1810 Pattern was worn on a shoulder belt and issued to naval bombardiers and gunners. The blade was of Turkish yataghan (forward-curved) style with a brass-hilt cross guard, wooden grip and swollen pommel.

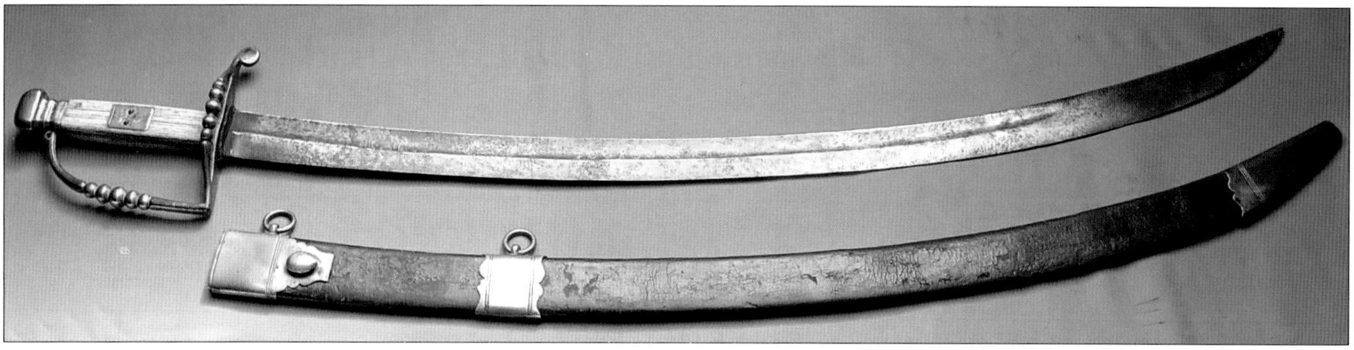

ABOVE An American officer's naval sword from *c.*1790. The blade is slightly curved and the grip is made from bone.

It was more of a hanger than a cutlass, and did not have the protective bowl guard or disc hilt more commonly associated with European naval cutlasses of this time. The Russian 1856 Pattern Boarding Cutlass was traditionally "western" in style and imitated British and French cutlasses. It had a blackened iron hilt with ribbed grip and matching blackened steel scabbard mounts. Cutlass design remained unchanged until 1940, when a new pattern was introduced for naval cadets. It had a double-edged, slightly curving blade and steel hilt with a pronounced guard and ribbed wooden grip. The need for a cutlass in the 1940s seems rather tenuous, although the Soviet Navy insisted on it being carried when outside the naval school. After 1958, it was only worn on ceremonial occasions.

Russian gallantry swords

Imperial Russian naval presentation swords were very popular in the 19th and early 20th centuries. They differed from standard naval patterns in having solid gilt, ribbed metal grips rather than the usual leather and brass twistwire wrapping. They were known as "Gold Swords" and featured engraved Cyrillic (Russian) lettering (normally with wording such as "For Gallantry") on the hilt bars. A number of grades, or orders, were also presented. An enamelled cross representing either the Order of St George or that of St Anne (before 1869) was also attached to the hilt pommel. Bullion sword knots were worn and their design differed according to the level of order attained.

American naval swords to the 20th century

Both during and after the American Revolutionary War (1775–83), American naval officers carried swords of traditional British or French style. Most were manufactured and exported from these countries to the United States during periods of peace between the two countries. In 1841, an eagle-headed naval officer's sword was introduced and its design closely followed sword styles already prevalent in the army. The Model 1852 Naval Officer's Sword was inspired by European (particularly French) solid, half-basket-hilted naval swords and it is still carried today. Cutlasses of English style were issued in 1797 and 1808.

The Model 1841 and Model 1860 USN cutlasses were both designed by the N.P. Ames sword company of Springfield, Massachusetts. The Model 1841 was derived from contemporary French "gladius" short swords, and the Model 1860 was an interpretation of the French Model AIX (1801–02), albeit with brass hilt and scabbard mounts, rather than the blackened sheet iron used in the French version.

Unusually, there was also an officer's model, differing from the ordinary seaman's cutlass in having the letters "USN" or "US" cut out of the hilt. This cutlass had a long service life and was only replaced in 1917 by a new model based on the Dutch army klewang (machete-style) cutlass. There are two versions: the early model has a solid iron bowl guard while the 1941 variation has a guard with separate branches.

BELOW The Model 1917 cutlass was carried on US Navy ships until the beginning of World War II. It was declared obsolete in 1949.

Swords of the two World Wars

Despite significant advances in warfare technology during the latter half of the 19th century, including the development of ever-more destructive firearms and artillery, many military commanders entered the first years of the new century still believing that the use of massed cavalry and the flash of steel would easily overcome the new machine guns and rapid-firing rifles. They would be sadly mistaken.

World War I swords

Paradoxically, the very first recorded casualty inflicted by a serving British soldier in Europe during World War I occurred when Captain Charles Hornby of the 4th Royal Irish Dragoon Guards killed a German Uhlan with his sword on 22 August 1914. He was leading a charge against four troopers of the 2nd Kurassier Regiment near the village of Casteau, north of Mons, in Belgium.

Both British and German officers continued to wear swords in the early stages of World War I but it soon became apparent that this was an anachronism totally unsuited to the practicalities of trench warfare. Officers also realized that the carrying of a sword

ABOVE The retreat from Mons during World War I in August to September 1914. Notice that the British cavalry are carrying lances.

The final British cavalry sword of 1908

Probably one of the most radical of all known sword designs is the 1908 Pattern Cavalry Trooper's Sword. It comprised a thin, rapier-like blade, large enclosed bowl-hilt and unique pistol grip. It was as far removed from traditional sword design as could be possible. Its very uniqueness finally resolved the argument within the British military establishment of whether to use a thrusting or cutting blade. The pattern was unashamedly thrusting and designed for the shock of a cavalry charge. The grip was also manufactured in a new composite material, dermatine (the 1912 Pattern Officer's version retained a fishskin covering), and included a thumb depression on the backpiece to enable the carrier to grip the sword in a fashion similar to the gripping of a lance.

Despite the fact that King Edward VII (*r.*1901–10) described this new design as "hideous", the 1908 Pattern went into full production and was soon standard issue in British cavalry regiments. The advent of World War I (1914–18) was regarded by the military as the ideal testing ground for this new pattern of sword, but the conflict actually sounded its death knell. Confronted with grinding trench warfare and an immovable battlefield typified by the Western Front, the opportunity for massed mobile cavalry action had simply disappeared.

BELOW 1908 Pattern Cavalry Trooper's Sword. Note the solid steel bowl guard and the pistol grip. The blade is rapier-like and designed for thrusting rather than cutting.

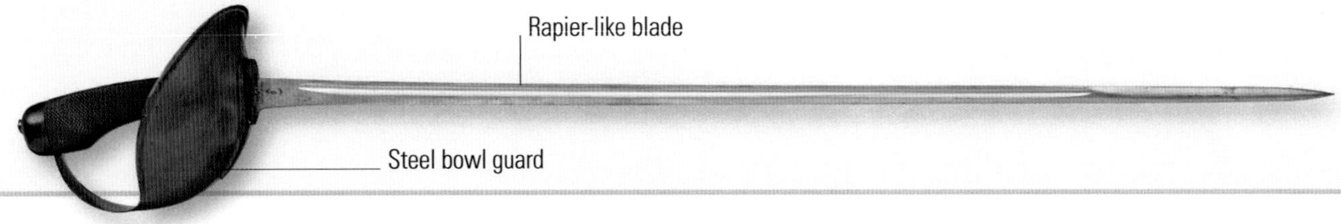

Russian cavalry swords

The active use of the sword within cavalry regiments in eastern Europe, and particularly Russia, was still commonplace throughout World War I and well into the 1930s. The vast, open terrain of the Russian landscape was well suited to the use of massed cavalry, and the Russian Cossack troops of both the Czarist and post-Revolutionary Soviet period wielded their favourite shasqua swords (a slightly curved sabre with a single-edged blade) against both German and Bolshevik enemies. The Soviets of the 1920s and 1930s continued issuing swords to Cossack troops (now "integrated" into the Soviet Republic), and these weapons were last called upon during the German invasion of Russia in 1941, when they were recorded as being used by troops undertaking brave but ultimately futile massed attacks against advancing German tanks.

ABOVE Cossack troops charge against German forces in 1942.

made them an obvious and prized target for machine gunners and snipers from both sides. Swords were still purchased but only for dress occasions.

The last massed British cavalry charge was at the Battle of Mughar, near Jerusalem, on 13 November 1917, when a combined force of the Buckinghamshire Hussars, supported by the Dorset and Berkshire Yeomanry Regiments, overran a significant Turkish position, capturing hundreds of prisoners.

British Air Force swords in the 20th century

The 1920s witnessed the emergence of a unique sword for a new branch of the British Army. This was the British 1920 Pattern Royal Air Force Officer's Sword, the last official regulation pattern sword of the British Army. Designed by the Wilkinson Sword Company of London, the hilt was based on the 1897 Pattern Infantry Officer's Sword. This was an acknowledgement of the crucial role played by the Royal Engineers' Balloonist Unit (raised in 1878) in establishing the future Royal Flying Corps (RFC) in 1912 and the Royal Naval Air Service (RNAS) in 1914. They were later merged in 1918 to form the Royal Air Force (RAF). British airmen from the RFC or the RNAS would have originally been posted from different army or naval units, and consequently they would have carried a dress sword appropriate to their original branch of service or regiment. The need for a standardized pattern was therefore obvious. The 1920 Pattern had a gilt-brass, half-basket hilt with eagle-head pommel and crowned winged albatross inset into the hilt cartouche. The grip was white sharkskin. This pattern of ceremonial sword is still carried by serving officers of the RAF.

Italian/German Air Force swords in the 20th century

Both Italy and Germany produced their own air force swords, with both nations drawing heavily on the contemporary Art Deco influences of the 1920s and 1930s. The Italian Air Force officer's sword of the 1930s had a sweeping, gilt brass eagle-head hilt, and the German Model 1934 Air Force Officer's Sword exhibited a very modernistic hilt design, with dramatically downswept quillons and exaggerated pommel.

Nazi swords before World War II

The catastrophic defeat of Germany and its allies in World War I brought a temporary halt to the widespread promotion and wearing of swords in these countries. The size of the German Army during the Weimar Republic (1919–33) was also reduced significantly and the famous German sword-making town of Solingen experienced a drastic reduction in military orders for its edged weapons. Only when the Nazis came to power in 1933 were the fortunes of Solingen reversed. A delegation of officials from the town met the new German Chancellor, Adolf Hitler, and persuaded him that the production of swords and daggers for the Nazi Party (and the armed forces) would create new employment in a town badly hit by the worldwide economic slump of 1929 and the early 1930s (the Great Depression). Soon numerous government and quasi-military organizations within the new Nazi state had adopted edged weapons. The German Army (Heer), Air Force (Luftwaffe) and Navy (Kriegsmarine) all started to carry new sword designs created in the workshops of Solingen.

Japanese swords and polearms

The traditional Japanese Samurai sword is both a devastating weapon of armed combat and an object of great aesthetic beauty. This makes it rather unusual when compared with most military swords, which are primarily functional tools of war. The manufacture of Samurai swords was, for the master swordsmith, part religious ceremony and part spiritual journey. The Samurai warrior, clad in exotic lacquered armour and fearsome horned kabuko helmet, would always ensure that he went into battle armed with a range of swords and daggers, most notably the katana and wakizashi.

Mythical beginnings

The history of the Japanese sword begins with the traditional mythology of Shinto (the native religion of Japan). The Sun Goddess, Amaterasu Omikami, is said to have given her grandson, Ninigi-no Mikoto, a special sword when he was sent down to reign on Earth. The Shinto religion and the worship of the Japanese sword have always been closely linked.

Japanese swords were thought to have miraculous spiritual powers and even a personal identity of their own. Japanese soldiers who were defeated in battle would pray at the shrines of the war god Hachiman, asking why their swords had lost their martial spirit.

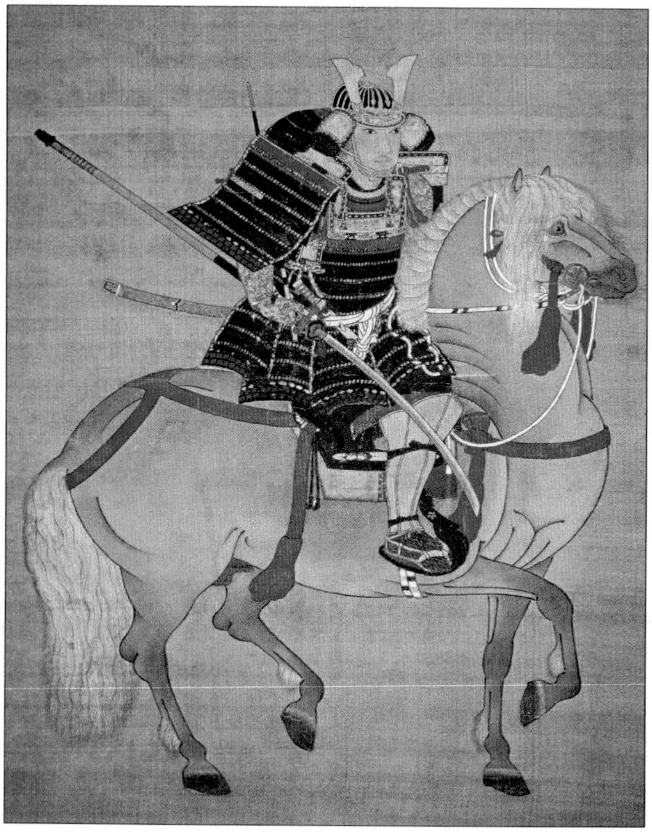

This extreme personalization of a Japanese warrior's sword resulted in the application of a strict code of etiquette for the handling and maintenance of swords.

Influence of China and Korea

In historical terms, the origin of the Japanese sword has a timeline of nearly 2,000 years. Japanese sword design mirrored very much the designs in China and Korea during the first two millennia. Swords that have been found in Japanese burial mounds and dated to *c.* AD300 have blades that were long and single-edged, very much like the Chinese jian, with a simple tsuba mount (a disc-shaped swordguard at the end of the handle).

Japanese clansmen warriors from this early period were predominantly horsemen who needed a long-bladed sword that could be used against infantry. Many Japanese swords were actually imported from China and Korea. A truly Japanese home-based sword-making industry only developed later.

The Heian period (AD794–1192)

During the early medieval period, the classic Japanese Samurai sword style started to become more recognizable. This process evolved through the gradual change of the blade shape from straight to slightly curved. During the Heian period, Japanese swordsmiths also began to mark their own work on the blade "tang" (the plate of metal that secures the blade to the sword handle), so enabling future generations to identify both the date of manufacture and the name and province in which the swordsmith lived. The appearance of a more distinctive "hamon", or pattern to the blade, is also evident during this period.

LEFT A 15th-century depiction of a Japanese Samurai warrior carrying sword and polearm. He lived by a code of honour, bravery and loyalty.

RIGHT 19th-century print of a Samurai holding his sword. Note the wakizashi (short sword or side arm) in his belt.

The Heian period, under the direction of Emperor Kammu (AD781–806), produced blades that are regarded as some of the most perfect ever manufactured and they have now acquired an almost mythical status. During this period the Fujiwara class of military nobility began to emerge and adopt this distinctive style of sword.

Other important periods of sword manufacture include the Kamakura period (1192–1333), Shoshino or Namboku Cho period (1333–93), Muromachi period (1338–1573), Edo period (1603–1867) and Showa period (1926–89). These periods relate to dynasties or clans that were based in separate areas of Japan, some at the same time.

The "way of the warrior"

Any history of the Samurai and his association with the sword must first begin with an explanation of bushido, or "the way of the warrior". This was a strict code of behaviour that had to be followed with honour, bravery and utmost loyalty. The Samurai was also taught to live with "freedom without fear". Allied with this moral philosophy was a strong reliance on training in the art of combat (bujutsu).

Early Samurai used a combination of bows and arrows, and swords. Later Samurai used swords, spears and naginata (halberds). Samurai often named their swords as a mark of personal devotion, and believed that their own warrior spirit was actually contained within these swords.

The Kamakura Period (1192–1333)

Samurai warrior culture developed from a series of territorial wars during the Kamakura period amongst the Minamoto, Fujiwara and Taira clans. These feudal groups were constantly at war with each other, and the Samurai (literally meaning "to serve") were drawn from these battle-hardened warriors.

This period of Japanese history is viewed as the highpoint of the Samurai warrior, with many stories chronicling their honour, bravery and stoicism in battle. Ironically, this period also allowed the Samurai, as privileged members of society, to kill any unfortunate peasants who offended them. It is also no surprise that some of the best Japanese swords were manufactured during this period.

The Muromachi period (1338–1573)

An interesting period in Samurai history is the Muromachi period, as it witnessed the emergence of the Samurai as an artist-warrior. The culture of the Samurai had now developed to such a degree that it was considered necessary for training to include the ritualized tea ceremony and flower arranging. These rituals were considered to add refinement and balance to the usually warrior-like persona of a Samurai.

BELOW An 18th-century Samurai sword. Training in its use was complex and required great skill. It was traditionally worn by the Samurai with the blade edge-up.

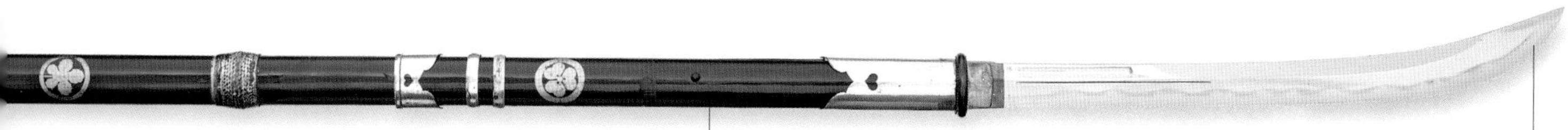

ABOVE The naginata polearm was commonly used by the Samurai warriors.

The decline of the Samurai (1603–1867)

During the Edo period (1603–1867) the gradual decline of the Samurai began. The unusual absence of any wars in Japan during a period of about 250 years meant that the Samurai were unable to play a warlike role in Japanese society. Although they were allowed to wear their traditional swords in public, they now had to accept civilian jobs to survive. The last Shogun, or Governor of Japan, resigned during the Meiji Restoration (1868–1912), and dissatisfied Samurai then led a revolt against a progressive and pro-Western government, which promptly abolished feudalism and in 1871, finally stripped the Samurai of all their special privileges. The carrying of Samurai swords in public had already been outlawed in 1867, resulting in a rapid decline in the number of working swordsmiths.

Changes in sword design in the 19th century

After the demise of the Samurai class in the late 19th century, Japan entered into an unprecedented period of contact with the West. This was reflected by dramatic changes in sword design for regular army forces. Although the traditional Samurai sword was still being made during this period (albeit in very small numbers), military swords from the 1870s to the 1900s were heavily influenced by European designs, most notably the French military. Some Japanese officers' swords were virtual copies of contemporary French military swords.

The Showa period (1926–89)

With the revival of Japanese nationalism during the Showa period, a parallel revival in sword making also occurred. One of the most common Japanese sword styles of the Showa period is the kyu-gunto pattern. It retained the long grip associated with traditional Samurai swords, but had a knuckle bow and pommel of European design. There were many variations of this pattern, including a version for both officers and non-commissioned officers. From the 1920s, when a rebirth of Japanese nationalism brought with it a new-found interest in their Samurai past, many officers reverted back to the classic Samurai sword form. This was the new shin-gunto pattern. Blades were either machine-made or hand-forged, or earlier family or ancestral blades were attached to new hilts. These swords were carried by all branches of the Imperial Japanese Army. Large numbers were destroyed at the end of World War II, but significant quantities were also brought home as souvenirs by the victorious Allied forces.

Indigenous Japanese sword making came to an abrupt end with the defeat of Japan in 1945, but the craft revived again from the 1970s, with great demand for particular swordsmiths.

The naginata polearm

This was a common polearm used by Samurai warriors and is most commonly associated with the Kamakura and Muromachi Periods (1338–1573). The naginata comprised a lacquered (sometimes inlaid with mother-of-pearl) wooden pole approximately 2m (6.5ft) in length. Onto this was forged a curved blade in very much the same way as traditional katana blades – and, indeed, many naginatas were actually mounted with recycled katana blades. The blade, or nakago, of a naginata was secured onto the pole by a single peg, or mekugi.

The yari

A short lance or spear, the Japanese yari was not intended to be thrown in the traditional Western military fashion. It was used by both the Samurai and the common Japanese foot-soldier, or ashigaru. There are many different styles of yari. The two main types are the su yari (straight-bladed) and the kama yari (with horizontal crossbars on the blade).

ABOVE The yari, or short lance or spear, was used by Japanese infantry soldiers and the Samurai.

Types of Japanese edged weapons

There are four main types of Samurai edged weapon.

Tachi (longsword)
This is the original historic sword of the Samurai and had a typical blade length ranging from 60–70cm (23.6–27.5in). It was worn with the blade edge downwards and suspended from a belt with two straps. It was later replaced by the daisho (a combination of the katana and wakizashi worn together) but continued to be worn at ceremonial events and when attending the Imperial Japanese Court. Many tachi were considered important family heirlooms and stored with great care.

Katana (standard sword)
This sword type had an average blade length of over 60cm (23.6in), and was generally used for outdoor combat. The single-edged blade was slightly curved. The sword was developed in the 10th century to accommodate the growing use of Japanese cavalry and was worn hung from the belt, with the cutting edge facing upwards.

Wakizashi (side arm or short sword)
With a blade length of around 30–40cm (11.8–15.7in), this sword was also worn indoors as it provided more ease of movement than the longer katana. Its shorter blade functioned as a side arm, and was well suited for stabbing at close quarters. It was also used to decapitate beaten opponents and take their heads from the battlefield. The traditional Samurai form of ritual suicide (*seppuku*, sometimes known as *hara-kari*, or "cutting the belly") was normally conducted with this type of short sword.

Tanto (short knife)
This is a small knife used in much the same manner as a wakizashi. The average length is 15–30cm (5.9–11.8in). Unlike other traditional Japanese swords that feature a sharpened edge, the tanto was used primarily as a stabbing weapon and was also designed to pierce armour.

Accessories are:

Saya (scabbard)
A Japanese sword is sheathed in a scabbard called a saya, usually made of magnolia wood and lacquered for weatherproofing. A sageo, or length of strong braid, attaches the scabbard to the owner's belt.

Tsuba (guard)
The tsuba is a rounded (sometimes squared) guard placed at the end of the grip of a traditional Japanese sword. The swordsman would place his right index finger on the tsuba to aid his balance and so control the blade more easily.

Tsuba

Tanto

Wakizashi

Katana

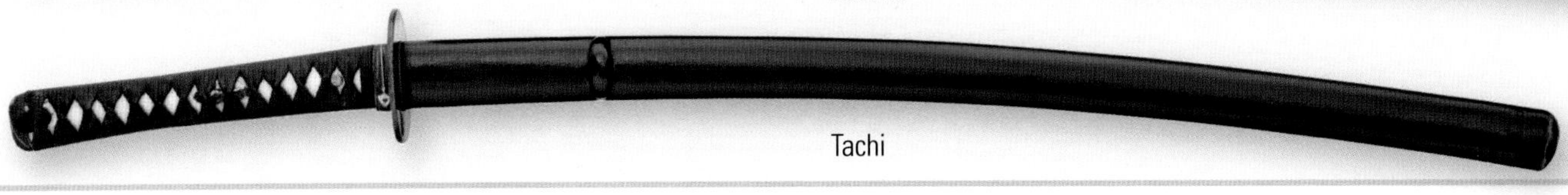
Tachi

Chinese and Central Asian swords

The origins of the Chinese sword are rooted in ancient legend. Solid-gold dao swords were reputedly made for the mythical San Huang emperors Fu-Xi-Shi, Shen-Nong-Shi and Sui-Ren-Shi (*c.*3000–2700BC). These swords were said to have extraordinary powers: they could glow in the dark, utter sounds, frighten evil spirits and even change into dragons. Their spiritual powers were embodied in the personal (or perhaps supernatural) strength of their owners. Like Viking swords, these weapons were sometimes accorded individual names.

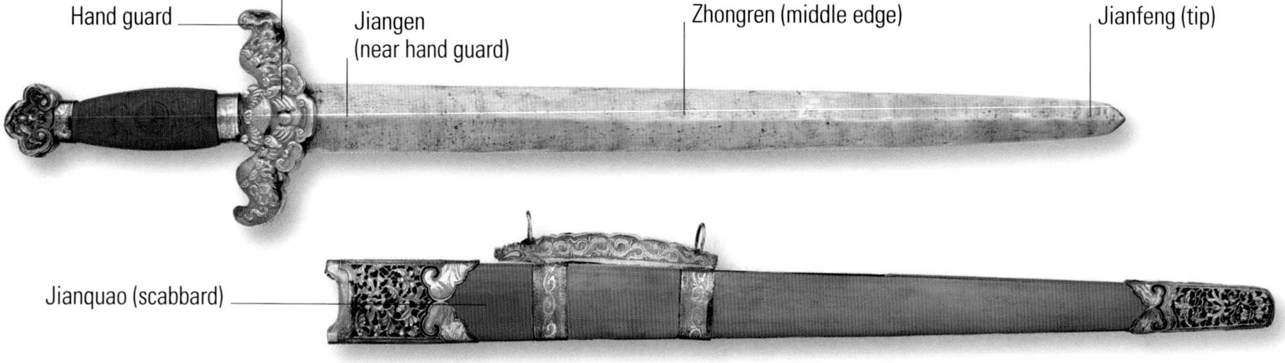

ABOVE The jian is a straight, double-edged sword used for over 2,500 years in China. The blade itself is normally divided into three sections for use in different techniques of attack and defence.

The jian

With a history dating back well over 2,500 years, the oldest type of Chinese sword is the jian. The earliest jian had short, double-edged and straight blades about 35cm (13.8in) in length and were made of bronze. Iron and steel had replaced bronze by the time of the Tang Dynasty (AD618–906), and during the Northern Song Dynasty (AD960–1127) notable jian of high quality were being produced in the Longquan area of Zhejiang province (on China's north-east coast). Raw materials such as iron ore and good access to water helped these swordsmiths to produce very fine blades.

The hilt

A jian hilt comprised a grip of either bound cord, carved wood, horn or wood covered in ray skin (sometimes stained green), with a wide ring or ferrule at each end of the grip. A large, stepped pommel was added for balance. The use of fish skin (normally the rough, dried-out skin of a ray or shark) provided an excellent non-slip surface on which to place a hand. The use of a tassel (a tuft of dyed cotton threads) placed through a hole in the pommel was popular during the Ming Dynasty (1368–1644), and during the Qing Dynasty (1644–1912) a tassel hole was driven through the grip itself.

Hilt fittings were usually made of brass, bronze or silver, and, on rare occasions, gold. Either the hilt was cast as a whole or both the hand guard and pommel were cast separately and then forged together. Decorated sheet metal was also applied to the hilt, and traditional motifs such as dragons and interlaced designs were punched or incised onto the metal.

The blade

A jian blade was divided into three distinct areas. Each had a specific function. The tip of the blade, or jianfeng, had a spear point designed for stabbing and rapid cuts. The middle section was known as the zhongren, and was effective at long cleaving cuts and deflection of the opponent's bade. The last section of blade (closest to the hand guard) was called the jiangen and would have been used for defensive blocking.

The dao – "Marshal of all Weapons"

In China, the dao was regarded as one of the four major Chinese weapons of combat, alongside the qiang (spear), jian (straight sword) and gun (staff

Sabres of the Mongols

When the Mongols invaded China in the early 13th century, they brought with them a curved, one-handed and single-edged cavalry sabre that had been used by Turkic peoples (from central Eurasia) since the 8th century. The curved design of the sabre influenced the shape of the Chinese dao, superseding the straight-bladed jian. During the Ming Dynasty, (1368–1644) sabres of increased curvature appeared, primarily for mounted troops.

RIGHT A 19th-century illustration of the Mongols in China. They are carrying long spears and sabres. Their horsemanship skills and ferocious fighting spirit were greatly feared by the Chinese forces of the Ming Dynasty.

or pole). Described as the "Marshal of all Weapons", it was an effective wide-bladed sword with excellent slashing or chopping capabilities. The word "dao" simply means "knife", and is also used to describe a whole range of single-edged and broad-bladed knives and tools.

Early history

Swords of dao form first emerged during the Shang Dynasty (*c.*1700–1100BC) and were initially manufactured in bronze, but by the time of the late Warring States (*c.*221– 5BC) iron and steel would have been utilized by Chinese swordsmiths to produce stronger and more durable blades.

During the Tang Dynasty (AD618–906) of southern China, dao were exported to both Korea and Japan, and became an important influence on the future development of the traditional Japanese Samurai sword, particularly the tachi (long sword) and the katana (standard sword).

BELOW Dao blades have varied greatly over the centuries but most are moderately curved and single-edged. Guards are typically disc-shaped with grips bound in cord.

Characteristics of the dao

Dao blades were broad, slightly curved and single-edged, with canted (angled) hilts, usually bound in cord, leather, wood or ray skin (fish skin). If a dao was to be used in battle, grips would be wrapped in silk, and the colours chosen were specified by strict military regulation. In Chinese culture, the use of particular colours and types of knots was considered to bring their owner luck and bravery.

Most dao had one or more fullers, or "blood grooves", deeply cut into the blade. This would have given the blade extra strength and flexibility. The sword bearer's hand was also protected by a disc-shaped and cupped guard. When the blade entered the scabbard, the "cup" acted as a barrier against rainwater penetrating it, or blood dripping down to the grip and so making the sword difficult to handle. Blade lengths averaged around 65–75cm (25.5–29.5in).

Dao scabbards were usually made of wood, covered with thick lacquer or fish skin, although sometimes they were made from lacquered leather, and many had heavily embossed and gilded panels. The scabbard was mounted with two rings that were attached to a belt.

Two-handed swords

Introduced into China around 2,000 years ago, two-handed swords have a long history in Chinese swordsmanship. Although not common, there was a two-handed jian of up to 1.6m (5.2ft) in length. It was known as a shuangshou jian (literally meaning two hands placed together). The dao sword also had a two-handed equivalent, the dadao, or "great sword". This comprised a massive falchion-type blade and simple cord-bound metal hilt with ring pommel. The dadao was used well into the 20th century and there are many photographs showing Chinese Nationalist forces carrying this weapon during the Second Sino-Japanese War (1937–45). Chinese troops boasted that it could sever the head of a Japanese soldier with one blow.

BELOW Emperor Chu Yuan-Chang (1328–98), founder of the Ming Dynasty. During this period the military began to use polearms in favour of the dao sword.

Ring-pommelled sword

The eastern Chinese Han Dynasty (AD23–220) adopted a unique type of sword – the single-edged huanshou dao, or "ring-pommelled sword". The blade was quite narrow, with a length of around 90cm (35.4in). The tang was very broad and forged with an integral and distinctive ring pommel. A peg was used to hold both tang and grip together. These ring-pommelled swords were still being used right up until the end of the 19th century. During the Boxer Rising of 1900, these swords were particularly popular amongst the rebel forces who besieged the European contingent in Beijing (Peking).

Polearms and percussive weapons

With the overthrow of the Mongols (or the Yuan Dynasty, 1279–1368) and the establishment of the Ming Dynasty, the Chinese Army began to rely more heavily on the use of long polearms and percussive weapons for their infantry soldiers. In purely economic terms, these weapons were much cheaper to produce and the training required to use them was minimal, unlike the prolonged training necessary to develop a proficient swordsman.

These polearms were still regarded as forms of the dao sword, but in this case the dao blade was attached to a wooden staff or pole. Their names highlight the close relationship they bore to the dao family of swords and included halberds (pointed axes) such as the jidao, and long-bladed glaives (axes) such as the yanyue dao, meijian dao and quadao. In keeping with European military staff weapons of this period, the long reach of the polearm was considered more effective when used by massed infantry formations in battle.

Double or paired swords

In 1644, the last Ming emperor Chung-Chen committed suicide after Beijing (Peking) was captured by the Manchus (from Manchuria, on

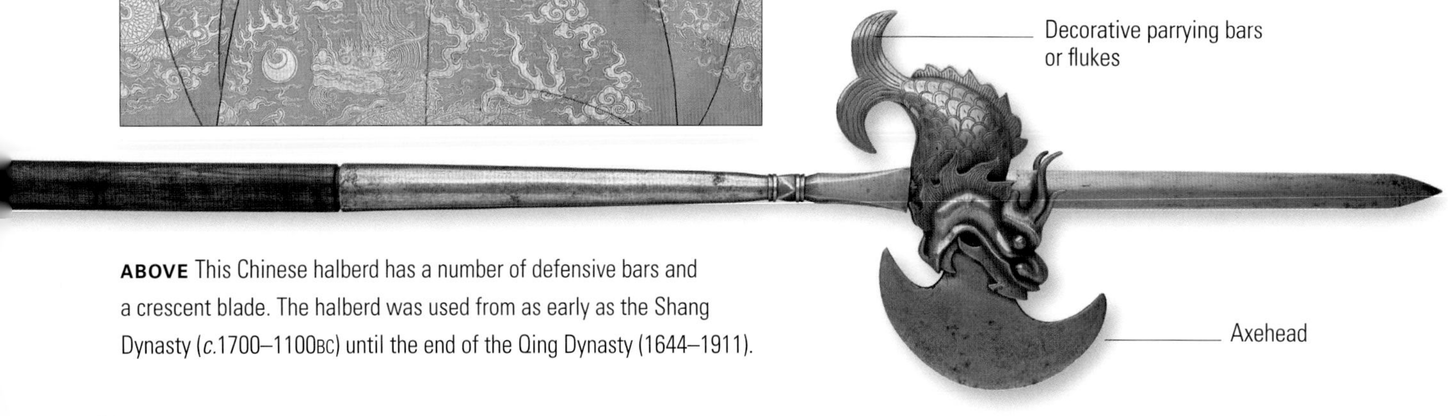

ABOVE This Chinese halberd has a number of defensive bars and a crescent blade. The halberd was used from as early as the Shang Dynasty (*c.*1700–1100BC) until the end of the Qing Dynasty (1644–1911).

China's eastern seabord). The new emperor Qing Shunzhi, of the Qing (Manchu) Dynasty, did not alter the design of Chinese swords in any radical way, and Ming-style swords, including the traditional jian and dao, continued to be worn until the end of the Qing Dynasty.

However, the Qing Dynasty (1644–1912) did witness the appearance of shuang jian, or paired swords. They are also known as "butterfly knives". These innovative swords were designed in such a way that they fitted back-to-back in the same scabbard and had half hilts that fitted on top of each other. The swordsman could quickly draw these short, double-edged swords out of their scabbard, wielding one in each hand. Hilt and blade design remained similar to the traditional jian.

ABOVE Chinese "Big Sword" troops wield their dao swords during a battle to defend the old Chinese province of Jehol (west of Manchuria) from the attacking Japanese army in March 1933.

BELOW A pair of butterfly swords. The butterfly sword was usually wielded in pairs. They were held side by side within the same scabbard, to give the impression of a single weapon.

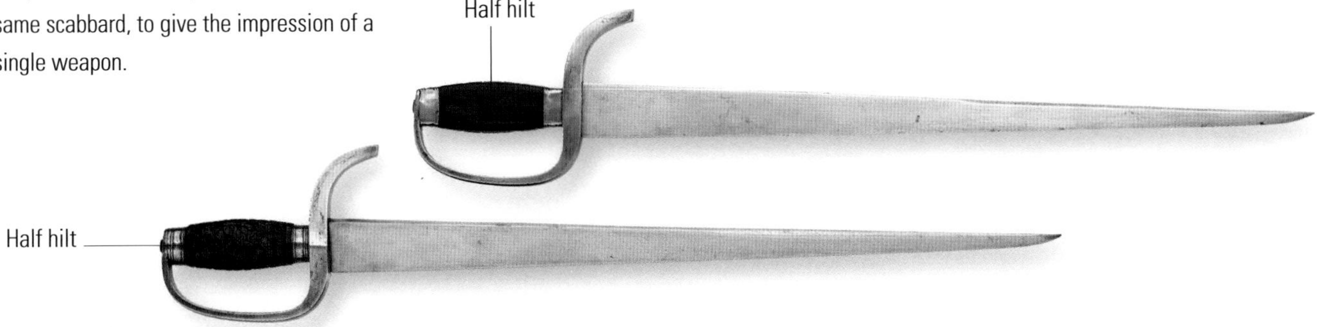

Swords of Tibet

The Tibetan longsword was called the ke tri (pronounced "kay dreh") or patang. These single-edged blades had a short-angled tip with an average blade length of up to 65cm (25.6in). They were usually worn with their edge facing upwards and diagonally across the front of the body, with the hilt located so that the right hand could rest upon it. The sword and scabbard were tucked into a long woollen-fabric waist belt worn with traditional costume. Belt attachments are seldom seen on scabbards. Decoration is quite ornamental, with extensive use of carved turquoise and inlaid coral to the hilt and scabbard. Incised silver work, including filigree (silver wire), is a common decorative feature.

BELOW 19th-century Tibetan longsword. Similar to the Chinese jian, it has a hilt embellished with turquoise and coral and includes an embossed silver scabbard.

African swords

In some African cultures the sword was regarded not merely as a weapon of war but also as an important element in ritual ceremonies. In the hands of a monarch it symbolized divine kingship and power over his subjects. There are great differences in sword design between North Africa, with its distinctively Arabic-inspired swords, and the eastern and Central African empires of the Yoruba, Benin and Asante, where strong beliefs in local spirits encouraged extravagant swords that were symbolic rather than weapons of war.

ABOVE This 19th-century flyssa was the traditional sword of the Berber people.

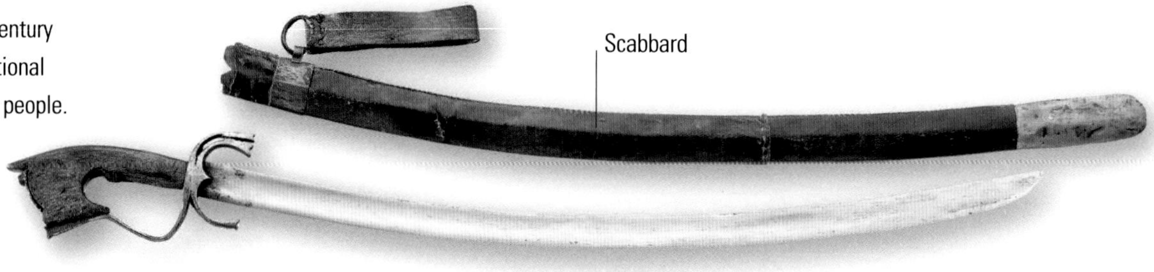

ABOVE The Moroccan nimcha sword (and scabbard) was often fitted with a European blade.

Swords of North Africa

The influence of the Islamic Arabic world had a profound effect on the indigenous peoples of North Africa. Arab armies began a series of invasions of North Africa after AD600, and with them they brought Islam and new weapons. They introduced both curved and straight-bladed swords over time, some directly influenced by earlier medieval designs, while new hilt and blade forms were developed that became emblematic of distinct regions, peoples and cultures.

The flyssa

This is the traditional sword of the Berber peoples of north-eastern Algeria and parts of Morocco. Swords of this type have single-edged, swelling blades of great length, up to 95cm (37.4in). They feature deeply incised and inlaid brass decoration and pommels of animal heads. The blade point is extremely long and needle-like. This sharp point was effective for piercing chain mail, which was still worn in North Africa well into the 19th century. The flyssa sword grip is without a conventional guard and normally manufactured in iron.

The nimcha

From the 15th century, a unique type of single-handed sword hilt was developed in north-western Africa, especially Morocco. The hilt displayed downward pointing quillons and a wooden or inlaid metal handle with squared-off or "hooked" pommels. From the cross guard, a thin knuckle guard began beneath the quillons and ran to the bottom of the pommel, although not actually joined to it.

Nimcha blades were usually sourced from older, European broadsword blades and many nimcha have Solingen (German), Venetian and Genoese blades from as early as the 17th century. The use of European rather than locally manufactured blades highlights the unique geographical position of this part of North Africa, as it had been an important area of both trade and conflict with the West for many centuries.

The takouba

This sword was used by the nomadic Tuareg tribes of the middle and western Sahara from the 16th century, and is still carried to this day. Up to 1m (3.3ft) in length, the takouba blade is wide and double-edged with three or more hand-ground fullers, or grooves, and a rounded point. The hilt is of simple, cruciform shape. The sword and scabbard are normally worn with a long tasselled baldric (shoulder belt) slung over the right shoulder.

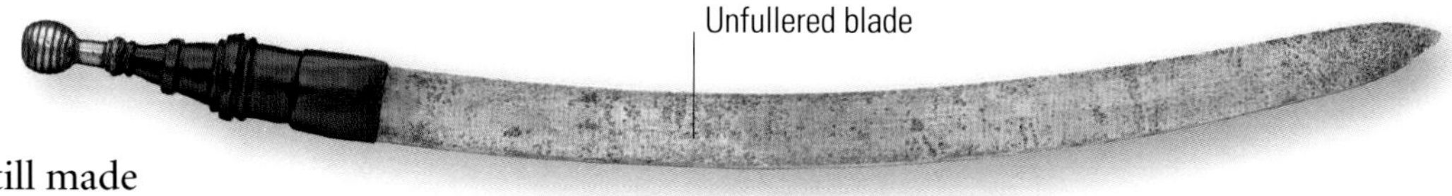

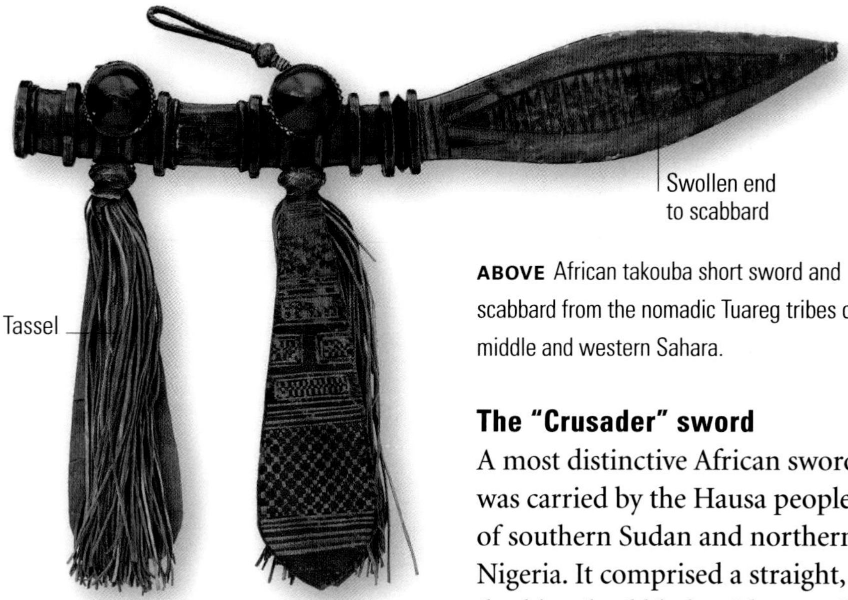

ABOVE African takouba short sword and scabbard from the nomadic Tuareg tribes of the middle and western Sahara.

The takouba sword is still made for the Tuareg by a special sword-making caste, known as the Ineden, who are reputed to have come originally from the Sudan. The Ineden speak their own language, Ténet. They are not allowed to intermarry and are regarded as having magical powers.

Swords of Sudanic West and Central Africa

The ancient empires of the western Sudan and Central Africa (also known as the Sahel) rose to prominence during the medieval period because of the success of their mounted horsemen. Using these horsemen for both raiding and trading parties, they procured large numbers of slaves, gold and ivory from Central Africa, and in return received weapons, most notably swords, spears and lances, from both indigenous peoples and European traders.

The "Crusader" sword

A most distinctive African sword was carried by the Hausa peoples of southern Sudan and northern Nigeria. It comprised a straight, double-edged blade with a cruciform cross guard and disc-shaped pommel. There have been many theories over the years concerning these cruciform-hilted swords, based mainly on the misguided belief that their overtly European and medieval style was introduced into this region by Crusaders of the 12th and 13th centuries.

The kaskara

This sword is readily identified with the Sudan. Blades are double-edged, with a spatulate, or spoon-shaped, tip and a blade length of around 95cm (37.4in). A broad central fuller, or "blood groove", is found on some examples, with others exhibiting multiple fullers. Interestingly, many blades are heavily stamped with spurious European swordsmith marks. Imported European blades were attached to kaskara blades from the 17th and 18th centuries, but most examples still surviving date from the 19th century and these marks were actually added by local sword makers to increase the perceived value and quality of a blade.

The cross guard is usually composed of forged iron although brass examples are also known. It also exhibits a long and thin langet (an extension of the guard). Pommels are of flat, disc form, and the grip is round and normally bound in leather. The 19th-century kaskara sword of the Sultan Ali Diner of Darfur has a hilt of solid gold and the blade is decorated with incised Koranic invocations or prayers.

BELOW A Sudanese kaskara, *c.*1898, with an Italian blade. This sword was owned by Sultan Ali Dinar of Darfur. It has a highly decorated blade and a gold hilt.

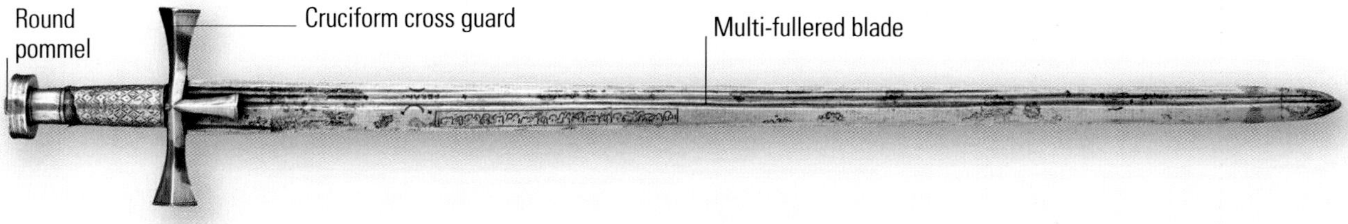

The African blacksmith

In traditional African societies, the blacksmith is still widely regarded as a figure of mystery and magic, possessed of supernatural powers. As such, he is considered ethnically distinct.

His mythology and status can be traced back to the acquisition by sub-Saharan blacksmiths of the knowledge to work iron. This probably derived from ancient Egypt and moved steadily southwards, so that by the 3rd and 4th centuries BC, iron was being worked in north-western Tanzania, northern Nigeria and the Sudan.

There was no Bronze Age in Africa; therefore, the blacksmiths' leap from producing stone and wood tools and weapons to iron must have seemed revolutionary (even supernatural).

A blacksmith's appearance in a village would initiate great excitement. A forge was set up and he would use a stone or iron anvil, iron tongs, bellows of stitched animal skins and clay tubes to funnel air to stimulate the fire. He produced a range of weapons, most notably daggers, swords and spearheads. The scarcity of reliable, durable weapons to subjugate rival tribes made him a revered figure. He would also manufacture agricultural tools to help sustain the village in more peaceful periods.

RIGHT These 18th–19th-century iron-bladed swords with wooden handles were characteristic of the weapons made by local blacksmiths.

Swords of eastern Africa

Originating in Abyssinia (ancient Ethiopia), the shotel is an extremely curved sword that is very reminiscent of a large sickle. The blade is diamond-sectioned and usually flat-backed or with a central ridge. The blade length is about 80cm (31.5in) and the wooden hilt is simple, smooth and undecorated. There is no guard. This sword would have been carried in a close-fitting leather scabbard.

Shotel swords were not very practical for slashing an opponent, but the extremely curved blade was used primarily to hook the enemy by reaching around his shield and then stabbing him in vital areas, such as the kidneys, heart or lungs.

Swords of West Africa

By AD900 the Yoruba people, originally located in central Nigeria, had slowly begun to move southwest. This was a reaction to northern Hausa expansion southwards into their lands, combined with long periods of devastating drought. The Yoruba finally settled in an area now comprising south-west Nigeria, Benin and Togo. They were noted swordsmiths and were involved in the mining and smelting of iron ore before AD800.

Yoruba and Edo swords

Between 1100 and 1700, the Yoruba kingdom of Ife flourished in conjunction with the neighbouring Edo kingdom of Benin, and part of this cultural cross-fertilization saw the introduction of the ada sword. This was an all-iron longsword (used either one-handed or double-handed), with a narrow and then greatly widening leaf-shaped and double-edged blade, designed for hacking and cutting. The oral tradition of the Edo people says that the ada sword was used primarily for ceremonial purposes and it would have been presented to the early rulers of Benin. They were known as the Ogiso, or "rulers of the sky".

RIGHT The shotel – the traditional curved sword of Ethiopia. This particular weapon was presented to Benito Mussolini following Italy's conquest of Abyssinia (Ethiopia) in 1936.

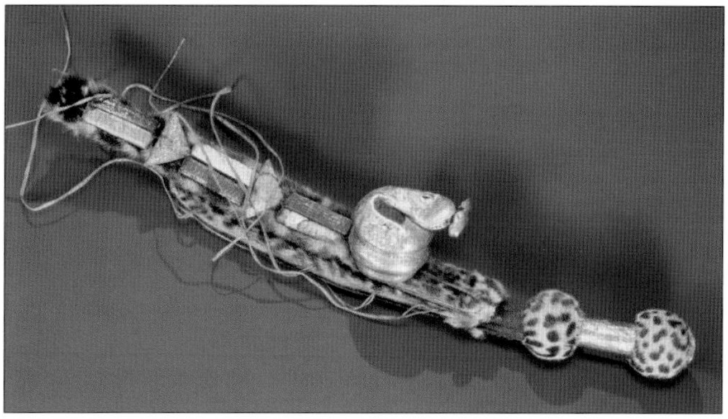

RIGHT An Asante oath-taking sword or mponponsuo from Ghana, with a gold and leopard skin handle.

In the 15th and 16th centuries, when Yoruba kings, or Obas, had taken over the rule of Benin, the ordinary soldier began to carry a short sword called an opia. This was a double-edged and smaller version of the ada. Benin tribal chiefs carried a specific sword called an eben. It was seen as a symbol of authority and comprised a broad blade with looped handles, elaborately decorated with openwork and brass inlays. If a neighbouring kingdom was at war with Benin and captured a Benin blacksmith, he would not automatically be executed (which was the usual fate for ordinary warriors). His metalworking skills were highly prized and he would quickly be put to use producing tools and weapons for his captors.

Asante state swords

The empire of the Asante (a federation of Akan-speaking and neighbouring tribes) was located in present-day Ghana. During the mid-18th century its influence began to replace that of the Benin empire. The Asante's divine king, or Ansantehene, was given a state sword, or afena. This was recognized as the supreme symbol of kingly power. The iron blade was curved, with a broad point gradually tapering towards the tang where a hilt of wood was covered in gold. The rounded grip expanded into a sphere at both ends. On both the hilt and the sheath there were a number of elaborate gold castings called abosodee. They had great symbolic importance and represented complex stories within the culture of the Asante kingdom. The decoration included grotesque human heads, knots, shells, fighting warriors and fantastical creatures.

ABOVE Dating probably from the 17th century, this bronze plaque from Benin depicts the Oba of Benin with attendants.

There were also a number of derivations of the afena sword. These included the asomfofena. This would be carried by representatives of the Asantehene (king), whose primary role would be to disseminate the king's will throughout the land. If an Asante was in the presence of this sword, he would know that the royal bearer deserved great respect and that the judgement of the king imparted through this instrument of the state could have both benign and fearful consequences.

The "keteanofena" was a term used to describe a group of important Asante state swords. The akrafena sword was associated with the religious and spiritual well-being of the community and was always carried on the right side during official processions. The bosomfena represented political and secular authority and would be carried on the left during official processions. The mponponsuo was the largest of the state swords and it was used to swear allegiance to the king. The bosommuru was used to swear allegiance to the Asante nation.

The afenatene was a most unusual ceremonial sword that comprised three widening blades that splayed outwards. The blade had a cut-out of fretwork decoration with animal motifs. The long iron shaft sometimes represented the body of a snake, links of a chain, or a series of complex, entwined knots. This sword would have been placed behind the king as he sat in state in his palace at Kumase, in present-day Ghana.

Indian swords

Distinguished by the sheer variety and uniqueness of their design, Indian swords are totally unlike Western swords. They reveal a strong visual extravagance that perfectly mirrors the huge size of the Indian subcontinent and its diffuse melting pot of cultural influences. From the Arabic-inspired north Indian talwar, sword of the Mughal princes, to the European-bladed south Indian firangi, or "foreign" sword, Indian sword makers were constantly producing weapons to amaze and instil terror in their enemies.

ABOVE An Indian sword of the Mughal era, 1526–1857, when most of the Indian subcontinent was ruled by a dynasty founded by the Mongol conqueror, Babur. The jade hilt is decorated with rubies.

The Indian dynasties

From around 180BC, ancient Hindu India experienced a number of invasions from Central Asia. The Indo-Parthians (from the area now known as Afghanistan), the Kushans (from what is now Tajikstan, Afghanistan and Pakistan), the Scythians (from Central Asia) and even the Greeks (under Alexander the Great) all established either kingdoms or strong cultural influences, particularly in northern India.

ABOVE Indian troops depicted using curved talwars against the English at Khurkowhah, 15 August 1857, during the Indian Mutiny.

The Maurya Empire (184BC–*c.* AD320) drove out these foreign invaders, and their pan-religious empire stretched from the Himalayas in the far north to the extreme southern Indian provinces of what are now Karnataka and Kerala. By the early 4th century AD, India had experienced a series of devastating internal wars, and, despite another period of internal unity (under the Gupta Dynasty, AD320–*c.*550), dynastic wars continued for the next few hundred years.

Militarily, however, the Indian subcontinent appears to have lagged somewhat behind the West and it is interesting to note that iron weapons did not appear in India until *c.*500BC. The sword was not even regarded as an important weapon and infantry were largely composed of bowmen. India's greatest military treatise, the *Siva-Dhanur-Veda* (*c.*500BC), concentrated on describing the important role of archers and their bows and arrows, to the detriment of any other bladed weapons.

To explain this anomaly, we must first consider the benign influence of Hindu religious culture in the conduct of war. Hand-to-hand conflict was usually avoided, as was mass slaughter. Nevertheless, despite

RIGHT Members of Indian royalty of the 19th century would have carried swords of great artistry and value.

the constraints imposed by religious beliefs, some astonishing edged weapons would be produced in the following centuries.

During the 11th and 12th centuries, India witnessed continuous and devastating invasions from Muslim Turks, Arabs and Afghans. In 1206 the Mamluk Dynasty (the first Muslim dynasty) was established, and there followed three centuries of Muslim rule throughout northern India. The south of the continent was not affected by this Muslim invasion and remained independent under the Hindu Vijayanagara Dynasty (1336–1646). In 1526, Babur Timurid, a Central Asian emperor and descendant of Genghis Khan, established the highly influential Mughal Empire (1526–1857), which reigned successfully over most of India and Afghanistan until its dissolution under British rule in the 19th century following the Indian Mutiny of 1857–58.

The British Raj

During the late 18th and early 19th centuries, the British East India Company had extended its control over most of India, paving the way for the establishment of the British Raj. These political changes had a limited impact on Indian swordsmiths, who continued to produce swords in a great diversity of forms. These included not only mainstream swords in the Muslim and Hindu traditions, such as the talwar and the khanda made for the princely states that survived under British rule, but also many regional or tribal variants.

The talwar

One of the most common of Indian swords, the origins of the talwar (*war*, or *vaar*, means "strike", as in "strike a blow") can be traced back to Central Asian invaders (the Saka-Jushans, ancestors of the Turks) who established their kingdoms in north-western India during the 13th century. They brought with them a curved sword of scimitar shape which was soon adopted by the indigenous Indian warrior clans, ancestors of the future Rajputs (a Hindu warrior dynasty, *c.* AD700–1947, originally from Rajasthan, a north Indian region bordering present-day Pakistan).

The all-metal talwar includes a disc pommel and a curved knuckle bow of inverted S-shape that is a continuation of the cross guard but does not actually attach itself to the pommel. Hilt quillons are usually globulous (rounded) and the middle part of the knuckle bow splays outwards towards the blade, forming pointed langets (the central area of the cross guard).

Scabbards are normally made of wood with leather or bright velvet covering.

BELOW This Indian talwar sword from the late 18th or early 19th century is all steel. Typically, it has a curved blade of up to 76cm (30in) and a disc-shaped pommel. It was used for slashing and thrusting.

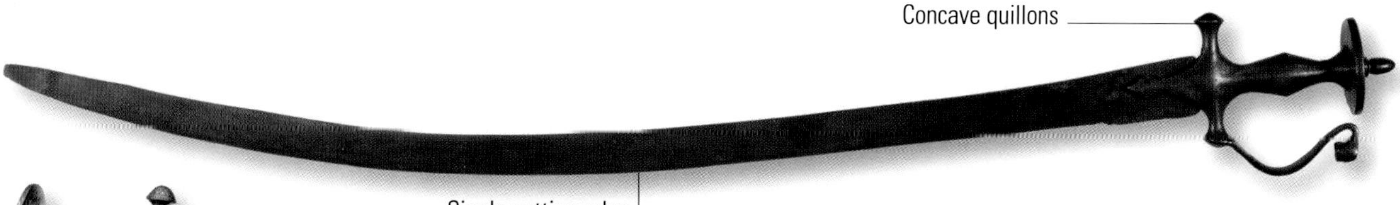

ABOVE A talwar sword with a shamshir blade.

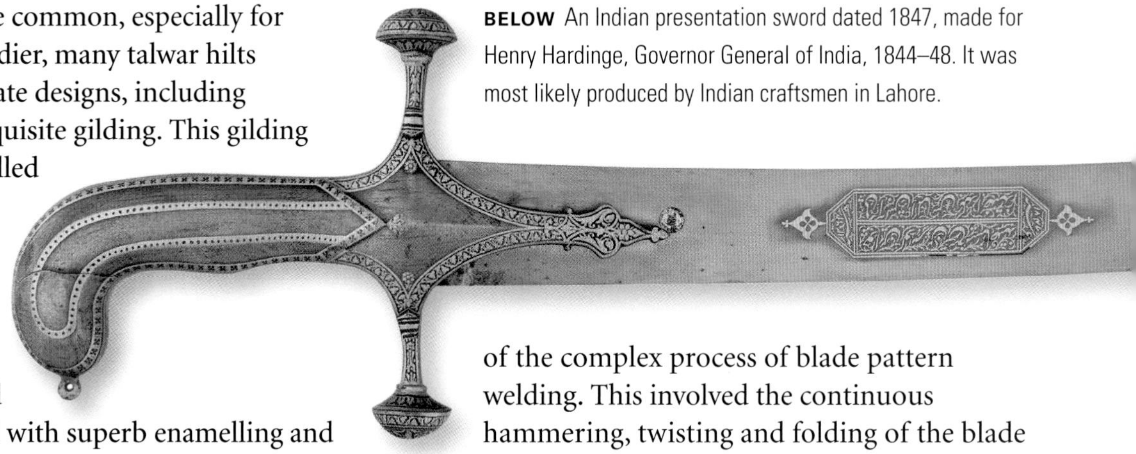

BELOW An Indian presentation sword dated 1847, made for Henry Hardinge, Governor General of India, 1844–48. It was most likely produced by Indian craftsmen in Lahore.

Although plain hilts were common, especially for the ordinary infantry soldier, many talwar hilts were decorated with ornate designs, including intricate chiselling or exquisite gilding. This gilding was done by a process called kofgari (meaning "goldbeating") or damascening (the complex inlaying of steel and gold). Hilts made for local rulers and people of rank are found with superb enamelling and inset jewels. Decoration was not just limited to the hilt. Blades were also decorated with fine incising (metal carving) or damascening.

Persian talwar blades

In the medieval period, blades made in Persia (modern-day Iran) were highly prized in India. Persian swordsmiths were recognized as being masters of the complex process of blade pattern welding. This involved the continuous hammering, twisting and folding of the blade to produce not only a very hard and durable weapon but also one that exhibited a finely textured and patterned surface.

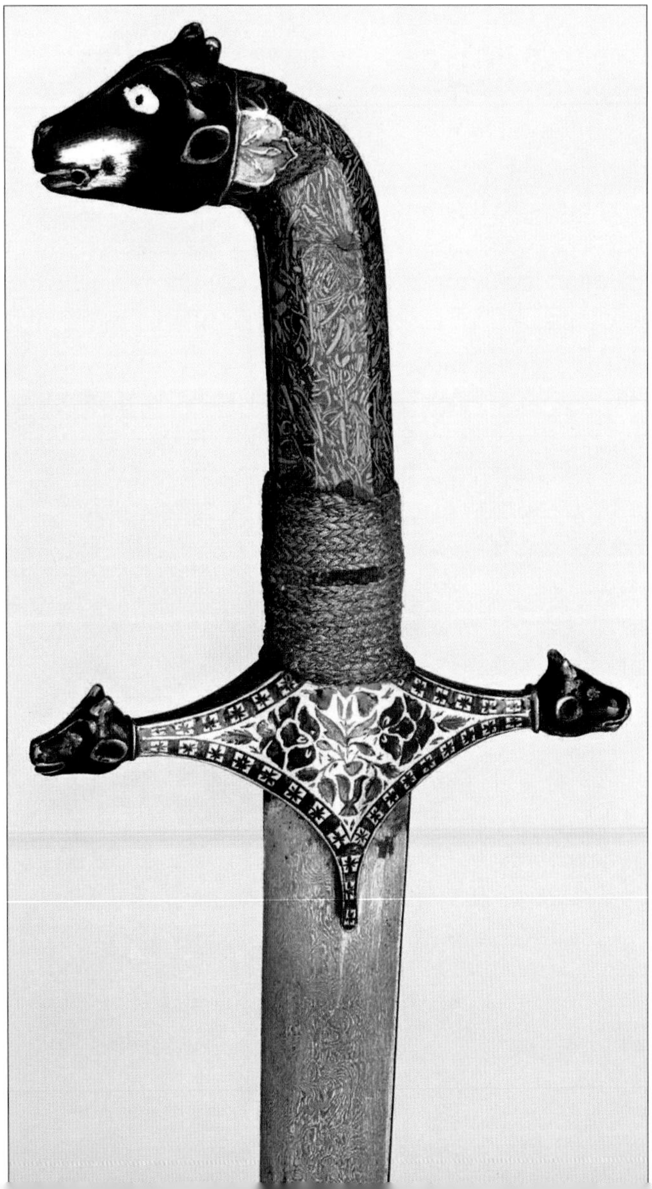

The "forty steps"

One specific pattern that was held to be superior to all others was known as the Ladder of the Prophet, or kirk nardaban (forty steps). It was a highly skilled effect and exhibited an application of a number of decorative chevrons, or stripes, down the blade. The bidr or qum (gravel) effect was another type of patterning applied to the blades of talwar swords.

Indian-made talwar blades

By the 16th century, the supply of blades from Persia and Damascus (Syria) had virtually dried up, and so Indian swordsmiths had to start producing their own work rather than rely solely on imported blades. They did this by introducing their own unique patterned steel, known as wootz (meaning "steel" in some south Indian languages). Importantly, the production of wootz blades replaced the time-consuming method of folding and hammering the steel. This was because the local iron ore naturally produced crystallized structures in the steel that local craftsmen were able to enhance by simple polishing.

Talwar blade marking

Blades of high quality were invariably marked by their makers in the form of a cartouche or tablet in the area just below the hilt (the forte). A gilded bedouh, or

LEFT An 18th-century Indian shamshir from Jaipur. The ends of the quillons and the pommel are modelled as animals' heads, which have been coated with blue enamel.

square, was also applied to this part of the blade and then divided into four quarters, each quarter displaying one of the Arabic numerals for the numbers 2, 4, 6 and 8. These numbers were thought to bring good fortune to the sword's owner.

Rounded cartouches inlaid in gold and carrying invocations or prayers from the Koran were also added. Another decoration that is common to many Indian swords is bidri, a combination of black-stained pewter and silver. This produced a dramatic contrasting effect. Bidri decoration originated in the city of Bider, northwest of Hyderabad (now capital of the present-day southern Indian state of Andhura Pradesh).

The talwar in battle

Being a curved sword, the talwar was useful when striking against bone or armour because it would not easily become embedded, as in the case of straight blades. The Rajput horsemen had a fearsome reputation for wildly attacking infantry formations, and, at close quarters, the short, spiked end on some talwars was efficient at stabbing an opponent in his face if unprotected.

The talwar in Indian culture

An extremely important symbol of Rajput traditions and customs, the talwar sword also became an inseparable part of their culture. It was used to bestow honours and titles to tribal chiefs and it symbolized prestige and honour. In the case of a groom being unable to attend his own wedding due to illness, his personal talwar sword could be sent along to take his place and so enable the wedding rituals to continue without him.

An oath of allegiance to a tribal clan was also sworn on a talwar sword by Rajput warriors. It comprised the words *dhal talwar ki aan* ("by the honour of my sword and shield").

ABOVE A mid-17th-century Indian miniature from Bijapur showing a warrior with talwar and pata, or gauntlet sword.

Afghan pulwar or talwar

Due to the talwar's growing popularity within the Mughal Empire, its influence spread northwards, and its design was interpreted by Afghan warriors who produced their own version, the Afghani talwar, or pulwar. Despite this acceptance of an "enemy's" sword, the Afghan and Rajput regions were constantly at war with each other, and contemporary Rajput texts frequently state how "...the Afghan army's sword broke under the Rajput talwar."

BELOW By the 16th century, the supply of superior blades from Persia and Damascus had virtually ceased. In response, Indian swordsmiths produced their own patterned blades. This Persian sword would have been made with Damascus steel.

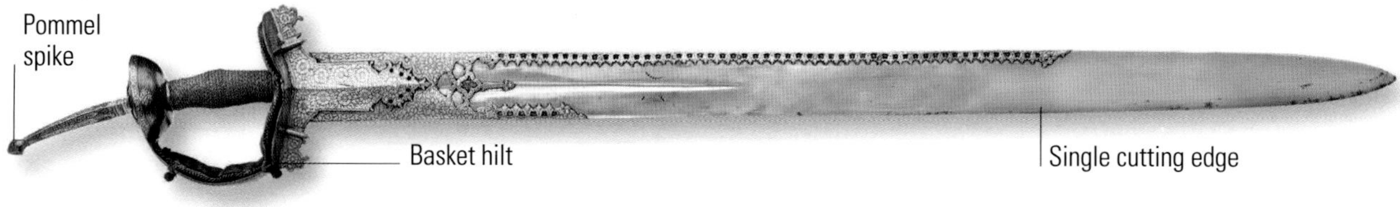

The khanda

It is thought that the origins of the khanda can be traced back to the Gupta Dynasty (AD320–550), as khanda-type swords have been recognized on period sculptures. During the medieval period, Rajput kings are depicted in wall paintings wielding this type of sword. The name "khanda" is thought to originate in the Sanskrit word for sword, *khanda*.

The khanda has a distinctive, wide and straight, watered steel (pattern-welded) blade that widens towards a spear-pointed tip. A light, flexible blade is characteristic of the khanda, as are two stiffened, ribbed reinforcements that run alongside the blade edge on either side; one is almost the length of the blade and the other is much shorter, to allow a cutting edge. This reinforcement produced a much lighter sword, having greater manoeuvrability than a thick, heavy blade.

TOP A khanda sword from around 1800 with a light and flexible spatulate blade, from Malabar in south-west India. It has a reinforcement bar that runs part of the way down the blade.

ABOVE Late 18th-century khanda sword with a typical Hindu basket hilt. It has a pronounced spiked pommel which was used if the swordsman needed a two-handed grip.

The khanda's hilt and pommel are similar to firangi swords, but with the addition of a wide, disc-like cross guard and knuckle bow. The hilt is also more basket-like in form than other open-hilted Indian swords. The long, spiked and canted (slightly curved) pommel that is found on khandas is thought to have a double use, both producing a double-handed option and acting as a handy walking stick (when unsheathed) or hand rest (when sheathed).

The pata (gauntlet sword)

One of the most unusual of Indian edged weapons, the pata comprises a long, straight-bladed and doubled-edged sword attached to an armoured, half-gauntlet hilt. The overall length could be up to 110cm (44in). In order to wield the sword effectively, the wearer gripped a concealed cross bar inside the gauntlet. Pata swords were favourite weapons of the southern and central Indian Maharatta Empire. The extended grip provided by the encasing of the forearm also allowed the user a very powerful, sweeping blow. Some warriors chose to carry a pata on each hand and would adopt the stance of a whirling windmill as they attacked swathes of infantry or even armoured cavalry.

Shivaji Bhosle (1627–80), founder of the Maharatta Empire, was known to be a practised exponent of this sword. It is said that one of his famous generals, Tanaji Malusare, wielded a pata in each hand during the Battle of Sinhagad (1670), a now legendary encounter between the Maharattas and Mughal forces besieged in a hilltop fort, near Pune (the present-day western Indian state of Maharashtra).

BELOW Indian pata, 18th century. It was considered a highly effective weapon for the infantry and also used against armoured cavalry.

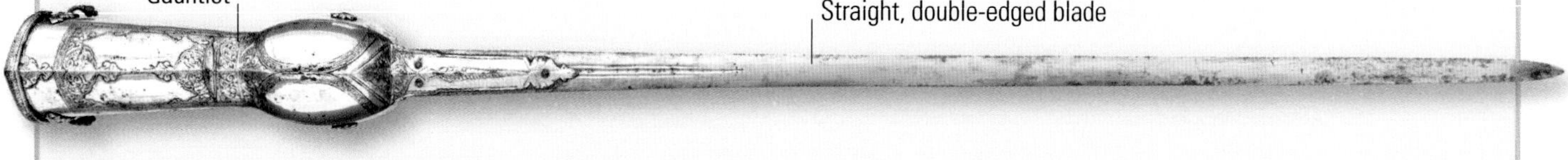

LEFT The kora is the national sword of Nepal. It has a curved steel blade ending in a flared tip.

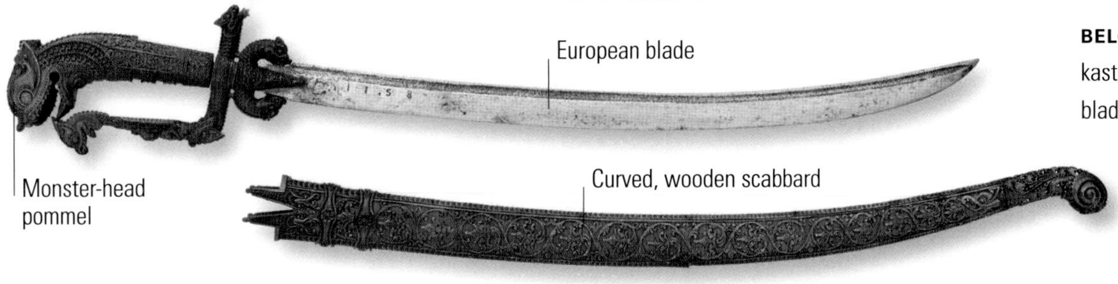

BELOW The Sri Lankan kastane with a European blade and scabbard, *c.*1758.

Weapon of last resort

To a Rajput horseman, the khanda was very much a lethal weapon of last resort. If unhorsed and surrounded by the enemy, he would quickly draw the large blade and begin swinging it around his head, taking full advantage of its estimable hacking and slashing functions. Because of the great width of the khanda blade, it was never perceived as an efficient thrusting sword.

The khanda was effective against the leather and chain-mail armour of the Mughal invaders, as its great strength (especially when wielded with two hands) could cut through these materials with considerable ease. When carried by infantrymen, this sword gave them a chance against horse-mounted soldiers.

The firangi

This was a typical sword of the Hindu southern and central Indian Maharatta Empire (1674–1818). The firangi had a narrow, straight blade, commonly made from imported European blades (the word "firangi" literally means "foreigner") and sometimes decorated with kofgari-worked inlaid gold or silver. When it was fitted with a home-made blade, it was called a sukhela, and in the Deccan (comprising the south Indian plateau), a dhup.

Like the khanda, the firangi blade is also reinforced along the blade edge, combined with a disc-shaped pommel terminating in a long spike used for a two-handed blow. Kofgari or inlaid gold ornamentation frequently decorated the hilt. The large, basket-type hilt is also padded and embroidered with silk or coloured velvet. In the 17th and 18th centuries, the Maharattas of the Western Deccan relied heavily on imported European trade goods and especially sword blades. The Maharattas' preference was for German and Italian blades, since they regarded English blades as very inferior.

The shamshir

Translated literally as "curved like a lion's tail", the shamshir was a distinctively curved sword introduced into India during the 16th century. Persian (Iranian) in origin, its fine pattern-welded or watered blades are some of the finest blades ever to have been produced.

The kora

Nepalese edged weapons were strongly influenced by the medieval Indian Rajputs, who brought Indian weapon styles into the region. Alongside the legendary kukri knife (a heavily curved tool and weapon), the kora is the traditional weapon of the Gurkhas (from Nepal and northern India). Its simple all-metal design comprises a wide and heavy blade with a massive flared tip. The grip was tubular, including a thin, disc-shaped pommel and cross guard. Decoration of koras includes chiselling and mounting of precious metals to the hilt.

The kastane

Sri Lanka's national sword, this distinctive weapon has a short, flat-backed or unfullered blade. The hilt is usually highly ornamented and includes fantastical creatures located at the end of multiple quillons. Gold and silver decoration is richly applied throughout, including the blade, where gilt damascening is worked for most of its length. European blades were frequently mounted on kastane hilts of the 17th and 18th centuries, highlighting the strong commercial ties with the West, particularly Portugal, which established successful trading bases in the country.

Swords and daggers come in an incredible variety of forms, depending on their historical period and place of origin.

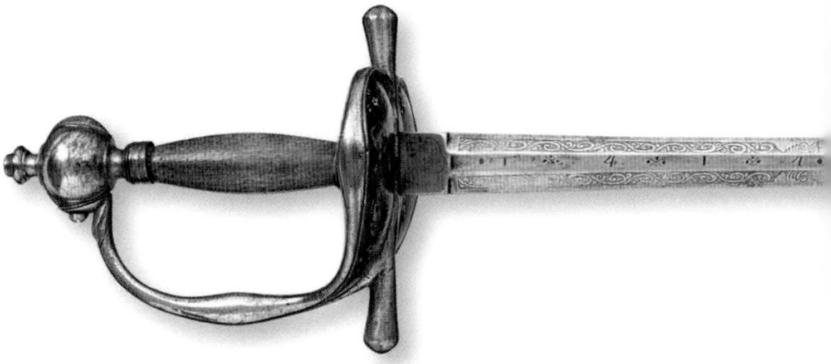

A directory of swords and sabres

In this substantial catalogue, you will find details of some of the most important weapons from around the world and throughout history, along with information about their manufacture and use. Arranged chronologically as well as by geographical area, each of the weapons has a description and a specification that lists its country of origin, date and length.

TOP A Swedish cavalry trooper's sword, *c.*1700.

TOP RIGHT British infantry officer's sword, Pattern 1895, with a three-quarter basket hilt.

MIDDLE German cavalry officer's dress sword, *c.*1700.

BOTTOM RIGHT Scottish basket-hilted broadsword, *c.*1720, with exquisite brass inlay to the hilt.

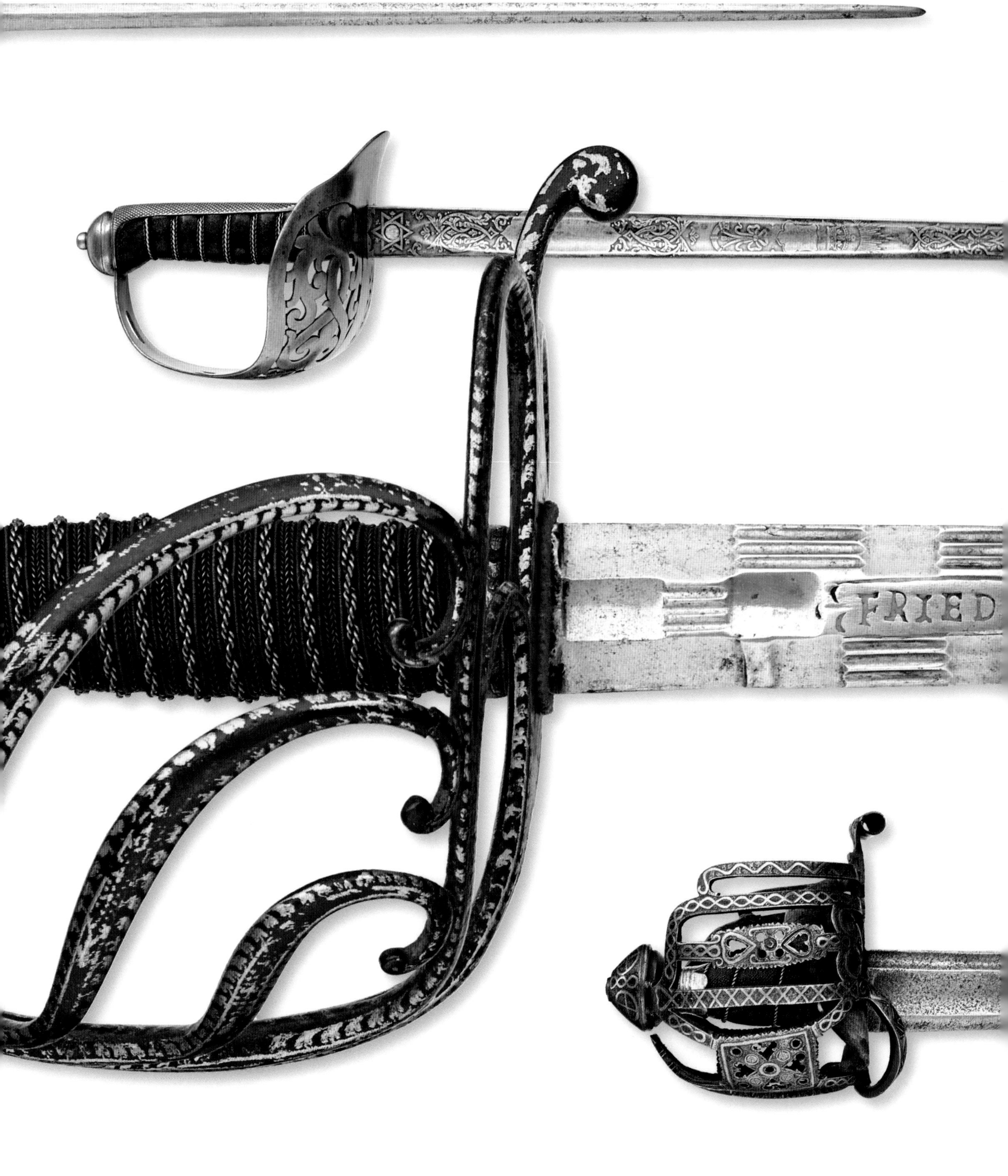
FRIED

Design of the sword

Over the centuries, the sword has evolved into many different forms and styles, but there is general agreement concerning how its parts should be named. From the hilt pommel that provides balance, to the blade fullers that give both strength and flexibility, sword makers have defined both types and parts of the sword in a way that makes it easier for us to understand this most universal of weapons.

Types of swords

Light cavalry officer's sword

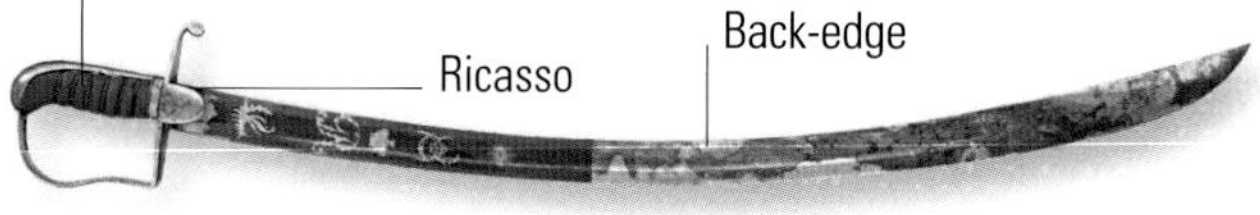

The curved blade of this cavalry sword was designed to provide the mounted horseman with an effective slashing and cutting weapon.

Rapier

Rapiers are defined by their long, needle-like blades and complex, multi-bar hilts. They were purely thrusting swords and most effective when used in the duel.

Basket-hilted broadsword

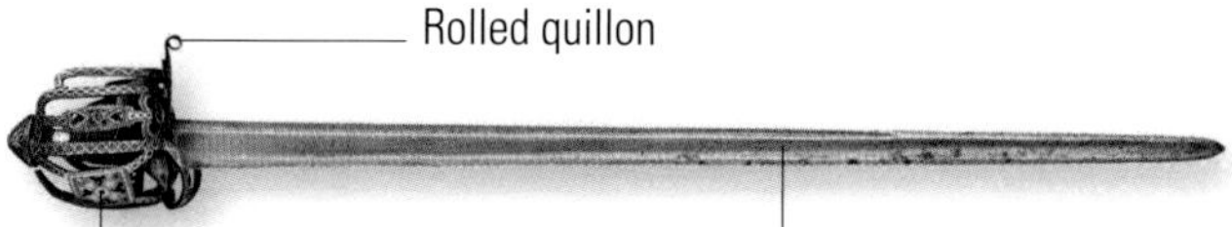

The large, enclosed basket hilt protected the swordsman's hand, and the wide, double-edged, slashing blade was devastating at close quarters.

Smallsword

The smallsword developed from the earlier rapier and usually took the form of a trefoil or three-sided blade. This blade shape provided exceptional strength.

Parts of a sword

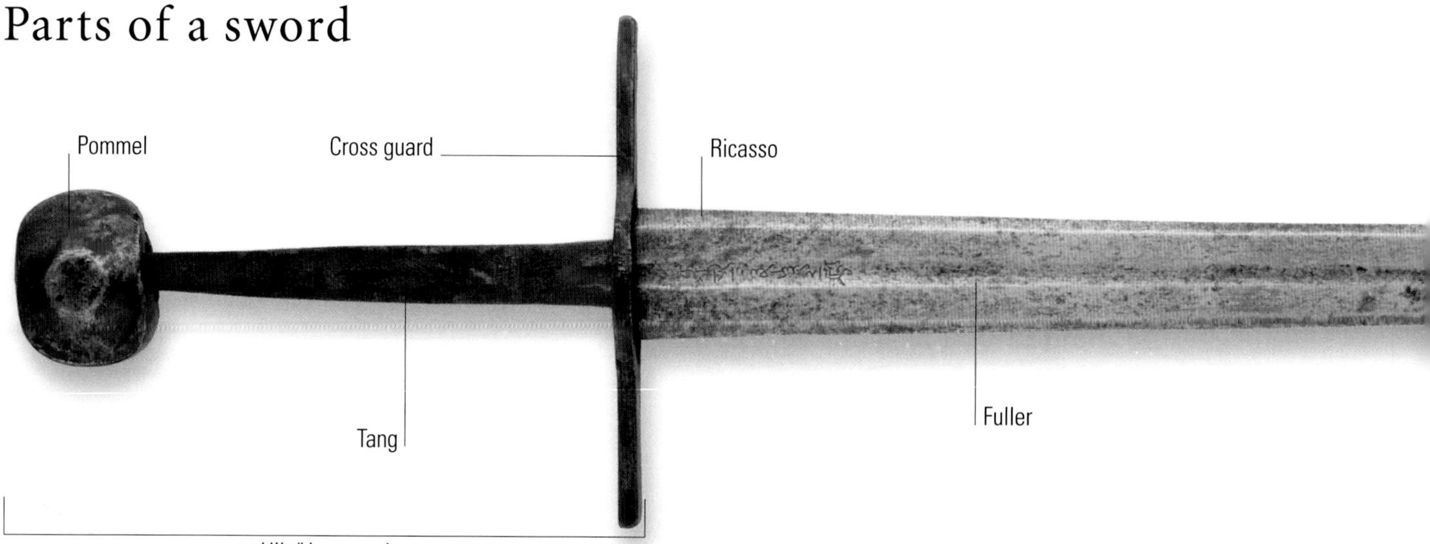

Types of blades

The sheer range of blade types that have been produced throughout history and across vast geographical areas is testament to the variety of functions that a sword could perform. Within any army or cultural group, different blades performed specific tasks. For example, cavalry swords were required to be of considerable length to enable the trooper to reach down and attack foot-soldiers. Blades were either curved or straight, depending on whether a thrusting or slashing motion was desired.

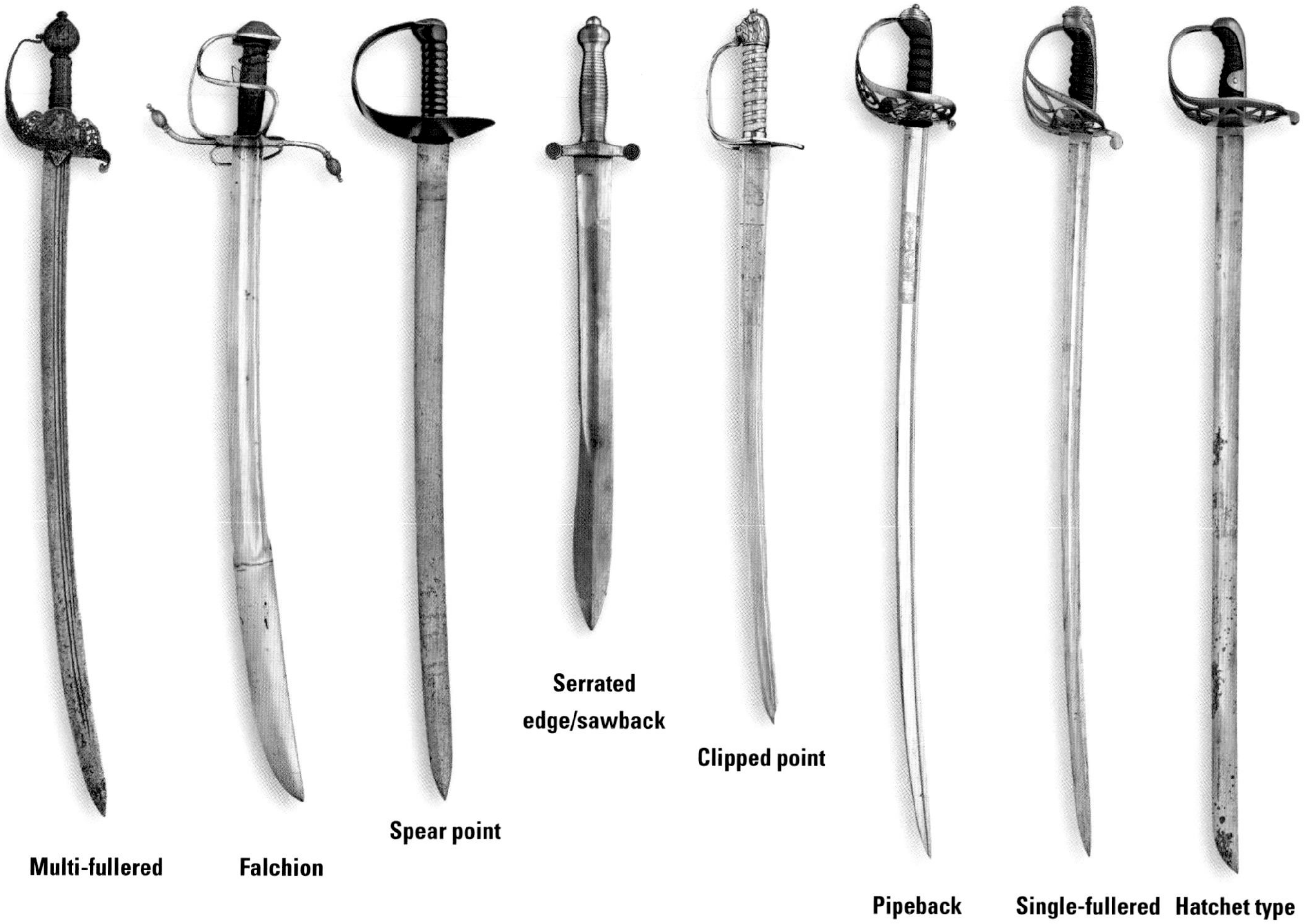

A sword is a bladed hand weapon comprising a blade and a handle. The blade is usually manufactured in metal, with at least one sharp edge and a pointed tip for thrusting. The handle, called the hilt, can be made of many materials, but the material most commonly used is wood covered by leather, fishskin or metal wiring. A cross guard prevents the user's hand from slipping onto the blade.

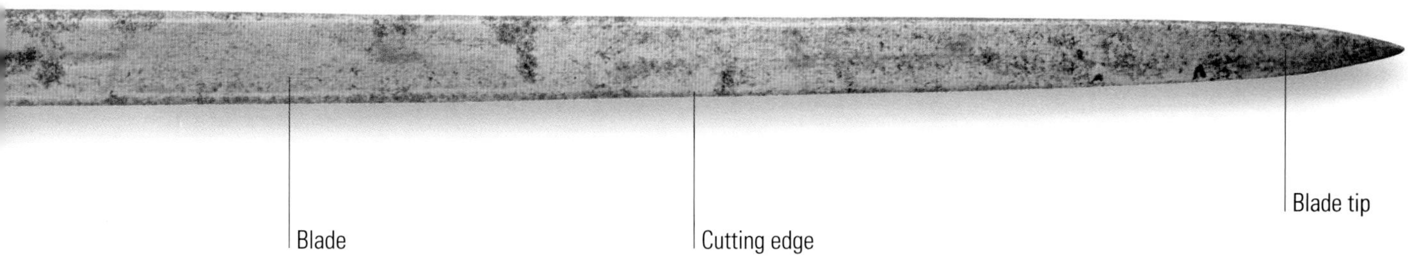

Early stone weapons

Flint axes and points were the practical day-to-day tools of the Stone Age and not designed to be weapons of war. They were for hunting, dissection of carcasses and manufacture of basic domestic tools. Only when a tribe was threatened by outsiders would these tools be transformed into weapons of defence.

Acheulean flint hand axes, 1.4 million BC

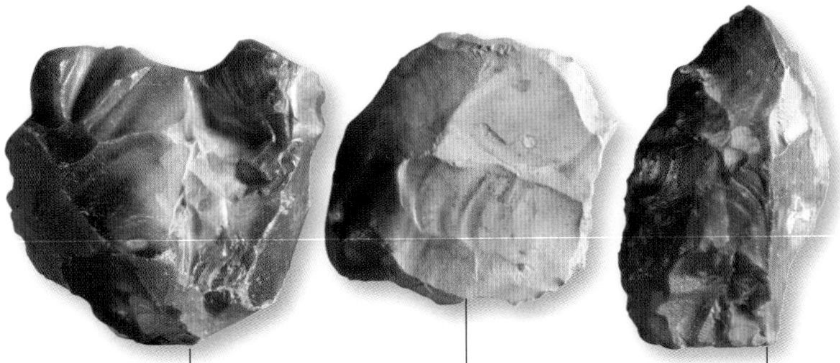

Over one million years ago, early humans (*Homo erectus*) moved from Africa to Eurasia and created these distinctive oval and pear-shaped flint hand axes. Some of the first examples were found in St Acheul (northern France) during the late 19th century.

DATE	1.4 MILLION BC
ORIGIN	EURASIAN
LENGTH	UNKNOWN

Solutrean laurel-leaf flint spear point, 28,000BC

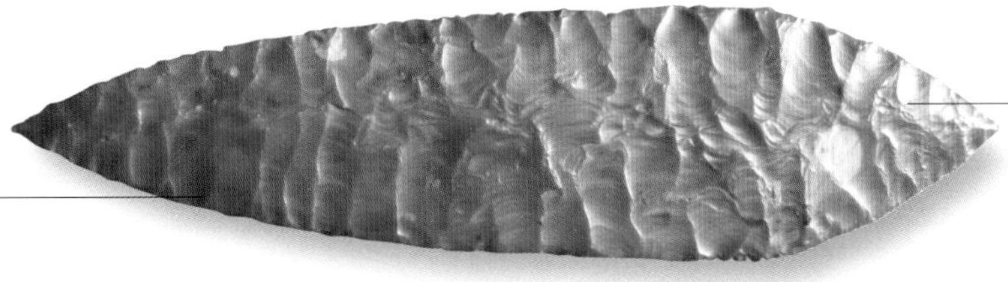

The Solutrean culture (named after Solutré, in central France) produced distinctive chipped flint points that are symmetrical and very finely crafted. Most examples date from around 17,000 years ago and were produced by pressure flaking. Slim, leaf-shaped projectile heads are characteristic of this type of flint point.

DATE	28,000BC
ORIGIN	FRENCH
LENGTH	UNKNOWN

Atlatl, 23,000BC

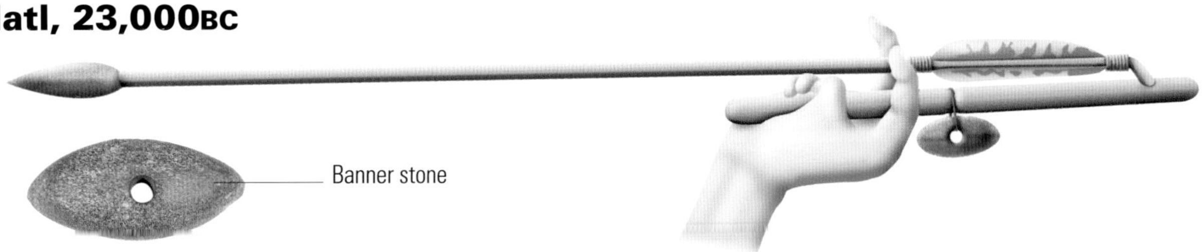

The atlatl was an effective hunting tool that used the leverage of the human arm to project a flint dart or spear at great speed against a moving target. The flint was placed on a hollowed shaft and the power of the upper arm and wrist was engaged to instantaneously propel the flint. A banner stone could be added as a weight to increase resistance. A range of up to 100m (328ft) could be achieved.

DATE	23,000BC
ORIGIN	EUROPEAN/AMERICAN
LENGTH	UNKNOWN

Clovis spear point, 11,500BC

DATE	11,500BC
ORIGIN	NORTH AMERICAN
LENGTH	19.6cm (7.7in)

First discovered in Clovis, New Mexico, in 1931, these small flint points have been dated to about 13,500 years ago, during the time of the Paleo-Indians. Created by pressure flaking, they were very thin and fluted in shape, and would have been effective at piercing animal (or human) flesh.

Full grooved axe, 8,000–1,000BC

DATE	8,000–1,000BC
ORIGIN	NORTH AMERICAN
LENGTH	13.9cm (5.5in)

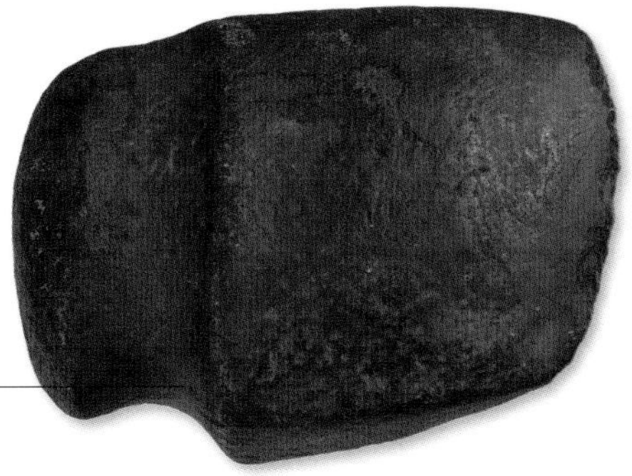

Early stone axes had grooves chiselled into them so the axe could be attached with twine to a wooden handle. The Archaic peoples (7,000–1,000BC) were also responsible for the development of the atlatl (hand-held weapon that fired darts) and the net sinker (notched pebbles used to sink fishing nets).

Yadkin point, 8,000–1,000BC

DATE	8,000–1,000BC
ORIGIN	NORTH AMERICAN
LENGTH	5cm (2in)

American archaeologists unearthed these flint arrowhead points from the Yadkin River, in Stanly County, North Carolina. This example has a serrated edge that has been finely knapped (chipped or broken with sharp blows), to produce a sawing tool.

Oakville arrowheads, 1,000BC–AD1,000

These projectile points were used in the south-eastern part of the United States (Alabama). Like their Archaic predecessors, Woodland Indians hunted small game and foraged in the forests. With the adoption of the bow and arrow came the need for smaller projectile points.

DATE	1,000BC–AD1,000
ORIGIN	NORTH AMERICAN
LENGTH	4.4–5cm (1.7–2in)

Bronze Age weapons

Leaf-shaped sword blades and riveted hilts are the defining features of many swords of the Bronze Age. The anthropomorphic and free-flowing style of these weapons, typical of European Celts, was also found in Eurasia, particularly Persia (Iran), where swords of great originality and elegance were made.

Turkish bronze sword, 3,350–3,000BC

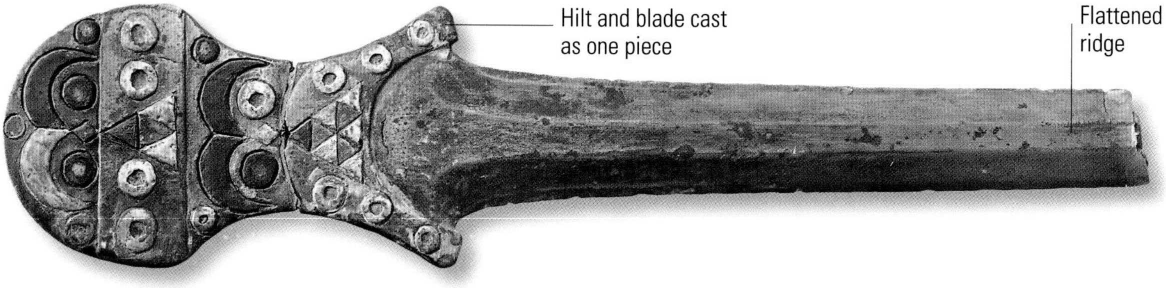

This sword is one of the earliest identified sword types in Europe. It was excavated in Turkey and is of one-piece construction, with the hilt and the blade cast together. The domed hilt has been hammered, ground and polished, and is also inlaid with silver roundels and pyramids. The blade has a slightly flattened central ridge that would have added extra strength.

DATE	3,350–3,000BC
ORIGIN	TURKISH
LENGTH	39.5cm (15.5in)

European bronze sword, 1,500BC

Of a type that was carried throughout western Europe, this sword has a series of false rivets worked into the hilt cross guard, indicating that it was cast in one piece. Many swords of this period do have separate hilts and blades that were attached to each other by means of large rivets.

DATE	1,500BC
ORIGIN	WESTERN EUROPEAN
LENGTH	60.5cm (23.8in)

German bronze sword, 1,100BC

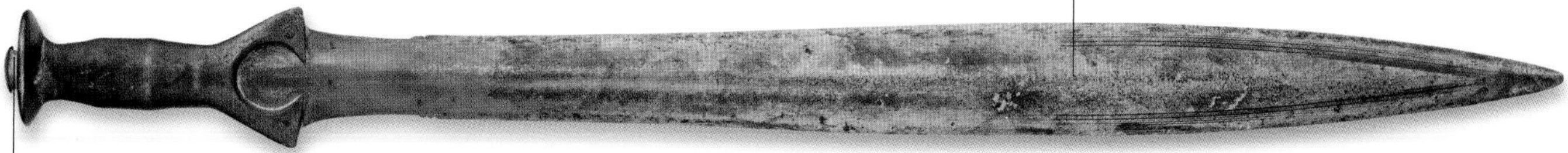

Before the introduction of iron into the sword-making process, bronze dominated sword manufacture. This sword has a typical leaf-shaped and double-edged blade. Flattened, disc-shaped pommels were also extremely common. An incised pattern has also been worked around the blade point.

DATE	1,100BC
ORIGIN	GERMAN
LENGTH	85cm (33.5in)

Persian bronze sword, 1,000BC

DATE	1,000BC
ORIGIN	PERSIAN
LENGTH	85cm (33.5in)

This bronze sword features an unusually long blade of lenticular (outwardly bulging) shape. The tang is rectangular, engraved with geometric patterns. The pommel has distinctive ear-shaped or antennae-like projections. The shoulders of the cross guard are squared and the whole sword has been cast as one piece.

Persian bronze sword, 1,000BC

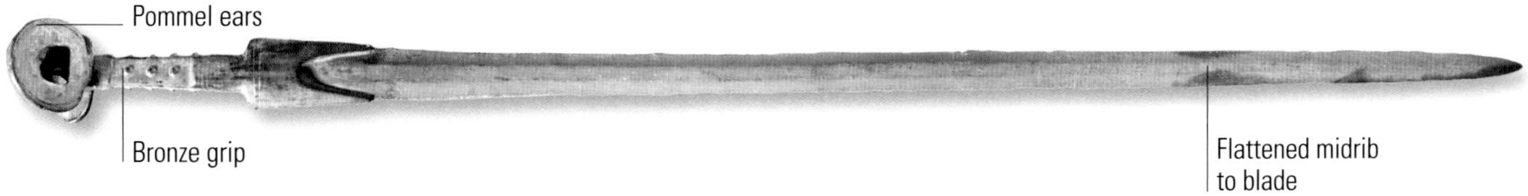

DATE	1,000BC
ORIGIN	PERSIAN
LENGTH	94.5cm (37.2in)

The bronze grip on this sword has been covered in decorative nubs that would have provided its owner with a rudimentary grip and more adhesion for the hand. There is a flattened midrib to the centre of the blade, a hollow, ear-shaped pommel and traces of a geometric design to the cross guard.

Italian large bronze spearhead, 500BC

DATE	500BC
ORIGIN	ITALIAN
LENGTH	47.5cm (18.7in)

The pronounced median, or central, strengthening ridge on this socketed spearhead would have provided its user with considerable thrusting power and strength. It is likely that its large size meant it would have been particularly effective against armour or mounted troops.

Chinese bronze sword, 500BC

DATE	500BC
ORIGIN	N.W. CHINESE
LENGTH	56cm (22in)

The earliest Chinese swords come from north-western China and this example is typical of a bronze jian (straight-bladed sword). The wide blade is diamond-sectioned, with a solid tang reinforced by a central ring in the centre of the grip. The cross guard has inlaid decoration and the pommel is flat and rounded.

Weapons of early civilizations

The ancient Greek and Egyptian armies fought in massed ranks and did not regard the sword as their primary weapon of war. The spear or javelin, bow and arrow and axe were all regarded as superior and were proven in battle. The sword was still carried but used more as a weapon of last resort. Conversely, the Roman and Celtic soldier held the sword in high regard and understood its supreme effectiveness in battle.

Egyptian sickle sword or khepesh, 1,400–1,200BC

DATE	1,400–1,200BC
ORIGIN	EGYPTIAN
LENGTH	65cm (25.6in)

The sickle sword, or khepesh, was a distinctive curved sword that was adopted from the Hyksos ("Sea peoples") invaders from Palestine, in the 17th century BC. It was used as an infantry weapon and, because of its extremely curved blade, was primarily a chopping sword. It was also the favoured weapon of Egyptian Pharoahs.

Egyptian khepesh, 1,250BC

The handle of this khepesh was originally inlaid with ivory. Its sickle-shaped blade was sharpened on either the inside or the outside edge of the blade. The outside edge was extremely effective at producing deep, slashing wounds, while the inside edge was utilized for hacking at an opponent.

DATE	1,250BC
ORIGIN	EGYPTIAN
LENGTH	Unknown

Ancient Greek spear

The Greek hoplite was a part-time soldier who normally carried a long spear (doru) and rounded shield (aspis). One battle tactic was to hold the spear overarm and lock the shield over the left forearm. The hoplites then pushed forward with their shields, confronting the enemy with a seemingly impenetrable wall.

RIGHT Greek hoplites, *c.*500BC.

Celtic sword, *c.*400–350BC

DATE	*c.*400–350BC
ORIGIN	CELTIC
LENGTH	69cm (27.2in)

This is a Celtic sword from the early La Tène period, which has been cleaned following excavation. It has an iron blade with short, tapered tang (the area near the hilt) that has become fused into the scabbard. There are three strengthening ridges to the scabbard and a decorated chape (tip).

Celtic sword, 300–100BC

DATE	300–100BC
ORIGIN	CELTIC
LENGTH	89cm (35in)

The absence of any remains to the grip of this sword probably indicates that it was made with a wood-based material and has simply decomposed over time. The blade is stuck in the scabbard but is recognizable as a broad-bladed weapon with a typically downward-curved, iron cross guard. The scabbard has a number of narrow rings that would have provided extra strength for the sheath.

Roman sword, AD14–37

DATE	AD14–37
ORIGIN	ROMAN
LENGTH	57.5cm (22.6in)

This Roman gladius sword was worn by a senior military officer during the reign of Emperor Tiberius (AD14–37). The scabbard mounts are decorated in fine gold and silver engraving, including depictions of Tiberius. The gladius was employed in a stabbing, thrusting motion and Roman soldiers were repeatedly trained to use the sword in a close, fighting formation.

Frankish, Viking and Saxon weapons

Both the Vikings and the Saxons had a deep reverence for the sword. Death in battle was seen as a great honour and a dead warrior's sword would be passed down the generations. Warriors also carried the spear and the great bearded war axe. In the right hands, these were devastating weapons of war and conquest.

Francisca throwing axe, *c.*600

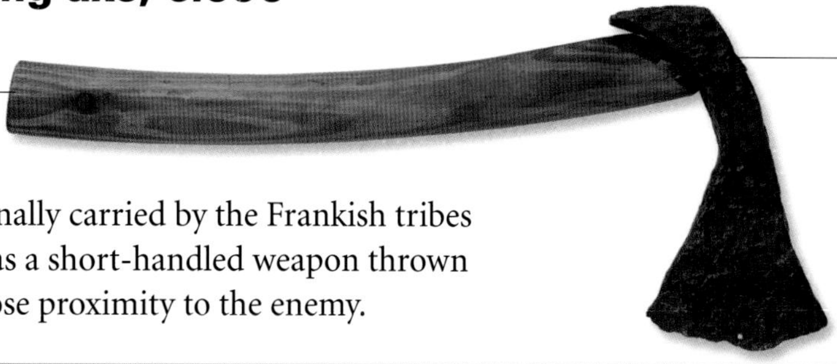

This type of axe was originally carried by the Frankish tribes of western Germany. It was a short-handled weapon thrown with great force and in close proximity to the enemy.

DATE	*c.*600
ORIGIN	GERMAN
LENGTH	37.5cm (14.8in)

Viking bearded battle-axe, *c.*900

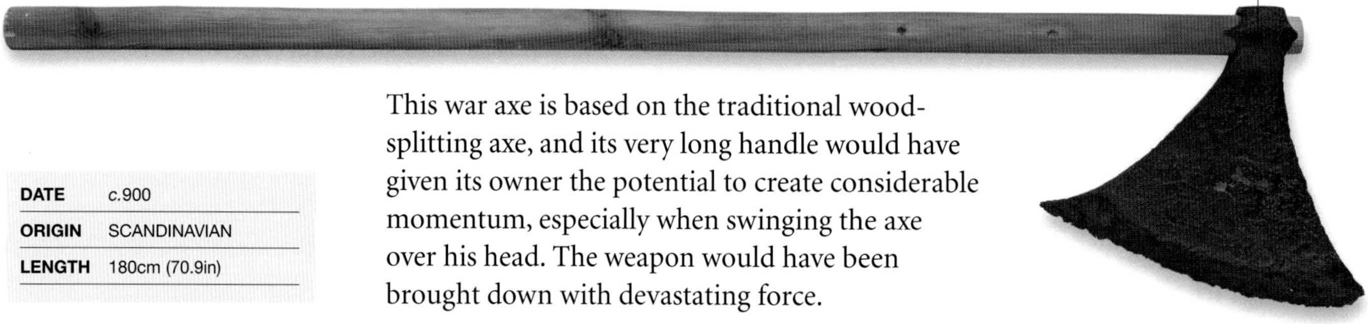

DATE	*c.*900
ORIGIN	SCANDINAVIAN
LENGTH	180cm (70.9in)

This war axe is based on the traditional wood-splitting axe, and its very long handle would have given its owner the potential to create considerable momentum, especially when swinging the axe over his head. The weapon would have been brought down with devastating force.

Anglo-Saxon scaramax, *c.*900

DATE	*c.*900
ORIGIN	BRITISH
LENGTH	74cm (29.1in)

The scaramax or seax (meaning "knife" in Anglo-Saxon) was a radical departure from typical blade design. It was more of a large and extended knife, and would have been used in a chopping or hacking fashion. The seax seems to have been used primarily as a tool but larger ones may also have been employed as weapons.

Viking socketed spearhead, *c.*900

The very slim and long profile of this spearhead was designed to enable the warrior to drive his weapon through most armour or defensive clothing and penetrate deep into an opponent's body.

DATE	*c.*900
ORIGIN	SCANDINAVIAN
LENGTH	70.5cm (27.7in)

Viking winged spearhead, *c*.900

Winged or lugged spearheads were used for both war and hunting. The leaf-shaped blade included double wings at the bottom of the socket that would have been effective at parrying sword blows or stopping an opponent's blade travelling down the spear and injuring the user's hands.

DATE	*c*.900
ORIGIN	SCANDINAVIAN
LENGTH	44.8cm (17.6in)

Viking sword, *c*.900

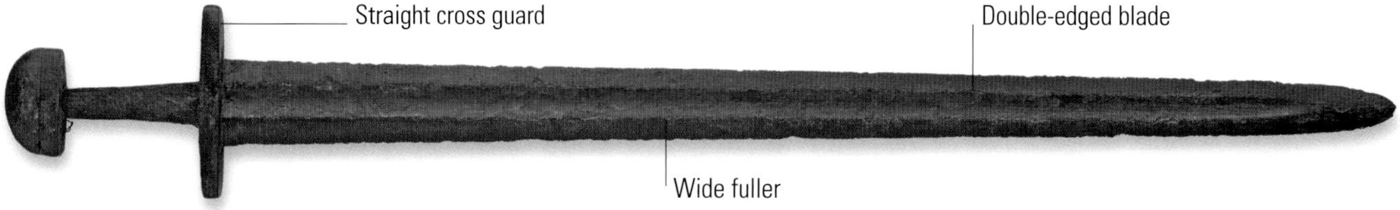

DATE	*c*.900
ORIGIN	SCANDINAVIAN
LENGTH	95.5cm (37.6in)

The deep, single fuller (the rounded or bevelled groove on the flat side of a blade) of this double-edged blade was not designed to allow an opponent's blood to channel down the blade, but was carefully crafted by the sword maker to give the blade less overall weight and consequently, more flexibility.

Viking sword, *c*.900

This sword has a wide, double-edged, pattern-welded blade that would have given it superb strength and durability. The pommel, which forms an ornament on the end of the hilt, is rounded in shape and very typical of late Viking sword hilts. The pommel needed to be heavy to counterbalance the heavy blade.

DATE	*c*.900
ORIGIN	SCANDINAVIAN
LENGTH	89cm (35in)

Late Viking sword, *c*.900–1150

DATE	*c*.900–1150
ORIGIN	SCANDINAVIAN
LENGTH	90.1cm (35.5in)

The large, rounded iron pommel of this sword acted as the perfect counterweight to its long and wide blade. At this late stage of Viking sword development, the blade has now become tapered towards the end and is in contrast to earlier Viking swords that had blades of equal width and more rounded points.

Medieval swords

The wide-bladed and double-edged knightly sword had developed into a highly effective weapon of war and important signifier of social rank. It could slice through chain mail with ease. Only at the end of the medieval period were swords developed with especially hardened points to penetrate plate armour.

Scandinavian late Viking/early medieval sword, *c.*1050

This sword has a distinctive "brazil nut" pommel that was common in the early medieval period. Unlike earlier Viking swords of the 900s, the cross guard has now increased considerably in width. The blade is also more finely tapered. This sword is very much a transitional piece.

DATE	*c.*1050
ORIGIN	SCANDINAVIAN
LENGTH	82cm (32.3in)

English late Viking/early medieval sword, *c.*1100–50

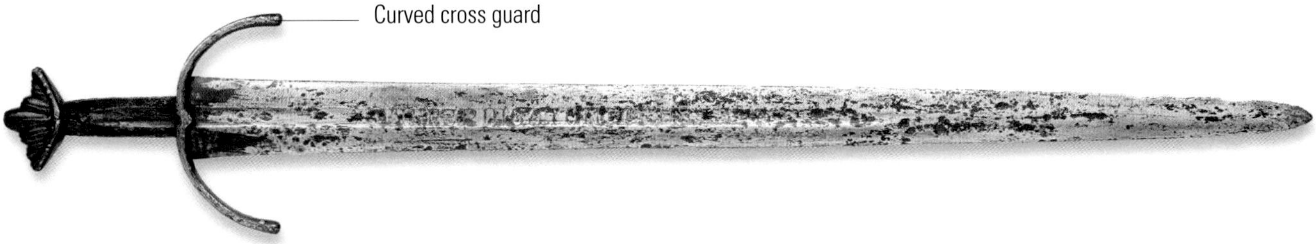

Although this sword was excavated from a river in southern England, it is in a remarkable state of preservation. The distinctive late Viking, lobated style of the pommel is clearly evident, but the sharply downswept cross guard has resulted in many authorities wrongly dating this sword to the later medieval period.

DATE	*c.*1100–50
ORIGIN	ENGLISH
LENGTH	92cm (36.2in)

European knightly sword, *c.*1150

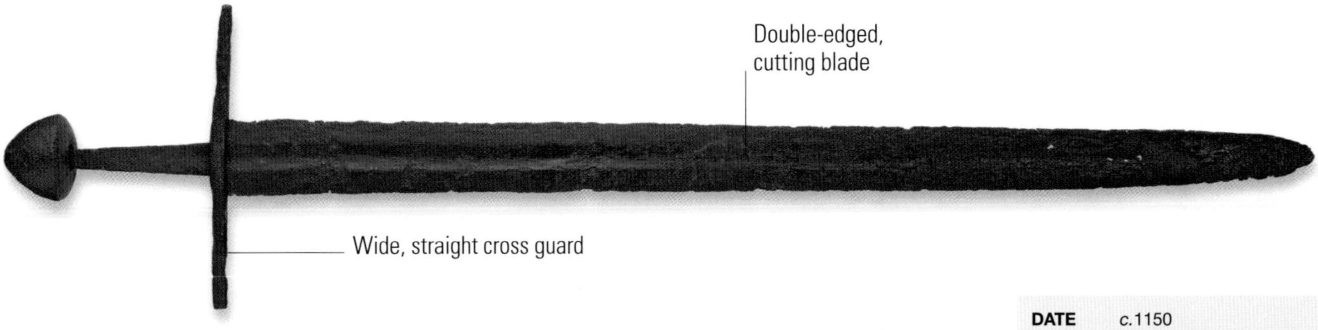

This is representative of the type of broadsword that would have been carried by a mounted knight during the Crusades (1095–1291). Pommel design was evolving from earlier triangular shapes to more rounded or "wheel" forms.

DATE	*c.*1150
ORIGIN	EUROPEAN
LENGTH	96.5cm (38in)

German knightly sword, *c.*1250–1300

DATE	*c.*1250–1300
ORIGIN	GERMAN
LENGTH	112cm (44in)

This sword has a spear-point blade with impressive cutting and thrusting capabilities. Its narrow blade and the consequent reduction in weight are likely to have provided its knight with considerable flexibility and agility, particularly when fighting on foot.

European knightly sword, *c.*1250–1300

DATE	*c.*1250–1300
ORIGIN	EUROPEAN
LENGTH	91.4cm (36in)

Although the blade is of relatively common form, it is the highly unusual hilt design that sets this sword apart from all other contemporary examples. Where most medieval swords display a wheel pommel, this sword features a two-pronged pommel and sharply angled quillons. This hilt design is rarely seen in contemporary medieval illustrations of knights, and the only two recorded visual references are represented in the royal seals of King Edward I of England (1239–1307) and Charles of Anjou, King of Sicily (1227–85).

The Crusades

When the Christian and Muslim forces clashed in battle during the Crusades (1095–1291), their sword types were quite varied in style and manufacture. The European knight carried a sword with a wide, single-fullered and double-edged blade, with rounded pommel and straight cross guard. When King Richard I of England (1157–1199) battled against the forces of Saladin, or Salah al-Din Yusuf ibn Ayyub (1137–1193), many Muslim troops carried the scimitar, a curved, single-edged sword with a much wider blade than the European weapon. Scimitar blades of very high quality were made from Damascus steel.

ABOVE A battle between Crusaders and Muslims. The Crusaders fought with double-edged blades against the curved scimitars.

English knightly sword, *c.*1300–1400

DATE	*c.*1300–1400
ORIGIN	ENGLISH
LENGTH	81.5cm (32.6in)

The rounded pommel on this sword is unusually large and acted both as a counterweight to the blade and as an additional downward force when thrusting with the blade. The sharp point has now evolved from the sword blades of the previous century that had been more rounded in profile. The short cross guard is a distinctive feature of knightly swords of this period. As we move further into the medieval period, cross guards become much wider.

European knightly sword, *c.*1300–25

DATE	*c.*1300–25
ORIGIN	EUROPEAN
LENGTH	96.5cm (38in)

This knightly sword has a wide, single-fullered and doubled-edged blade. The grip appears to be a modern, wooden replacement. The original grip would have had a wooden core overlaid with leather. Very few of these have survived the centuries.

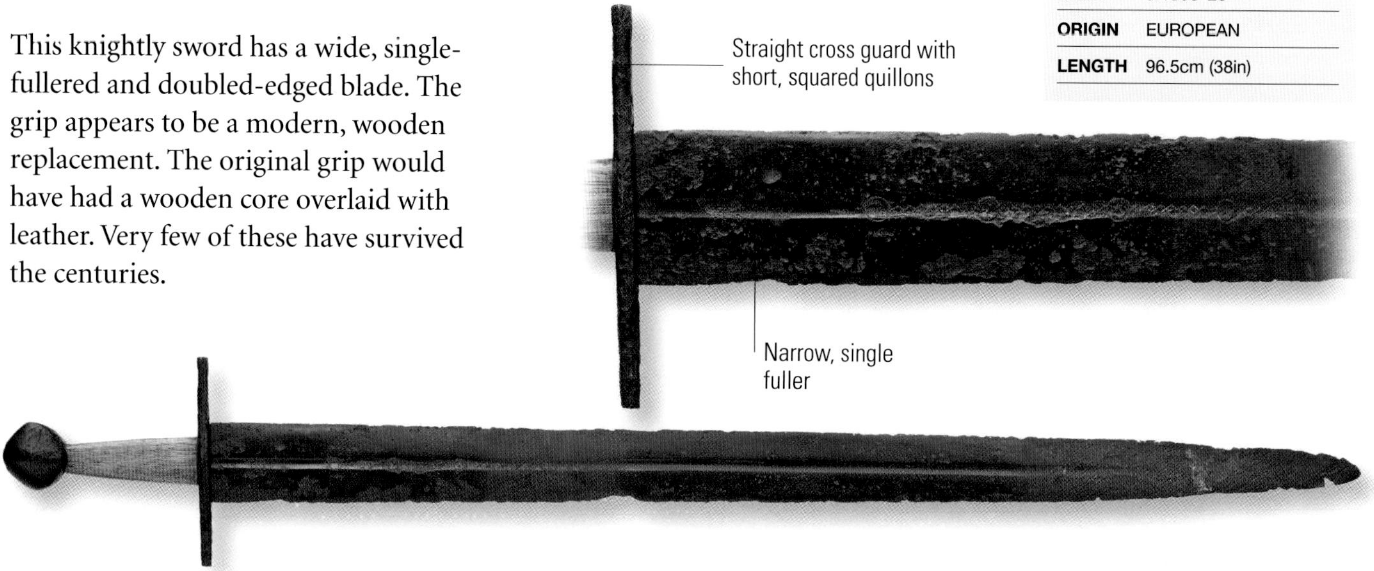

European knightly sword, *c.*1300–50

This sword has an unusually wide cross guard and a long, double-edged blade. Considerable hand and arm strength would have been required to wield the sword effectively. The owner might have used two hands to control this weapon.

DATE	*c.*1300–50
ORIGIN	EUROPEAN
LENGTH	121.5cm (47.8in)

English knightly sword, *c.*1325

DATE	*c.*1325
ORIGIN	ENGLISH
LENGTH	80cm (31.5in)

The sword is heavily corroded and was found in the River Nene, in the east of England. The rounded pommel is covered in a copper alloy and the decoration includes a raised shield with incised coat of arms (unidentified). It is of "riding sword" proportions (swords with a lighter, more flexible blade), worn at court or on a hunt rather than in battle.

European knightly sword, *c.*1350

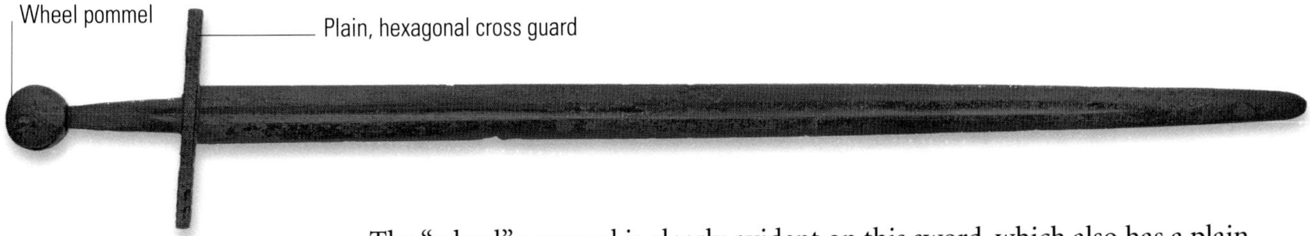

DATE	*c.*1350
ORIGIN	EUROPEAN
LENGTH	105.4cm (41.5in)

The "wheel" pommel is clearly evident on this sword, which also has a plain, hexagonal cross guard. This would become an extremely common sword style throughout Europe during the medieval period. Against lightly armoured opponents (such as those encountered in the Middle East), this heavy, double-edged sword could be quite devastating.

European knightly sword, *c.*1350–80

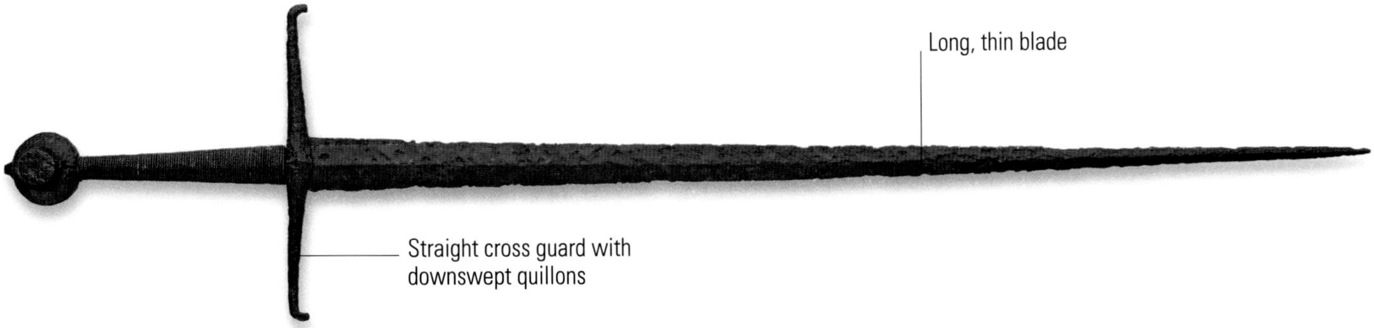

DATE	*c.*1350–80
ORIGIN	EUROPEAN
LENGTH	112.4cm (44.2in)

This sword has a needle-like blade specifically designed to penetrate plate armour. Held aloft and brought down with considerable force against an opponent, this type of sword would expose any inherent weaknesses in the armour, particularly under the arms (where armour had to be jointed to allow the wearer freedom of movement). Its thin, strong blade could also be pushed through the slits in closed helmets.

European riding sword, *c.*1380

The downswept cross guard of this sword is a new departure and is a style that was particularly common in medieval France and Germany. The pommel is globular, with a pronounced tang "button" at the top. The blade is shorter than the regular knightly sword of the period. This type of sword is normally categorized as a "riding sword", and it was worn mostly for civilian occasions such as a hunt or while at court.

DATE	*c.*1380
ORIGIN	EUROPEAN
LENGTH	90cm (35.4in)

European knightly sword, *c.*1380

The extremely tapered blade of this sword is evidence of its transitional role from a purely hacking and slashing weapon to one that had both cutting and thrusting capabilities. In the late 14th century, improved plate armour was beginning to appear and a new kind of sword was now required to successfully penetrate this all-encompassing protection. This type of longsword would become important during the Renaissance period.

DATE	*c.*1380
ORIGIN	EUROPEAN
LENGTH	126cm (49.6in)

German knightly sword, *c.*1380

The long, thin blade of this sword was designed solely for penetration of plate armour and it is likely that use of the blade edge in combat was minimal. The weapon is in a heavily corroded condition and is likely to have been excavated. It is very fortunate that such a fragile blade from this period survives.

DATE	*c.*1380
ORIGIN	GERMAN
LENGTH	128.5cm (50.6in)

English knightly sword, *c.*1400

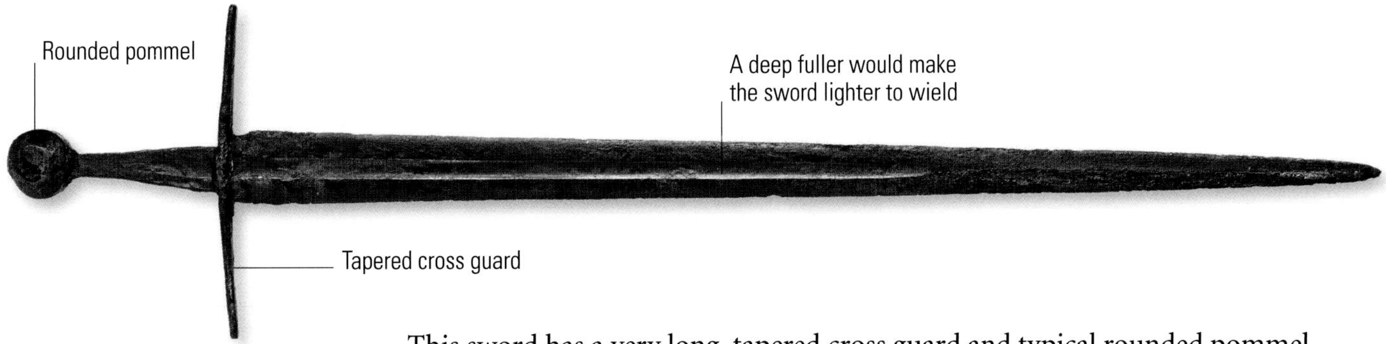

DATE	*c.*1400
ORIGIN	ENGLISH
LENGTH	83.2cm (32.8in)

This sword has a very long, tapered cross guard and typical rounded pommel. The fuller is short and quite deep, with some of the "dead" weight removed from the blade, giving the user a much more flexible weapon to wield. The grip is also quite short and would have meant that the purchase on the grip was stronger, enabling greater accuracy. This sword would be most effective as a stabbing weapon, particularly against an armoured opponent.

German knightly sword, *c.*1450

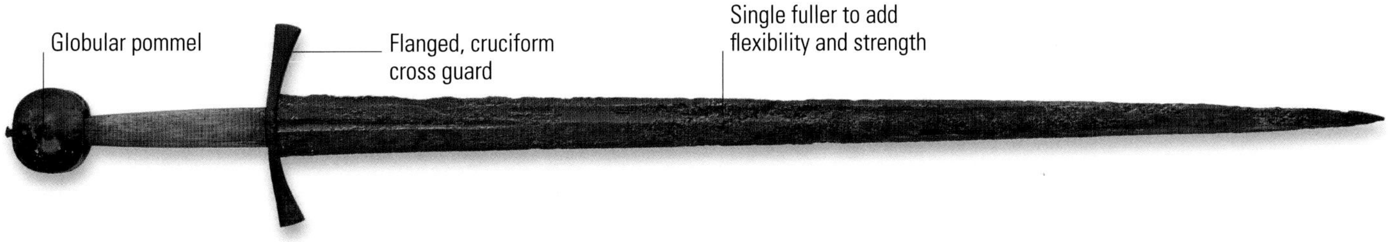

DATE	*c.*1450
ORIGIN	GERMAN
LENGTH	107.9cm (42.5in)

The flanged and slightly cruciform-shaped cross guard of this sword is a popular style found in many German swords of this period. The pommel is extremely globular and exhibits a raised tang button at the top. This sword would probably have been very flexible and lightweight to handle.

European knightly sword, *c.*1450

DATE	*c.*1450
ORIGIN	EUROPEAN
LENGTH	117.4cm (46.2in)

With a blade of diamond-shaped cross-section and a very sharp point, this late medieval weapon is representative of the changing battlefield role of the sword. The blade is now shorter than swords from the beginning of the century, and this deliberate reduction in length highlights the new-found requirement for penetration. Both knights and the ordinary soldier had begun to move away from fighting solely on horseback, and many previously mounted knights now chose to fight on foot. This sword would have been an ideal weapon at close quarters.

Late medieval and Renaissance swords

By the end of the 15th century, the nature of warfare had changed dramatically. The introduction of sophisticated plate armour had made the effective use of the traditional double-edged cutting broadsword more difficult. Consequently, sword makers now produced weapons with extremely hardened points for deep penetration into the armour. Great hand-and-a-half and two-handed broadswords also emerged and became important weapons against massed ranks of pikemen.

English cross-hilted sword, *c.*1450

DATE	*c.*1450
ORIGIN	ENGLISH
LENGTH	94.4cm (37.2in)

A group of 80 similar swords was found on the battlefield site of Castillon, near Bordeaux, France, where English and French forces met in 1453. The pommel is quite unusual, and is known as a "scent-stopper" type. The cross guard has globular finials, unlike the usual plain, squared cross guard which is found on swords of the period.

English two-handed sword, *c.*1450

DATE	*c.*1450
ORIGIN	ENGLISH
LENGTH	148.3cm (58.4in)

The pommels on two-handed swords of this period tend to be of flaring or fluted shape, and less pronounced than the earlier rounded or globular pommels of the knightly sword. The thin grip on this sword would have provided a comfortable two-handed grip. The narrow blade has a prominent thrusting point.

European two-handed sword, *c.*1450

DATE	*c.*1450
ORIGIN	EUROPEAN
LENGTH	119cm (46.8in)

Found in the River Thames, London, this sword is likely to have a German-made blade and hilt. Most blades were manufactured in Germany, Italy or Spain. Although there were established manufacturing facilities in England, they were not as well organized as in countries such as Germany, where sword makers had formed themselves into specialist sword guilds from the early medieval period.

German broadsword, *c.*1450

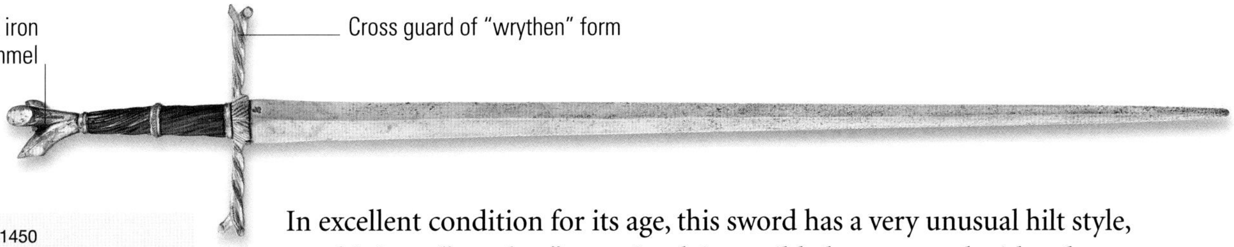

DATE	*c.*1450
ORIGIN	GERMAN
LENGTH	109.9cm (43.3in)

In excellent condition for its age, this sword has a very unusual hilt style, combining a "wrythen", or twisted, iron-gilded cross guard with a three-pronged pommel. This distinctive style became common during the 15th century, particularly in Germany.

German two-handed sword, *c.*1500

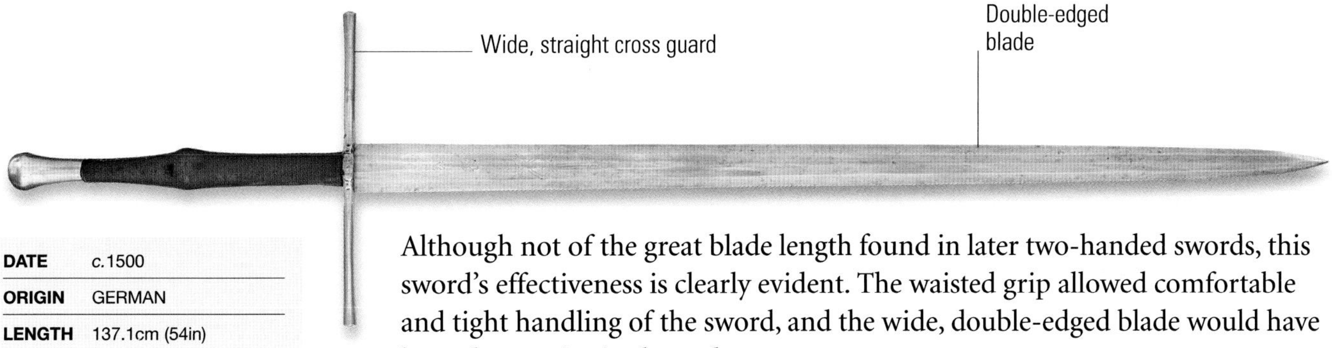

DATE	*c.*1500
ORIGIN	GERMAN
LENGTH	137.1cm (54in)

Although not of the great blade length found in later two-handed swords, this sword's effectiveness is clearly evident. The waisted grip allowed comfortable and tight handling of the sword, and the wide, double-edged blade would have been destructive in the melee.

German Landsknecht-type sword, *c.*1500

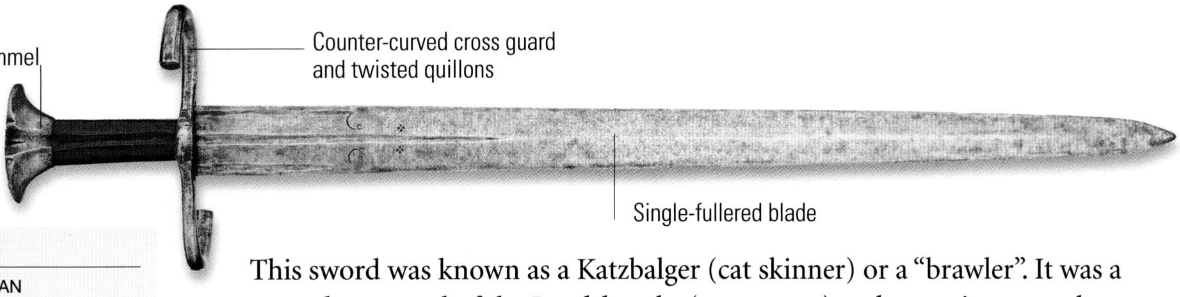

DATE	*c.*1500
ORIGIN	GERMAN
LENGTH	71.1cm (28in)

This sword was known as a Katzbalger (cat skinner) or a "brawler". It was a secondary sword of the Landsknecht (mercenary) and sometimes acted as a weapon of last resort when his larger, two-handed sword was unavailable.

Swiss ceremonial broadsword, *c.*1500

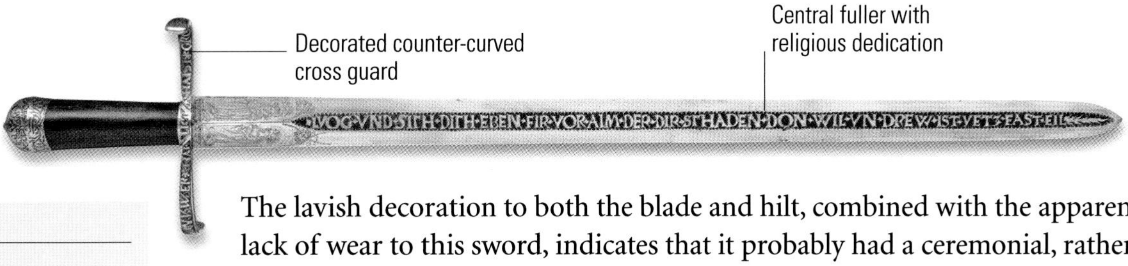

DATE	*c.*1500
ORIGIN	SWISS
LENGTH	71.1cm (28in)

The lavish decoration to both the blade and hilt, combined with the apparent lack of wear to this sword, indicates that it probably had a ceremonial, rather than a combat, function. Engraved religious images and devotional messages were common on sword blades throughout the Renaissance period.

German two-handed Landsknecht sword, *c.*1500

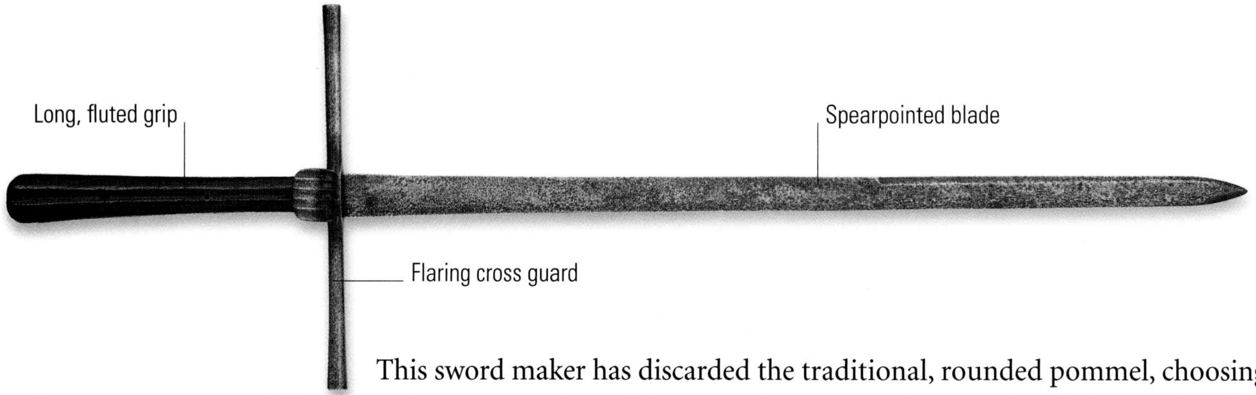

This sword maker has discarded the traditional, rounded pommel, choosing to incorporate the weight needed to balance the sword by fitting a grip of heavy, fluted wood. The cut-steel *écusson* (escutcheon) block (in the middle of the cross guard) has by now become a significant design feature and heralds a change that would become common on swords later in the century.

DATE	*c.*1500
ORIGIN	GERMAN
LENGTH	103.5cm (40.7in)

Italian cinquedea, *c.*1500

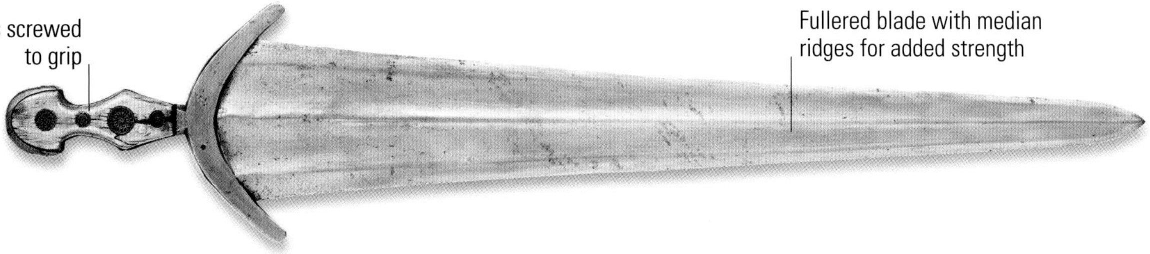

The Italian cinquedea is an extremely handsome sword type of the early 16th century. It was carried extensively in Italy during the Renaissance but found little favour outside its borders. The name is derived from the five deep fullers, or "fingers", on the blade. Many fine examples have blades with elaborately engraved and gilded decoration. The opportunity for the Renaissance craftsmen to embellish such an unusually wide area on a sword blade was rarely ignored.

DATE	*c.*1500
ORIGIN	ITALIAN
LENGTH	71.1cm (28in)

German hand-and-a-half sword, *c.*1520

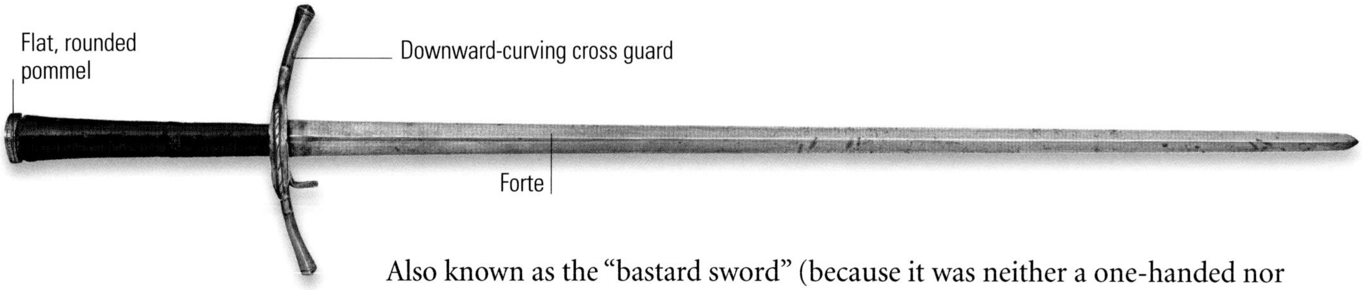

Also known as the "bastard sword" (because it was neither a one-handed nor a two-handed sword), its slightly shorter grip accommodated one hand, while the fingers of the second hand would be placed on the blade forte to allow extra leverage and positional control when swinging the blade. The pommel is flattened and rounded, with a leather and wood grip that is of gradually flaring form.

DATE	*c.*1520
ORIGIN	GERMAN
LENGTH	123.2cm (48.5in)

German Landsknecht broadsword, *c.*1550

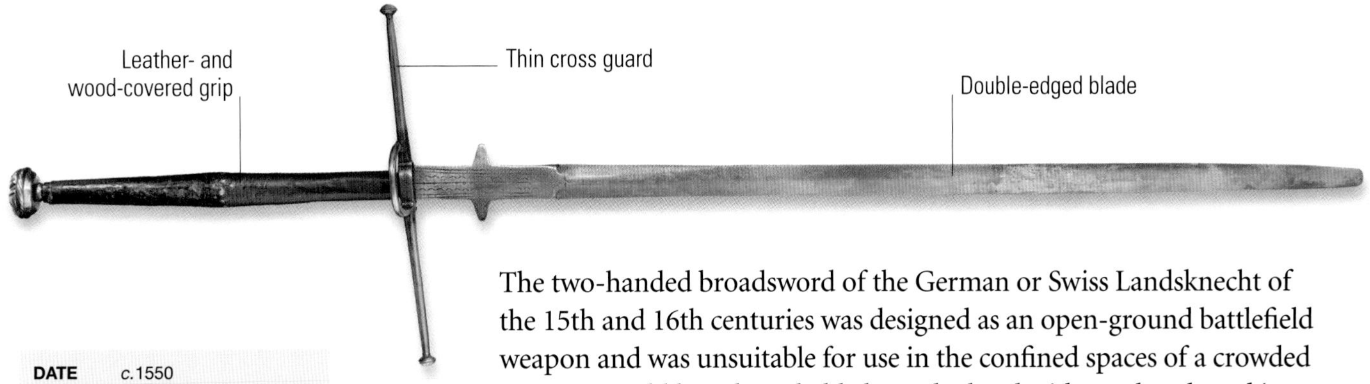

DATE	*c.*1550
ORIGIN	GERMAN
LENGTH	104.2cm (41.6in)

The two-handed broadsword of the German or Swiss Landsknecht of the 15th and 16th centuries was designed as an open-ground battlefield weapon and was unsuitable for use in the confined spaces of a crowded town. It would have been held above the head with two hands and its long, double- or single-edged blade engaged to wildly hack into packed formations of enemy pikemen or infantry, clearing a passage for the cavalry.

German two-handed Landsknecht sword, *c.*1550

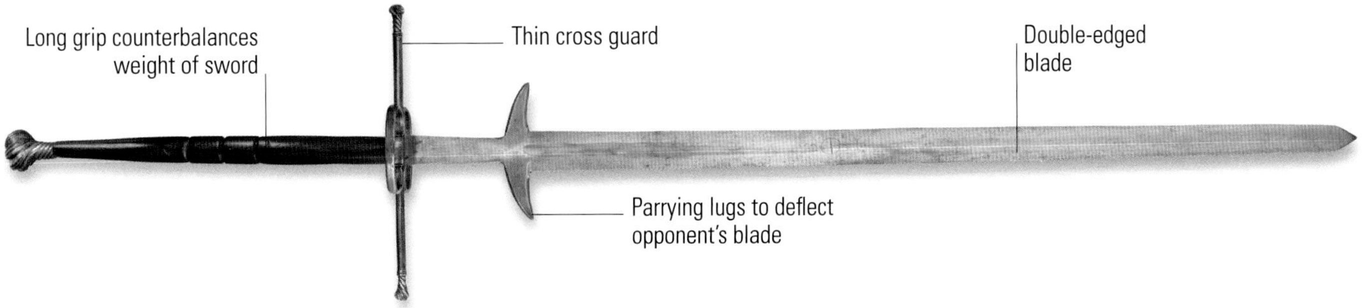

DATE	*c.*1550
ORIGIN	GERMAN
LENGTH	175.8cm (69.2in)

Two-handed Landsknecht swords of the 16th century are commonly found with downwardly curved parrying lugs positioned near the blade forte. Their function was to deflect an opponent's blade or polearm. A primitive ringed counterguard at the middle of the hilt cross guard began to appear at this time. It gave the swordsman's hand some protection when he gripped the sword with his fingers extended at the bottom of the grip.

German sword of the State Guard of the Duke of Brunswick, 1573

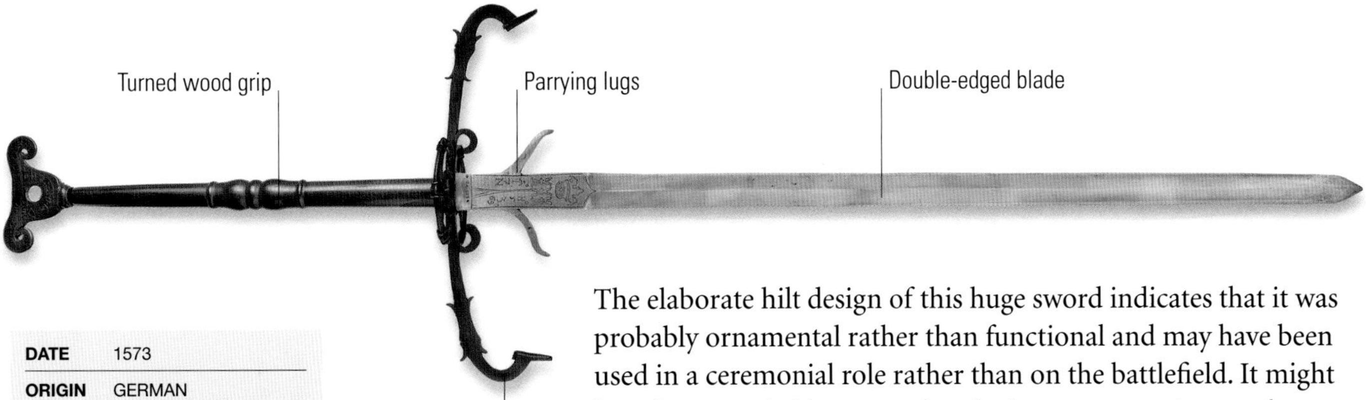

DATE	1573
ORIGIN	GERMAN
LENGTH	203.2cm (80in)

The elaborate hilt design of this huge sword indicates that it was probably ornamental rather than functional and may have been used in a ceremonial role rather than on the battlefield. It might have been carried in procession during state occasions such as royal marriages or investitures.

Rapiers

The elegant profile of the rapier is a striking image often associated with the Renaissance gentleman. It was not just an effective weapon and the first choice for duels but it also signified a person's social rank and wealth. Its origins were in 15th-century Spain and Italy, and the name derives from the Spanish term *espada ropera* (sword of the robes), meaning it could be worn with civilian clothing.

Italian transitional rapier, *c.*1520

This sword is a transitional piece and not yet a fully formed rapier. The blade is similar to wide, pre-1500 broadsword blades, and the large, rounded pommel, although stylishly fluted (to reflect Renaissance tastes), still echoes earlier knightly swords. It is only when we view the "swept" and flowing hilt guards that a more traditional, albeit simple, rapier shape is becoming apparent.

DATE	*c.*1520
ORIGIN	ITALIAN
LENGTH	111.5cm (43.9in)

German rapier, *c.*1550

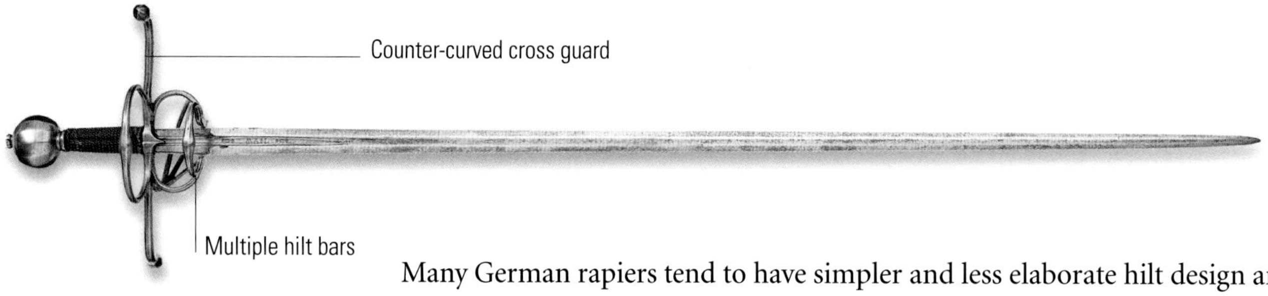

DATE	*c.*1550
ORIGIN	GERMAN
LENGTH	96.3cm (37.9in)

Many German rapiers tend to have simpler and less elaborate hilt design and decoration than their Italian and Spanish counterparts. This example has a large, plain, rounded pommel that acted to counterbalance the weight of its long, double-edged blade. The hilt bars, although elaborately formed, are not unnecessary. They are designed to protect the wearer's hand.

Italian rapier, *c.*1590

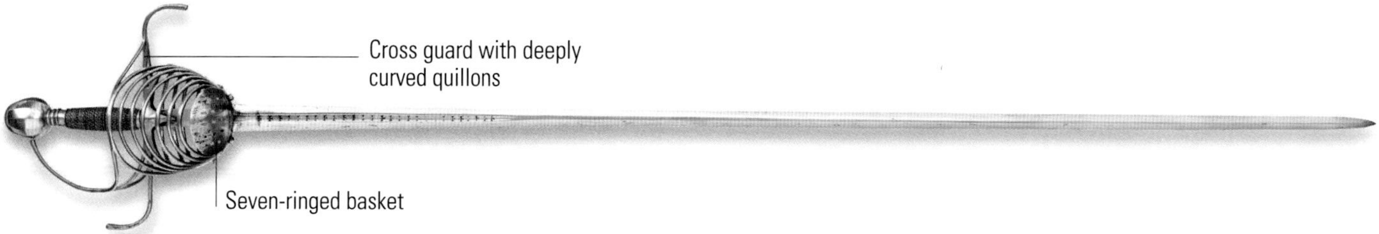

Multi-ringed rapiers are quite common but most surviving examples have a maximum of three to four hilt rings. Seven-ringed rapiers like this piece are rare. Many of these rapiers feature a scalloped or ribbed bowl or plate which is located at the bottom of the hilt.

DATE	*c.*1590
ORIGIN	ITALIAN
LENGTH	136.9cm (53.9in)

Rapiers and parrying daggers in duels

The duelling era commenced in the fifteenth or sixteenth centuries and continued well into the nineteenth century. The rapier and left-handed parrying dagger were edged weapons used while opponents were engaged in a duel.

The dagger was held by placing four fingers around the grip, while the thumb was placed firmly behind the blade near the quillons. By using the dagger in this way, the duellist was able to parry the rapier for a crucial moment while his own rapier thrust could be made at his opponent's body.

ABOVE Two gentlemen engaged in a duel, *c.*1600. Both are using left-handed parrying daggers.

Italian swept-hilt rapier, *c.*1610

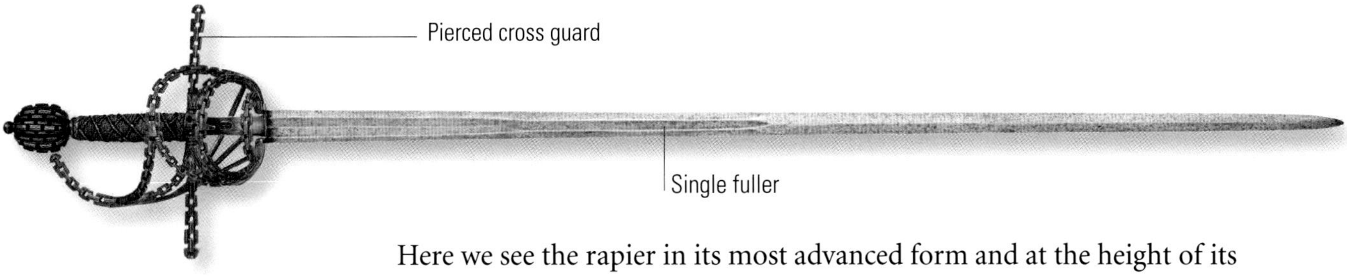

DATE	*c.*1610
ORIGIN	ITALIAN
LENGTH	119.4cm (47in)

Here we see the rapier in its most advanced form and at the height of its development. The extensively pierced and chiselled hilt is of superb "swept-hilt" design, with the "sweep" beginning at the knuckle guard and moving downwards and around the guard, with three branches, or bars, detaching away and re-connecting at the shell guard just above the ricasso.

Italian swept-hilt rapier, *c.*1610

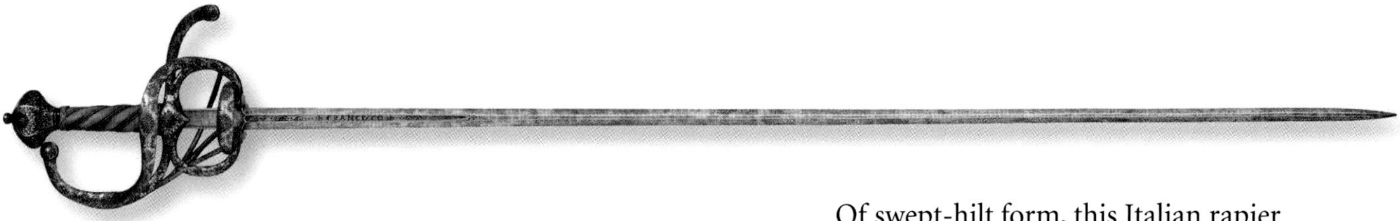

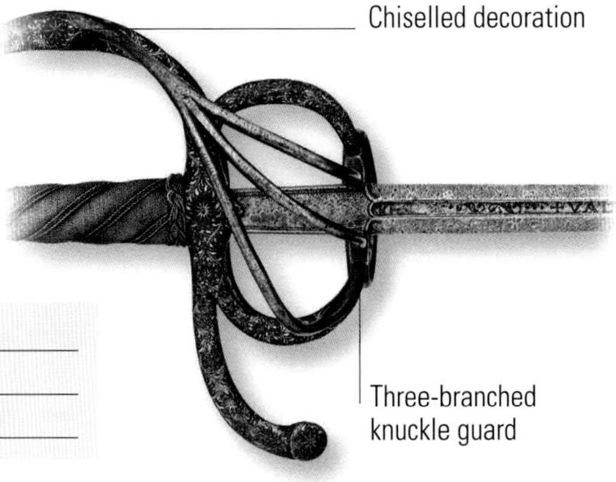

DATE	*c.*1610
ORIGIN	ITALIAN
LENGTH	120.3cm (47.4in)

Of swept-hilt form, this Italian rapier highlights the superb artistry of the sword maker, particularly his phenomenal skills as a metalworker. The hilt is profusely decorated with deeply cut chiselled embellishments and the large pommel lends a perfect, symmetrical balance to the subject. The grip would have been manufactured from a wooden core, overlaid with a complex pattern of fluted silver twistwire and "Turk's-head" finials to each end of the grip.

German swept-hilt rapier, *c.*1610

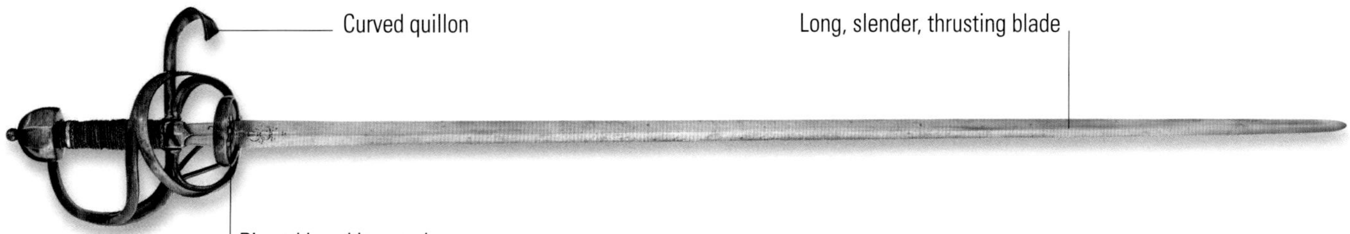

The hilt of this rapier features a flat, inwardly curving quillon. The open nature of the hilt and the large gaps between the bars probably afforded little protection to the sword hand. It was hoped that the great length of a rapier's blade would ensure a sufficiently safe and constant distance from any opponent, so reducing the threat of any injuries or even potentially fatal thrusts.

DATE	*c.*1610
ORIGIN	GERMAN
LENGTH	121.4cm (47.8in)

German swept-hilt rapier, *c.*1620

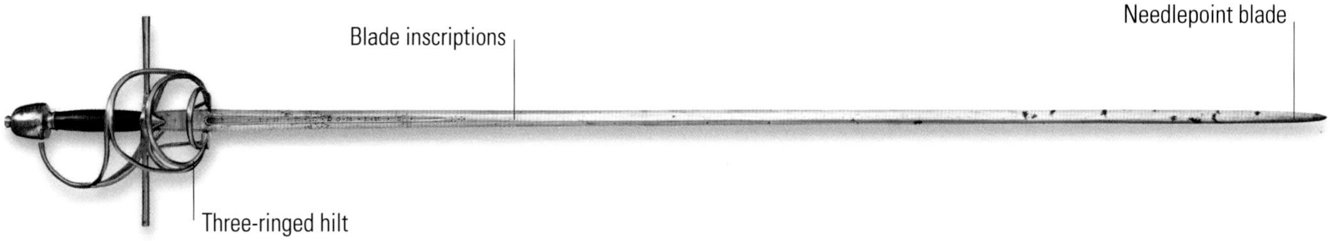

The plain, yet functional styling of this three-ringed swept-hilt rapier probably indicates a German origin. The blade has numerous armourer's marks and a religious inscription. Swordsmiths and armourers marked their swords in many different ways, with the cross motif being very common amongst European sword makers. They also stamped their names into the blade fuller. This blade has "Francesco" inscribed on it.

DATE	*c.*1620
ORIGIN	GERMAN
LENGTH	130.3cm (51.3in)

English Littlecote rapier, *c.*1630

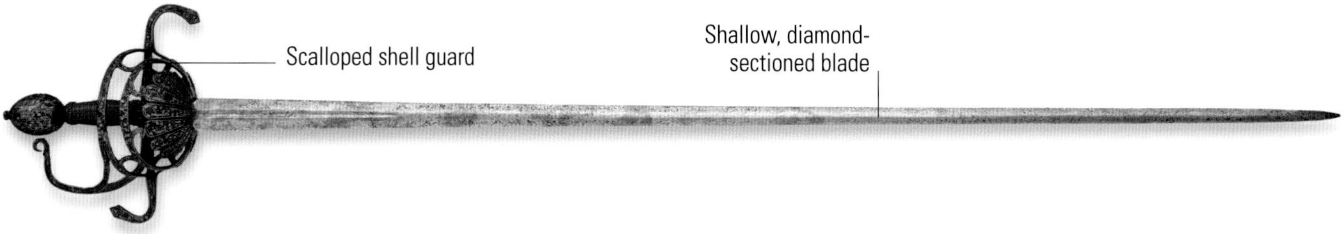

This sword is from Littlecote House, in Wiltshire, southern England. This was the Elizabethan mansion of Sir John Popham (1531–1607), who was Speaker of the House of Commons and Lord Chief Justice of England. The scalloped shell guard would have afforded better protection for the hand, coupled with an extra two rows of open and linked hilt bars placed just above. There is a large ovoid pommel that would have been effective at providing the balance required to wield a sword with such a long blade.

DATE	*c.*1630
ORIGIN	ENGLISH
LENGTH	133.8cm (52.7in)

Flemish "Pappenheimer" rapier, *c.*1630

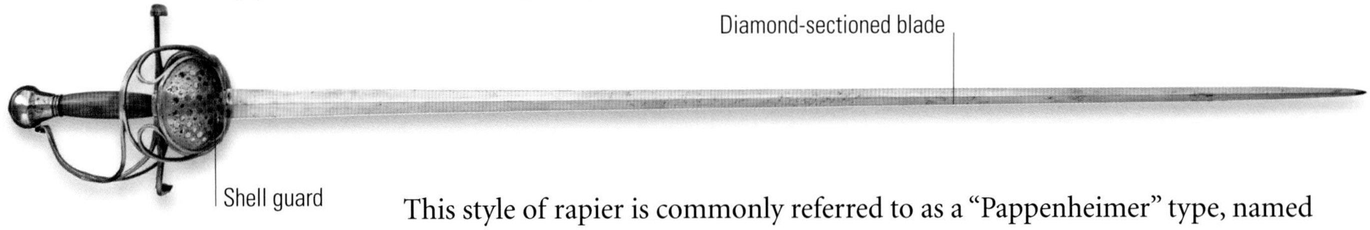

DATE	*c.*1630
ORIGIN	FLEMISH
LENGTH	127cm (50in)

This style of rapier is commonly referred to as a "Pappenheimer" type, named after the German Count Gottfried Heinrich, Graf von Pappenheim, an illustrious commander of cavalry forces during the Thirty Years' War (1618–48). His regiment of cuirassiers carried this type of military rapier, distinguished by its large, pierced shell guard.

English duelling rapier, *c.*1640

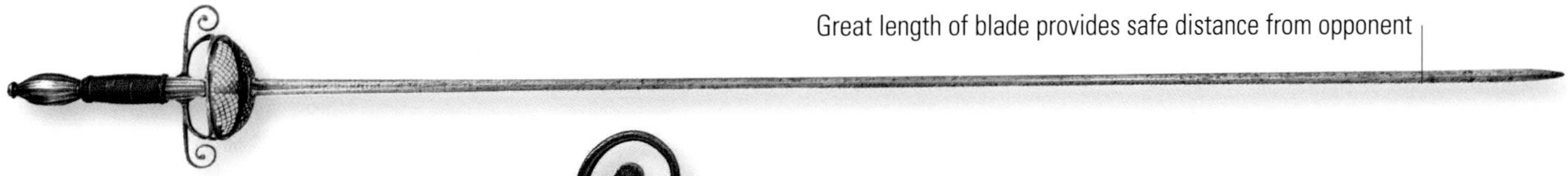

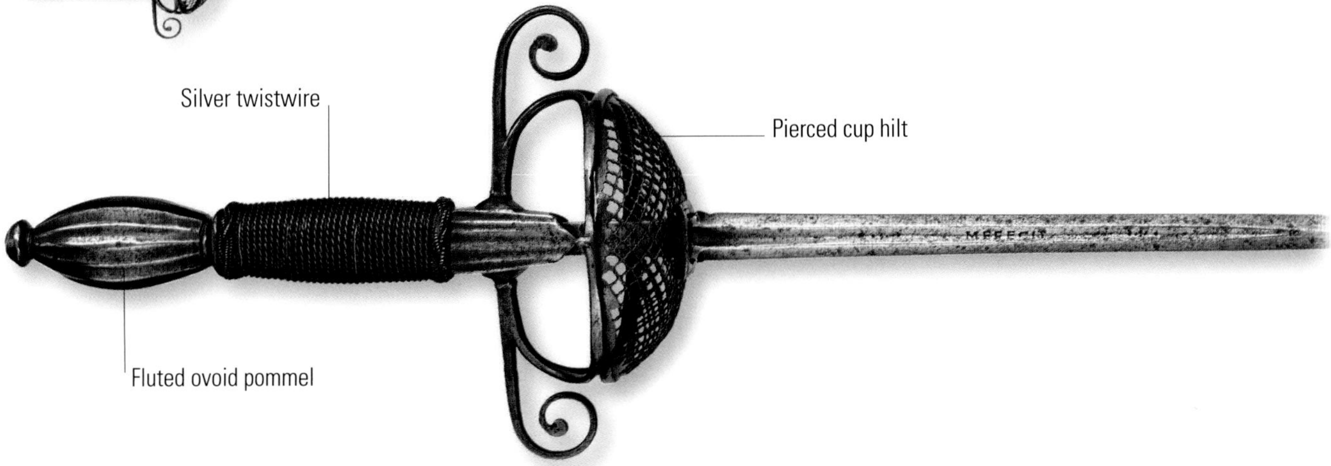

DATE	*c.*1640
ORIGIN	ENGLISH
LENGTH	141.6cm (55.7in)

Rapiers of this type are normally referred to as "duelling rapiers", and are characterized by a "dish hilt" and an extremely long, diamond-sectioned blade. The shallow "dish", or guard, is located at the bottom of the hilt, and is of delicately pierced and cross-hatched form. The coiled quillons and the *pas d'âne* – the two curved bars that branch from the cross guard and rest on the dish – are a precursor to a hilt style found on later smallswords.

English rapier, *c.*1640

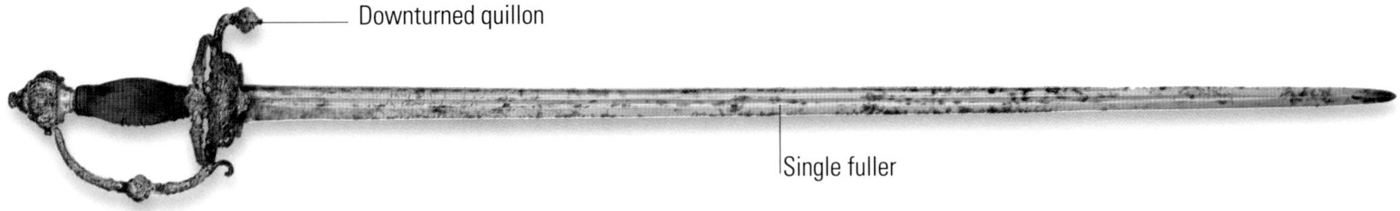

DATE	*c.*1640
ORIGIN	ENGLISH
LENGTH	97cm (38.2in)

Dating from the time of the English Civil War (1642–51), this is a very fine example of an English rapier. Many English sword makers of this period were noted for their ability to produce intricate, chiselled-steel decoration on the sword hilts.

English rapier, *c.*1650

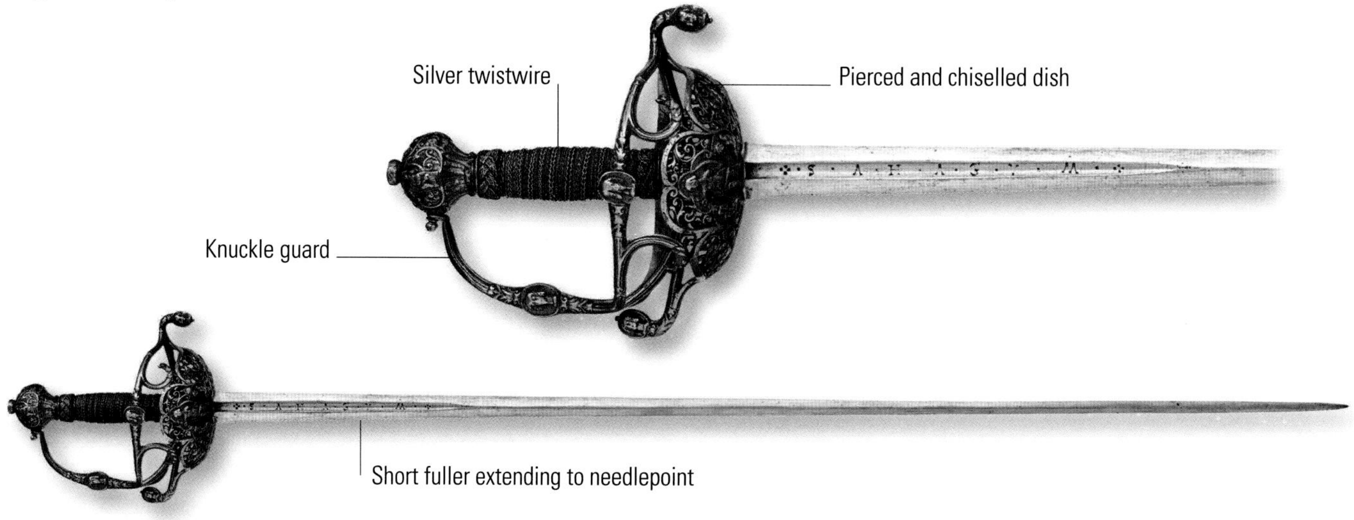

A superb example of an English Civil War period rapier, with a large, chiselled-steel ovoid pommel and pierced, scalloped shell guard. This style was influenced by "mortuary" broadswords of the period, and is particularly evident in the application of chiselled human faces to the hilt bars.

DATE	*c.*1650
ORIGIN	ENGLISH
LENGTH	108.2cm (42.6in)

Spanish cup-hilt rapier, *c.*1650

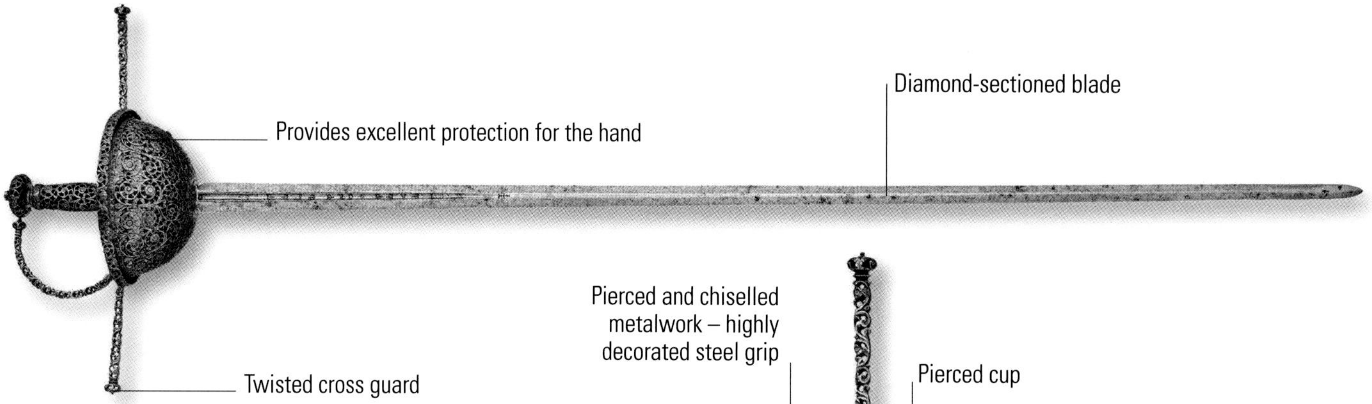

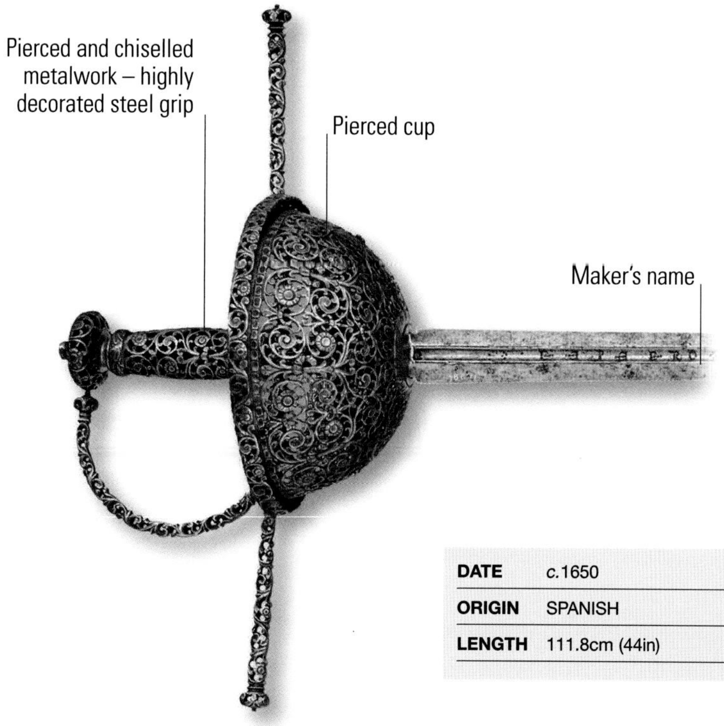

Spanish rapiers introduced an enclosed form of hilt known as the cup hilt. Designed primarily as a duelling sword, the cup-hilt rapier was not meant for military use, although it was sometimes carried into battle. This high-quality example was more likely to have been made for a gentleman and probably used as a duelling rapier. The cup is pierced with scrolled decoration and the cross guard is of a twisted, spiral form. The blade is deeply engraved with a maker's name within the fuller.

DATE	*c.*1650
ORIGIN	SPANISH
LENGTH	111.8cm (44in)

Spanish swept-hilt rapier, *c.*1650

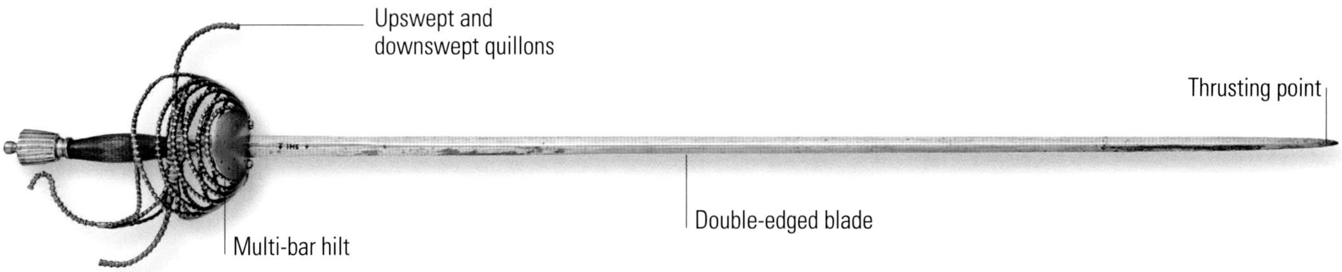

DATE	*c.*1650
ORIGIN	SPANISH
LENGTH	116.6cm (45.9in)

Spanish rapiers of the 17th century represent the height of the sword maker's art and are invariably of flamboyant and extravagantly fluid style. In this example, the many flowing hilt bars are present for both practical and aesthetic reasons.

Spanish swept-hilt rapier, *c.*1650

This is a rapier of very high quality, characterized by a distinctive cut-steel pattern to the hilt bars and an unusual faceted or layered ovoid pommel. The blade is deeply stamped with the sword maker's name and there is also a punched mark just below the ricasso.

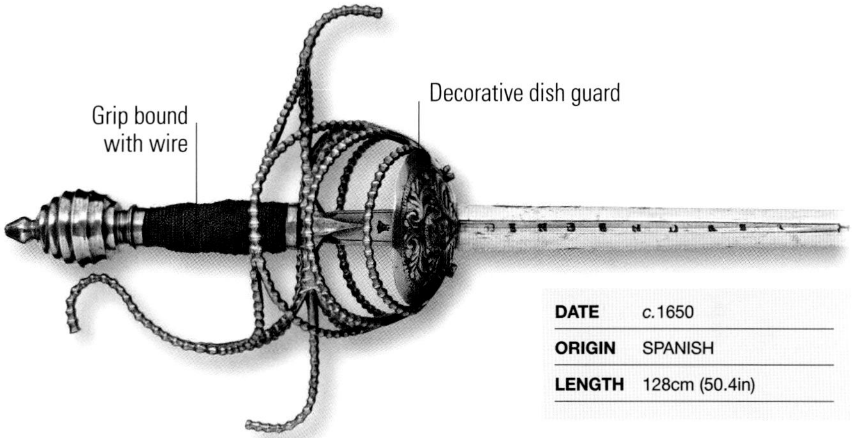

DATE	*c.*1650
ORIGIN	SPANISH
LENGTH	128cm (50.4in)

Rapiers in action

The chaotic scenes depicted in so-called "swashbuckling" movies, in which the protagonists attack each other with rapiers in a violent and rapid series of lunging thrusts and desperate parrying, is not actually how an Elizabethan or Jacobean swordsman would have handled his rapier. Rather, the action of a fight with rapiers would have involved a series of premeditated and ferociously quick lunges from a standing position that would have been "voided", or dodged, by the opponent, and the process continued until an opening was found by one or other rapier.

ABOVE These two protagonists have chosen to use a cloak as a method of parrying each other's rapier. It was hoped that the rapier would be caught and dragged away in the cloak, providing an opportunity for a thrust.

Halberds

Developed primarily as an edged weapon that could vastly extend a soldier's reach, combined with the cutting capabilities of an axe and the thrusting, penetrative function of a spear point, the halberd reached its zenith during the massed battles of the medieval and Renaissance periods. The halberd gave the ordinary soldier an opportunity both to unhorse and to kill mounted troops.

Swiss/German halberd, *c.*1480

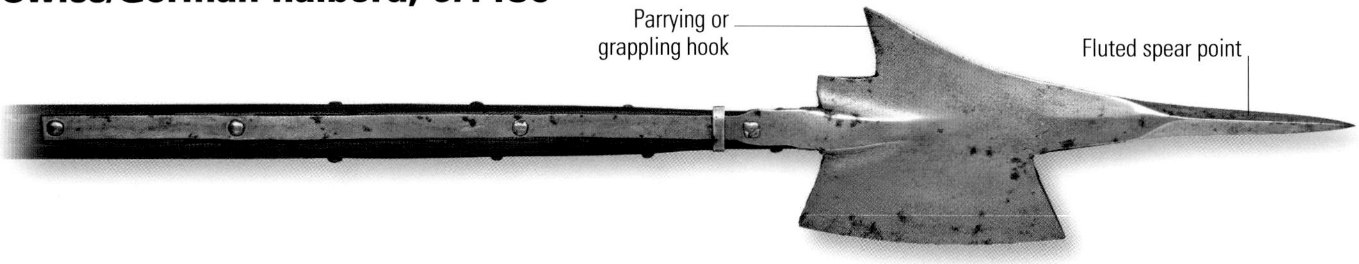

This is an early form of halberd, comprising a large rectangular cutting blade with a short, fluted spearhead. The hook for dismounting or parrying an opponent's blade is still very crude and it would have taken great skill and practice to wield effectively.

DATE	*c.*1480
ORIGIN	SWISS/GERMAN
LENGTH	226.7cm (89.3in)

Halberd, *c.*1550

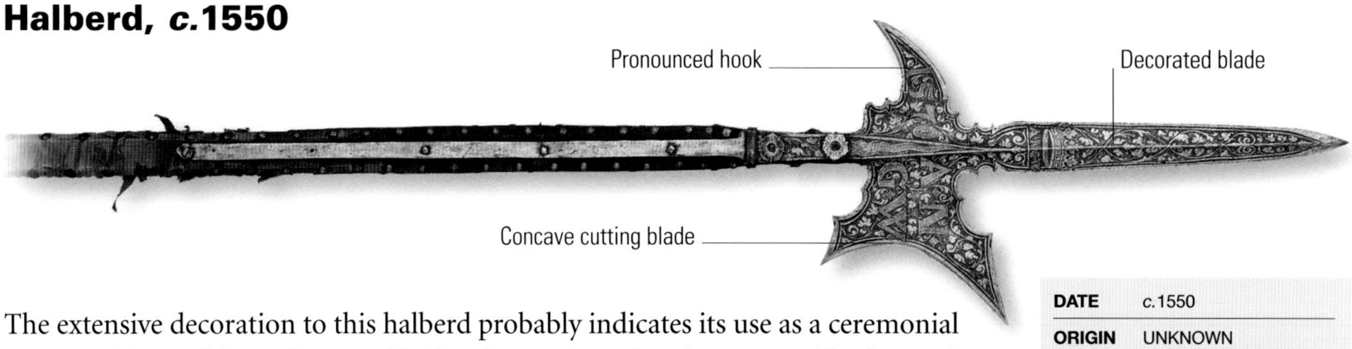

The extensive decoration to this halberd probably indicates its use as a ceremonial weapon. Many of these decorated halberds were issued to the personal bodyguard of a ruler and were deliberately designed to impress.

DATE	*c.*1550
ORIGIN	UNKNOWN
LENGTH	227.5cm (89.6in)

German halberd, *c.*1550

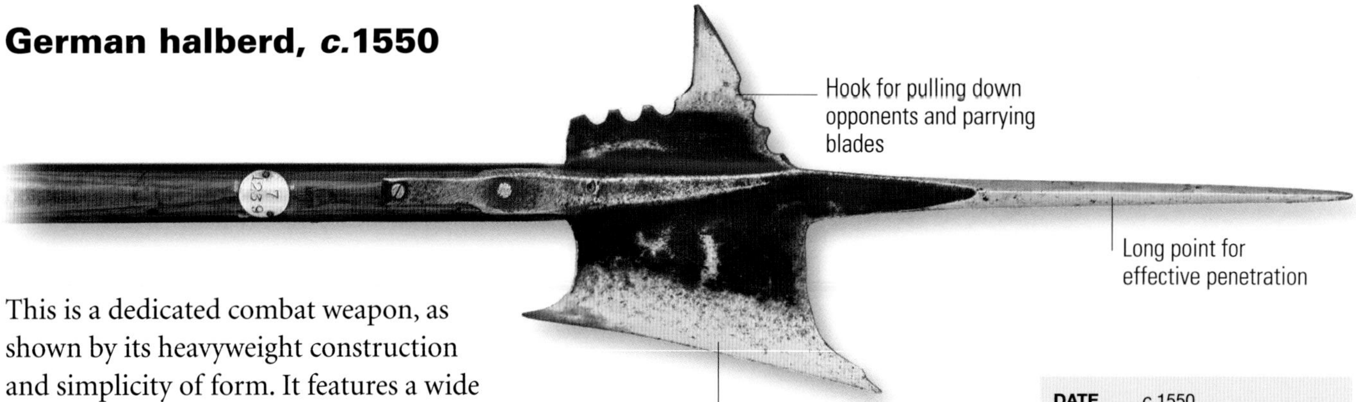

This is a dedicated combat weapon, as shown by its heavyweight construction and simplicity of form. It features a wide cutting edge to the axe and a complex system of larger and smaller parrying hooks. The spear point is long and designed for deep penetration.

DATE	*c.*1550
ORIGIN	GERMAN
LENGTH	55.4cm (21.8in) head

Italian halberd, *c.*1570

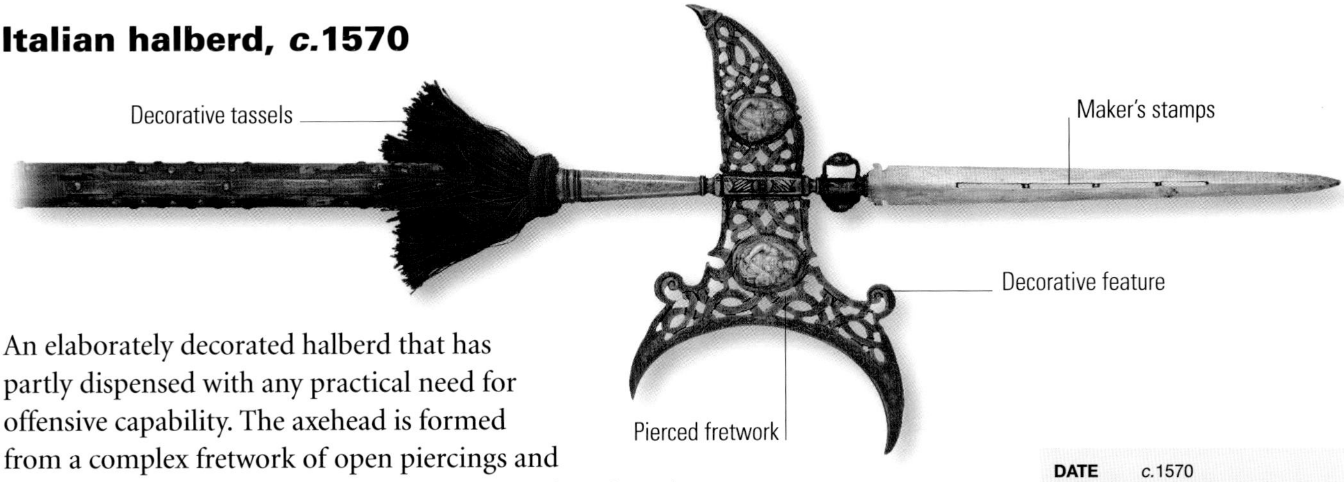

An elaborately decorated halberd that has partly dispensed with any practical need for offensive capability. The axehead is formed from a complex fretwork of open piercings and would have been easily vulnerable to damage if used on the battlefield. The most practical part of this halberd is the long, almost sword-like blade, but its use must have been mainly ceremonial.

DATE	*c.*1570
ORIGIN	ITALIAN
LENGTH	64.5cm (25.4in) head

German halberd, *c.*1580

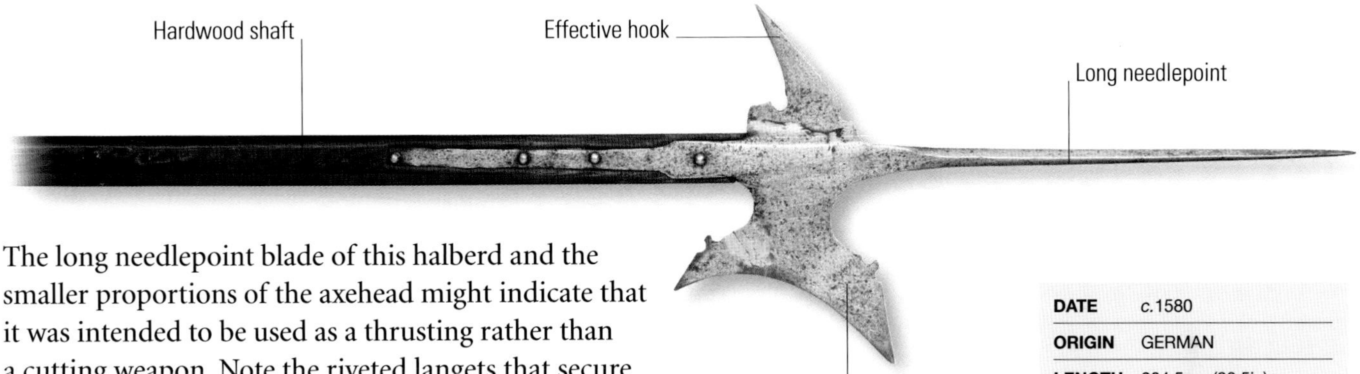

The long needlepoint blade of this halberd and the smaller proportions of the axehead might indicate that it was intended to be used as a thrusting rather than a cutting weapon. Note the riveted langets that secure the head of the halberd to the heavy wooden shaft.

DATE	*c.*1580
ORIGIN	GERMAN
LENGTH	204.5cm (80.5in)

English halberd/partizan, *c.*1700

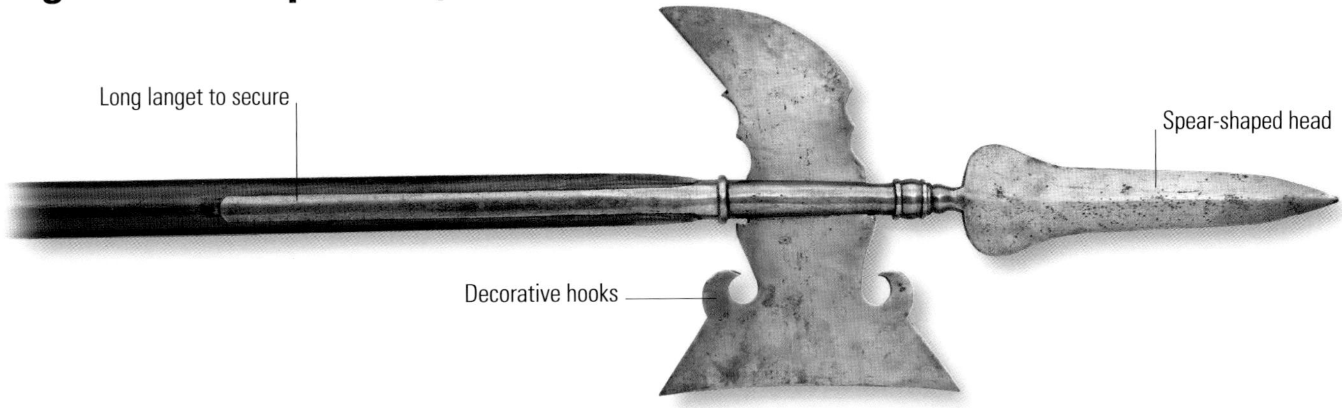

DATE	*c.*1700
ORIGIN	ENGLISH
LENGTH	239.7cm (94.4in)

The halberd had become militarily superfluous by the end of the 18th century, particularly with the advent of more close-range firearms and artillery. This example is very much a transitional piece and would still have been quite effective as a polearm, especially when employing the sharpened axehead and spear-shaped, double-edged head.

Partizans and glaives

Both the partizan and glaive were common staff weapons on the battlefields of Europe from the late medieval period (approximately the 13th to 14th centuries). However, the glaive had ceased to be used by the 18th century, by which time the partizan had become more of a symbolic weapon and signifier of military rank, being carried by officers and non-commissioned officers (NCOs).

Italian glaive, *c.*1550

The glaive was a significant cutting polearm, consisting of a long convex blade with a small parrying hook. This glaive also had twin parrying hooks, or lugs, at the bottom of the blade, just above the socket. Many early glaives were simply sword or knife blades mounted onto long wooden shafts.

DATE	*c.*1550
ORIGIN	ITALIAN
LENGTH	75.5cm (29.7in) head

French glaive, 1564

This particularly fine example was made for a soldier in the service of the Duke of Burgundy. The deeply etched blade features the ducal coat of arms and two intertwined letter "M"s representing Maximilian II (Holy Roman Emperor, 1564–1576) and Maria of Spain (1528–1603).

DATE	1564
ORIGIN	FRENCH
LENGTH	71cm (27.9in) head

Yeomen of the Guard

The Yeomen of the Guard are the oldest established military corps in the British Army. They were formed by Henry VII after the Battle of Bosworth in 1485, and they still wear uniforms based on those worn at the time of the Tudor monarchy (1485–1603). The tunic displays the Tudor crown, the Lancastrian rose, shamrock and thistle and the motto DIEU ET MON DROIT (God and my right). Originally, the Yeomen carried the pike of the the ordinary foot-soldier but later they carried a decorated (blue and gilt) partizan, which is still carried today while they perform their ceremonial duties.

RIGHT The Yeomen of the Guard searching the crypt of the Houses of Parliament, 1894. The uniform and the partizan remain unchanged to this day.

French partizan of the Burgundian Ducal Guard, 1618

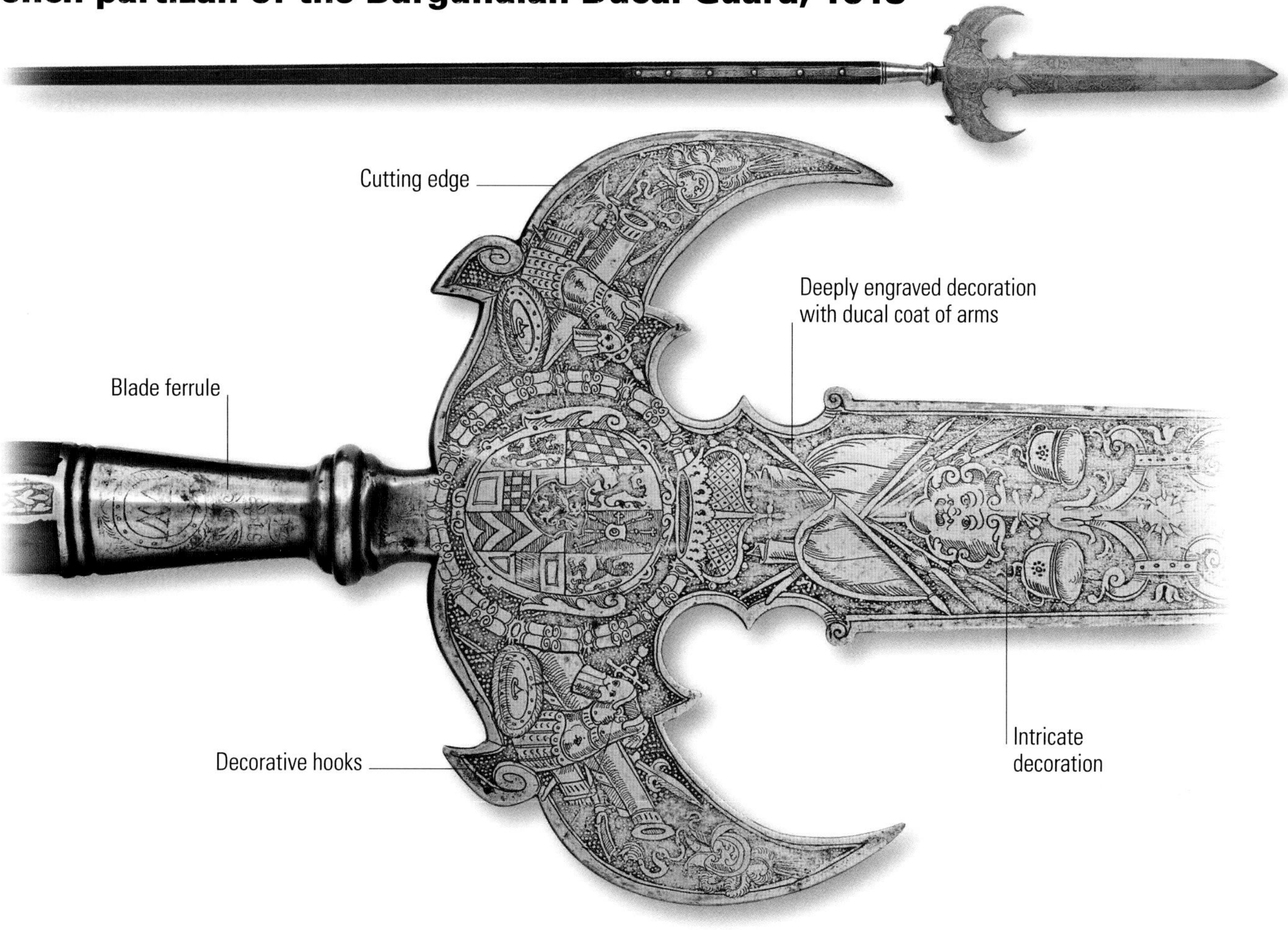

DATE	1618
ORIGIN	FRENCH
LENGTH	64.2cm (25.3in) head

This elaborately decorated partizan would have been carried by a member of the Burgundian Ducal Guard. It would have been an extremely expensive weapon to produce and therefore only issued to a very limited number of carefully selected troops.

French partizan, *c.*1680

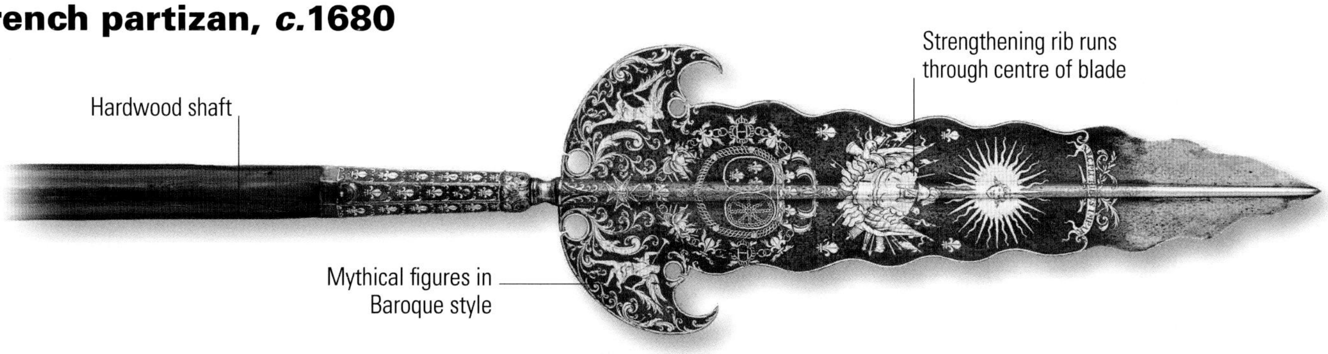

DATE	*c.*1680
ORIGIN	FRENCH
LENGTH	192.1cm (75.6in)

The increasing use of gilt decoration to both sword and polearm blades during the 17th and 18th centuries is clearly evident in this superb piece. It was produced for ceremonial and guard duties, and it features the French royal crown, coat of arms and classically inspired figures in the Rococo style. The sun motif on the blade is probably an allusion to Louis XIV (1638–1715), who was known as the "Sun King".

Pikes, bills and spontoons

The sight of massed ranks of opposing pike and billmen pushing against each other with their bills, pikes and spontoons was common during the battles of the 16th and 17th centuries. The average length of a pike during the English Civil War (1642–51) was around 4.9m (16.1ft) which was an obvious asset in keeping a safe distance, but the long, heavy, wooden shaft could also make it cumbersome and unwieldy.

Italian pike or lance, *c.*1550

The simple military spear has a history stretching back millennia and its use as an offensive military weapon was still undiminished in the 16th century. The only discernible change was to the length of the shaft, which had increased over the centuries in response to the prevalent use of massed ranks of infantrymen and the important need to keep a relatively safe distance from the enemy in front.

DATE	*c.*1550
ORIGIN	ITALIAN
LENGTH	182cm (71.6in)

Italian pike, *c.*1550

Even with the introduction of improved matchlock firearms during the 17th century, the only effective defence against a concerted cavalry charge was still a row of disciplined pikemen. Ironically, more time was needed to train a pikeman than a musketeer to fire his matchlock musket. This was due to the complex drilling manoeuvres required and the great physical strength needed.

DATE	*c.*1550
ORIGIN	ITALIAN
LENGTH	65.7cm (25.9in) head

English bill, *c.*1550

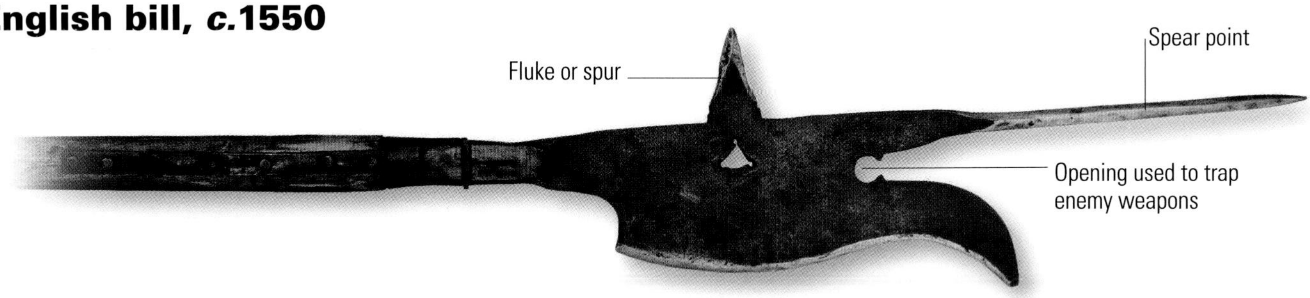

English bills of the 16th century tend to be quite plain in form but robust in their manufacture. This bill has a number of projections that all serve different functions. The curved axehead would be a good cutting weapon, the long spear point had great penetrative capabilities and the pronounced parrying hook could deflect blows and bring down mounted soldiers and hamstring horses.

DATE	*c.*1550
ORIGIN	ENGLISH
LENGTH	195.5cm (77in)

Italian bill, *c.*1550

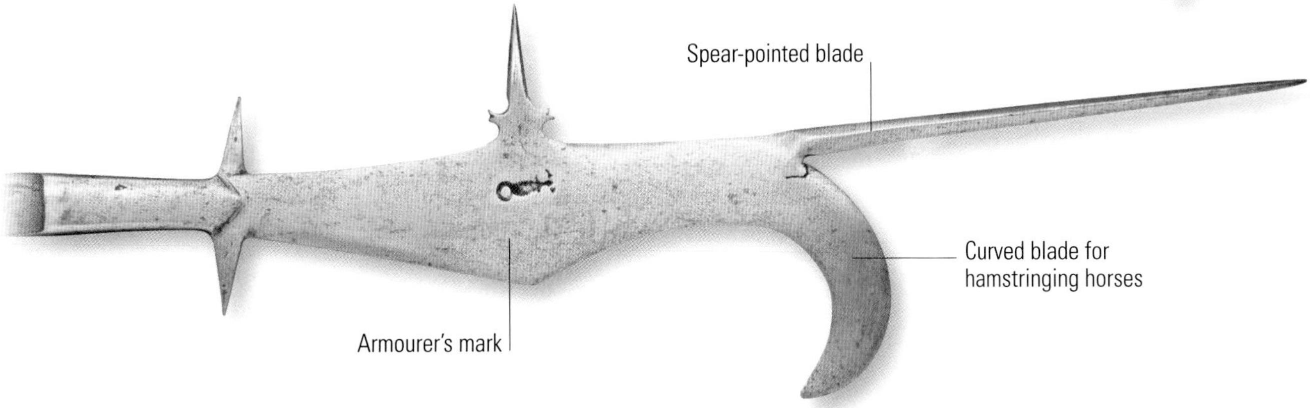

DATE	*c.*1550
ORIGIN	ITALIAN
LENGTH	67.3cm (26.5in) head

The curved hook just below the spear point of this bill would have been used to hamstring the enemy's horses and consequently bring down their horsemen. The bill's needlepoint spear could then be employed to finish off the now vulnerable opponent on the ground.

Italian bill, *c.*1560

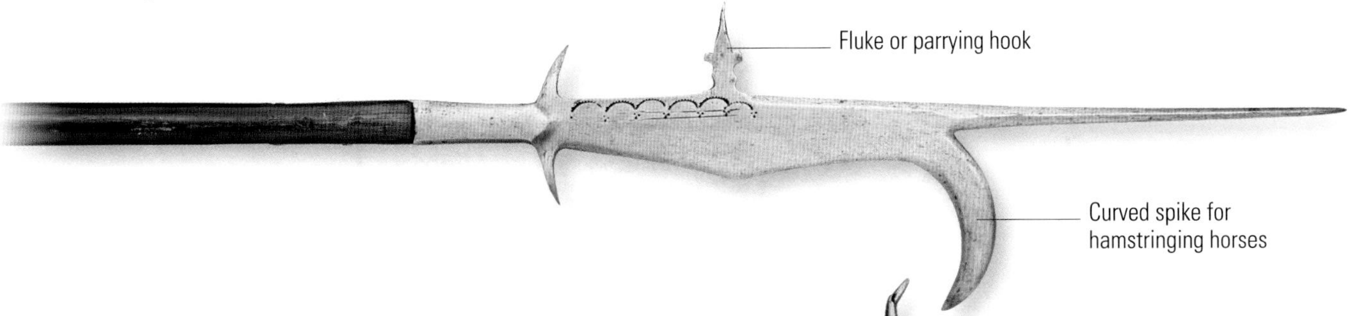

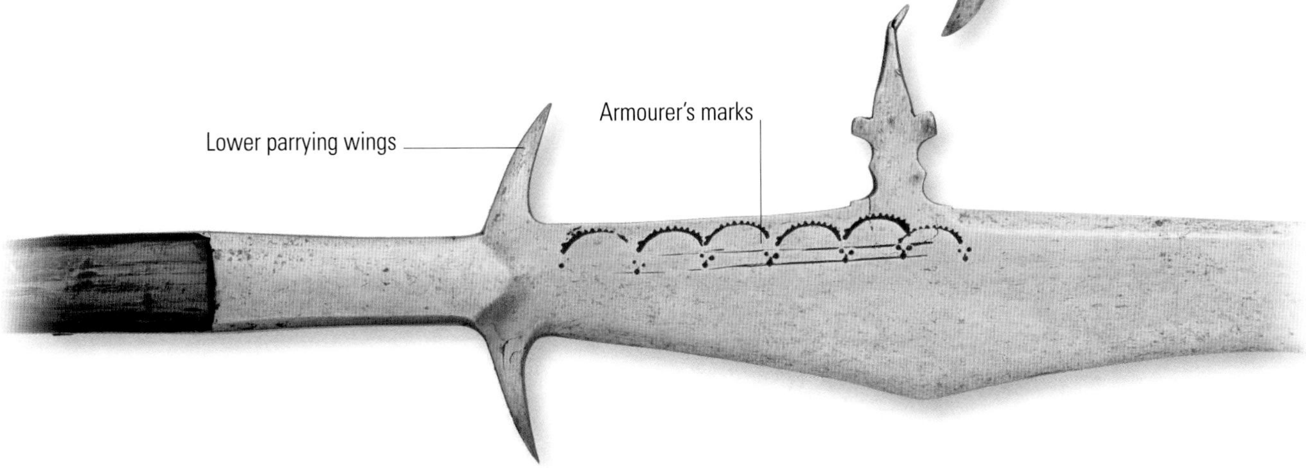

DATE	*c.*1560
ORIGIN	ITALIAN
LENGTH	70.6cm (27.8in) head

Italian bills (roncone) were far more sophisticated in design than their English counterparts and tended to have longer heads with more piercing points. The blade on this bill has armourer's stamps of repeated crescent shape. Armourers used a wealth of different marks and many are quite obscure and bizarre in shape, making identification very difficult.

English bill, *c.*1580

This style of bill was carried throughout Europe but was especially popular in England, where it was used well into the 17th century. This example is of a very early and simple design. It is reminiscent of civilian agricultural tools and it is from this source that many polearm forms were derived.

DATE	*c.*1580
ORIGIN	ENGLISH
LENGTH	19.2cm (7.5in) head

English bill, *c.*1580

The very long head of this bill is particularly unusual. It was probably used more as a thrusting than as a cutting weapon. Two winged parrying lugs are located near the bottom of the head and there is another effective parrying hook, or fluke, which is placed just above.

DATE	*c.*1580
ORIGIN	ENGLISH
LENGTH	217.2cm (85.5in)

English spontoon, *c.*1790

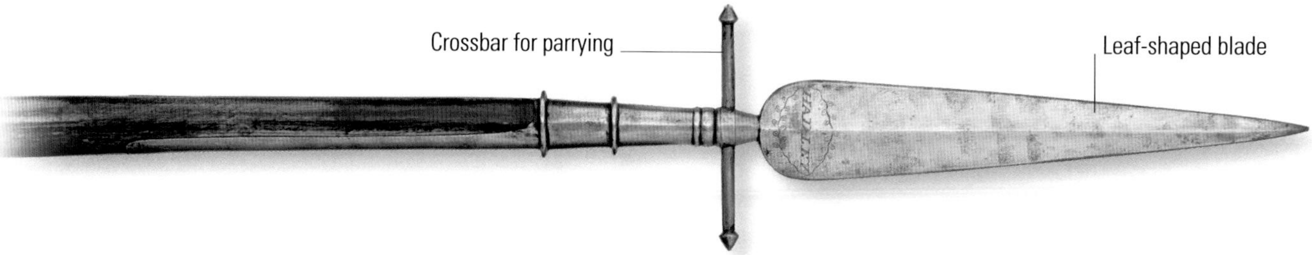

By this time, the spontoon was purely a weapon signifying military rank and only carried by officers and NCOs. The curved parrying bars, or flukes, of earlier polearms have now disappeared, to be replaced by a simple crossbar with decorative finials or quillons.

DATE	*c.*1790
ORIGIN	ENGLISH
LENGTH	157.5cm (62in)

French officer's spontoon, *c.*1780

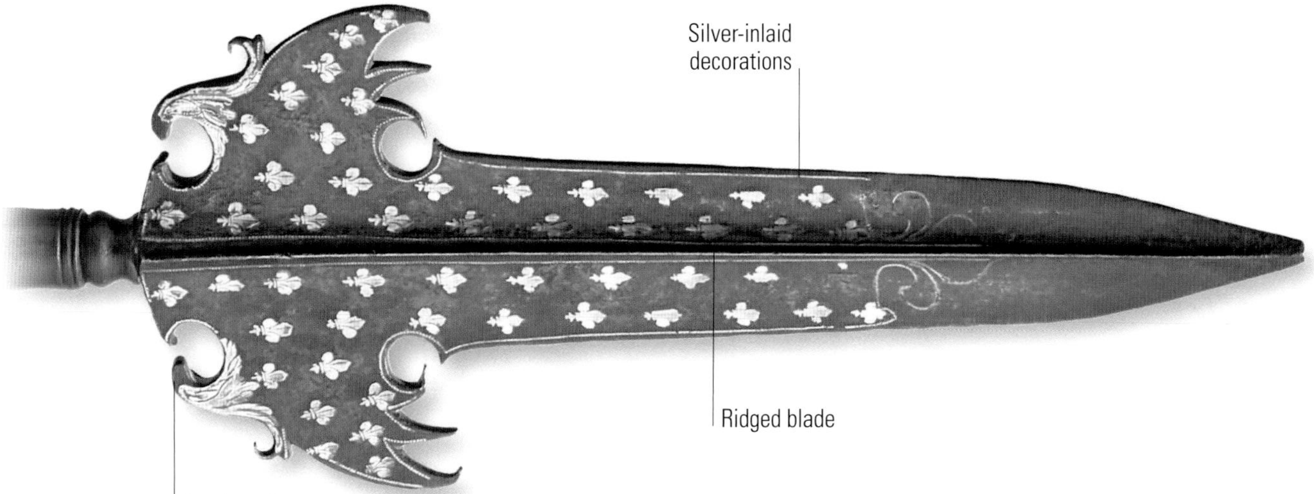

DATE	*c.*1780
ORIGIN	FRENCH
LENGTH	40.3cm (15.9in) head

This is a spontoon made of forged iron and used by the guards of French king Louis XVI (*r.* 1774–91). The blackened blade has a strong ridge on each side and approximately two thirds of its surface is decorated with silver-inlaid lilies and fine bead bands.

English spontoon, *c.*1800

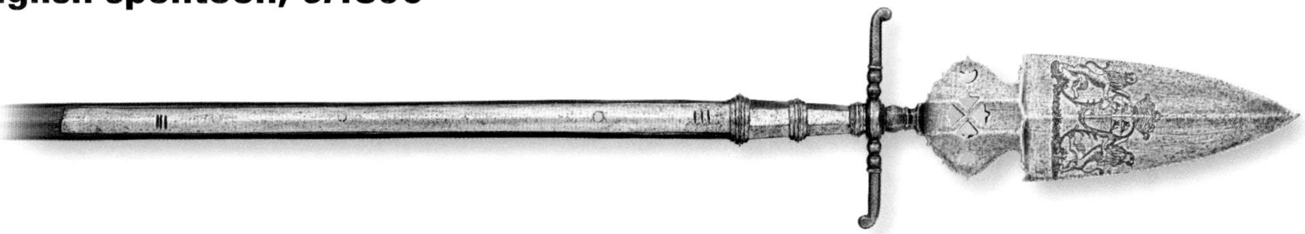

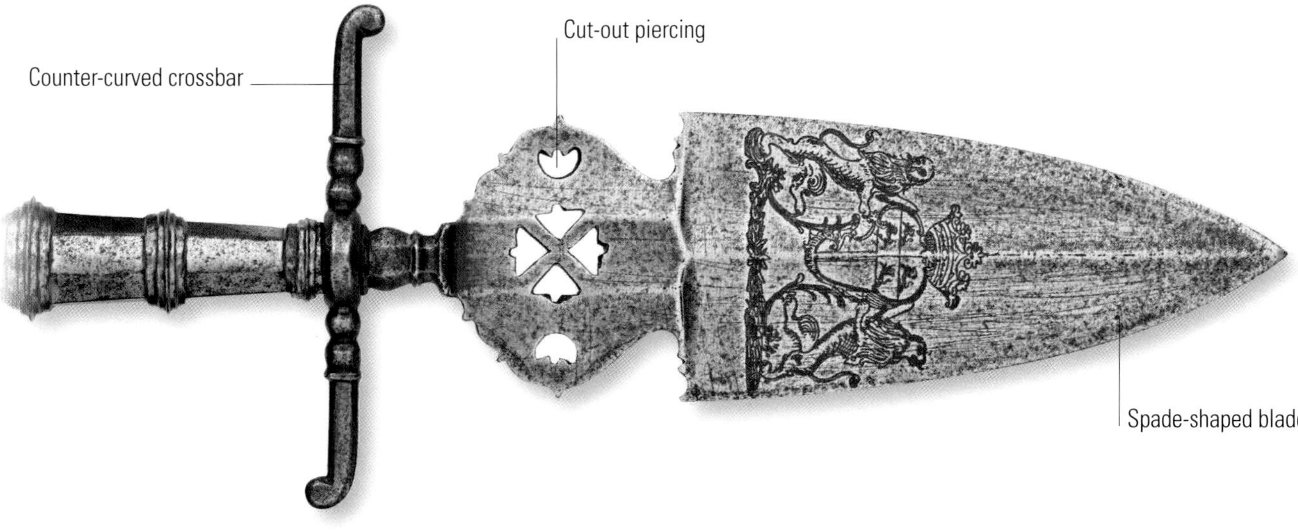

DATE	*c.*1800
ORIGIN	ENGLISH
LENGTH	23.5cm (9.2in) head

The use of cut-out piercings and engraved decoration on the blade indicate that this spontoon was probably more of a ceremonial weapon, although its construction is still robust and durable enough for combat. The spontoon head is attached to the wooden shaft by long, riveted langets.

Spears, guisarmes and bardiches

The spear was used in battle long before recorded history and this longevity bears witness to its simple effectiveness. By the medieval and Renaissance periods, it was no longer thrown like a javelin but used more like a short, thrusting polearm. The guisarme was a more sophisticated development of a peasant's agricultural tool. The bardiche was very much the weapon of the ordinary peasant soldier, with its long and heavy crescent-shaped blade that functioned as a devastating war axe.

German winged, or lugged, spear, *c.*1480

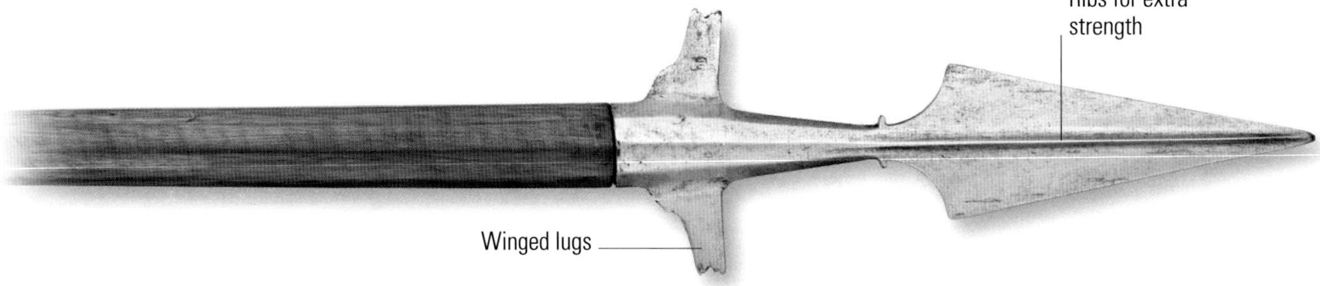

The winged, or lugged, spear had a leaf-shaped blade with triangular side projections that acted as a barrier to stop the spearhead sinking too deeply into an opponent, thus becoming difficult to withdraw. This was to be avoided as it rendered the soldier vulnerable.

DATE	*c.*1480
ORIGIN	GERMAN
LENGTH	109.2cm (43in)

Italian military spear, *c.*1500

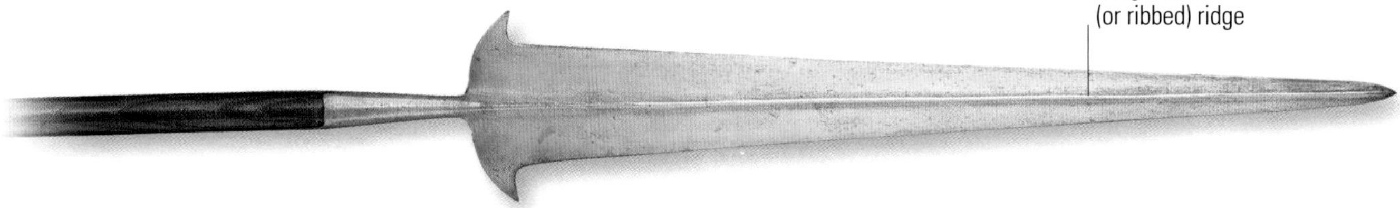

The long, triangular blade of this military spear has a pronounced median or strengthening ridge down the centre of the blade to ensure that it can withstand the great force that would be generated by heavy penetration, particularly into armour or protective clothing.

DATE	*c.*1500
ORIGIN	ITALIAN
LENGTH	240cm (94.5in)

Italian military spear, *c.*1520

Of very simple form, this late Renaissance military spear would not have looked out of place at the Battle of Hastings (1066) some five hundred years earlier. Its function was still the same, except that it would not have been thrown but used instead as a short polearm.

DATE	*c.*1520
ORIGIN	ITALIAN
LENGTH	46.3cm (18.2in) head

English small spear, *c.*1550

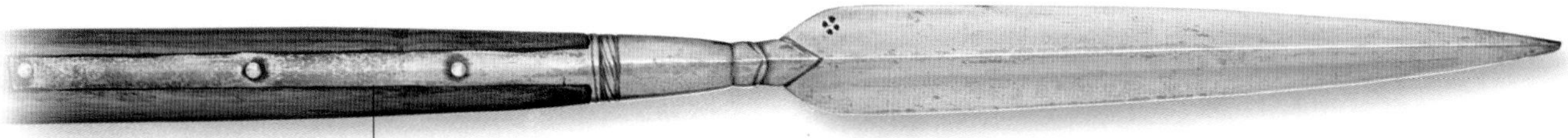

DATE	*c.*1550
ORIGIN	ENGLISH
LENGTH	33.2cm (13.1in) head

The riveted langets attached to the wooden staff of this spear are similar to those used on halberds and other polearms of the period, and they would certainly have added extra strength to the socket. It is likely that this is a smaller version of the military pike.

English guisarme, *c.*1580

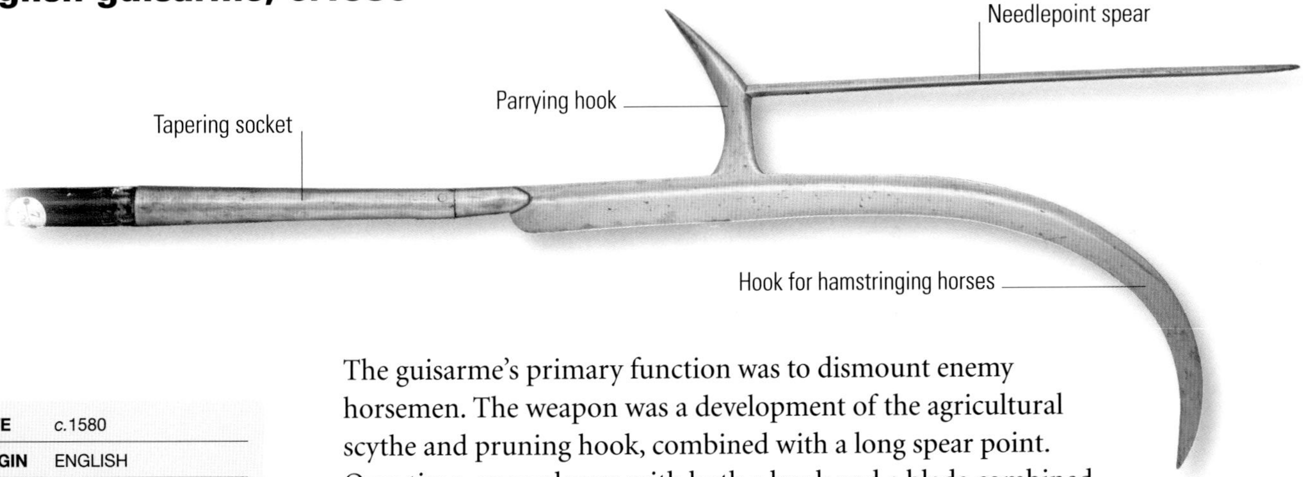

DATE	*c.*1580
ORIGIN	ENGLISH
LENGTH	99.1cm (39in) head

The guisarme's primary function was to dismount enemy horsemen. The weapon was a development of the agricultural scythe and pruning hook, combined with a long spear point. Over time, any polearm with both a hook and a blade combined together was normally termed a guisarme.

North European bardiche, *c.*1480

DATE	*c.*1480
ORIGIN	NORTH EUROPEAN
LENGTH	76.2cm (30in) head

A warrior would have required considerable strength to wield this weapon. The combined weight of the heavy axehead and thick wooden shaft would probably have created some manoeuvrability problems, unless used by an experienced soldier. The bottom of the axehead was secured to the shaft by strong rivets to ensure stability of the long blade. The bardiche was a standard infantry weapon in eastern Europe, particularly Russia and Poland, where 17th-century musketeers (an early form of infantryman armed with a musket) used the end of the pole at the back of the bardiche to rest their guns while firing. Presumably, a long spike would have been fitted into the bottom of the pole to secure it into the ground.

Poleaxes

The poleaxe's function was to smash and cut its way through armour and flesh. By the late 15th century, it had become the preferred battlefield weapon of the knight, who now fought primarily on foot, and had relegated the sword to a secondary role. The poleaxe usually comprised an axe, hammer and long spike. Effective training enabled a knight to dispatch any opponent with a series of well aimed, ruthless blows.

European poleaxe, *c.*1480

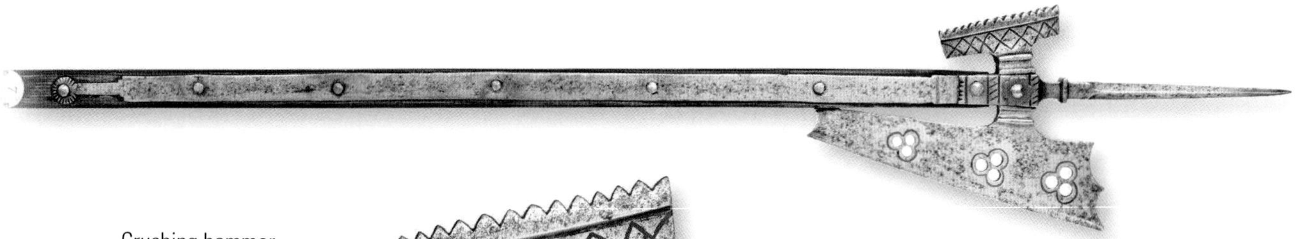

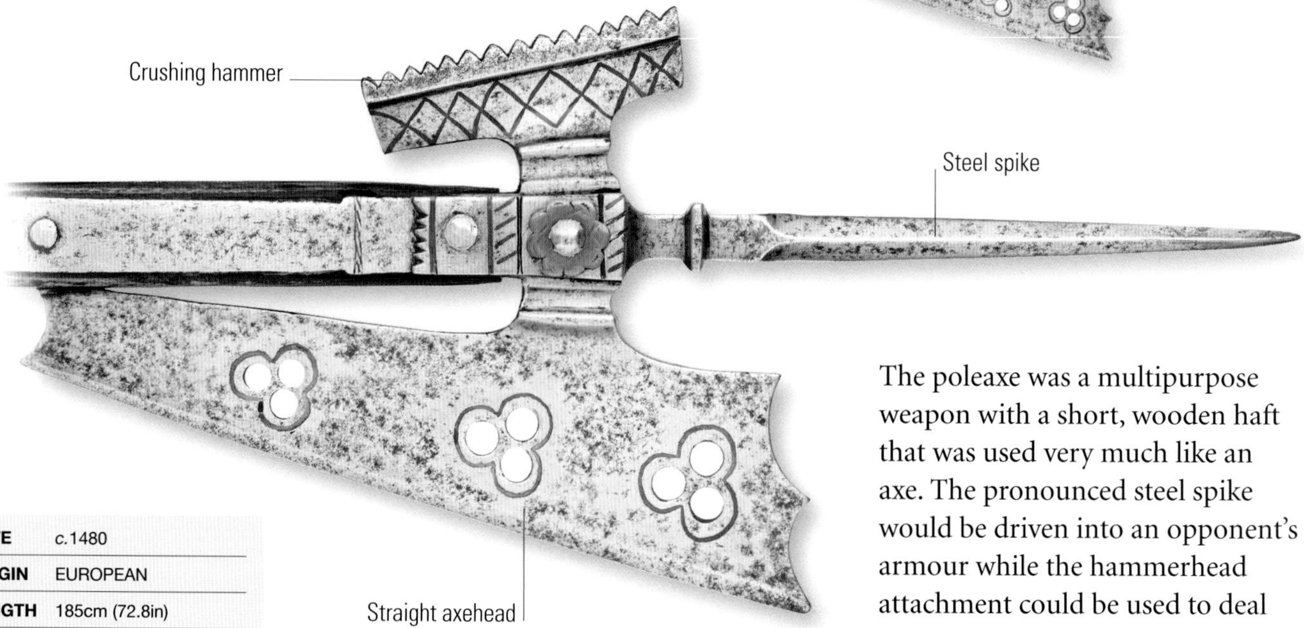

DATE	*c.*1480
ORIGIN	EUROPEAN
LENGTH	185cm (72.8in)

The poleaxe was a multipurpose weapon with a short, wooden haft that was used very much like an axe. The pronounced steel spike would be driven into an opponent's armour while the hammerhead attachment could be used to deal crushing blows.

North European poleaxe, *c.*1480

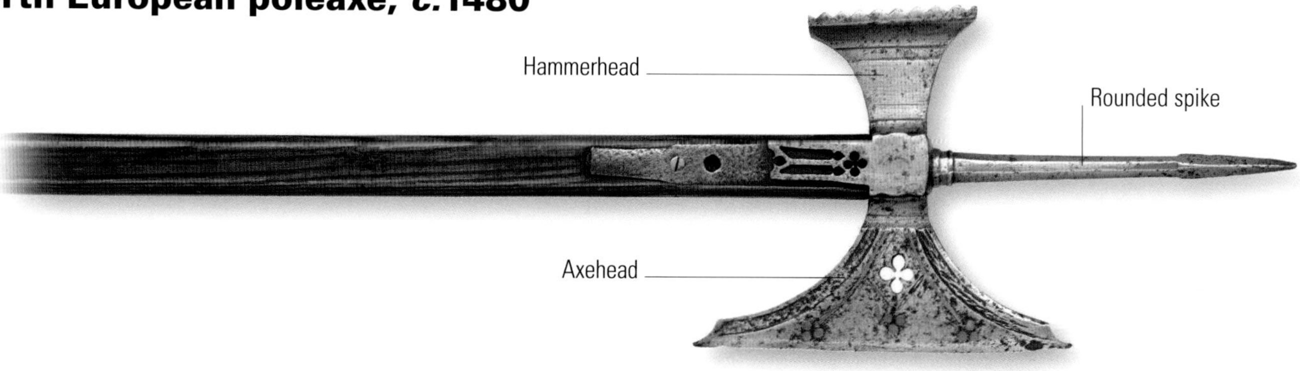

Many poleaxes were decorated but this example is fairly plain. The spike has a rounded profile, unlike the usual triangular type that is normally encountered on a poleaxe. The name "poleaxe" is derived from the word "poll" which is the Old English name for head.

DATE	*c.*1480
ORIGIN	NORTH EUROPEAN
LENGTH	35cm (13.7in) head

Poleaxes on the battlefield

By the 15th century, English knights fought predominantly on foot and the poleaxe was their primary weapon of choice. A two-handed grip was essential when holding the poleaxe, and it was held at shoulder height with elbows tucked close to the body in order to protect the knight from blows to his vulnerable sides, particularly the underarm area where plate armour was normally absent. While engaged in the melee of battle, the knight would dodge and parry enemy blades, and carefully wait for the right moment to strike with his poleaxe. Although any effective blow to the body that could maim or kill was the main priority of any attacker with a poleaxe, a shattering strike to the face was the most coveted. Incapacitated (or sometimes killed outright on the spot), the victim would be finished off by the poleaxe's hammerhead.

ABOVE 15th-century hand-to-hand fighting. Both knights are using poleaxe-type weapons.

North European poleaxe, *c.*1500

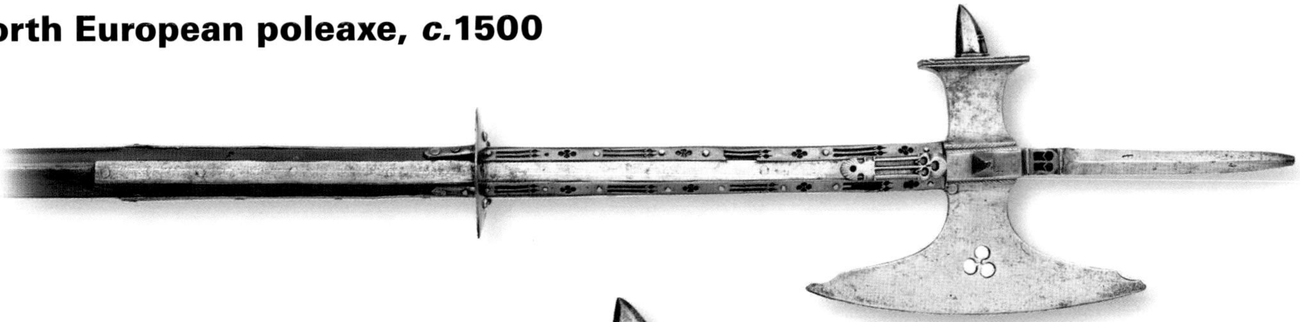

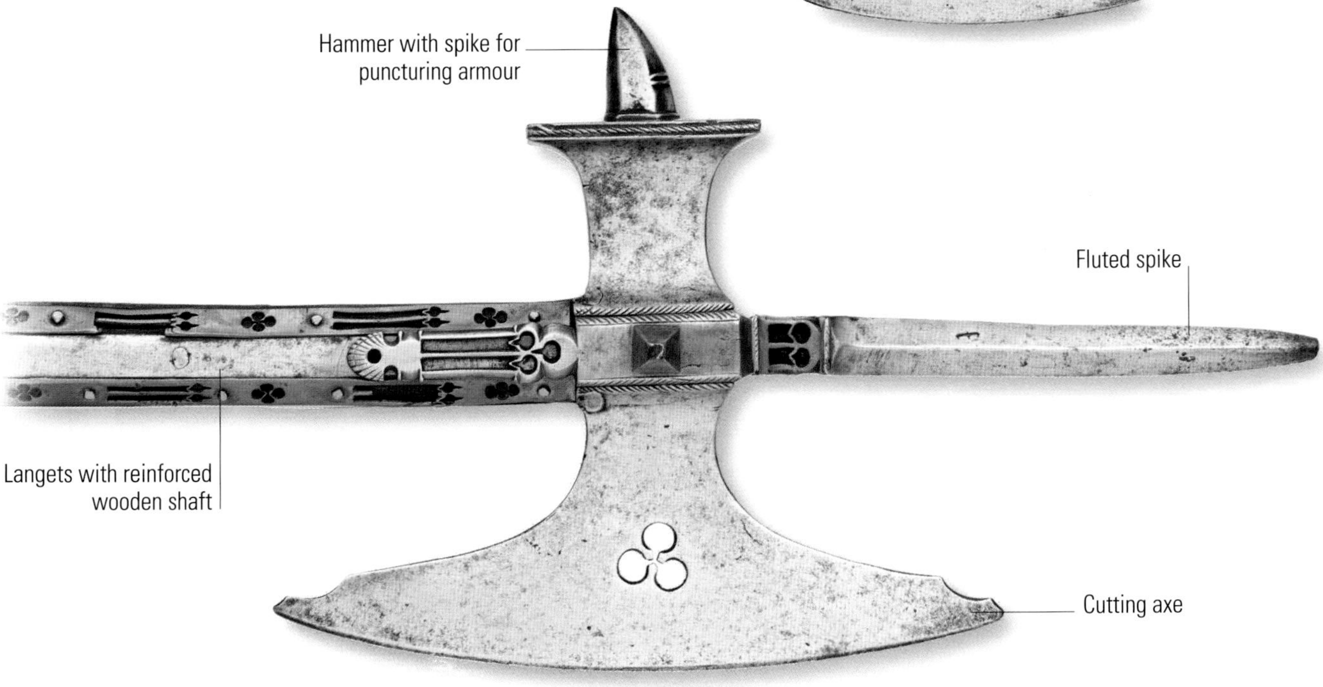

DATE	*c.*1500
ORIGIN	NORTH EUROPEAN
LENGTH	177.8cm (70in)

This poleaxe has a spike attached to the hammerhead. Made of solid steel, this tooth-shaped addition would have been highly effective at puncturing armour, providing the user with an opening in which to drive in the long spike at the end of the axehead.

Other polearms

As well as the halberd, pike and poleaxe, a number of lesser known polearms were used by the infantry soldier. They included the batwinged chauve souris (meaning "bat" in French) and the crudely effective war scythe, a development of the agricultural scythe and a tool familiar to the conscripted peasant soldier.

German war scythe, *c.*1480

The war scythe was little more than an adapted agricultural scythe used for harvesting wheat. The main difference was that the war scythe had a less pronounced curve than its agricultural counterpart. Swung with sufficient momentum, the war scythe could literally cut a swathe through opponents.

DATE	*c.*1480
ORIGIN	GERMAN
LENGTH	250.2cm (98.5in)

Italian corseque, *c.*1500

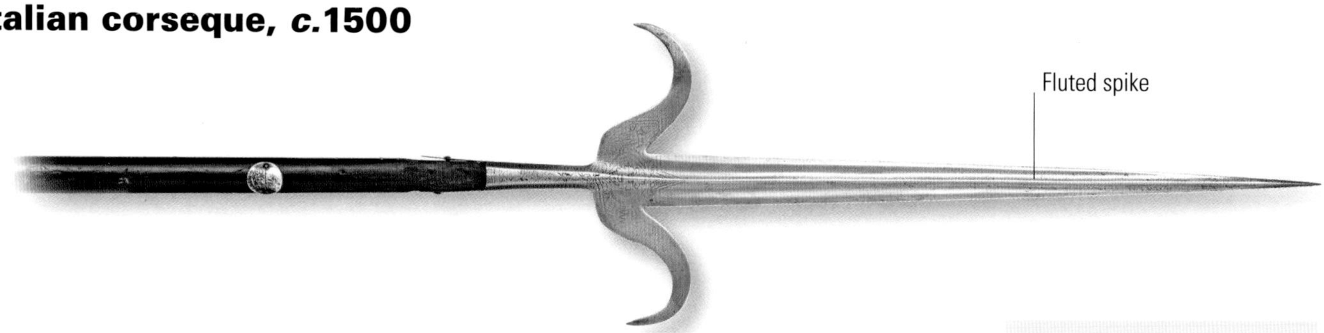

The corseque had curved wings bending back towards the handle of the weapon. It was similar to the partizan but exhibited a fluted spike rather than the typical leaf-shaped blade more commonly associated with the partizan.

DATE	*c.*1500
ORIGIN	ITALIAN
LENGTH	74.9cm (29.5in) head

Italian chauve souris, *c.*1550

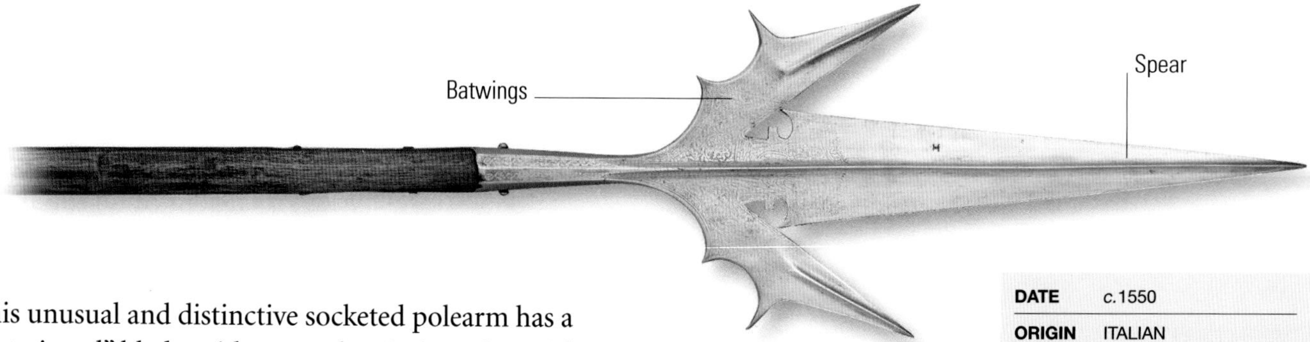

This unusual and distinctive socketed polearm has a "batwinged" blade, with upward-pointing wings either side of a spear point. Below this are notched spikes.

DATE	*c.*1550
ORIGIN	ITALIAN
LENGTH	193.1cm (76in)

Italian chauve souris, *c.*1550

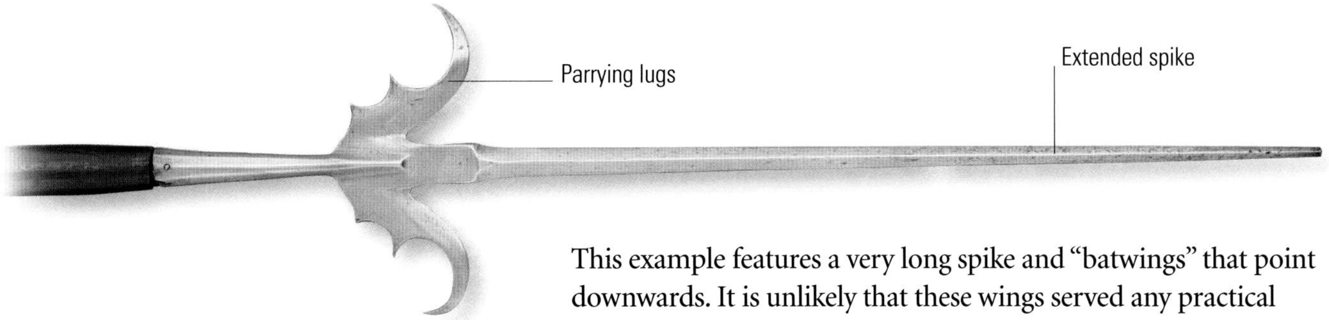

DATE	*c.*1550
ORIGIN	ITALIAN
LENGTH	83.8cm (33in) head

This example features a very long spike and "batwings" that point downwards. It is unlikely that these wings served any practical purpose as the robust, extra-long spike made this a thrusting, rather than cutting weapon. Also, the hooked blade points could easily become entangled in clothing. This polearm is also known as a Runka or Ranseur.

English war scythe, *c.*1600

DATE	*c.*1600
ORIGIN	ENGLISH
LENGTH	99.1cm (39in)

This is a very crude example of the type of peasant weapon that would have been carried from the early medieval period. Unlike the double-edged bill or halberd, the war scythe had a single-edged blade on the concave side. This weapon was very common in eastern Europe, particularly Russia and Poland, where the need to quickly raise peasant armies (in the face of the constant Ottoman threat) and therefore produce simply manufactured weapons meant that the war scythe would always be one of the first weapons to be called upon in a national crisis.

German military fork, *c.*1650

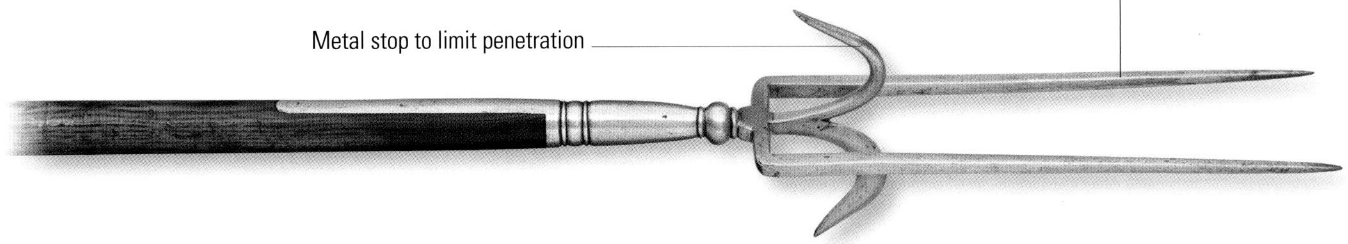

DATE	*c.*1650
ORIGIN	GERMAN
LENGTH	41.1cm (16.2in) head

An adaptation of the agricultural pitchfork, the military fork had a variety of uses on and off the battlefield. Its two long prongs, or tines, could easily dismount riders and enable their swift dispatch or capture. Many enemy knights were subsequently held to ransom following the application of the military fork to lever them unharmed off their horses. It could also be utilized as a practical tool during a siege when the prongs were used to raise up siege ladders or deliver supplies to ramparts.

Hunting swords and hangers

The use of a short-bladed sword for hunting has its origins in the late medieval period and reached its height of popularity during the 18th century, when this sword changed from being a handy tool to dispatch and carve up an animal to an overt excuse for displaying the wealth and status of its owner. The hanger was adopted by the military, particularly the foot-soldier, and was also a common weapon for naval officers.

English hanger, *c.*1640

DATE	*c.*1640
ORIGIN	ENGLISH
LENGTH	93.5 cm (36.8in)

Towards the end of the 17th century, some English hangers began to adopt zoomorphic, or animal-head, pommels. Two of the most common types were the lion's-head and the dog's-head pommel. Contemporary interpretations of what the head of a lion or dog should look like ranged from the highly realistic to the weirdly grotesque. It is the innocent naivety of the sword maker that makes these pommels so attractive to modern eyes.

English hanger, *c.*1645

The hanger was a common infantry sword during the 17th century, particularly in England where it was combined with many hilt types. This example has a pierced, steel shell guard with a slightly curved and single-fullered blade. There is also a pronounced tang button at the top of the flattened pommel.

DATE	*c.*1645
ORIGIN	ENGLISH
LENGTH	81cm (31.9in)

English/German hanger, *c.*1650

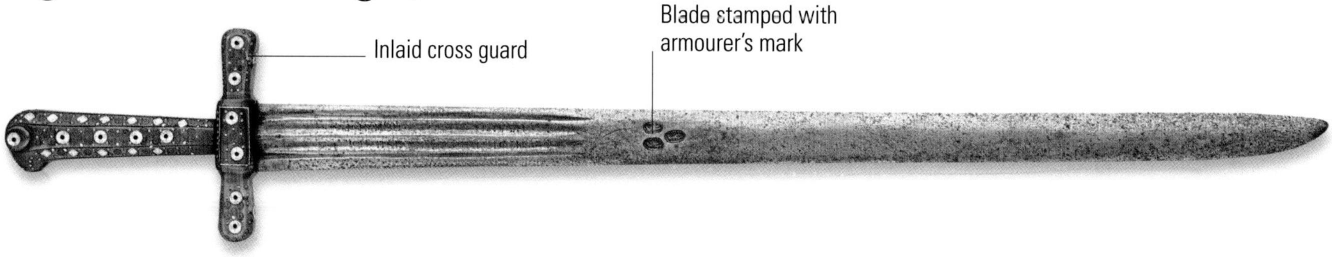

The cruciform hilt of this hanger is made from cow horn, with an inlay of metal studs in either silver or pewter, combined with stag-horn or ebony roundels. The blade was manufactured in Germany and imported into England, where it was mounted onto this hilt.

DATE	*c.*1650
ORIGIN	ENGLISH/GERMAN
LENGTH	78.8cm (31in)

English hanger, *c.*1650

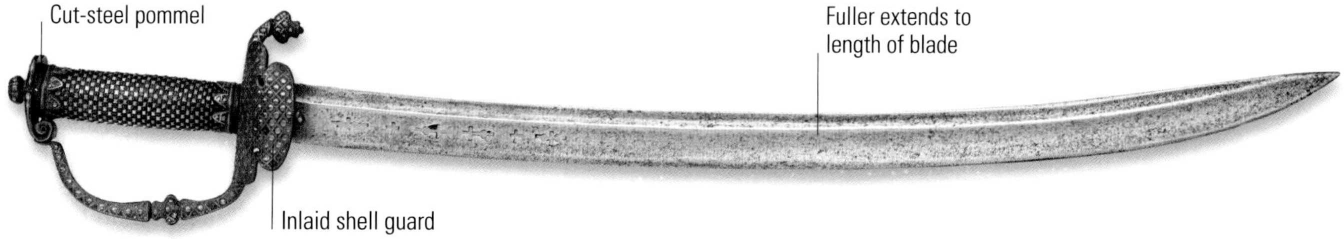

DATE	*c.*1650
ORIGIN	ENGLISH
LENGTH	73.2cm (28.8in)

This is a very fine example of an English infantry hanger of the English Civil War (1642–51) period. The hilt is deliberately blackened to highlight the superb inlaid silver chequering. This would have been an expensive sword to purchase and was probably worn by a person of considerable means. It is likely that the leather scabbard would have had decorative mounts to match the hilt.

English hanger, *c.*1650

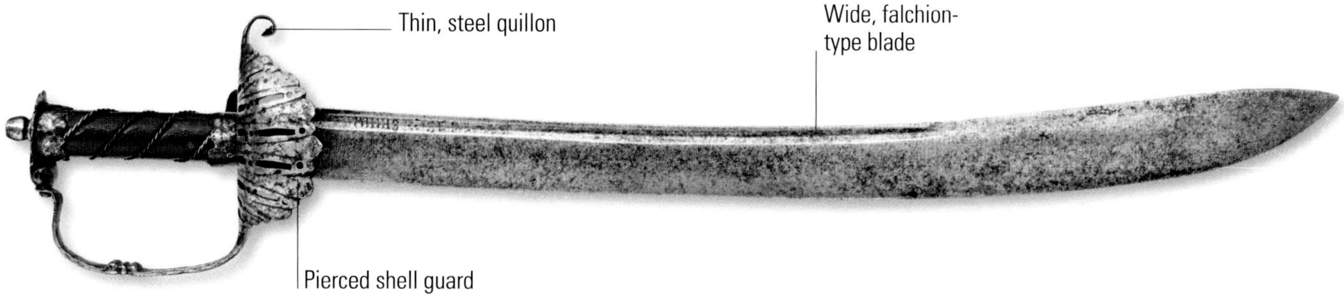

DATE	*c.*1650
ORIGIN	ENGLISH
LENGTH	70cm (27.5in)

One of the most common blade types to be found on hangers of this period is the falchion. This is a curved blade that widens considerably near the point, sometimes ending with a false edge on the back of the blade. The shell guards are of pierced form and a thin knuckle guard is attached to the pommel by means of a flat-headed screw.

English hanger, *c.*1680

DATE	*c.*1680
ORIGIN	ENGLISH
LENGTH	84.6cm (33.3in)

This hanger is typical of the type carried by huntsmen and naval officers of the 17th and 18th century. It was a practical choice for naval officers, as the short length of the blade meant that it was less likely to get caught up in the rigging and could be wielded within the limited space available on board a ship at war. The grip is made of stag-horn and the hilt is brass. Pommels tended to be slightly domed with the tang button prominent.

European hunting sword, *c.*1680

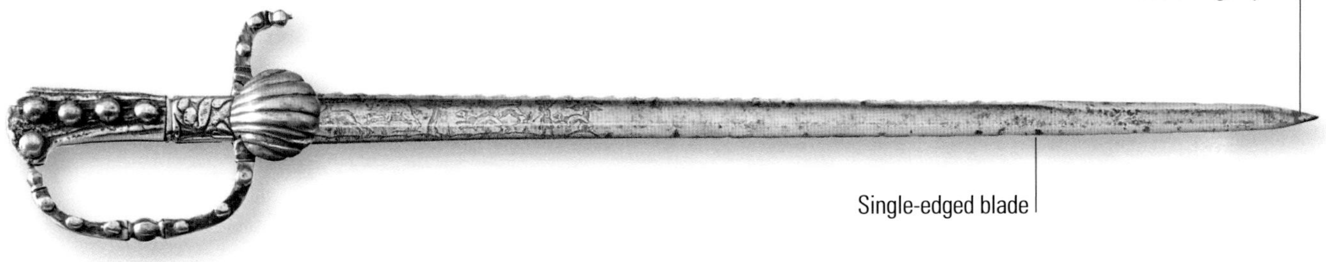

This hunting sword has a fullered single-edged blade with a double-edged point. Each side of the upper third of the blade is etched with hunting scenes. It has a simple, iron, knucklebow hilt with clam shell and stag-horn plates, partially replaced. The grip ferrule is florally cut, and the grip panels are stag-horn with large, hemispherical rivets, one of which has been replaced.

DATE	1680
ORIGIN	EUROPEAN
LENGTH	84cm (33in)

English/German hanger, *c.*1690

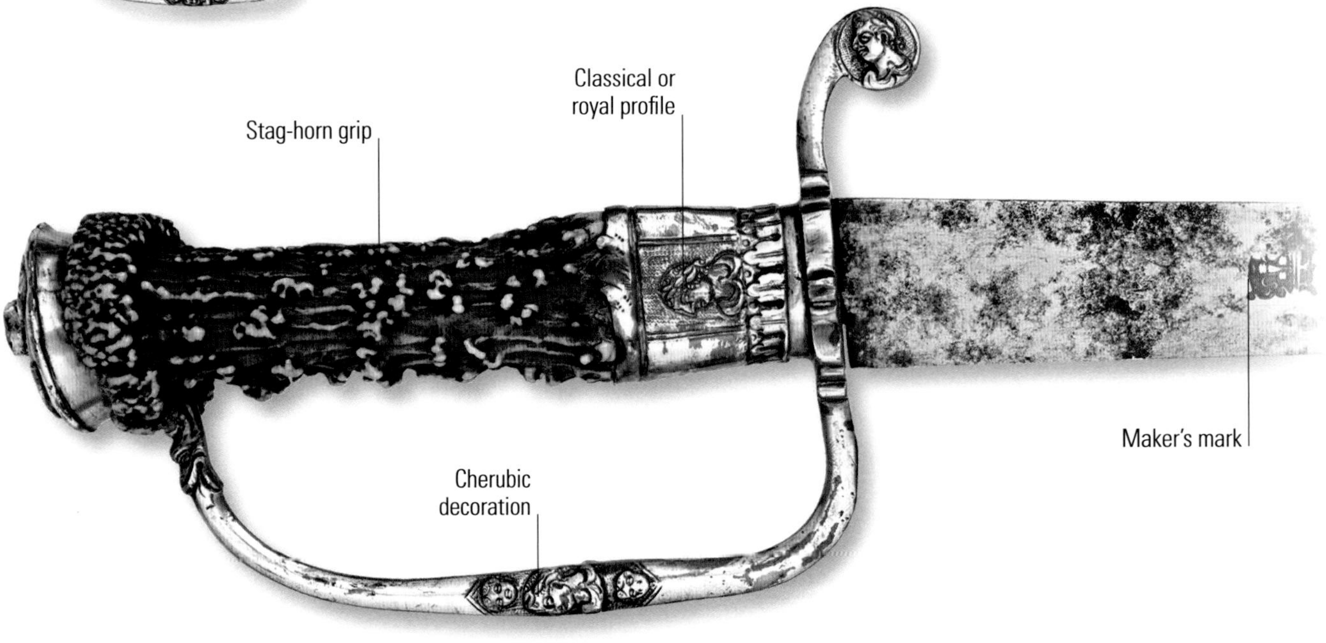

This fine hanger is marked on the hilt with the initials of Richard Fuller (*c.*1670–1731), a noted English sword cutler working in London. He was a skilled hilt maker and in this sword we can see the finely crafted detail he has applied to the pommel, knuckle guard, cross guard and ferrule (the metal band at the bottom of the grip). This stag-horn grip would have been specially chosen because of its gnarled properties and ability to keep the wearer's hand firmly in place. The grip's unusual shape is also aesthetically pleasing. The blade has the king's head-impressed stamp of the Wundes sword-making family of Solingen, Germany.

DATE	*c.*1690
ORIGIN	ENGLISH/GERMAN
LENGTH	63.5cm (25in)

English hanger, *c.*1700

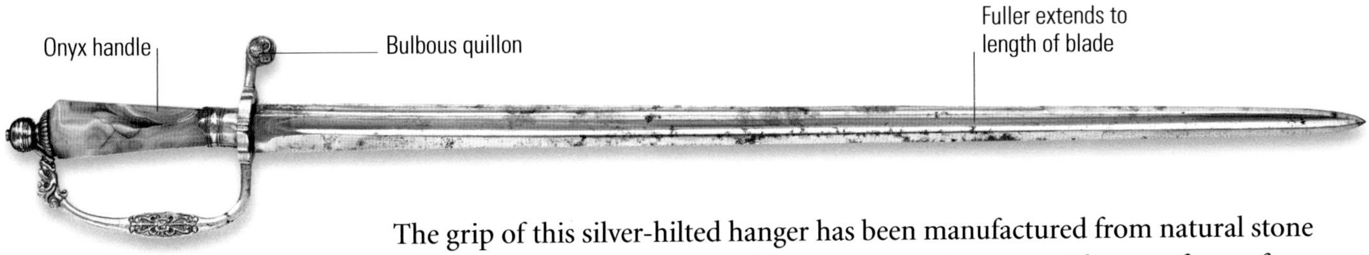

DATE	*c.*1700
ORIGIN	ENGLISH
LENGTH	69.2cm (27.2in)

The grip of this silver-hilted hanger has been manufactured from natural stone agate and would have been highly distinctive when worn. The use of onyx for sword grips was very popular during the first half of the 18th century. The hilt mounts are solid silver and the long, straight blade has a fuller that extends for most of the blade length, giving the sword flexibility and strength.

English hanger, *c.*1730

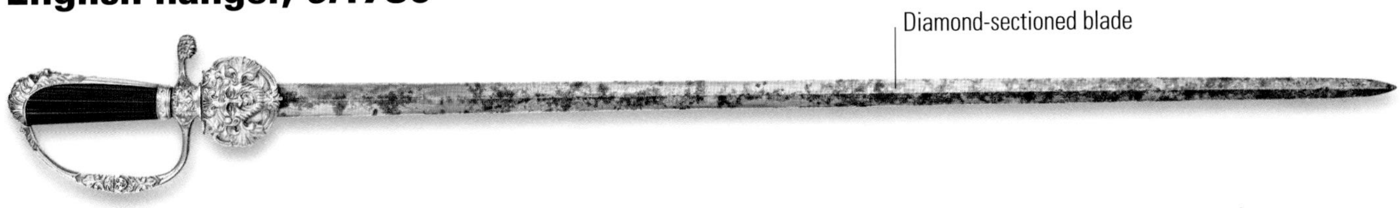

DATE	*c.*1730
ORIGIN	ENGLISH
LENGTH	92.1cm (36.2in)

The shell guard of this silver-hilted hanger is decorated in the form of a bearded human face. It is probably an interpretation of the pagan Green Man (also known as "the wild man of the woods") and was a popular hunting motif in mid-18th century England.

Russian hanger, *c.*1750

DATE	*c.*1750
ORIGIN	RUSSIAN
LENGTH	70.2cm (27.6in)

This hanger was made at the Imperial Russian armoury in the town of Tula, about 165km (102 miles) south of Moscow. The first factory was opened by Peter the Great (1672–1725) in 1712, and it soon became the centre of both sword and armaments making. This dress sword was probably made for a civilian gentleman, as indicated by the use of multiple cut-steel ornamentation to the hilt.

English hanger, *c.*1750

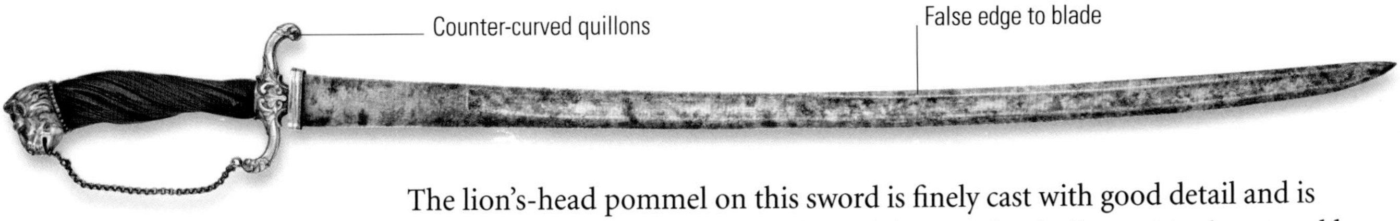

DATE	*c.*1750
ORIGIN	ENGLISH
LENGTH	80.3cm (31.6in)

The lion's-head pommel on this sword is finely cast with good detail and is combined with an ebony grip of spiral design. The shell guard is absent and has been replaced by a simple cross guard. From the mid-18th century, the normally solid knuckle guard was sometimes replaced by a linked metal chain guard. Chain guards were easily prone to damage and many have been lost over time.

English Civil War swords

Although the importance of firearms on the battlefield was beginning to be felt at the start of the English Civil War (1642–51), the sword was still the principal edged weapon of the mounted horseman. One of the most distinctive swords to emerge from this conflict was the so-called mortuary sword, a peculiarly English broadsword that featured a bowl or half-basket guard with extensive, decorative chiselling to the hilt. It would have been carried by Royalist (Cavalier) and Parliamentarian (Roundhead) troops.

English broadsword, *c.*1620

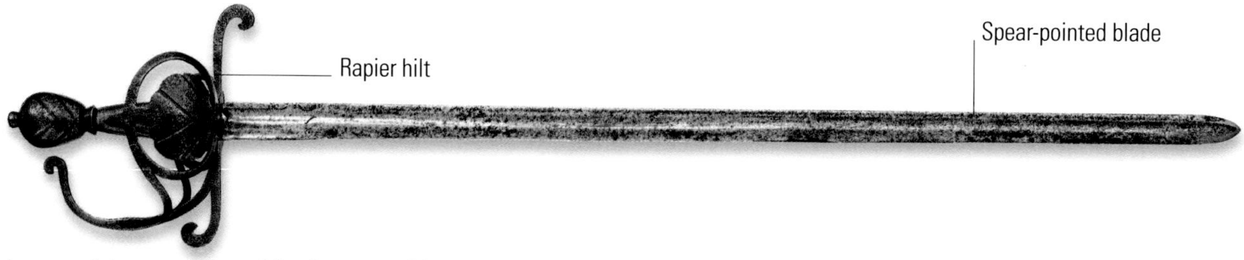

This sword is transitional in form and has a typical Renaissance "swept" rapier hilt and a long, broadsword blade. Protection for the hand is minimal and although this type of sword was still carried during the English Civil War (1642–51), the hilt was being superseded by mortuary-style basket hilts.

DATE	*c.*1620
ORIGIN	ENGLISH
LENGTH	94cm (37in)

English backsword, *c.*1640

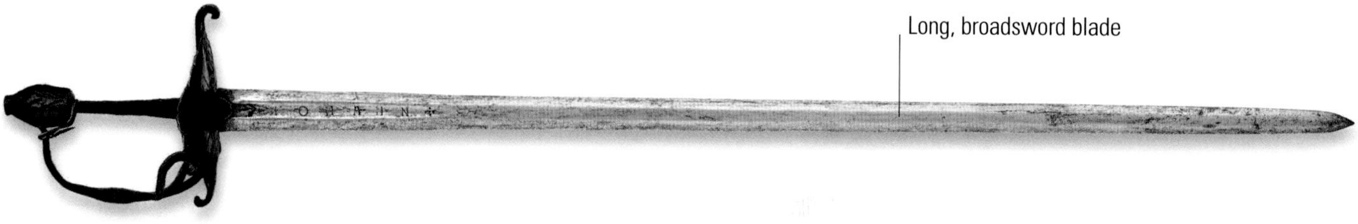

This sword would probably have been carried by a mounted officer. The hilt design has echoes of contemporary rapiers but differs in that the blade is much broader and flatter, having a double-edged cutting function, in contrast to the thrusting capabilities of a rapier.

DATE	*c.*1640
ORIGIN	ENGLISH
LENGTH	90.6cm (35.7in)

English mortuary-type sword, *c.*1640

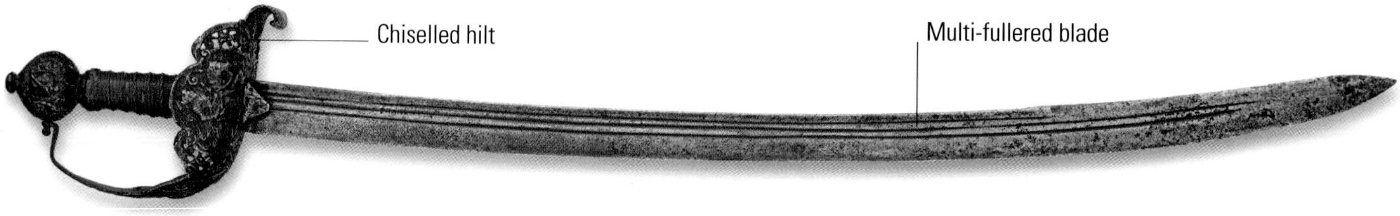

Although the blade is longer than a hanger, its curved shape is similar to short-bladed English hangers or hunting swords of the period. The guard, knuckle guard and pommel have been heavily encrusted in silver.

DATE	*c.*1640
ORIGIN	ENGLISH
LENGTH	92.5cm (36.4in)

English cavalry broadsword, 1640

An early form of lion's-head pommel marks out this cavalry sword as being quite unusual. It is a very early example of an animal-headed pommel on an English broadsword. The hilt has a deeply chiselled half basket.

DATE	1640
ORIGIN	ENGLISH
LENGTH	112.7cm (44.4in)

English mortuary-hilted broadsword, *c.*1640

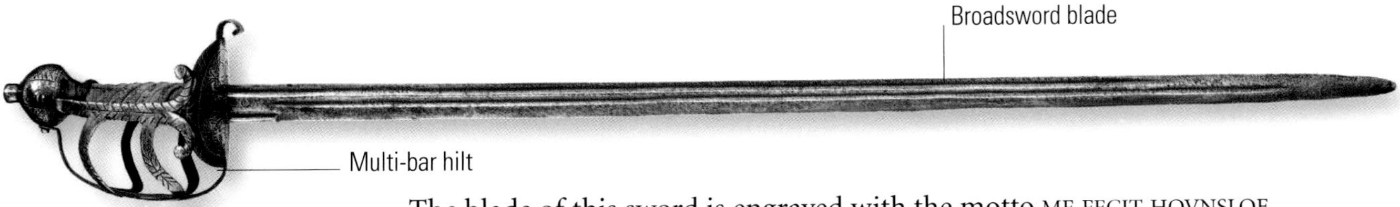

DATE	*c.*1640
ORIGIN	ENGLISH
LENGTH	102.9cm (40.5in)

The blade of this sword is engraved with the motto ME FECIT HOVNSLOE ("Hounslow made me") and is a reference to the west London borough that was a major sword-making town during the 17th century. Many diverse sword types, from hunting hangers to broadswords, were manufactured in Hounslow, and they are characterized by the use of chiselled and inlaid metalwork on the hilt.

English mortuary-hilted broadsword, *c.*1640

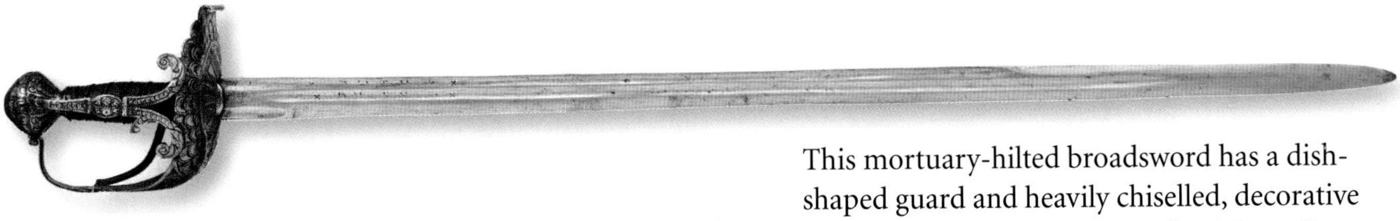

This mortuary-hilted broadsword has a dish-shaped guard and heavily chiselled, decorative metalwork. Two knuckle guards with smaller side branches are also screwed into the pommel. The grip is bound with silver twisted wire. Most swords of this age are likely to have been re-bound more than once during their lifetime, as grip wire can become unravelled quite easily.

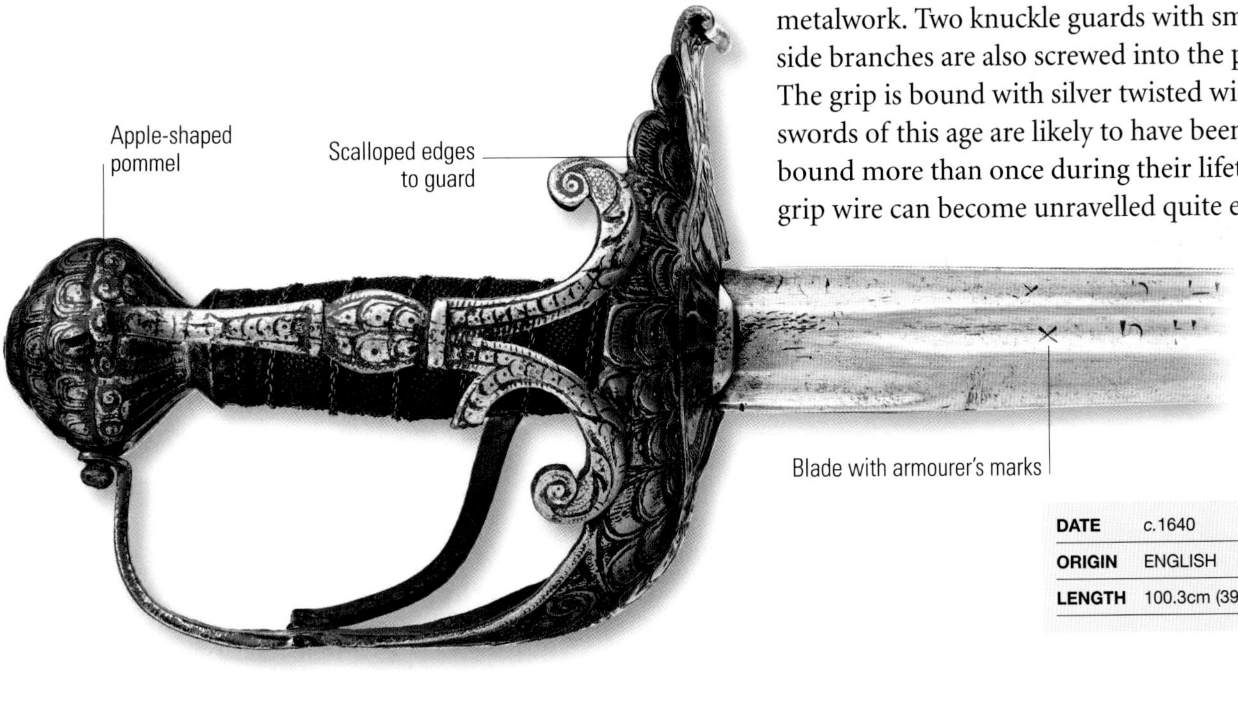

DATE	*c.*1640
ORIGIN	ENGLISH
LENGTH	100.3cm (39.5in)

English mortuary-hilted broadsword, *c.*1650

The mortuary sword is so named because of the application of stylized, chiselled human heads to the decoration of many of these sword hilts. The title "mortuary" was erroneously given by Victorian sword collectors who believed that the likenesses of King Charles I (1600–49) and Queen Henrietta (1609–69) had been applied to the hilts by English sword makers as a form of silent memorial following his execution in 1649. The hilt of this sword is made from iron with a dish- or boat-shaped guard. Two side knuckle guards are linked to a central guard that screws into the pommel.

DATE	*c.*1650
ORIGIN	ENGLISH
LENGTH	109.7cm (43.2in)

English mortuary-hilted broadsword, *c.*1650

A common feature of mortuary swords is the attachment of the hilt knuckle bow to the pommel by way of a securing screw. In this case, there is just one knuckle guard, but some mortuary hilts exhibit several knuckle guards screwed around a large apple-shaped pommel.

DATE	*c.*1650
ORIGIN	ENGLISH
LENGTH	104.4cm (41.1in)

English proto-mortuary sword, *c.*1650

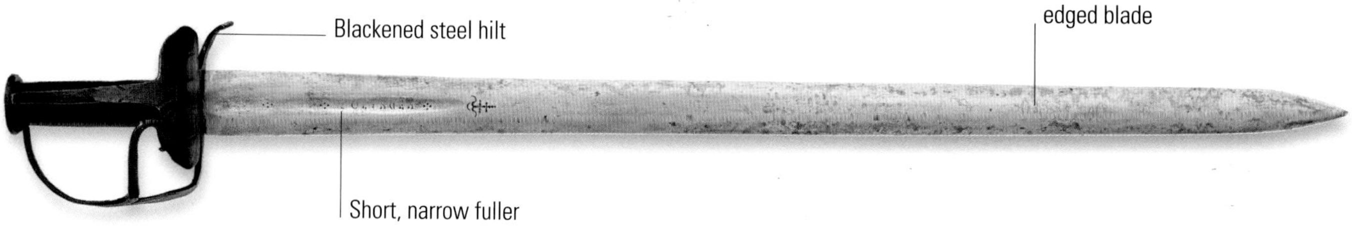

The term "proto-mortuary" normally refers to a group of English swords that was present in England just before the introduction of the fully developed mortuary sword in the mid-17th century. They are usually distinguished by their simple hilt design. In this case, the plain shell and knuckle guard indicate that this sword is of "munition" quality, meaning that it would have been produced for an ordinary soldier (to a prescribed pattern) rather than an officer.

DATE	*c.*1650
ORIGIN	ENGLISH
LENGTH	84.4cm (33.2in)

English mortuary-hilted sword, *c.*1650

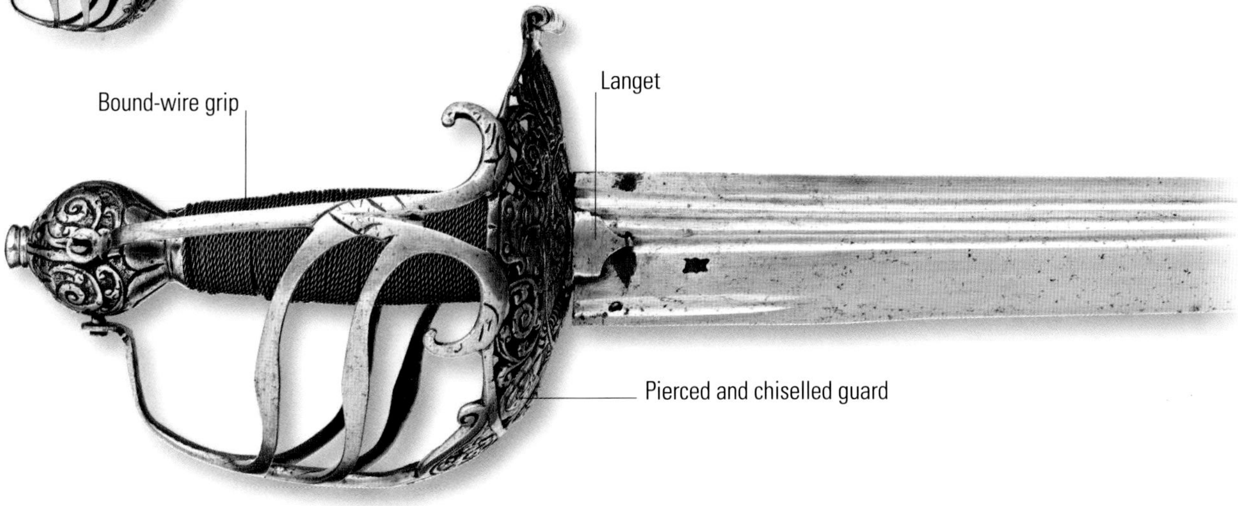

DATE	*c.*1650
ORIGIN	ENGLISH
LENGTH	100.3cm (39.5in)

This sword has a wide, double-edged blade, probably German. One of the characteristic features of a mortuary hilt is the positioning of two shield-shaped langets on either side of the blade, where it enters the dish guard. It is thought that their function was to add extra strength and stability to the blade.

English mortuary sword, *c.*1650

DATE	*c.*1650
ORIGIN	ENGLISH
LENGTH	102.9cm (40.5in)

Although one of the main types of decoration found on mortuary-hilted swords is a chiselled human head, other forms of decoration are present. This can include family coats of arms, armed figures, floral motifs, geometric patterns and even nautical motifs such as stylized dolphins and sea creatures.

English mortuary sword, *c.*1650

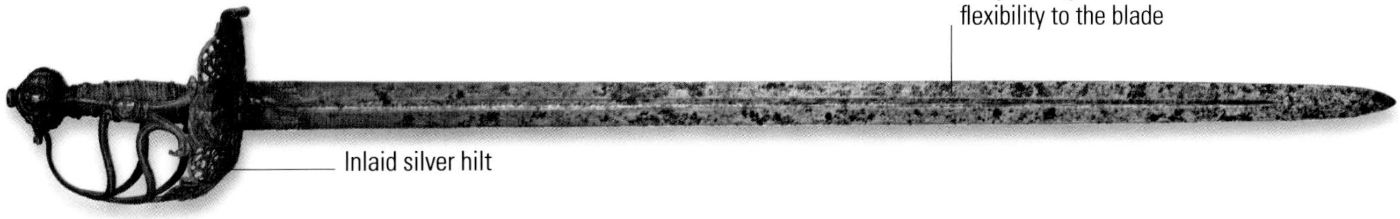

DATE	*c.*1650
ORIGIN	ENGLISH
LENGTH	99.8cm (39.3in)

The use of inlaid silver decoration was a common feature in mortuary-hilted swords. This example is covered with small pieces of solid silver that have been hammered into the blackened steel hilt. Two extra side branches on either side of the hilt are attached to the knuckle guard, giving the user extra protection.

Broadswords and sabres

Following the Renaissance, a number of distinctive sword types began to emerge. By the late 15th century, a diverse range of broadsword hilts and blades are noted. Swords with wide blades, both curved and straight, were used by cavalrymen as well as infantry soldiers. They had great slashing capabilities and were very robust. They largely replaced the medieval cruciform-hilted, double-edged knightly sword.

German broadsword, *c.*1550

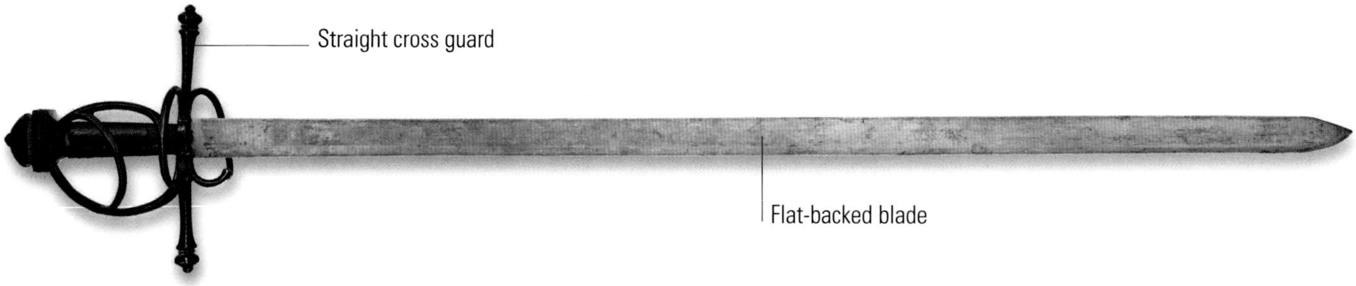

These German fighting swords were extremely common during the 16th century and were carried throughout Europe. The sweeping hilt bars and straight cross guard are reminiscent of contemporary rapiers but differ in having a flattened pommel (as opposed to the traditionally ovoid rapier pommel) and a wide, broadsword blade.

DATE	*c.*1550
ORIGIN	GERMAN
LENGTH	108.5cm (42.7in)

German Dussäge or Sinclair sabre, *c.*1580

DATE	*c.*1580
ORIGIN	GERMAN
LENGTH	101.9cm (40.1in)

This sword derives its Scottish name from an incorrect association by Victorian collectors with Colonel George Sinclair, the leader of a group of Scottish mercenaries, who led a doomed military expedition to Sweden in 1612. It was falsely believed the swords were brought to Sweden from Scotland by Sinclair's men. Supplies of this sword type were actually sent into Norway by Christian IV of Denmark (1577–1648).

German clamshell sabre, *c.*1600

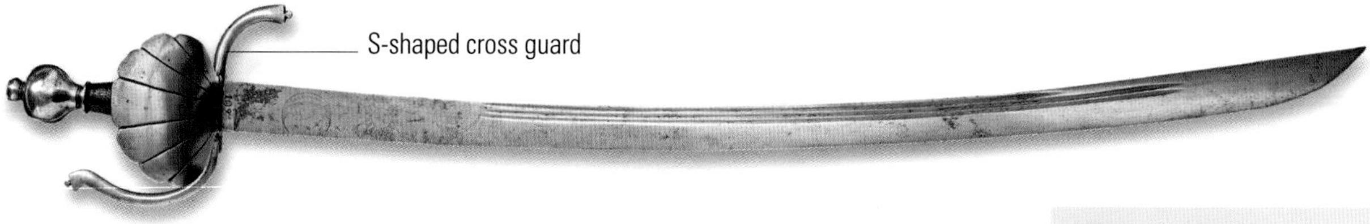

Of simple yet well-constructed manufacture, these robustly made broadswords have a large clamshell guard and S-shaped cross guard. Their weight would have made them an effective slashing sword, if wielded at speed and on horseback.

DATE	*c.*1600
ORIGIN	GERMAN
LENGTH	78.7cm (31in)

German sabre, *c.*1600

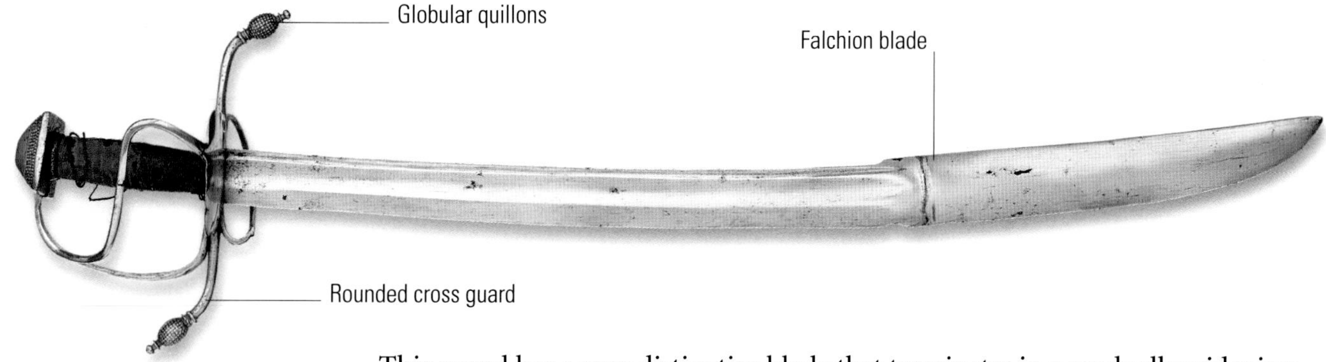

DATE	*c.*1600
ORIGIN	GERMAN
LENGTH	83.8cm (33in)

This sword has a very distinctive blade that terminates in a gradually widening, double-edged, stepped back. It is of falchion shape, with a wide fuller running down the middle of the blade. The pommel has a squared base with a domed top. The sword was probably carried by an infantry soldier. The very long recurved quillons branch out from the cross-guard and terminate in a globular shape.

Italian/Spanish broadsword, *c.*1600

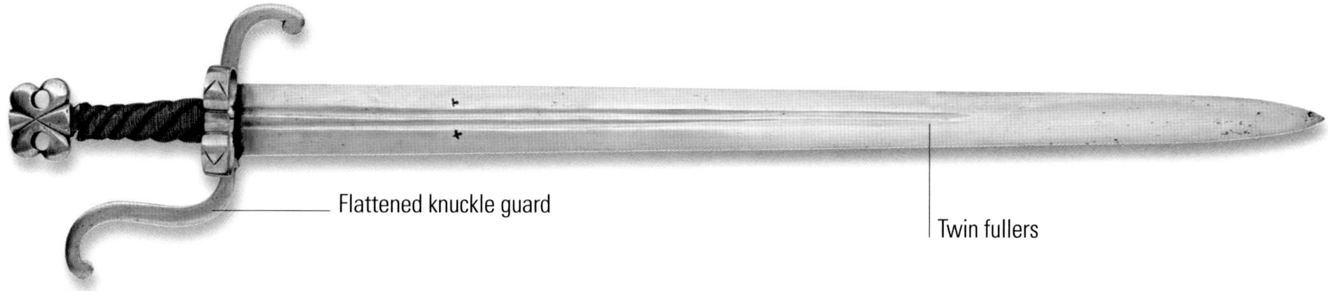

DATE	*c.*1600
ORIGIN	ITALIAN/SPANISH
LENGTH	82.5cm (32.5in)

The requirement for adequate hand protection was evidently not regarded as a priority in the manufacture of this sword and it is likely that it would have been carried by a soldier wearing full armour, particularly gauntlets. The pommel and ringed cross guard have simple, cut-steel decoration. The blade is wide, with twin fullers running down the centre of the blade and is double-edged.

German "crab claw" broadsword, *c.*1620

DATE	*c.*1620
ORIGIN	GERMAN
LENGTH	94cm (37in)

The addition of extra "crab claws" to the hilt guard of this sword makes it an interesting piece. The purpose of these down-curving quillons was to parry or trap an opponent's blade. The long, thrusting blade indicates that it was probably carried by a mounted soldier.

Italian "crab claw" broadsword, *c.*1620

This sword is another variation of the "crab claw" hilted broadsword and features an enclosed, solid hilt. This is quite unusual as sword hilts of this period tended to be open, with an exposed knuckle guard and widely spaced hilt bars. The hilt would have given far more protection to the sword hand and is a precursor of much later sword types.

DATE	*c.*1620
ORIGIN	ITALIAN
LENGTH	92cm (36.2in)

English cavalry broadsword, *c.*1620

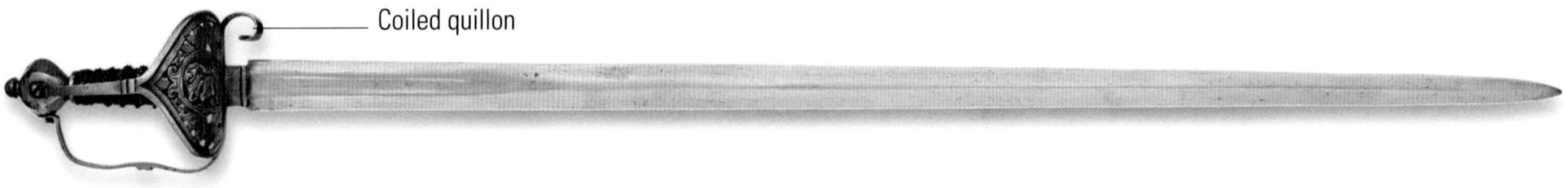

The emphasis of this sword is very much on the blade. Of considerable length and width, it would have been carried by a heavily armoured horseman or cuirassier. The user would need a strong arm to wield this sword. If used correctly, a weapon of these proportions could sever limbs with ease.

DATE	*c.*1620
ORIGIN	ENGLISH
LENGTH	101.8cm (40.1in)

Italian broadsword, *c.*1620

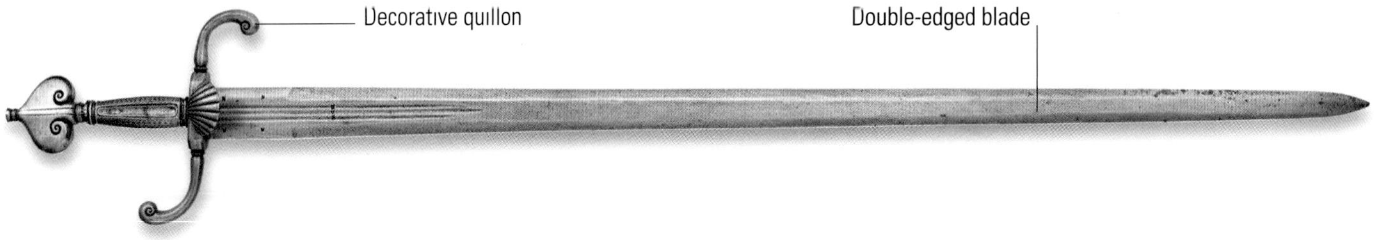

The hilt and blade style of this sword is reminiscent of medieval sword types. There are some subtle differences though, including the Renaissance-inspired classical styling to the cross guard and pommel. The small, clamshell guard is the only indicator that we are looking at a sword of the 17th century.

DATE	*c.*1620
ORIGIN	ITALIAN
LENGTH	102.1cm (40.2in)

Swiss cavalry broadsword, *c.*1620

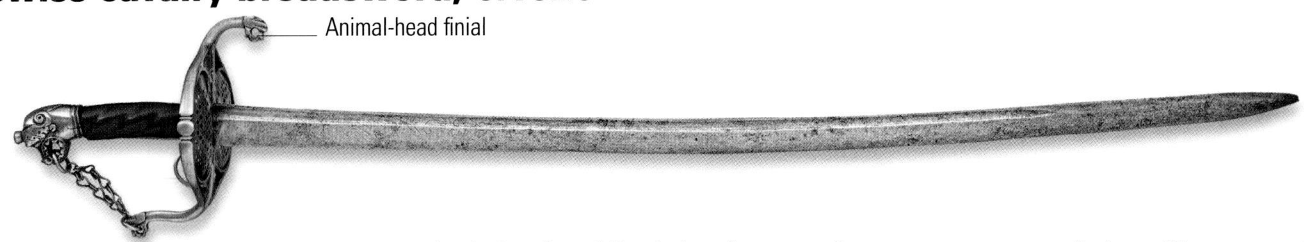

DATE	*c.*1620
ORIGIN	SWISS
LENGTH	93.7cm (36.9in)

Brass dog's-head and lion's-head pommels were common on Swiss military swords of the 17th and 18th centuries. Embossed (or raised) panels were also inserted into the hilt guards. This example has a loose chain knuckle guard in place of the normally rigid bar, a rather impractical form of defence for this military sword.

German cavalry broadsword, *c.*1640

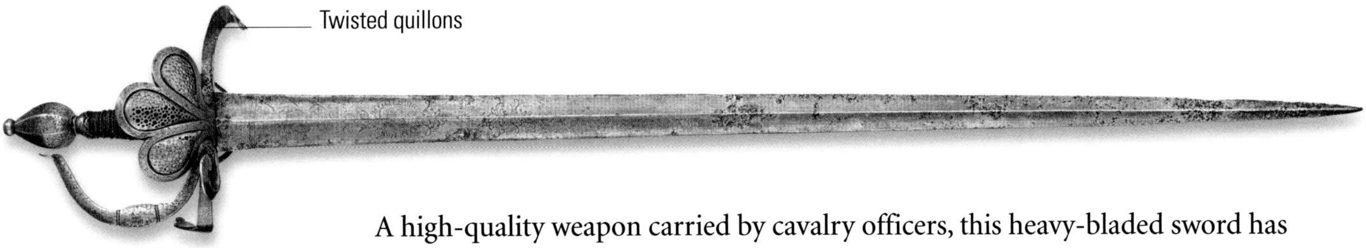

DATE	*c.*1640
ORIGIN	GERMAN
LENGTH	111.8cm (44in)

A high-quality weapon carried by cavalry officers, this heavy-bladed sword has a simple elegance that is characteristic of many swords of this period. It is also a transitional piece, combining the sweeping beauty of the declining rapier hilt with the new pierced and scalloped guard that had become a fashionable design feature on swords of the mid-17th century.

German broadsword, *c.*1640

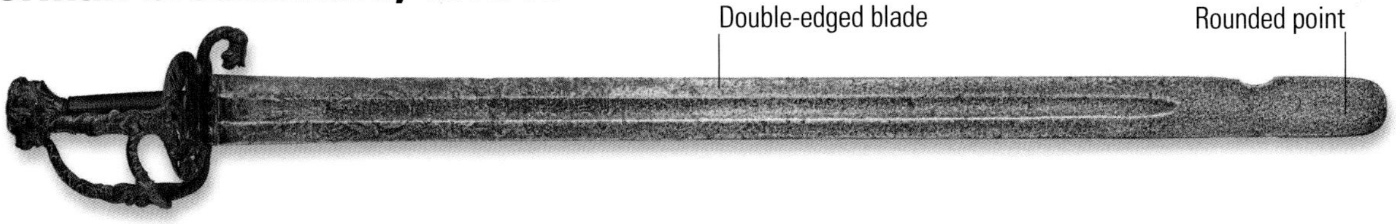

DATE	*c.*1640
ORIGIN	GERMAN
LENGTH	101.8cm (40.1in)

This is a sword of large proportions. The rounded point at the end of a huge, double-edged blade gives us a clue that it was possibly once used as an executioner's sword, although it might not have started out as one. Executioners' swords, particularly German examples, tend to have a simple cruciform hilt.

German cavalry officer's broadsword, *c.*1690

DATE	*c.*1690
ORIGIN	GERMAN
LENGTH	98cm (38.6in)

This is a superb example of the sword maker's art. The name "Clemens" is found on the blade. He was a highly regarded German sword maker of the 17th century and his name was extensively copied on sword blades of the period. A blade of this quality is most definitely a Clemens original.

Cavalry lances

The cavalry lance was a popular weapon of the medieval mounted soldier and was used throughout Europe for many hundreds of years. It had fallen out of favour by the time of the Renaissance but was adopted again in the Napoleonic Wars (1799–1815), when the Imperial French Army established an elite regiment of Polish lancers. By the 1800s, most European nations had established regiments of lancers.

European lance head, *c.*1400

The war lance comprised a solid wooden shaft (usually made of ash, though cedar and poplar were also used), and the lance head was similar in shape to that of a spear.

DATE	*c.*1400
ORIGIN	EUROPEAN
LENGTH	15cm (5.9in)

British cavalry lance, 1840 Pattern

DATE	1840
ORIGIN	BRITISH
LENGTH	277cm (109in)

The long, riveted steel langets of this lance had a two-fold purpose. They secured the lance head to the shaft but were also effective at parrying sword blows. The lance head is larger than earlier patterns and more fluted.

British cavalry lance, 1846 Pattern

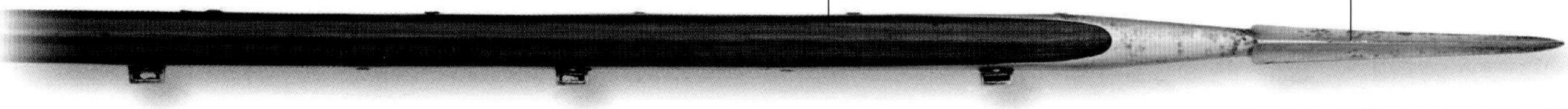

This lance has a thin, fluted head and was attached to the wooden shaft by means of two long, riveted langets. The thin profile of the lance head would have eased penetration. The shaft was normally manufactured in ash.

DATE	1846
ORIGIN	BRITISH
LENGTH	119.7cm (47.1in) head and langets only

British cavalry lance, 1846 Pattern

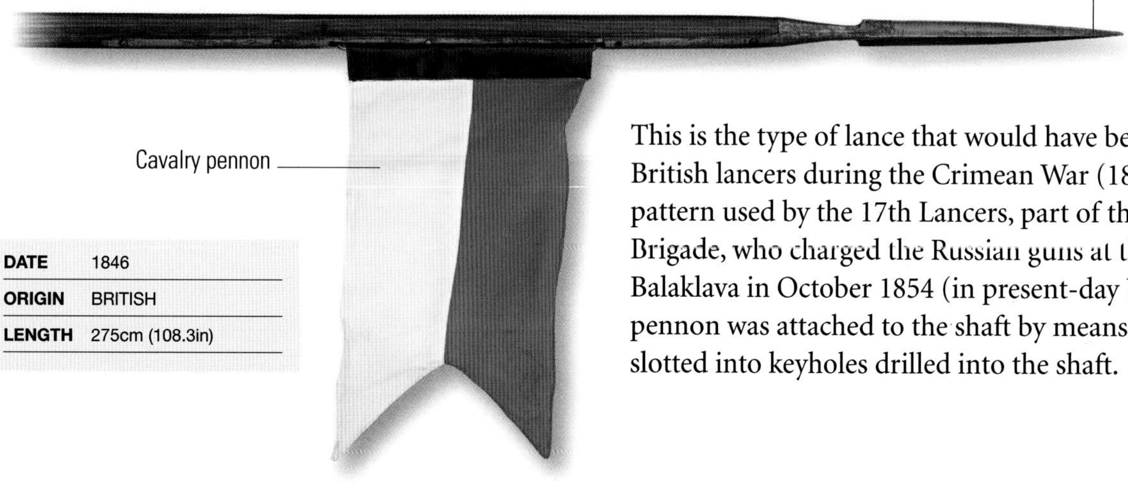

DATE	1846
ORIGIN	BRITISH
LENGTH	275cm (108.3in)

This is the type of lance that would have been carried by British lancers during the Crimean War (1853–56). It was a pattern used by the 17th Lancers, part of the ill-fated Light Brigade, who charged the Russian guns at the Battle of Balaklava in October 1854 (in present-day Ukraine). The pennon was attached to the shaft by means of studs that slotted into keyholes drilled into the shaft.

British cavalry lance, 1868 Pattern

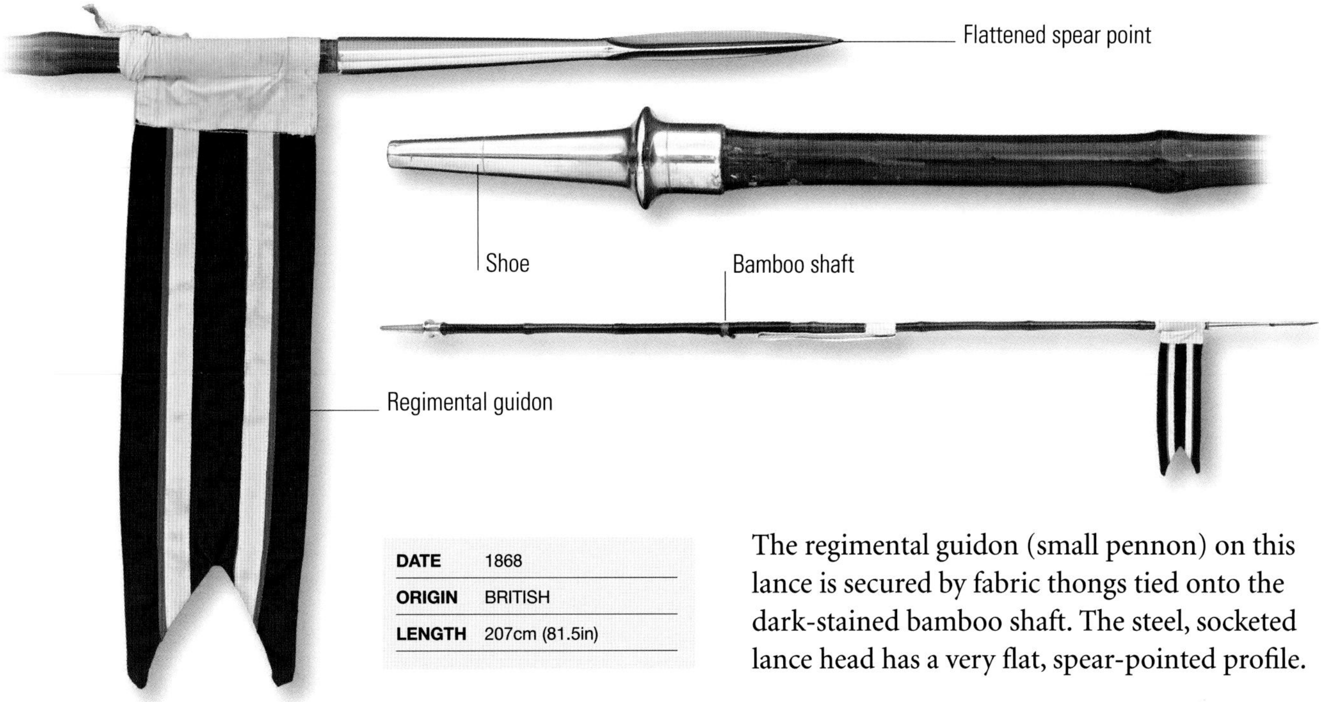

DATE	1868
ORIGIN	BRITISH
LENGTH	207cm (81.5in)

The regimental guidon (small pennon) on this lance is secured by fabric thongs tied onto the dark-stained bamboo shaft. The steel, socketed lance head has a very flat, spear-pointed profile.

British cavalry lance, 1885 Pattern

The swallow-tail design of this lance pennon indicates that it is the last pattern of British cavalry lance. Pennon design changed between patterns and this particular design was carried through to the eventual withdrawal of lances from the British Army in the 1920s. Although it might be assumed that pennons were unfurled in battle, it was normal practice for them to be rolled up when on active service. The unravelled pennon was most commonly seen during parades.

DATE	1885
ORIGIN	BRITISH
LENGTH	275cm (108.3in)

British practice cavalry lance, *c.*1890

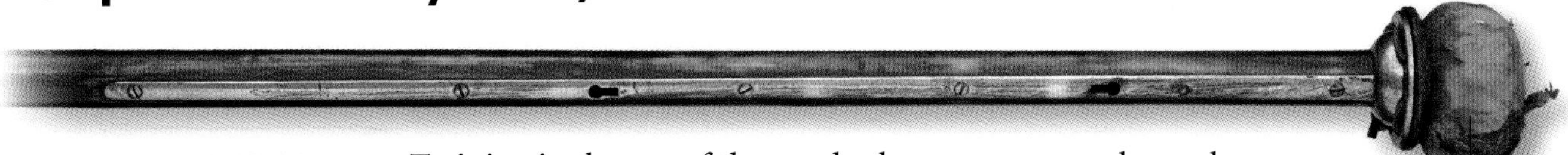

DATE	c.1890
ORIGIN	BRITISH
LENGTH	277cm (109in)

Training in the use of the cavalry lance was a complex and time-consuming process, and involved instruction in how to hold the lance correctly and lunge with accuracy while mounted on a charging horse.

Military and tournament lances

The spectacle of a massed group of heavily armoured mounted knights, long lances couched under their arms, galloping towards a line of infantry, would have been an awe-inspiring sight. There would have been no defence against them if the opposing archers had failed to stop their advance. Outside of war, the jousting tournament was another opportunity to improve a knight's prowess with sword and lance.

English carousel lance, *c.*1600

By the 17th century, the lance as a weapon was restricted to the jousting field, with more emphasis on the exhibition of a knight's equestrian skills. This example is typical of a design carried for over 300 years. It is constructed from solid hardwood, although some lances were hollow to allow easier splintering.

DATE	*c.*1600
ORIGIN	ENGLISH
LENGTH	363.7cm (143.2in)

Italian lance head for jousting, *c.*1600

The aim of jousting was not to kill an opponent but to unhorse him or shatter his lance. To do this in relative safety, lances had to be fitted with a blunt end, or head. The weight and momentum of the charge could nevertheless still cause serious injury and occasionally death.

DATE	*c.*1600
ORIGIN	ITALIAN
LENGTH	12.7cm (5in)

Jousting knights

By the end of the 13th century, a Statute of Arms for Tournaments had been established to provide a series of rules and guidance for knights participating in jousts. Under the statute, knights were considered to be gentlemen and required to abide by the ideals of chivalry, including fair play and honour. Jousting tournaments became organized events and the introduction of blunted weapons massively reduced fatalities. If a knight was killed at the joust, it was not only deeply unfortunate but also considered to be dishonourable. Ironically, if a knight killed a horse, the public ire was even greater.

The main object of a knight participating in the joust was to unhorse as many fellow knights as possible and, crucially, to break the highest number of lances. If he could do this without injury or death, the audience would regard him as displaying great skill with the lance and excellent horsemanship.

ABOVE Medieval jousting knights, *c.*1445. Note the limited vision available when wearing a closed helm (helmet).

English jousting or carousel lance, *c.*1600

DATE	*c.*1600
ORIGIN	ENGLISH
LENGTH	363.7cm (143.2in)

By the beginning of the 17th century, interest in the combative side of the joust had waned and an alternative form of equestrian entertainment was developed. This was the carousel (from the Italian *garosello* and the Spanish *carosella*, meaning "little war"). The lance was used in such games as "catching the ring", which involved lancing a swinging dummy or small rings suspended from a revolving apparatus. Later, brightly painted wooden horses and mounted figures were added as targets and this became the precursor to today's carousel rides.

European fluted cavalry lance, *c.*1620

DATE	*c.*1620
ORIGIN	EUROPEAN
LENGTH	353.8cm (139.3in)

The military lance was not a common battlefield weapon in the 17th century. This example is similar to later lances, especially with regard to the long, riveted langets, but it still retains the earlier, medieval, rounded hand grip. The massed ranks of infantrymen armed with pikes and other polearms would have made it difficult to use this lance with any great effect.

English jousting lance, *c.*1850

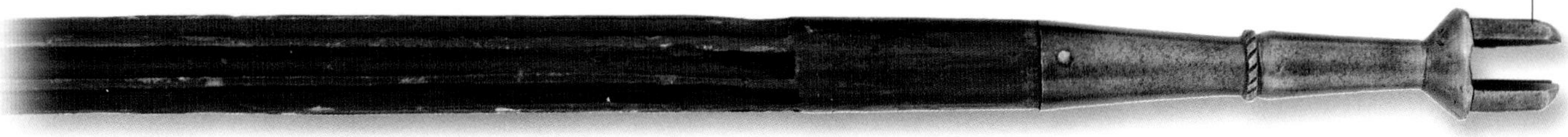

DATE	*c.*1850
ORIGIN	ENGLISH
LENGTH	353.8cm (139.3in)

A medieval revival in Britain during the early 1800s, boosted by the popular romantic novels of Sir Walter Scott (1771–1832), encouraged the restaging of many jousting tournaments. This lance has a two-pronged head (the coronal) and was designed to catch on an opponent's shield and then hold it fast, making it much easier to unhorse him. The wooden shaft is probably hollow, as this would make it shatter more easily.

17th- to 19th-century cavalry swords

The cavalry swords of the 17th to 19th centuries were designed to inflict maximum injury on their victims. They were wide-bladed, with either straight or curved double- and single-edged blades. Their great length would enable a galloping horseman to reach down and strike with devastating ease.

German cavalry officer's dress sword, 1697

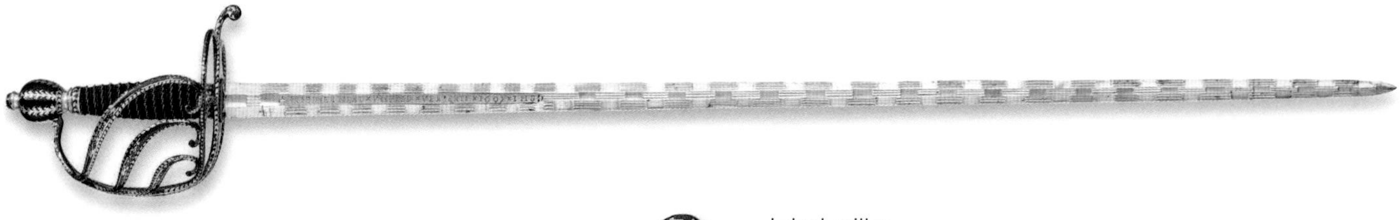

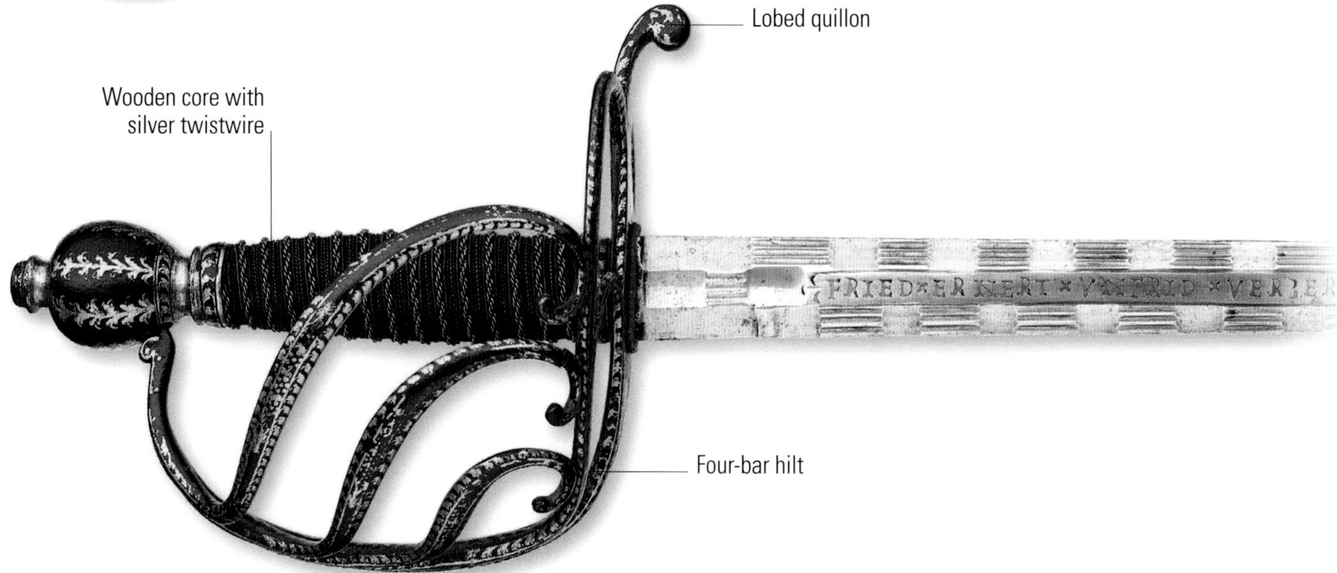

Although the blade of this fine-quality cavalry officer's sword is definitely German in manufacture, the hilt is possibly English. In many cases, sword blades were purchased directly from Germany and then attached to a hilt in a separate country. German blades were highly prized throughout Europe during this period. The four-bar hilt of this sword is finely decorated in silver inlay and the hilt has been deliberately blackened to highlight the silver. The blade is double-edged and comprises a series of cut-steel, chiselled niches that are purely decorative in nature. It is likely that it would have been carried in a leather scabbard with blackened steel or silver mounts.

DATE	1697
ORIGIN	GERMAN
LENGTH	96.5cm (38in)

French cavalry trooper's sword (Swedish style), *c.*1700

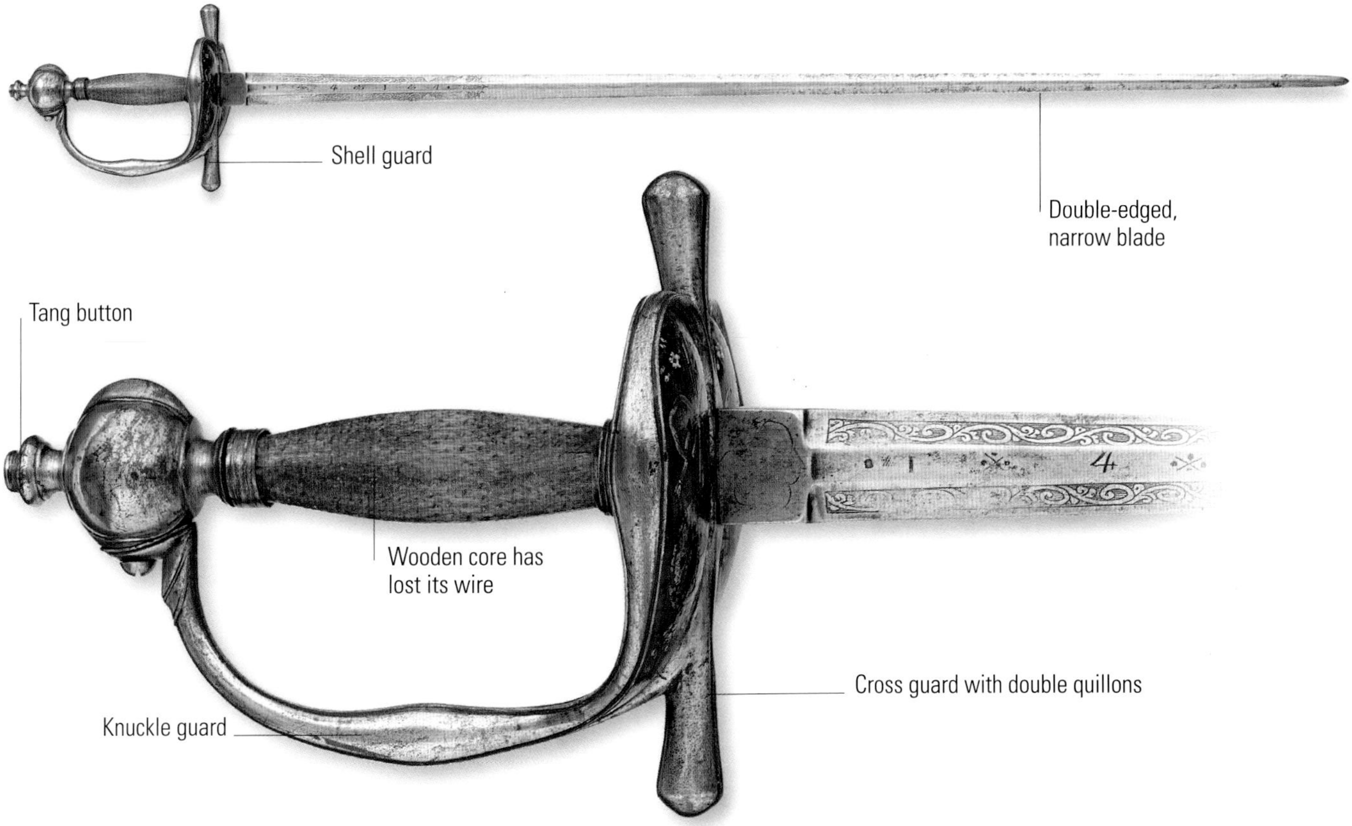

DATE	*c.*1700
ORIGIN	SWEDISH
LENGTH	111.5cm (43.9in)

This sword has an open hilt that would have left the swordsman's hand quite exposed. Sweden was one of the first nations in Europe to begin standardizing swords into specific patterns during the 17th century. The shell guards on this sword still have the distinctive piercings that are reminiscent of earlier, mid-17th century "Walloon" broadswords and indicate that this particular sword is a transitional piece. The hilt style is more in keeping with the new smallswords that were just beginning to become popular at this time.

British cavalry officer's sword, *c.*1740

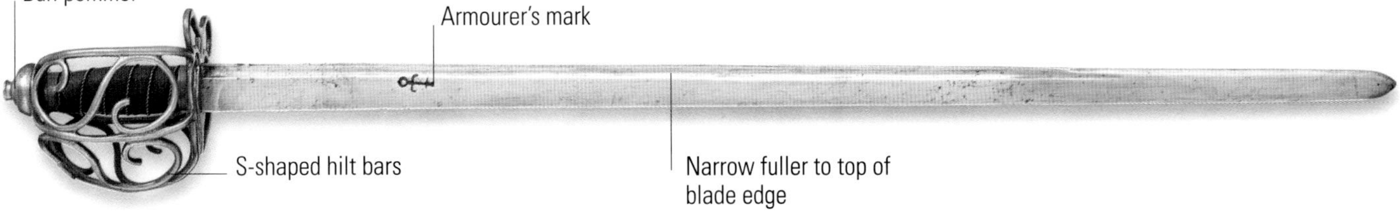

DATE	*c.*1740
ORIGIN	BRITISH
LENGTH	87.6cm (34.5in)

This is a type of broadsword carried by British heavy dragoon officers during the Battle of Culloden in 1746. It has a substantial, single-edged backsword blade that would have been effective at hacking and slashing while on horseback. The guard has decorative, S-shaped hilt bars and a large bun-shaped pommel.

Austrian cavalry officer's sword, 1745

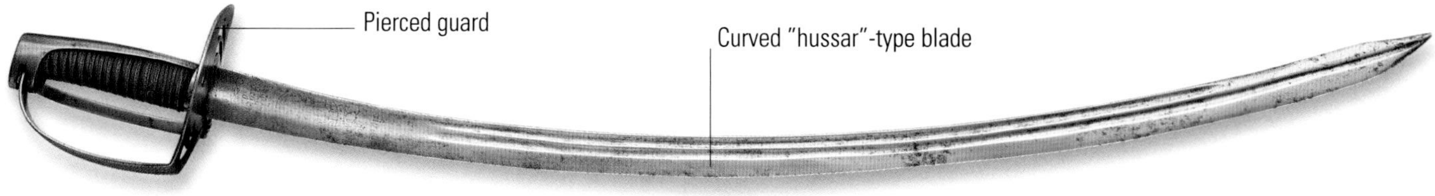

Many cavalry swords of this period tend to have long, straight blades, but this example features a curved, double-fullered blade that ends in a distinctive spear point. It has a folding attack hilt that pivots by means of a hinge underneath the hilt plate. Curved blades were popular with hussar regiments.

DATE	1745
ORIGIN	AUSTRIAN
LENGTH	90.2cm (35.5in)

French cavalry sword, *c.*1750

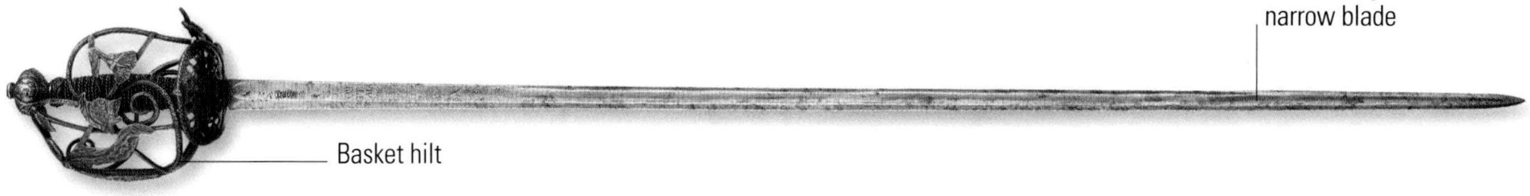

This rather unique and unusual cavalry officer's sword has an intricate multi-bar hilt with a pierced dish guard. The extremely long, double-edged blade has a pronounced point that would have been used as a kind of short, thrusting lance.

DATE	*c.*1750
ORIGIN	FRENCH
LENGTH	118.1cm (46.5in)

Russian cavalry trooper's sword, *c.*1750

Carried by Imperial Russian dragoons from the mid-18th century, this impressive sword has a brass hilt and bird's-head pommel. This hilt guard comprises a number of intersecting brass bars. Blades of this period are normally engraved with the monogram of the Empress Elizaveta Petrovna ("EPI"), also known as the Empress Elizabeth (1709–62).

DATE	*c.*1750
ORIGIN	RUSSIAN
LENGTH	104.9cm (41.3in)

French cavalry trooper's sword, "à la Suédoise", *c.*1770

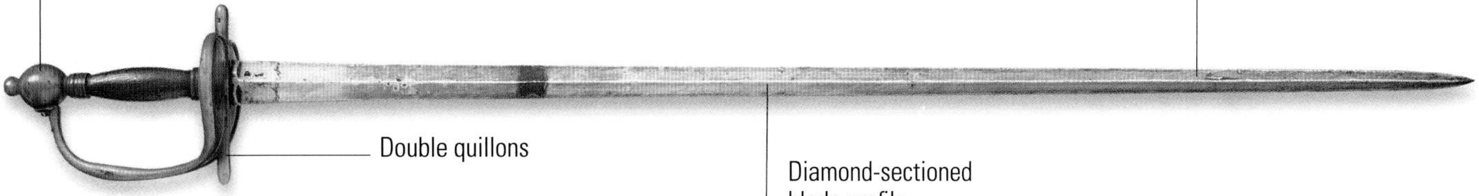

DATE	*c.*1770
ORIGIN	FRENCH
LENGTH	109.2cm (43in)

Based on the hilt styles of contemporary Swedish cavalry swords, this French version has a brass hilt, with ovoid pommel, double quillons and a solid hilt plate. The blade is double-edged, with a slightly diamond-sectioned profile. The grip is wooden but would originally have had a twistwire binding. The open hilt would provide little protection to the sword hand and an opponent could easily disable his enemy by making a cut towards his hand.

Danish heavy cavalry trooper's sword, Model 1774

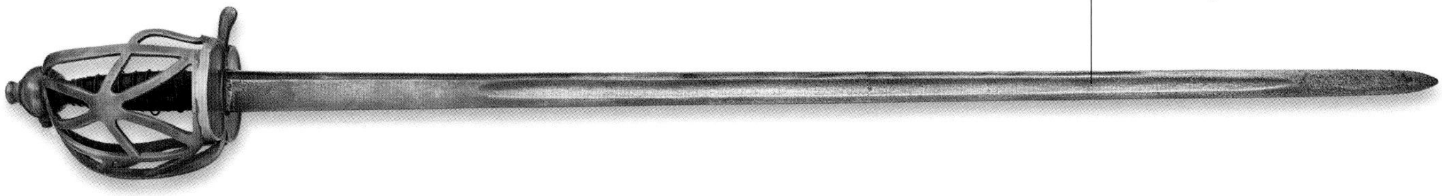

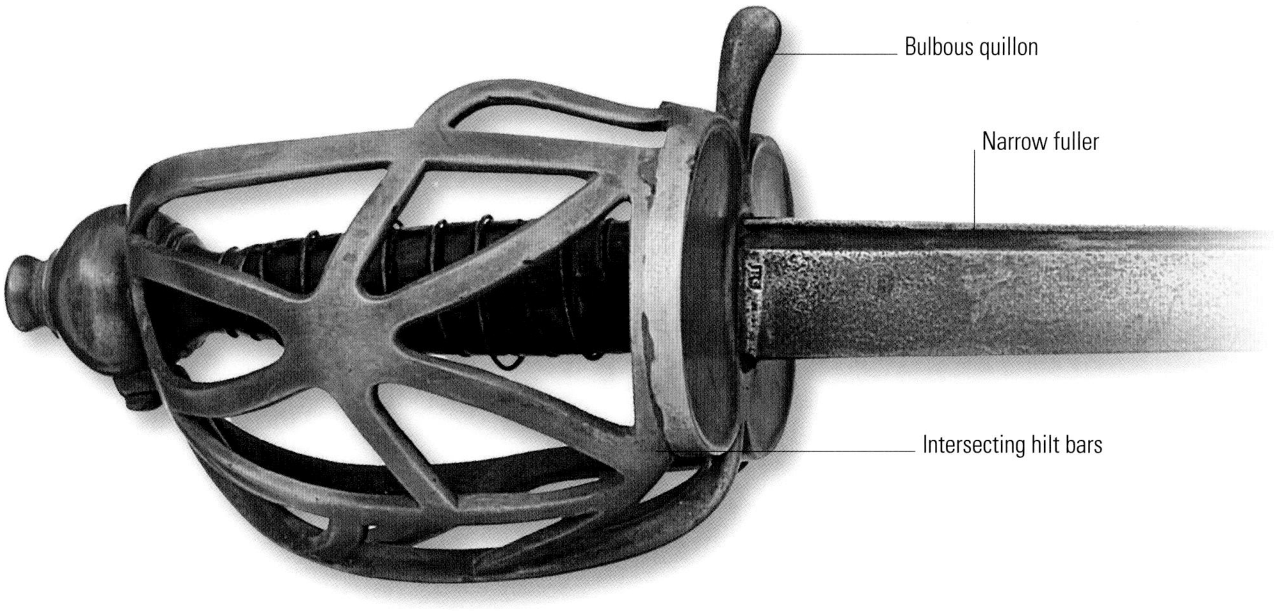

DATE	1774
ORIGIN	DANISH
LENGTH	117.3cm (46.2in)

This large broadsword has a single-fullered, double-edged blade (towards the point) and would have been most effective as both a thrusting and a slashing weapon. The large brass basket hilt incorporates a series of intertwined bars with a thick and solid hilt plate at its base. During this period, a number of Scandinavian and North European armies adopted these heavy basket-hilted broadswords. They were popular within Cuirassier regiments.

French cavalry officer's sword, *c.*1780

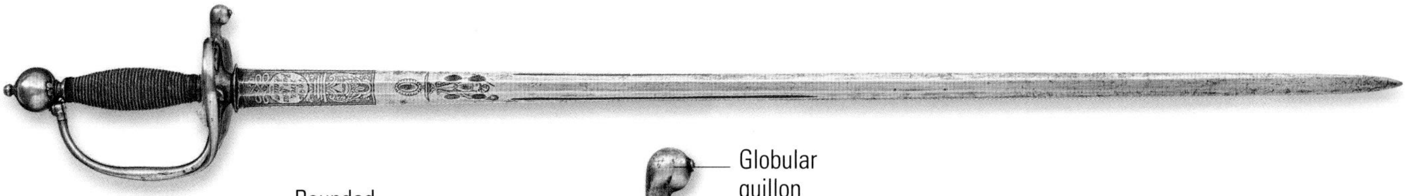

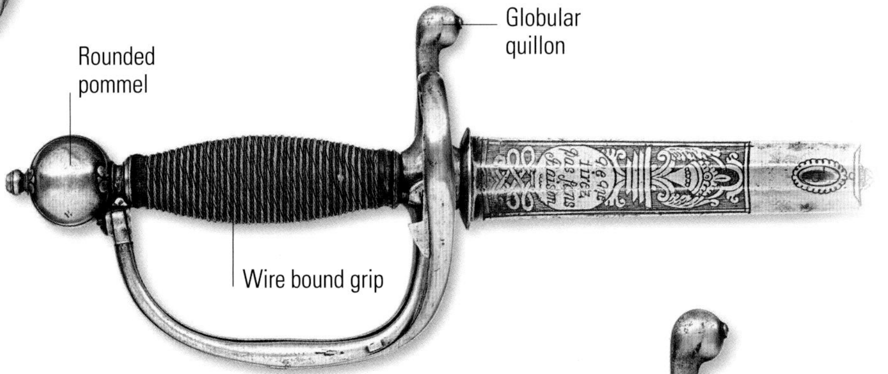

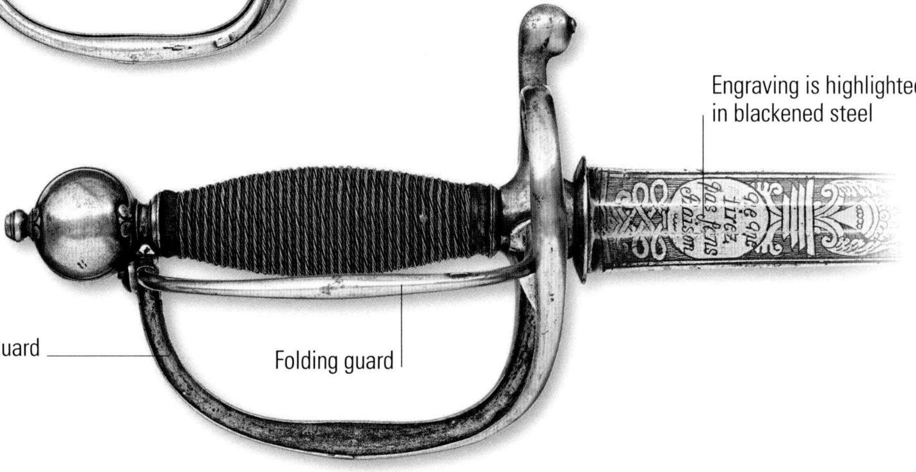

This is an interesting early example of a so-called folding "attack hilt". Introduced during the 18th century, it comprises a traditional one- or two-bar hilt with an additional bar that could be opened out for use in combat and then retracted afterwards. The relative thinness of this folding guard would not have made an enormous difference to hand protection.

DATE	*c.*1780
ORIGIN	FRENCH
LENGTH	102.8cm (40.5in)

British light cavalry officer's sword, 1788 Pattern

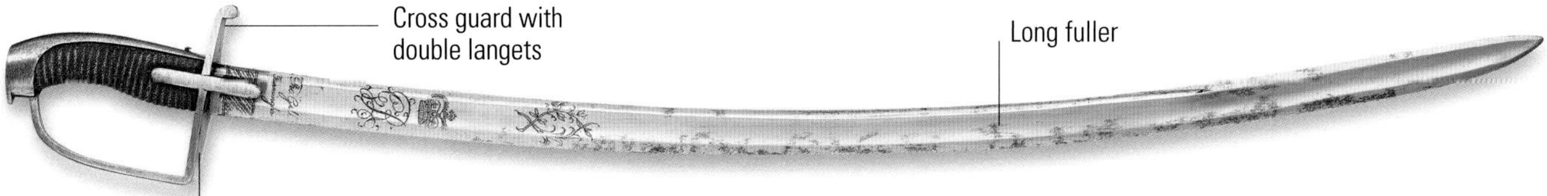

The British Army introduced this light cavalry sword at a time when there was great debate within the army as to whether a curved or straight-bladed sword was the most effective cutting weapon. It was decided that heavy cavalry regiments would continue to carry a straight-bladed sword but light cavalry regiments were issued with this new sword. Its design was based on Austrian and German "hussar" swords that had been carried since the early 18th century. It features a stirrup-shaped hilt with flattened pommel and distinctive double langets. The sword was very effective at close-quarter slashing and cutting.

DATE	1788
ORIGIN	BRITISH
LENGTH	102.8cm (40.5in)

French dragoon trooper's sword, *c.*1790

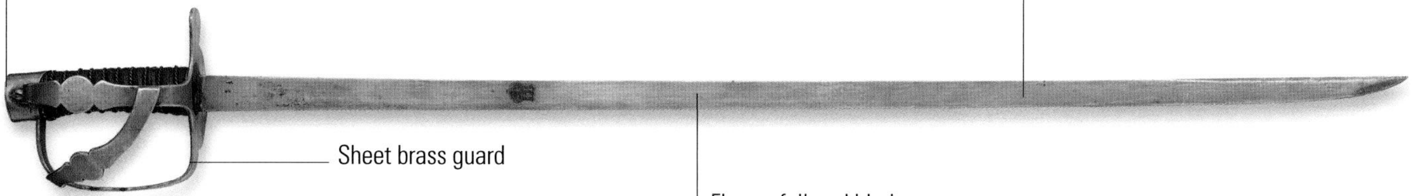

DATE	*c.*1790
ORIGIN	FRENCH
LENGTH	108cm (42.5in)

This sword was carried by mounted *chasseurs* (meaning "hunters"), light cavalry soldiers who were engaged in various roles, primarily as skirmishers and shock troops. The blade is straight, single-edged and would have been most effective at thrusting. The hilt is brass and typical of swords carried by French cavalry at the time of the French Revolution (1789–99) and during the early years of the Napoleonic Wars (1799–1815).

British heavy cavalry officer's sword, 1796 Pattern (undress)

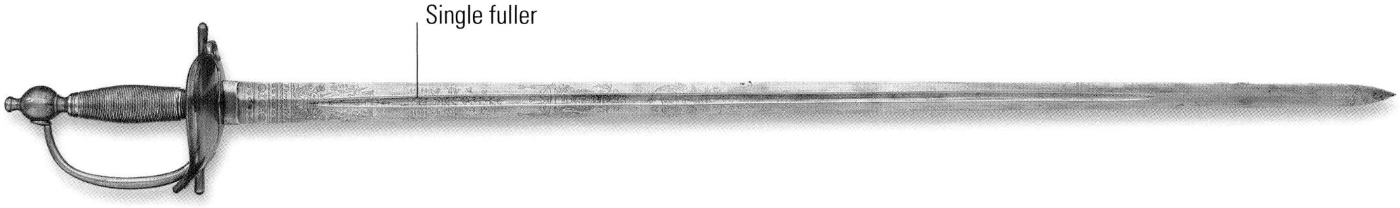

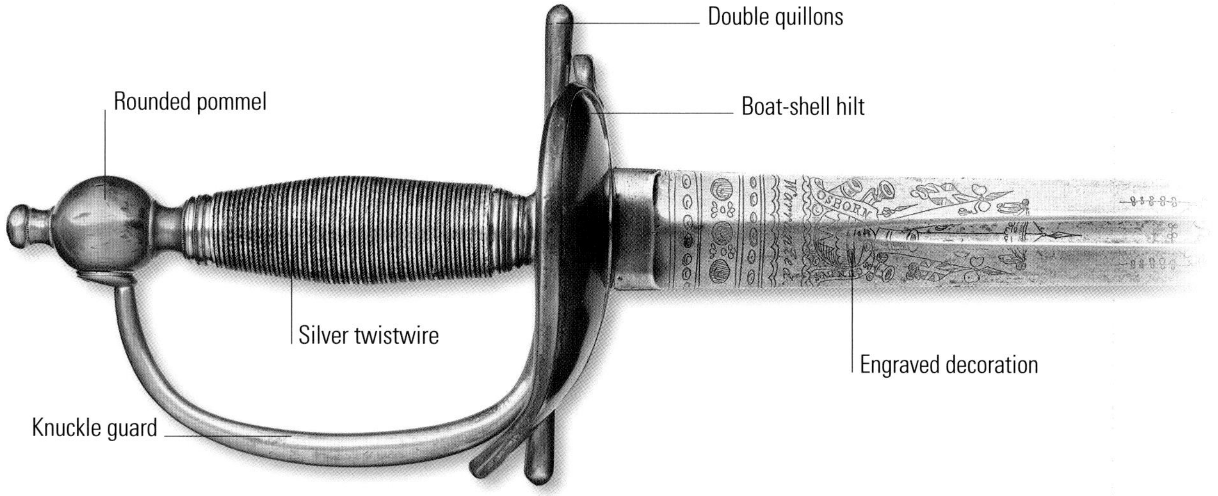

DATE	1796
ORIGIN	BRITISH
LENGTH	101.8cm (40.1in)

This elegant sword would have been worn for more formal dress occasions, including regimental parades and social functions. The hilt is of boat-shell type, with a solid, upwardly curving shell guard and double quillons. The knuckle guard is secured to the pommel by means of a screw. Many blades were left plain but in this case there is extensive engraving of military trophies and decorative foliage. While in the field, heavy cavalry officers would have carried a much more sturdy sword with a wide, cutting blade and basket-type hilt. This sword can be found with either a leather or a steel scabbard.

British Royal Horseguards trooper's sword, *c.*1796

The Royal Horseguards was an elite cavalry regiment established in 1650 by Oliver Cromwell (1599–1658). Their primary function was to protect the reigning monarch, although they were also present at many of the most famous battles of the British Army. The regiment adopted their own sword designs and this weapon was a variation of the 1796 Heavy Cavalry Trooper's Sword. It differed in having an open guard, with a "star" pattern to the underside of the hilt. Hilt bars branch out and meet to form one thick knuckle guard that enters the pommel. The wide blade is single-edged with a hatchet point.

DATE	*c.*1796
ORIGIN	BRITISH
LENGTH	102.3cm (40.3in)

Danish mounted infantryman's sword, Royal Guards Model 1799

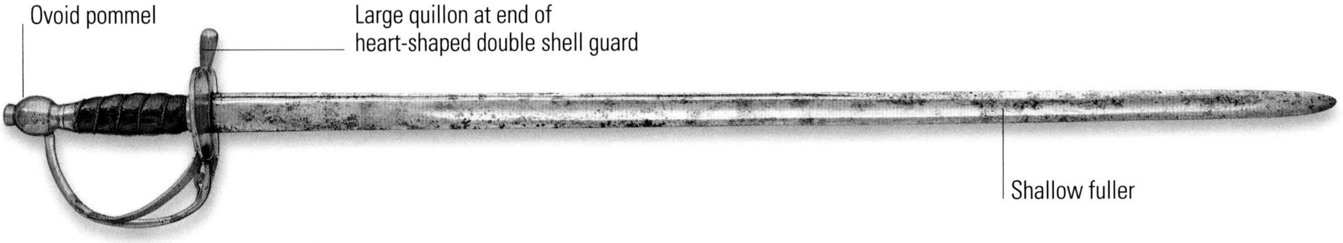

The Danish Royal Guards regiment is one of the oldest guards regiments in Europe (established in 1658 by King Frederick III, 1609–70). Although ostensibly an infantry regiment, some infantry had mounted duties. The blade has a shallow fuller that begins around a third of the way down from the ricasso and is complemented by another narrow fuller that runs just below the top edge of the blade. The hilt is simple in design, with two side branches that emerge from the hilt plate and join the knuckle guard.

DATE	1799
ORIGIN	DANISH
LENGTH	107.3cm (42.2in)

Spanish cavalry trooper's sword, Model 1799

Spanish cavalry forces carried the traditional and rather archaic cup-hilt rapier ("Bilbo") until the end of the 18th century and this model was quite a departure from previous Spanish sword types. The hilt and blade style is similar to other European swords of the period (particularly French). The hilt has a pronounced bowl guard, with three hilt bars leading to the domed pommel. The blade is unfullered and has a raised strengthening ridge that forms the ricasso. Grips were covered in leather and would not have been bound.

DATE	1799
ORIGIN	SPANISH
LENGTH	106.9cm (42.1in)

Spanish heavy cavalry officer's sword, *c.*1800

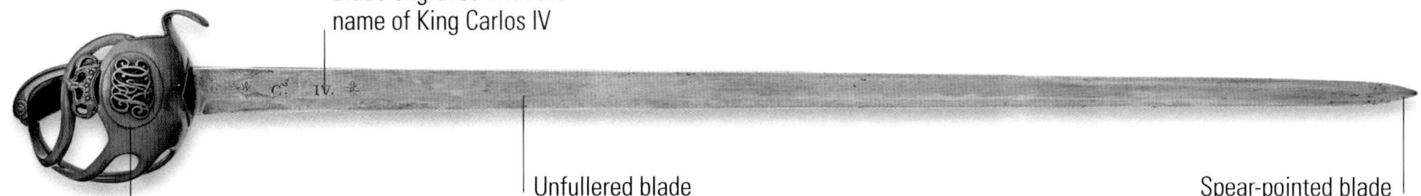

DATE	*c.*1800
ORIGIN	SPANISH
LENGTH	98.2cm (38.7in)

This is a more elaborate version of the Model 1799 Cavalry Trooper's Sword and incorporates the Spanish royal crown and cypher inserted into the brass hilt. The flat-backed, double-edged blade is also engraved with the initials of King Carlos IV of Spain (1748–1819). The enclosed half-basket hilt would have provided a reasonable amount of protection for the hand.

Spanish cavalry trooper's sword, Model 1825

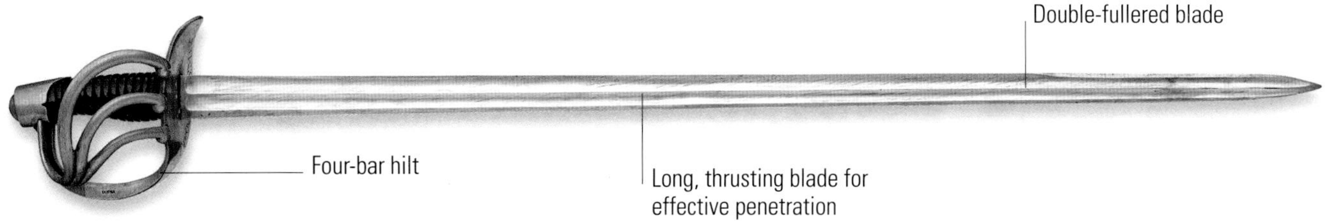

DATE	1825
ORIGIN	SPANISH
LENGTH	109.2cm (43in)

This sword is very similar to French Napoleonic heavy cavalry swords and it is likely that the Spanish Army simply copied the design. It has a brass, four-bar hilt and a slightly canted, or angled, pommel. The blade is double-fullered and was carried in a heavy, iron scabbard. When used in the charge, the sword would have been held in an outstretched position and used as a type of short lance. The grip has a wooden core wrapped in leather and brass twistwire.

German cavalry trooper's sword, Model 1852

DATE	1852
ORIGIN	GERMAN
LENGTH	64cm (25.2in)

A cage-like hilt is the distinctive feature of this sword and would have provided a certain amount of protection for the sword hand, although the gaps between the hilt bars could still allow the penetration of a well-directed sword point. There is also a leather thumb strap within the hilt that allowed the trooper to grip the sword more effectively, especially when at the charge. It would have been contained in a plated steel scabbard.

17th- to 19th-century infantry swords

During this time, the role of the infantry soldier changed and he became more reliant on the musket and socket bayonet as his primary weapons. Despite this, infantrymen still carried swords and popular styles included the short-bladed, brass-hilted hanger. Officers also chose short hangers and smallswords.

English infantry hanger, *c.*1700

The heavy pitting and corrosion on this sword indicate that it was probably excavated. This sword is of a general type that was carried by both infantry troops and even naval seamen (where it would have been used as a cutlass). The short, falchion-type blade was effective at close-quarter fighting, particularly amongst the close rigging of a ship's deck.

DATE	*c.*1700
ORIGIN	ENGLISH
LENGTH	85.7cm (33.7in)

Prussian hanger, *c.*1750

This style of short hanger was popular throughout Europe from the early 18th century. The hilt is cast brass and the blade is single-fullered and double-edged towards the point. Many of these Prussian swords are regimentally marked.

DATE	*c.*1750
ORIGIN	PRUSSIAN
LENGTH	79.3cm (31.2in)

British grenadier's hanger, *c.*1760

There were many hanger types carried by British infantry regiments during the mid-18th century. This sword has a substantial iron hilt that is reminiscent of heavy cavalry (dragoon) swords of this period. The well-enclosed hilt would have provided a good level of protection to the hand.

DATE	*c.*1760
ORIGIN	BRITISH
LENGTH	110.3cm (43.4in)

British infantry private's hanger, *c.*1760

DATE	*c.*1760
ORIGIN	BRITISH
LENGTH	78.2cm (30.8in)

The introduction of brass-hilted infantry hangers to the British Army was probably influenced by contemporary continental designs, particularly German and French hangers. What they all have in common is a heart-shaped dish guard and a cast brass, ribbed grip. The hilt of this example is marked "Lancashire Militia" and the blade is stamped with the initials "SH" (for Samuel Harvey), a noted Birmingham sword maker who manufactured a large number of swords for the British Army.

British infantryman's sword with monster-head pommel, *c.*1760

DATE	*c.*1760
ORIGIN	BRITISH
LENGTH	Unknown

Monster-head or grotesque pommels were common on British military hangers for a brief period during the early to mid-18th century. They were superseded by the traditional lion's-head pommel before the end of the century. The slightly curved blade has a single sharpened edge, with a narrow fuller present at the top of the blade. The brass grip has an unusual simulated rope design. Swords of this hilt type are known to have been carried by grenadier companies.

British infantry officer's sword, *c.*1770

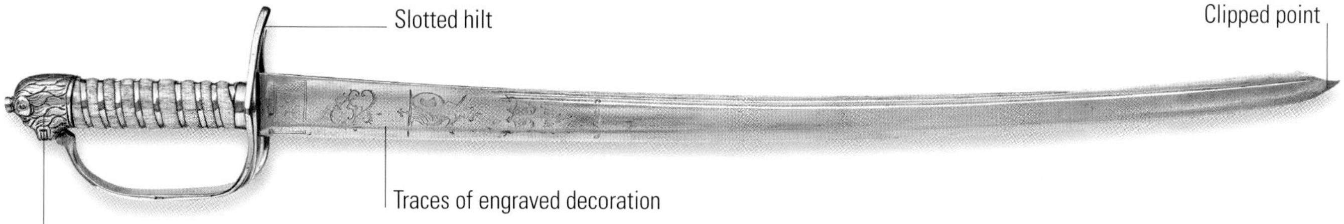

DATE	*c.*1770
ORIGIN	BRITISH
LENGTH	Unknown

The lion's head was a common pommel shape on British officers' infantry hangers during the 18th century, and this sword is a fine example. It has a well crafted, solid brass, "slotted" hilt, comprising a hilt guard split into open geometric, or slotted, sections. The slotted hilt did not have any particular defensive function and was probably more of a decorative statement. The engraved blade is slightly wider than contemporary military hangers and its profile is similar to hunting swords of the period.

British infantry officer's hanger, *c.*1780

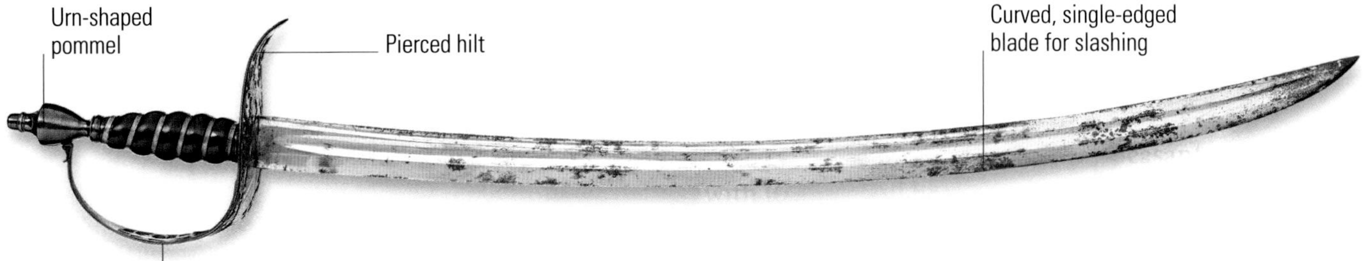

DATE	*c.*1780
ORIGIN	BRITISH
LENGTH	80.3cm (31.6in)

The short, curved sabre was very popular with British infantry officers during the late 18th century. The hilt is pierced with cut-out sections and the grip is carved ebony, bound with silver twistwire. The use of urn-shaped pommels was influenced by the contemporary Neo-classical revival of the decorative arts throughout Europe. The curved, single-edged blade features both wide and narrow fullers or grooves.

British Tower Hamlets volunteer infantry officer's sword, *c.*1803–14

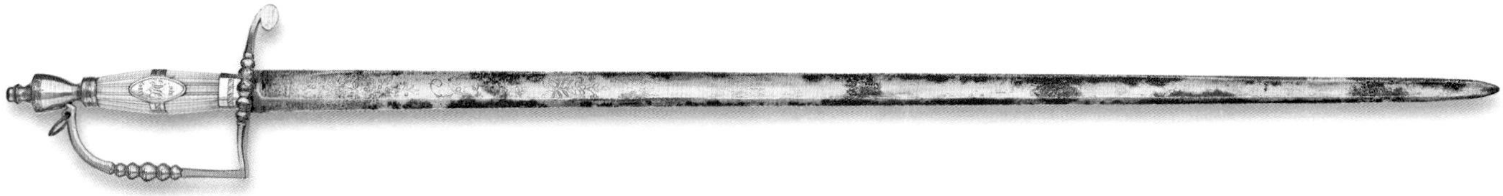

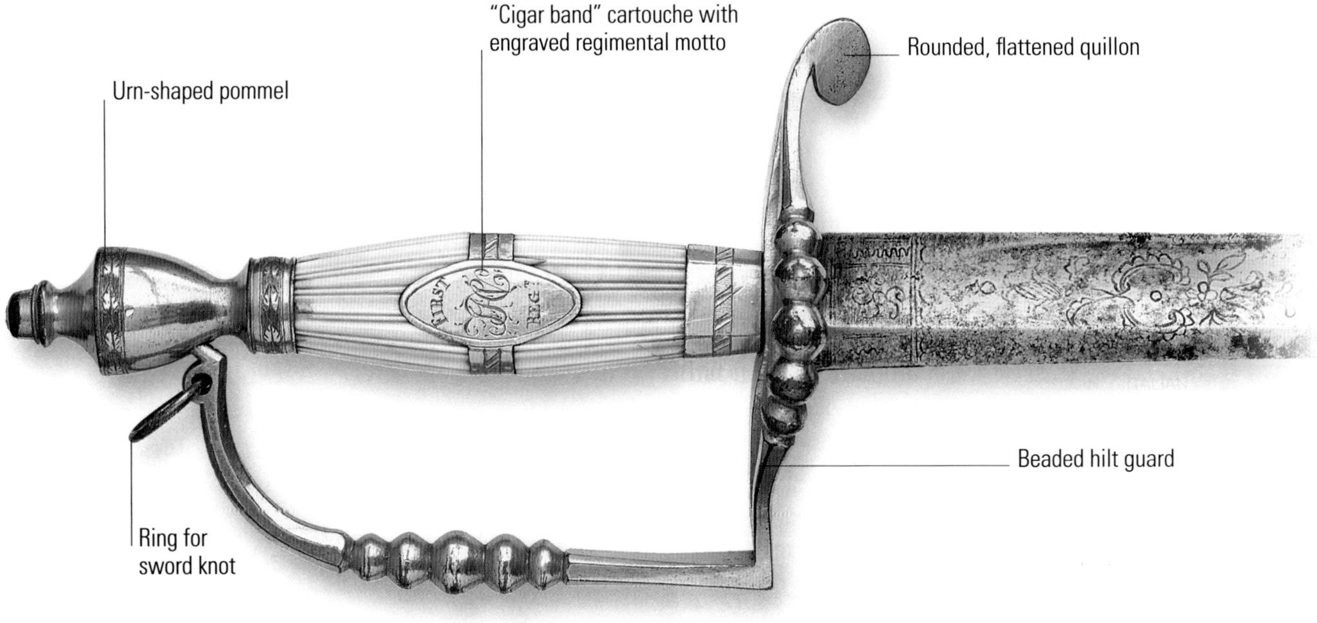

DATE	*c.*1803–14
ORIGIN	BRITISH
LENGTH	97.8cm (38.5in)

The Tower Hamlets Volunteer Militia was one of many volunteer cavalry and infantry units that were raised during the Napoleonic Wars (1799–1815). The primary role of the militia was to protect Britain from an anticipated French invasion. Militia officers would have carried swords identical to those of the regular army. This rare example has a gilt-brass "five-ball" beaded hilt and a ribbed ivory grip with a "cigar band" cartouche wrapped around the centre. A regimental device is engraved onto the band.

British infantry officer, 1812

The British infantry officer did not carry a regulation infantry sword until 1786. Before this, a series of smallswords or hangers were carried into battle and some officers even chose to arm themselves with a short polearm or spontoon. Its fighting capabilities must surely have been dubious and it was used more as a symbol of rank or a signpost to gain attention when the officer was rallying his troops. The spontoon was also issued to senior NCOs.

The 1786 Pattern Infantry Officer's Sword brought in a measure of uniformity with regard to blade and hilt specifications, but it was not until 1796 that a universal design of infantry officer sword became standard within the British Army. And, even then, elite infantry regiments such as the Rifle Corps and some Scottish lowland regiments still chose to wear swords of a completely different design.

RIGHT Officer of the King's Own Scottish Borderers, *c.*1812. He is carrying a sword of mameluke design that became popular after the Egyptian campaigns of 1798–1801.

Batavian Republic infantry officer's sword, *c.*1810

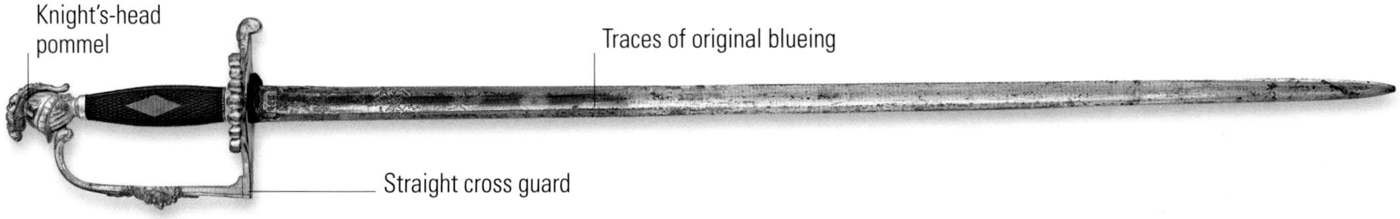

In 1795, William V (1748–1806), the Prince of Orange and the Netherlands, fled to England and a republic was subsequently declared in the Netherlands. Napoleon Bonaparte (1769–1821) invaded the new country and it became a vassal of France until 1806, when he installed his younger brother Louis Napoleon (1778–1846) as King of Holland (1806–10). The hilt style of this sword clearly shows the influence of French sword styling, particularly on the Neo-classical knight's-head pommel that is typically French Napoleonic.

DATE	*c.*1810
ORIGIN	DUTCH
LENGTH	89.7cm (35.3in)

French pioneer or sapper's sword, *c.*1810

DATE	*c.*1810
ORIGIN	FRENCH
LENGTH	81cm (31.9in)

The cast-brass hilt of this particular sword is surmounted by an impressive crowing French cockerel. The blade is slightly curved and serrated on one edge. It would have been used by pioneer or sapper troops to construct fascines. These are sticks or brushwood which are firmly bound together to be used for filling up trenches or ditches, and constructing batteries or creating other lines of defence.

Basket-hilted swords

The basket-hilted sword developed as a particular type of weapon that gave the swordsman much greater protection to his sword hand. From the 17th century onwards, this would be adopted by most European nations and it found its apogee in the superbly crafted basket hilts of the Scottish Highlander. In most examples, the basket hilt was attached to a wide, double-edged blade.

English basket-hilted sword, *c.*1590

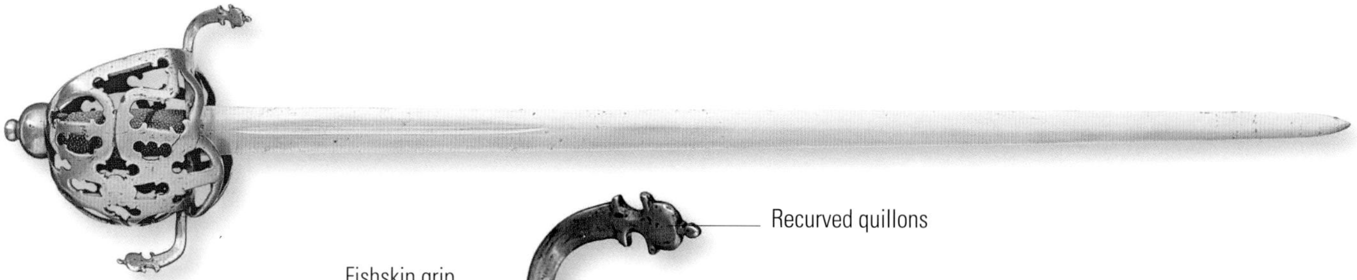

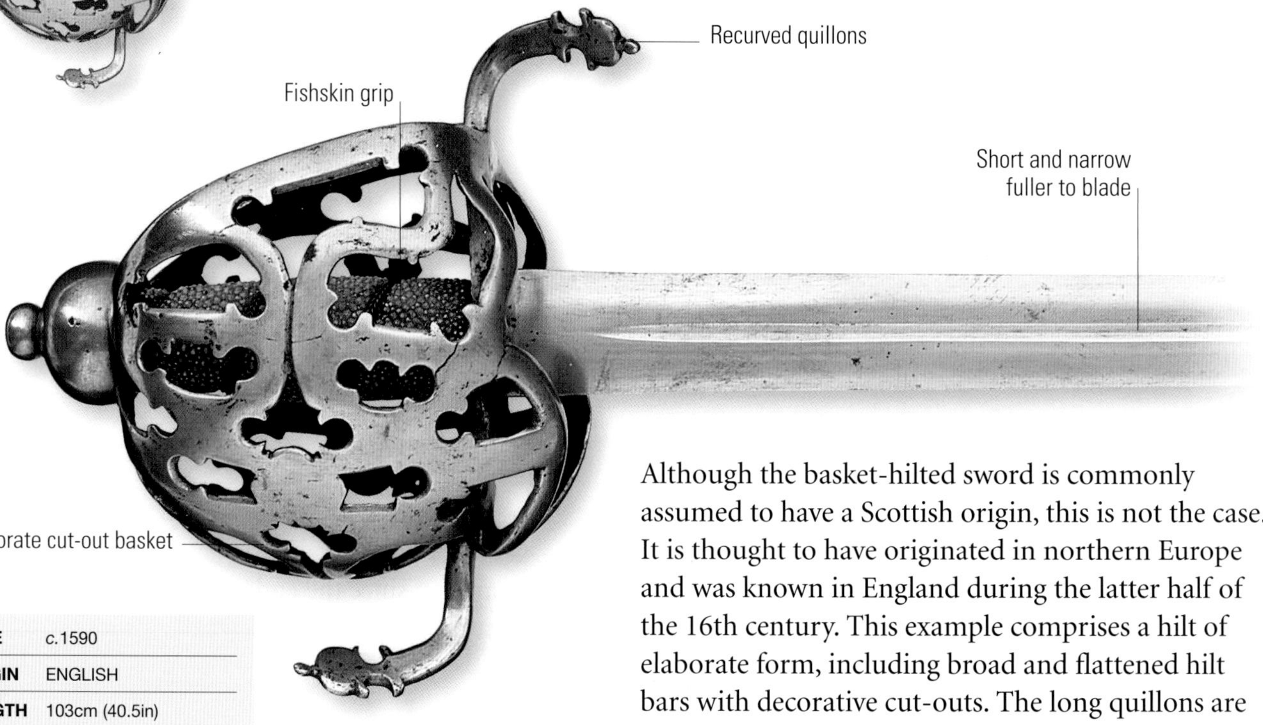

Although the basket-hilted sword is commonly assumed to have a Scottish origin, this is not the case. It is thought to have originated in northern Europe and was known in England during the latter half of the 16th century. This example comprises a hilt of elaborate form, including broad and flattened hilt bars with decorative cut-outs. The long quillons are recurved and terminate with finials of a violin shape.

DATE	*c.*1590
ORIGIN	ENGLISH
LENGTH	103cm (40.5in)

Scottish basket-hilted broadsword, *c.*1680

This type of basket hilt is Scottish in origin and referred to as a "ribbon hilt". This description comes from the flat and ribbon-like appearance of the hilt bars. These weapons are also known as "beaknose" or "snoutnose" swords, because of the small counter-curved quillons that project from the bottom of the hilt.

DATE	*c.*1680
ORIGIN	SCOTTISH
LENGTH	92.9cm (36.6in)

English basket-hilted cavalry broadsword, *c.*1680

DATE	*c.*1680
ORIGIN	ENGLISH
LENGTH	104cm (40.9in)

This is a late 17th-century English basket-hilted sword of superb quality. With typical apple-shaped pommel and inlaid silver hilt, these swords are commonly mistaken for Scottish basket hilts; the pommel, hilt plate and bar shape are what differentiate the sword types.

English basket-hilted broadsword, *c.*1680

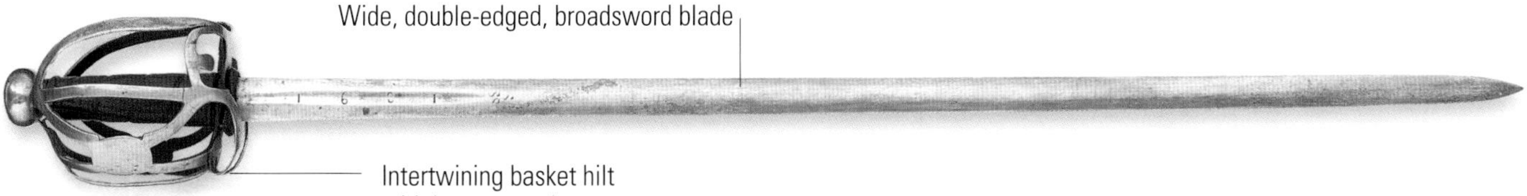

DATE	*c.*1680
ORIGIN	ENGLISH
LENGTH	96.5cm (38in)

Basket hilts of this style had been common since the end of the 16th century and were carried by English cavalry troopers throughout the English Civil War (1642–51) and for some time afterwards. This example is of "munition" quality, meaning that it was produced relatively cheaply and lacks decoration.

Italian schiavona broadsword, *c.*1700

DATE	*c.*1700
ORIGIN	ITALIAN
LENGTH	94.2cm (37.1in)

The schiavona (meaning "Slavonic") sword is a weapon that is closely associated with mercenaries from eastern Europe who served both Spain and the Republic of Venice from the 16th to the 18th century. The complex cage-like arrangement of the basket hilt is a consistent feature of these swords. There are great variations in both quality of manufacture and decoration, some being very plain and functional while others have superb chiselling and applied brasswork.

Scottish basket-hilted broadsword, *c.*1720

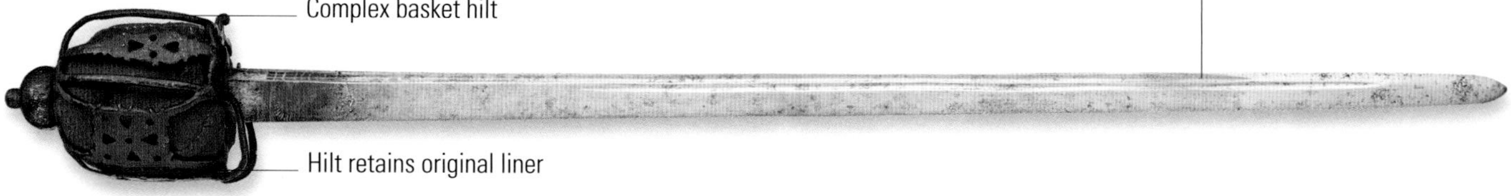

This Scottish basket hilt still retains its original red-felt and buff-leather hilt liner. The liner would have protected the swordsman's hand from chafing against the hilt bars. The blade is double-edged with an incised bun-shaped pommel to the hilt and heart-shaped piercings to the hilt plates.

DATE	*c.*1720
ORIGIN	SCOTTISH
LENGTH	96.2cm (37.9in)

Scottish basket-hilted broadsword, *c.*1720

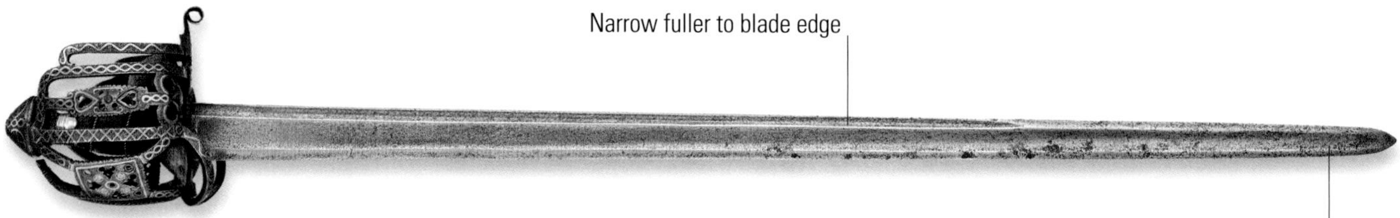

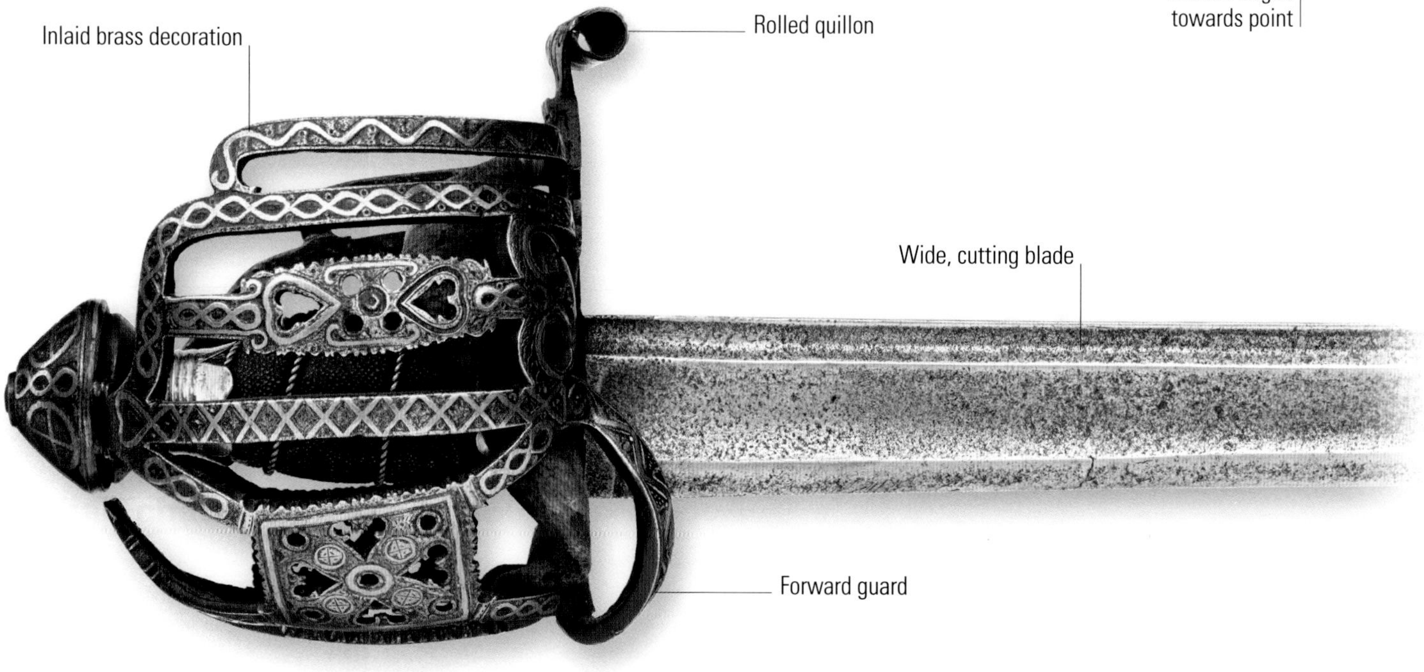

The intricate and superb brass inlay to the hilt marks this out as a sword of historic importance. It would have been made in either Glasgow or Stirling (in the Scottish Lowlands), where a number of sword-making "schools" were successfully established in the 17th and 18th centuries. These sword-making families spanning a number of generations created hilts of rare artistry and quality. Most surviving examples are to be found in museums or prominent private collections.

DATE	*c.*1720
ORIGIN	SCOTTISH
LENGTH	104.1cm (41in)

Italian schiavona sword, *c.*1730

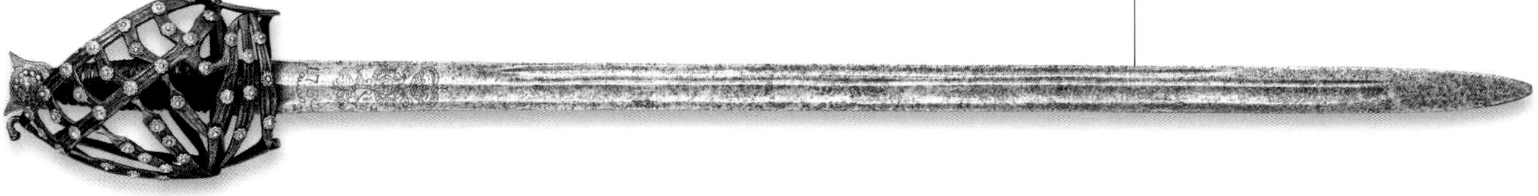

DATE	*c.*1730
ORIGIN	ITALIAN
LENGTH	99.3cm (39.1in)

The schiavona has its origins as the sword type carried by Dalmatian (eastern European) mercenaries recruited to fight for Spain and the Republic of Venice during the 17th and 18th centuries. The complex arrangement of the hilt bars and the "cat's-head" pommel are characteristic features of this sword. These double-edged broadswords would have been relatively lightweight and easy to handle, thus making them very effective fighting weapons.

English basket-hilted cavalry broadsword, *c.*1740

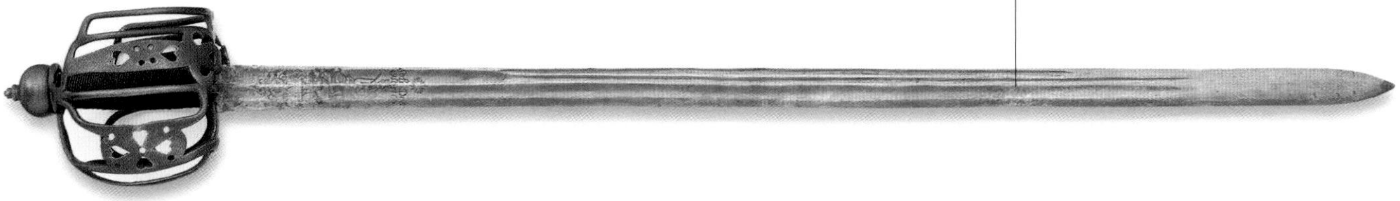

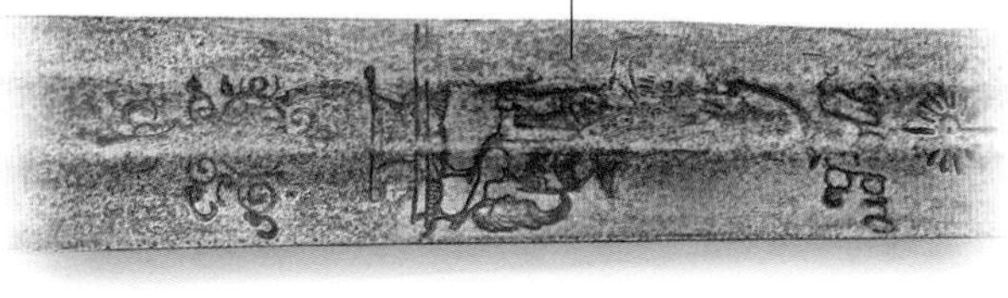

DATE	*c.*1740
ORIGIN	ENGLISH
LENGTH	104.1cm (41in)

The long, double-edged blade of this broadsword would have made it an effective slashing and cutting weapon. English basket hilts tended to have more widely spaced hilt bars compared with Scottish basket hilts, which were manufactured with thicker bars and more solid and protective hilt plates. The use of engraved depictions of mounted cavalrymen became more common after this period.

English basket-hilted broadsword, *c.*1750

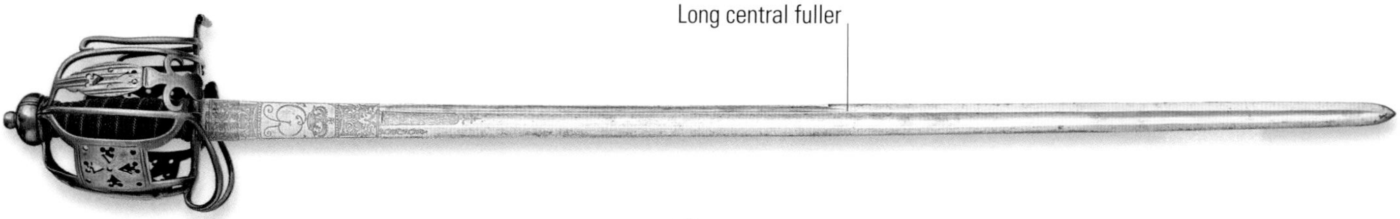

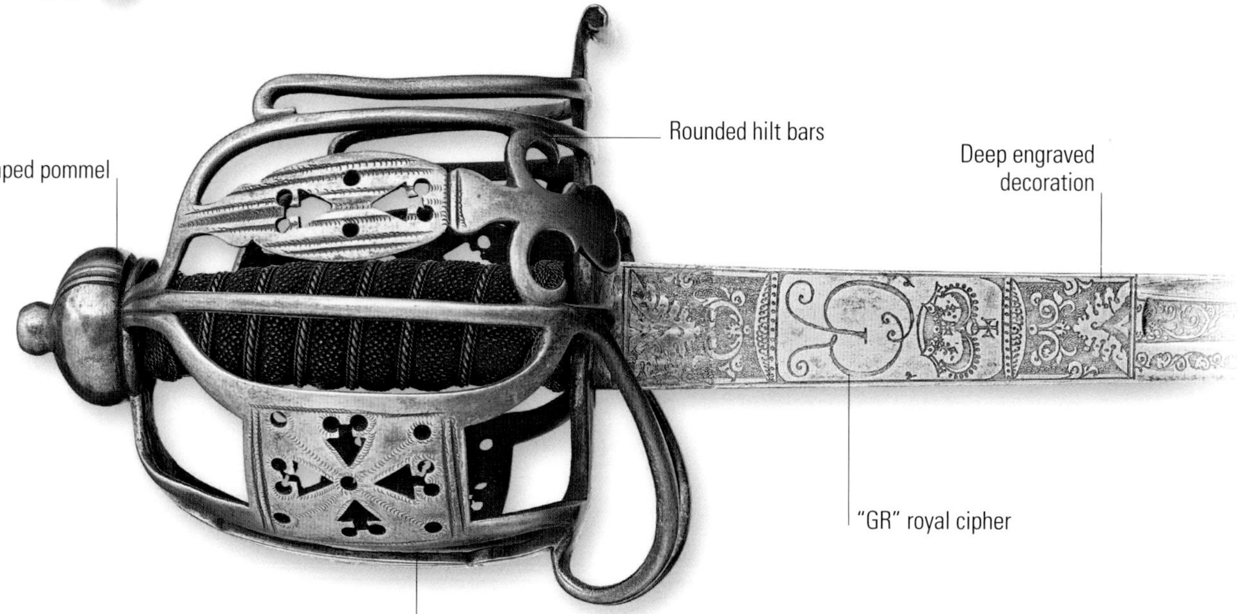

This is an interesting sword as the hilt has all the characteristics of a Scottish-made basket hilt, although it is not. This sword would have been manufactured in England for a heavy dragoon officer in a British cavalry regiment. The blade is etched with the "GR" royal cipher of King George II (*r.*1727–60).

DATE	*c.*1750
ORIGIN	ENGLISH
LENGTH	99cm (39in)

Scottish basket-hilted broadsword, *c.*1750

Scottish Jacobite Highlanders (followers of the House of Stuart, 1371–1714) purchased their basket-hilted swords with blades that were invariably manufactured outside of Scotland. This example is likely to be fitted with a German blade, manufactured in Solingen, and then exported to Scotland where a local hilt maker would have attached it to the hilt.

DATE	*c.*1750
ORIGIN	SCOTTISH
LENGTH	101cm (39.8in)

English basket-hilted broadsword, *c.*1780

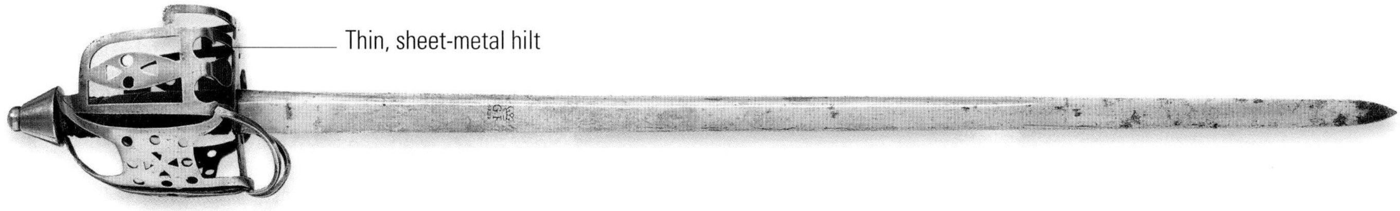

DATE	*c.*1780
ORIGIN	ENGLISH
LENGTH	97.5cm (38.4in)

Although easily mistaken for a Scottish Highland sword, this sword was actually issued to English troops serving in Highland regiments during the latter half of the 18th century. The blade is marked "Drury" and would have been made in Birmingham, England. The quality of these swords tended to be quite poor.

British regimental basket-hilted broadsword, *c.*1860

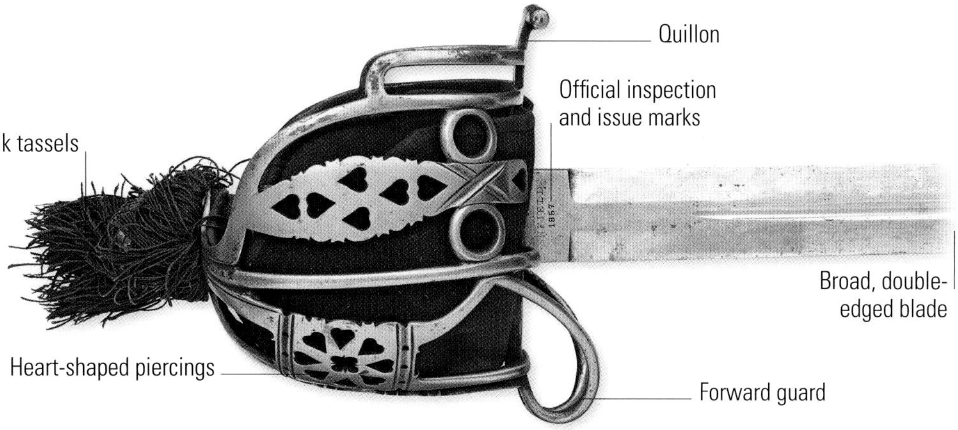

DATE	*c.*1860
ORIGIN	BRITISH
LENGTH	98cm (38.6in)

This sword would have been carried by a sergeant (Non-Commissioned Officer) of one of the Scottish Highland regiments. Unlike officers who had to purchase both uniform and sword through private means, this sword would have been issued to the NCO by the British Army. Government-issue swords tended to be passed around the regiment over a long period of time and, consequently, very few now survive because of this heavy service wear.

Highland regiments

The Highland regiments of the British Army were established after the defeat of the Jacobite cause under Prince Charles Edward Stuart (1720–88), also known as the "Young Pretender" or Bonnie Prince Charlie, at the Battle of Culloden (1746). The British realized that some form of permanent and substantial garrisoning of Scotland would be required. Before this time, Scottish landed gentry loyal to the English Crown had raised independent companies to protect the government's interests and keep the peace amongst rival clans.

RIGHT An officer of the Gordon Highlanders, *c.*1854. He is carrying a regulation basket-hilted broadsword that is attached to his belt by white leather slings.

17th- and 18th-century smallswords

The smallsword was a natural evolution of the rapier into a more manageable weapon and an acknowledgement that a gentleman no longer required both armour and a large sword for everyday protection. Its smaller proportions meant that it could be worn comfortably with civilian clothes and it soon became a fashion accessory and signifier of rank and status. The development of the three-sided colichemarde blade in the 17th century also made the smallsword surprisingly strong, especially when fencing.

English smallsword, *c.*1660

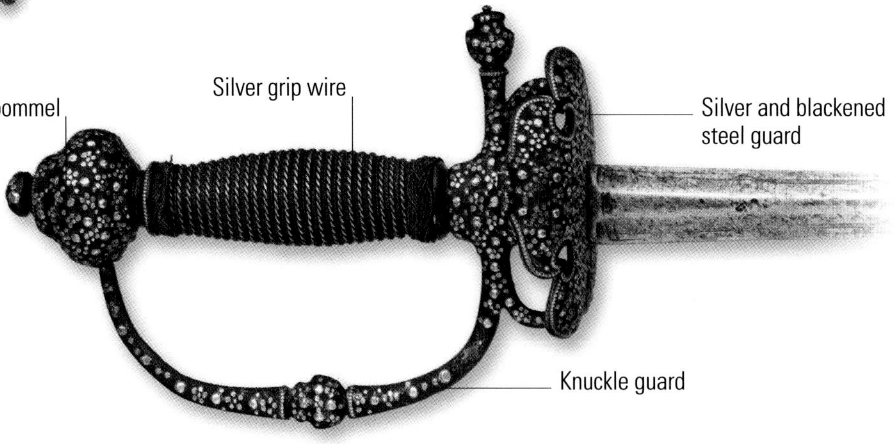

English sword makers of the 17th and 18th centuries were noted for their particular skills at mounting precious metals into sword hilts. This sword is an excellent example of their artistry. All available surfaces have been inlaid with small pieces of silver individually hammered into the hilt. The blackened background of the metal brings out the silver in a superb fashion.

DATE	*c.*1660
ORIGIN	ENGLISH
LENGTH	98.7cm (38.8in)

English smallsword, *c.*1690

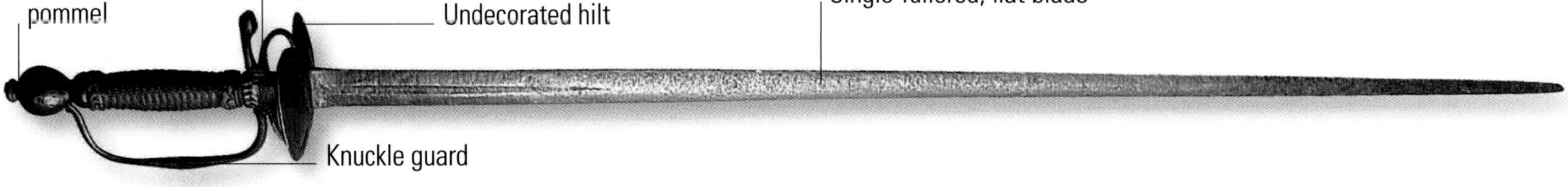

This early smallsword is quite simple in design and very much of transitional form. The single-fullered, flat blade is reminiscent of earlier rapiers, although it does not have the extended length found in these earlier swords. The undecorated hilt is made from iron and displays a globular pommel, D-shaped knuckle guard and swollen quillon. Distinctive features include the two curling arms that reach down to the slim dish guard, which became a common stylistic addition to smallswords.

DATE	*c.*1690
ORIGIN	ENGLISH
LENGTH	UNKNOWN

Italian smallsword, *c.*1690

DATE	*c.*1690
ORIGIN	ITALIAN
LENGTH	99.2cm (39.1in)

The transitional nature of this sword is clearly evident as it shows design characteristics of both a rapier and a smallsword. The long, rapier blade is attached to a hilt that is of early smallsword form. The two downward-pointing arms that reach from under the cross guard are known as a *pas d'âne.*

English smallsword, *c.*1690

DATE	*c.*1690
ORIGIN	ENGLISH
LENGTH	98cm (38.6in)

The unusually wide blade of this smallsword indicates that it was probably carried by a military officer, as it is more robust than the standard "civilian" examples found on smallswords of this period. The pierced guard and bulbous pommel are reminiscent of earlier rapier styles and highlight its transitional nature.

French smallsword, *c.*1720

DATE	*c.*1720
ORIGIN	FRENCH
LENGTH	100.2cm (39.4in)

This smallsword was produced at the height of the Rococo period in the early 18th century, when French decorative influence spread throughout Europe. The hilt is blued steel and encrusted with gold decoration, including helmets, stands of arms and delicate flowers. The top of the blade (the forte) shows traces of the original applied blue and gilt wash, and the remainder of the blade etching is highlighted in gilt. Sheathed in a stiff leather scabbard, the mounts would have repeated the style of decoration already present on the sword hilt.

English smallsword, *c.*1730

From the end of the 17th century onwards, smallswords are found with the addition of two *pas d'âne* rings or arms, which form from the cross guard and terminate with an inward curl at the top of the dish guard. Their purpose was mainly one of decoration, although they probably also added some strength to the hilt. They became a common design feature in smallswords.

DATE	*c.*1730
ORIGIN	ENGLISH
LENGTH	92.3cm (36.3in)

English silver-hilted smallsword, *c.*1745

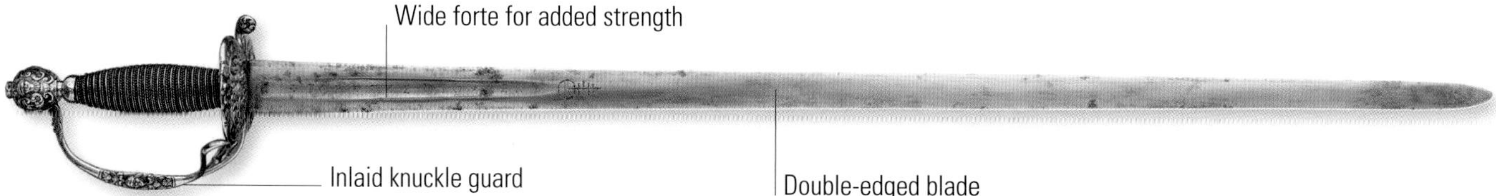

This is a typical example of a high-quality solid silver-hilted gentleman's smallsword of the mid-18th century. It is assayed (silver marked) for London and stamped with the initials "W.G.", probably for William Garrard. Unusually, the leather and silver mounted scabbard has survived.

DATE	*c.*1745
ORIGIN	ENGLISH
LENGTH	75cm (29.5in)

English smallsword, 1756

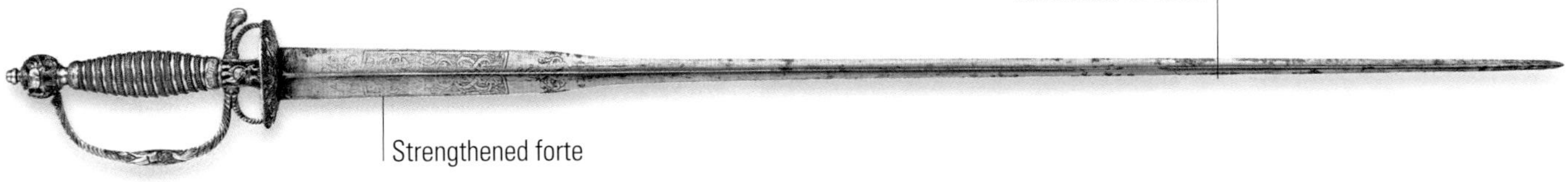

DATE	1756
ORIGIN	ENGLISH
LENGTH	99.6cm (39.2in)

The silver hilt is marked with the initials of the silversmith John Carman II (*c*.1721–64), who worked in London. On his trade card he describes himself as making and selling "all Sorts of Gold and Silver Work at ye lowest prices Likewise Choice Swords and Cuteaus…". The sword has a distinctive colichemarde blade that comprises a wide, triangular forte and needle point.

French smallsword, *c*.1770

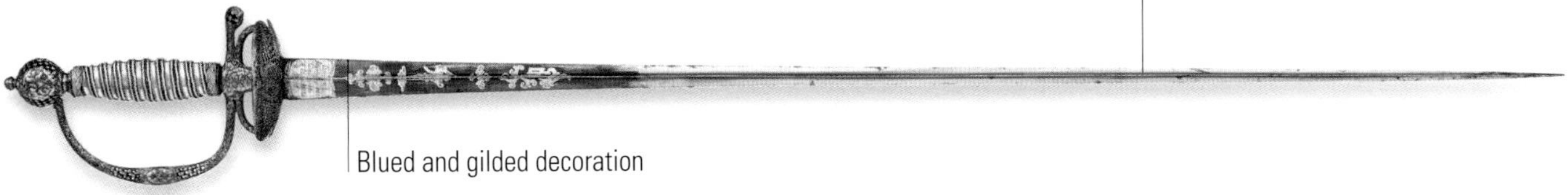

DATE	*c*.1770
ORIGIN	FRENCH
LENGTH	100.3cm (39.5in)

This is an elegant smallsword and very typical of the restrained Neo-classical style encountered in late 18th-century smallswords. The trefoil, or three-sided blade, has been blued and gilded near the forte, and the decoration includes fanciful embellishments. Pommels of this period tended to be spherical in shape.

English smallsword, *c*.1770

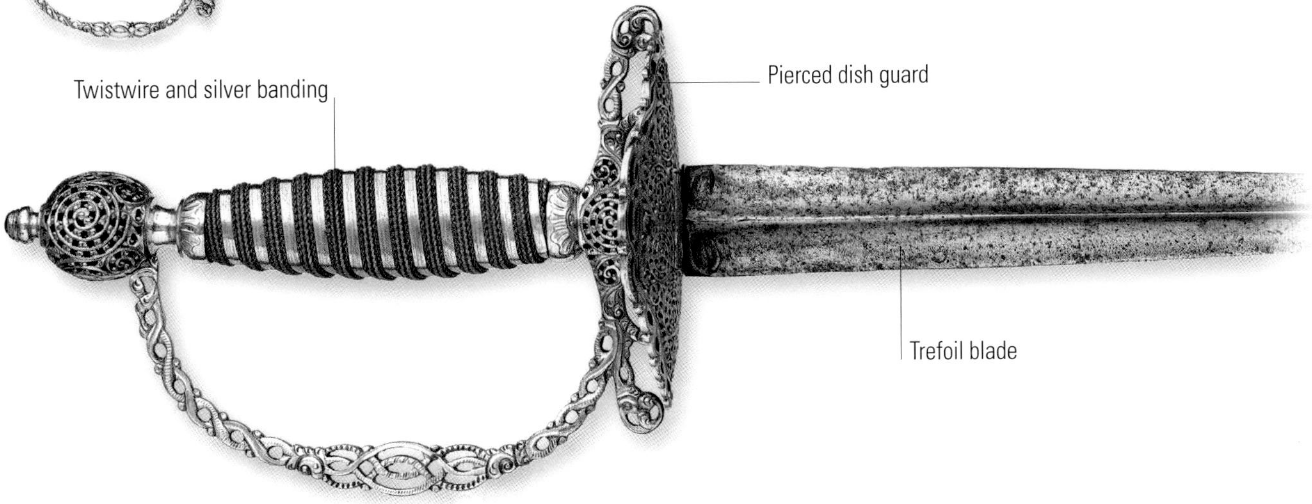

DATE	*c*.1770
ORIGIN	ENGLISH
LENGTH	95cm (37.4in)

This is a fine silver-hilted smallsword that is marked "IR" on the hilt. These letters represent John Radborn (1737–80), who was a gifted sword cutler and silversmith of London. The delicate hilt piercings of this sword are executed with great craftsmanship. This is very much a dress sword and would have been worn on special occasions.

French smallsword, *c.*1780

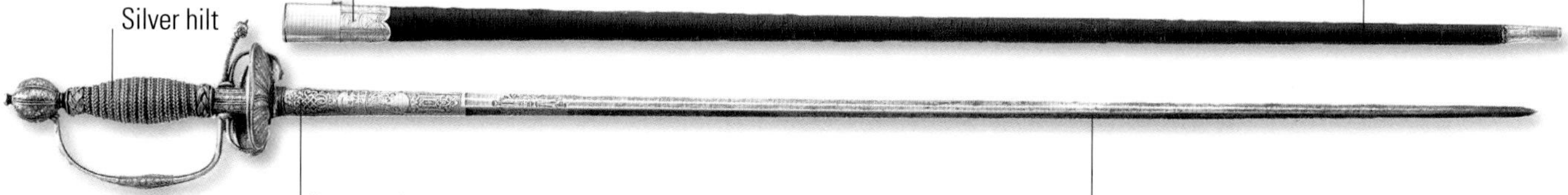

The slim, thrusting blade of this smallsword is engraved with the following motto: *"La Prudence se fait voir dans le vin."* Roughly translated it means: "Prudence is shown in the wine," a cautionary warning for the owner to not use the sword unnecessarily when intoxicated.

DATE	*c.*1780
ORIGIN	FRENCH
LENGTH	92cm (36.2in)

English smallsword, *c.*1790

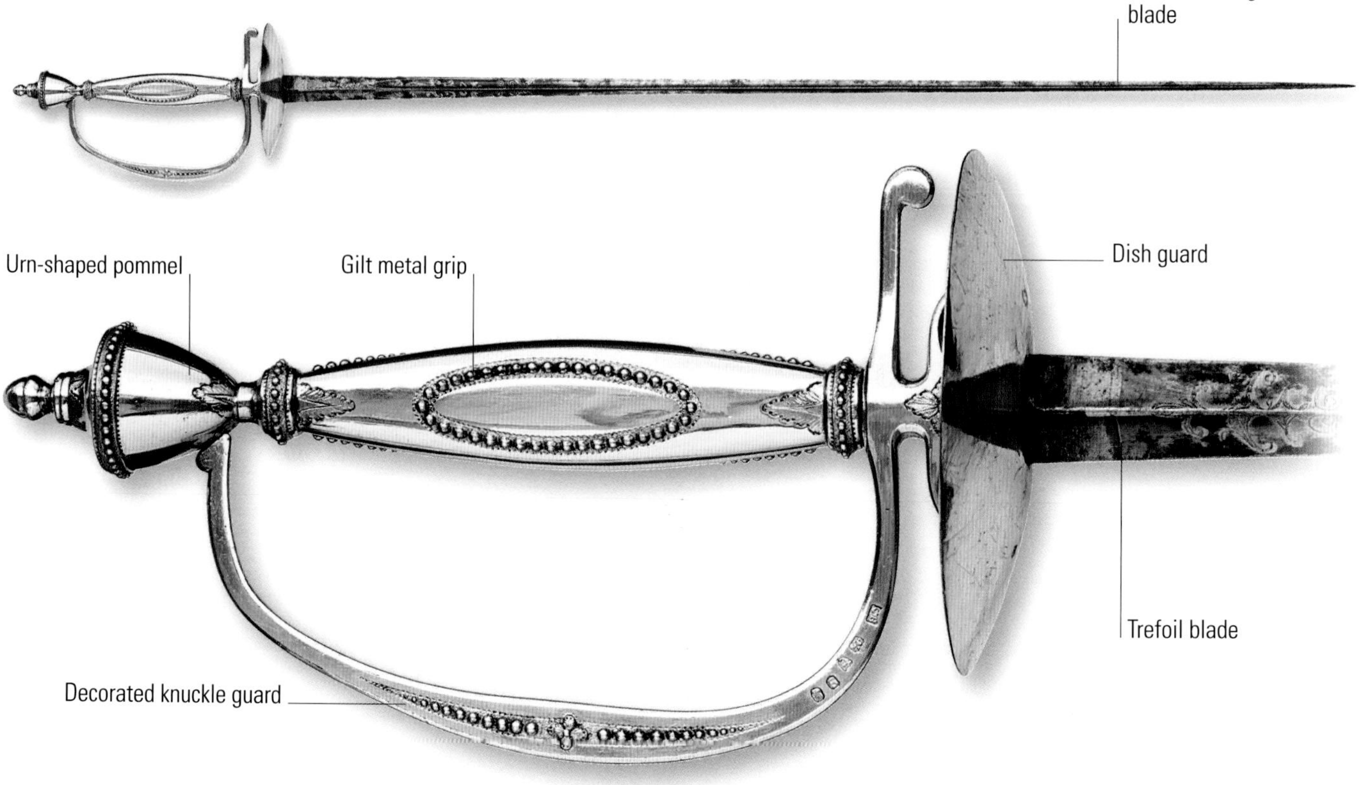

A vogue for urn-shaped pommels on English smallswords is evident during the last quarter of the 18th century. This was a reaction to the influence of such Neo-classical architects as Robert Adam (1728–92), who used the design of the classical Roman urn on many of his decorative features. The grip of this sword does not have a normal wooden core bound in twisted wire but is made of silver gilt. This sword was manufactured by Cornelius Bland of London (1748–94). The silver hallmarks, including the maker's initials, have been clearly punched into the bottom of the knuckle guard.

DATE	*c.*1790
ORIGIN	ENGLISH
LENGTH	95.2cm (37.4in)

English mourning smallsword, *c.*1800

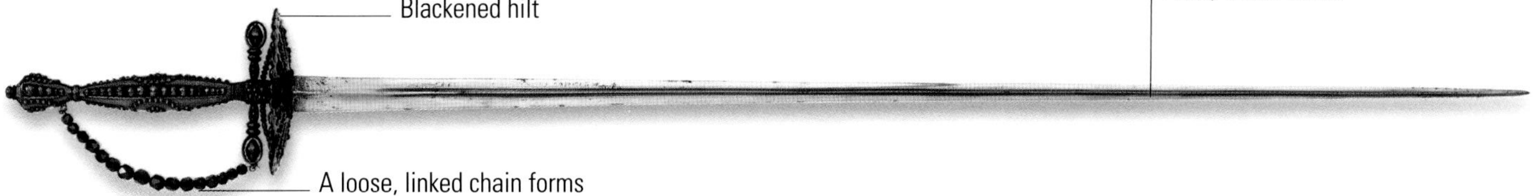

DATE	*c.*1800
ORIGIN	ENGLISH
LENGTH	93cm (36.6in)

Towards the end of the 18th century, a specific type of smallsword was designed to be worn by gentlemen while they were attending a funeral and then during an appropriate period of mourning. The steel hilt was deliberately blackened and many examples have cut-steel or faceted decoration. Scabbard mounts would also have been blackened. Most examples of this type of sword feature a loose chain in place of the normally rigid knuckle guard.

English smallsword, *c.*1800

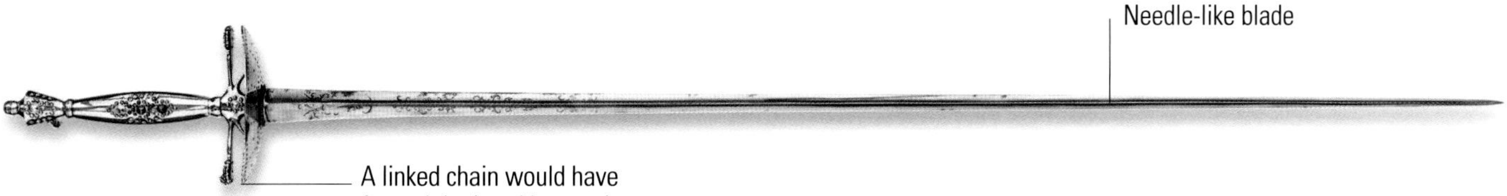

DATE	*c.*1800
ORIGIN	ENGLISH
LENGTH	97.8cm (38.5in)

Although now absent, this dress sword would have had a thin, gilt metal chain knuckle guard strung from the end of the cross guard quillon and terminating at the bottom of the pommel. Because of the inherent fragility of these knuckle guards, many have become detached and lost over the intervening years.

Late 18th-century gentleman

The carrying of a smallsword by a late 18th-century gentleman was both a necessary evil and an opportunity to display his wealth and status. In sword-making centres such as London, numerous small workshops produced high-quality smallswords for discerning gentlemen customers. London gained a reputation for manufacturing silver hilts of exceptional quality. Most blades would have been imported from such blade-making countries as Germany and then mounted to the hilt. Accessories such as the scabbard and sword belt would also have been made locally. Most English silver smallswords were hallmarked with a number of impressed stamps that indicated the city of manufacture, year of production and the maker's initials.

LEFT Late 18th-century gentleman equipped with a smallsword.

North American swords

The influence of Europe on American sword design was quite profound. Most of the cavalry and infantry swords carried by the US Army after 1840 were interpretations or direct copies of European swords, particularly French designs. At the beginning of the American Civil War (1861–65), both Confederate and Union forces had to import a large number of their swords from Europe.

US militia NCO's sword, *c.*1840

Many US states raised their own militias and each officer and NCO carried their own particular sword style. Swords with knight's-head pommels were popular throughout the US and heavily influenced by French sword designs of the period. The grip on this example is either ribbed ivory or bone and the sword would have been carried in a plain or engraved brass scabbard.

DATE	*c.*1840
ORIGIN	AMERICAN
LENGTH	90.1cm (35.5in)

US infantry NCO's sword, Model 1840

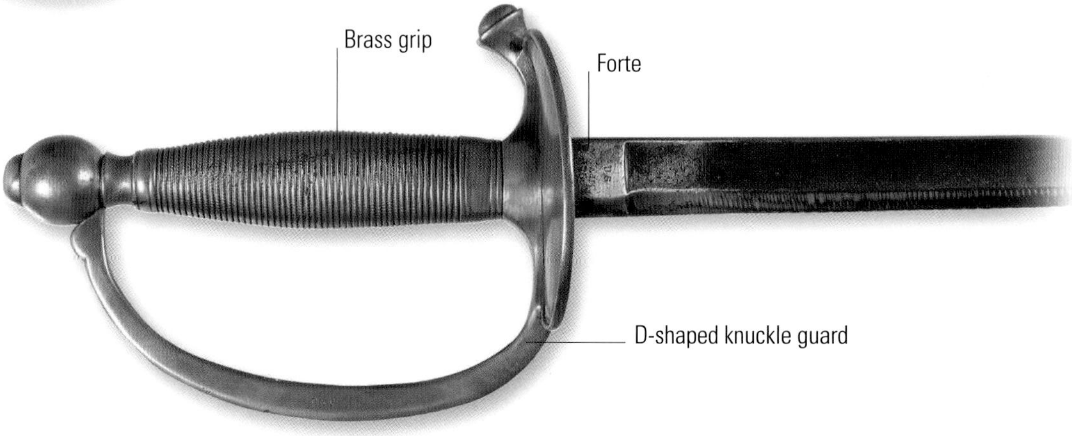

Of rather limited use in battle, this sword was very similar to French infantry swords of the mid-19th century. The hilt was cast brass, with an ovoid pommel, plain shell guard and D-shaped knuckle guard. Most examples were produced in the North for Union forces. This sword would have been sheathed in a brass and leather mounted scabbard.

DATE	1840
ORIGIN	AMERICAN
LENGTH	94cm (37in)

US cavalry trooper's sword, Model 1860

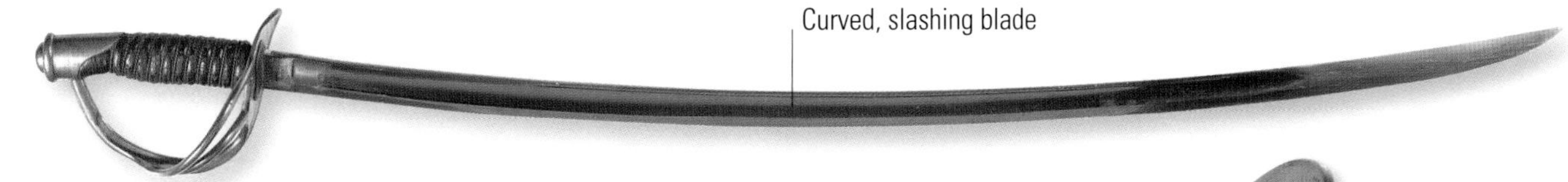

This was the standard cavalry trooper's sword for Union forces during the American Civil War. It was a direct copy of the French Model 1822 Cavalry Trooper's sword, and its slightly curved, single-edged blade was effective at slashing and cutting.

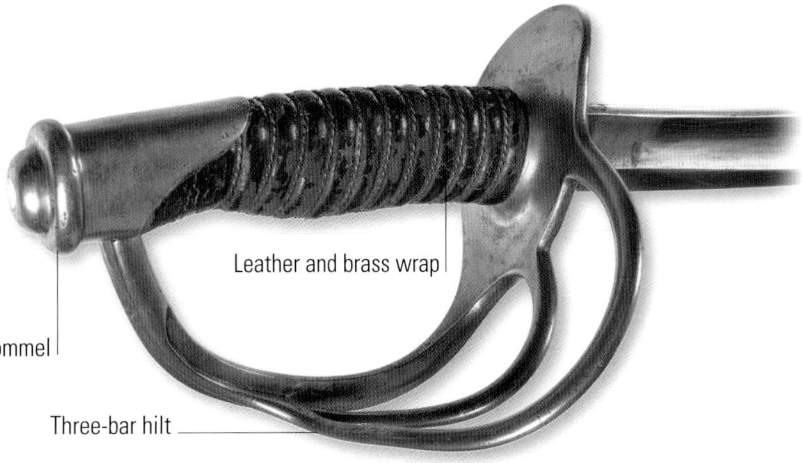

DATE	1860
ORIGIN	AMERICAN
LENGTH	101.6cm (40in)

US Confederate States field officer's sword, *c.*1864

DATE	*c.*1864
ORIGIN	AMERICAN
LENGTH	101.6cm (40in)

At the outbreak of civil war in 1861, most Confederate officers would have carried the same sword models as their Union adversaries. This sword is loosely based on a contemporary US infantry field officer's sword but it would have been manufactured in the South. Overall quality was generally poorer than examples in the North.

US Army infantry officer's sword, Model 1902

This sword is still carried by serving infantry officers of the US Army. Early models had grips manufactured in black-stained wood or horn, while later examples were moulded in early forms of plastic (bakelite or thermoplastic).

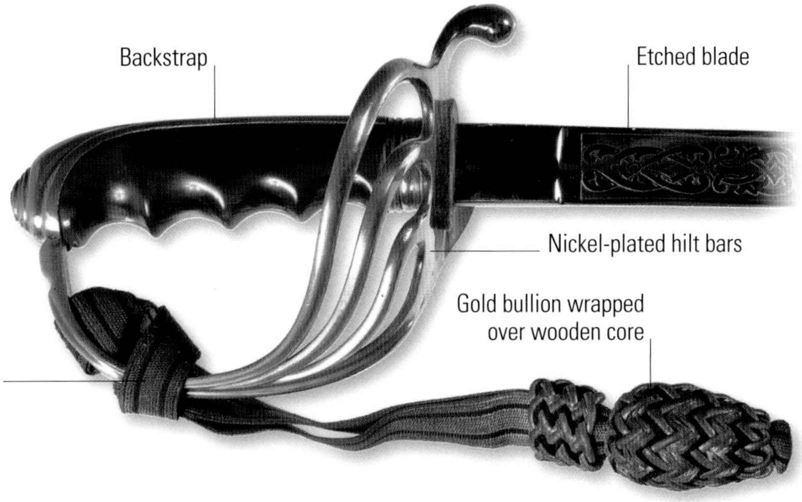

DATE	1902
ORIGIN	AMERICAN
LENGTH	97.7cm (38.5in)

Fencing swords

The art of fencing has its origins in the Spanish and Italian fencing schools of the 15th century. It was regarded as an important element in the training of a gentleman and an important signifier of social rank. During the 18th century, the blunted fencing foil was developed in France and fencing became extremely popular among university students, particularly in Germany, where the large-hilted Schlager fencing sword was used extensively. New schools of fencing emphasized finger control over arm strength.

French fencing foil, *c.*1890

This is a typical late 19th-century French fencing foil and comprises a double-ringed hilt guard, with velvet protective liner. The grip is bound cord and terminates in a plain pommel. The blade is of rectangular section, unsharpened and with a blunted point.

DATE	*c.*1890
ORIGIN	FRENCH
LENGTH	107cm (42.1in)

German fencing Schlager, *c.*1890

The Schlager (meaning "hit") fencing sword was a popular design in German academic fencing schools of the 19th century. This example has a large, multi-bar hilt with a canted, or angled, grip, which allowed better manoeuvrability while fencing. The blade is unfullered and blunted.

DATE	*c.*1890
ORIGIN	GERMAN
LENGTH	106cm (41.7in)

German fencing Schlager, *c.*1890

Complex hilt design is a regular feature of German Schlager swords, and this example exhibits an extravagant series of hilt bars that form near the base and expand into a large basket hilt. The hilt liner is multi-coloured and possibly represents the colours of a particular fencing school.

DATE	*c.*1890
ORIGIN	GERMAN
LENGTH	90cm (35.4in)

Italian fencing sabre, *c.*1900

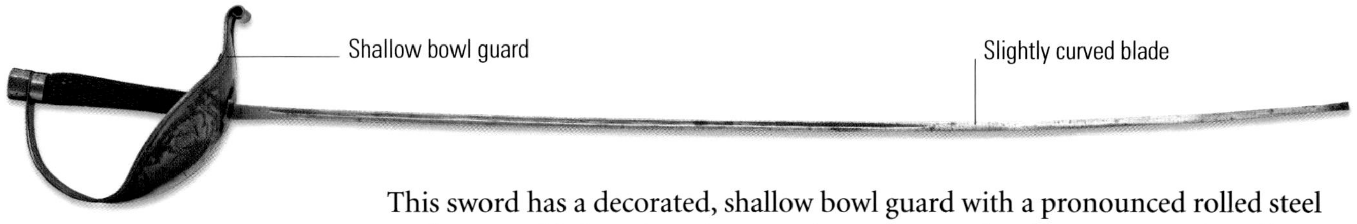

DATE	*c.*1900
ORIGIN	ITALIAN
LENGTH	106cm (41.7in)

This sword has a decorated, shallow bowl guard with a pronounced rolled steel quillon. It is likely to have been used in military schools to train cavalry officers. The blade is slightly curved and the hilt design mirrors full-size cavalry swords of the period. These military fencing swords would not have had a scabbard and were probably hung up in racks in the fencing hall.

British fencing épée, *c.*1980

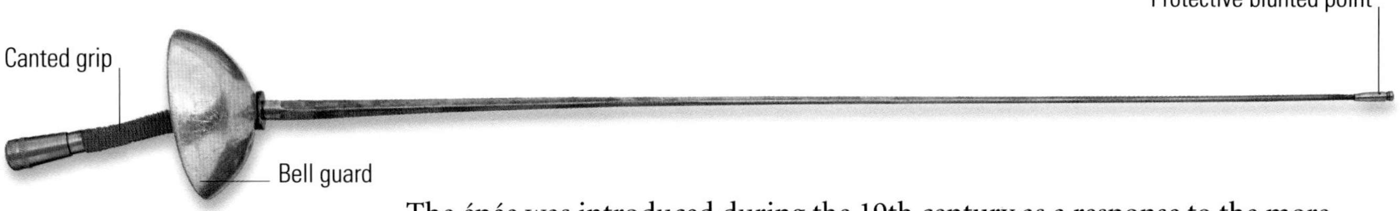

DATE	*c.*1980
ORIGIN	BRITISH
LENGTH	111cm (43.7in)

The épée was introduced during the 19th century as a response to the more common, lighter foil that was regarded by some fencers as not providing a realistic enough experience of duelling with a proper rapier sword. It is slightly heavier than the fencing foil and features a larger bell guard. During a fencing bout, the combatants can aim for the whole body and double hits are allowed.

British fencing foil, *c.*1980

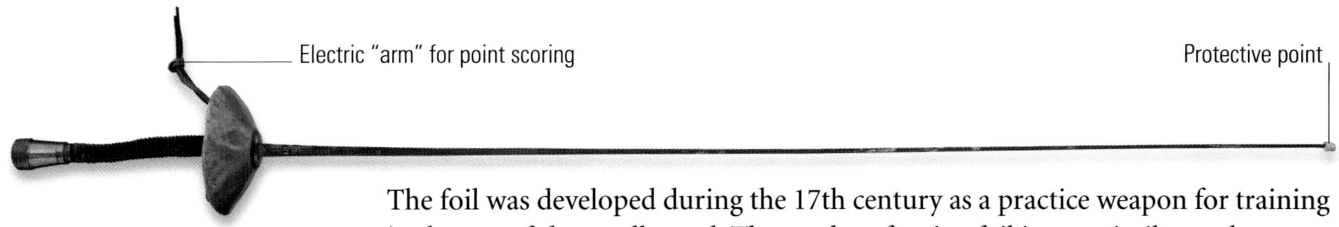

DATE	*c.*1980
ORIGIN	BRITISH
LENGTH	109cm (42.9in)

The foil was developed during the 17th century as a practice weapon for training in the use of the smallsword. The modern fencing foil is very similar to those carried by fencers of a hundred years earlier. This lightweight sword is used during fencing competitions. The torso is the only area of the body permitted to be struck and only single (rather than double) hits are allowed.

British electric fencing foil, 1994

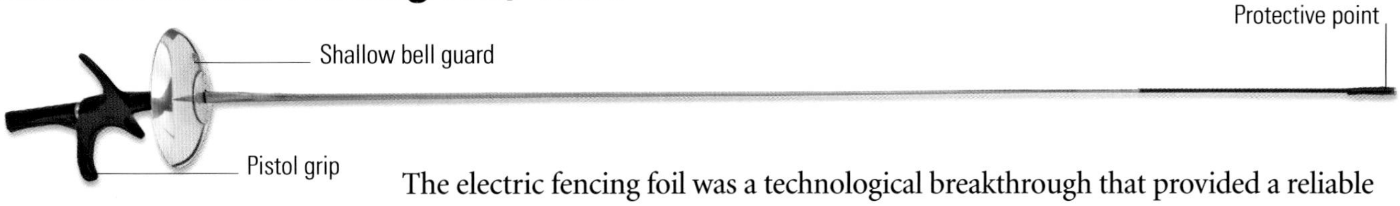

DATE	1994
ORIGIN	BRITISH
LENGTH	105.5cm (41.5in)

The electric fencing foil was a technological breakthrough that provided a reliable method of scoring while in competition. The fencer wears a metallic vest (lamé) with a flexible body cord that is attached to the foil, which has a button in the grip with electric wires that then run down the blade. When a touch is made, a buzzer goes off and a light illuminates on the side of the fencer who has been touched.

Naval weapons

A dedicated sword for naval use was not evident until the 17th and 18th centuries and its introduction coincided with the more efficient organization of European navies into proper fighting branches of the nation state. The cutlass, pike and axe were specialist naval weapons and ideally suited to fighting in the confused close-quarter conditions found on board a fighting ship from the age of sail.

Imperial Russian naval officer's hanger, *c.*1760

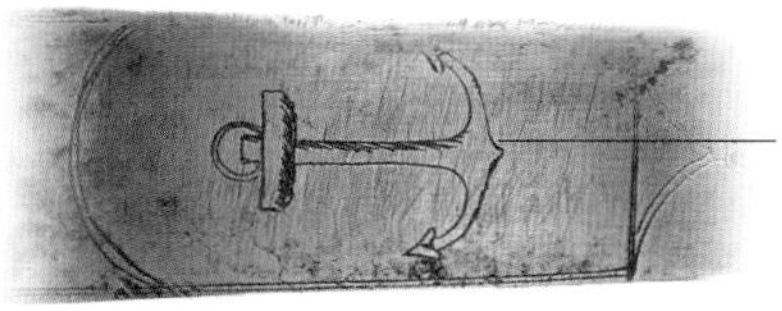

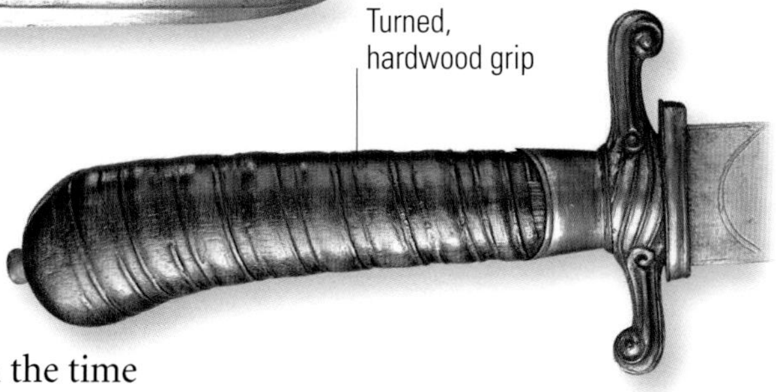

This is a very rare Imperial Russian Naval Officer's hanger from the time of Empress Elizabeth Petrovna (1709–62). It has a turned wooden grip and gilt-brass hilt mounts. The blade is etched on one side with the royal cypher of Elizabeth Petrovna, coupled with the double-headed eagle symbol of Russia. A simple anchor is etched to the other side, which provides the only indication that it is naval in origin.

DATE	*c.*1760
ORIGIN	RUSSIAN
LENGTH	52cm (20.5in)

British boarding pike, *c.*1800

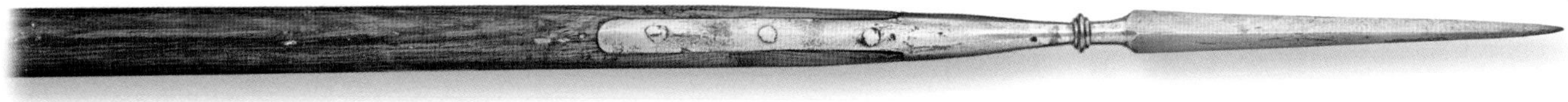

This is an early type of British boarding pike and has a distinctive, decorative brass band around the neck of the pikehead. There were no official patterns of British boarding pikes until well into the 19th century.

DATE	*c.*1800
ORIGIN	BRITISH
LENGTH	254cm (100in)

British boarding pike, *c.*1800

From the 1800s, British boarding pikes tended to adopt a wider, leaf-shaped head with a more squared profile. This example has dispensed with the long retaining langets of earlier pikes and relies on a sturdy brass socket. The regulation of British boarding pikes was quite haphazard and it was only after the Napoleonic Wars (1799–1815) that a form of standardization was introduced.

DATE	*c.*1800
ORIGIN	BRITISH
LENGTH	251.4cm (99in)

British "tomahawk" boarding axe, *c.*1800

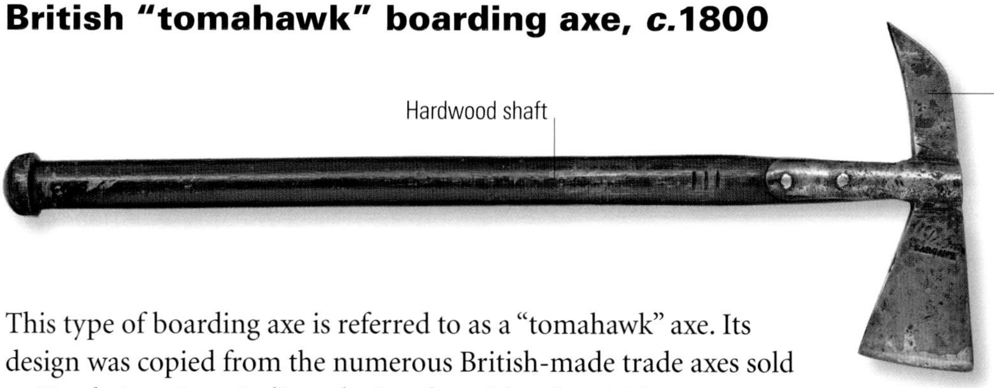

This type of boarding axe is referred to as a "tomahawk" axe. Its design was copied from the numerous British-made trade axes sold to North American Indians during the mid-to-late 18th century. Most British tomahawk boarding axes were covered in a thick layer of black japanning (black enamel paint) to protect them from seawater rust. Alternatively, a number were scraped and oiled. The choice was up to the captain of the ship.

DATE	*c.*1800
ORIGIN	BRITISH
LENGTH	102.9cm (40.5in)

British naval officer's sword, *c.*1800

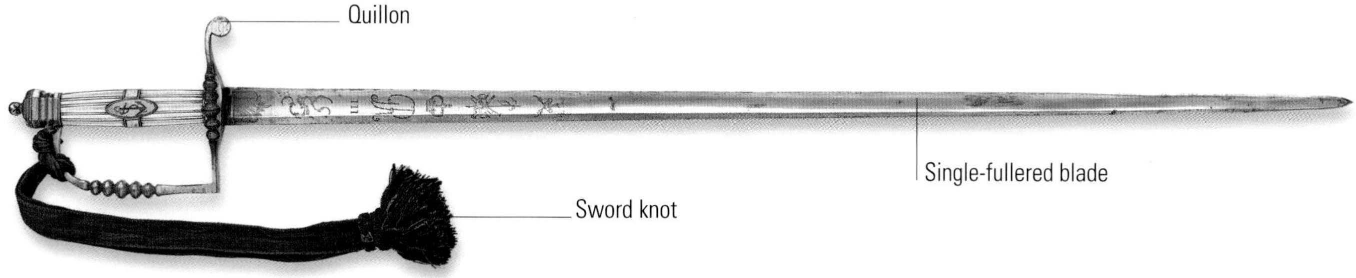

DATE	*c.*1800
ORIGIN	BRITISH
LENGTH	99cm (39in)

British naval officers began to carry this type of sword at the end of the 18th century. It has a "five-ball", beaded knuckle guard and a side ring with an inset brass anchor. The hilt is virtually identical to an infantry officer's sword and features a brass cushion pommel, ribbed ivory grip and sword knot. The scabbard was normally leather with gilt brass mounts.

British cutlass, *c.*1805

DATE	*c.*1805
ORIGIN	BRITISH
LENGTH	85cm (33.5in)

This iron-hilted cutlass is known as a "figure-of-eight" cutlass due to the shape of its hilt guard, which resembles a solid figure eight. It was introduced in 1804, became standard issue to sailors of the Royal Navy and was carried throughout the Napoleonic Wars. The hilt would have been blackened or "japanned" to protect it from the risk of saltwater corrosion. The straight, flat-backed blade is impressed with the "GR" (George III) acceptance mark, indicating that it had been approved for military service.

British naval officer's sword, *c.*1815

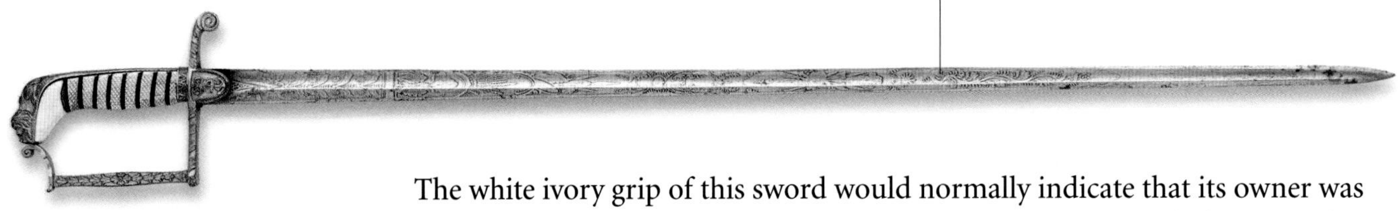

The white ivory grip of this sword would normally indicate that its owner was of commander rank. Its Neo-classical hilt design is very typical of army and navy swords of the Napoleonic period. This is not a fighting sword and would have been carried as a dress weapon, reserved for social occasions such as balls and formal dinners. By this time, the use of a pommel in the form of a lion's head had become standard on most swords in the Royal Navy. Blades were sometimes etched with nautical motifs and many had blue and gilt decoration. Scabbards were leather and gilt brass mounted.

DATE	*c.*1815
ORIGIN	BRITISH
LENGTH	84.5cm (33.3in)

British midshipman's sword, *c.*1825

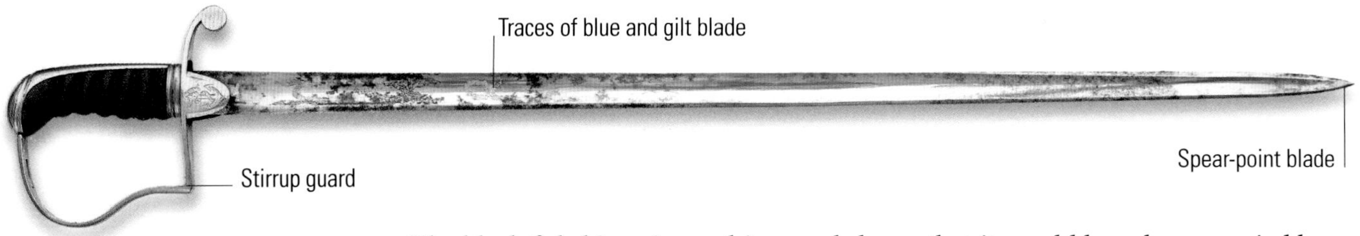

The black fishskin grip on this sword shows that it would have been carried by a Royal Navy midshipman, of junior rank, on board a British fighting ship. Higher ranks normally carried ivory or white sharkskin grips. The hilt is gilt brass with a "stirrup" knuckle guard and is very similar to British cavalry hilts of the period. In the middle of the cross guard is a shield-shaped langet with an engraved fouled anchor. The sword would have been kept in a black leather and gilt brass mounted scabbard with two carrying rings.

DATE	*c.*1825
ORIGIN	BRITISH
LENGTH	68.5cm (27in)

French naval cutlass, *c.*1840

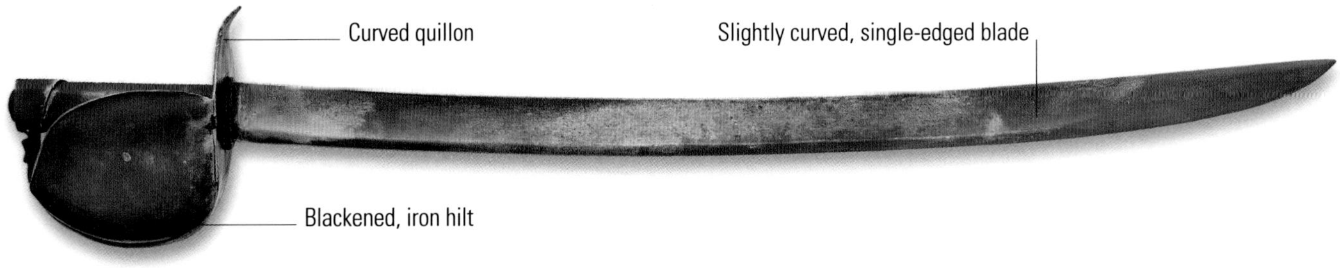

This is a French Model 1833 Naval Cutlass and is an evolution of the Model IX (1800–01) Naval Cutlass that was introduced during the Napoleonic period. The blade is slightly narrower than the original and normally included the engraved anchor. The large, blackened iron hilt would have afforded excellent protection for the hand.

DATE	*c.*1840
ORIGIN	FRENCH
LENGTH	80.5cm (31.7in)

British naval cutlass, *c.*1850

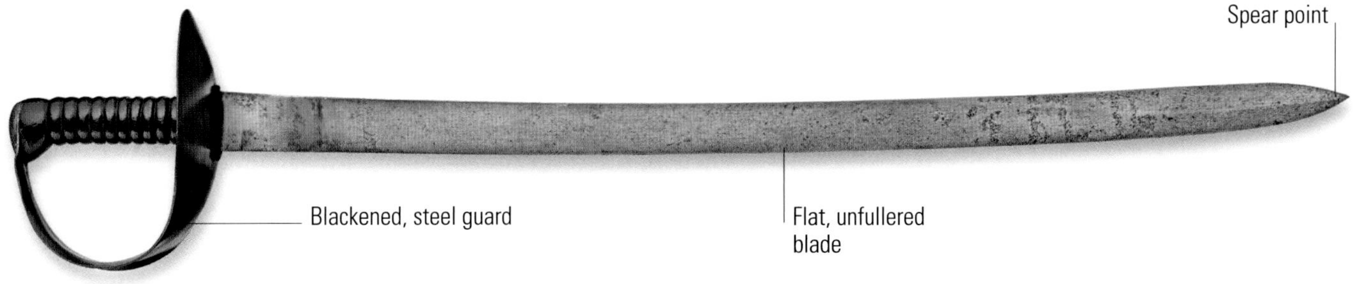

The British Napoleonic "figure-of-eight" cutlass was replaced in 1845 with a new pattern of British naval cutlass. It had a shallow bowl guard with a ribbed iron grip and was very similar to contemporary British cavalry troopers' guards. Originally, it would have had a straight, flat-backed blade, but in 1887, all cutlass blades were changed to a slightly curved and single-fullered profile. This was thought to provide the seaman with a better-cutting sword.

DATE	*c.*1850
ORIGIN	BRITISH
LENGTH	84.5cm (33.3in)

French naval cutlass, *c.*1880

DATE	*c.*1880
ORIGIN	FRENCH
LENGTH	82.5cm (32.5n)

This is a Model 1833 French Naval Cutlass that has had the original iron bowl guard removed. This was done after the 1880s in order to reduce the space taken up by the cutlass while in storage on board ship, and was also deemed more practical when carried on land. The cutlass would have been sheathed in a leather and brass mounted scabbard. During the 1900s, quantities of these cutlasses were sold by the government to private companies.

US Navy cutlass, 1917

DATE	1917
ORIGIN	AMERICAN
LENGTH	76.2cm (30in)

When the US Navy decided to adopt a new naval cutlass in the first half of the 20th century, they chose a sword design that was already available. The Model 1917 US Navy Cutlass is a copy of a Dutch Army "klewang", or double-edged machete, which had been developed following colonial experience in the Dutch East Indies. The grips are held in place by three recessed screw nuts. A later US model features an open hilt, with a two-branched guard. This cutlass was still carried on US Navy ships until the beginning of World War II.

French Napoleonic swords

The French Revolution (1789–99) and the subsequent accession of Napoleon Bonaparte (1769–1821) brought with it a renewed feeling of pride in the Imperial French Army. This resulted in the rapid development of a great variety of military swords, many designed for individual regiments and heavily influenced by the contemporary vogue for Neo-classical decoration.

French dragoon trooper's sword, *c.*1790

Most French cavalry swords of this period are found with hilts of either brass (for troopers) or gilt brass (for officers). This sword has a decorative S-shaped hilt bar that begins at the cross guard, forming a branch that joins the knuckle guard. Flat-topped pommels were common on French Napoleonic swords.

DATE	*c.*1790
ORIGIN	FRENCH
LENGTH	143.1cm (56.3in)

French cuirassier officer's sword, *c.*1790

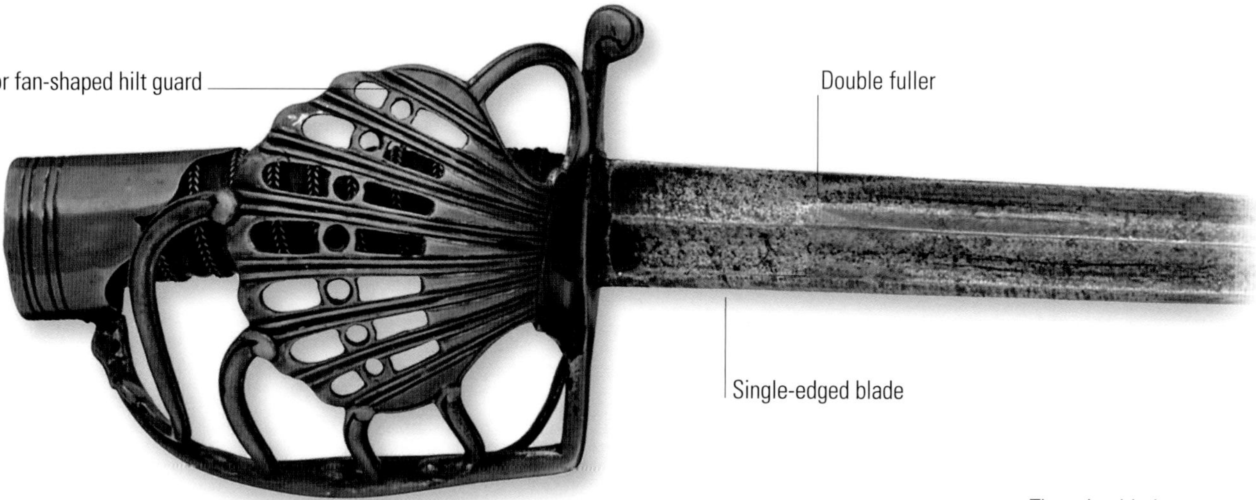

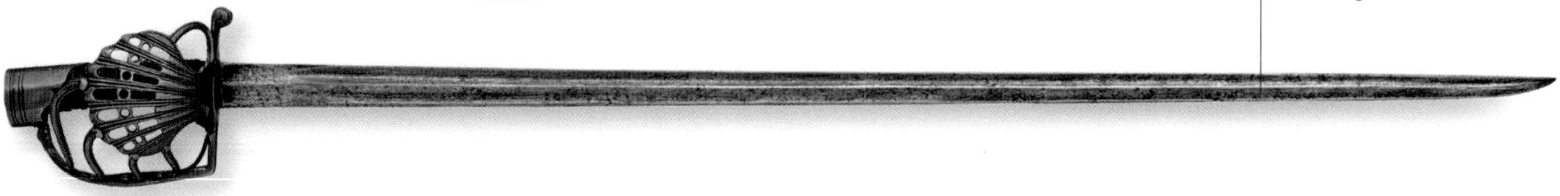

This sword has a distinctive fan-shaped and pierced hilt guard. The long, single-edged blade would have been used primarily as a thrusting weapon. French heavy cavalry troops inflicted more fatal wounds with this type of sword than their English counterparts, who carried a long, slashing sword.

DATE	*c.*1790
ORIGIN	FRENCH
LENGTH	103.7cm (40.8in)

French cadet's sword, École de Mars, *c.*1790

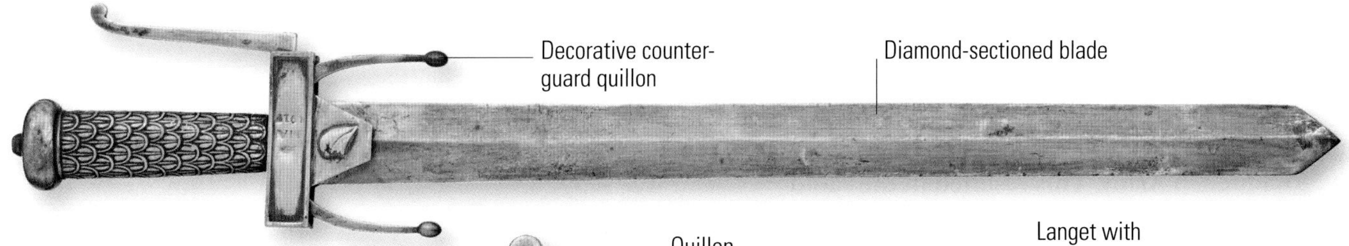

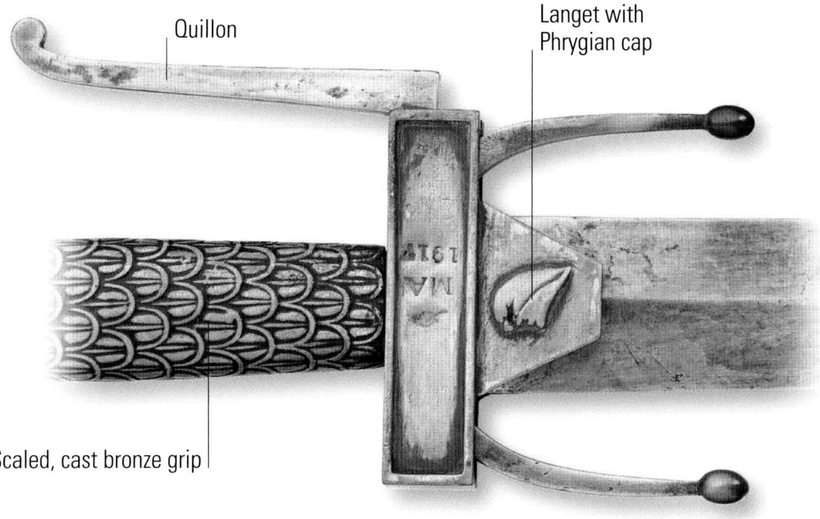

Designed by the painter Jacques-Louis David (1748–1825), this unique gladius-style sword was carried by army cadets in the elite École de Mars, a Napoleonic military academy in Paris. Note the revolutionary Phrygian (liberty) cap emblem to the hilt langet.

DATE	*c.*1790
ORIGIN	FRENCH
LENGTH	67cm (26.4in)

French light cavalry officer's sword, *c.*1800

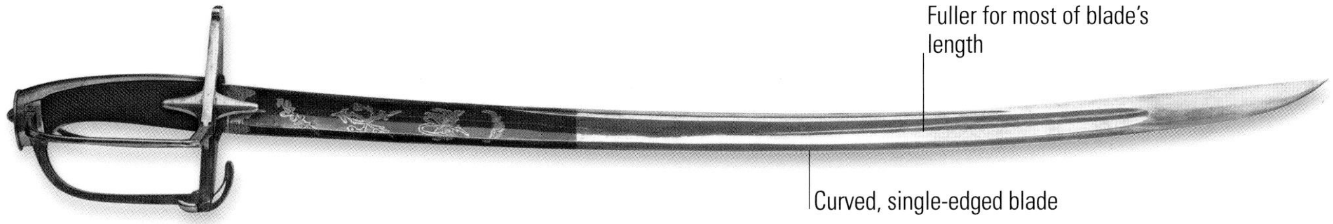

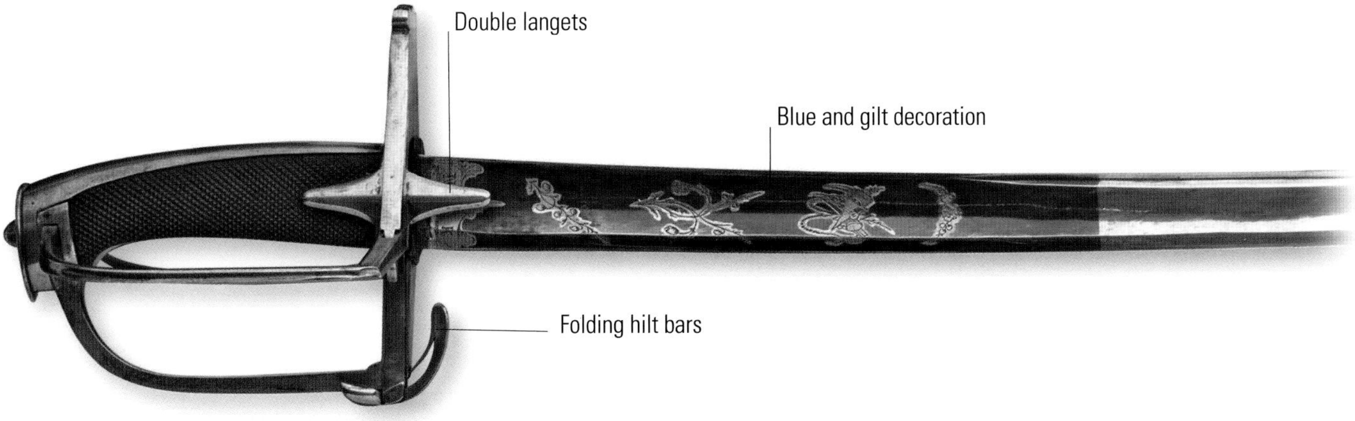

DATE	*c.*1800
ORIGIN	FRENCH
LENGTH	88.5cm (34.8in)

Unlike their British counterparts, the French favoured the "attack hilt" sword. This comprised a series of one or two sliding hilt bars that could be engaged during battle and then folded away afterwards. This sword retains a considerable amount of its original blue and gilt decoration to the blade, and would have been sheathed in a gilt brass and leather mounted scabbard.

Napoleon Bonaparte

During his military career, Napoleon Bonaparte (1769–1821) carried a wide range of swords and we are able to document a number of them through their depiction in famous paintings. One of the most notable is a ceremonial sword designed and made by the goldsmith Martin-Guillaume Biennais (1764–1843). The gold hilt is elaborately decorated with classical and imperial themes, including a Napoleonic eagle with outstretched wings and a profile of Napoleon. Interestingly, the sword is of rather small proportions and reflects the French emperor's small stature. Jacques-Louis David (1748–1825), a French painter at the forefront of Neo-classicism, produced a series of paintings of Napoleon, including the study featured right. His most famous work is Napoleon at St Bernard (1800). In this painting, the young Napoleon is astride his horse and carries a sword of distinctly eastern or mameluke style, no doubt influenced by his recent campaigns in Egypt.

ABOVE Napoleon Bonaparte in his study. To his left can be seen a smallsword in its scabbard. It is likely that he would have carried this sword while on campaign.

Napoleon's smallsword, 1780

DATE	1780
ORIGIN	FRENCH
LENGTH	99.7cm (39.2in)

This officer's smallsword was presented to Napoleon Bonaparte by his contemporary, Alexandre Desmazis, with whom he attended the École Militaire. They were later comrades at the Régiment de La Fère, where they both served as lieutenants at Valence in 1775. The engraved blade has a flattened, diamond-section profile with a narrow, central fuller. There is an engraved inscription to one of the hilt shell guards and also on the blade.

French infantry briquet (sword), *c.*1800

DATE	c.1800
ORIGIN	FRENCH
LENGTH	47cm (18.5in)

This brass-hilted short sword was one of the most common French infantry swords of the Napoleonic Wars (1799–1815) and would have been carried by infantry privates. It had a heavy, ribbed brass grip, with a D-shaped knuckle guard and a slightly curved, flat-backed, single-edged blade. It was copied by most European nations, although rejected by Britain.

French hussar officer's sword, *c.*1800

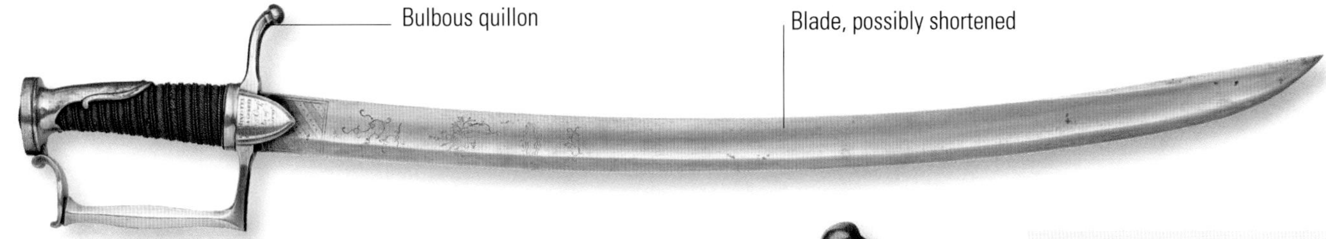

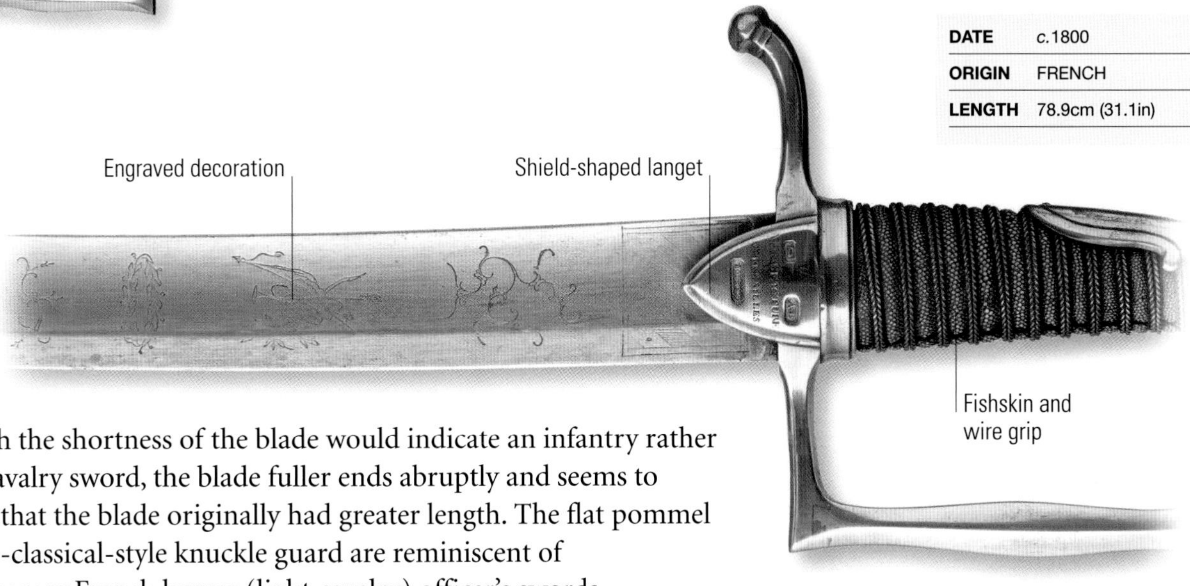

DATE	*c.*1800
ORIGIN	FRENCH
LENGTH	78.9cm (31.1in)

Although the shortness of the blade would indicate an infantry rather than a cavalry sword, the blade fuller ends abruptly and seems to indicate that the blade originally had greater length. The flat pommel and Neo-classical-style knuckle guard are reminiscent of contemporary French hussar (light cavalry) officer's swords.

French heavy cuirassier trooper's sword, *c.*1810

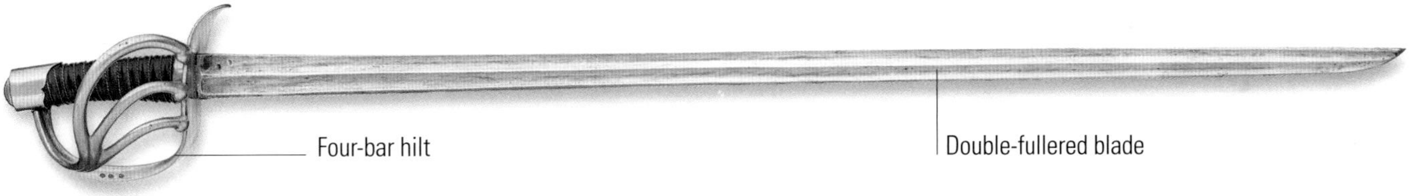

DATE	*c.*1810
ORIGIN	FRENCH
LENGTH	113cm (44.5in)

This is a Model AN XIII Cuirassier Trooper's Sword and was issued to heavy cavalry regiments. The sword has a straight, single-edged and double-fullered blade. The large, brass, four-bar hilt has a domed pommel cap. These swords are normally engraved with the date and place of manufacture on the blade's edge.

French light cavalry officer's sword, *c.*1810

These swords were originally carried by officers of German hussar regiments and later adopted by French cavalry officers. The double langet is a design feature commonly encountered on Napoleonic swords. The end of the blade is double-edged, with a clipped point.

DATE	*c.*1810
ORIGIN	FRENCH
LENGTH	95.3cm (37.5in)

British Napoleonic swords

By the end of the 18th century, the British Army was embroiled in a global conflict with Napoleon Bonaparte of France (1769–1821) and his allies. The British Army began to re-arm on a massive scale. The old haphazard and corrupt system of sword purchasing by regimental colonels was ended and a new range of officially approved "pattern" swords was introduced for all branches of the Army and Navy.

British heavy cavalry officer's sword, 1788 Pattern

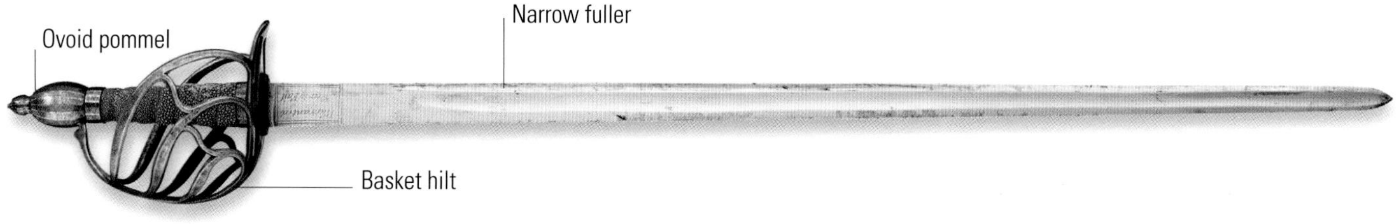

This basket-hilted sword has a large, enclosed iron hilt made up of a number of inter-linked bars. The long, double-edged blade would have been counter-balanced by the heavy, ovoid pommel.

DATE	1788
ORIGIN	BRITISH
LENGTH	102.8cm (40.5in)

British heavy cavalry officer's sword, 1788 Pattern

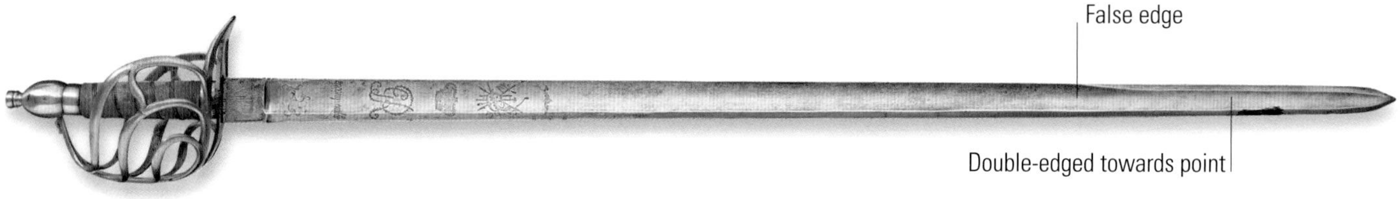

While a sword of this great size and weight would have been effective at the charge, contemporary accounts of British cavalry troopers constantly bemoan its cumbersome handling and the brittleness of the blades. This blade is engraved with the royal cypher ("GR") and crown.

DATE	1788
ORIGIN	BRITISH
LENGTH	120.6cm (47.5in)

British light cavalry officer's sword, 1788 Pattern

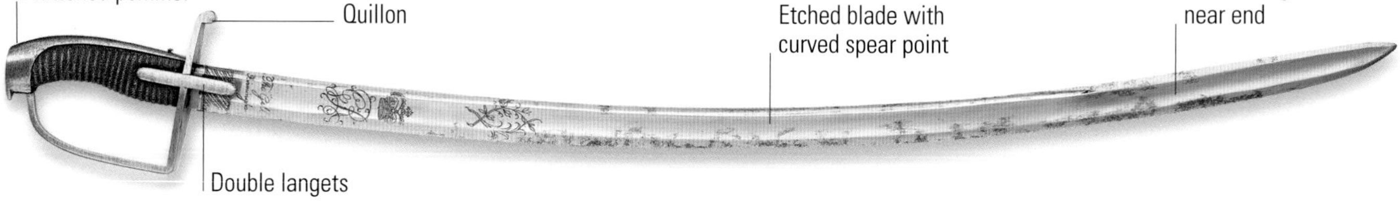

This sword has a straight knuckle guard, double langets and a slightly curved blade, double-edged for the last 15cm (6in). The grip consists of a wooden core, bound with either cord or string and then wrapped in wet fishskin or leather. While drying, the covering would shrink over the cord, producing a tight, ribbed grip.

DATE	1788
ORIGIN	BRITISH
LENGTH	63.5cm (25in)

The Duke of Wellington

As a general officer in the British Army, the Duke of Wellington (1769–1852) was normally obliged to carry a sword of regulation pattern. He certainly purchased or recieved a 1796 Pattern General Officer's Sword (see below) but it is unlikely that he carried this pattern sword while on campaign. He is actually more well known for carrying a mameluke-style sword and his decision to wear this eastern-inspired sword design was directly influenced by the campaign he fought in Egypt (1798–1801). Fellow British officers soon copied their commanding officer and the mameluke sabre became de rigueur within the British Army of the 1800s.

RIGHT Equestrian portrait of the Duke of Wellington with British hussars on a battlefield, 1814. He carries a sword of mameluke style.

General Officer's 1796 Pattern sword of the Duke of Wellington

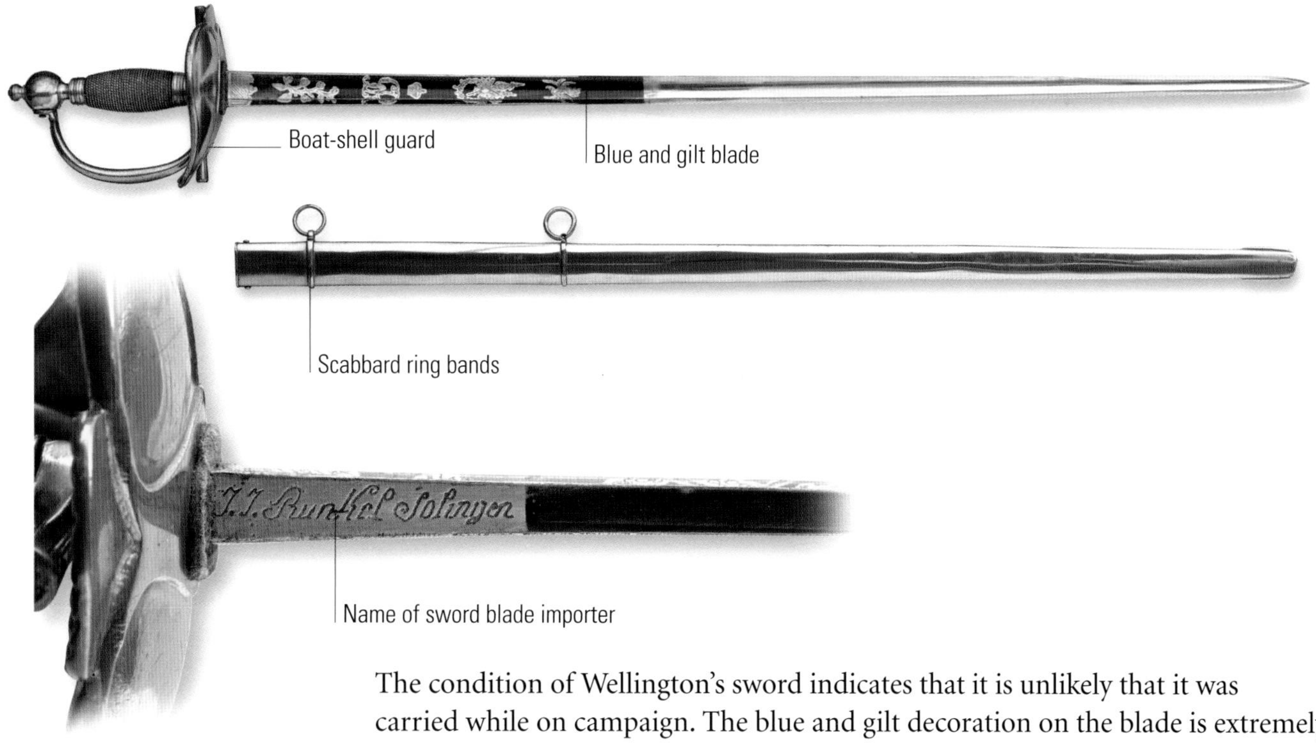

The condition of Wellington's sword indicates that it is unlikely that it was carried while on campaign. The blue and gilt decoration on the blade is extremely fresh and has not been exposed to weather or poor storage conditions. Its provenance dates from a post held by the Duke of Wellington at the Tower of London. The constable of the Tower of London holds one of the most ancient offices in England. The Duke of Wellington was constable of the Tower from 1825 to 1852 and presented this sword to the Tower Armouries.

DATE	1796
ORIGIN	BRITISH
LENGTH	99.8cm (39.3in)

British heavy cavalry trooper's sword, 1796 Pattern

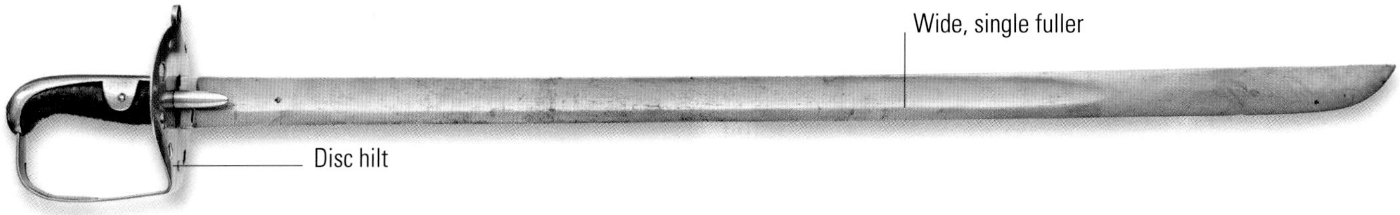

The 1796 Pattern Heavy Cavalry Trooper's Sword was based on an earlier Austrian design and featured a distinctive disc hilt. The blade was single-edged with a wide, single fuller. The hatchet point at the end of the blade was most effective as a slashing and cutting weapon.

DATE	1796
ORIGIN	BRITISH
LENGTH	101.5cm (40in)

British light cavalry trooper's sword, 1796 Pattern

The light cavalry regiments of the British Army were issued with a sword that had a blade of "hussar" shape. This comprised a stirrup hilt, leather-bound grip and slightly curved, broad-fullered blade. It would have been carried in a heavy plain iron or steel scabbard with two carrying rings.

DATE	1796
ORIGIN	BRITISH
LENGTH	94cm (37in)

British light cavalry officer's sword, 1796 Pattern

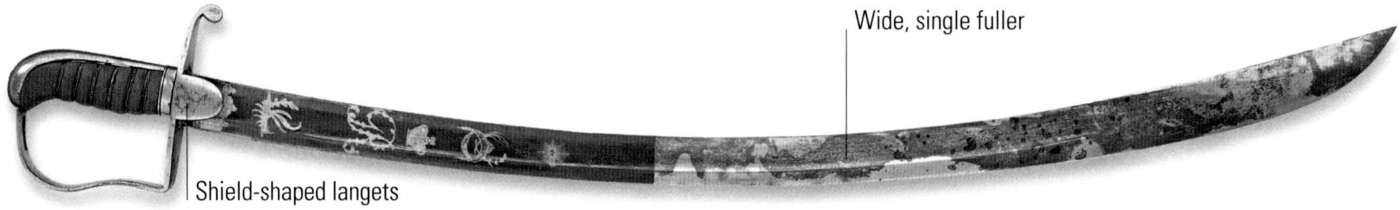

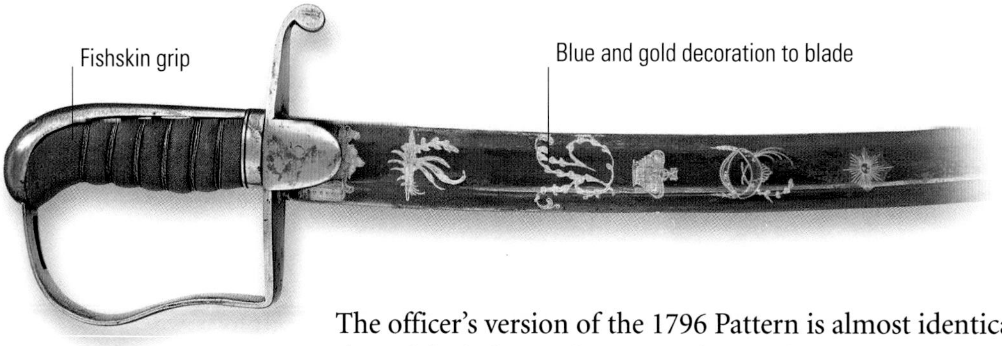

DATE	1796
ORIGIN	BRITISH
LENGTH	94.7cm (37.3in)

The officer's version of the 1796 Pattern is almost identical in shape and form to that of the light cavalry trooper's sword, but was generally lighter in weight and better finished. Blue and gilt decorated blades were very popular at the end of the 18th century and invariably featured stands or arms, floral motifs and the "GR" royal cypher of King George III (1738–1820). The hilt has a "stirrup" knuckle guard and shield-shaped target.

British infantry officer's sword, 1796 Pattern

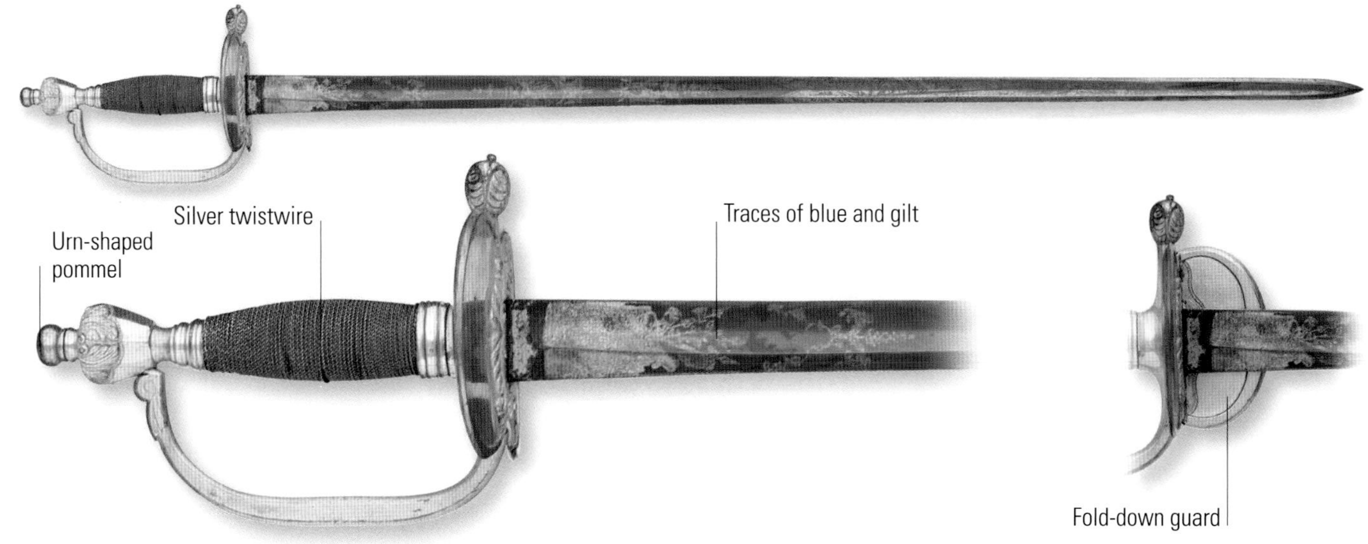

DATE	1796
ORIGIN	BRITISH
LENGTH	100cm (39.3in)

Inspired by the Neo-classical designs of Georgian architects, such as Robert Adam (1728–92), the urn-shaped pommel and acanthus-leafed decoration on this infantry officer's sword would appear very elegant alongside an officer's uniform. Unfortunately, it was far too flimsy to be an effective battlefield weapon.

British infantry officer's sword, 1803 Pattern

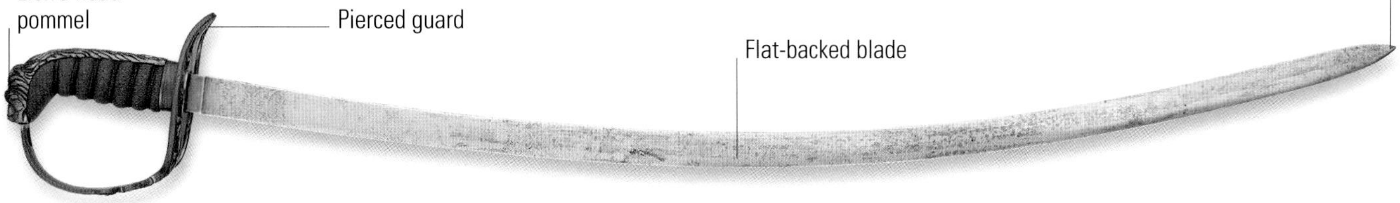

DATE	1803
ORIGIN	BRITISH
LENGTH	94.2cm (37.1in)

The 1803 Pattern was a considerable departure from its previous incarnation (the 1796 Pattern) and answered the request by British infantry officers for a stronger sword that had good slashing capabilities. With a lion's-head pommel, slotted hilt, slightly curved blade and a knuckle guard featuring an inset royal cypher and crown, this was an elaborate and attractive sword for officers.

British rifle officer's sword, 52nd Regiment, *c.*1810

The elite 52nd (Oxfordshire) Light Infantry Regiment served with Wellington during the Peninsular Campaigns (1808–13) and at the Battle of Waterloo (1815). The strung bugle motif of a rifle regiment is placed on the fishskin grip.

DATE	*c.*1810
ORIGIN	BRITISH
LENGTH	90.1cm (35.5in)

Swords of the British Empire

The British Army experimented with many new sword designs during the 19th century and army committees were regularly established to design the perfect sword: one with both cutting and thrusting capabilities. The designs were never wholly successful and often proved to be unsatisfactory in the field. Despite this, the sword was still used extensively in battle throughout the British Empire.

British Life Guards trooper's sword, 1820 Pattern

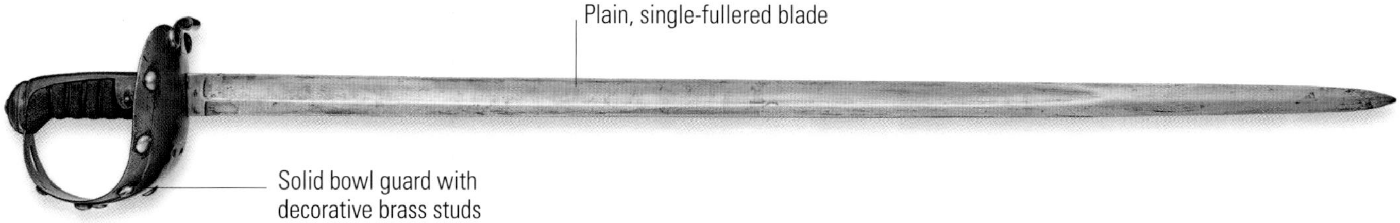

The distinguishing feature of this sword is a solid bowl guard and 12 decorative brass studs placed around the outside edge. The single-edged blade was unusually long (about 95cm, or 37.4in) and could be quite effective (albeit a little unwieldy) if used correctly by a strong sword arm.

DATE	1820
ORIGIN	BRITISH
LENGTH	110.5cm (43.5in)

British Royal Horse Guards trooper's sword, 1820 Pattern

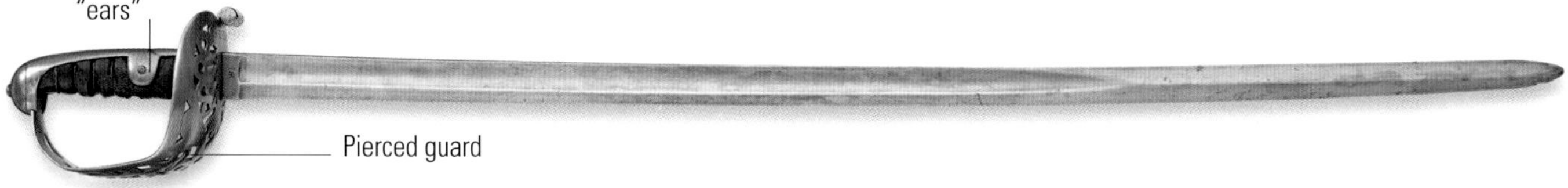

Similar to heavy cavalry officers' swords of this period, the Royal Horse Guards Trooper's Sword has a "honeysuckle" hilt, with the hilt bars arranged to give the appearance of a stylized, trailing plant. Unlike an officer's sword, the backstrap has strengthening "ears" riveted through the tang.

DATE	1820
ORIGIN	BRITISH
LENGTH	111.3cm (43.8in)

British heavy cavalry officer's sword, 1821 Pattern

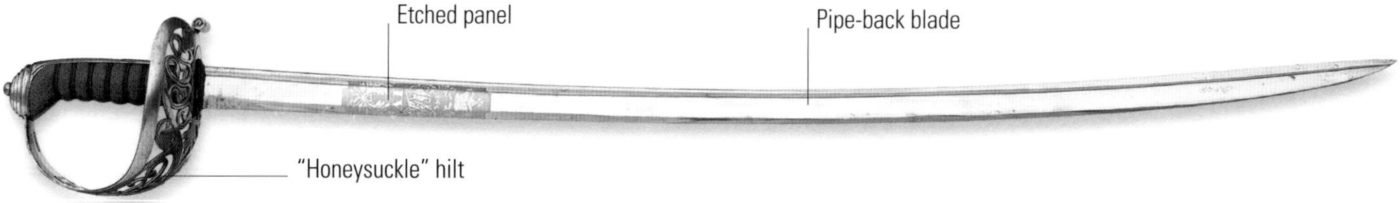

The introduction of this pattern coincided with the development of a new kind of service blade, known as the "pipe back". This blade has a tubular strengthening "pipe" that runs down the top edge of the blade, terminating in a quillpoint. The bowl guard was pierced and decorated with a "honeysuckle" pattern.

DATE	1821
ORIGIN	BRITISH
LENGTH	92.1cm (36.2in)

British light cavalry trooper's sword, 1821 Pattern

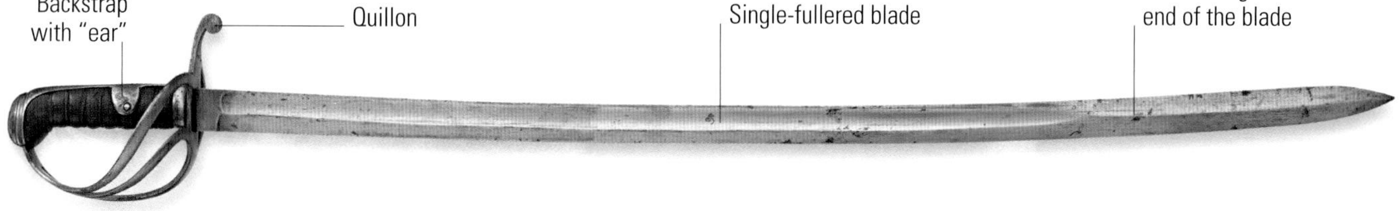

DATE	1821
ORIGIN	BRITISH
LENGTH	103.6cm (40.8in)

The arrival of the 1821 Pattern was a deliberate attempt to produce a true cut-and-thrust sword. It had a slightly curved, spear pointed and single-fullered blade that was double-edged towards the end. The leather-covered grip had a strengthening "ear" that was formed from the backstrap and riveted into the grip.

British heavy cavalry trooper's sword, 1821 Pattern

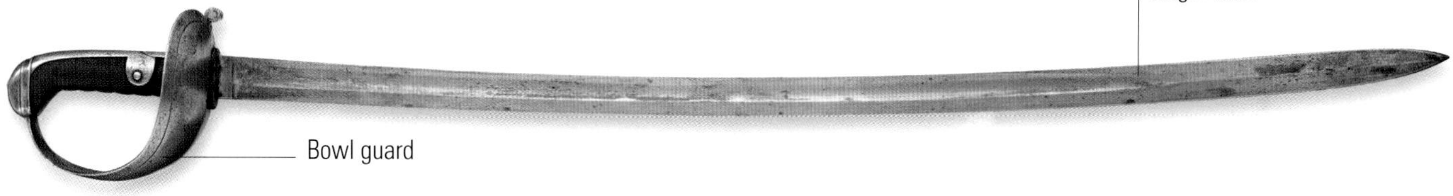

DATE	1821
ORIGIN	BRITISH
LENGTH	107cm (42.1in)

The 1821 Pattern Heavy Cavalry Trooper's Sword was part of a new generation of cut-and-thrust bladed swords that were introduced in the 1820s by the British Army to counter complaints that previous patterns were not effective in either requirement. Unfortunately, the solid bowl guard was too thin and the blades were prone to break in combat.

Light dragoons

The light dragoon regiments of the British Army were formed during the mid-18th century with the primary function of providing a reconnaissance and skirmishing role for the main army before a battle. They did not take part in the initial charge (normally reserved for the heavy cavalry), but by the time of the Napoleonic Wars (1799–1815) this strategy had changed and light dragoons now took an active part in any major battle. They gained particular experience and acclaim during the long campaigns of the Peninsular War (1808–14). Occasionally, they were also known to fight dismounted if the occasion required it. The 22nd Dragoons fought on foot during the Anglo-Dutch Java (Dutch East Indies) Campaign of 1811. The main sword pattern carried by British light dragoons during the Napoleonic period would have been the stirrup-hilted 1796 Pattern light cavalry trooper's sword.

ABOVE Light dragoons at the charge in the East Indies, *c.*1821.

British infantry officer's sword, 1822 Pattern

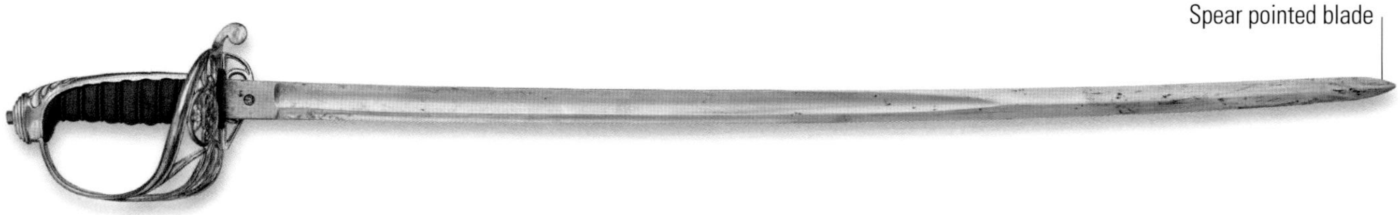

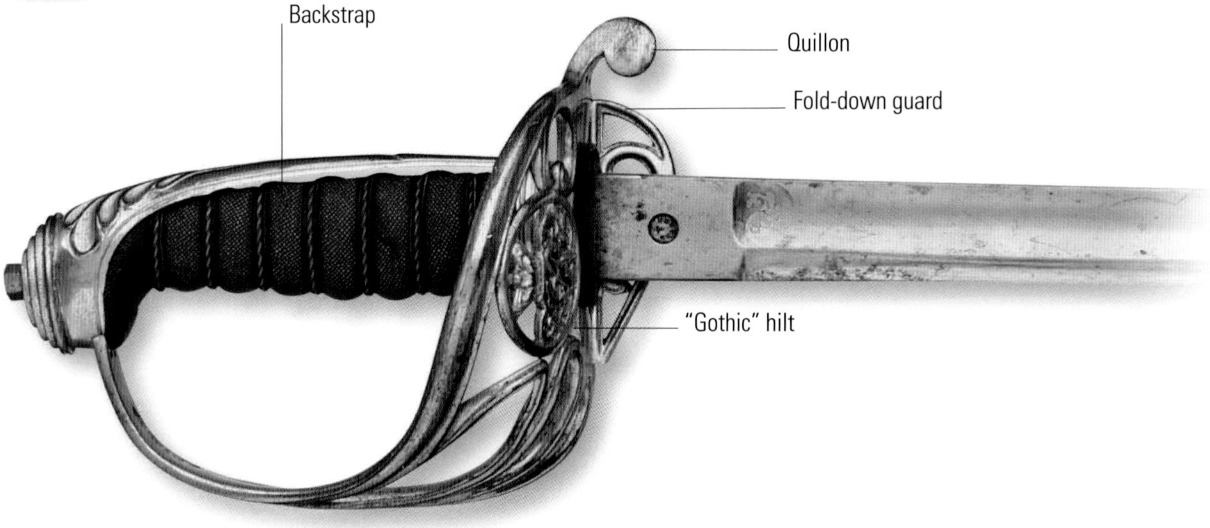

This sword was a radical departure from previous British infantry swords and displayed a pierced brass "Gothic" style, half-basket hilt. The term "Gothic" refers to the hilt design, which closely resembled the shape of church windows in the medieval Gothic style, a design motif popular in Britain during the first half of the 19th century. Within the hilt is an open-work cartouche with the royal cypher of the reigning monarch.

DATE	1822
ORIGIN	BRITISH
LENGTH	89.3cm (35.1in)

British 5th Dragoon Guards sword, *c.*1825

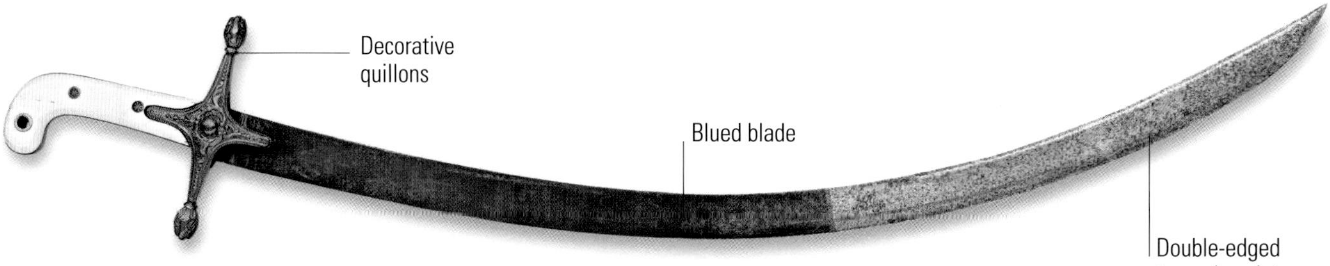

The French invasion of Egypt (1798–1801) by Napoleon Bonaparte was an attempt to protect French trade interests and hinder Britain's access to India. The involvement of the British Army during this campaign meant that many officers came into contact with eastern swords and led to British cavalry officers adopting the mameluke sword. Many officers brought home curved eastern swords and they became extremely fashionable, especially within hussar regiments. This example is typical and comprises an ivory-slab grip, double quillons, langets and an *écusson* (cartouche) in the middle of the cross guard. Blades are always curved.

DATE	*c.*1825
ORIGIN	BRITISH
LENGTH	83.9cm (33in)

British rifle officer's sword, Madras Native Infantry, 1827 Pattern

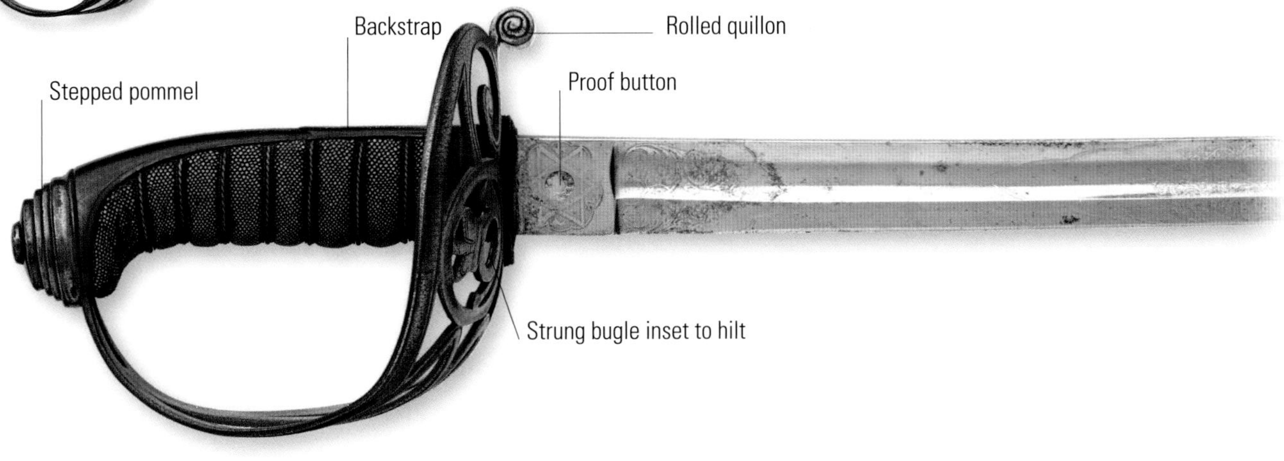

DATE	1827
ORIGIN	BRITISH
LENGTH	100cm (39.4in)

Formed in 1800, the Rifle Brigade (95th Regiment) carried this 1827 Pattern Rifle Officer's Sword throughout the 19th century. It has a steel Gothic hilt, with a strung bugle (symbolizing the use of a bugle to control troops) in the centre of the hilt. The strung bugle motif is usually repeated on the blade.

British Life Guards officer's dress sword, *c.*1840

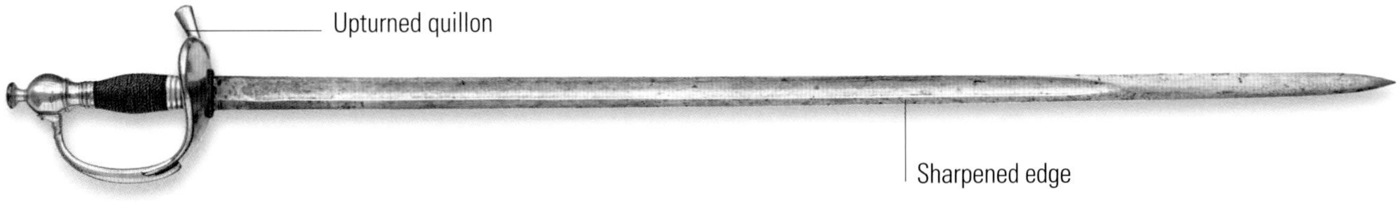

DATE	*c.*1840
ORIGIN	BRITISH
LENGTH	104cm (41in)

This sword would have been worn for evening (levee) or parade use. It is based on the 1796 Pattern Heavy Cavalry Officer's Dress Sword and has a boat-shell hilt, straight, single-edged blade and a distinctive, flattened pommel. The scabbards have unusually long frog lockets (used to secure the scabbard to a sword belt).

British infantry officer's sword, *c.*1860

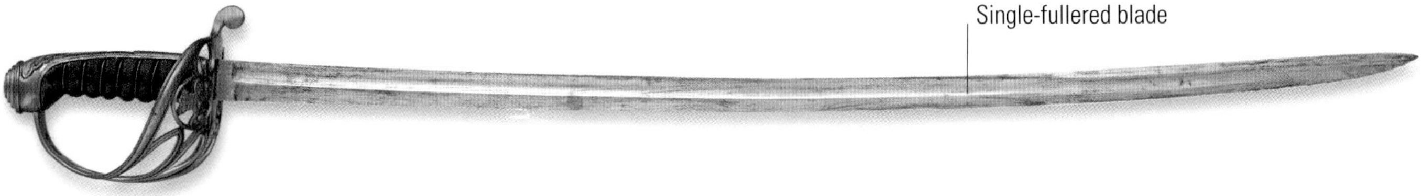

DATE	*c.*1860
ORIGIN	BRITISH
LENGTH	96.5cm (38in)

This is a later variation of the 1822 Pattern Infantry Officer's Sword and comprises a Gothic pierced gilt-brass, half-basket hilt. By this time, the fold-down guard had been removed and the pipe-back blade had been substituted with a single-fullered and spear-pointed version.

British cavalry trooper's sword, 1853 Pattern

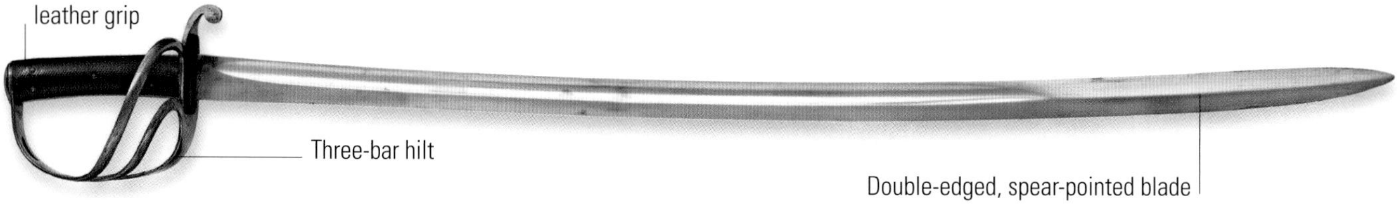

This sword was an attempt by the British Army to combine the hilt and blade characteristics of both the light and the heavy trooper's sword into one universal pattern. The chequered leather grip was riveted into the tang, giving the sword much more strength. Troopers using the sword often complained that the three-bar hilt allowed an enemy to thrust his sword point through the gaps.

DATE	1853
ORIGIN	BRITISH
LENGTH	104.6cm (41.2in)

British cavalry trooper's sword, 1864 Pattern

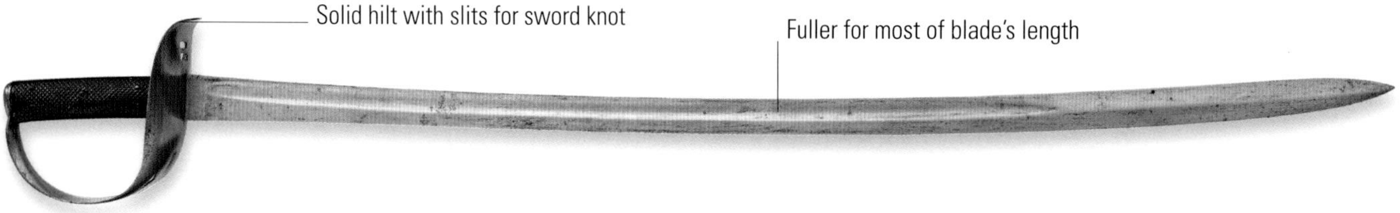

This is quite a scarce sword as relatively few were manufactured. It uses the blade from an 1853 Pattern Cavalry Trooper's Sword but the open, three-bar hilt of the previous pattern has been replaced by a shallow, solid hilt, with a cut-out Maltese Cross design. Unusually, two small slits (for sword knots) were placed at the back of the hilt, in imitation of contemporary Austrian cavalry swords.

DATE	1864
ORIGIN	BRITISH
LENGTH	107.5cm (42.3in)

British cavalry trooper's sword, 1882 Pattern

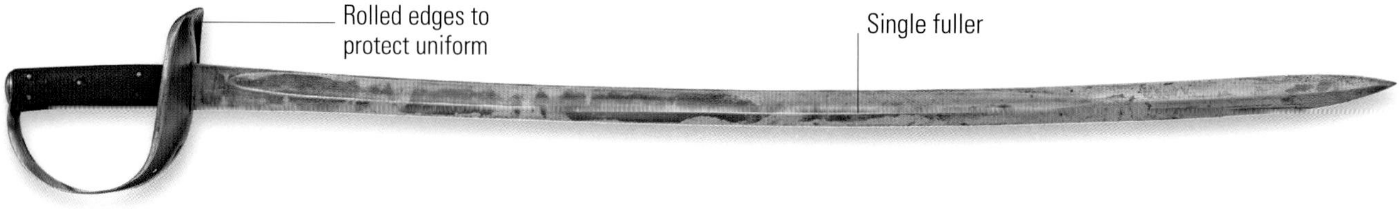

There were two blade lengths for this pattern, termed either "short" or "long". The reason for the different lengths is unclear, although it has been suggested that certain regiments recruited taller troopers and the longer pattern was needed for these soldiers. In any case, the pattern was changed three times due to constant blade and hilt failings. Despite these drawbacks, the pattern was widely issued to cavalry regiments and German sword companies had to make up the shortfall when British suppliers could not produce enough swords for the British Army.

DATE	1882
ORIGIN	BRITISH
LENGTH	101.6cm (41.3in)

British infantry officer's sword, 1895 Pattern

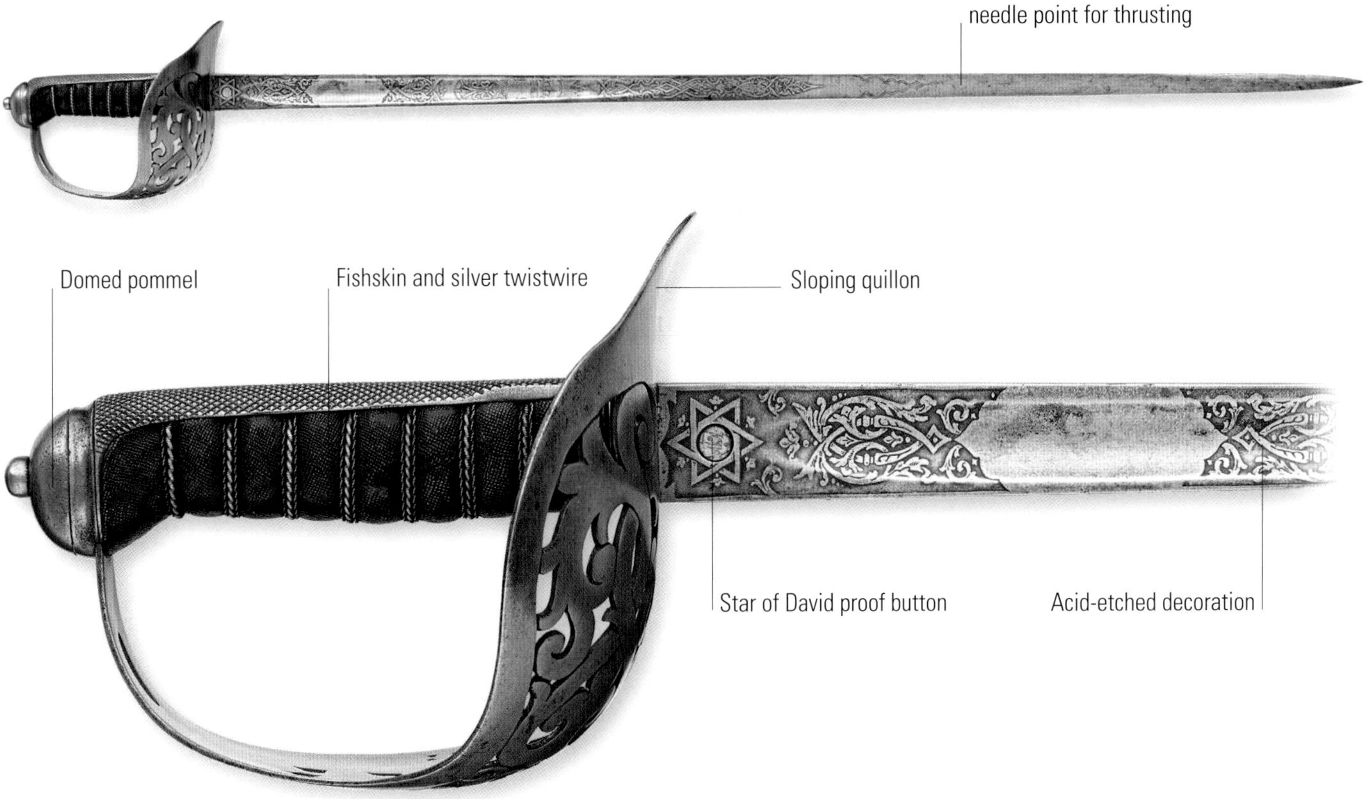

DATE	1895
ORIGIN	BRITISH
LENGTH	97.3cm (38.3in)

This sword was a considerable improvement on previous patterns as the design afforded much better protection for the wearer's hand through the provision of a three-quarter basket hilt. Combined with a more robust blade introduced in 1892 and boasting a ruthless thrusting point, the sword proved quite effective on the battlefield. An alteration was made in 1897, with the addition of a small, turned-down, inner guard to prevent fraying of the uniform. Most swords of this pattern are found with either a fishskin or leather-wrapped grip.

British cavalry trooper's sword, 1899 Pattern

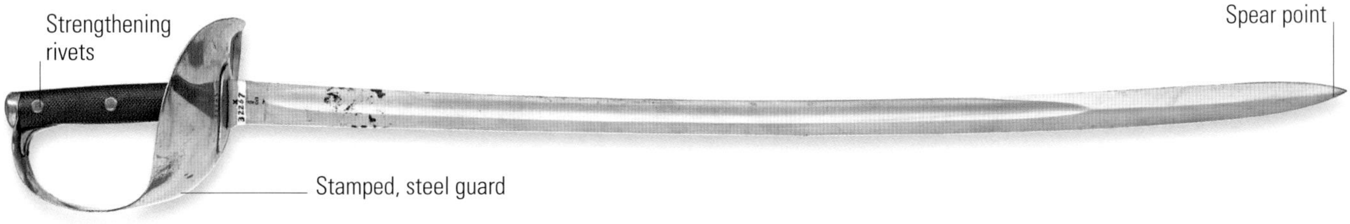

DATE	1899
ORIGIN	BRITISH
LENGTH	101.8cm (40.1in)

A solid guard made from thin sheet metal distinguishes this pattern, coupled with an unusually long, stamped, leather grip. The serving soldier, however, soon complained that the long grip slipped out of his hand (particularly in the hotter climes of the British Empire) and the thin guard was prone to breaking once it had been struck by a sword blade. It was also issued with a thin, steel scabbard that tended to be easily damaged. This was a pattern loathed by cavalry troopers and it necessitated a radical re-evaluation of British military sword design.

Swords of the Russian Empire

Before the Napoleonic Wars (1799–1815), Russian swords were heavily influenced by eastern sword design. During the 19th century, European-inspired swords became more common in Russia. Swords from her one-time enemy, France, were also heavily copied and large stocks of captured French swords were reissued to Russian troops following Napoleon's disastrous march on Moscow, in 1812.

Russian cavalry trooper's sword, Model 1826

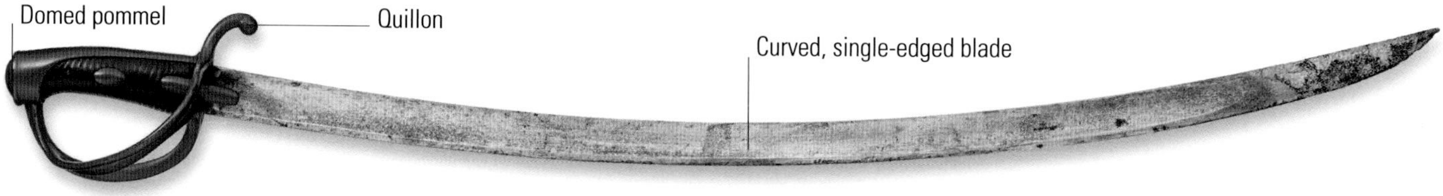

This sword is a later copy of the French Model AN XI Light Cavalry Trooper's Sword. It has a wide, single-edged, slightly curved blade, brass three-bar hilt and double langets. Overall, it was quite a robust sword and would have been an effective close-quarter, hacking weapon.

DATE	1826
ORIGIN	RUSSIAN
LENGTH	101.8cm (40.1in)

Russian pioneer sword, Model 1827

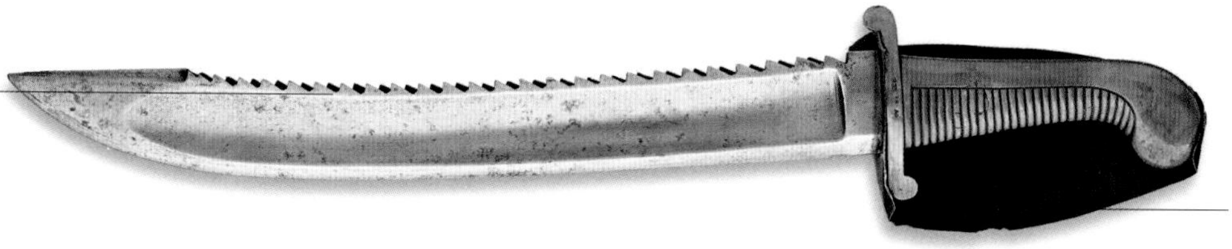

The enormous saw-back blade of this sword was used by pioneer troops to cut away undergrowth and construct defensive works. The cast brass hilt was extremely heavy and it must therefore have been a cumbersome weapon to carry for any great distance.

DATE	1827
ORIGIN	RUSSIAN
LENGTH	67.9cm (26.7in)

Russian artillery short sword, Model 1847

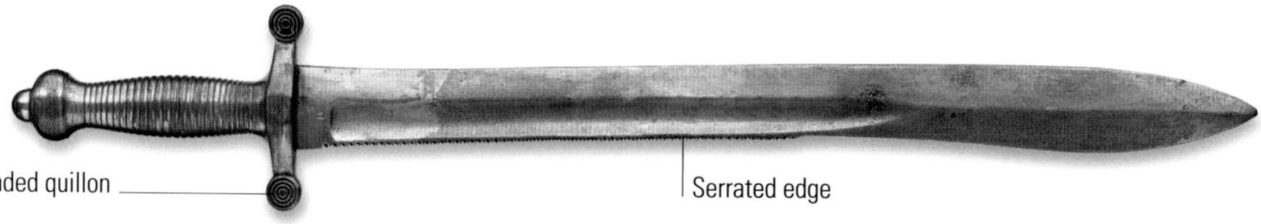

This is the successor to the Model 1827 Pioneer Sword and has a "gladius" style identical to contemporary French designs. It still incorporated a saw-back blade, although it is doubtful whether these swords were actually used in combat. The end of the blade is double-edged and bulbous. The sword was carried in a leather and brass mounted scabbard. Most are in good condition, indicating little use.

DATE	1847
ORIGIN	RUSSIAN
LENGTH	63.5cm (25in)

Napoleon's invasion of Moscow

The French Army that invaded Russia in 1812 comprised many different European nationalities and, consequently, they would have carried a wide range of edged weapons. During this period Napoleon raised several regiments of lancers who would have frequently clashed with the Russian Cossack cavalry during the retreat from Moscow.

RIGHT The entry of French forces into Moscow on 14 September 1812. The troops are carrying a wide range of weapons.

Russian infantry/artillery officer's sword, Model 1865

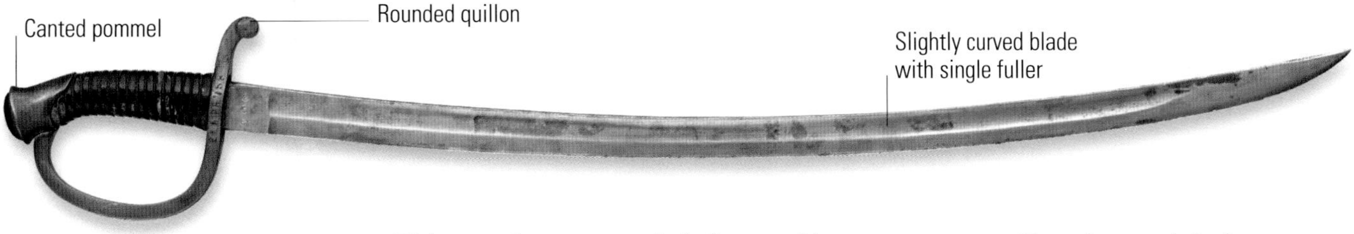

This sword was strongly influenced by contemporary French sword designs. The hilt has a canted, or angled, pommel that is also seen on French swords, coupled with a D-shaped knuckle guard. Most Russian infantry swords of this period display single knuckle guards lacking extra hilt bars, thus affording little protection to the hand. Russian sword blades tended to be well made and robust, and they stood up well to battle conditions when compared with contemporary European (particularly British) sword blades.

DATE	1865
ORIGIN	RUSSIAN
LENGTH	89.7cm (35.3in)

Russian cavalry trooper's sword, Model 1881

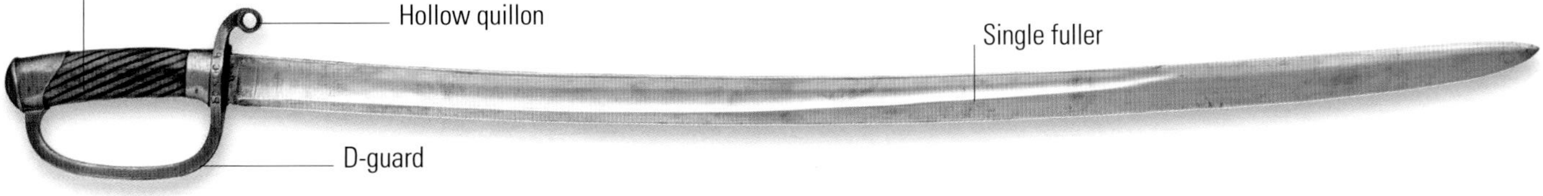

These swords were produced in vast quantities for the Imperial Russian Army. Later models have an attachment on the scabbard for the provision of a socket bayonet (Model 1891 Moisin-Nagant). The hilt comprises a ribbed wooden grip and a D-shaped knuckle guard. The quillon is unusual in being hollow. Many swords are regimentally marked on the cross guard, although it is common for this designation to be defaced. The post-1917 revolutionary Bolsheviks regularly erased any traces they could find of the Imperial Russian monarchy on both swords and weapons.

DATE	1881
ORIGIN	RUSSIAN
LENGTH	101.6cm (40in)

Swords of the German Empire

Before the unification of Germany in 1871, independent German states carried their own distinctive sword styles and models, with most following the sword fashions of the day in Europe. After unification, more standardized patterns were developed for use in all branches of the new Imperial German Army, although individual state emblems were still incorporated into the design of the sword.

Prussian infantry officer's dress sword, *c.*1870

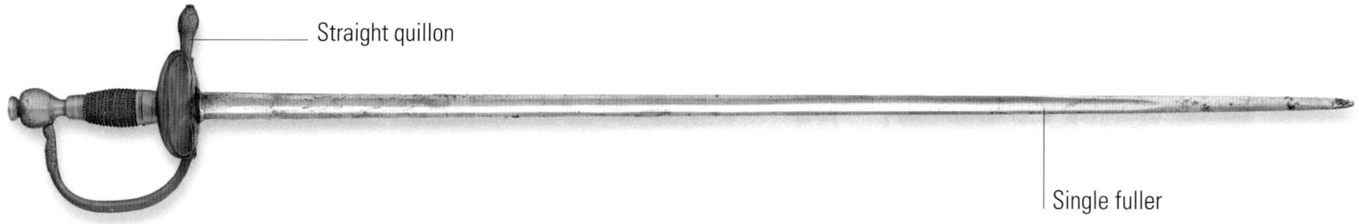

This style of sword was influenced by earlier Napoleonic smallswords and featured a double shell guard, D-shaped knuckle guard and ovoid pommel. The blade was straight and single-edged. It was not an effective combat weapon and would have been relegated for use as a dress sword.

DATE	*c.*1870
ORIGIN	PRUSSIAN
LENGTH	100.3cm (39.5in)

German officer's sword, *c.*1880

The dove-head pommel is a common feature on German swords of this period. In this case it is combined with a stirrup hilt and shield-shaped langets that display a silver badge of oak leaves and crossed swords. This indicates use by a cavalry officer.

DATE	*c.*1880
ORIGIN	GERMAN
LENGTH	92.2cm (36.3in)

Bavarian infantry officer's sword, Model 1889

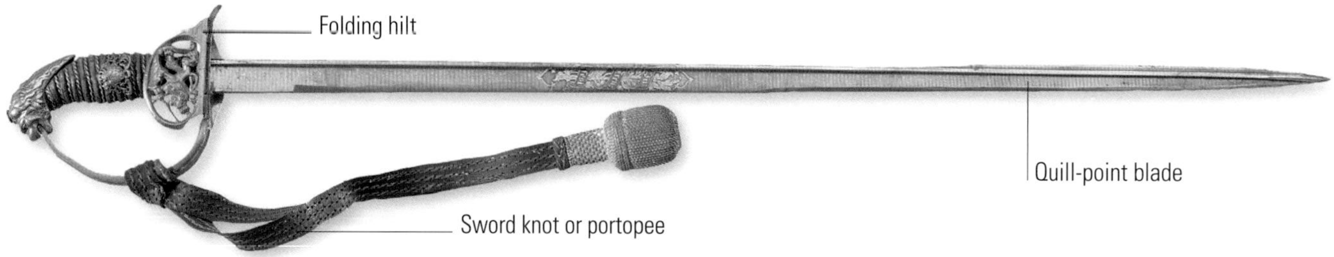

This is a very high-quality example of a late 19th-century Bavarian infantry officer's sword. It is etched with the Bavarian national motto *In Treue Fest* (Firm in Loyalty). The lion's-head hilt is gold plated and has a folding guard. It still retains its original green and silver bullion sword knot.

DATE	1889
ORIGIN	GERMAN
LENGTH	94cm (37in)

Prussian cavalry trooper's sword, Model 1889

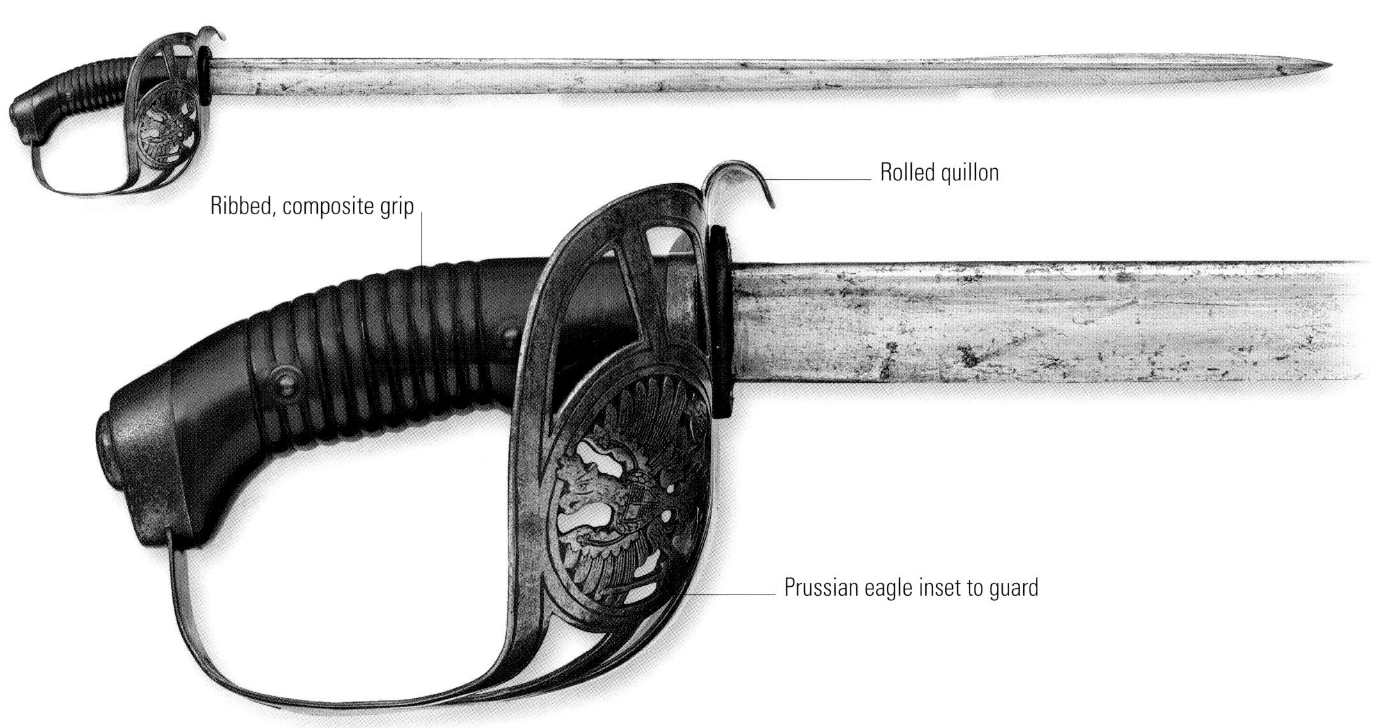

DATE	1889
ORIGIN	PRUSSIAN
LENGTH	96cm (37.8in)

This is a very common German cavalry sword and was widely issued to mounted regiments from the end of the 19th century and right through World War I. It incorporates an angled pistol grip (for better lunging) of composite material and has a steel guard inset with the Prussian eagle.

Bavarian regimental sword of Kaiser Wilhelm II, *c.*1900

DATE	*c.*1900
ORIGIN	GERMAN
LENGTH	92cm (36.2in)

This sword was carried by Kaiser Wilhelm II (1859–1941) and worn with his Bavarian regimental uniform. The engraved, double-fullered blade is of watered, or patterned, steel, with a gold-plated hilt. The Bavarian national coat of arms is embossed on the hilt back plate and the grip is covered in sharkskin, bound with gilt wire. The scabbard is nickel-plated iron. The screw pommel cap bears the engraved royal cipher "WII" beneath a crown.

Swords of the Austro-Hungarian Empire

The Austro-Hungarian Empire (1700–1915) stretched across a large area of central Europe and was second in size only to the Russian Empire. There were many different cultures within the empire and this melting pot also influenced sword design. One of the most striking sword designs was the curved, stirrup-hilted, light cavalry sword of the Hungarian hussar. Over time, it would be adopted by most European armies.

Austro-Hungarian hussar officer's sword, *c.*1750

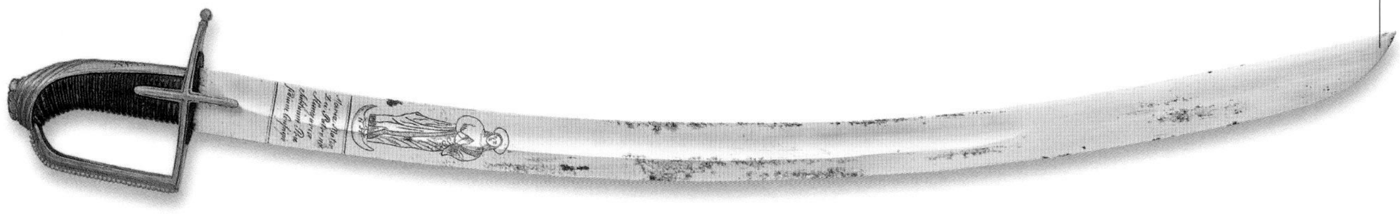

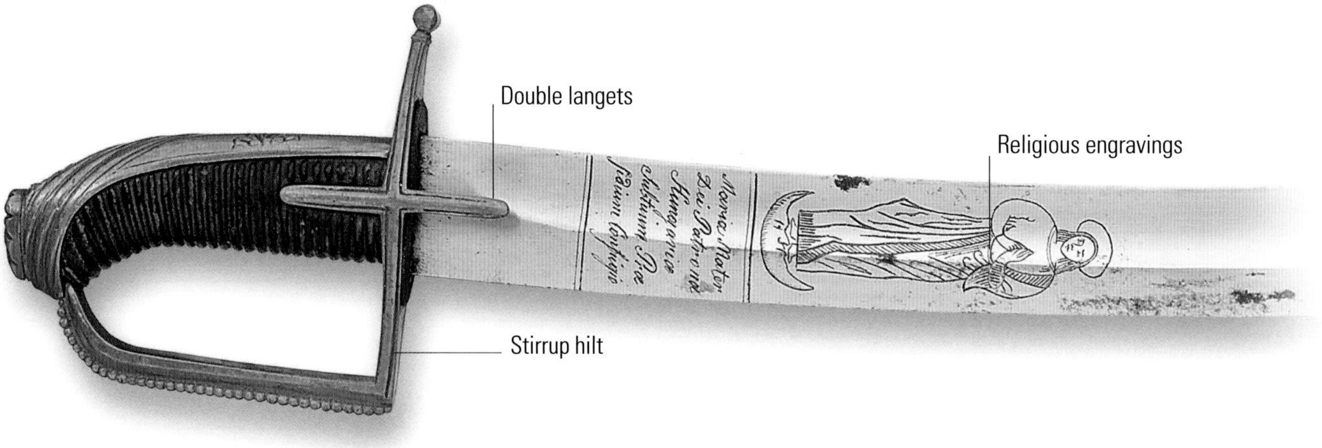

Hussars were lightly equipped, mounted soldiers, known for their speed and mobility. The "stirrup" hilt is a design that was first recognized on hussar swords, combined with double langets positioned in the centre of the cross guard. The blade is of substantial width, and single-edged with a hatchet point. Religious themes, particularly representations of saints and invocatory prayers, were commonly engraved into blades.

DATE	*c.*1750
ORIGIN	AUSTRO-HUNGARIAN
LENGTH	93.4cm (36.8in)

Austrian infantry pioneer's sword, *c.*1780

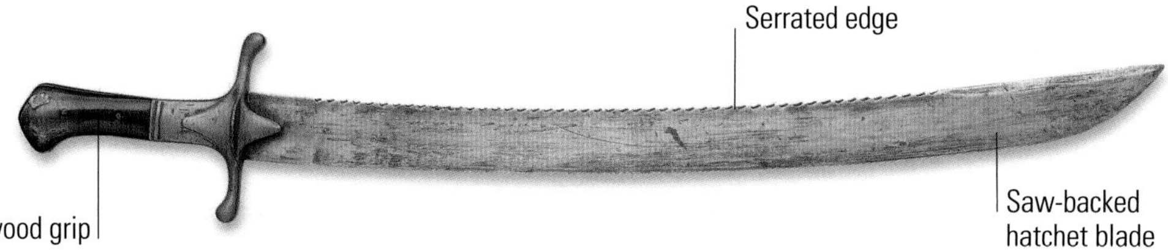

This short hanger was carried by sappers or pioneers. The row of teeth on top of the blade would have been used for sawing through wood and constructing rudimentary defences. The brass and hardwood grip is reminiscent of eastern or Ottoman (Turkish) swords.

DATE	*c.*1780
ORIGIN	AUSTRIAN
LENGTH	85.7cm (33.7in)

Austrian infantry officer's sword, *c.*1800

DATE	*c.*1800
ORIGIN	AUSTRIAN
LENGTH	91.7cm (36.1in)

Of smallsword style, this infantry officer's sword has a boat-shell hilt that mirrors contemporary European designs. The blade is double-edged and has a rapier-like profile. As a thrusting weapon, it would have been quite effective.

Austrian infantry officer's sword, Model 1837

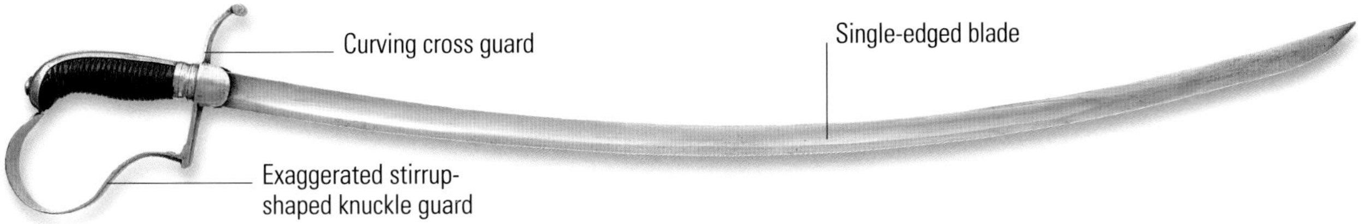

DATE	1837
ORIGIN	AUSTRIAN
LENGTH	96.7cm (38.1in)

A bulging and exaggerated knuckle guard was fashionable on infantry swords of this period and is also seen on contemporary infantry swords from Prussia, Bavaria and Saxony. A spring catch was normally fitted to the top of the blade to prevent it slipping out of the scabbard.

Austrian cavalry officer's sword, Model 1850

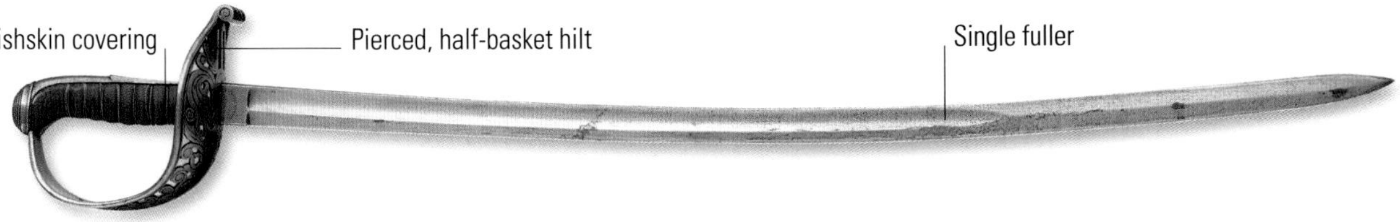

DATE	1850
ORIGIN	AUSTRIAN
LENGTH	97.8cm (38.5in)

This Austrian cavalry officer's sword of the mid-19th century has a slightly curved blade and a pierced, half-basket, or shallow, cup hilt. The grip is made of wood, wrapped in fishskin and twistwire. The sword would have been carried in a plain iron scabbard with two loose rings.

Austrian cavalry trooper's sword, Model 1861

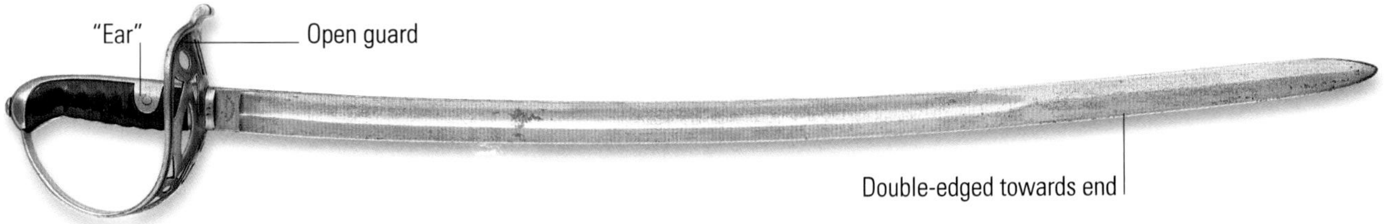

DATE	1861
ORIGIN	AUSTRIAN
LENGTH	97.8cm (38.5in)

The iron hilt of this sword is ornamented with circular and triangular perforations, and there are two slits at the back for placing a sword knot. The backstrap has a side projection, or "ear", with a rivet driven into the tang to further strengthen the grip and blade.

Swords of the French Empire

French sword design had considerable influence over military swords throughout Europe and beyond. During the 19th century, French hilt and blade styles were adopted by the armies of many countries.

Brass, three-bar hilts and domed pommels were common features on French cavalry swords, with infantry officers' swords displaying quill-pointed or spear-pointed blades and ribbed horn grips.

French infantry officer's sword, Model 1821

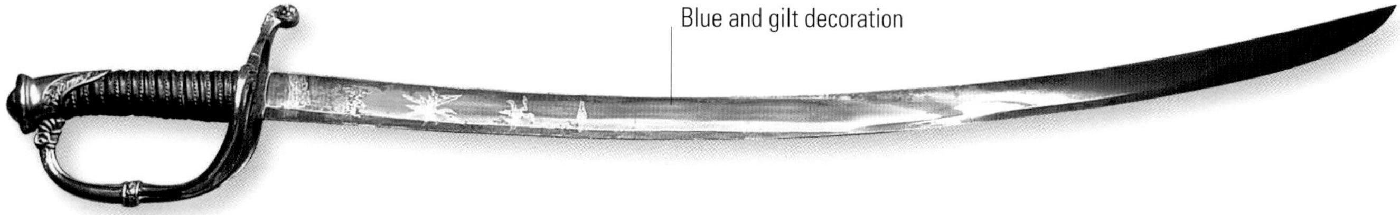

This is an interesting example of an infantry officer's sword with a fine blade decorated with blue and gilt. By the time that this model was introduced, the use of blue and gilt was beginning to lose favour within the French Army and subsequent models of this sword had completely plain blades.

DATE	1821
ORIGIN	FRENCH
LENGTH	105.9cm (41.7in)

French light cavalry trooper's sword, Model 1822

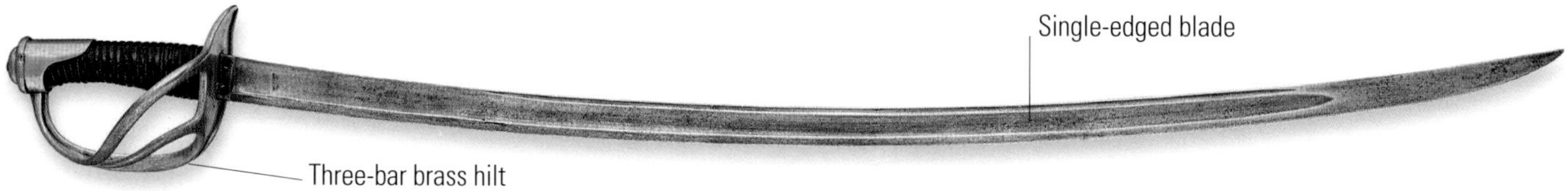

The Model 1822 was a lighter version of the sword carried by heavy cavalry troopers and featured a three-bar brass hilt, with leather and brass twistwire on the grip. The blade was slightly curved and single-edged. The sword was carried in a heavy, iron scabbard.

DATE	1822
ORIGIN	FRENCH
LENGTH	105.9cm (41.7in)

French artilleryman's short sword, Model 1831

Known as a "cabbage chopper", this short sword has its design origins in the ancient Roman "gladius" short sword. It had a solid brass, ribbed grip and a wide, spear-pointed blade. This sword is marked with an anchor and was probably carried by soldiers in the marine artillery. It is unlikely that it would have been used in a combat situation.

DATE	1831
ORIGIN	FRENCH
LENGTH	63.5cm (25in)

French infantry officer's sword, Model 1845

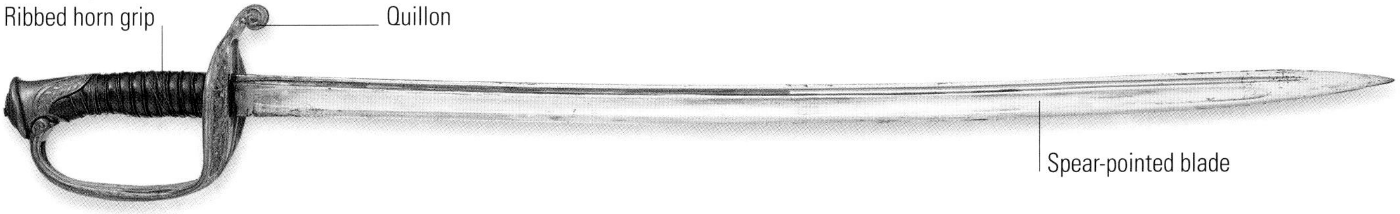

DATE	1845
ORIGIN	FRENCH
LENGTH	89.3cm (35.1in)

French infantry swords of this period were normally fitted with slightly curved, spear-pointed blades. Invariably, the blades were plain and without engraved decoration. Grips were manufactured from either dark stained horn or from a wooden core wrapped in leather and bound with brass twistwire.

French dragoon officer's sword, Model 1854

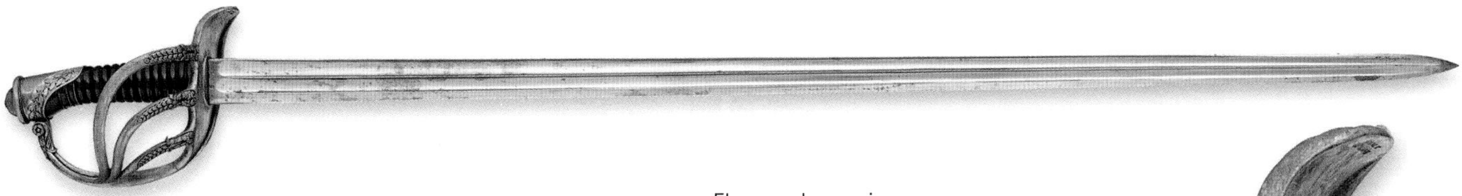

This officer's sword differs from the trooper's version in having a decorated hilt. The blade is straight, with double fullers. The straight, thrusting blade had been out of favour after the Napoleonic Wars (1799–1815) but was reintroduced during the mid-19th century as it was an effective battlefield weapon.

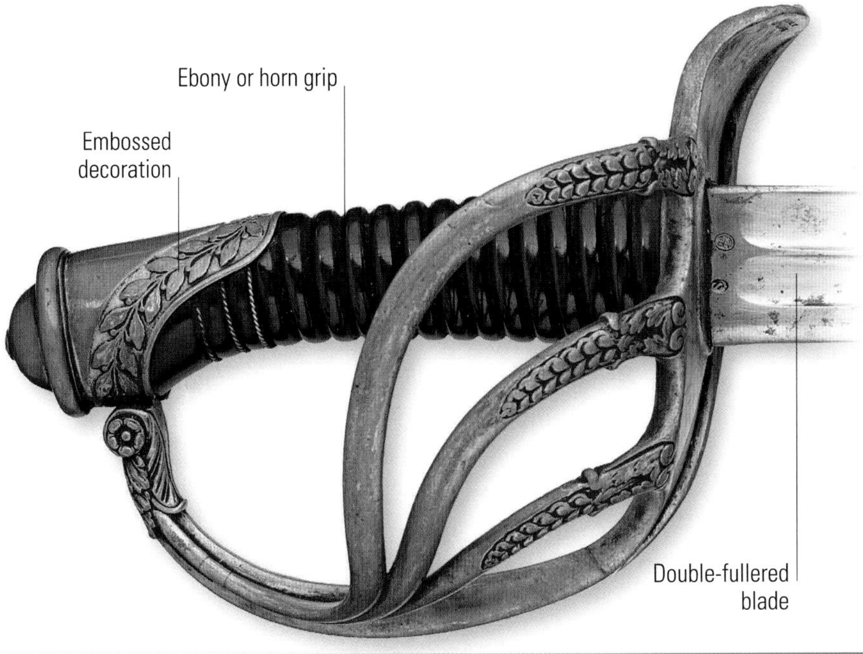

DATE	1854
ORIGIN	FRENCH
LENGTH	106.1cm (41.7in)

French cavalry officer's sword, Model 1896

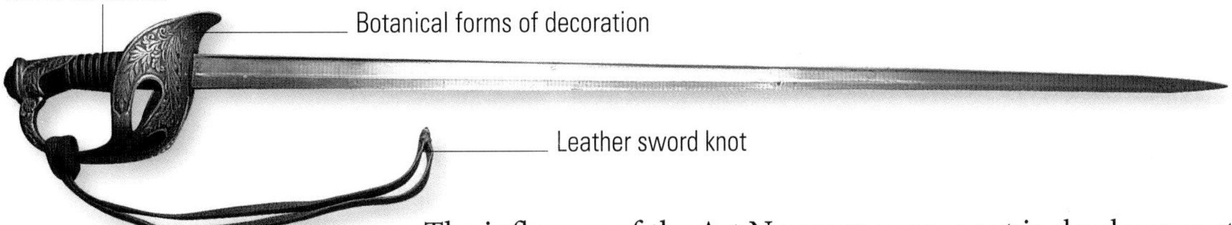

DATE	1896
ORIGIN	FRENCH
LENGTH	91.7cm (36.1in)

The influence of the Art Nouveau movement is clearly present in the design of this sword hilt. It was designed by the sculptor Jean Alexandre Falguiére, a professor at the School of Fine Arts in Paris. The free-flowing curves and expressive botanical forms are evidence of the contemporary vogue for natural themes, even in military decoration. The grip is made of buffalo horn, wrapped in silver twistwire.

Swords of the Ottoman Empire

At one time, the Ottoman Empire covered a vast geographical area in eastern Europe and the Middle East and was at the height of its power from the 15th to the 17th centuries. One of the most recognizable sword types of these Turkic peoples was a curved sabre, the inspiration for the Mamluk or mameluke sword, later to be adopted by European armies during the Napoleonic Wars (1799–1815).

Turkish sword (kilij), *c.*1770

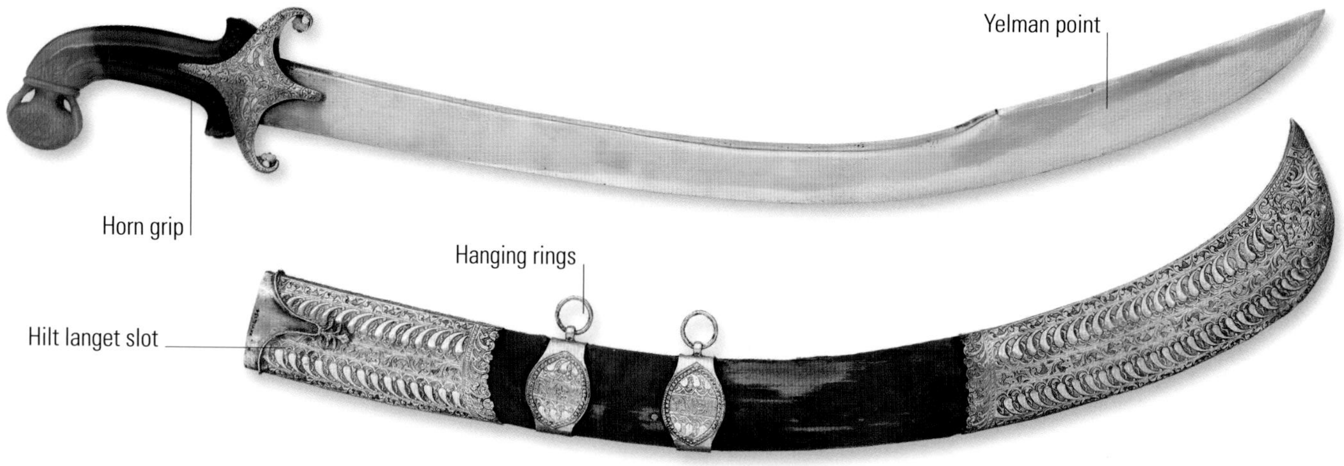

The kilij (meaning literally "sword") is a variation of the Turko-Mongolian wide-bladed and curved cavalry sabre that was carried throughout Eurasia from the 13th century. The end of the blade is flared and double-edged. This is known as the yelman. It added greater heft towards the front and substantial slashing power.

DATE	*c.*1770
ORIGIN	TURKISH
LENGTH	84cm (33.1in)

Persian sword (shamshir), *c.*1800

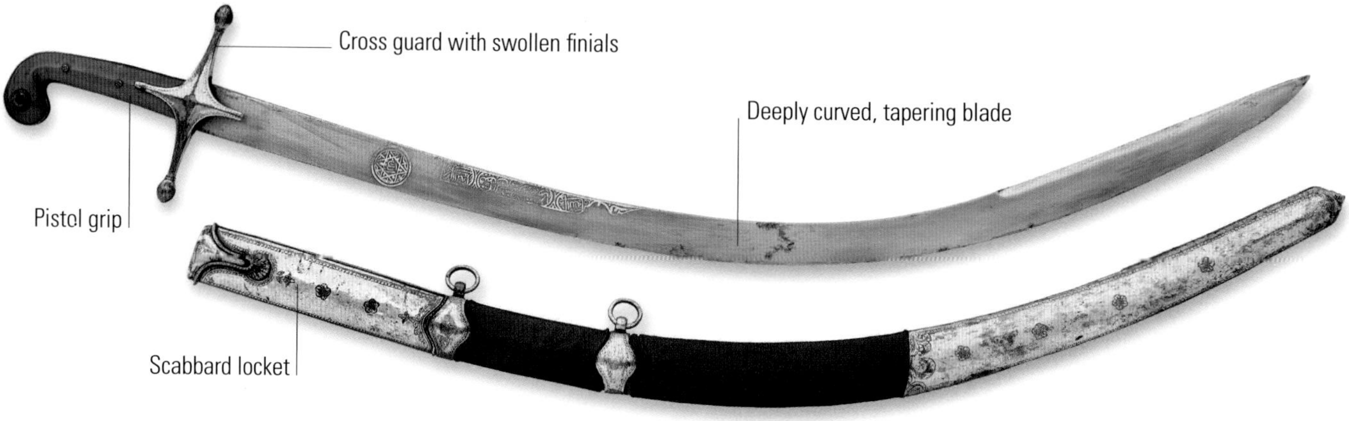

DATE	*c.*1800
ORIGIN	PERSIAN
LENGTH	90.9cm (35.8in)

Persian sword makers were long acknowledged as the undisputed masters of their craft and their blades exhibited superb tempering, sharpness and exquisite gold koftgari (inlaid gold on steel) decoration. This sword has a mameluke-style horn hilt with typical double langets and a cross guard that terminates in swollen finials. The blade flares into a double-edged yelman towards the point. The scabbard is brass and leather mounted, with an inset for the hilt langet.

Turkish sword (yataghan), *c.*1800

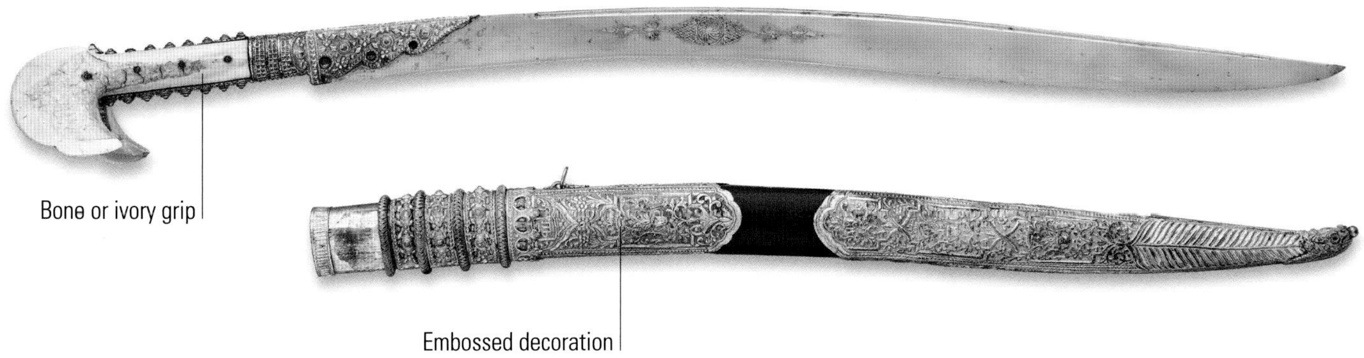

DATE	*c.*1800
ORIGIN	TURKISH
LENGTH	83cm (32.7in)

The yataghan is a distinctive sword with a forward-curving blade and very reminiscent of the kopis blade carried by the ancient Greeks. The yataghan was the standard weapon of the famous Turkish Janissaries (Turkish infantry), whereas the cavalry tended to carry the kilij. The handle of this sword is probably made from walrus ivory or bone, secured by a series of rivets. Scabbards were usually heavily decorated.

Turkish sword (yataghan), *c.*1800

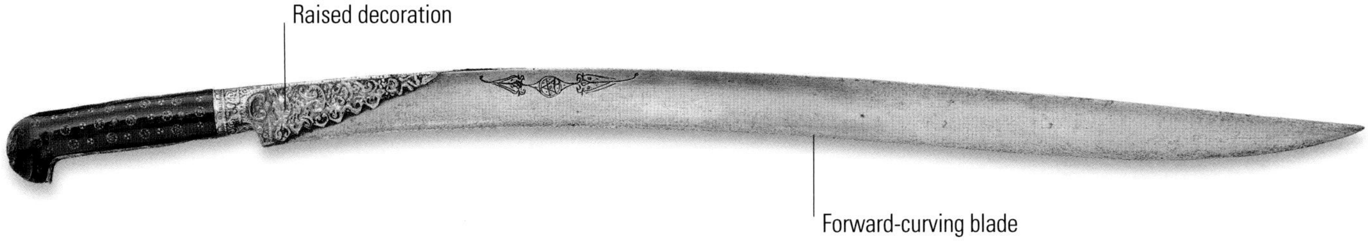

DATE	*c.*1800
ORIGIN	TURKISH
LENGTH	78.8cm (31in)

The Turkish yataghan blade is similar in profile to the Indian sosun pattah (with a forward-curving, leaf-shaped blade) and the Nepalese kukri, and has a forward-curving blade that would have been used like a large chopper, hacking and slashing with devastating effect. The raised decoration that flows from the end of the handle and on to the blade ricasso is a common feature on these swords. The decoration was usually made from inlaid gold or silver and the pattern was often repeated on the scabbard mounts.

Turkish sword (yataghan), *c.*1800

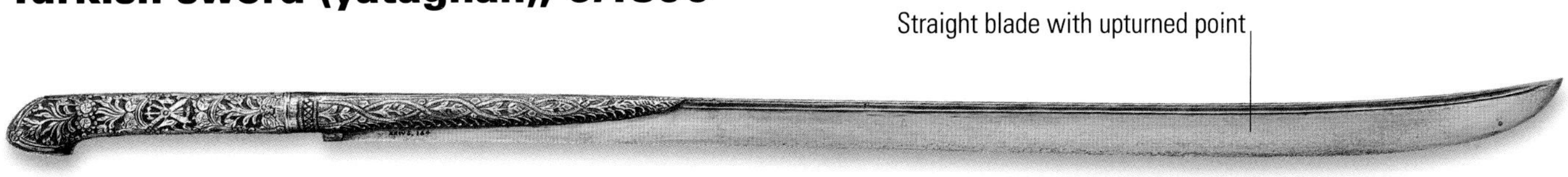

DATE	*c.*1800
ORIGIN	TURKISH
LENGTH	85cm (33.5in)

This sword is quite unusual in that the blade shape is not typical of most yataghans. Instead of the usual forward-curving blade, this version has a straight blade that ends with an upturned point. This blade is similar in shape to those used on Russian or Cossack swords.

Japanese swords

The production of a Japanese sword blade is the result of a complex and ritualized process, involving the creation of a blade that has a hard, cutting edge and a softer, more durable core and back. The sword maker undertakes a careful process of enfolding a number of steel layers and then selectively cooling different areas of the blade to produce a distinct range of qualities and a unique pattern (hamon). Japanese sword blades are considered to be amongst the finest ever created.

Japanese sword (nagamaki) by Unji, *c.*1300

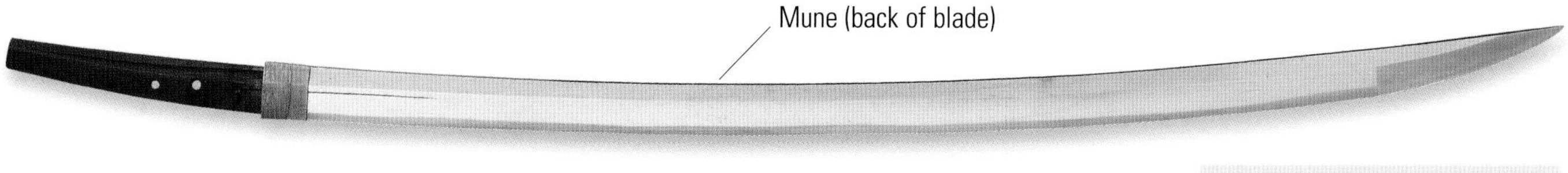

This sword blade was manufactured for use on a two-handed polearm, known as a nagamaki (translated as "long wrapping"). The weapon would have had a long metal or lacquered-wood handle, mounted with a katana-type blade.

DATE	*c.*1300
ORIGIN	JAPANESE
LENGTH	85.8cm (33.8in)

Japanese sword (katana) by Masamitsu, *c.*1370

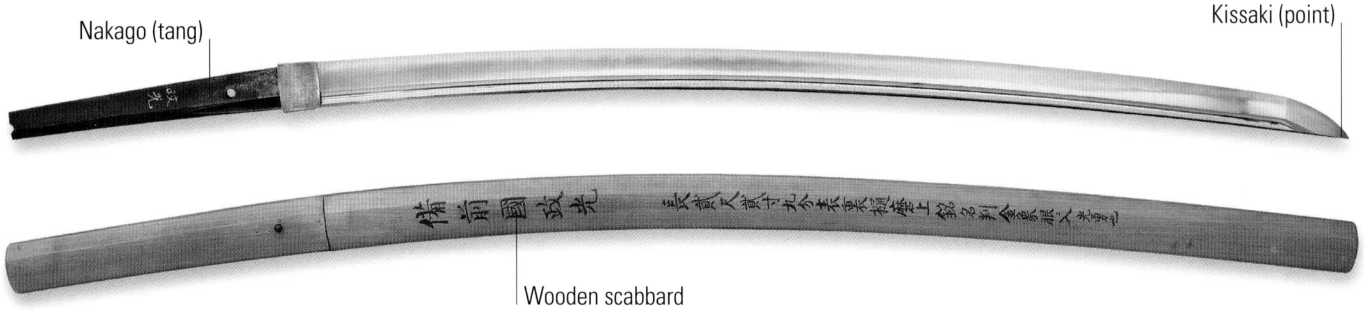

This is a very early katana sword made by the swordsmith Masamitsu. He was from Takano, in Geishu (near present-day Hiroshima), and was a notable smith. His blades were known for their superb cutting qualities. This sword is housed in a protective wooden scabbard which is likely to be a later addition.

DATE	*c.*1370
ORIGIN	JAPANESE
LENGTH	76.4cm (30.1in)

Japanese sword (wakizashi) by Kanesada, *c.*1550

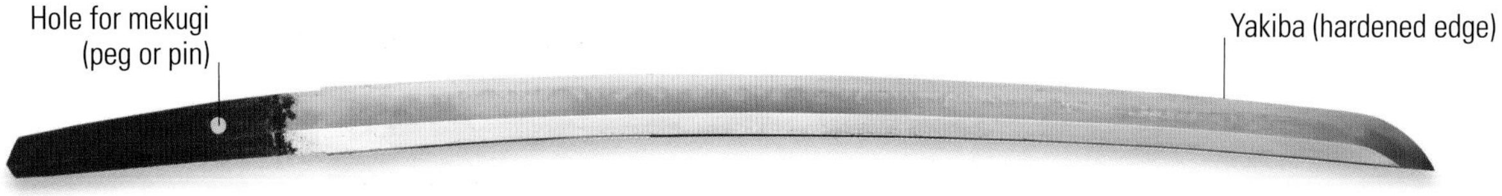

The swordsmith Kanesada was working in the town of Seki (between Tokyo and Osaka) during the 16th century. Known as the "City of Swords", Seki was a sword-making centre of excellence for well over 800 years. Kanesada gained a reputation for producing robust and practical blades. This is a wakizashi, or short sword, and would have been carried with a katana.

DATE	*c.*1550
ORIGIN	JAPANESE
LENGTH	59cm (23.2in)

Japanese sword (wakizashi) by Kaneyasu, *c.*1550

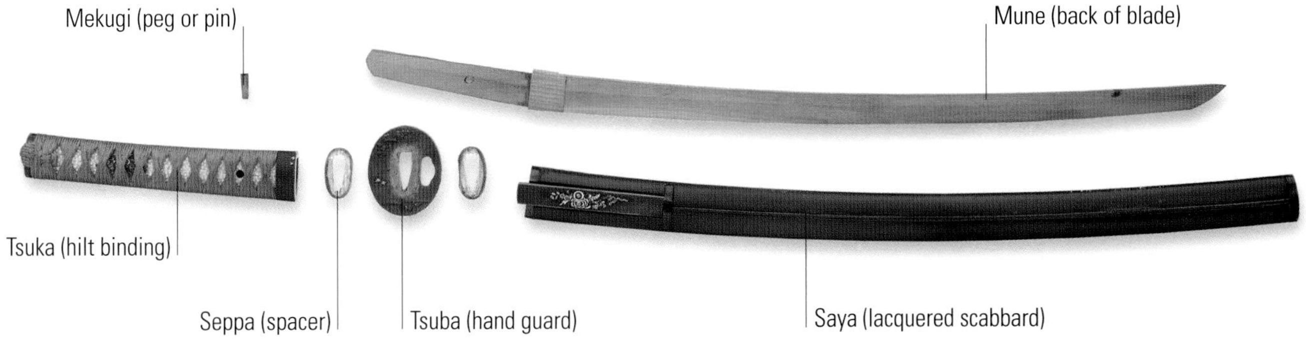

DATE	*c.*1550
ORIGIN	JAPANESE
LENGTH	62cm (24.4in)

Here we see the disassembled parts of a wakizashi sword. In order of importance, the blade – the heart of the sword – always came first. The blade's cutting qualities were the first consideration. Fittings such as the grip, hand guard and scabbard were always regarded as decorative (albeit important) extras, and were usually decorated with traditional Japanese motifs.

Japanese sword (katana) by Kunitsugu, *c.*1550

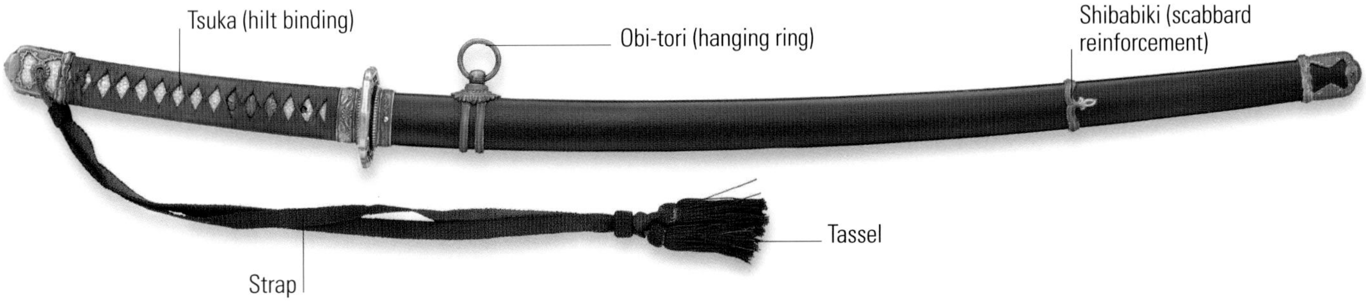

DATE	*c.*1550
ORIGIN	JAPANESE
LENGTH	97cm (38.2in)

Many katana swords were carried by high ranking Japanese officers. This sword was the property of Major-General Murai, who was a commander of the Japanese forces during the Battle of Pelelui, east of the Phillipines, in 1944. Although it is mounted in a scabbard that dates from this time, the blade was originally produced by Takeda Kunitsugu, a swordsmith working in Aizu, near Tokyo, during the 16th century. Many Japanese swords have hilts and scabbards that were made at a much later date than their blades.

Japanese sword (katana) by Sadayuki, *c.*1650

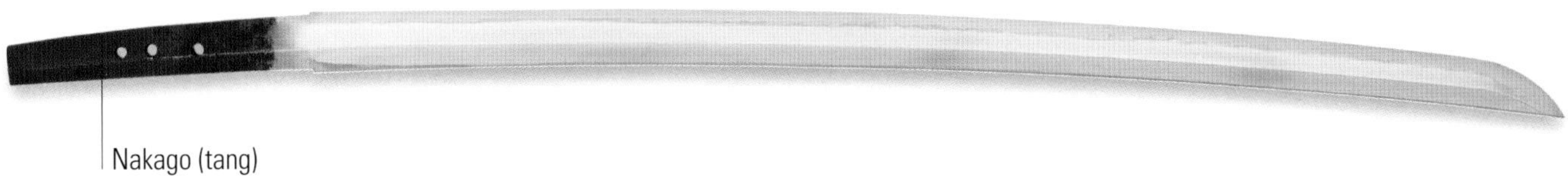

DATE	*c.*1650
ORIGIN	JAPANESE
LENGTH	93.9cm (37in)

The tang (nakago) of a handmade Japanese sword was normally marked with the maker's name, date of manufacture and province in which the maker lived. Yamato Dairoku Sadayuki is on a list of 228 great katana swordsmiths published in a work of 1805 (the *Kaihokenshaku*) by the Samurai Yamada Asaemon, who worked as a tester of Japanese sword blades.

Japanese sword (wakizashi) by Kanemoto, *c.*1650

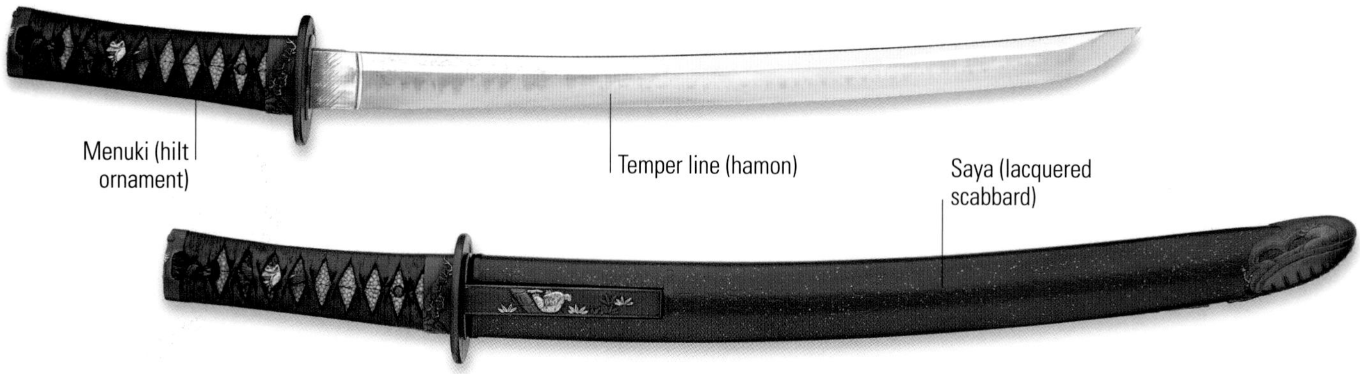

The wakizashi was a short sword favoured by the Samurai and worn with civilian dress or in combination with his longer katana sword. The wakizashi was more comfortable to wear indoors than the katana, which the Samurai would place on a sword rack upon arrival. An owner's status and wealth were signified by how elaborately the hilt mountings were made. The hamon or temper line is clearly visible on this sword. This is a pattern created during the tempering process when the sword was made.

DATE	*c.*1650
ORIGIN	JAPANESE
LENGTH	57.6cm (22.7in)

Japanese sword (katana), *c.*1780

This sword is a good example of an early blade carried by a Japanese officer during World War II. This is evident in the military issue leather scabbard cover. Large numbers of these were either captured or surrendered by Japanese officers to Allied forces at the end of the war. Regrettably, a great number were destroyed.

DATE	*c.*1780
ORIGIN	JAPANESE
LENGTH	71.2cm (28in)

Japanese sword (katana) *c.*1850

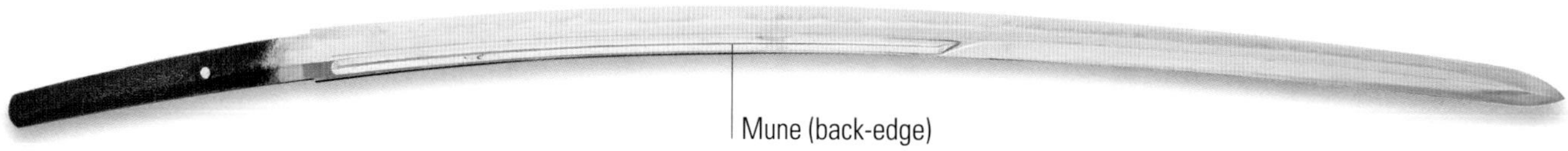

This sword blade was manufactured not long before the demise of the Samurai warrior class. This resulted in the carrying of Samurai swords in public being made illegal in 1867. After this date, the Japanese military chose to adopt swords of a western design instead.

DATE	*c.*1850
ORIGIN	JAPANESE
LENGTH	74cm (29.1in)

Japanese weapon (tanto) and scabbard, *c.*1890

DATE	*c.*1890
ORIGIN	JAPANESE
LENGTH	30cm (11.8in)

The tanto (meaning "short sword") is a short-bladed weapon that was used for thrusting rather than cutting. Blades tend to be flat and unfullered, with some displaying considerable thickness near the hilt, enabling a blade to pierce through armour. This example has a decorated ivory hilt and scabbard. It was probably a souvenir for Western travellers to Japan.

Japanese sword (shin-gunto), *c.*1930

DATE	*c.*1930
ORIGIN	JAPANESE
LENGTH	86.4cm (34in)

Japan experienced a period of rising nationalism during the 1930s and army officers adopted a sword very similar to the Samurai tachi, called the shin-gunto. Most of these swords were fitted with machine-made blades, although much older blades were also attached to military hilts. Scabbards were made from either leather or painted steel.

Japanese sword (tachi) by Kanesane, *c.*1940

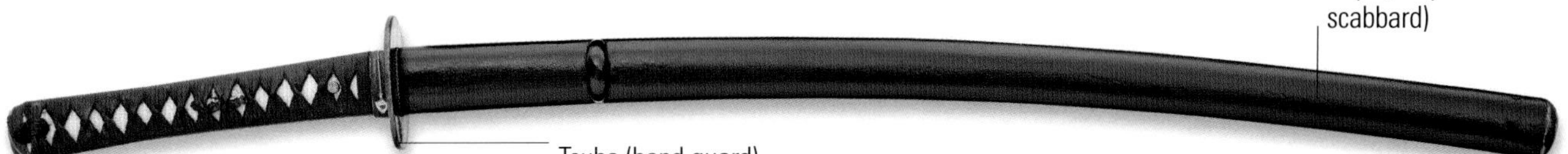

DATE	*c.*1940
ORIGIN	JAPANESE
LENGTH	91.6cm (36in)

Asano Kanesane was a swordsmith during the Showa era (1926–89). Born in 1910 in Seki, known as the "City of Swords", he was apprenticed to master swordsmith Kojima Kanemichi in 1923 and worked in Seki all his life. The tachi shown here has a blade of great length. Earlier versions of this sword would have been worn slung over a Samurai's shoulder.

Japanese polearms

The Japanese Samurai warrior was not solely reliant on the sword as his primary battlefield weapon. Polearms, including spears and sword blades attached to shafts (naginata), were regularly carried by Japanese warrior clans. The effective use of such arms involved considerable training. The production of polearms became a specialist skill and some Japanese sword makers only produced naginata blades.

Japanese polearm (nagamaki), *c.*1450

The nagamaki is a polearm associated with the warring Samurai clans of the Kamakura (1192–1333) and Muromachi (1338–1573) eras. This example comprises a long sword blade (similar to a katana blade) attached to an all-metal shaft. Blades had lengths upwards of 75cm (29.5in), and the overall length varied from 1–1.5m (3.2–4.9ft).

DATE	c.1450
ORIGIN	JAPANESE
LENGTH	195cm (76.8in)

Japanese spear (yari), Edo period (1603–1867)

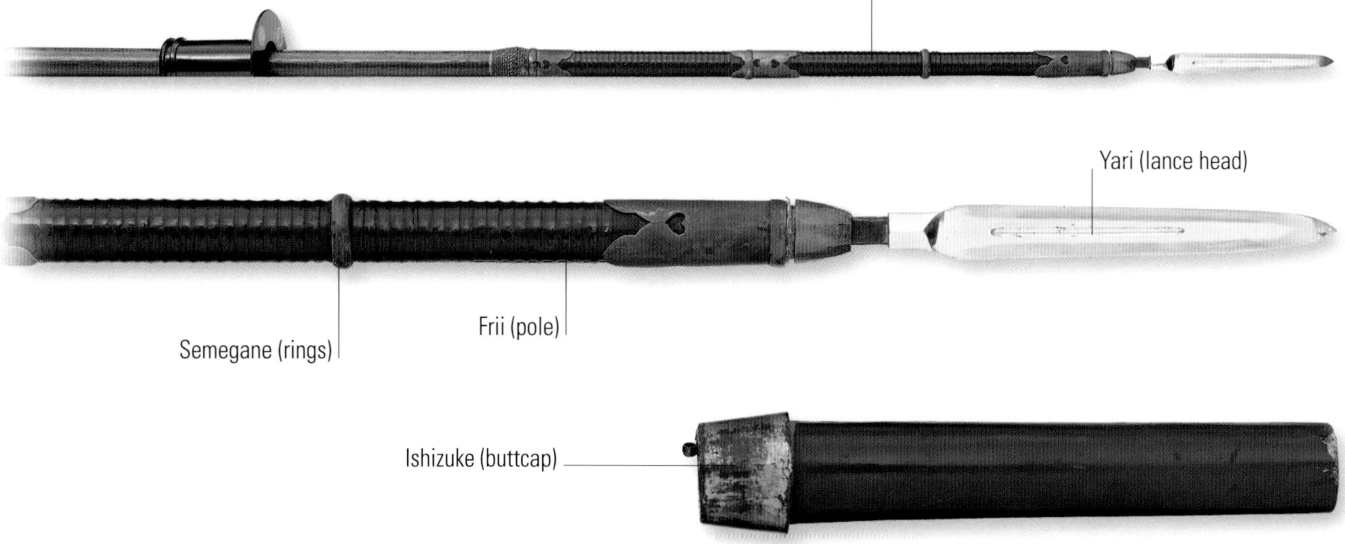

The Japanese yari is a spear or short lance that was not intended to be thrown but to be used as a thrusting weapon. It was carried by both Samurai warriors and the ordinary foot-soldier. This yari is known as a su yari, which is a reference to its straight blade, and is the most common type of Japanese spear. Some yari have horizontal crossbars on the blade (kama yari) and very long yari are known as omi no yari. The quality of yaris varies considerably. Yaris manufactured by swordsmiths exhibit fine, tempered blades with a hamon pattern across the blade and are of a two-piece construction, while others are one-piece and crudely wrought.

DATE	EDO (1603–1867)
ORIGIN	JAPANESE
LENGTH	368.5cm (145.1in)

Japanese staff weapon (naginata), *c.*1650

DATE	*c.*1650
ORIGIN	JAPANESE
LENGTH	105cm (41.3in)

This weapon is very reminiscent of the European glaive and consists of a curved blade with a very long metal tang attached to a wooden shaft by means of a series of wooden pegs driven through the handle. This example is of fine quality and would have been produced by a master swordsmith.

Japanese catch pole (sode garami), *c.*1850

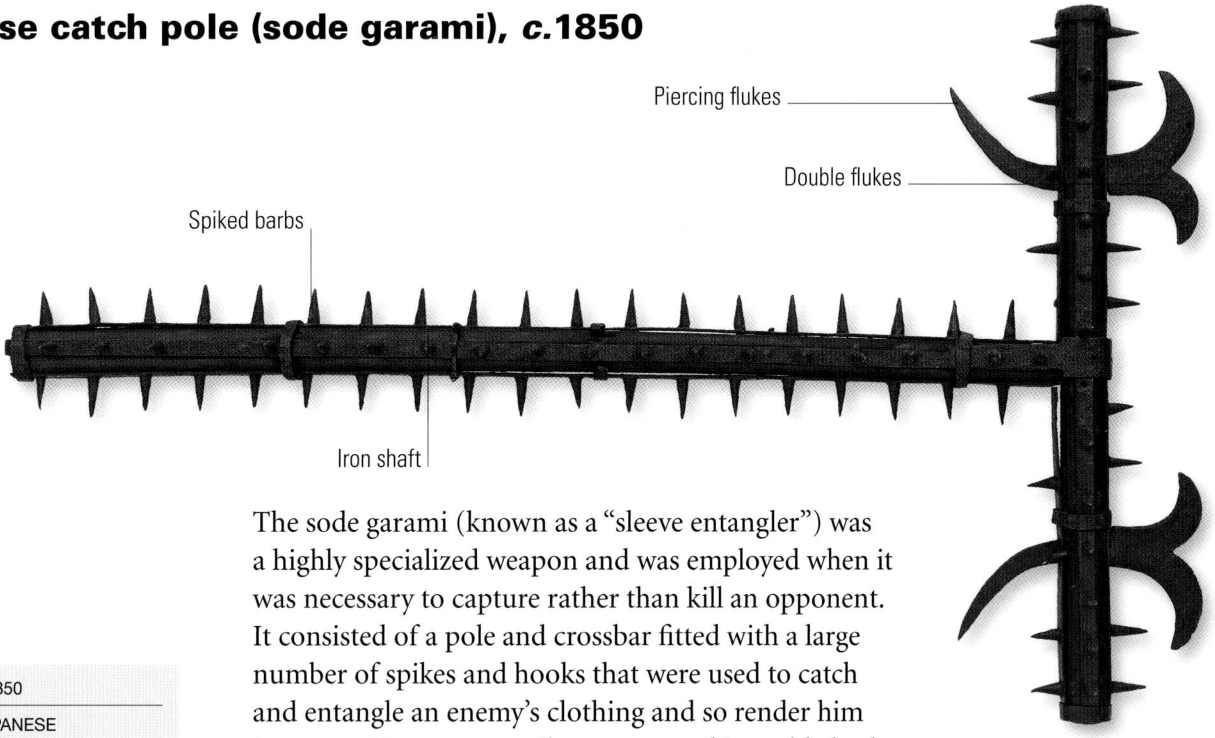

The sode garami (known as a "sleeve entangler") was a highly specialized weapon and was employed when it was necessary to capture rather than kill an opponent. It consisted of a pole and crossbar fitted with a large number of spikes and hooks that were used to catch and entangle an enemy's clothing and so render him impotent. It was a versatile weapon and it could also be used as a lethal spiked and bladed polearm if required.

DATE	*c.*1850
ORIGIN	JAPANESE
LENGTH	70.3cm (27.7in)

Japanese staff weapon (naginata), *c.*1850

DATE	*c.*1850
ORIGIN	JAPANESE
LENGTH	211.4cm (83.2in)

To use a naginata effectively, a series of swift, propeller-like moves were directed at all parts of the enemy's body. So successful was the naginata during the Muromachi period (1338–1573) that it hastened the introduction of protective armour for the legs and lower body parts. The wives of Samurai warriors were particularly skilled in the naginata's use and Japanese women still use the naginata in martial arts sports.

Chinese and Tibetan swords

The straight-bladed jian and the curved-bladed dao are some of the most recognizable Chinese sword types and were used for many centuries. The jian is regarded as the most venerable of Chinese swords and has its origins in antiquity. Unlike in western Europe, where sword design went through discernible changes in form and function, Chinese swords remained virtually unchanged over millennia.

Chinese/Tibetan sword, *c.*1420

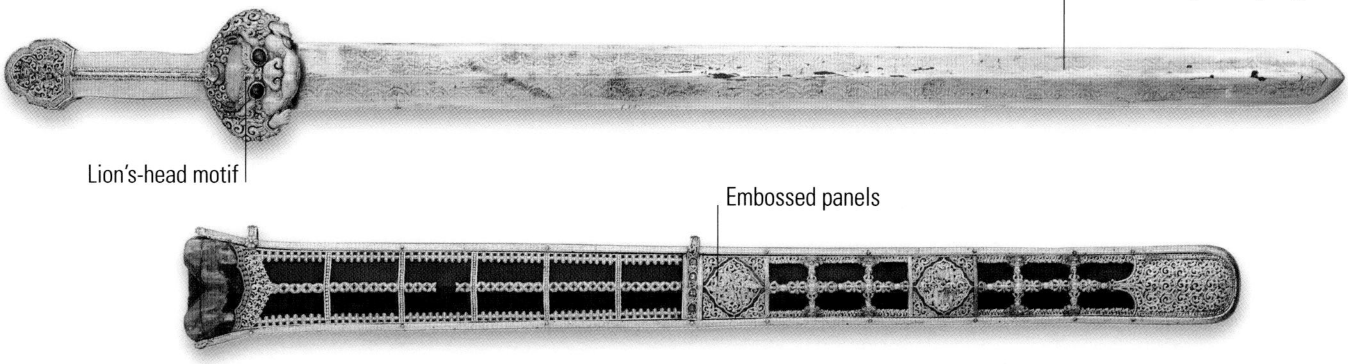

This sword is of exceptional quality and was presented by the Yongle Ming emperor (1326–1424) to the ruler of Tibet. The blade has a central strengthening ridge and is typically plain. The cross guard includes an impressive lion's-head motif and the scabbard displays a fretwork pattern, with embossed panels.

DATE	*c.*1420
ORIGIN	CHINESE/TIBETAN
LENGTH	90.3cm (35.5in)

Chinese sword (qibing dao), *c.*1800

This long-bladed dao was probably carried by a mounted soldier and has a single-edged blade that ends in an upturned point which was particularly effective at thrusting. The cutting edge was made of harder steel, while the back of the blade was forged in softer steel to avoid the blade becoming too brittle.

DATE	*c.*1800
ORIGIN	CHINESE
LENGTH	95.3cm (37.5in)

Chinese sword (fang), *c.*1850

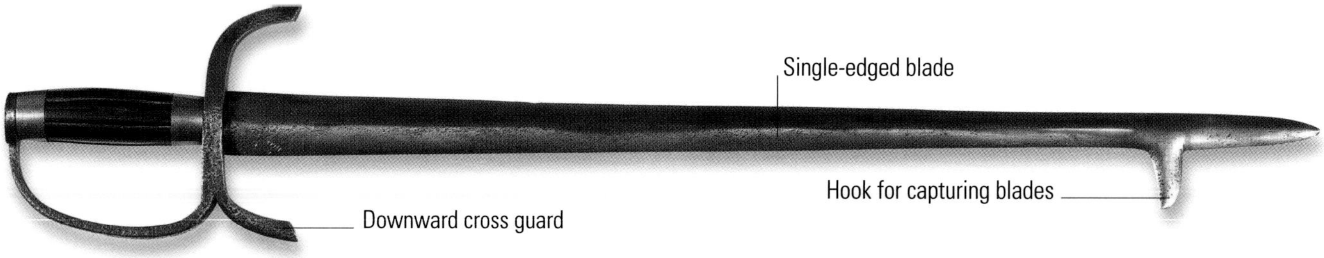

The simple construction of this unusual sword indicates that it was a weapon of the ordinary soldier. A downturned crossguard served the function of blocking or trapping an opponent's blade. There is another projecting bar near the end of the blade. The blade itself is of rather crude manufacture.

DATE	*c.*1850
ORIGIN	CHINESE
LENGTH	73.1cm (28.8in)

Chinese double, or butterfly, swords, *c.*1850

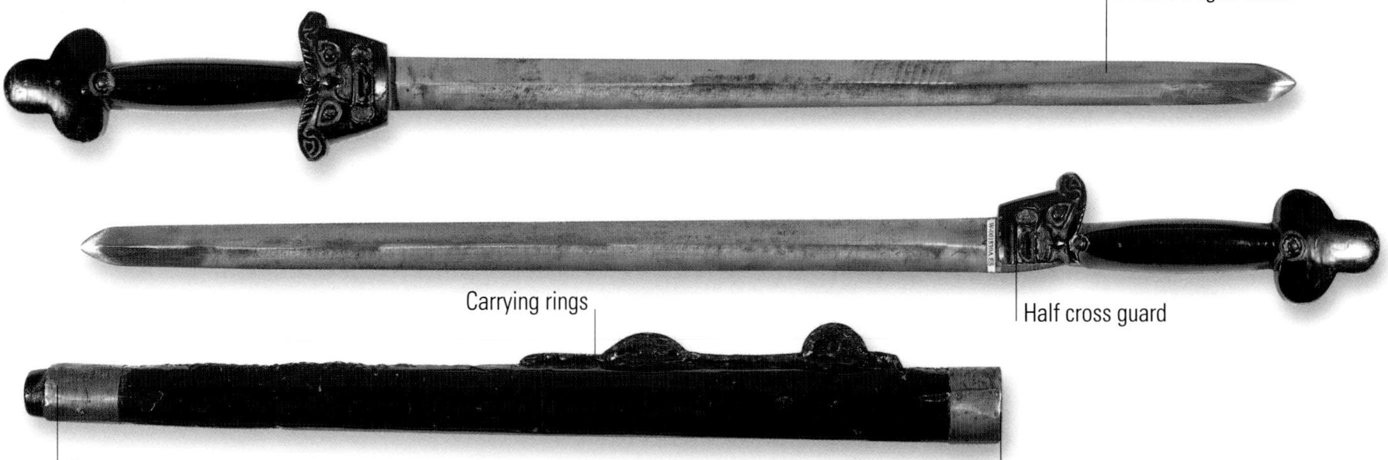

DATE	*c.*1850
ORIGIN	CHINESE
LENGTH	67.3cm (26.5in)

The double sword is uniquely Chinese and was designed to provide the user with a two-handed combination of weapons housed in just one sheath. Hilt and blade design is based on the traditional straight-bladed jian. Blades are invariably plain and diamond-sectioned, although some examples are found with inlaid copper or brass roundels. This sword is of a higher quality than normally encountered and has a well-carved hilt and scabbard.

Chinese double, or butterfly, swords, *c.*1850

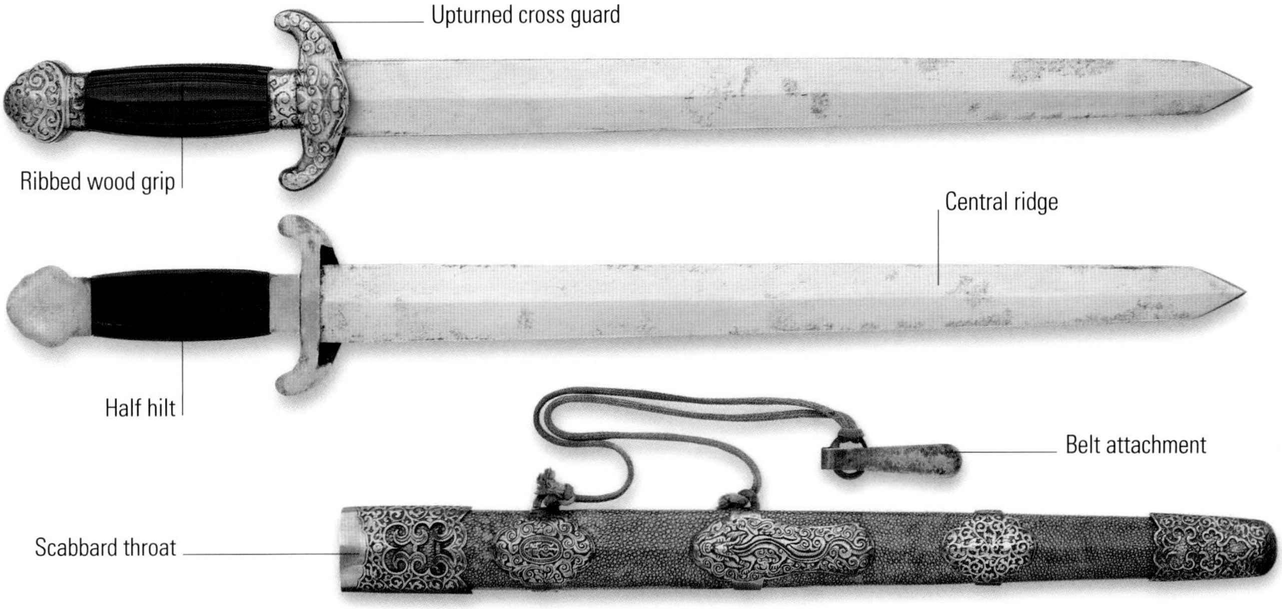

DATE	*c.*1850
ORIGIN	CHINESE
LENGTH	56.8cm (22.3in)

These double, or butterfly, swords are of above-average quality and feature a decorated, brass mounted hilt with ribbed wooden grips. The blade is double-edged with a central ridge. The scabbard still retains the original carrying cord and metal clip that would have been attached to a belt. Although these swords were effective as close-combat weapons, the shortness of the blades meant that against wider broadswords they were rather ineffective.

Chinese double, or butterfly, swords, *c.*1850

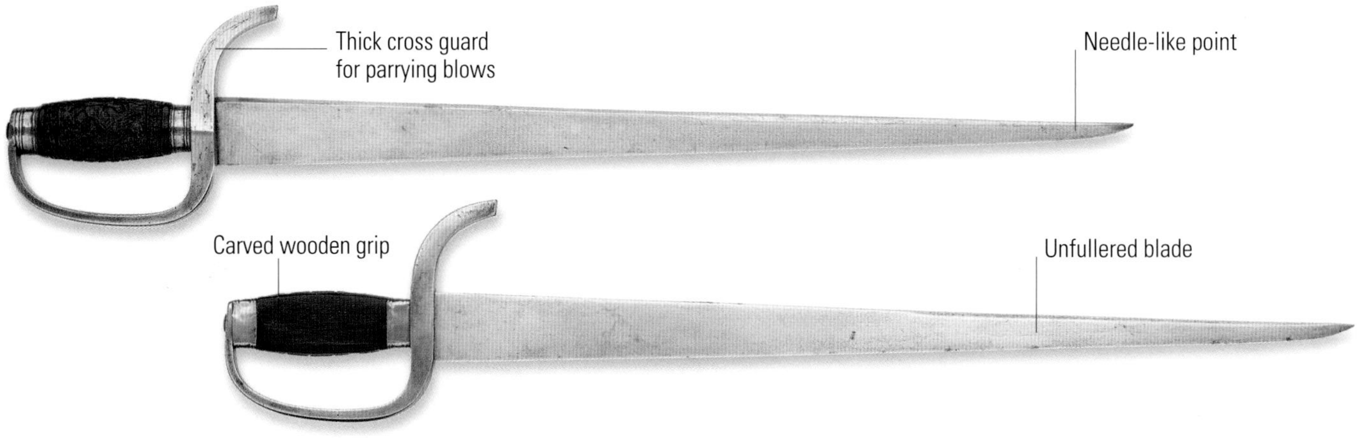

The needle-like shape of these sword blades indicates that they were used more as long, thrusting knives, while the thick cross guard and knuckle guard could also be used as an effective knuckleduster. The blade was normally only sharpened from halfway down, so that the unhoned part could be used for blocking.

DATE	*c.*1850
ORIGIN	CHINESE
LENGTH	62.3cm (24.5in)

Chinese sword (jian), *c.*1850

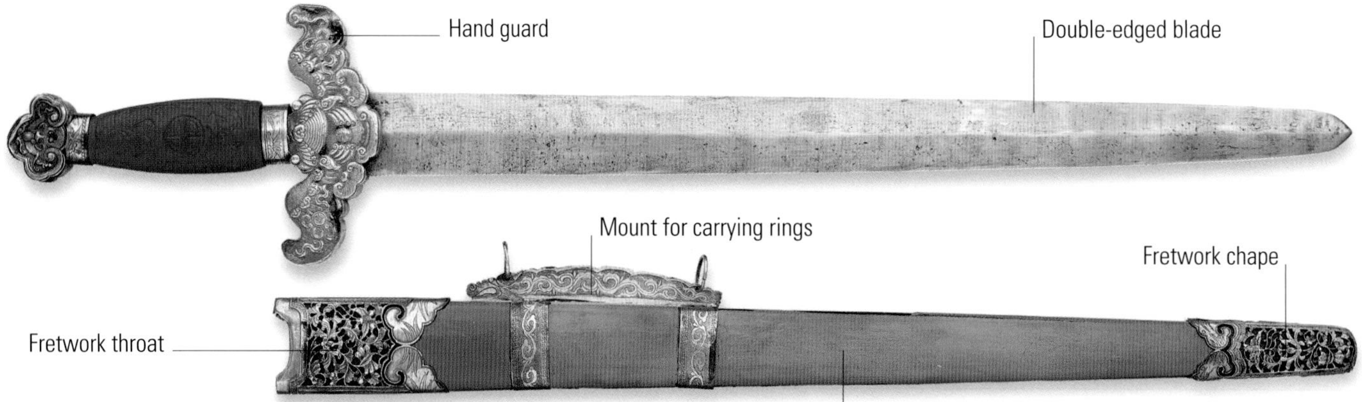

As the 19th century progressed, the Qing Empire (1644–1911) laid more emphasis on the use of firearms over edged weapons. This jian sword highlights how the need for elaborate decoration had overtaken the practical necessities of producing an effective combat weapon. The short, flimsy blade would have been useless against any kind of heavy, broad-bladed sword.

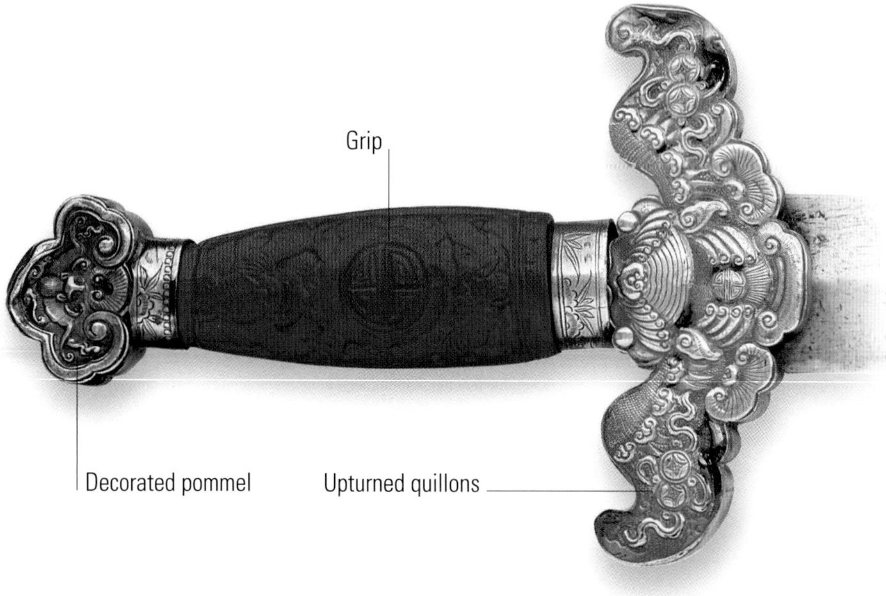

DATE	*c.*1850
ORIGIN	CHINESE
LENGTH	77.8cm (30.6in)

Tibetan/Chinese sword, *c.*1850

DATE	*c.*1850
ORIGIN	TIBETAN/CHINESE
LENGTH	71.2cm (28in)

Tibetan swords are usually highly decorated, particularly on hilts and scabbards, where the application of heavy gilding, silver wire, carved turquoise and inlaid coral is a common theme. Blades tend to be plain. Quality varies considerably, although this example is better than most. There is a possibility that this sword was actually manufactured in China, in the Tibetan style.

Chinese sword *c.*1850

DATE	*c.*1850
ORIGIN	CHINESE
LENGTH	67.3cm (26.5in)

The blade of this broadsword is very much designed as a chopping weapon and could have been used with both hands as the grip is quite long. It would probably have been sheathed in a plain leather scabbard.

Chinese sword (jian), *c.*1870

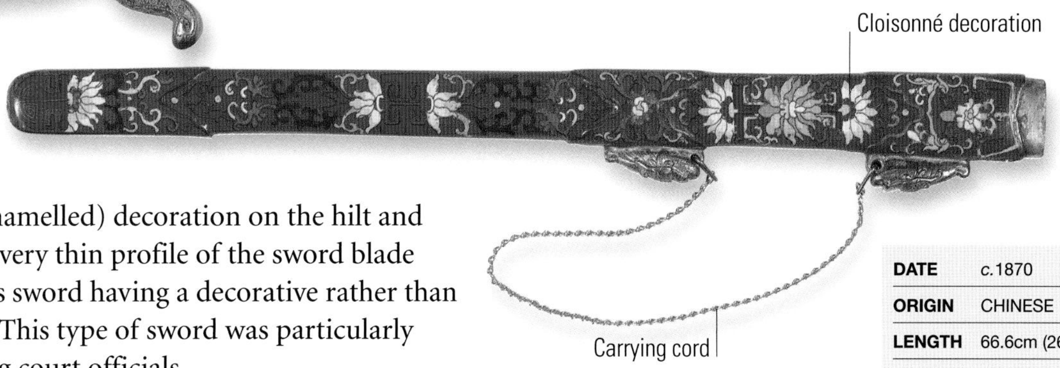

The cloisonné (enamelled) decoration on the hilt and scabbard and the very thin profile of the sword blade point towards this sword having a decorative rather than a functional role. This type of sword was particularly popular with Qing court officials.

DATE	*c.*1870
ORIGIN	CHINESE
LENGTH	66.6cm (26.2in)

Chinese polearms

The polearm was an important weapon of the Chinese infantry and the sheer range and variety of polearms that have survived are a testament to this. Most of them are similar in function to western European polearms such as the glaive and halberd, but their designs are radically different, incorporating motifs such as dragon-head sockets and features such as extremely curved blades.

Chinese polearm (yan yue dao), *c.*1840

Also more commonly known as the guan dao, the yan yue dao (meaning "reclining moon blade") is similar to the European fauchard and comprises a heavy, single-edged blade that terminates with an exaggerated curve. Serrations and notches on the top edge of the blade were used to catch an opponent's blade. This weapon would have been effective at sweeping cuts to the lower body.

DATE	*c.*1840
ORIGIN	CHINESE
LENGTH	251.4cm (99in)

Chinese polearm (yan yue dao), *c.*1850

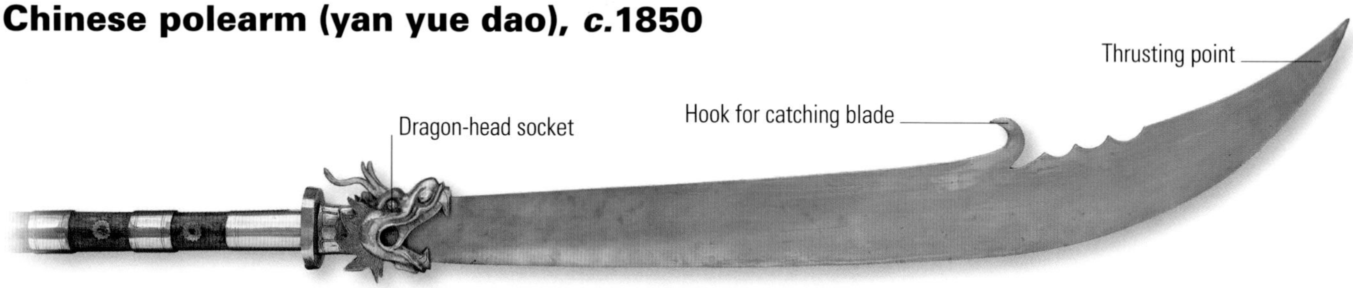

DATE	*c.*1850
ORIGIN	CHINESE
LENGTH	252.5cm (99.4in)

This type of polearm was usually mounted on a wooden or metal pole, 1.5–2.5m (4.9–8.2ft) in length, with a heavy counterweight at the bottom that balanced the great weight of the blade and could also be used as a bludgeoning weapon. The dragon's head was a common motif on Chinese polearms.

Chinese halberd, *c.*1850

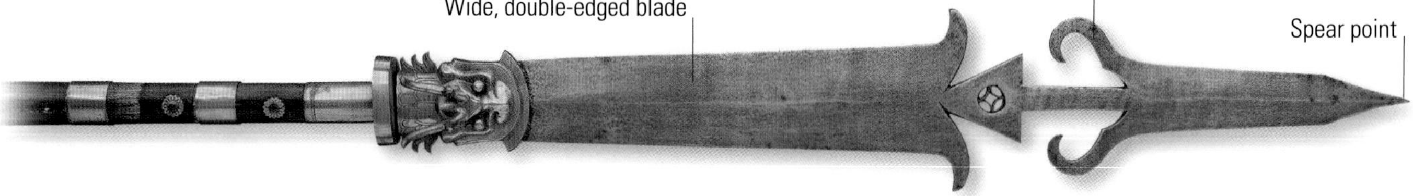

This is a complex weapon and would have served several functions. The blade has a needle-like spear point that could easily pierce armour. At the base of the point are two downward projections, or flukes, that would catch an opponent's blade. Another wide, double-edged blade is below this and used for parrying.

DATE	*c.*1850
ORIGIN	CHINESE
LENGTH	250.5cm (98.6in)

Chinese halberd, *c.*1850

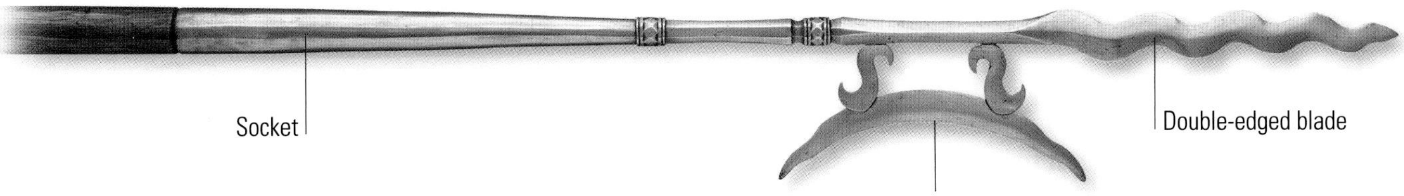

The very long socket and blade of this halberd were designed to keep an opponent at a safe distance. It has a "flamboyant", or snake-like, double-edged blade to the head as well as a crescent-shaped blade just below, which was employed as both a parrying and a cutting weapon.

DATE	*c.*1850
ORIGIN	CHINESE
LENGTH	256.8cm (101.1in)

Chinese halberd, *c.*1850

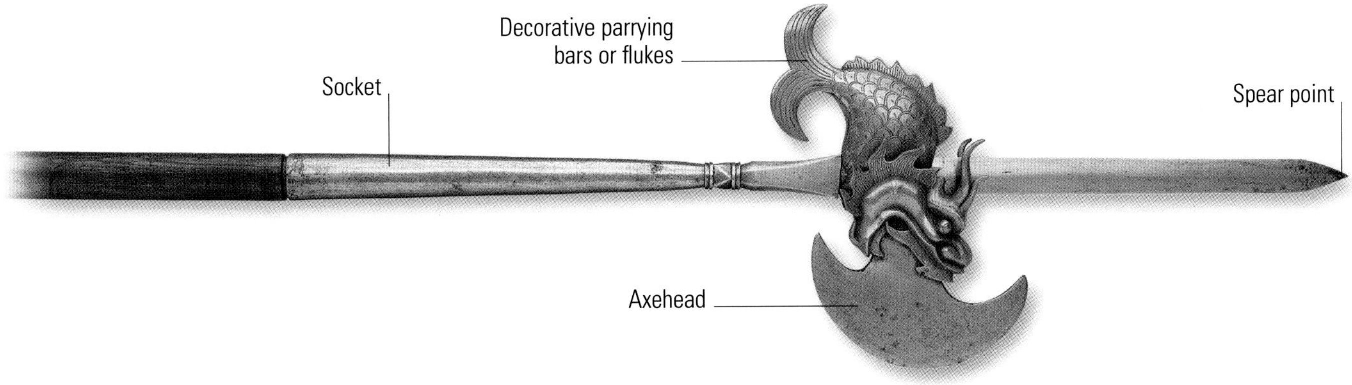

This unusual halberd has a distinctive brass axehead in the shape of a snake-fish. It is likely that the long, double-edged, spear-pointed blade was the most effective part of this halberd, with the axehead serving a more decorative rather than functional role. Many Chinese polearms had tassels hanging from where the pole and the blade were joined. They were coloured red as this is regarded as an auspicious colour in Chinese culture.

DATE	*c.*1850
ORIGIN	CHINESE
LENGTH	250cm (98.4in)

First Sino-Japanese war

The Chinese and Japanese forces that faced each other during the First Sino-Japanese War over the control of Korea (1894–95) carried a wide variety of edged weapons. The Chinese soldier still used a range of polearms, while Japanese troops adopted more western swords. The war demonstrated Japan's military and technical superiority over China and its new-found ability to compete with, rather than be dominated by, the Western powers.

RIGHT Detail from battle scene, Sino-Japanese War. Note the polearms being used by the Chinese forces.

African weapons

Swords from the African continent vary according to both geographical and cultural factors. North African sword design was heavily influenced by the Arabic Muslim invaders of the medieval period, while central and west African swords tended to be produced on a very small scale, with the local blacksmith forging swords and edged weapons primarily for his village.

North African sword (saif), *c.*1800

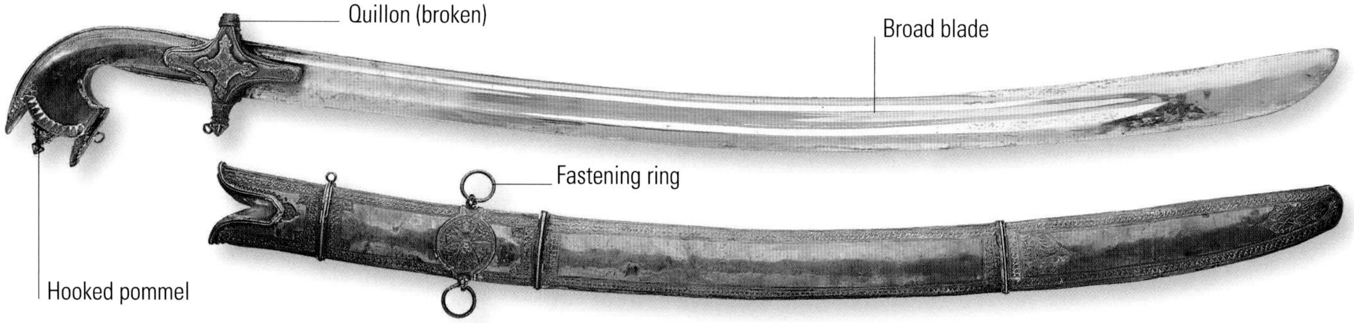

The saif is an Arab sword type that was brought into North Africa by Arabic invaders. It comprises a broad, curved blade and hooked pommel. It was carried in front of the body, slung from two rings fastened to a wide band around the scabbard. It may have had a chain knuckle guard (now missing).

DATE	*c.*1800
ORIGIN	NORTH AFRICAN
LENGTH	83.5cm (32.8in)

Sudanese spear, *c.*1850

DATE	*c.*1850
ORIGIN	SUDANESE
LENGTH	113.2cm (44.6in)

The African spear was used primarily as a throwing weapon. It would be thrown at the beginning of a skirmish and was only used in close combat conditions when an opponent was badly injured and could be finished off easily. This Sudanese spear has a leaf-shaped blade and long, iron shaft, which is then mounted on a further wooden shaft.

Somalian sword, *c.*1850

The long, slightly curved blade of this sword probably indicates that it could have been used while on horseback. The blade shape is similar to European Napoleonic cavalry swords, particularly the hatchet point. Weapons such as these had a dual function. They were obviously implements of war but could also be utilized as everyday tools of the home and the field.

DATE	*c.*1850
ORIGIN	SOMALIAN
LENGTH	84.6cm (33.3in)

Kenyan short sword, *c.*1850

DATE	*c.*1850
ORIGIN	KENYAN
LENGTH	53.3cm (21in)

This Masai short sword is of machete type and has a distinctive double-edged blade that widens towards the point. The weapon would have been used more for chopping rather than thrusting and no doubt would also have had an agricultural function if required. The sword's scabbard is made from heavy, stitched leather, as is the carrying strap.

Tunisian short sword, *c.*1850

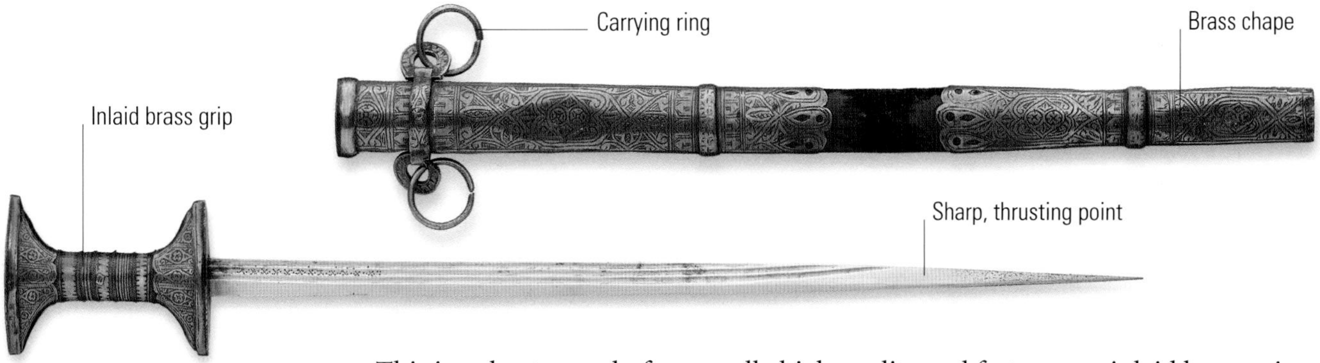

DATE	*c.*1850
ORIGIN	TUNISIAN
LENGTH	70.4cm (27.7in)

This is a short sword of unusually high quality and features an inlaid brass grip and scabbard with matching mounts. The blade appears to be European in origin and is probably a cut down European rapier blade. Commercial contact over many centuries between North Africa and mainland Europe meant that large quantities of European sword blades were introduced into Africa.

South African Zulu spear (umKhonto), *c.*1870

DATE	*c.*1870
ORIGIN	SOUTH AFRICAN
LENGTH	77cm (30.3in)

The umKhonto (meaning "spear" in Zulu) has a leaf-shaped head and is fixed to the shaft by means of a tang. The shaft is wound with cord to prevent it splitting. It is also known as the assegai and was designed for throwing, although there are shorter versions (made in iron), for stabbing.

Moroccan sword (flyssa), *c.*1880

The flyssa is the national sword of the Kabyles tribe of North Africa, part of a confederation of tribes that form the Berber race. Blades are straight and very long, with a pronounced needle-like point. Many are engraved with inlaid brass decoration on the top of the blade edge. Animal-head pommels are common.

DATE	*c.*1880
ORIGIN	MOROCCAN
LENGTH	101.3cm (39.9in)

Sudanese sword (kaskara), *c.*1880

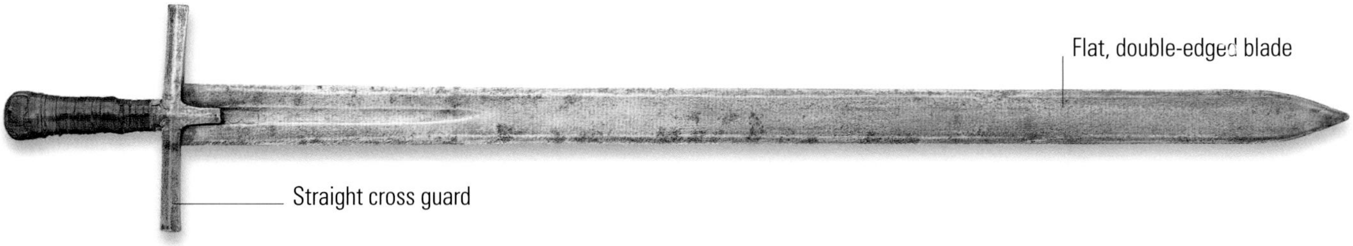

The Sudanese kaskara sword is sometimes confused with medieval Crusader swords, as the cruciform hilt and wide, fullered blade is similar to European broadswords. Some blades were heavily etched for most of their length with Koranic verses. The rounded grip is wrapped in strips of leather.

DATE	*c.*1880
ORIGIN	SUDANESE
LENGTH	106.4cm (41.8in)

Nigerian sword (takouba type), *c.*1880

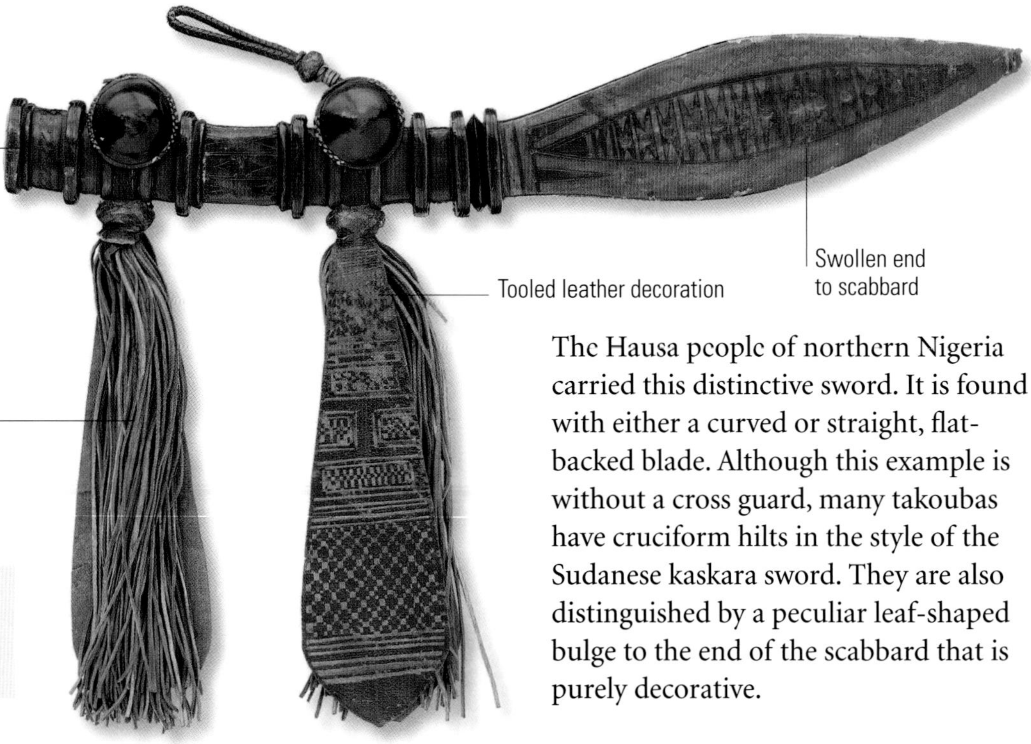

The Hausa people of northern Nigeria carried this distinctive sword. It is found with either a curved or straight, flat-backed blade. Although this example is without a cross guard, many takoubas have cruciform hilts in the style of the Sudanese kaskara sword. They are also distinguished by a peculiar leaf-shaped bulge to the end of the scabbard that is purely decorative.

DATE	*c.*1880
ORIGIN	NIGERIAN
LENGTH	80cm (31.5in)

Kenyan sword (seme), *c.*1880

The Masai people were traditionally armed with a spear, short sword (seme) and occasionally a shield. In a lion hunt, the seme was a weapon of last resort and also used as a side-arm if the spear was lost in combat.

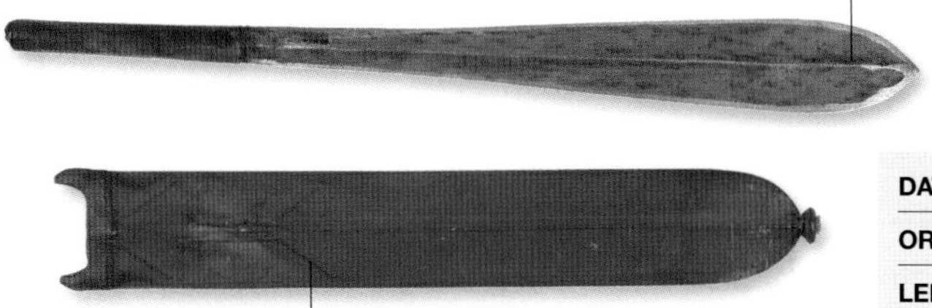

DATE	*c.*1880
ORIGIN	KENYAN
LENGTH	32.6cm (12.8in)

Zairean sword, *c.*1880

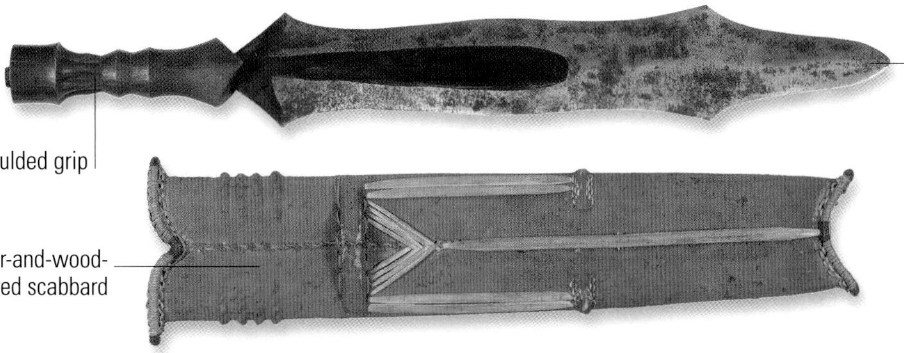

DATE	*c.*1880
ORIGIN	ZAIREAN
LENGTH	57.1cm (22.5in)

The Salampasu people of southern Zaire used this iron-bladed sword. It has a carved black wood grip and a blade of waisted shape. The scabbard is wood, covered with raw hide and reinforced with rattan fibre at its mouth and tip. The double-edged blade has a pronounced thrusting point.

Sudanese sword (kaskara), *c.*1890

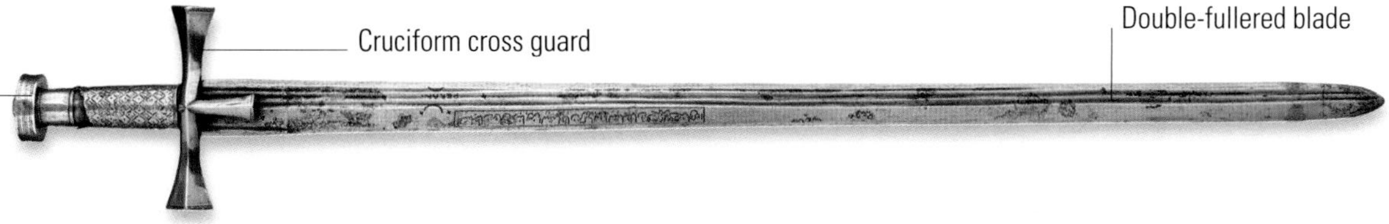

DATE	*c.*1890
ORIGIN	SUDANESE
LENGTH	99.5cm (39.2in)

This kaskara sword was owned by the Sultan Ali Dinar of Darfur (Sudan), who was khalifah or "caliph" (the country's civil and religious leader) until he was killed by the British in 1916. The cruciform hilt is wrapped in sheet gold and the blade has false European armourer's marks. These were thought to add an element of quality.

South African pair of swords, *c.*1910

DATE	*c.*1910
ORIGIN	SOUTH AFRICAN
LENGTH	79.4cm (31.2in)

These swords are likely to be of southern African origin and have male and female matching hardwood pommels. The blades are double-edged and were probably made by a local blacksmith, with the pommel carving done separately.

Sri Lankan and Indian swords

Despite the enormous cultural influence of the British Raj (1858–1947), Indian sword makers continued to produce a wide variety of indigenous designs with little regard to their new Western rulers. Muslim, Hindu and Sikh traditions had become solidly entrenched following centuries of invasion and assimilation, and sword forms reflected these established cultures.

Sri Lankan sword (kastane), *c.*1750

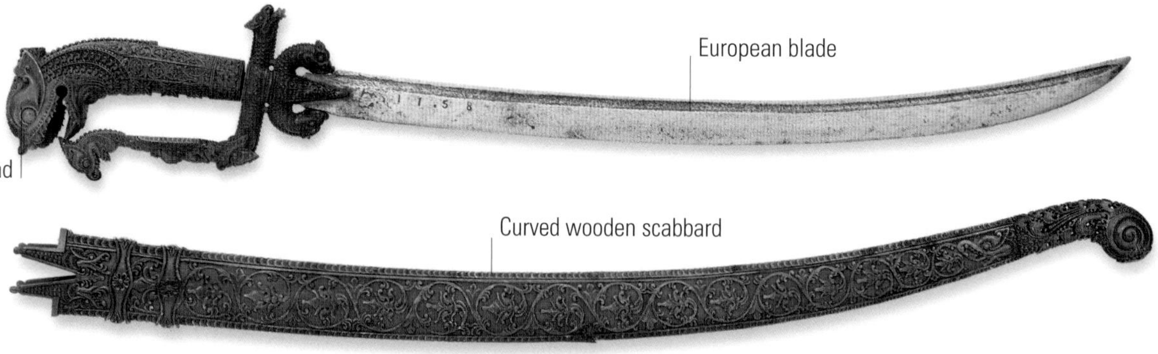

This Sri Lankan kastane has a typical monster-head pommel and a short, slightly curved European blade. Many kastane blades bear the marks of the Dutch East India Company (1602–1800), a commercial trading company of the Netherlands.

DATE	c.1750
ORIGIN	SRI LANKAN
LENGTH	66.7cm (26.2in)

Indian ritual sword, *c.*1750

DATE	c.1750
ORIGIN	INDIAN
LENGTH	80cm (31.5in)

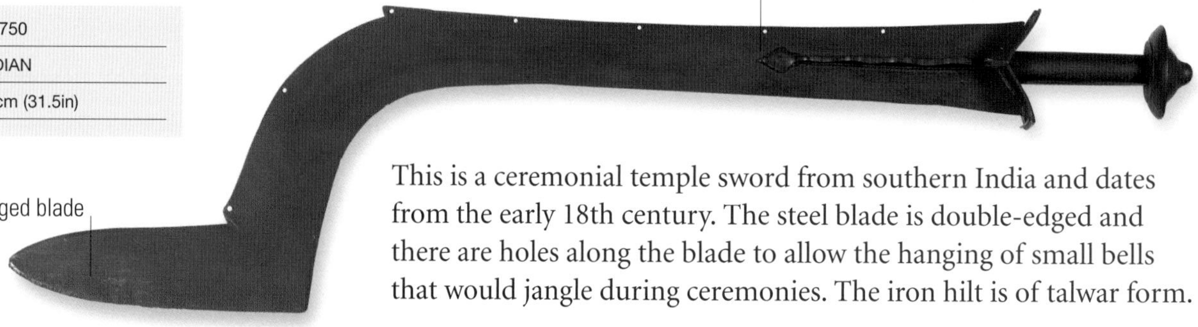

This is a ceremonial temple sword from southern India and dates from the early 18th century. The steel blade is double-edged and there are holes along the blade to allow the hanging of small bells that would jangle during ceremonies. The iron hilt is of talwar form.

Indian two-handed sword, *c.*1750

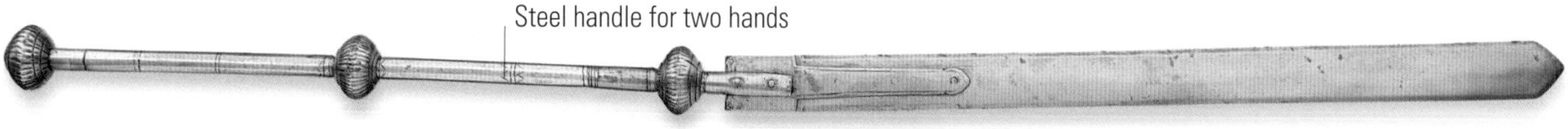

DATE	c.1750
ORIGIN	INDIAN
LENGTH	150.2cm (59.1in)

Indian warriors brought a wide range of swords and polearms on to the battlefield. This all-steel, two-handed sword has an unfullered, double-edged blade with spear point. It is likely that it would have been swung over the head in the same way as a battle-axe. The blade is similar in form to a khanda blade and is secured to the metal handle by means of a long, rivetted flange or hinge.

Indian sword (khanda), *c.*1790

DATE	*c.*1790
ORIGIN	INDIAN
LENGTH	108cm (42.5in)

The khanda was a Hindu sword from the Maratha culture (originally a Hindu warrior class based in present-day Marahashtra, south-west India). This example has extensive brass reinforcement bars on both sides of the blade, to give support and strengthen the sword.

Indian sword (khanda), *c.*1790

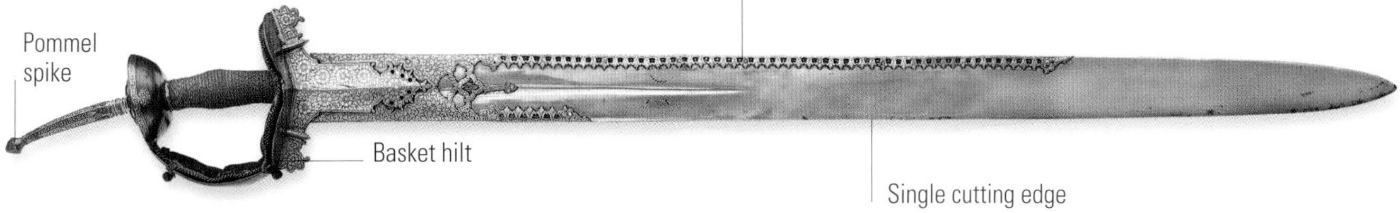

DATE	*c.*1790
ORIGIN	INDIAN
LENGTH	105.3cm (41.4in)

Here we have a fine example of a khanda with typical Hindu basket hilt. The blade is straight with the back-edge strengthened by a metal rib. A curved spike projected from the centre of the pommel and could be used as an effective penetrative weapon. The hilt and strengthening rib are covered with gilt brass.

Indian sword (khanda), *c.*1800

DATE	*c.*1800
ORIGIN	INDIAN
LENGTH	91.5cm (36in)

Khandas are normally encountered with a straight, watered (or patterned) blade that swells towards the tip. Blades are relatively thin and flexible and require reinforcement bars that run part-way down the blade. The spiked projection on the top of the pommel normally served as an extra grip for two-handed use but could also be engaged as a convenient hand rest when the sword was sheathed. The hilt shape of this khanda is unusual. Many khandas have a cushioned velvet liner to the basket hilt. The khanda was a heavy weapon designed to inflict damage through sheer force and was used for hacking rather than thrusting.

Indian sword (pata) *c.*1800

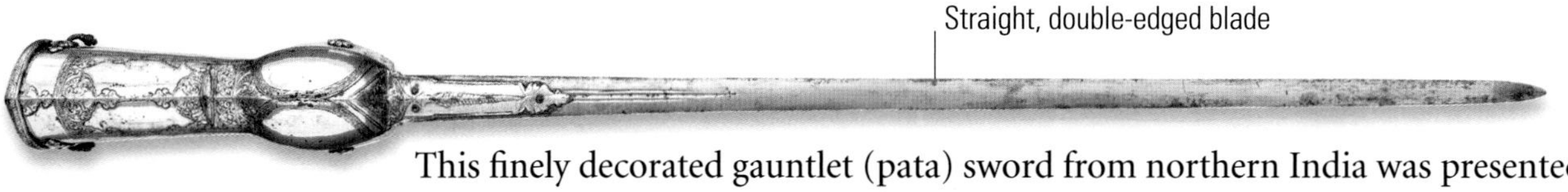

DATE	*c.*1800
ORIGIN	INDIAN
LENGTH	133.5cm (52.5in)

This finely decorated gauntlet (pata) sword from northern India was presented to Alexander Cunningham (1814–93), an officer in the Bengal Engineers and founder of the Indian Archaeological Survey. The sword would have been held by grasping a bar inside the gauntlet. Some warriors carried one of these swords in each hand and attacked the enemy with a whirling, windmill-like action.

Indian sword (tegha), *c.*1800

DATE	*c.*1800
ORIGIN	INDIAN
LENGTH	88.3cm (34.8in)

This sword has a tulwar-style hilt and a very wide, double-edged blade. They were carried by the Mahrattas (south-west India) and the Rajputs, who ruled much of pre-Mughal India. Because of the great width and thickness of the blade, many are thought to have been used as executioner's swords.

Indian sword (talwar), *c.*1800

DATE	*c.*1800
ORIGIN	INDIAN
LENGTH	95.5cm (37.6in)

Known as a talwar, talwaar or tulwar, this Indian sword type has its origins in 13th-century Persian (Iranian) swords such as the shamshir and the Turkish kilij. Blades tend to be wider than Persian swords and it has a distinctive, flat disc pommel. Hilts are all metal and many of them are decorated with exquisite koftgari (inlaid gold) designs.

Indian sword (talwar), *c.*1800

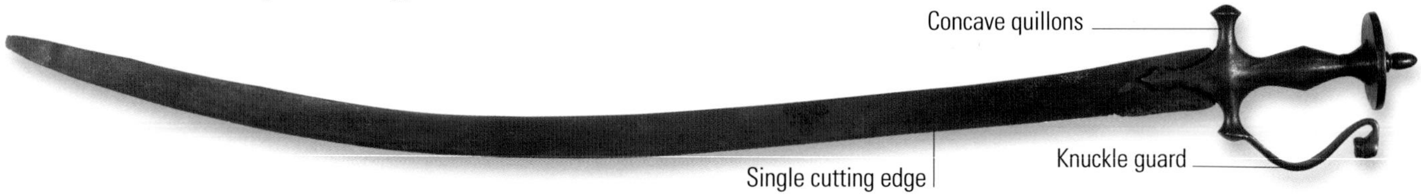

DATE	*c.*1800
ORIGIN	INDIAN
LENGTH	95.3cm (37.5in)

This talwar dates from the late 18th and early 19th century and is of all-steel construction. It has a curved blade, disc-shape pommel and a knuckle guard that curves away from the pommel. It was both a slashing and thrusting weapon.

Indian sword (kora), *c.*1800

DATE	*c.*1800
ORIGIN	INDIAN
LENGTH	27.9cm (11in)

This is the national sword of Nepal and features a uniquely shaped, dramatically curved blade that terminates with a flared point. Koras of this great size are sometimes attributed to ceremonial use, although some were also employed as executioners' swords.

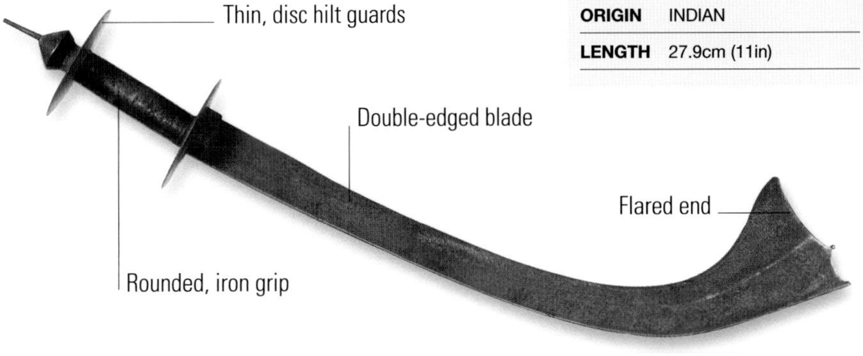

Mughal sword, *c.*1800

DATE	*c.*1800
ORIGIN	INDIAN
LENGTH	91cm (35.8in)

The Mughal Dynasty (1526–1857) ruled a great part of India (particularly the northern areas) for many centuries and the strong influence of earlier Mongol sword design is evident in this sword. The hilt is made from jade and decorated with rubies. The end of the blade has a typical yelman, or double-edged, swelling.

Indian sword (shamshir), *c.*1840

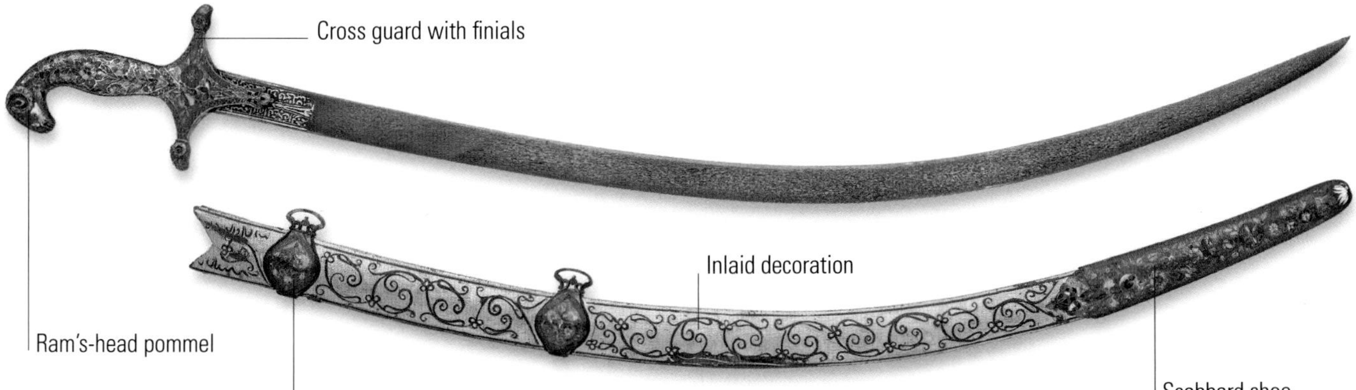

DATE	*c.*1840
ORIGIN	INDIAN
LENGTH	97.7cm (38.5in)

The shamshir is Persian (Iranian) in origin and functions purely as a cutting weapon, due to the curved point being inadequate for thrusting. This sword is of extremely high quality, and comprises an enamelled, ram's-head pommel and heavily decorated scabbard. Blades tend not to be decorated except for the name of the maker and possibly the date of manufacture. Blades of this status are invariably made in watered (pattern-welded) steel, a process of repeated forging that produced a unique pattern on the surface of the blade that was highly prized.

Indian polearms

The use of the polearm in India continued long after it had become obsolete in Europe and it was still carried into battle during the 19th century. The long spear was a particular favourite and was used as a thrusting, rather than throwing, weapon in massed infantry formations. Tridents, great battle-axes and spiked maces were all brought into play during Indian battles of the 18th and 19th centuries.

Indian lance, *c.*1750

Despite the pre-eminence of infantry formations over cavalry in Indian armies, mounted soldiers, particularly Mughal cavalry, used the lance or spear with notable success. The heavy weight of the wooden shaft would have added considerable power and striking impetus.

DATE	*c.*1750
ORIGIN	INDIAN
LENGTH	38.8cm (15.3in) head

Indian spear, *c.*1800

This Indian spear is more reminiscent of a European pike and would have served the same purpose, being used as a thrusting weapon in massed infantry formations. The large ball at the end of the spearhead would have stopped the spear travelling too far into an opponent and becoming difficult to extract.

DATE	*c.*1800
ORIGIN	INDIAN
LENGTH	31.1cm (12.2in) head

Indian spear, *c.*1800

The wickedly sharp, triangular point of this spear would have been driven through the light armour of Indian warriors with relative ease. The spearhead is secured to the shaft by means of a flange. The mounts are in silver and probably indicate that it had a possible ceremonial role, perhaps as the weapon of a royal guard. Indian cavalry also carried spears of this great length, and they were used primarily as lances.

DATE	*c.*1800
ORIGIN	INDIAN
LENGTH	233.2cm (91.8in)

Indian spear, *c.*1800

DATE	*c.*1800
ORIGIN	INDIAN
LENGTH	277.3cm (109.2in)

Indian infantry of the early 19th century would have faced British and European forces with this simple weapon. Against disciplined musket and artillery fire, it would have been quite useless, although if a warrior could get within close enough range of his opponent the extremely long spike would have been driven through an unarmoured Western military uniform with ease.

Indian javelin, *c.*1800

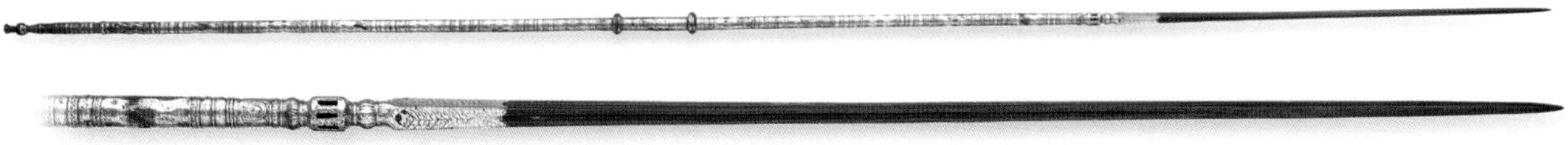

DATE	*c.*1800
ORIGIN	INDIAN
LENGTH	228cm (89.8in)

This javelin has a very long, iron shaft with a needle-like spiked end. It was probably carried by a horseman and used very much like a traditional cavalry lance. Although Indian armies tended to be composed mainly of infantry, the use of cavalry was not uncommon and these long polearms would have been very effective at charging massed ranks of foot-soldiers.

Indian trident, *c.*1800

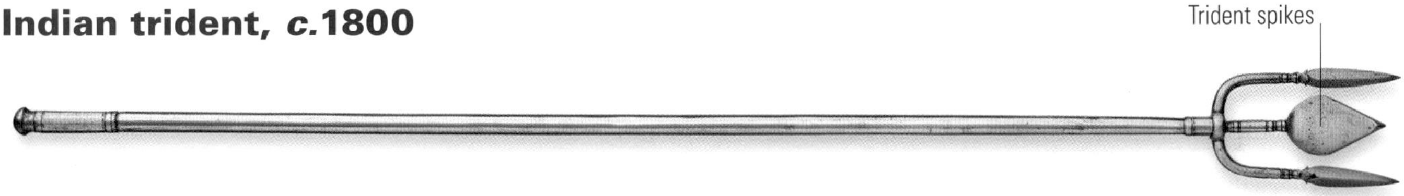

DATE	*c.*1800
ORIGIN	INDIAN
LENGTH	92.5cm (36.4in)

The trident has great religious significance in the Hindu faith and is depicted as the favoured weapon of Lord Shiva, "the Destroyer". It was probably most effective at pulling down a horseman and the two spikes were used to finish off an opponent. It could also be employed to trap an enemy's blade.

Indian battle-axe, *c.*1800

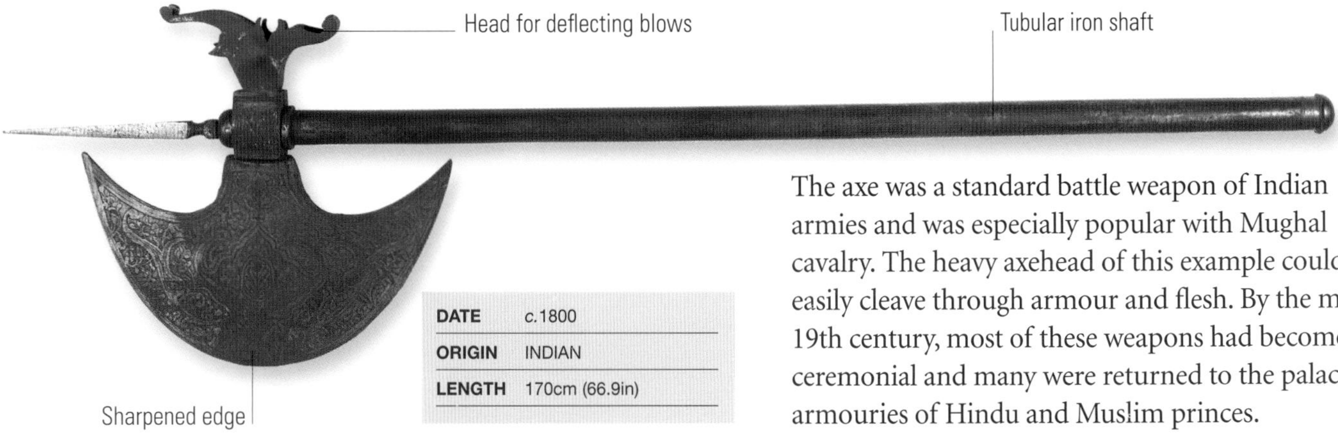

DATE	*c.*1800
ORIGIN	INDIAN
LENGTH	170cm (66.9in)

The axe was a standard battle weapon of Indian armies and was especially popular with Mughal cavalry. The heavy axehead of this example could easily cleave through armour and flesh. By the mid-19th century, most of these weapons had become ceremonial and many were returned to the palace armouries of Hindu and Muslim princes.

Weapons of South-east Asia

The variety of hilted weapons in South-east Asia is surprisingly large; and many are peculiar to certain distinct areas and cultures. One sword that is common throughout this region is the kris or keris, a sword design that appears to have no imitators and comprises an unusual, hand-forged blade. The Burmese dha and the Naga dao also bear a passing resemblance to the traditional Japanese sword.

Malayan spear, *c.*1800

Traditionally, Malayan spears had wooden or steel heads – the wooden heads were used for throwing and the steel heads for thrusting. The best examples are beautifully made and inlaid. This spear has a shaft carved to imitate bamboo.

DATE	*c.*1800
ORIGIN	MALAYAN
LENGTH	216.9cm (85.4in)

Philippine sword (kris), *c.*1850

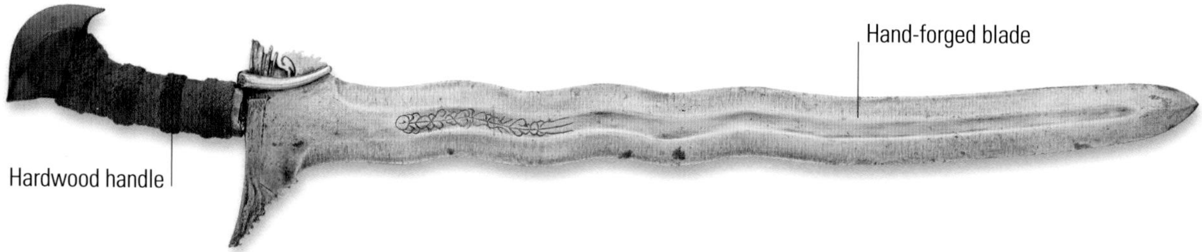

Kris blades are straight and wavy in profile with a surface that is rough and coarse to the touch. This is the result of a complex and laborious process of manufacture that sees many different types of iron forged, re-forged and then folded on to each other. A distinctive and unique pattern is then produced for each sword. The surface is left unpolished.

DATE	*c.*1850
ORIGIN	PHILIPPINE
LENGTH	60cm (23.6in)

Burmese sword (dha), *c.*1850

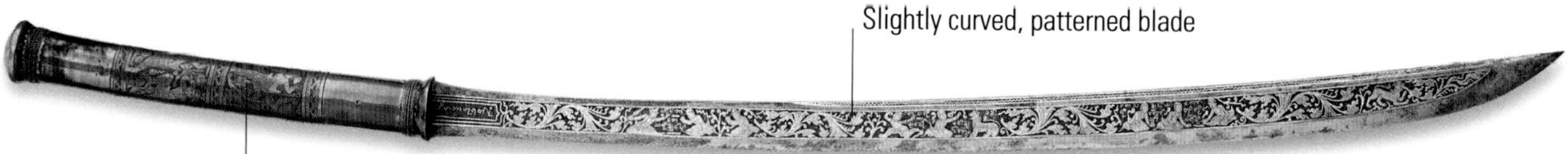

This is the national weapon of Burma and similar to a Japanese katana sword, although there is no comparison in terms of the quality. The blade is slightly curved, single-edged and terminates in a narrow point. The rounded brass handle is without a guard. Most dhas are carried in wooden sheaths, with some of them decorated in sheet silver.

DATE	*c.*1850
ORIGIN	BURMESE
LENGTH	85.5cm (33.7in)

Malayan sword (mandau), *c.*1850

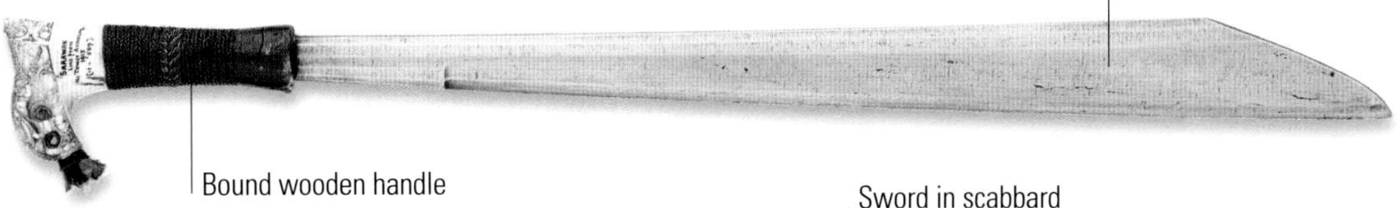

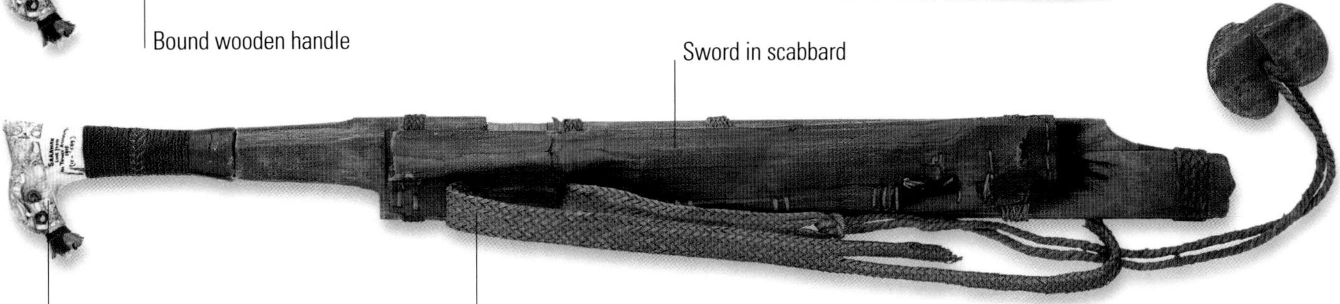

DATE	*c.*1850
ORIGIN	MALAYAN
LENGTH	67cm (26.4in)

This Dayak head-hunter's sword has a finely carved, horn, animal-head pommel (they usually depict either demons or dragons), wooden grip and heavy, double-edged blade. The scabbard is made from two shaped, wooden boards (normally teak) and bound with cane and rattan. Pommels are frequently found with tufts of human hair, purportedly from slain opponents. A large number of these swords were brought back to Europe during the colonial period.

Malayan sword (mandau), *c.*1880

DATE	*c.*1880
ORIGIN	MALAYAN
LENGTH	27cm (10.6in)

The mandau was a sword used by the Dayak peoples of Borneo (now modern-day Malaysia). The blade has an unusual profile, with one face slightly convex and the other slightly concave. The Dayaks were known as prolific head-hunters and the small knife that accompanies this sword was said to have been used to clean heads taken from the enemy. It is likely that the blade would have been used in a chopping motion in the manner of a machete.

Presentation swords

The presentation of a sword to an individual for either gallantry in the field of battle or loyal service to a monarch or state has a long history going back to the medieval period. Usually the sword is extensively decorated and in a number of cases, a presentation inscription is also added. During the Napoleonic Wars (1799–1815), the presentation sword became very popular, particularly in Britain, where the grateful nation regularly presented highly decorated and valuable swords to officers who had shown exceptional courage and leadership in the face of the enemy.

Royal Persian scimitar presented to Catherine the Great, *c.*1600

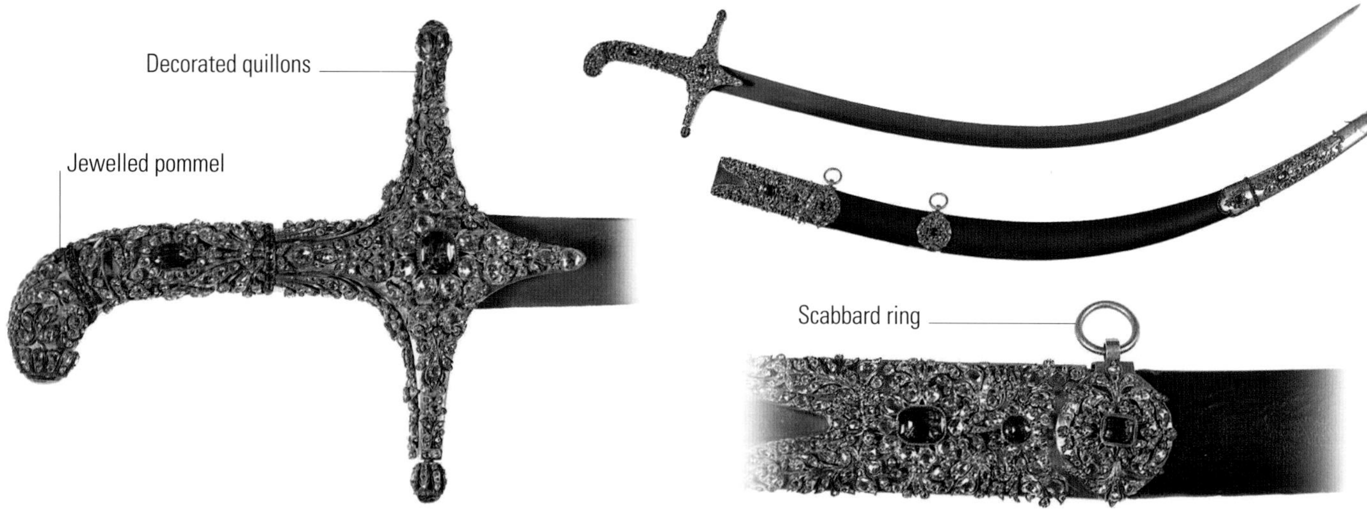

This opulent scimitar was originally a Persian court sword commissioned by Abbas the Great, Shah of Persia (1571–1629). It is decorated with 1,295 diamonds and 50 karats of rubies, finished with an 11-karat emerald set into the hilt. The Ottoman Turkish government presented this sword to Empress Catherine the Great of Russia (1729–96).

DATE	*c.*1600
ORIGIN	PERSIAN, IRAN
LENGTH	100cm (39.4in)

British Patriotic Fund sword presented to James Bowen, *c.*1803

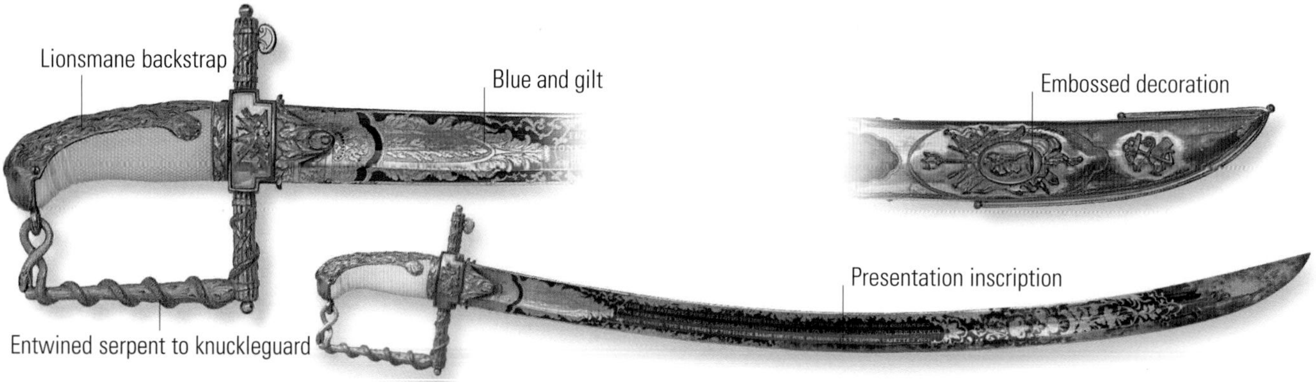

The Lloyds Patriotic Fund, comprising a group of London bankers, presented this sword to Lieutenant James Bowen of HMS *La Loire*, after a successful engagement with the French brig (a ship with two, square-rigged masts), Venteux. The hilt and scabbard mounts are richly covered in fire-gilt and the blade has extensive use of blue and gilt decoration.

DATE	*c.* 1803
ORIGIN	BRITISH
LENGTH	89cm (35in)

Corporation of the City sword presented to VA Lord Collingwood, *c.*1805

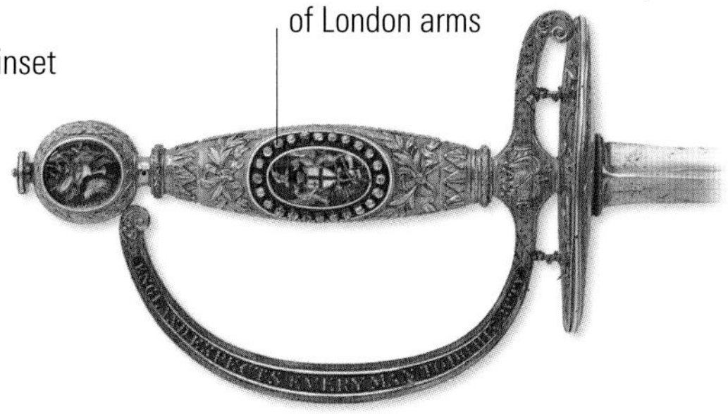

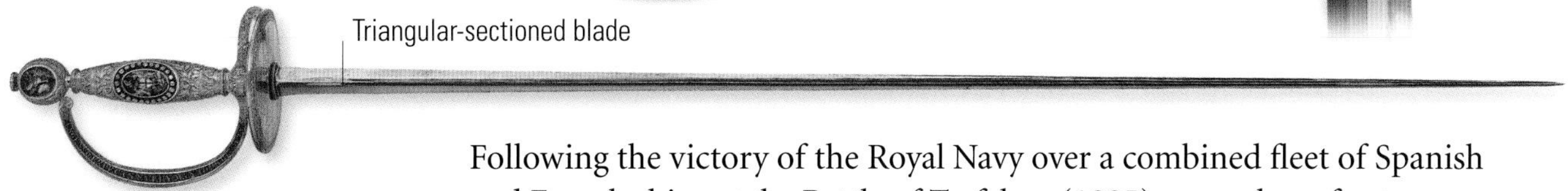

DATE	*c.*1805
ORIGIN	BRITISH
LENGTH	101.6cm (40in)

Following the victory of the Royal Navy over a combined fleet of Spanish and French ships at the Battle of Trafalgar (1805), a number of extravagant presentation swords were commissioned by British commercial institutions. This smallsword was presented to Vice Admiral Lord Collingwood and comprises a hilt of gold, inset with enamel plaques, surrounded with diamonds. The knuckle guard and oval shell guard are also inscribed.

King of Sweden, Charles XIV sword presented to Lord Bloomfield, *c.*1822

DATE	*c.*1822
ORIGIN	SWEDISH
LENGTH	Unknown

Charles XIV, king of Sweden (1763–1844), presented this sword to the 1st Lord Bloomfield (1768–1844), British Ambassador to Sweden. Its design is very reminiscent of the French Napoleonic Empire style that was popular throughout Europe during the early 1800s. The cut steel hilt includes distinctive piercings to the cross guard and pommel. The grip is made from porphyry (a form of crystal) and the blade is frost-etched. It would have been worn during formal occasions.

Legislature of Nova Scotia sword presented to Sir Fenwick Williams, 1856

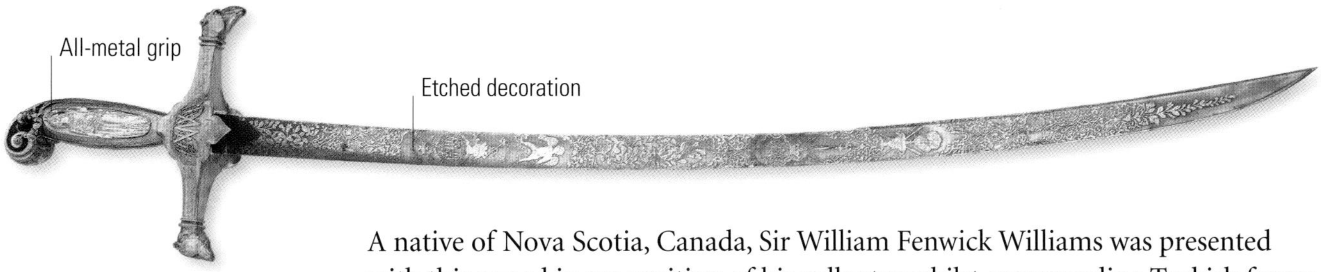

DATE	*c.*1855
ORIGIN	BRITISH
LENGTH	89cm (35in)

A native of Nova Scotia, Canada, Sir William Fenwick Williams was presented with this sword in recognition of his gallantry whilst commanding Turkish forces during the Siege of Kars (1855). The hilt is made from silver gilt with bands of engraved leaf scrolls and the quillons terminate with animal-head finials. The blade is frost-etched with a selection of motifs including a classical urn, crossed swords, crowned "VR" (Queen Victoria), winged angels and trophies of arms.

Civilian and regimental swords

One of the main driving forces behind the production of a civilian or regimental sword is the desire to produce a distinctive and memorable sword that can encompass either the history or the ethos of an organization or regiment. Regimental swords usually incorporate the regiment's badge or battle honours on both the hilt and the blade. Civilian swords are not designed to be used in battle, so they are normally of a lightweight form and are produced mainly for dress purposes.

Knights of Malta sword and scabbard, *c.*1800

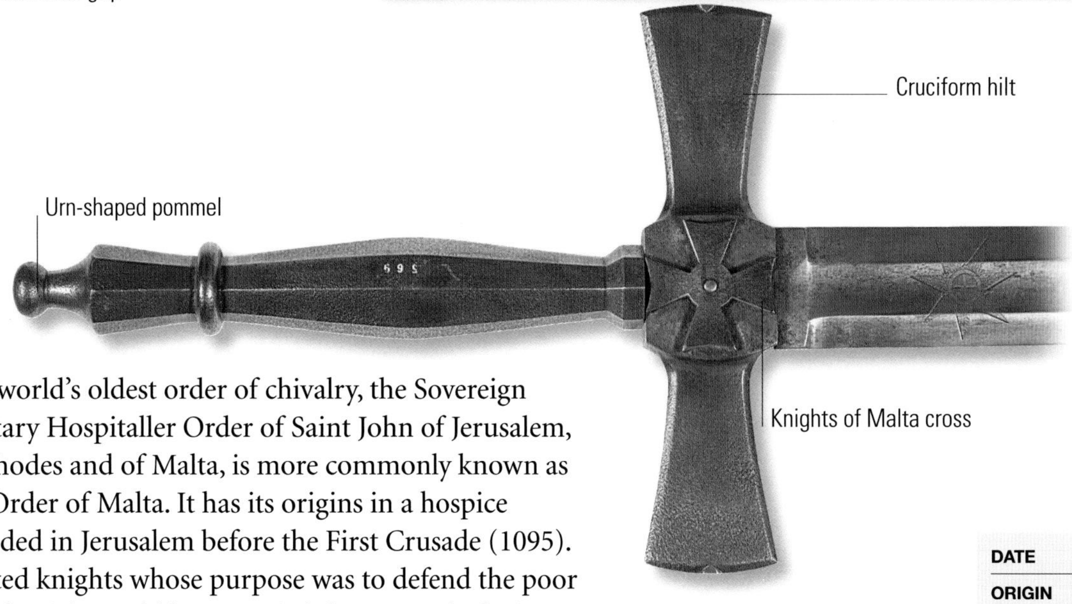

The world's oldest order of chivalry, the Sovereign Military Hospitaller Order of Saint John of Jerusalem, of Rhodes and of Malta, is more commonly known as the Order of Malta. It has its origins in a hospice founded in Jerusalem before the First Crusade (1095). Elected knights whose purpose was to defend the poor and the sick would have carried these swords during ceremonial occasions.

DATE	*c.*1800
ORIGIN	MALTESE
LENGTH	82cm (32.3in)

British Coldstream Guards officer's sword, 1854 Pattern

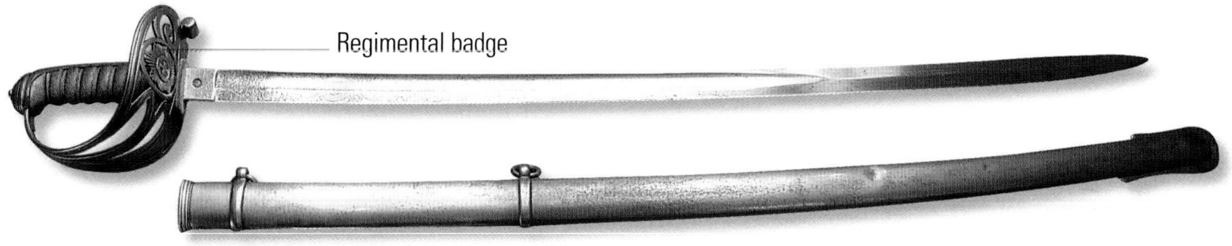

The Coldstream Guards is the oldest serving regiment in the British Army and was founded by Oliver Cromwell (1599–1658) in 1650. A specific regimental sword was issued in 1854 and includes a regimental badge in the middle of the hilt cartouche.

DATE	1854
ORIGIN	BRITISH
LENGTH	109cm (42.9in)

British officer's sword, the Border Regiment, *c.*1870

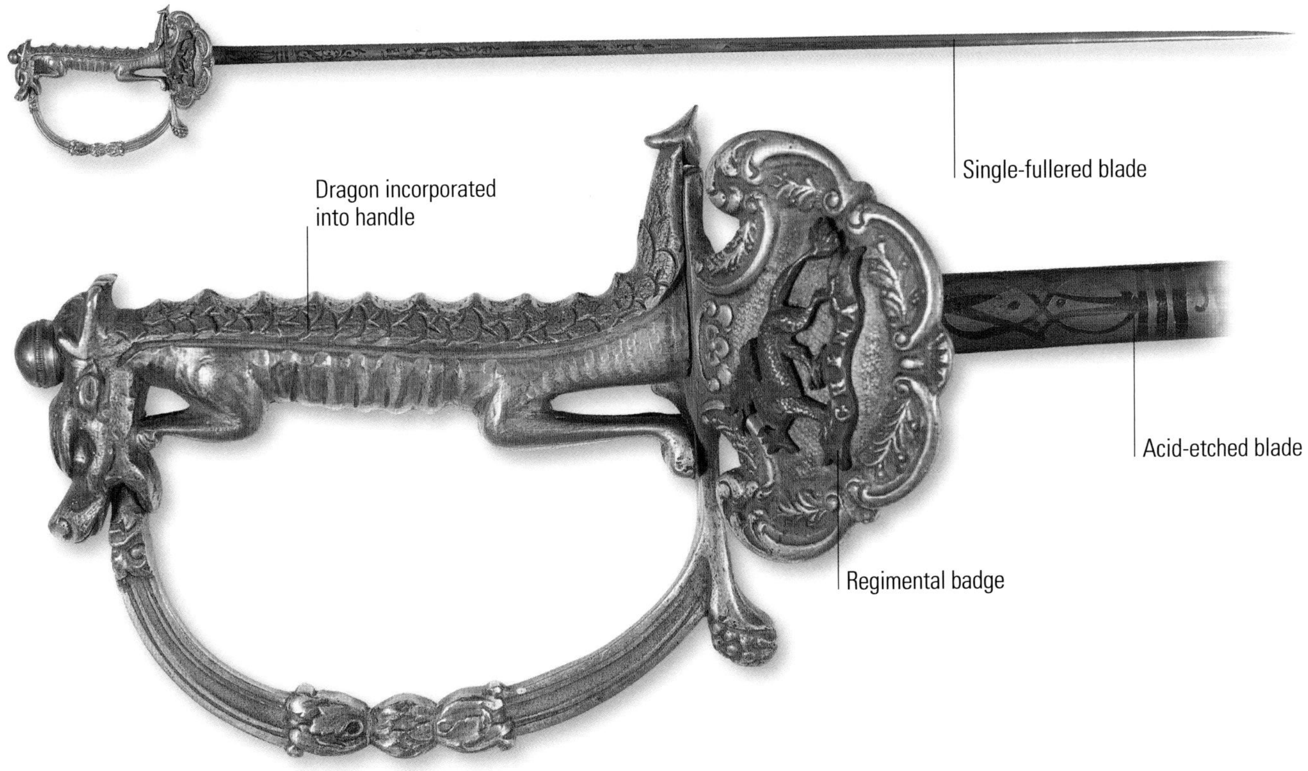

DATE	*c.*1870
ORIGIN	BRITISH
LENGTH	85cm (33.5in)

This extraordinary sword was carried by British infantry officers of the Border Regiment during the 19th century. Their regimental badge featured a dragon and this has been incorporated into the hilt. This sword was for dress purposes rather than being used in battle.

Scottish Royal Company of Archers short sword, 1910

DATE	1910
ORIGIN	SCOTTISH
LENGTH	56cm (22in)

The Royal Company of Archers was founded in 1676 and acted as a personal bodyguard to the monarch while in Scotland. This sword would have been carried by a bodyguard of below officer rank. The hilt is heavy cast brass with an acid-etched blade. This sword design was developed during the late 19th century: the influence of Gothic Victorian style is evident in the handle and cross guard.

Dress swords

The wearing of dress swords became popular after the demise of the rapier in the late 17th century, and was also hastened by the introduction of the smallsword soon after. These lightweight swords were not meant for battle conditions and their role was primarily one of dress and ornamentation. Military officers, diplomats and government officials all had the right to wear one and the range of designs is simply enormous.

English dress sword, *c.*1790

The rather distinctive hilt styling of this sword is very similar to designs manufactured by Matthew Boulton (1728–1809), a sword maker and engineer from Birmingham, England, who is famous for his collaboration with the steam-engine engineer, James Watt. In his earlier career, Boulton established a factory making cut steel and marcasite (imitation diamond) buttons and sword hilts.

DATE	*c.*1790
ORIGIN	ENGLISH
LENGTH	97cm (38.2in)

French dress sword, *c.*1800

This dress sword represents the height of late 18th-century smallsword ornamentation. The hilt, guard and pommel are all encrusted with paste (artificial) diamonds. The sword would have been carried by a person of very high social rank and worn at only the most formal of occasions.

DATE	*c.*1800
ORIGIN	FRENCH
LENGTH	73.5cm (28.9in)

French infantry officer's dress sword, *c.*1800

DATE	*c.*1800
ORIGIN	FRENCH
LENGTH	92.5cm (36.4in)

The hilt styling of this dress sword is typically Napoleonic. The inlaid brass Egyptian motifs on the grip were clearly inspired by Napoleon's Egyptian campaigns (1798–1801). French Napoleonic smallswords had a wide range of pommel styles, including knight's-helmet, tri-lobed, urn-shaped, globular and lion's head.

French infantry officer's dress sword, *c.*1815

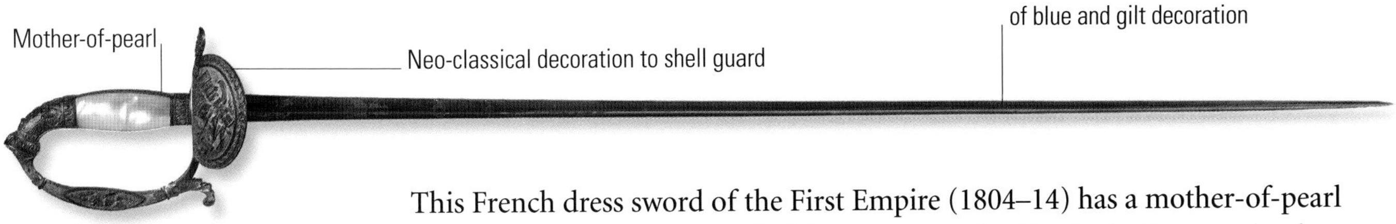

DATE	*c.*1815
ORIGIN	FRENCH
LENGTH	95.5cm (37.6in)

This French dress sword of the First Empire (1804–14) has a mother-of-pearl grip and extensive Neo-classical decoration to the hilt, including stands of arms, a combed helmet and scrolling foliage. The canted, or angled, pommel was a popular style during the early 19th century. Although of dress appearance, this sword was probably also carried in the field.

French dress sword, *c.*1820

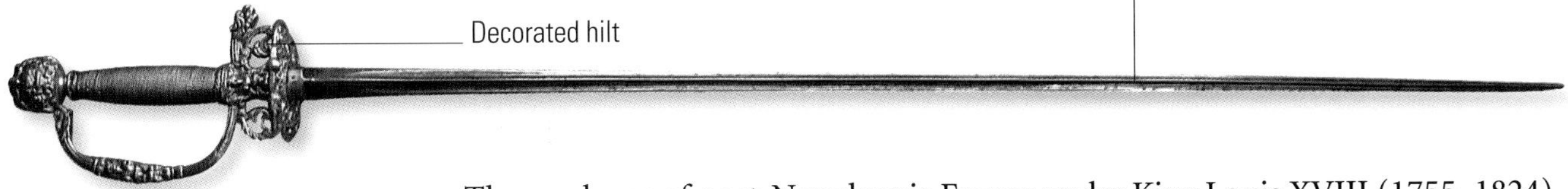

DATE	*c.*1820
ORIGIN	FRENCH
LENGTH	96cm (37.5in)

The opulence of post-Napoleonic France under King Louis XVIII (1755–1824) is evident in this dress sword, particularly the fantastical and classically inspired decoration to the gilt-brass hilt. The sword would have been carried by a senior military officer or official. The shell guard features mythical sea monsters and this might allude to a naval origin.

English court sword, *c.*1890

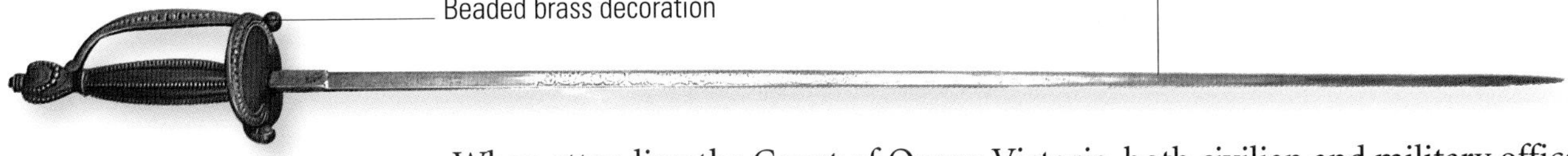

DATE	*c.*1890
ORIGIN	ENGLISH
LENGTH	92.5cm (36.4in)

When attending the Court of Queen Victoria, both civilian and military officers carried a smallsword. This example is likely to have been carried by a civilian official and comprises a cast brass hilt with "beaded" decoration. Blades were normally flat-backed and plain, although some were etched with the royal crown and floral decoration.

Swords of the two World Wars

During the 19th century, the sword was a crucial part of any soldier's list of equipment. As the century progressed and the rapid firing rifle and pistol became the predominant first weapons of choice within the major armies of Europe and beyond, the use of the sword in battle became rather anachronistic. At the commencement of World War I in 1914, the sword had been relegated to a very marginal role and by 1939, it had become a purely decorative or dress item in officers' wardrobes.

German naval officer's sword, *c.*1914

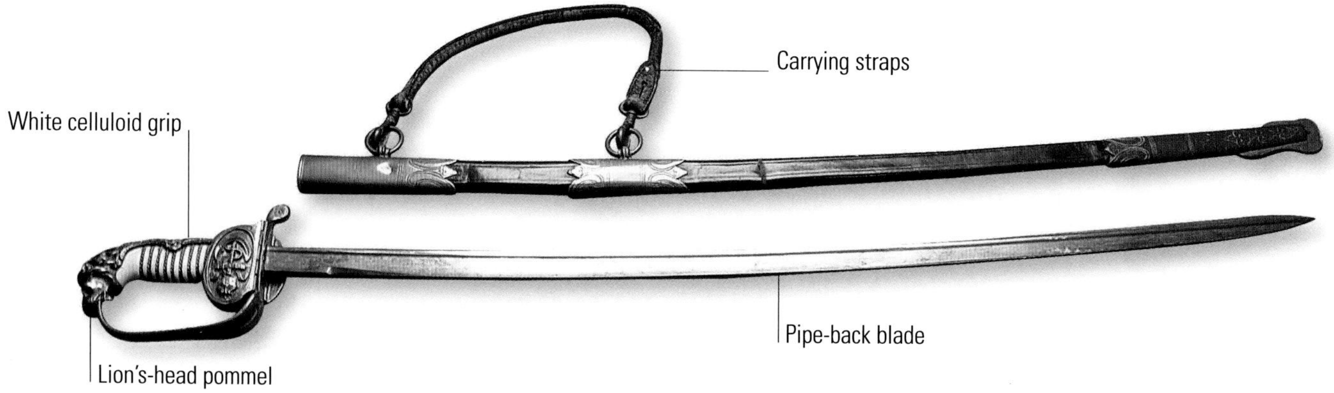

Officers' swords of the Imperial German Navy followed the Army's tradition of having a lion's-head pommel but differed in the design of the hilt guard. This took the form of a hinged, folding guard. Grips were normally made from ivory, bone or simulated ivory. Blades were often etched with nautical scenes, including crowned anchors and battleships.

DATE	*c.*1914
ORIGIN	GERMAN
LENGTH	90cm (35.5in)

Turkish infantry NCO's sword, *c.*1915

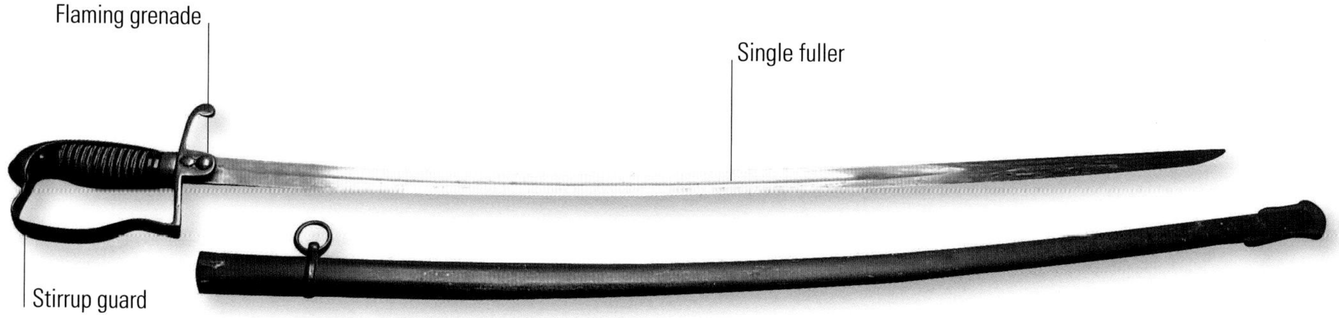

The Turkish military tended to emulate the sword designs of its Axis partners (Germany, Austria-Hungary, the Ottoman Empire and Bulgaria), with many Ottoman swords actually manufactured in Germany. This sword would have been carried by an NCO of sergeant rank and features a flaming grenade, probably signifying a grenadier or artillery regiment. The scabbard is black painted steel and has one carrying ring.

DATE	*c.*1915
ORIGIN	TURKISH
LENGTH	92.5cm (36.5in)

German Army officer's sword, *c.*1940

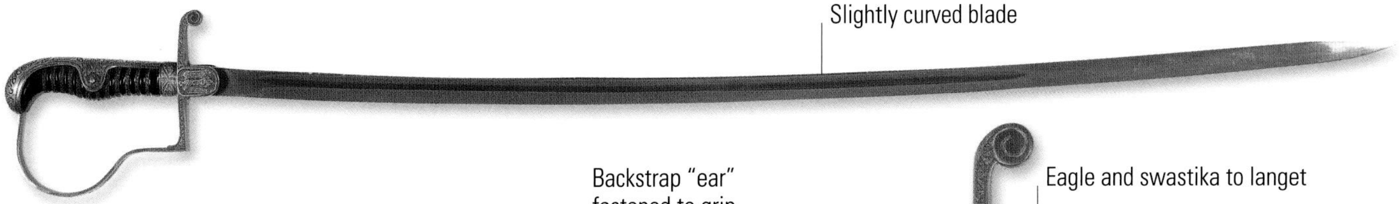

Many German infantry swords of this period have a lion's-head pommel, but some also feature a dove's-head or rounded pommel. The Nazi regime added an eagle and swastika to the hilt langet where previously the branch of service, such as crossed cannons for artillery or crossed lances for cavalry officers, would have been seen.

DATE	*c.*1940
ORIGIN	GERMAN
LENGTH	93.5cm (36.8in)

German Luftwaffe sword, *c.* 1941

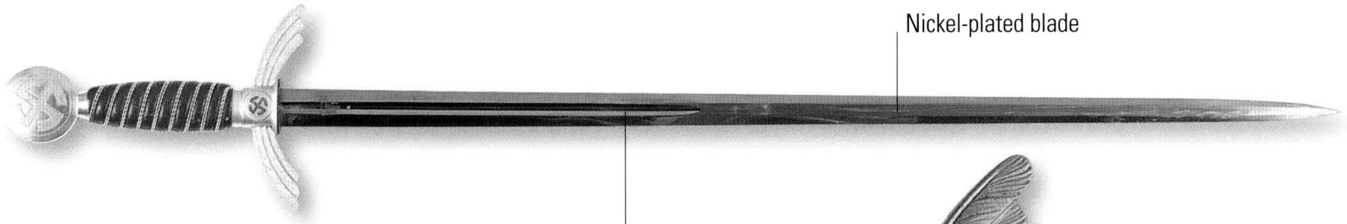

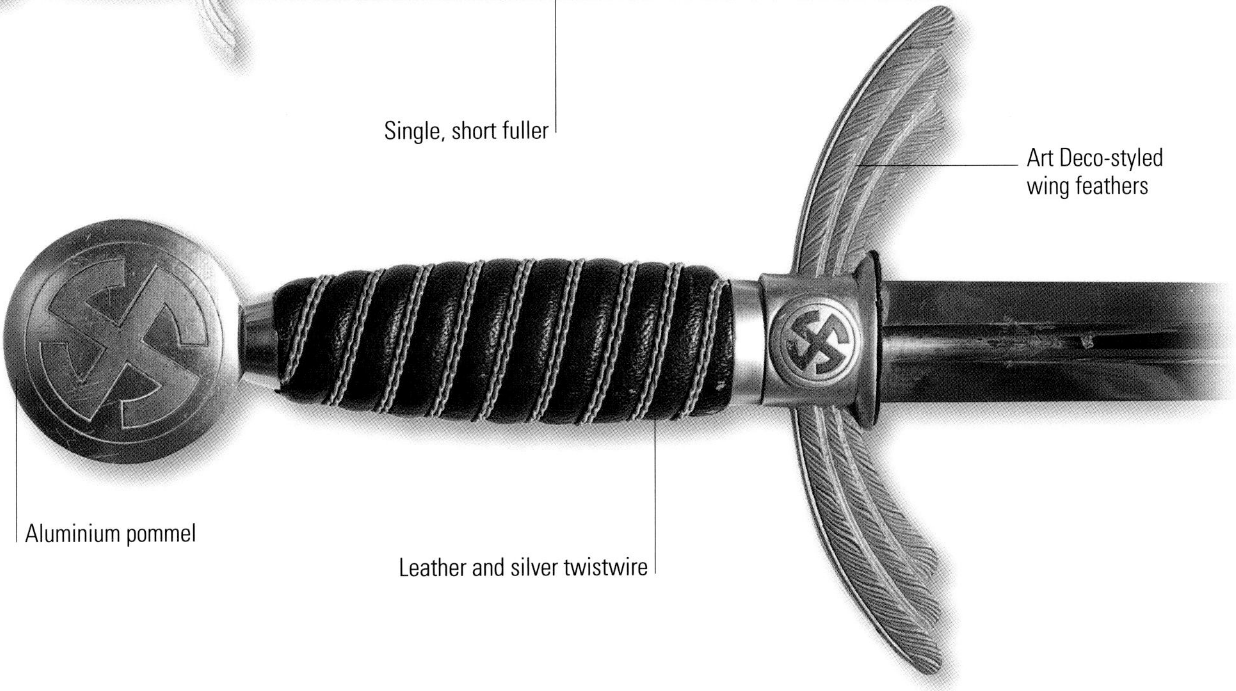

DATE	*c.*1941
ORIGIN	GERMAN
LENGTH	93.5cm (36.8in)

The styling of this sword was directly influenced by the Art Deco movement of the 1930s, and especially its obsession with speed and air flight. The downswept cross guard is typical Art Deco inspired design. The hilt and scabbard mounts are manufactured in aluminium. The Nazi swastika is depicted in an unusual form on the rounded pommel.

Marks and decorations

Swords and edged weapons have been marked and decorated since ancient times. From the crude engraving of a sword maker's name on a Roman gladius, to the bold lettering found on a Viking pattern-welded broadsword, and through to the fanciful blue and gilt styling of a Napoleonic sword blade, the need for recognition and decoration has always been paramount. Swords were also marked to ensure continuity of quality, and many are found with official stamps of approval. Identifying the marks of sword makers who practised their trade many centuries ago has become a difficult process, and many are now completely lost in the mists of time.

German knightly sword, *c.*1050

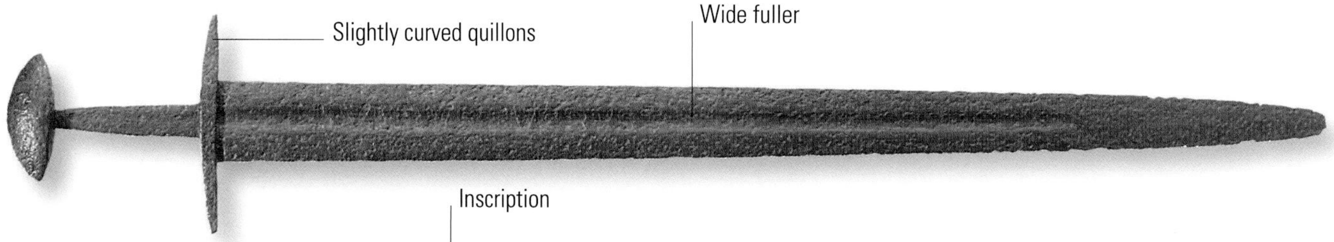

This is a typical broad-bladed knightly sword with a single, wide fuller. On one side of the blade there are remnants of an inscription "VERUSFVERUSF". Its meaning is unknown but could relate to the maker. The quillons are of square section, curved slightly downwards and ending in conical finials. The tang terminates with a large, mushroom-shaped pommel.

DATE	*c.*1050
ORIGIN	GERMAN
LENGTH	102.5cm (40.3in)

German knightly sword, *c.*1250–1300

This sword has a pronounced spear-point blade that would have had impressive cutting and thrusting capabilities. The blade is narrow and the consequent reduction in weight enabled the knight to wield the sword with flexibility and agility. The blade has a crude running wolf mark on both sides. This indicates manufacture in Passau, Germany, and was a common mark used by many sword makers in that region.

DATE	*c.*1250–1300
ORIGIN	GERMAN
LENGTH	112cm (44.1in)

German knightly sword, *c.*1300

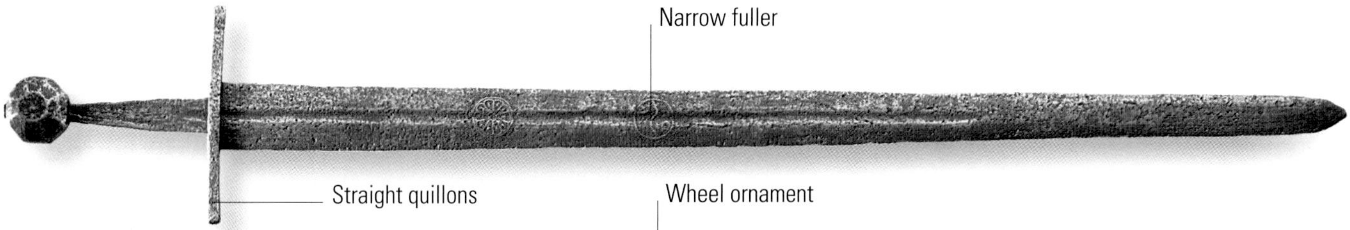

DATE	*c.*1300
ORIGIN	GERMAN
LENGTH	112cm (44.1in)

The heavy double-edged, cutting blade of this sword would have been quite devastating when wielded on horseback. The blade has two inlaid silver wheel ornaments. Their meaning is unknown, although they might be armourer's marks or armourial symbols.

French/German knightly sword, *c.*1450

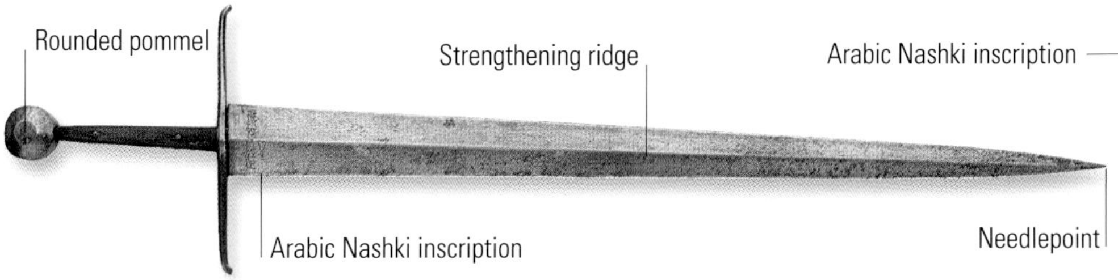

DATE	*c.*1450
ORIGIN	FRENCH/GERMAN
LENGTH	117.2cm (46.1in)

This European sword was captured by Ottoman (Turkish) forces and stored in a government armoury in Alexandria, Egypt. There is an Arabic Nashki inscription on the blade forte detailing its origins and new owner.

N. European Halberd, *c.*1450

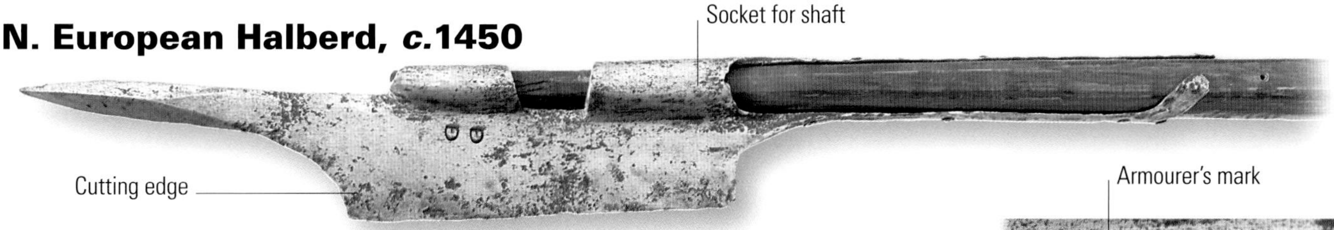

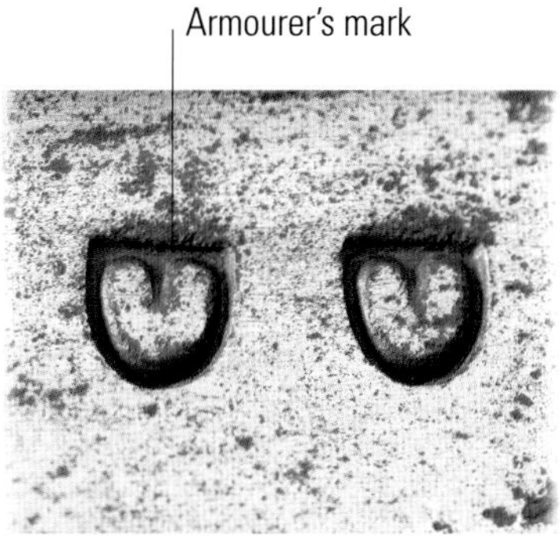

Two armourer's marks are deeply impressed on the blade of this early halberd. It is likely to be northern European in origin, although the halberd does bear a resemblance to the Scottish Lochaber axe, a standard infantry weapon of the Highland clans right through until the Battle of Culloden (1746).

DATE	*c.*1450
ORIGIN	NORTHERN EUROPEAN
LENGTH	198cm (77.9in)

German hand-and-a-half sword, *c.*1520

DATE	*c.*1520
ORIGIN	GERMAN
LENGTH	120cm (47.2in)

This is a good example of a Renaissance hand-and-a-half, or "bastard," sword. The blade is double-edged with wide and shallow fullers on both sides. A stylized brass orb and running wolf mark is present at the blade forte and probably indicates manufacture in the Solingen-Passau area of Germany.

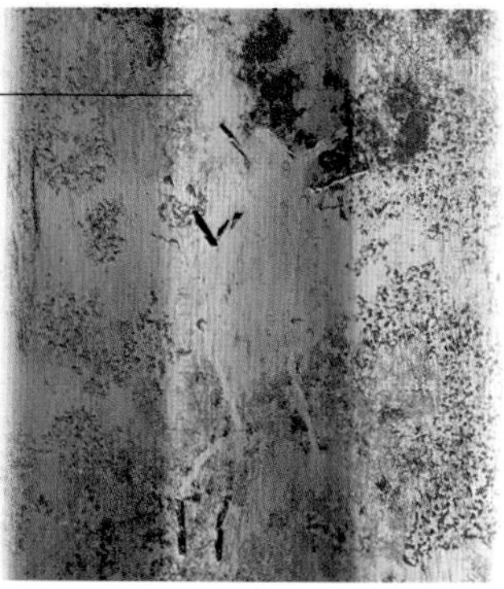

German halberd, *c.*1570

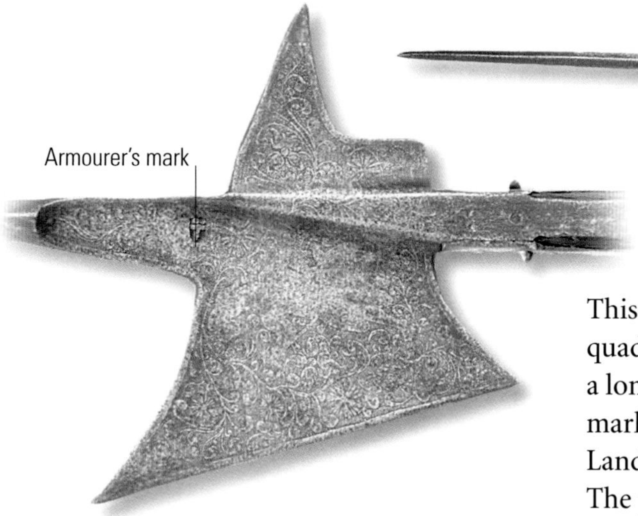

DATE	*c.*1570
ORIGIN	GERMAN
LENGTH	187cm (73.6in)

This is an etched ceremonial halberd with an enormous quadrangular spike. The blade is straight-edged and has a long, heavy fluke, or beak, to one side. There is an armourer's mark to one side. The engraving includes standing Landsknechte (mercenaries) amidst flowers and vines. The polygonal socket has four broad rivets.

German rapier, *c.*1600

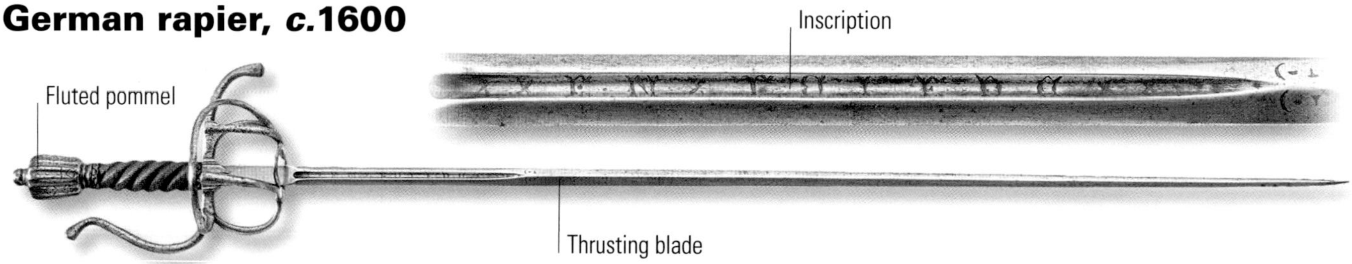

The simple yet functional hilt design of this rapier indicates a probable German origin. Although the hilt is German, the blade is Spanish in origin and inscribed with the words "In Toledo" within the central fuller. Toledo, in central Spain, was an important manufacturing centre for sword blades, which were noted for their exceptional quality and exported throughout Europe.

DATE	*c.*1600
ORIGIN	GERMAN
LENGTH	106.5cm (41.9in)

Dutch "Walloon" broadsword, *c.*1660

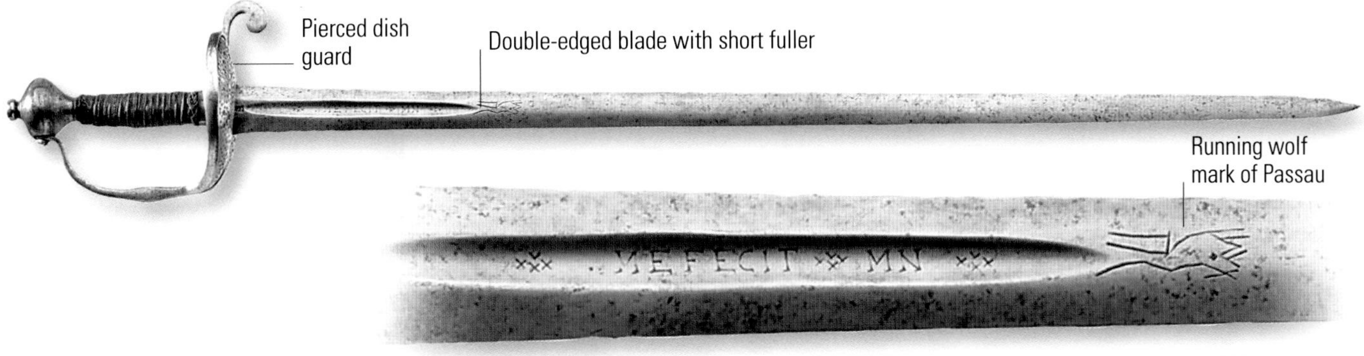

DATE	*c.*1660
ORIGIN	DUTCH
LENGTH	109cm (42.9in)

This style of north European broadsword is commonly known as a "Walloon" type and has its origins in the Netherlands. The blade displays the running wolf mark of Passau, Germany, and a crowned "P". There are also impressed inspection marks for the city of Amsterdam on the blade forte. The hilt is constructed in iron, with a heart-shaped and pierced, double-shell guard. It retains the original iron twistwire to the grip.

German broadsword, *c.*1695

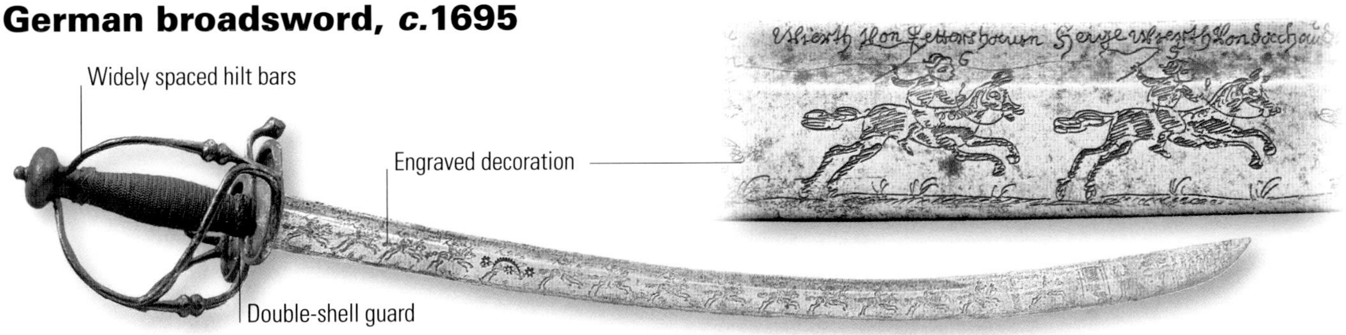

DATE	*c.*1695
ORIGIN	GERMAN
LENGTH	87cm (34.2in)

The curved blade of this broadsword has an unusual and rare depiction of a 17th-century horse race. There are 15 numbered riders, each designated by their individual names. The blade features crescent marks on both sides, a common symbol used by sword makers of this period. The open hilt has widely spaced bars, enabling the user to hold the grip with a large, leather, military riding gauntlet.

Polish estoc, *c.*1700

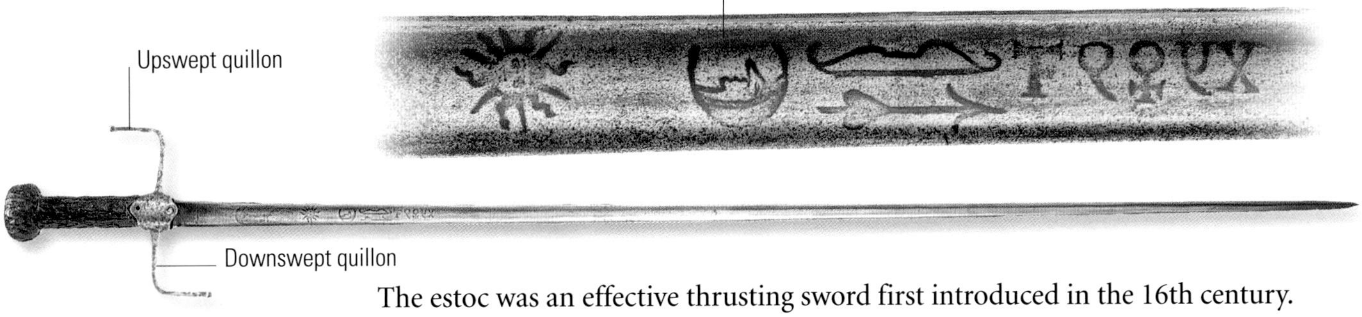

DATE	*c.*1700
ORIGIN	POLISH
LENGTH	158cm (62.2in)

The estoc was an effective thrusting sword first introduced in the 16th century. During the 16th and 17th centuries, it was adopted by Austrian and Polish hussars. This example has a long, narrow blade etched with depictions of the sun, moon, crossed sabres, bow and arrow, and cabalistic (mystical) inscriptions that were thought to bring luck to the owner of the sword.

German sword, *c.*1700

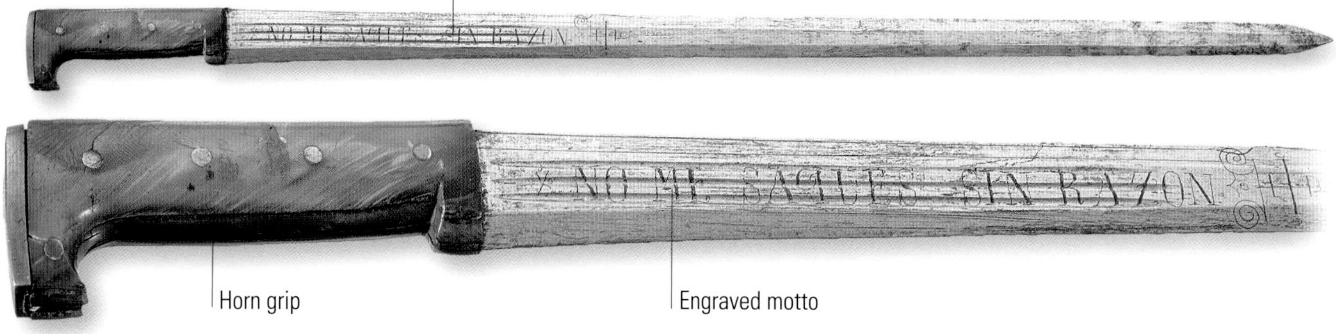

The blade of this sword is engraved with the motto NO ME SAQUES SIN RAZON–NO ME ENTRAINES SEN HONOR. Literally translated, it means: "Do not draw me without reason. Do not sheath me without honour". This is a common motto found on many European swords of the 18th and 19th centuries.

DATE	*c.*1700
ORIGIN	GERMAN
LENGTH	80.5cm (31.7in)

Venetian schiavona, *c.*1700

This is a very fine Venetian schiavona sword with typical complex basket hilt and cat's-head pommel. There is only one small armourer's mark on the blade that cannot be identified. This is the case with many marks of this period, where armourers or sword makers used a number of sometimes obscure symbols to mark their work. Unfortunately, time has erased all knowledge of who these people were.

DATE	*c.*1700
ORIGIN	VENETIAN
LENGTH	107.5cm (42.3in)

Spanish cup-hilt rapier, *c.*1700

The blade of this Spanish cup-hilt rapier is clearly engraved with the signature of Abraham Stamm, a member of a noted Solingen (German) family of sword makers. They were established in the late 16th century and continued production until the 1920s.

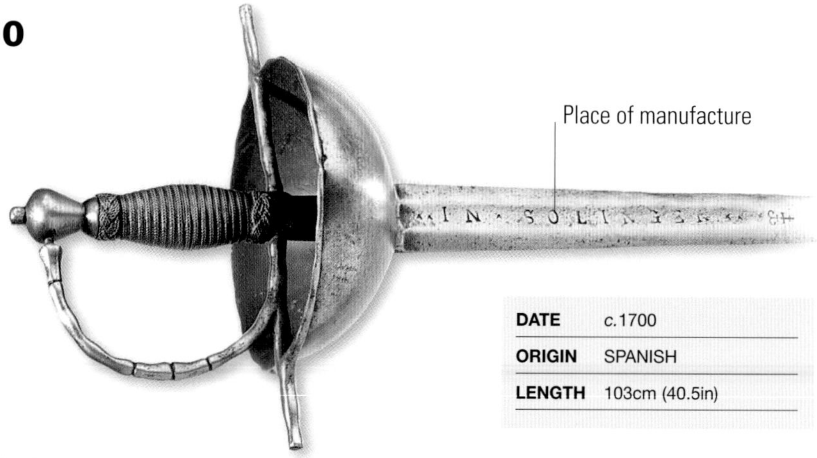

DATE	*c.*1700
ORIGIN	SPANISH
LENGTH	103cm (40.5in)

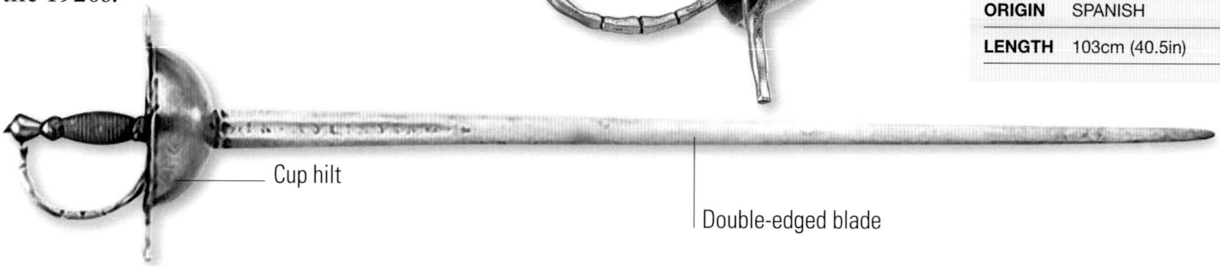

German hunting sword, *c.*1740

The quality of this hunting sword is quite exceptional. The slightly curved, double-fullered blade is etched on both sides with flowers and tendrils. The whale ivory grip is thought to be an earlier piece (*c.*1660) and comprises sculptured figures of hunting dogs fighting a bear and a male goat. The pommel and open shell guard are gilt brass. The ivory carving is attributed to the Maucher family of ivory sculptors, who worked in Germany during the late 17th century.

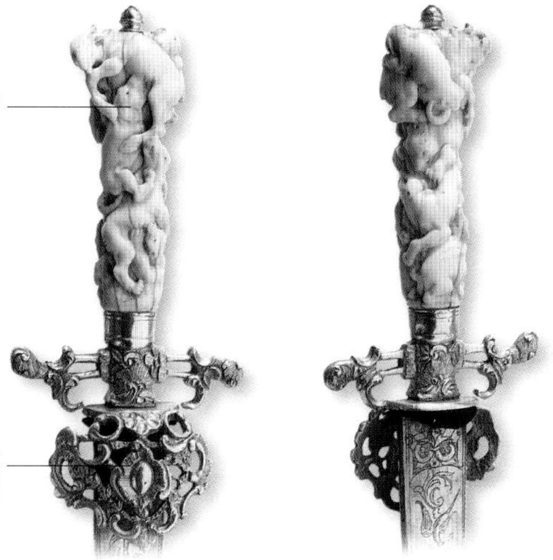

DATE	*c.*1740
ORIGIN	GERMAN
LENGTH	78cm (30.7in)

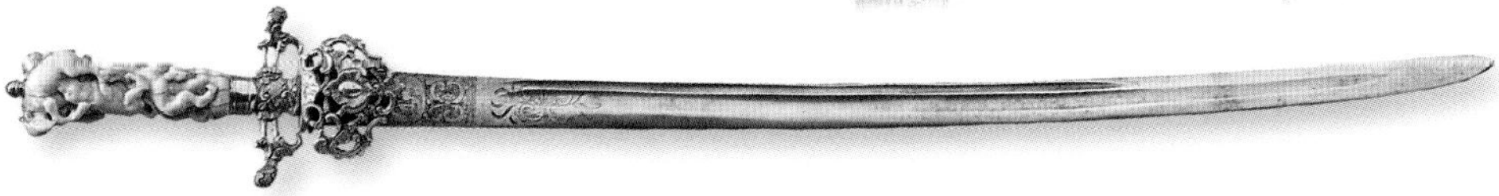

Spanish cup-hilt rapier, 1769

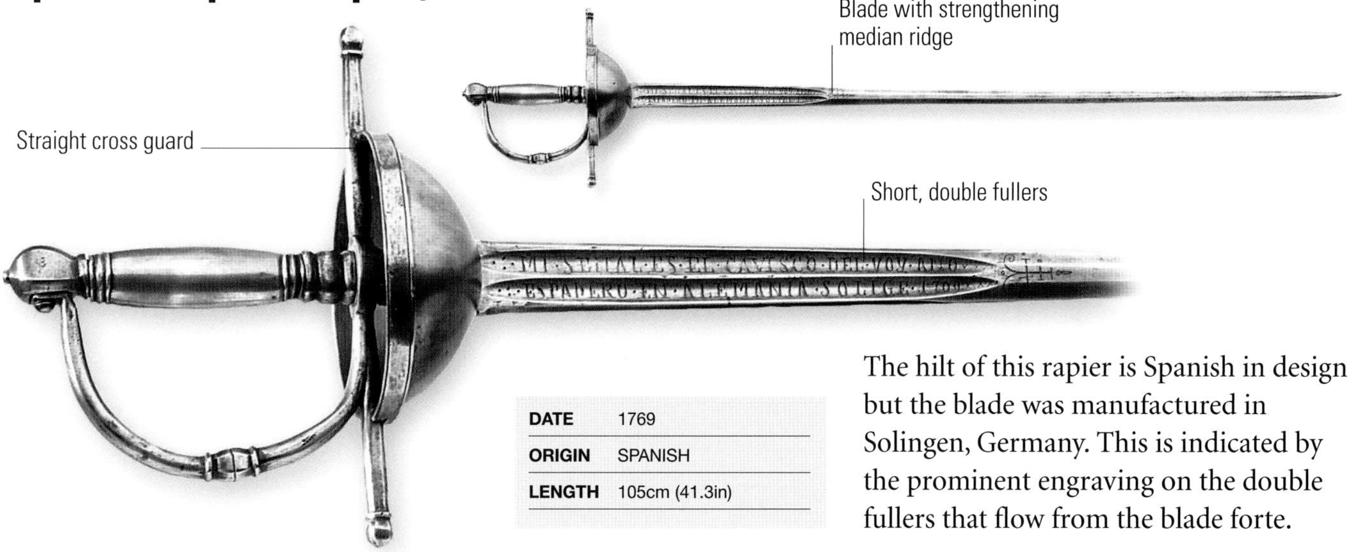

DATE	1769
ORIGIN	SPANISH
LENGTH	105cm (41.3in)

The hilt of this rapier is Spanish in design but the blade was manufactured in Solingen, Germany. This is indicated by the prominent engraving on the double fullers that flow from the blade forte.

Spanish broadsword, 1774

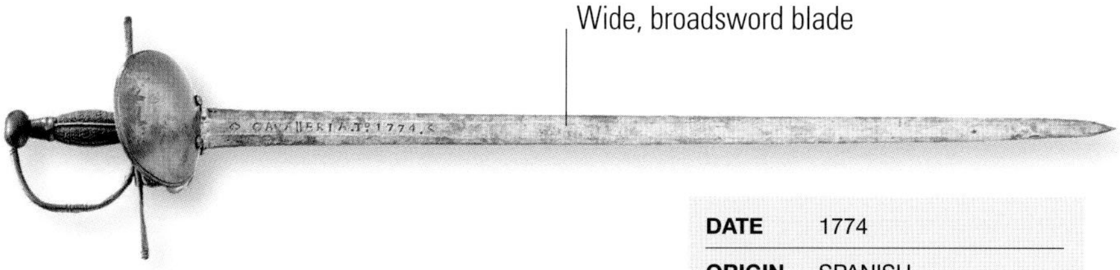

DATE	1774
ORIGIN	SPANISH
LENGTH	106cm (41.7in)

The Spanish military began issuing officially approved pattern swords from the late 18th century. This cavalry trooper's sword has been engraved with the date of manufacture or issue and *"Por El Rey Carlos III"*. This refers to King Carlos III of Spain (1716–1788).

Glossary

Atlatl Hunting tool that uses the leverage of the human arm to project a flint dart or spear at great speed against a moving target.

Back-edge The unsharpened edge on a single-edged weapon.

Backpiece Metal plate at the back of the grip that meets the pommel.

Backsword Straight or curved, single-edged broadsword.

Baldric Belt (leather or cloth) worn across the shoulder as a carrier for a sword.

Bardiche Long poleaxe used in medieval or Renaissance Europe.

Baselard Straight-bladed short sword carried by infantry during the late medieval period.

Basket hilt Large sword guard that was designed to enclose the hand through a series of interconnecting hilt bars.

Bastard sword Also known as the "hand-and-a-half" sword. It was a long, straight-bladed sword first introduced in the 15th century. Used with one hand and fingers of free hand for extra grip.

Bearing swords Large, two-handed broadswords carried during public ceremonies to signify the authority of the individual, state or institution.

Belt frog A leather or cloth sleeve in which a sword scabbard is held.

Bidr (qum) A form of Arabic blade patterning that results in a gravel effect – mainly applied to the blades of talwars.

Bill A polearm with various projecting spikes or flukes at the end of a shaft. It was especially popular in England during the 16th century.

Boar sword Introduced during the 14th century. A double-edged sword with stiffened blade and spear point. Designed to withstand the power of a charging boar or large animal.

Broadsword Straight, wide and single-edged sword. Popular from the 17th–18th centuries. Often attached to a basket hilt.

Buckler Small, rounded defensive shield worn on the wrist and used in conjunction with a sword. Common in Europe from the 13th–17th centuries.

Cartouche Oblong or oval space, surrounded by scrollwork, often with a dedication or image in the centre. It usually appears on the pommel, hilt or blade of a sword.

Chape Top of the scabbard shoe or drag.

Cinquedea Wide-bladed Italian short sword of the Renaissance. The name derived from the "five fingers" width of the blade.

Claymore Two-handed Scottish "great sword" of the 15th–17th centuries.

Clipped point Blade type with short, upturned point.

Colichemarde blade Sword blade of the 17th and 18th centuries. It is noted for its triangular profile. Designed with wide and long forte for added strength.

Coronal Crown-shaped metal cap (of three or more metal prongs) at the end of a lance. It was used during a joust to catch on to an opponent's shield.

Cross guard An extended bar across the bottom of the hilt to prevent slippage of the hand. It also protects the hand from sword blows.

Cuirassier Mounted cavalry soldiers of the 17th–19th centuries who wore a cuirass breastplate and a helmet. They were armed with firearms as well as a sword.

Cup hilt Round hilt cup protecting the sword hand on a rapier.

Cutlass Short sword with straight or slightly curved, single-edged blade. It normally refers to a sword used on board a ship.

Cutler Sword or edged-weapon maker.

Dadao Chinese heavy sword. Its name means "big knife". It has a large, machete-like blade, based on the style of agricultural knives.

Daisho Pair of Japanese swords including the katana and wakizashi.

Dao Straight-bladed sword of the Naga peoples of Assam, north-east India. The blade is squared off at the point.

Dirk A small, typically Scottish dagger. Used as a backup to the broadsword, and carried on a waistbelt.

Doru Traditional spear of the hoplites, with a large, leaf-shaped spearhead.

Ear Securing strap leading from the hilt backstrap that is riveted into the grip.

Épée Duelling sword used by fencers.

Estoc A forerunner to the rapier, and designed to puncture plate armour or cut the links of chain mail. It featured a long, triangular and heavily pointed blade.

Falcata Sword of the ancient Celts, with a kukri-type, single-edged blade.

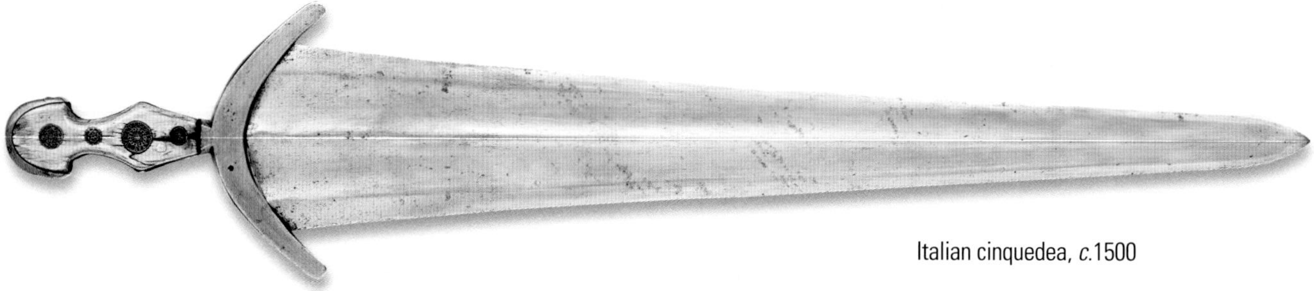

Italian cinquedea, *c.*1500

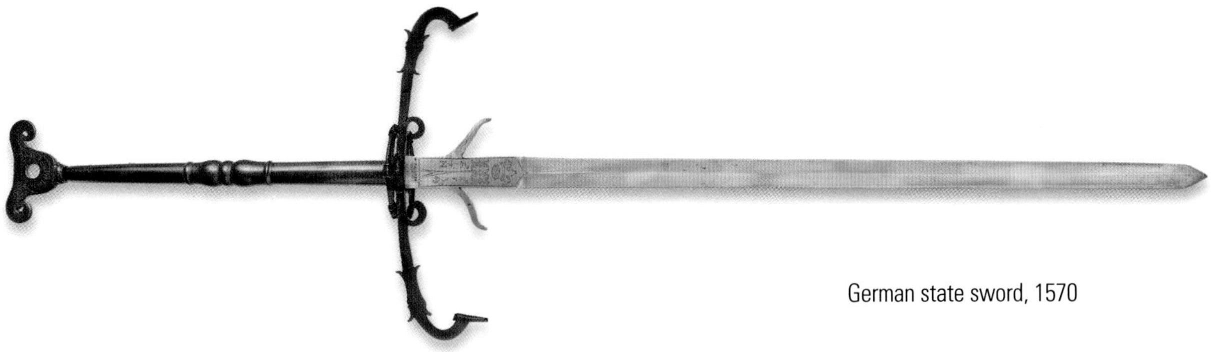

German state sword, 1570

Falchion Short sword with a broad, slightly curved blade. It was popular during the medieval and Renaissance periods and used mainly by archers and infantry soldiers.

False edge Usually seen on longer, single-edged swords. The final section of the blade was sharpened to make penetration and withdrawal easier.

Ferrule Metal protective band at bottom of sword hilt, fitted just above the cross guard.

Fluke Pointed projections at end of a polearm blade.

Flyssa A heavy-bladed sword, used to cut apart chain mail. It was the traditional sword of the Kabyles tribe of Algeria. The sword was in use until the 19th century.

Foil Modern fencing sword with a quadrangular blade and blunted tip.

Forte Strongest section of the sword blade and the part nearest the hilt.

Francisca axe Short, throwing axe used by Germanic tribes from around AD300.

Fuller Straight and shallow ridges on a sword blade that provide flexibility and strength.

Garniture (trousse) Set of carving tools, including knife and fork, found with hunting sword. Sheathed in a pocket within the scabbard alongside the main sword blade.

Gladius Ancient Roman double-edged, straight-bladed short sword.

Glaive Polearm with single-edged blade. Sometimes fitted with small hook to dismount riders. Used from the 13th to the 16th centuries.

Grip Part of the sword hilt grasped by the hand. Usually covered in either leather or metal, or a combination of both.

Guard Protective metal plate at the bottom of handle.

Haft Wooden pole/handle attached to both axes and polearms.

Halberd Polearm with cleaver-like blade and extended spike. It was used from the 16th to the 17th centuries.

Hamon Blade patterning on Japanese sword blades created by tempering.

Hanger Short infantry or hunting sword with a single-edged, curved or straight blade.

Hatchet point Cleaver-type end to blade point.

Hilt Upper part of the sword that includes the guard, grip, tang and pommel.

Hoplites Greek heavy infantry, formed from a citizen militia. They were armed with spears for use in the phalanx formation and they also carried a short sword.

Hunting sword Short sword with either curved or straight blade (some with saw-back edges). Popular from the 17th century, they were used during the hunt to carve up the kill.

Hussar Lightly armoured horseman, who normally carried curved sabres. They were considered the elite soldiers of their time and usually wore ornate and decorative uniforms.

Javelin A lightweight throwing spear.

Jian Chinese sword with straight, double-edged blade.

Kastane National sword of Sri Lanka, with a short, curved blade and monster-head pommel. Blades are normally of European origin.

Katana Traditional Japanese Samurai sword. With a very slightly curved, single-edged blade. Used with either one or two hands.

Katzbalger Short sword of the 16th to the 17th centuries, with a figure-of-eight guard. It was popular with Landsknechte (mercenaries).

Khanda Indian sword of the Marathas. It has a distinctive broad blade that widens towards the tip. The hilt is of basket form with a long, spiked pommel.

Khepesh Extremely curved, single-edged sword of the ancient Egyptians and the favoured weapon of the Pharaohs.

Kilij Persian scimitar sword with pronounced flared point, or yelman.

Klewang Traditional, single-edged, machete-type sword from Indonesia.

Knuckle bow This is also known as the knuckle guard. Normally a thin, curved bar that extends from the hilt, designed to protect the hand from sword cuts.

Kopis An ancient Greek short sword with a heavy, forward-curving blade for chopping or cleaving blows.

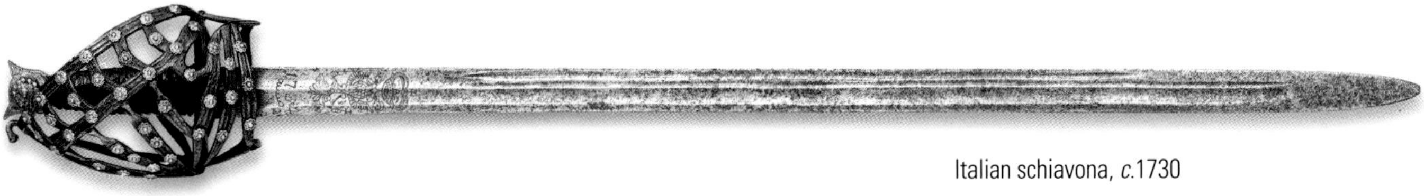

Italian schiavona, *c.*1730

North European poleaxe, *c.*1500

Kora National sword of Nepal and also used in northern India. It has a heavy blade that flares towards the tip.

Kris Short sword or long dagger from South-east Asia. It has a distinctive wavy blade that is forged from many different types of metal, giving a watered appearance.

Lance A long cavalry spear used by mounted horsemen both in battle and during jousts or tournaments.

Langets A downward extension of the cross guard that fits into the scabbard and protects the sword. It also refers to a long metal strip attached to the shaft of a polearm.

Lochaber axe Scottish infantry polearm used from the 17th century. It has a wooden shaft with heavy axe blade similar to a bardiche.

Locket Metal fitting where the blade enters the scabbard.

Longsword A late medieval and early Renaissance broadsword which had a cruciform hilt and two-handed grip.

Lowland sword Scottish two-handed broadsword of the 16th century, similar to the claymore.

Main gauche Left-handed dagger used in conjunction with a rapier. It was a popular weapon in the 16th-century duel.

Mameluke Sword with curved scimitar-shaped blade.

Mandau National short sword/knife of the Dayak peoples of Borneo.

Mortuary sword English basket-hilted broadsword of the mid-17th century. The hilt is commonly decorated with human heads.

Mouthpiece Protective metal lip at the top of a scabbard.

Nagamaki Japanese two-handed polearm with a blade similar to that of a katana sword.

Nimcha Single-handed sword used primarily in Morocco from the late 18th century onwards. It usually has forward-pointing quillons, and squared-off, "hooked" pommels.

Pappenheimer Military rapier of the 17th century. It was named after a German Field Marshal of the Thirty Years' War (1618–48).

Partizan Polearm with a broad, triangular blade and projections at its base. It was used from the 16th century.

Pas-d'âne Two curling arms that reach down to a dish guard – a common stylistic addition to smallswords.

Pata Indian sword, with the handle encased by a gauntlet-like cover. Traditionally used by specialized infantrymen against armoured cavalry.

Pattern welding Forging of several different types of metal that are twisted to form a pattern on a sword blade.

Pike Long infantry spear with a small head mounted on a wooden shaft. It was popular from the medieval period to the 17th century.

Pilum Ancient Roman heavy javelin, normally with a triangular head.

Pipe-back blade Rounded, tubular section on the back-edge of a blade, which was believed to provide extra strength to the sword. It is found on swords from the late 18th century.

Polearm Close-combat infantry weapon comprising a wooden shaft upon which is placed a bladed head.

Poleaxe Short infantry polearm with combination of axe, hammer or spiked head. It was common during the medieval period.

Pommel A metal weight at the top of the hilt. Acts as a counter-balance for the sword and, when screwed into the tang, ensures that the sword is solid, without any looseness or wobble.

Pulwar Single-handed Afghan sword. Heavily inspired by Indian tulwar designs, the hilt features two short quillons turned to face the direction of the blade.

Quillon Usually a swollen finial at the end of the hilt cross guard.

Rapier Thrusting sword of the mid-16th and 17th centuries. It is noted for its long, narrow blade.

Ricasso Squared-off and flattened part of the sword blade near the hand guard. It was originally designed to allow a finger to hook around it to improve the user's grip.

Sabre Cavalry or infantry sword with a curved blade.

Sageo Cord for tying a Japanese Samurai sword scabbard into belt.

Saif Arabic word loosely translated to mean "sword". It is usually attributed to curved sabres.

Saya Japanese sword scabbard.

Scabbard Sheath in which a sword blade is placed.

Scaramax Sword version of the Anglo-Saxon seax or knife. The blade is shaped like a machete.

Schiavona Renaissance, double-edged broadsword with a complex cage-like hilt. It was associated with Dalmatian mercenaries of the 16th to the 18th centuries.

Scimitar Middle Eastern sabre with curved blade.

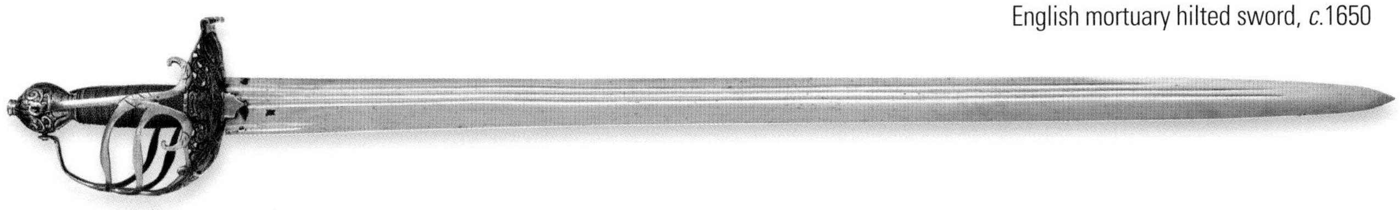

English mortuary hilted sword, *c.*1650

Scutum The large, rectangular shield carried by Roman legionaries. It was made of wood and calfskin, with a heavy, iron rim and centrepiece.

Seax Anglo-Saxon knife.

Seme Short sword used by the Maasai peoples of East Africa. Traditionally used to hunt lions, it features a simple wooden handle, with a scabbard covered with red rawhide and tipped with a coin.

Seppa Copper spaces fitted on each side of a Japanese Samurai sword guard.

Shamshir A Persian sabre with a curved blade.

Shell guard Defensive guard placed on sword hilts in the shape of a clamshell. It was popular from the 16th century.

Shin-gunto Japanese sword based on the Samurai tachi. Introduced during the 1930s and normally manufactured with machine-made blades.

Shoe Protective metal extension at the end of the scabbard.

Shotel Large, sickle-like sword from Abyssinia. It features a simple, wooden hilt with no guard and a heavily curved blade.

Shoulder This is the unsharpened cutting edge of a blade near the hand guard and is designed to protect the user's hand if it slips over the guard.

Smallsword Light, one-handed sword developed from the rapier. It was common from the late 17th century and often worn for dress purposes. Designed primarily for thrusting.

Sosun Pattah Traditional form of Indian sword with forward-curving blade.

Spadroon Light infantry sword designed for cutting and thrusting. Introduced in Europe and carried from the mid-18th century.

Spatha Ancient Roman, straight, double-edged sword with a long blade.

Spear point Sharpened point of a sword that resembles a spearhead.

Spiculum Ancient Roman throwing spear or javelin.

Spontoon European polearm of the 17th and 18th centuries, with a spear-shaped head. Used primarily by officers and NCOs as a symbolic or rallying weapon on the battlefield.

Stirrup-hilted Knuckle guard of sword hilt that resembles a horse's stirrup. Popular on cavalry swords (particularly British) from the late 18th century.

Swept hilt Type of rapier hilt guard formed by a number of intertwining bars that "swept" around the hand. Introduced during the late 16th century.

Tachi Long Japanese Samurai sword which is worn slung over the shoulder.

Takouba Traditional sword of the Saharan Tuareg tribe. Typically, it has a brass grip due to their owners' traditional aversion to touching iron. It usually features three or more fullers and a rounded point.

Talwar Wide-bladed Indian sword with distinctive dish pommel and one-piece grip of lozenge-shaped cross-section.

Tang Part of the blade that fits through the grip.

Tang button The end of the tang that is hammered (peened) over the top of the pommel. It adds stability and strength. Some tang buttons are screwed into the pommel and attached to the tang.

Tanto Japanese dagger with diamond-sectioned blade.

Targe Old English word for a concave shield. It was traditionally carried by Scottish Highlanders alongside their broadsword. Highlanders carried targe shields throughout the 17th century.

Trefoil Three-sided or triangular blade most commonly seen on smallswords.

Tsuba Metal guard (either rounded or square) found on Japanese Samurai swords.

Tuck (estoc in French) Late medieval variation of the longsword with strengthened point to penetrate plate armour.

Wakizashi Japanese Samurai short sword. It is normally carried in combination with a katana.

Wootz Indian method of patterning a sword blade with iron ore, charcoal and glass.

Yataghan Ottoman (Turkish) sword with a forward-curving blade.

Yelman The flared end of a Persian sword blade which gave the blade greater heft or weight when cutting. It is found on Persian kilij swords.

Xiphon The short sword carried by the Greek hoplites. It had a large, leaf-shaped blade and was normally only used after the spear had been discarded.

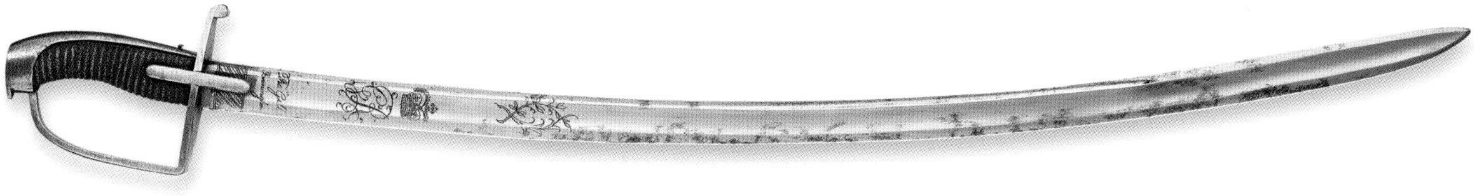

British light cavalry sword, 1788

Further information

BIBLIOGRAPHY

Annis, P.G.W., *Naval Swords: British and American Naval Edged Weapons 1660–1815* (Arms and Armour Press, London, 1970).

Aylward, J.D., *The Smallsword in England* (Hutchinson, London, 1960).

Bosanquet, H.T., *The Naval Officer's Sword* (H.M.S.O., London, 1955).

Burton, Richard, *The Book of the Sword* (Dover Publications Inc., New York, 1987).

Dolinek, Vladimir and Durdik, Jan, *The Encyclopedia of European Historical Weapons* (Hamlyn, London, 1993).

Evangelista, Nick, *The Encyclopedia of the Sword* (Greenwood Press, London, 1995).

Ffoulkes, Charles and Hopkinson, E. C., *Sword, Lance and Bayonet* (Arms and Armour Press, London, 1967).

Gilkerson, William, *Boarders Away: With Steel-Edged Weapons and Polearms 1626–1826* (Andrew Mowbray Publishers, Lincoln RI, 1991).

Gyngell, D.S.H., *Armourer's Marks* (Cambridge University Press, New York, 1963).

Hayward, J.F., *Swords and Daggers* (H.M.S.O., London, 1964).

Hutton, Capt. Alfred, *The Sword and the Centuries* (Grant Richards, London, 1901).

Kulinsky, A.N., *European Edged Weapons* (Atlant, St Petersburg, 2003).

May, W.E. and Annis, P.G., *Swords for Sea Service* (H.M.S.O., London, 1970).

May, W.E. and Kennard, A.N., *Naval Swords and Firearms* (H.M.S.O., London, 1962).

National Trust for Scotland, Culloden, *The Swords and the Sorrows* (NTS Trading Company, Edinburgh, 1996).

Neumann, George C., *Swords and Blades of the American Revolution* (Rebel Publishing Co., Inc., Texarkana TX, 1991).

Norman, A.V.B., *The Rapier and Smallsword, 1460–1820* (Arms and Armour Press, London, 1980).

Oakshott, Ewart, *Records of the Medieval Sword* (The Boydell Press, New York, 1991).

Peterson, Harold, *The American Sword 1775–1945* (Riling Arms Books, Philadelphia, PA, 1996).

Robson, Brian, *Swords of the British Army. The Regulation Patterns, 1788 to 1914* (National Army Museum, London, 1996).

Southwick, Leslie, *London Silver-Hilted Swords* (Royal Armouries, Leeds, 2001).

Stone, George Cameron, *A Glossary of the Construction, Decoration and Use of Arms and Armor in all Countries and in all Times* (Jack Brussel, Southworth Press, New York, 1961).

Valentine, Eric, *Rapiers* (Stackpole Books, Harrisburg, PA, 1970).

Various authors, *Swords and Hilt Weapons* (Weidenfeld and Nicolson, London, 1989).

Wagner, Eduard, *Cut and Thrust Weapons* (Spring Books, London, 1967).

Wallace, John, *Scottish Swords and Dirks, An Illustrated Reference Guide to Scottish Edged Weapons* (Arms and Armour Press, London, 1970).

Wilkinson, Frederick, *Swords and Daggers: An Illustrated Reference Guide for Collectors* (Arms and Armour Press, London, 1985).

Wilkinson, Frederick, *Swords and Daggers* (Ward Lock and Co. Ltd, London, 1967).

Wilkinson-Latham, John, *British Military Swords from 1800 to the present day* (Crown Publishers, Inc, New York, 1967).

Wilkinson-Latham, John, *British Cut and Thrust Weapons* (David and Charles Publishers, Newton Abbott, 1971).

Wilkinson-Latham, R.J., *Pictorial History of Swords and Bayonets* (Ian Allan, London, 1973).

Withers, Harvey, *British Military Swords 1786–1912. The Regulation Patterns. An Illustrated Price Guide for Collectors* (Studio Jupiter Military Publishing, Sutton Coldfield, 2003).

Withers, Harvey, *World Swords 1400–1945. An Illustrated Price Guide for Collectors* (Studio Jupiter Military Publishing, Sutton Coldfield, 2006).

MUSEUMS OF INTEREST

UNITED KINGDOM

The British Museum
Great Russell Street
London
WC1B 3DG
www.britishmuseum.co.uk

Fitzwilliam Museum
Trumpington Street
Cambridge
CB2 1RB
www.fitzmuseum.cam.ac.uk

National Army Museum
Royal Hospital Road
Chelsea
London
SW3 4HT
www.national-army-museum.ac.uk

National Museum of Scotland
Chambers Street
Edinburgh
EH1 1JF
www.nms.ac.uk

National War Museum
Edinburgh Castle
EH1 2NG
www.nms.ac.uk

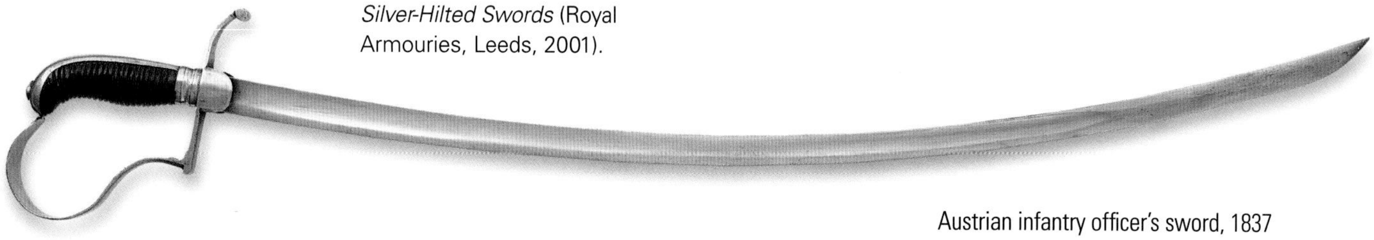

Austrian infantry officer's sword, 1837

Burmese dha sword, *c.*1850

The Royal Armouries, Leeds
Armouries Drive,
Leeds
LS10 1LT
www.royalarmouries.org

Victoria and Albert Museum
Cromwell Road
London
SW7 2RL
www.vam.ac.uk

The Wallace Collection
Hertford House
Manchester Square
London
W1U 3BN
www.wallacecollection.org

Windsor Castle
Berkshire
SL4 1NJ
www.royalcollection.org.uk

AUSTRIA
Historisches Museum der Stadt, Vienna
A-1040 Wien
Karlsplatz
www.wienmuseum.at

Landeszenghaus, Graz
Abteilung Landeszeughaus
Herrengassse16
A-8010
Graz
www.zeughaus.at

Waffensammlung, Vienna
A-1010 Wien
Maria Theresien-Platz
www.khm.at

BELGIUM
Porte de Hal, Brussels
Boulevard du Midi
Zuidlaan
1020
Brussels
www.kmkg-mrah.be

DENMARK
Tojhusmet, Copenhagen
Tøjhusgade 3
1214
København
www.thm.dk

FINLAND
National Museum of Finland
Mannerheimintie 34
Helsinki
www.nba.fi/en/nmf

FRANCE
Musée de l'Armée, Paris
Hôtel National des Invalides
129 Rue de Grenelle
75007
Paris
www.invalides.org

Musée du Louvre, Paris
34, Rue du Louvre
75001
Paris
www.louvre.fr

GERMANY
Historisches Museum, Dresden
Zwinger
Semperbau
D-01067
Dresden
www.skd-dresden.de

Museum für Deutsche Geschicte, Berlin
Unter den Linden 2
10117
Berlin
www.dhm.de

Württembergisches Landesmuseum
Schillerplatz 6
70173
Stuttgart
www.landesmuseum-stuttgart.de

ITALY
Museo Nazionale, Florence
Via della Ninna 5
50122
Firenze
www.polomuseale.firenze.it

Stibbert Collection, Florence
Via Frederick Stibbert 26
50134
Firenze
www.museostibbert.it

NETHERLANDS
Dutch Army Museum
Korte Geer 1
Delft
www.legermuseum.nl

NORWAY
Universitetets Oldsaksamling
Fredriks Gate 2
Oslo 0164
www.ukm.uio.no

POLAND
Wawel Armoury, Cracow
31-001 Kraków
Wawel 5
www.wawel.krakow.pl

SPAIN
Armoury, Palacio Réal de Madrid, Madrid
Calle Bailén
28071 Madrid
www.patrimonionacional.es

SWEDEN
Statens Historiska Museum
Narvavägen 13–17
114 84
Stockholm
www.historiska.se

SWITZERLAND
Historischemuseum, Basel
Steinenberg 4
CH–4051
Basel
www.hmb.ch

Schweizerisches Landesmuseum
Museumstrasse 2
8021
Zurich
www.musee-suisse.ch

UNITED STATES
Metropolitan Museum of Art
1000 Fifth Avenue
New York, NY
10028–0198
www.metmuseum.org

Smithsonian Institution
Several locations at
PO Box 37012
SI Building
Room 153
MRC 010
Washington, D.C.
20013–7012
www.si.edu

Allentown Art Museum
31 N. 5th Street
Allentown, Pennsylvania
PA 18101
www.allentownartmuseum.org

Brooklyn Museum
200 Eastern Parkway
Brooklyn
New York, NY
11238–6052
www.brooklynmuseum.org

Cleveland Museum of Art
1150 East Boulevard
Cleveland, OH
44106
www.clevelandart.org

Higgins Armory Museum,
100 Barber Avenue
Worcester, Massachusetts
01606–2444
www.higgins.org

RUSSIA
Hermitage Museum, St Petersberg
34 Dvortsovaya Naberezhnaya
St Petersburg
190000
www.hermitagemuseum.org

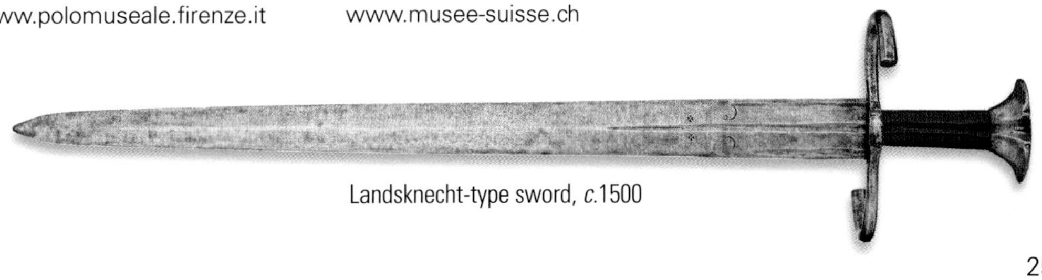

Landsknecht-type sword, *c.*1500

Index

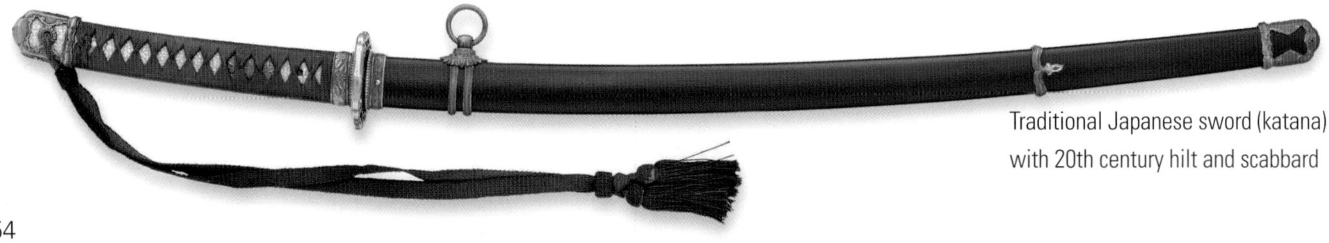

Traditional Japanese sword (katana) with 20th century hilt and scabbard

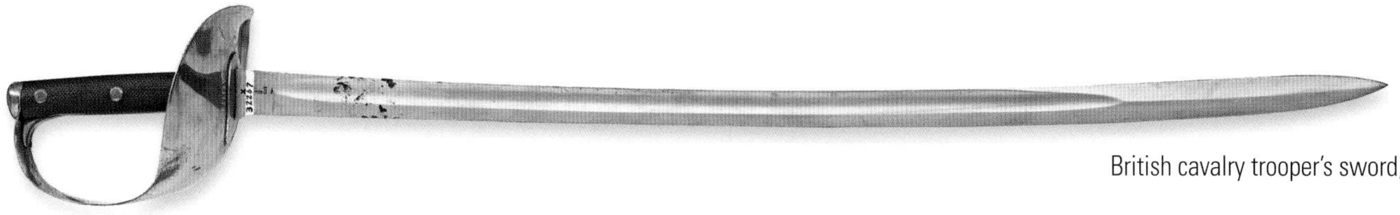

British cavalry trooper's sword, 1899

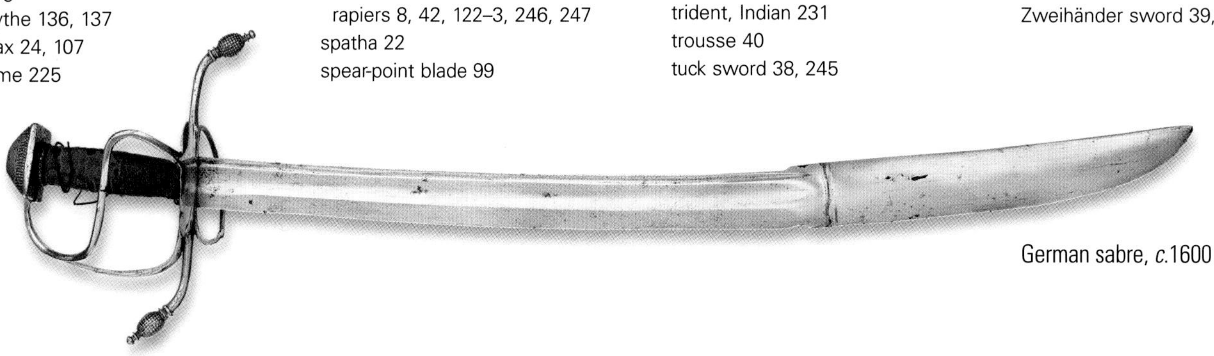

German sabre, *c.*1600

Picture credits

The publisher would like to thank the following for kindly supplying photos for this book: Alamy: 53br, 62bl, 83tr; AKG: 15br, 16bl, 18bl, 22tl, 26bl, 28tr, 31br, 35t, 36br, 37tr, 43br, 60tl, 93tr, 104b, 201tr; Ancient Art & Architecture: 17tr, 88tr; The Art Archive: 16tr, 20br, 21t, 23b, 48b, 59tl; Berman Museum of World History, Alabama: 7b, br, 9tr, 10br, 11b, 12t, 57b, 64t, t, b, 65m, 79b, 81br, 85b, 88br, 90t, 91b, 93b, 94b, 100bl, 101tr, m, mr, br, 178t, b, b, 179t, m, b, b, 185b, 206b, 212m, m, 213b, b, 216b, 217t, 219t, t, m, m, b, 223b, 225t, b, 228b, 229t, m, 231b, 234t, 236t, 238t, 241t, b, 242t, 243m,b, 244t, m, b, 245t, m, b; Bridgeman Art Library: 7tl, tr, 13m, 14bm, 21b, 24b, 27tr, 28br, 29tr, bl, 32tl, 40tl, 43tl, 44bl, 46tl, 50t, bl, 51tr, 57br, 58bl, 69mr, 73mr, 84bl, 89tr, 90bl, 105b, 123b, 188t, 195br, 221br; Corbis: 10t, 56mr, 109b, 78b, 177bl; Getty Images: 77ml, 79tr, 85tr ; Hermann Historica Auctioneers, Munich: 19tl, 19tm, tr, br, bl, 38t, b, 41t, mr, b, 80b, 86tm, 102t, m, 103t, t, b, 105t, m, 131b, 140t, 173t, 176t, 202b, 203b, b, 242t, t, 243t, t, 244t, t, t, m, m, b, b, 245t, t, m, m, b, b, 246t, t, m, m, b, b, 247t, t, t, m, m, b, b; Michael Holford: 15tr, 100tl, m, 104m; iStock: 171br; Jean Brink: 69tl, br; Jupiter Images Corporation: 15tl, 17br, 25tr, 30tl, 52tl, 55tl, 65tr; David Xavier Kenney, South Beach FL (www.RomanOfficer.com): 22bl, 23tr; TopFoto: 23ml, 45br, 47t, b, 67mr, 76tr, 88tr, 89bl, 91t, 92tr, bl, 126br; Harvey Withers: 60b, 63b, 73b, 75t, 165t, 172b, 182t, 206t, 207b, 236b, 238t, 239m, b, 240t, b. All other images from the Royal Armouries, Leeds in England. All artwork by Peters & Zabransky Ltd.